A Hands-On Introduction to Machine Learning

CHIRAG SHAH

University of Washington

CAMBRIDGE
UNIVERSITY PRESS

University Printing House, Cambridge CB2 8BS, United Kingdom

One Liberty Plaza, 20th Floor, New York, NY 10006, USA

477 Williamstown Road, Port Melbourne, VIC 3207, Australia

314–321, 3rd Floor, Plot 3, Splendor Forum, Jasola District Centre,
New Delhi – 110025, India

103 Penang Road, #05–06/07, Visioncrest Commercial, Singapore 238467

Cambridge University Press is part of the University of Cambridge.

It furthers the University's mission by disseminating knowledge in the pursuit of
education, learning, and research at the highest international levels of excellence.

www.cambridge.org
Information on this title: www.cambridge.org/highereducation/isbn/9781009123303
DOI: 10.1017/9781009122092

© Chirag Shah 2023

This publication is in copyright. Subject to statutory exception
and to the provisions of relevant collective licensing agreements,
no reproduction of any part may take place without the written
permission of Cambridge University Press.

First published 2023

Printed in the United Kingdom by TJ Books Limited, Padstow Cornwall

A catalogue record for this publication is available from the British Library.

ISBN 978-1-009-12330-3 Hardback

Additional resources for this publication at www.cambridge.org/shah-ML

Cambridge University Press has no responsibility for the persistence or accuracy of
URLs for external or third-party internet websites referred to in this publication
and does not guarantee that any content on such websites is, or will remain,
accurate or appropriate.

To my students who helped me, challenged me, and made me learn in ways that went far beyond my own education and research.

Contents

Preface	*page* xiii
Acknowledgments	xix
About the Author	xxi

Part I Basic Concepts

1 Teaching Computers to Write Programs — 3
- 1.1 What Is Machine Learning? — 3
- 1.2 Branches of Machine Learning — 9
- 1.3 What Do You Need for Machine Learning? — 11
  - 1.3.1 Skills — 11
  - 1.3.2 Tools — 13
- 1.4 Computational Thinking — 15
- 1.5 Issues of Ethics, Bias, and Privacy in Machine Learning — 18
- 1.6 Summary — 19
- Key Terms — 20
- Conceptual Questions — 20
- Hands-on Problems — 21
- Further Reading and Resources — 25

2 Python — 26
- 2.1 Introduction — 26
- 2.2 Getting Access to Python — 26
  - 2.2.1 Download and Install Python — 26
  - 2.2.2 Running Python through the Console — 27
  - 2.2.3 Using Python through an Integrated Development Environment — 27
- 2.3 Basic Examples — 29
- 2.4 Control Structures — 32
- 2.5 Functions — 34
- 2.6 Making Python Interactive — 36
- 2.7 Installing and Using Python Packages — 36
  - 2.7.1 Spyder — 37
  - 2.7.2 Jupyter Notebook — 37
  - 2.7.3 Google Colab — 37

2.8 Statistics Essentials ... 39
    2.8.1 Importing Data ... 42
    2.8.2 Plotting the Data ... 43
    2.8.3 Correlation ... 44
2.9 Summary ... 45
Key Terms ... 45
Conceptual Questions ... 46
Hands-on Problems ... 46
Further Reading and Resources ... 48

3 Cloud Computing ... 49
3.1 Cloud Computing ... 49
3.2 Google Cloud Platform ... 50
    3.2.1 Hadoop ... 53
3.3 Microsoft Azure ... 59
3.4 Amazon Web Services ... 66
3.5 Moving between Cloud Platforms ... 75
3.6 Summary ... 75
Key Terms ... 76
Conceptual Questions ... 76
Hands-on Problems ... 76
Further Reading and Resources ... 77

Part II Supervised Learning

4 Regression ... 81
4.1 Introduction ... 81
4.2 Linear Regression ... 82
4.3 Multiple Linear Regression ... 91
4.4 Ridge and Lasso Regression ... 96
4.5 Gradient Descent ... 98
4.6 Considerations for ML Modeling ... 110
    4.6.1 Accuracy ... 111
    4.6.2 Training–Testing ... 111
    4.6.3 Training Time ... 111
    4.6.4 Linearity ... 111
    4.6.5 Number of Hyperparameters ... 112
    4.6.6 Number of Features ... 112
    4.6.7 Choosing the Right Estimator ... 112
4.7 Summary ... 113
Key Terms ... 113
Conceptual Questions ... 114
Hands-on Problems ... 114
Further Reading and Resources ... 117

A Hands-On Introduction to Machine Learning

Packed with real-world examples, industry insights, and practical activities, this textbook is designed to teach machine learning in a way that is easy to understand and apply. It assumes only a basic knowledge of technology, making it an ideal resource for students and professionals, including those who are new to computer science. All the necessary topics are covered, including supervised and unsupervised learning, neural networks, reinforcement learning, cloud-based services, and the ethical issues still posing problems within the industry. While Python is used as the primary language, many exercises will also have the solutions provided in R for greater versatility. A suite of online resources is available to support teaching across a range of different courses, including example syllabi, a solutions manual, and lecture slides. Datasets and code are also available online for students, giving them everything they need to practice the examples and problems in the book.

Dr. Chirag Shah is Professor at the University of Washington (UW) in Seattle, USA. Before UW, he was at Rutgers University. His research focuses on intelligent information access systems that are also fair, transparent, and trustworthy. Dr. Shah received his M.S. in Computer Science from the University of Massachusetts Amherst, and his Ph.D. in Information Science from the University of North Carolina Chapel Hill. He directs the InfoSeeking Lab and co-directs the Center for Responsibility in AI Systems & Experiences (RAISE). His research is supported by awards from the National Science Foundation (NSF), the National Institute of Health (NIH), the Institute of Museum and Library Services (IMLS), as well as Amazon, Google, and Yahoo!. Dr. Shah teaches undergraduate, masters, and Ph.D. programs at UW, focusing on data science and machine learning. He has designed MOOCs and has taught several tutorials and short courses at international venues. Dr. Shah has written several books, including his textbook *A Hands-On Introduction to Data Science*. He has visited and worked with many tech companies, including Amazon, Brainly, Getty Images, Microsoft Research, and Spotify.

5 Classification 1 — 118

- 5.1 Introduction — 118
- 5.2 Classification with k-Nearest Neighbors — 119
- 5.3 Decision Tree — 123
  - 5.3.1 Decision Rule — 127
  - 5.3.2 Classification Rule — 127
  - 5.3.3 Association Rule — 128
- 5.4 Random Forest — 132
- 5.5 Summary — 137
- Key Terms — 137
- Conceptual Questions — 138
- Hands-on Problems — 138
- Further Reading and Resources — 143

6 Classification 2 — 144

- 6.1 Introduction — 144
- 6.2 Logistic Regression — 145
- 6.3 Softmax Regression — 152
- 6.4 Naïve Bayes — 154
- 6.5 Support Vector Machine — 159
- 6.6 Summary — 165
- Key Terms — 166
- Conceptual Questions — 166
- Hands-on Problems — 167
- Further Reading and Resources — 170

Part III Unsupervised Learning

7 Clustering — 175

- 7.1 Introduction — 175
- 7.2 Divisive Clustering — 176
  - 7.2.1 Divisive Clustering with k-Means — 179
  - 7.2.2 Divisive Clustering with k-Modes — 182
- 7.3 Agglomerative Clustering — 186
- 7.4 Expectation Maximization — 192
- 7.5 Density Estimation — 196
- 7.6 Summary — 199
- Key Terms — 200
- Conceptual Questions — 200
- Hands-on Problems — 200
- Further Reading and Resources — 204

8 Dimensionality Reduction — 206
    8.1 Introduction — 206
    8.2 Feature Selection — 207
    8.3 Principal Component Analysis — 214
    8.4 Linear Discriminant Analysis — 218
    8.5 Summary — 221
    Key Terms — 222
    Conceptual Questions — 222
    Hands-on Problems — 222
    Further Reading and Resources — 223

Part IV Neural Networks

9 Neural Networks — 227
    9.1 Mimicking the Human Brain — 227
        9.1.1 Basics of a Neural Network — 228
        9.1.2 Human vs. Artificial Neuron — 228
    9.2 Architectures of Basic Neural Networks — 229
        9.2.1 Feed-Forward Network — 231
        9.2.2 Perceptrons — 231
        9.2.3 Single-Layer Perceptron — 232
        9.2.4 Multilayer Perceptron — 235
    9.3 Autoencoders — 243
    9.4 Convolution Neural Network — 247
    9.5 Recurrent Neural Network — 251
    9.6 Long Short-Term Memory — 256
    9.7 Summary — 259
    Key Terms — 260
    Conceptual Questions — 260
    Hands-on Problems — 261
    Further Reading and Resources — 263

10 Deep Learning — 264
    10.1 Introduction — 264
    10.2 When and How to Use a Deep Model — 265
    10.3 Building Your First Deep Learning Model with Python — 266
    10.4 Building a Classifier with Deep Learning — 272
    10.5 Using Deep Models for Embeddings — 278
    10.6 Encoders and Transformers — 283
        10.6.1 Input Embeddings — 285
        10.6.2 Positional Encoding — 285
        10.6.3 Encoder Layer — 286
        10.6.4 Multi-headed Attention — 286
    10.7 Summary — 297

Key Terms		298
Conceptual Questions		298
Hands-on Problems		299
Further Reading and Resources		300

Part V Further Explorations

11 Reinforcement Learning — 303
- 11.1 Introduction — 303
- 11.2 Conceptualizing RL — 304
- 11.3 Doing RL by Hand — 306
- 11.4 Q-learning — 311
- 11.5 Bandits — 315
  - 11.5.1 Multi-arm Bandits — 316
  - 11.5.2 Contextual Bandits — 316
- 11.6 Summary — 322
- Key Terms — 323
- Conceptual Questions — 323
- Hands-on Problems — 323
- Further Reading and Resources — 324

12 Designing and Evaluating ML Systems — 326
- 12.1 Introduction — 326
- 12.2 Thinking through an ML Solution — 327
- 12.3 Evaluation — 331
  - 12.3.1 Offline Evaluation — 331
  - 12.3.2 User Research — 335
  - 12.3.3 A/B Testing — 337
  - 12.3.4 Counterfactual Evaluation — 340
  - 12.3.5 Adversarial Learning — 344
- 12.4 Summary — 344
- Key Terms — 345
- Conceptual Questions — 345
- Hands-on Problems — 346
- Further Reading and Resources — 347

13 Responsible AI — 348
- 13.1 Introduction — 348
- 13.2 Diversity vs. Misinformation: A Case Study — 349
- 13.3 Responsible AI in Academia, Industry, and Regulations — 352
- 13.4 Bias and Fairness — 353
  - 13.4.1 Where Does Bias Come From? — 353
  - 13.4.2 Bias Is Everywhere — 354
  - 13.4.3 Bias vs. Fairness — 355

13.5	Accountability and Auditing	356
13.6	Transparency and Explainability	358
13.7	Summary	361
	Key Terms	363
	Conceptual Questions	363
	Hands-on Problems	363
	Further Reading and Resources	364

Appendices 367
Index 405

Preface

Machine learning (ML) is everywhere. From the news that gets recommended in our feeds to diagnosing cancer, from which image to display on a movie poster for a user to forecasting storms. Because of this, there is high demand for people to fill ML-related jobs. This is not something new; ML has been in play for decades. So why is it that suddenly there is a lot more chatter about ML, coming from all sorts of people and places? I believe there are two primary reasons. First is technical advancement. There is a new availability of large-scale data, and of tools that can work on such large-scale data with striking effectiveness. Most ML algorithms, as you will see in this book, require data – often, a lot of it. Many of these algorithms do better with more data and more diverse data. But that's just one part of the equation. The others are computational power, and the tools and the techniques that can process that data to create insights. Since the beginning of the twenty-first century we have made amazing advancements in all of these areas. Not all techniques are new, but years ago they were limited in their applicability due to sparsity of data or lack of computational power. We have also developed new hardware components, programming tools, and rich software libraries that allow us to more effectively and efficiently implement ML solutions, making them more viable in a number of areas that were ignored before.

The second reason is more subtle, but much more potent. It is about the social acceptability of ML. When I was in grad school we worked on ML (and artificial intelligence in general) with a few specific applications in mind – speech, vision, robotics. We were fascinated by neural networks primarily as a way to try to hypothesize how a human brain worked. But now ML has made its way into every aspect of our lives, and, more importantly, we have all accepted that new reality. Why is this so important? Because that acceptance fuels more development and usage of ML, not just in traditional computer science fields, but in finance, healthcare, travel, business, education, and almost any field you can imagine. More acceptance and usage mean more data generated, and more data means better tuning of those ML algorithms. It is this cycle that has triggered unprecedented amounts of funding and efforts in this field. It is for this reason that ML is now being taught not only in computer science and engineering disciplines, but in all kinds of majors in colleges and graduate schools. And it is with this as a core principle that this book has emerged.

This book is not just for computer science majors, but also for those who want to understand ML and even build ML solutions for whatever they care about. It is organized in a way that provides a very easy entry point for almost anyone to become introduced to ML, but it also has enough fuel to take one from that beginning stage to a place where they feel comfortable applying learning algorithms to solve real-life problems. In addition to providing the basics of ML and intelligent systems, the book teaches standard tools and techniques for using them. It also examines the implications of the use of ML in areas such as privacy, ethics, and fairness. Finally, as the name suggests, this text is meant to provide a hands-on introduction to these topics. Almost everything presented in the book is accompanied by examples and exercises – sometimes done by hand and other times using the tools taught here. In teaching these topics myself, I have found this to be a very effective method.

The rest of this preface explains how the book is organized, how it could be used for fulfilling various teaching needs, and what specific requirements a student needs to meet to make the most out of it.

Requirements and Expectations

This book is intended for advanced undergraduates or graduate students in information science, computer science, business, education, psychology, sociology, and related fields who are interested in ML. It is not meant to provide an in-depth treatment of any programming language, tool, or platform. One of the strengths of this book is the very low barrier it provides for anyone to enter the realm of ML.

The book assumes no prior exposure to programming or technology. It does, however, expect the reader to be comfortable with computational thinking (see Chapter 1) and the basics of statistics (covered in Appendix A). The reader should also have general computer literacy, including the ability to download, install, and configure software, do file operations, and use online resources. Each chapter lists specific requirements and expectations, many of which can be met by going over some other parts of the book (usually an earlier chapter or an appendix).

Almost all the tools and software used in this book are free. There is no requirement for a specific operating system or computer architecture, but it is assumed that the reader has a relatively modern computer with reasonable storage, memory, and processing power. In addition, a reliable and preferably high-speed internet connection is required for several parts of this book.

Structure of the Book

The book is organized in five parts. Part I provides enough background and basics for anyone coming from non-technical fields so that they can get the most out of the rest of the book. It starts by providing a clear introduction to ML and various related concepts, along with computational thinking. Immediately after that, a chapter on Python is provided. Remember, this is not a programming book, so while this part introduces Python, it is not meant to provide a comprehensive treatment to any programming platforms. Instead, the focus here is on giving a quick introduction with lots of examples and hands-on practice, and then showing how various ML functions can be used with appropriate packages. It is useful to know that the rest of the book uses Python as the standard language for most of the examples and problem-solving, but many of those exercises will also have solutions in R in case an instructor wants that option while teaching ML. In addition to Python, this part also has a chapter on using cloud-based services for doing ML. This is becoming increasingly popular as it circumvents the need to buy one's own high-end hardware or worry about scalability of one's ML apps. The three popular platforms – Amazon Web Services (AWS), Google Cloud, and Microsoft Azure – will be introduced here.

Parts II and III are for two main branches of ML: supervised learning and unsupervised learning, respectively. Each of these parts could be its own course, as they cover many techniques for solving a large variety of problems. For each technique or algorithm, an intuitive explanation is given first, sometimes with a helpful math derivation, followed by a couple of hands-on exercises to see how it allows us to solve real-life problems. There are also plenty of exercises provided at the end of each of the chapters that could be useful for homework assignments or hands-on projects.

Part IV is about neural networks. My students often think this subject is something very new or advanced in ML/AI. And I often tell them that it was already pretty old and well established when I was a student. Here, we assume no background, and start from the beginning – all the way back in the 1950s with basic neural architectures. We talk about learning laws and discuss how they are appropriate for different kind of problems – supervised or unsupervised learning. Then we continue moving through the landscape of various models, all the way to the new ones in deep learning that keep making the headlines, including CNN, RNN, LSTM, and BERT. Once again, the idea here is not to worry about the theoretical depths of these models, but to focus on understanding the intuitions behind them and learn when and how to apply them, with lots of hands-on exercises.

Finally, we come to Part V, which introduces reinforcement learning. This branch of ML has always been very important, but in the past it was primarily used within robotics. In recent years, as we have encountered problems involving large amounts of data and not enough labels or annotations, reinforcement learning has found its way into many interesting and important problems. In this part we will also see how ML is used in research and development – both in academia and industry. We will also look at some of the ways ML systems are evaluated, including A/B testing. The last chapter is one of the most important ones – it shows where ML fails, not in the technical realm, but at a societal level, where it introduces and propagates biases and a lack of fairness and equity. These issues have become very important in recent years, and I strongly recommend anyone studying or teaching ML not to ignore them.

The book is full of extra material that either adds more value and knowledge to the ML theories and practices being covered, or provides a broader and deeper treatment of some of the topics. Throughout the book there are several FYI boxes that provide important and relevant information without interrupting the flow of the text, allowing the student to be aware of various issues related to ML and AI without being overwhelmed by them. There are also "ML in Practice" boxes at several places that provide insights from how ML techniques covered in the book are used in industry. These insights stem primarily from my own experiences working at and with various tech companies.

The appendices of this book provide quick reference to various formulas from differential calculus and probability, as well as helpful pointers and instructions for installing and configuring various tools used in the book. Another appendix provides a listing of various sources for obtaining datasets to further practice ML, or even to participate in ML challenges to win some cool prizes and recognition. There is also an appendix that provides helpful information related to ML jobs in various fields and what skills one should have to apply for those jobs.

The book also has an online appendix (OA), accessible through the book's website at www.cambridge.org/shah-ML, which is regularly updated to reflect any changes in data and other resources. The primary purpose for this OA is to provide you with the most current and up-to-date datasets or links to datasets that you can download and use in the dozens of examples and try-it-yourself exercises in the chapters, as well as data problems at the ends of the chapters. Look for the OA icon 🌐 which will inform you that you can find the needed resource in the OA. In the description of the exercise you will see the specific number (e.g., OA 4.7) that tells you where exactly you should go in the OA. In addition to the OA document, at this website you will also find code and datasets used in Hands-On Exercises, as well as an errata document that will list any corrections in the book after its printing.

Using This Book in Teaching

The book is deliberately organized around teaching ML to beginner computer science (CS) students or intermediate to advanced non-CS students. The book is modular, making it easier for students and teachers to cover topics at the desired depth. This makes the book suitable for use as a main reference book or textbook for an ML curriculum. The following is a suggested curriculum path in ML using this book. It contains six courses, each lasting a semester or a quarter:

- preparation for ML (beginner): Chapters 2 and 3, appropriate appendices;
- introduction to ML (beginner): Chapters 1 and 2, with some elements from Parts II and III as needed;
- ethical issues in ML (beginner): Chapters 1 and 13;
- neural networks (intermediate): Chapters 9 and 10; and
- ML at scale (advanced): Chapters 3 and 12.

This book's website contains a Resources tab with a section labeled "For Instructors." This section contains sample syllabi for various courses that could be taught using this book, PowerPoint slides for each chapter, and other useful resources such as sample midterms and final exams. These resources make it easier for someone teaching this course for the first time to adapt the text as needed for his or her own ML curriculum.

Each chapter also has several conceptual questions and hands-on problems. The conceptual questions could be used for in-class discussions, homework, or quizzes. For each new technique or problem covered in this book, there are at least two hands-on problems. One of these could be used in the class and the other could be given for homework or as an exam. Most hands-on exercises in chapters are also immediately followed by hands-on homework exercises that a student could try for further practice, or that an instructor could assign as homework or as an in-class practice assignment.

Strengths and Unique Features of This Book

Machine learning has a very visible presence these days, and it is not surprising that there are currently several books and much material related to the field available. *A Hands-On Introduction to Machine Learning* is different from the other books in several ways:

- It is targeted at students with very basic experience with technology. Students who fit within that category are those majoring in information science, business, psychology, sociology, education, health, cognitive science, and indeed any area in which ML can be applied. The study of ML should not be limited to those studying CS or statistics. This book is intended for a broader audience.
- The book starts by introducing the field of ML without any expectation of prior knowledge on the part of the reader. It then introduces the reader to some foundational ideas and techniques that are independent of technology. This does two things: (1) it provides an easier access point for a student without a strong technical background; and (2) it presents material that will continue to be relevant even when tools and technologies have changed.
- Based on my own teaching and curriculum development experiences, I have found that most ML books on the market can be divided into two categories: they are either too technical, making them suitable only for a limited audience; or they are structured to be simply informative, making it hard for the reader to actually use and apply data science tools and techniques. *A Hands-On Introduction to Machine Learning* is aimed at a nice middle ground. On one hand, it does not simply describe ML, but also teaches real hands-on tools (Python, cloud computing) and techniques (from basic regression to neural networks and deep learning). On the other hand, it does not require students to have a strong technical background to be able to learn and practice ML.
- *A Hands-On Introduction to Machine Learning* also examines the implications of the use of data in areas such as privacy, ethics, and fairness. For instance, it discusses how unbalanced data used without enough care with an ML technique could lead to biased (and often unfair) predictions.
- The book provides many examples of real-life applications, as well as practices ranging from small to big data. For instance, Chapter 1 has an example of working with movie recommendations, and this one is done by hand, without using any tools or programming. In Chapter 5 we see how multiple linear regression can be easily implemented using Python to learn how advertising spending on various media could influence sales. Chapter 6 includes an example that uses Python to analyze data about wines to predict which ones are of high quality. Chapters 8–11 on supervised and unsupervised learning have many real-life and general interest problems from different fields. Many of the examples can be worked by hand or with everyday software, without requiring specialized tools. This makes it easier for a student to grasp a concept without having to worry about programming structures, which allows the book to be used for non-majors as well as professional certificate courses.

- Each chapter has plenty of in-chapter exercises where I walk the reader through solving a data problem using a new technique, homework exercises to do more practice, and more hands-on problems (often using real-life data) at the ends of the chapters. There are 51 hands-on solved exercises, 50 try-it-yourself exercises, and 81 end-of-chapter problems.
- The book is supplemented by a generous set of material for instructors. These instructor resources include curriculum suggestions (even full-length syllabi for some courses), slides for each chapter, datasets, program scripts, answers and solutions to each exercise, and sample mid-term exams and final projects.

Acknowledgments

While this book lists only one author, it was a result of many years of collaboration with many people – some of them gave inspiration, some provided raw material, and others made critical corrections. It is nearly impossible to list them all, but I would be remiss if I didn't at least attempt to thank a few.

I want to start by acknowledging the profound impact on my education and life that my late father, Rajendrakumar Shah, had. He encouraged and supported me to pursue my dreams even when he didn't understand them. He is still guiding me through my life.

Writing a book is a very arduous and often lonely task. But I could always count on my dear wife, Lori, to help me through it. She wrangled and even managed to hide many of life's complexities that allowed me to focus on this project. Her unconditional support is perhaps more than what I deserve but was necessary to make this book possible. My smart and sweet daughters – Sophie, Zoe, and Sarah – were just as much instrumental in this support. At the beginning of this summer, my oldest daughter, Sophie, who had just turned 10, asked me about AI and ML. As I proceeded to talk to her with excitement, I realized how widespread these technologies have become in our society today that elementary school kids are talking and learning about them. Thanks, sweetheart, for continuing to inspire and challenge me.

I started my journey on the path of AI at the Indian Institute of Technology (IIT) – first in Bombay (Mumbai) and then in Madras (Chennai). I'm grateful to Prof. Pushpak Bhattacharyya (IITB) and Prof. B Yegnanarayana (IITM) for introducing me to the wonderful worlds of natural language processing and neural networks. Thanks to their tremendous patience and support, I continued my appreciation and exploration of these topics even after I left India.

A big reason I could embark on this book journey is that I'm an educator myself. The first drafts of almost everything in this book have come from my own teaching and advising. I have been fortunate enough to have access to some of the brightest and most curious minds in the world at major US universities, such as the University of Washington and Rutgers University. My colleagues and students from these places over the last many years have contributed substantively to my understanding of the material presented here; I have learned a lot by teaching. I would specifically call out Andrea Berg, Smart Chang, Yuzhen Qu, Daniel Saelid, and Bingbing Wen for their contributions to some of the writeups, problems, and solutions.

I have also had the opportunity to spend time at tech industry places such as Amazon, Getty Images, Microsoft, and Spotify. Through my work in applied science at these places, I learned a lot about making machine learning work in real-life applications. Some of those lessons have been poured into this book, especially with the "ML in Practice" boxes. I'm thankful for these opportunities and the wonderful collaborators I had at these places, who are too many to list.

I am very grateful to the wonderful staff of Cambridge University Press for guiding me through the development of this book from the beginning. I would first call out Lauren Cowles and Stefanie Seaton. Having worked with them before for my textbook on data science, I knew how wonderful and supportive they were and decided to work with them again. They certainly did not disappoint! Through many rounds of feedback and design decisions, they once again ensured that the book meets the highest standards of quality and accessibility that one would expect from the Press. I am also grateful to Madelyn Glymour, who painstakingly not only proofread the whole manuscript, but also corrected several technical errors.

Finally, I want to thank the University of Washington iSchool and the Whiteley Center at Friday Harbor for supporting two writing retreats in 2021–2022 that allowed me to do critical writing work on this book.

I am almost certain that I have forgotten many more people to thank here, but they should know that it was a result of my forgetfulness and not ungratefulness.

About the Author

Dr. Chirag Shah is Professor in the Information School (iSchool) at the University of Washington (UW) in Seattle. He is also Adjunct Professor with the Paul G. Allen School of Computer Science & Engineering as well as the Human Centered Design & Engineering (HCDE) department. Before UW, he was at Rutgers University. He received his Ph.D. in Information Science from the University of North Carolina (UNC) Chapel Hill, and MS in Computer Science from the University of Massachusetts (UMass) Amherst.

Dr. Shah's research involves creating smart systems for search and recommendation. Examples include intelligent assistants and task managers. He also focuses on making these systems bias-free. He applies techniques from data science and ML for most of this work. He has published several books and peer-reviewed articles in these areas. He developed the Coagmento system for collaborative and social searching, IRIS (Information Retrieval and Interaction System) for investigating and implementing interactive IR activities, as well as several systems for collecting and analyzing data from social media channels, including the award-winning ContextMiner, InfoExtractor, TubeKit, and SOCRATES systems. He is the Founding Co-Director of Responsibility in AI Systems & Experiences (RAISE) at UW, a center focused on research and education around issues of bias, fairness, accountability, transparency, and ethics in AI. He is also the Founder and Director of the InfoSeeking Lab, where he investigates issues related to information seeking, interactive information retrieval, and social media. These research projects are supported by grants from the National Science Foundation (NSF), National Institute of Health (NIH), Institute of Museum and Library Services (IMLS), Amazon, Google, and Yahoo!. He has also served as a consultant to the United Nations Data Analytics on various data science projects involving social and political issues, peacekeeping, climate change, and energy.

He spent his sabbatical in 2018 at Spotify, working on voice-based search and recommendation problems. In 2019, as an Amazon Scholar, he worked with Amazon's Personalization team on applications involving personalized and task-oriented recommendations.

In 2020 he was a Visiting Researcher at Microsoft Research (MSR) AI and worked on an intelligent task manager. In 2021 he visited Getty Images to work on improving their search platform with embedding-based deep semantic approaches.

Dr. Shah teaches undergraduate, masters, and Ph.D. programs at UW, focusing on data science and ML. He teaches both on campus and online. He has also created a course for Coursera (Social Media Data Analytics) and taught several tutorials and short courses at international venues. Dr. Shah has written several books, including the textbook *A Hands-On Introduction to Data Science*, published by Cambridge University Press.

PART I

BASIC CONCEPTS

This part is meant to provide enough background and basic information to anyone coming from non-technical fields that they can get the most out of the rest of the book. It starts by providing a clear introduction to machine learning (ML) and various related concepts, along with computational thinking. At this point, all of these are quite conceptual, but we still work through some hands-on examples. Of course, to further our investigation in ML, we need to pick up some tools. We start this by learning Python. If you have worked with Python before you can skip this chapter or just skim over it quickly. Next, there is a chapter on using cloud-based services for doing ML. This is becoming increasingly popular as it circumvents the need to buy one's own high-end hardware or worry about scalability of one's ML apps. The three popular platforms – Amazon Web Services (AWS), Google Cloud, and Microsoft Azure – are introduced here.

1 Teaching Computers to Write Programs

What do you need?
- A general understanding of computer and data systems.
- Familiarity with a few basic computer apps, such as spreadsheets.

What will you learn?
- Definitions and example applications of machine learning.
- Solving a small machine learning problem by hand.
- Computation thinking – a way to solve problems systematically.
- Introduction to tools, techniques, and skills for doing machine learning.

1.1 What Is Machine Learning?

Before we answer the question of what machine learning (ML) is, let's consider learning itself. The *New Oxford American Dictionary* (third edition) defines "to learn" as: "To get knowledge of something by study, experience, or being taught; to become aware by information or from observation; to commit to memory; to be informed of or to ascertain; to receive instruction."

All these meanings have limitations when they are associated with computers or machines. With the first two meanings, it is virtually impossible to test whether learning has been achieved or not. How can you check whether a machine has obtained knowledge of something? You probably cannot ask it questions, and even if you could, you would not be testing its ability to learn but its ability to answer questions. How can you tell whether it has become aware of something? The whole question of whether computers can be aware is a burning philosophical issue.

As for the last three meanings, although we can see what they denote in human terms, merely committing to memory and receiving instruction seems to fall short of what we mean by ML. These tasks are too passive, and we know that they are trivial for today's computers. Instead, we are interested in improving computer performance, or at least in the potential for improving performance, in new situations. You can commit something to memory or be informed of something by rote learning without being able to apply the new knowledge to new situations. In other words, you can receive instruction without benefiting from it at all. Therefore, it is important to come up with a new operational definition of learning in the context of the machine, which we can formulate as:

> Things learn when they change their behavior in a way that makes them perform better in the future.

This ties learning to performance rather than knowledge. You can test learning by observing present behavior and comparing it with past behavior. This is a more objective kind of definition and is more appropriate for our purposes. Therefore, we are going to focus on the concept of learning that is connected to a change in knowledge (objectively defined in some way) or performance in a task. This is important for us to understand and accept, not just for the sake of philosophical or definitional discussions, but in order to envision what ML could and should do.

Learning usually involves a change in the system or person that is supposed to be learning. This change, presumably, should be in a positive direction – whatever "positive" means in the given context. Think about learning to play a piano. It requires knowing some basic rules about piano and music, a few pointers about where to start and what to do, and a goal, or at least some metric for improvement. Using this framework you can be said to be learning a piano if you follow those rules (maybe inventing a few new ones along the way), and with repeated practice, improve your performance. Here, performance could be simply being able to play the "Happy Birthday" song without any help or hesitation; or it could be qualifying to play with the London Philharmonic. The point is – you are doing something and improving your performance. You are learning.

Can we use that same idea for computers? This is what Tom Mitchell, a renowned scholar and a leader in the field of ML provided as a definition for computer (or any automated system) learning: "A computer program is said to learn from experience E with respect to some class of tasks T and performance measure P if its performance at tasks in T, as measured by P, improves with experience E." Think about this for a minute. While this definition is for machines (computer programs), it equally applies to humans. In the example above, the task (T) is to play a piano. The experience (E) is repeated practice, and the performance (P) is improvement toward the goal of being able to play a song or qualify for a professional entourage. If you are improving in doing that task with more practice, you are learning. If not, then perhaps you should reconsider your choice in the hobby, the career, or the teacher.

Now we understand what learning is. The next question is *why should a computer learn?* Imagine what happens in a typical programmable system. There is usually an algorithm – a set of rules and instructions – that drives that system. Think about a traffic light at a major intersection. There is an underlying algorithm that controls how each of the light-sets behave for different lanes and directions. Perhaps it changes the timing for them at night or during rush hour. No matter what, these algorithms are all pre-programmed. One could do a traffic study over several weeks to see if that program is working optimally and adjust its parameters (e.g., time to stay on, frequency of changes) as needed. In this case, a deterministic program is changed using human learning. But what if that system, that program, could figure out the optimal traffic light pattern by itself? In other words, can we have it adjust its own parameters? Figure 1.1 shows a simple schematic

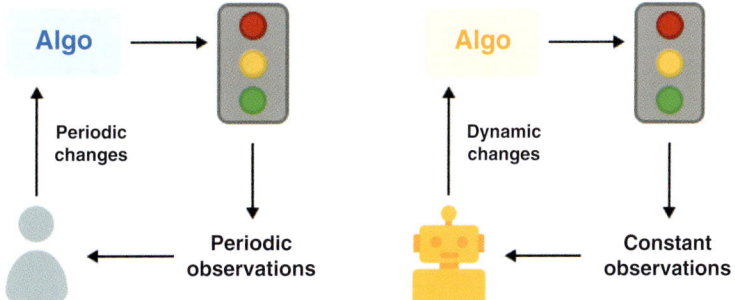

Figure 1.1 (Left) traditional (deterministic), human-operated changes to traffic light behavior; and (right) an ML-based approach to optimizing traffic light patterns.

difference between a traditional, deterministic program for traffic lights, and one where the program learns.

Hopefully you can see the difference between these two models. The first model (on the left) is costly as it involves human observations and could be less accurate since it may be prohibitive to patrol a team of humans for a very long time to observe every moment of every day and every season. The second model (on the right) may cost some extra hardware at first (e.g., cameras), but we can bypass costly observations and analysis by humans. Here, the ML-based agent or program is able to change the algorithm (and associated code) that drives the traffic light behavior.

In general, ML allows computational systems to write their own algorithms or tune the parameters for existing algorithms. According to Arthur Samuel (1959), an American pioneer in the field of artificial intelligence (AI), the goal of ML is to give "computers the ability to learn without being explicitly programmed."[1] Machine learning is a field of study that explores the use of algorithms that can learn from data and use that knowledge to make predictions on data they have not seen before. Such algorithms are designed to make data-driven predictions or decisions by building a model from sample inputs. While quite a few ML algorithms have been around for a long time, the ability to automatically apply complex mathematical calculations to big data in an efficient manner is a recent development. Following are a few widely publicized examples of ML applications you may be familiar with.

The first is the heavily hyped self-driving Google car (now rebranded as WAYMO). As shown in Figure 1.2, this car uses a real view of the road to recognize objects and patterns such as sky, road signs, and moving vehicles in a different lane. This process is quite complicated for a machine to do. A lot of things may look like a car (that blue blob in the bottom image is a car), and it may not be easy to identify where a street sign is. The self-driving car needs to not only do such object recognition, but also make decisions about navigation. There are so many unknowns involved here that it is impossible to come up with an algorithm for a car to execute. Instead, the car needs to know the rules for driving, have the ability to do object and pattern recognition, and apply these to making decisions in real time. In addition, it needs to keep improving. That is where ML comes into play.

Figure 1.2 Machine learning technology behind a self-driving car (source: YouTube: Deep Learning: Technology Behind Self-Driving Car[2]).

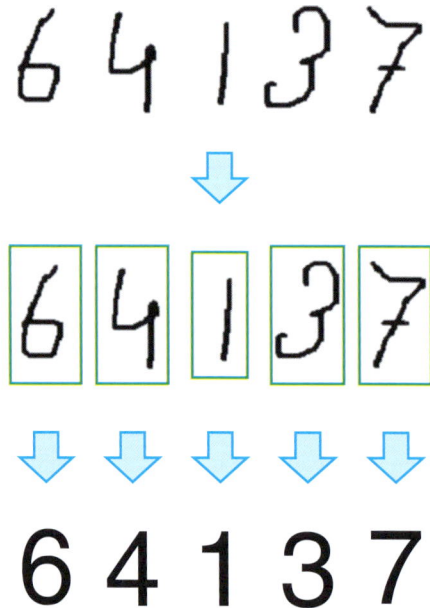

Figure 1.3 The problem of OCR.

Another classic example of ML is optical character recognition (OCR). Humans are good at recognizing handwritten characters, but computers are not. Why? Because there are too many variations in the way that any one character can be written, and there is no way we could teach a computer all those variations. There may also be noise – an unfinished character, a join with another character, some unrelated stuff in the background, uneven or disjoint lines or curves, etc. So, once again, what we need is to give the computer a basic set of rules that says what "A," "a," "5," etc., look like, and then have it make a decision based on pattern recognition. The way this happens is by showing many versions of a character to the computer so it *learns* that character, just like a child would through repetition, and then have it go through the recognition process (Figure 1.3).

This is an example of a classification problem. In such a problem, the objective is to learn how different patterns (here, handwritten characters) fall under one of the classes of interest (here, digits or characters). As a reference, classification falls under what is known as supervised learning. The self-driving car example we saw before represents unsupervised learning and reinforcement learning categories of ML. In the following section we will discuss these branches in more detail. Before that, let's work through a few examples for our hands-on practice.

Hands-on Example 1.1: Machine Learning by Hand

Let's take an example that is perhaps more relevant to everyday life. If you have used any online services, the chances are you have come across recommendations. Take, for instance, services such as Amazon and Netflix. How do they know what products to recommend? We understand that they are *monitoring* our activities, that they have our past records, and that is how they are able to give us suggestions. But how exactly? They use something called **collaborative filtering** (CF). This is a method that uses your past behavior and its similarities with the behaviors of other users in that community to figure out what you may like in the future.

Look at Table 1.1. There is data about four people's ratings for different movies. The objective for the system is to figure out if Person 5 will like a movie or not based on that data as well as her own movie ratings from the past. In other words, it is trying to *learn* what kinds of things Person 5 likes (and dislikes) based on what others similar to Person 5 like, and uses that *knowledge* to make new recommendations. On top of that, as Person 5 accepts or rejects its recommendations, the system extends its learning to include knowledge about how Person 5 responds to its suggestions, and further corrects its models.

Table 1.1 Machine learning-based CF for movie recommendations.

		Movie name				
		Sherlock Holmes	*Avengers*	*Titanic*	*La La Land*	*WALL-E*
Rating	Person 1	4	5	3	4	2
	Person 2	3	4	3	2	4
	Person 3	2	3	4	5	3
	Person 4	3	4	4	5	2
	Person 5	4	?	3	?	4

> Can we solve this by hand? Let's try. First off, what is your guess? Is there another person in this dataset that Person 5 is close to in terms of their movie tastes? We have data for only three movies for Person 5. They seem to like two of the movies (*Sherlock Holmes* and *WALL-E*), but not so much the third one (*Titanic*). Do we know anyone else with the same or similar taste? What about Person 2? It is not an exact match, but a close one. Based on that match, if we were to guess, we could recommend *Avengers* to Person 5, but not *La La Land*. Of course, in reality, things are not as straightforward, and we do not have to rely on a simple technique like the one we just used to figure out what to recommend. But I hope this simple exercise gave you a glimpse into how ML can work in real-life scenarios. What we just did is an example of applying a classification or clustering technique to a recommendation application. We will learn about classification in Chapters 5 and 6, clustering in Chapter 7, and practical recommendation systems in Chapter 12.

Movie recommendation is perhaps something we all encounter and can relate to as we can see those recommendations coming our way in an explicit manner, but there are many other applications where recommendations happen in subtle ways. For example, Facebook uses ML to personalize each member's news feed. Most financial institutions use ML algorithms to detect fraud. Intelligence agencies use ML to sift through mounds of information to look for credible threats of terrorism.

There are many other applications that we encounter in daily life that involve ML in one way or another. In fact, it is almost impossible to finish our day without having used something that is driven by ML. Did you do any online browsing or searching today? Did you go to a grocery store? Did you use a social media app on your phone? Then you have used ML applications.

Try It Yourself 1.1: Machine Learning by Hand

The recommendation example we tried above used CF, which uses data about similar people to make recommendations to a given person. But we can also use **content filtering**, which uses information about similar items to decide what to recommend. In Table 1.2 we have ratings for one person's movies and various characteristics of those movies. Based on this information, would you recommend *Avengers* to this person? Explain your process and reasoning.

Table 1.2 Machine learning-based filtering for movie recommendations.

			Characteristics		
		Rating	Year	Genre	Lead
Movies	*Sherlock Holmes*	4	2009	Action	Robert Downey, Jr.
	Avengers	?	2012	Action	Robert Downey, Jr.
	Titanic	3	1997	Drama	Leonardo DiCaprio
	La La Land	2	2016	Comedy	Ryan Gosling
	WALL-E	4	2008	Animation	Ben Burtt

In most cases the application of ML is entwined with the application of statistical analysis. Therefore, it is important to remember the differences in the nomenclature of these two fields:

- A variable in statistics is called a **feature** in ML.
- In statistics a target is called a dependent variable, whereas in ML it is called a **label**.
- A transformation in statistics is called **feature creation** in ML.

As we move through various chapters, especially Chapter 4, you will see more ML terminology used. If you are coming from a strong statistics background or even have taken an introductory level statistics class before, these differences are important to note to get you comfortable with ML. If you did not have a chance to learn basic statistics, or it has gotten a bit rusty, I strongly recommend you brush up on it before continuing, or refer to appropriate appendices in this book as needed.

1.2 Branches of Machine Learning

In the previous section we looked at different problems that we could solve using ML techniques. Now, let's look at these techniques within a systematic framework. Figure 1.4 shows the three main branches of ML: supervised, unsupervised, and reinforcement.

If we are trying to predict a value by learning (from data) how various predictors relate to the response variable, we are performing **supervised learning**. Within that branch, if the response variable is continuous, the problem is **regression**. Think about knowing someone's age and occupation and predicting their income. If, on the other hand, the response variable is **discrete** (having a few possible values or labels), this is a **classification** problem. For instance, using someone's age and occupation to learn whether they are a high-earner, medium-earner, or low-earner (three classes) is classification. We will cover regression in Chapter 4 and classification in Chapters 5 and 6.

Supervised learning problems require us to know the truth first. For example, in order to learn how age and occupation predict one's earning class, we need to know the true value

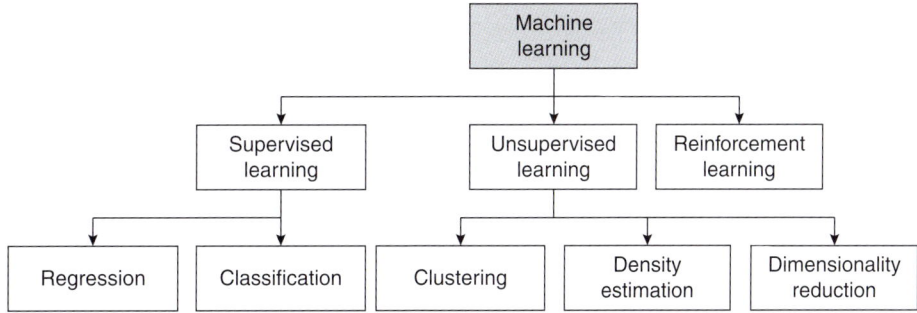

Figure 1.4 An outline of the core ML branches.

of someone's class – are they a high-earner, medium-earner, or low-earner? But there are times when the data given to us do not have clear labels or true values. And yet, we are tasked with exploring and explaining that data. In this case, we are dealing with an **unsupervised learning** problem. Within that, if we want to organize data into various groups, that is a **clustering** problem. Clustering is similar to classification, but unlike classification we do not know how many classes there are or what they are called. On the other hand, if we are trying to explain the data by estimating underlying processes that may be responsible for how the data is distributed, that is a **density estimation** problem. We will cover clustering and density estimation in Chapter 7.

There are times when the problem we are dealing with does not have labeled data (supervised learning), nor does it involve organizing the data or observations in some way (unsupervised learning). More specifically, there are situations where the given context or environment is so complex or dynamic that we have to learn on the go without having labels or clear boundaries. That brings us to the third branch of ML – **reinforcement learning**. This used to be exclusively popular in robotics, but has gotten a lot of attention in other kinds of ML applications due to its versatility and appeal in dynamically changing environments. For example, some of the best chess-playing programs in the world are built using reinforcement learning, and so are core components in self-driving cars. We will cover reinforcement learning in Chapter 11.

These branches will appear in the chapters on neural networks (Chapters 9 and 10) as well. A neural network model can be built for solving regression or classification (supervised learning) as well as clustering, density estimation, and dimensionality reduction (unsupervised learning). A neural network-based model can be combined with reinforcement learning processes to build a dynamic and adaptive intelligent system.

FYI: AI vs. ML

It is not uncommon to see many people and places using AI (artificial intelligence) and ML (machine learning) interchangeably. But it is important to understand that ML is typically understood to be a subset of AI. Of course, these days, ML techniques and applications have been so predominant and successful that they overwhelm the field of AI. Perhaps it may be better to think about what is in AI that is not in ML.

Areas of knowledge representation, constraint optimization, logical and probabilistic reasoning, and planning are examples of core AI that are typically outside of ML. Most expert systems and rule-based intelligent entities are also in AI, but are not considered to be in ML. In general, AI is about getting systems to perform tasks that typically require human cognition and decision-making abilities. A lot of this is being done using various ML techniques these days, but not all.

In the end, this difference may not matter much to most. Certainly, in this book, as our goal is to apply various techniques to solve problems, we would not be concerned about this. For the most part, we are focused on ML, but as we get more reflective and start contextualizing our work toward the end, we will reconnect with AI in the last chapter.

1.3 What Do You Need for Machine Learning?

Several things are required for a student to successfully learn and practice ML. One needs to, of course, be able to read, write, and think logically. But what are some of the specialized requirements? Here, we divide them up into two parts: skills and tools. In this book, we will cover both of those parts, but keep in mind that some skills are better covered in other parts of a curricula. For example, while we will cover some required math, especially statistics, it is expected that the reader has already received a comprehensive and formal education in statistics. Similarly, there are many tools for doing ML, but in this book we will cover only some of them – namely, Python and cloud computing. If you are interested in diving deeper into those tools or platforms you will have to find some other resources outside of this book. Some of these resources are listed at the end of the corresponding chapters.

1.3.1 Skills

Given that ML is about teaching computers to program themselves, one needs to know how to program in the first place. Programming is an essential skill for doing ML. But what else do you need? Historically, ML was almost exclusively taught in computer science (CS) programs. A lot of what is needed for ML is also already covered in any traditional statistics program. And this means, traditionally, the skills needed for ML were those that were typically found in CS and statistics programs.

Things have changed now. First, the entry barrier for ML has come down substantially. Before, one needed expensive hardware and sophisticated tools and programming skills to be able to develop ML solutions. That is no longer the case. Most ML techniques can be learned and practiced with nothing more than a modern laptop and online resources. There are existing libraries or packages that make building ML models as easy as writing your first "Hello, World!" program (see the next subsection). Lots of datasets are now available freely and easily for training and testing models. There are plenty of online forums and discussion groups where one can seek and receive help. ML is no longer reserved for the few and the privileged, nor should it be.

That brings us to the second point. Machine learning is not just about solving a few complex and sometimes abstract problems. Given how ML is integrated in our lives, solving ML problems and applying ML techniques goes way beyond traditional CS boundaries. In fact, as we will see in the section on ethics, bias, and privacy later in this chapter, and in the chapter on responsible AI (Chapter 13), we need people from different disciplines to join the ML revolution. We need people who can think not just with a computational lens, but also a social one. And while we are on that subject, I want to reiterate and remind you that this book is explicitly written with that premise in mind – lowering the barrier for ML entry and making ML accessible to a broad audience to engage them in the future of ML and AI.

With that vision in mind, let's talk some practicalities. What do you need to learn and practice ML these days? I can think of five categories of skills:

1. *Math*. Yes, you need at least some basics of mathematics – more specifically, statistics and probabilities. A lot of what ML builds on is statistics. In fact, a typical ML training starts with a refresher on statistics or simply starting with ML algorithms that are already found in statistics, such as regression. In this book I assume that you already have taken basic courses that cover statistics and probability theory, but if you need a refresher make sure to check out the appropriate appendices and recommended resources.
2. *Programming*. This is often an expectation that turns people from non-CS fields away from ML. But as I noted before, programming has gotten a lot easier and smarter than before. You may have seen elementary schools teaching coding, and I have seen kids able to code before they could even read or write very well. If you held back on doing ML because of worries about programming requirements, let me put your mind at ease. If you can think logically, you can program today. Even better, the programming language that we are going to use here and the one that is most used in ML and data science – Python – is extremely easy to learn and practice. The next chapter will introduce Python, with lots of exercises. Of course, just as with anything, you can get better with time and practice. So, while you will be able to pick up programming very quickly and easily for ML, you should keep practicing and improving.
3. *Computer and data literacy*. This one is not always obvious, but without it you will hit a lot of hurdles. Computer literacy involves knowing various computational tools and knowing when to use which ones. These tools include command line tools, programs and scripts, and cloud computing. We have devoted a whole chapter to cloud computing (Chapter 3). Data literacy involves understanding what data is appropriate in each situation or context, how to collect and store it, how to analyze it, and how to interpret and present the insights. Some of this requires technical skills, whereas the rest is about understanding contexts and communicating.
4. *ML algorithms*. Many of the techniques used for ML come straight from statistics, but there are also several distinct algorithms that are more squarely pegged in ML. These are broadly categorized, as we saw before, into supervised learning and unsupervised learning. We will explore both categories in this book, along with reinforcement learning.
5. *Critical thinking*. This is often a big part of our K–12 curriculum and tests for higher education (e.g., SAT, GRE). Simply put, critical thinking involves analyzing data, facts, and observations rationally, without bias, and with skepticism. According to Clarke (2019),[3] critical thinking is self-directed, self-disciplined, self-monitored, and self-corrective thinking. What does that mean for us? It means that when we are working with some data, it is our responsibility to question its validity and provenance. When we look at a problem or a situation, we need to ask a lot of "why" questions, in addition to the "what" and "how" questions. It is often easy to apply an ML technique to given data and get some results. But I have seen a lot of "garbage-in, garbage-out" with no thought to the appropriateness of the process. There is also a tendency to forcefully apply a given technique or tool to a problem without careful thinking just because of

one's high level of familiarity or comfort with it. Critical thinking asks us to rethink – not just about the solution or how we get there, but even about the problem or the question itself.

> **ML in Practice: What Do I Need to Get an ML Job?**
>
> If you have been watching tech news and reading job listings, you already know the importance of ML in various industries (not just software development). But if you lack foundational training in computer or information science or statistics, you may be wondering if you could ever get one of those jobs. Let me put your mind at ease – these days, those who do ML are coming from a lot more diverse backgrounds than ever before and we are only moving further in the direction of diversity. As you will see in the "skills" section of this chapter, not all skills expected from those doing ML are math or technical skills, and certainly none that you have to be "born with"! These skills can be learned; perhaps some may take more effort than others, but they are learnable. As I visit various tech companies and see their structures, projects, and, more importantly, employees, I am convinced even more that ML is not the privilege of a few STEM majors. I have seen excellent ML scientists coming from business, physics, and psychology majors and doing fantastic work.
>
> I am not promising that going through this book will get you an ML job, but if you are serious about a career in this field, this book should at least get you enough of the required skills and tools to build sufficient confidence and a resumé that can get you qualified for those jobs. The biggest objective this book has is to level the playing field. Don't forget to take a look at the last appendix in the book, where we review some of the career paths for ML.

1.3.2 Tools

In the previous subsection we discussed what kinds of skills one needs to have to be good at ML. We also know by now that a lot of what ML engineers/scientists do involves processing data and deriving insights. An example was given above, along with a hands-on practice problem. These things should at least give you an idea of what you may expect to do in ML. Going forward, it is important that you develop a solid foundation in statistical techniques (covered in the appendices) and computational thinking (covered in a later section of this chapter). Then you need to pick up a couple of programming and data processing tools. We will cover Python in the next chapter, and there is an appendix on R. But let's quickly review these here so we understand what to expect when we get to those chapters.

Let me start by noting that there are no special tools for doing ML; there just happen to be some tools that are more suitable for the kind of things one does in ML. And so, if you already know some programing language (e.g., C, Java, PHP) or a scientific data processing environment (e.g., MATLAB), you could use them to solve many or most of the problems and tasks in ML. Of course, if you go through this book you will also find that Python or R could generate a graph with one line of code – something that could take you a lot more effort in C or Java. In other words, while Python or R were not specifically designed for people to do ML, they provide excellent environments for quick implementation, visualization, and testing for most of what one would want to do in ML – at least at the level we are interested in for this book.

Python is a scripting language. That means the programs written in Python do not need to be compiled whole as you would do with a program in C or Java; instead, a Python program runs line by line. The language (its syntax and structure) also provides a very easy learning curve for beginners, while giving very powerful tools to advanced programmers.

Let's see this with an example. If you want to write the classic "Hello, World" program in Java, here is how it goes:

Step 1: Write the code and save as HelloWorld.java.

```
public class HelloWorld {
   public static void main(String[] args) {
      System.out.println("Hello, World");
   }
}
```

Step 2: Compile the code.

```
% javac HelloWorld.java
```

Step 3: Run the program.

```
% java HelloWorld
```

This should display "Hello, World" on the console. Do not worry if you have never done Java (or any) programming before and all this looks confusing. I hope you can at least see that printing a simple message on the screen is quite complicated (and we have not even done any data processing!).

In contrast, here is how you do the same in Python:

Step 1: Write the code and save as hello.py

```
print("Hello, World")
```

Step 2: Run the program.

```
% python hello.py
```

Again, do not worry about actually trying this now. We will cover detailed instructions in Chapter 2. For now, at least you can appreciate how easy it is to code in Python. And if you want to accomplish the same in R, you type the same – `print("Hello, World")` – in the R console.

Both Python and R are very easy to learn, and even if you have never done any programming before it is possible to start solving data problems from day 1 of using either. Both of them also offer plenty of packages that you can import to accomplish more complex tasks.

1.4 Computational Thinking

Many skills are considered "basic" for everyone. These include reading, writing, and thinking. It does not matter what profession or discipline one belongs to; one should have these abilities. In today's world, **computational thinking** is becoming an essential skill, not one reserved for computer scientists.

What is computational thinking? Typically, it means thinking like a computer scientist. But that is not a very helpful definition, even to computer scientists! According to Jeannette Wing (2006),[4] "Computational thinking is using abstraction and decomposition when attacking a large complex task or designing a large complex system." It is an iterative process based on the following three stages:

1. problem formulation (abstraction);
2. solution expression (automation); and
3. solution execution and evaluation (analyses).

The three stages and the relationships between them are schematically illustrated in Figure 1.5.

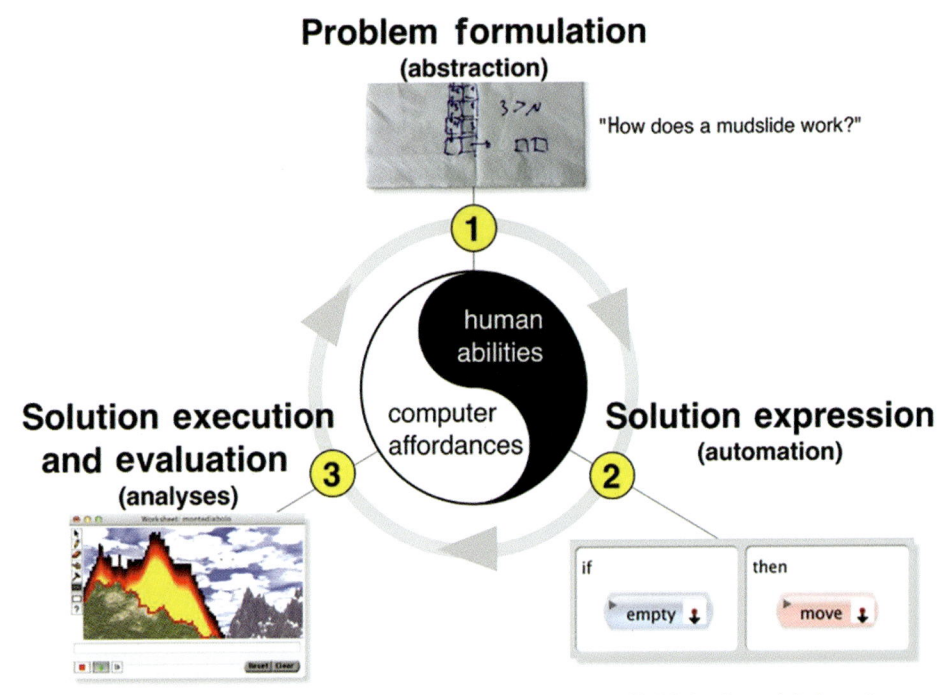

Figure 1.5 Three-stage process describing computational thinking. From Repenning, A., Basawapatna, A., & Escherle, N. (2016). Computational thinking tools. In *2016 IEEE Symposium on Visual Languages and Human-Centric Computing (VL/HCC)* (pp. 218–222).

Hands-on Example 1.2: Computational Thinking

Let's consider an example. We are given the following numbers and are tasked with finding the largest of them: 7, 24, 62, 11, 4, 39, 42, 5, 97, 54. Perhaps you can do it just by looking at it. But let's try doing it "systematically."

Rather than looking at all the numbers at the same time, let's look at two at a time. So, the first two numbers are 7 and 24. Pick the largest of them, which is 24. Now we take that and look at the next number. It is 62. Is it larger than 24? Yes, which means, as of now, 62 is our largest number. The next number is 11. Is it larger than the largest number we know so far (i.e., 62)? No. So we move on. If you continue this process until you have seen all the remaining numbers, you will end up with 97 as the largest. And that is our answer.

What did we just do? We broke down a complex problem (looking through 10 numbers) into a set of small problems (comparing two numbers at a time). This process is called *decomposition*, which refers to identifying small steps to solve a large problem.

More than that, we derived a process that could be applied to not just 10 numbers (which is not that complex), but to 100 numbers, 1000 numbers, or one billion numbers! This is called *abstraction* and *generalization*. Here, *abstraction* refers to treating the actual object of interest (10 numbers) as a series of numbers, and *generalization* refers to being able to devise a process that is applicable to the abstracted quantity (a series of numbers) and not just the specific objects (the given 10 numbers).

And there you have an example of computational thinking. We approached a problem to find a solution using a systematic process that can be expressed using clear, feasible computational steps. And that is all. You do not need to know any programming language to do this. Sure, you could write a computer program to carry out this process (an algorithm). But here, our focus is on the thinking behind this.

Let's take one more step with the previous example. Assume you are interested not just in the largest number, but also the second largest, third largest, and so on. One way to do this is to sort the numbers in some (increasing or decreasing) order. It looks easy when you have such a small set of numbers. But imagine you have a huge, unsorted shelf of books that you want to alphabetize. Not only is this a tougher problem than the previous one, but it becomes increasingly challenging as the number of items increases. So, let's step back and try to think of a systematic approach.

A natural way to solve the problem would be just to scan the shelf and look for out-of-order pairs – for instance Rowling, J.K. followed by Lee, Stan – and flipping them around. Flip out-of-order pairs, then continue your scan of the rest of the shelf, and start again at the beginning of the shelf each time you reach the end until you make a complete pass without finding a single out-of-order pair on the entire shelf. That will get your job done. But depending on the size of your collection and how unordered the books are at the beginning of the process it will take a lot of time. It is not a very efficient tactic. If you are curious, this approach is characterized as the bubble sort algorithm.[5]

Here is an alternative approach. Let's pick any author at random, say Lee, Stan, and reorder the shelf so that all the books that are earlier (letters to the left of "L" in the dictionary, A–K) than Lee, Stan are on the left side of it, and the later ones (M–Z) are on the right. At the end of this step, the Lee, Stan book is in its final position, probably near the middle. Next you perform the same steps to the sub-shelf of the books on the left and separately to the sub-shelf of books on the right. Continue this effort until every book is in its final position, and thus the shelf is sorted.

Now you might be wondering, what is the easiest way to sort the sub-shelves? Let's take the same set of numbers from the last example and see how it works. Assume that you have picked the first number, 7. So, you want all the numbers that are smaller than 7 on the left-hand side of it and the larger ones on the right. You can start by assuming 7 is the lowest number in the queue and therefore its final position will be first, which is its current position. Now you compare the rest of the numbers with 7 and adjust its position accordingly. Let's start at the beginning. Of the remaining numbers, 24 is at the beginning; 24 is larger than 7. Therefore, the tentative position of 7 remains at the beginning. Next is 62, which is, again, larger than 7; therefore, no change in the tentative position of 7. And the same for the next number, 11. Next, the comparison is between 4 and 7. Unlike the previous three numbers, 4 is smaller than 7. Here, your assumption of 7 as the smallest number in the queue is rendered incorrect, so you need to adjust your assumption of 7 from smallest to second smallest.

Here is how to perform the adjustment. First, you have to switch the place of 4 and the number in second position, 24. As a result the queue becomes 7, 4, 62, 11, 24, 39, 42, 5, 54, 97. And the tentative position of 7 has shifted to the second position, right after 4, making the queue 4, 7, 62, 11, 24, 39, 42, 5, 54, 97.

Now you might be thinking, why not swap between 7 and 4 instead of 24 and 4? The reason is that you started with the assumption that 7 is the smallest number in the queue. And so far during comparisons you have found just one violation of the assumption (i.e., 4). Therefore, it is logical that at the end of the current comparison you will adjust your assumption to 7 as the second smallest element and 4 as the smallest one, which is reflected by the current queue.

Moving on with comparisons, the next numbers in the queue are 39 and 42, both of which are larger than 7, and thus there is no change in our assumption. The next number is 5, which is, again, smaller than 7. So you follow the same procedure as you did with 4. Swap the third element of the queue with 5 to readjust your assumption as 7 is the third smallest element in the queue and continue the process until you reach the end of the queue. At the end of this step, your queue is transformed into 4, 5, 7, 11, 24, 39, 42, 62, 54, 97, and the initial assumption has evolved, as now 7 is the third smallest number in the queue. So now 7 has been placed in its final position. Notice that all the elements to the left of 7 (4, 5) are smaller than 7, and all the elements to the right are larger.

If you now perform the same set of previous steps with the numbers on the left and separately with the numbers on the right, every number will fall into the right place, and you will have a perfectly ordered list of ascending numbers.

Once again, a nice characteristic that all these approaches share is that the process for finding a solution is clear, systematic, and repeatable, regardless of the size of the input (number of numbers or books). That is what makes it computationally feasible.

Now that you have seen these examples, try finding more problems around you and see if you can practice your computational thinking by devising solutions in this manner. Below are some possibilities to get you started.

> **Try It Yourself 1.2: Computational Thinking**
>
> For each of the following problem-solving situations, explain how you apply computational thinking – that is, how you abstract the situation, break the complex problem into small sub-problems, and bring together sub-solutions to solve the problem.
>
> 1. Find a one-hour slot in your schedule when the preceding or following event does not take place at home.
> 2. Visit five different places while you are running errands with the least amount of travel time and not crossing any road, sidewalk, or location more than once.
> 3. Strategize your meetings with potential employers at a job fair so that you can optimize (meet as many people as possible) connecting with both high-profile companies (long lines) and startups (short lines).

1.5 Issues of Ethics, Bias, and Privacy in Machine Learning

This chapter (and this book) may give the impression that ML is all good, that it is the ultimate path to solve all of society's and the world's problems. I hope you do not buy such exaggerations. Even at its best, ML, and in general anything that deals with data or employs data analysis using a statistical-computation technique, bears several issues that should concern us all – as users or producers of data, or as data and ML scientists. Each of these issues is big enough and serious enough to warrant its own separate book (and such books exist), but lengthy discussions will be beyond the scope of this book. Instead, we will briefly mention these issues here and call them out at different places throughout this book when appropriate. In addition, we have a whole chapter devoted to these issues (Chapter 13), which talks about issues of bias, fairness, transparency, accountability, privacy, and ethics under the larger umbrella of "responsible AI."

A lot of what ML systems build on is data. But what if the data is flawed in some way? How will that affect the ML system built using such data? Many ML scientists fail to ask that question. In fact, many of the issues related to privacy, bias, and ethics can be traced back to the origin of the data. Ask how, where, and why the data was collected. Who collected it? What did they intend to use it for? More important, if the data was collected from people, did these people know (1) that such data was being collected about them, and (2) how the data would be used? Often those collecting data mistake availability of data for the right to use that data. And then there are inherent biases found in the data. For instance, most facial recognition systems are trained on datasets that contain predominantly White people. This makes it difficult for a system trained on that data to do well on non-White faces.

Such limitations with regard to racial disparity in ML systems have real-life consequences. For example, Larson, Mattu, Kirchner, and Angwin (2016)[6] found when studying a system used by law enforcement authorities in the USA that Black defendants were far more likely than White defendants to be incorrectly judged to be at a higher risk of recidivism, while White defendants were more likely than Black defendants to be incorrectly flagged as low risk. This was due to the dataset that was used for training the system containing biased information about Black people.

There are many cases throughout our digital life history where data about users has been intentionally or unintentionally exposed or shared, causing various levels of harm to the users. And this is just the tip of the iceberg in terms of ethical or privacy violations.

Many data and technology companies are trying to address these issues, as we will see in Chapter 13, often with very little to no success. But it is admirable that they are trying. And while we also cannot be successful at fending off all biases and prejudices or being completely fair, we need to try. So, as we proceed in this book with data collection and analysis methods, keep these issues at the back of your mind. And wherever appropriate, I will present some pointers in FYI boxes like the one below.

> **FYI: Fairness in ML**
>
> Understanding the gravity of ethics in practicing ML, Google, a company that has thrived during the last two decades guided by ML, recently acknowledged the biases in traditional ML approaches in one of its blog posts. You can read more about this announcement here: https://developers.google.com/machine-learning/fairness-overview/.
>
> In this regard, computational social science has a long way to go to adequately deal with ordinary human biases. Just as with the field of genomics, to which computational social science has often been compared, it may well take a generation or two before researchers combine high-level competence in data science with equivalent expertise in anthropology, sociology, political science, and other social science disciplines.
>
> There is a community, called Fairness, Accountability, and Transparency (FAT, or now called FAccT), that has emerged in recent years that is trying to address some of these issues, or at least to shed light on them. This community, thankfully, has scholars from the fields of data science, ML, AI, education, information science, and several branches of the social sciences.
>
> This is a very important topic in ML, so we will continue discussions throughout this book at appropriate places with FYI boxes like this.

1.6 Summary

Machine learning is a subset of AI. As we saw in this chapter, before we dive into understanding and building ML systems, it is important that we understand what *learning* is and what makes a system *intelligent* if that is what we are after. I often see people being careless about the terminology and generously calling many systems AI systems when all they do is some pre-defined, deterministic computational operations. While that may not harm anyone, it is important for us to understand what earns a system the "ML" or "AI" title. That is because as we study different algorithms and techniques in this book, we will be mindful about how and what they are learning. This will be useful in not only building those ML systems, but also being aware of certain ethical issues with them.

Learning involves change, typically in a positive direction. What that means is that with more learning (change), we should get better at performing the given task we are supposedly learning. This applies to humans as well as machines. With this in mind, we can turn our attention to the categories of learning.

Machine learning algorithms are organized into a taxonomy, based on the desired outcome of the algorithm. Common algorithm types include the following:

- **Supervised learning**: when we know the labels on the training examples we are using to learn.
- **Unsupervised learning**: when we do not know the labels (or even the number of labels or classes) from the training examples we are using for learning.
- **Reinforcement learning**: when we want to provide feedback to the system based on how it performs with training examples.

We will cover supervised learning in Part II of the book and unsupervised learning in Part III. These are the two main branches of ML. Part IV, which is devoted to neural networks, will touch on both of these branches. We will cover reinforcement learning in Chapter 11.

Key Terms

- **Artificial intelligence (AI)** is a field of research and development that aims to build computational systems that could perform tasks that normally require human intelligence, such as visual perception, speech recognition, decision-making, and language translation.
- **Machine learning (ML)** is a subfield of AI that focuses on building systems that are able to learn and adapt, using statistical methods, without being explicitly programmed.
- **Supervised learning**: A class of algorithms that use a set of examples from previous records that are labeled to make predictions about the future.
- **Unsupervised learning**: A problem where the outcomes of test cases are based on the analysis of training samples for which explicit class labels are absent.
- **Reinforcement learning**: A class of ML problems where a system takes feedback for various actions performed and learns or makes a decision for subsequent actions based on optimizing some reward.

Conceptual Questions

1. What is ML? Give two examples of systems you see in everyday life that use ML and two systems that do not.

2. What are the two primary branches of ML? How do they differ?

3. What is computational thinking? Give an example of how computational thinking is applied to solve a problem.

4. While ML has made a lot of things possible and better, it has also created new problems. List two such problems and give a couple of lines of description for each.

5. For each of the following problem-solving situations, explain how you apply computational thinking. Your response to each problem should be about two paragraphs and should clearly identify the three stages of computational thinking. Overall, the submission should be no more than two pages in length.

   a. You want to color the days on your calendar using the three primary colors (red, green, blue), such that no subsequent days have the same color within a month. Once the month changes, you can restart coloring. For example, January 29, 30, and 31 may be colored green, red, and blue. It is okay for February 1 to also be blue. Assuming you start your pattern with red, how many red, green, and blue colors will you have used in a year? Think about leap year and non-leap year configurations as well.

   b. In the US coin system there are pennies (1 cent), nickels (5 cents), dimes (10 cents), and quarters (25 cents). How many ways can you break a dollar (100 cents) using different combinations of these coins?

Hands-on Problems

Problem 1.1

In Table 1.3, heights for 12 different groups of people and their average weights are provided. Using this data, what would be your guesses for weight for those who are 60 inches and 73 inches tall? How about someone who measures 65.5 or 68.5 inches?

Describe your process for making these guesses or deriving the weights for these people for whom we do not have the data. Can you relate this to the idea of regression that we talked about in this chapter?

Problem 1.2

Imagine you see yourself as the next Harland Sanders (the founder of KFC) and want to learn about the poultry business at a much earlier age than Mr. Sanders did. You want to figure out what kind of feed can help grow healthier chickens. Table 1.4 presents a dataset that might help. The dataset is sourced from OA 1.1.

Based on this dataset, which type of chicken feed appears the most beneficial for a thriving poultry business? For this exercise, let's assume that the bigger the chicken (in weight), the better.

Table 1.3 Height–weight chart for Problem 1.1.

Height (inches)	Weight (lb.)
61	122
62	124
63	125
64	132
65	145
66	151
67	157
68	165
69	172
70	176
71	178
72	180

Table 1.4 Weight–feed chart for Problem 1.2.

#	Weight (lb.)	Feed
1	179	Horsebean
2	160	Horsebean
3	136	Horsebean
4	227	Horsebean
5	217	Horsebean
6	168	Horsebean
7	108	Horsebean
8	124	Horsebean
9	143	Horsebean
10	140	Horsebean
11	309	Linseed
12	229	Linseed
13	181	Linseed
14	141	Linseed
15	260	Linseed
16	203	Linseed
17	148	Linseed
18	169	Linseed
19	213	Linseed
20	257	Linseed
21	244	Linseed
22	271	Linseed
23	243	Soybean
24	230	Soybean
25	248	Soybean
26	327	Soybean
27	329	Soybean

Table 1.4 (cont.)

#	Weight (lb.)	Feed
28	250	Soybean
29	193	Soybean
30	271	Soybean
31	316	Soybean
32	267	Soybean
33	199	Soybean
34	171	Soybean
35	158	Soybean
36	248	Soybean
37	423	Sunflower
38	340	Sunflower
39	392	Sunflower
40	339	Sunflower
41	341	Sunflower
42	226	Sunflower
43	320	Sunflower
44	295	Sunflower
45	334	Sunflower
46	322	Sunflower
47	297	Sunflower
48	318	Sunflower
49	325	Meatmeal
50	257	Meatmeal
51	303	Meatmeal
52	315	Meatmeal
53	380	Meatmeal
54	153	Meatmeal
55	263	Meatmeal
56	242	Meatmeal
57	206	Meatmeal
58	344	Meatmeal
59	258	Meatmeal
60	368	Casein
61	390	Casein
62	379	Casein
63	260	Casein
64	404	Casein
65	318	Casein
66	352	Casein
67	359	Casein
68	216	Casein
69	222	Casein
70	283	Casein
71	332	Casein

Table 1.5 Auto-insurance ratings for Problem 1.3.

#	Insurance provider	Rating (out of 10)
1	GEICO	4.7
2	GEICO	8.3
3	GEICO	9.2
4	Progressive	7.4
5	Progressive	6.7
6	Progressive	8.9
7	USAA	3.8
8	USAA	6.3
9	USAA	8.1

Table 1.6 Movie-review dataset for Problem 1.4.

Lead actor	Movie name	IMDB rating (out of 10)
Irfan Khan	*Knock Out*	6.0
Irfan Khan	*New York*	6.8
Irfan Khan	*Life in a... Metro*	7.4
Anupam Kher	*Striker*	7.1
Anupam Kher	*Dirty Politics*	2.6
Anil Kapoor	*Calcutta Mail*	6.0
Anil Kapoor	*Race*	6.6

Problem 1.3

Table 1.5 presents an imaginary dataset of auto-insurance providers and their ratings as provided by the last three customers. If you had to choose an auto-insurance provider based on these ratings, which one would you opt for? Why?

Problem 1.4

Imagine you have grown to like Bollywood movies recently and started following some of the well-known actors from the Hindi film industry. You want to predict which of these actors' movies you should watch when a new one is released. Table 1.6 is a movie-review dataset from the past that might help. It consists of three attributes: movie name, leading actor in the movie, and its IMDB rating. Assume that a better rating means a more watchable movie.

Further Reading and Resources

- https://docs.microsoft.com/en-us/learn/modules/introduction-to-machine-learning/.
- www.digitalocean.com/community/tutorials/an-introduction-to-machine-learning.
- www.geeksforgeeks.org/introduction-machine-learning/.

There are several books for beginner ML students. Some are more theory-focused and some are more practice-focused. The following are some that are worth exploring.

Abu-Mostafa, Y. S., Magdon-Ismail, M., & Lin, H. T. (2012). *Learning from data*. AML-Book.

Alpaydin, E. (2020). *Introduction to machine learning*. MIT Press.

Barber, D. (2012). *Bayesian reasoning and machine learning*. Cambridge University Press.

Bishop, C. M., & Nasrabadi, N. M. (2006). *Pattern recognition and machine learning*. Springer.

Boehmke, B., & Greenwell, B. (2019). *Hands-on machine learning with R*. Chapman & Hall/CRC.

Deisenroth, M. P., Faisal, A. A., & Ong, C. S. (2020). *Mathematics for machine learning*. Cambridge University Press.

Flach, P. (2012). *Machine learning: the art and science of algorithms that make sense of data*. Cambridge University Press.

Gareth, J., Daniela, W., Trevor, H., & Robert, T. (2013). *An introduction to statistical learning: with applications in R*. Springer.

Géron, A. (2019). *Hands-on machine learning with Scikit-Learn, Keras, and TensorFlow: Concepts, tools, and techniques to build intelligent systems*. O'Reilly Media.

Kelleher, J. D., MacNamee, B., & D'arcy, A. (2020). *Fundamentals of machine learning for predictive data analytics: algorithms, worked examples, and case studies*. MIT Press.

Watt, J., Borhani, R., & Katsaggelos, A. K. (2020). *Machine learning refined: foundations, algorithms, and applications*. Cambridge University Press.

Notes

1. Samuel, A. L. (1967). Some studies in machine learning using the game of checkers. II: Recent progress. *IBM Journal of Research and Development*, *11*(6), 601–617.
2. YouTube (2015). Technology behind the self-driving car. www.youtube.com/watch?v=kMMbW96nMW8.
3. Clarke, J. (2019). *Critical dialogues: thinking together in turbulent times*. Policy Press, p. 6.
4. Wing, J. M. (2006). Computational thinking. *Communications of the ACM*, *49*(3), 33–35.
5. Upadhyay, S. (2022). Bubble sort algorithm: overview, time complexity, pseudocode and applications. www.simplilearn.com/tutorials/data-structure-tutorial/bubble-sort-algorithm.
6. Larson, J., Mattu, S., Kirchner, L., and Angwin, J. (2016). How we analyzed the COMPAS recidivism algorithm. www.propublica.org/article/how-we-analyzed-the-compas-recidivism-algorithm.

2   Python

> **What do you need?**
> - Computational thinking (refer to Chapter 1).
> - The ability to install and configure software.
> - Knowledge of basic statistics, including correlation and regression.
> - Ideally, prior exposure to any programming language.
>
> **What will you learn?**
> - Basic programming skills with Python.
> - Using Python to do statistical analysis, including producing models and visualizations.
> - Loading data in Python dataframes and doing basic analyses.

2.1   Introduction

Python is a simple-to-use yet powerful scripting language that allows one to solve data problems of varying scale and complexity. It is also the most used tool in machine learning (ML) and most frequently listed requirement in ML job postings. Python is a very friendly and easy-to-learn language, making it ideal for beginners. At the same time, it is very powerful and extensible, making it suitable for advanced ML needs.

This chapter starts with an introduction to Python and then dives into using the language for addressing various data problems using statistical processing and ML.

2.2   Getting Access to Python

One of the appeals of Python is that it is available for almost every platform you can imagine, and it is free. In fact, in many cases – such as on a UNIX or Linux machine – it is likely to be already installed for you. If not, it is very easy to obtain and install.

2.2.1   Download and Install Python

For the purpose of this book, I will assume that you have access to Python. Not sure where it is? Try logging on to the server (using SSH) and run the command `python -version` at the terminal. This should print the version of Python installed on the server.

It is also possible that you have Python installed on your machine. If you are on a Mac or using Linux, open a terminal or a console and run the same command to see if you have Python installed, and if you do, what version.

Finally, you can install an appropriate version of Python for your system by downloading it directly from the Python website (www.python.org/downloads) and following the installation and configuration instructions. See Appendix D for more detail.

2.2.2 Running Python through the Console

Assuming you have access to Python – either on your own machine or on the server – let us now try something. In the console, first enter `python` to enter the Python environment. You should see a message and a prompt like this:

```
Python 3.7.4 (default, Aug 13 2019, 15:17:50)
[Clang 4.0.1 (tags/RELEASE_401/final)] :: Anaconda, Inc. on darwin
Type "help", "copyright", "credits" or "license" for more information.
>>>
```

At this prompt (the three "greater than" signs), write `print ("Hello, World!")` and hit enter. If things go right, you should see "Hello, World!" printed on the screen:

```
>>> print ("Hello, World!")
Hello, World!
```

Let us now try a simple expression: Type `2+2`. You see 4? Great!

Finally, let us exit this prompt by entering `exit()`. If it is more convenient, you could also use Ctrl + d to exit the Python prompt.

2.2.3 Using Python through an Integrated Development Environment

While running Python commands and small scripts using the console is fine, there are times when you need something more sophisticated. That is when an **integrated development environment (IDE)** comes in. An IDE lets you not only write and run programs, but can also provide help and documentation, as well as tools to debug, test, and deploy your programs – *all in one place* (thus, "integrated").

There are several decent options for Python IDE, including using a Python plug-in for a general-purpose IDE such as Eclipse. If you are familiar with and invested in Eclipse, you might get the PyDev Python plug-in for it and continue using Eclipse for your Python programming.[1]

If you want to try something new, then look up Anaconda, Spyder, and Jupyter (more in Appendix D). Most beginners waste a lot of time trying to install and configure packages needed for running various Python programs. To make your life easier, I recommend using Anaconda as the platform and Spyder on top of it.

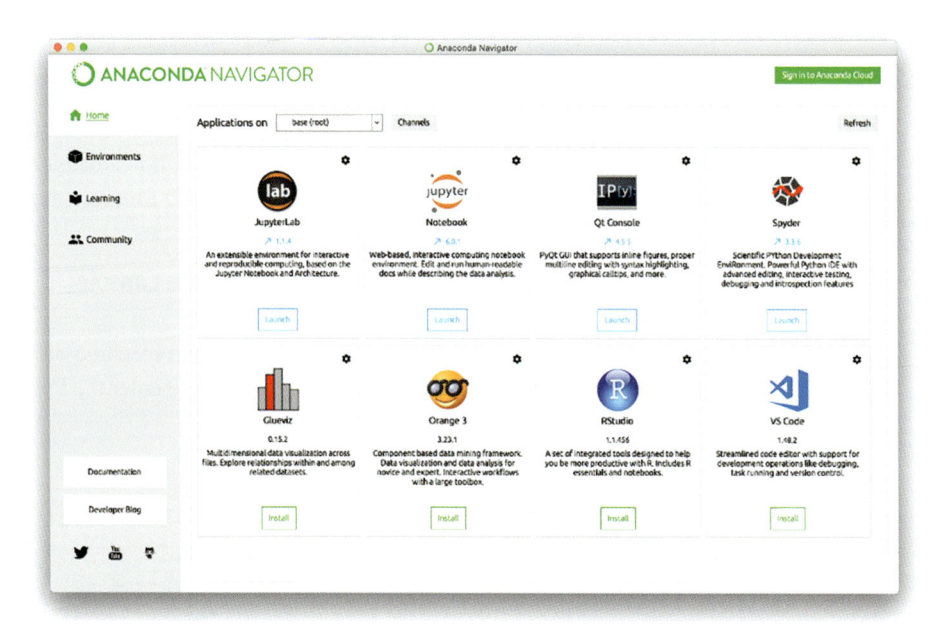

Figure 2.1 A screenshot of Anaconda Navigator.

There are three parts to getting going. The good news is that you will have to do this only once. First, make sure you have Python installed on your machine. Download and install an appropriate version for your operating system from the Python link above. Next, download and install Anaconda Navigator.[2] Once ready, go ahead and launch it. You will see something like Figure 2.1. Here, find the panel for "Spyder." In the screenshot you can see a "Launch" button because I already have Spyder installed. For you, it may show "Install." Go ahead and install Spyder through Anaconda Navigator.

Once installed, the "Install" button in the Spyder panel should become "Launch." Go ahead and launch Spyder. Figure 2.2 shows how it may look – it will probably not have all the stuff that I have showing here, but you should see three distinct panes: one occupying the left half of the window and two on the right-hand side. The left panel is where you will type your code. The top-right panel, at the bottom has the Variable Explorer, File Exploration, and Help. The bottom-right panel is where you will see the output of your code.

That is all for now in terms of setting things up. If you have made it thus far, you are ready to do *real* Python programming. The nice thing is that whenever we need extra packages or libraries for our work, we can go to Anaconda Navigator and install them through its nice IDE rather than fiddling with command line utilities (many of my students have reported wasting hours doing that).

Rather than doing any programming theory, we will learn basic Python using hands-on examples.

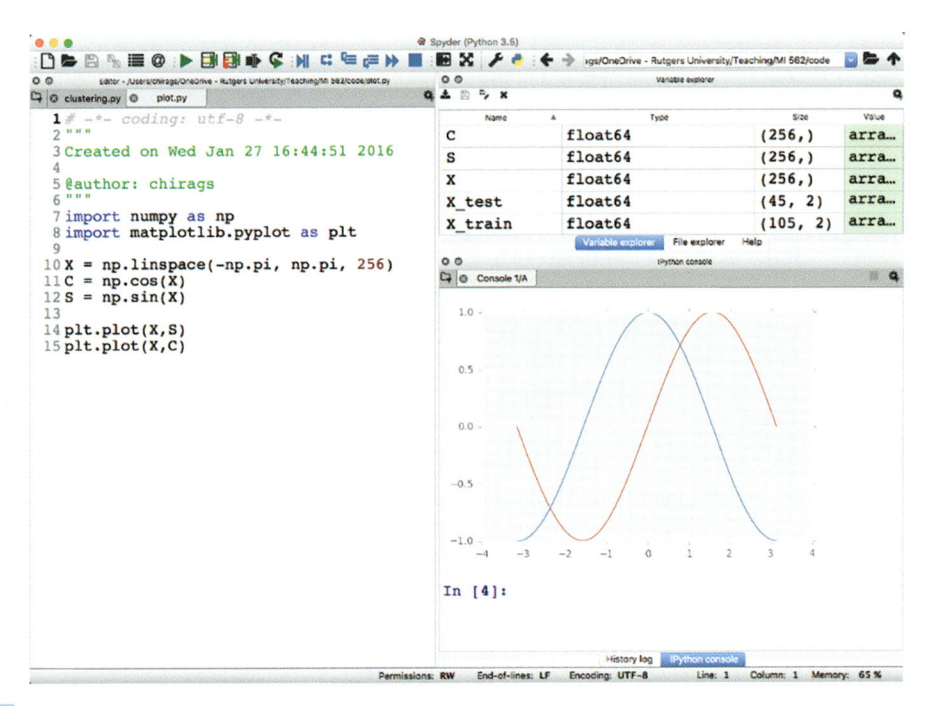

Figure 2.2 A screenshot of Spyder IDE.

2.3 Basic Examples

In this section we will practice with a few basic elements of Python. If you have done any programming before, especially if it involved scripting, this should be easy to understand.

The following screenshots are generated from a Jupyter notebook. Refer to Appendix D if you want to learn more about this tool. Here, "In" lines show you what you enter, and "Out" lines show what you get in return. But it does not matter where you are typing your Python code – directly at the Python console, in the Spyder console, or in some other Python tool – you should see the same outputs.

In the earlier section we began with a couple of commands that we tried when we first started up Python. Then, we did variable assignments. Entering x = 2 defines variable x and assigns the value 2 to it. In many traditional programming languages, doing this much could take two or three steps as you have to declare what kind of variable you want to define (in this case, an integer – one that can hold whole numbers) before you can use it to assign values. Python makes it much simpler: Most of the time you do not have to worry about declaring **data types** for a variable.

After assigning values to the variables x and y, we performed a mathematical operation when we entered z = x + y. But we do not see the outcome of that operation until we enter z. This should convey one more thing to you – generally speaking, when you want to know the value stored in a variable, you can simply enter that variable's name on the Python prompt.

Continuing on, let us see how we can use different **arithmetic operators**, followed by the use of **logical operators**, for comparing numerical quantities.

Practicing arithmetic operators

```
In [16]: 2 + 3, 2 - 3, 2 * 3, 2 / 3, 2**3
Out[16]: (5, -1, 6, 0.6666666666666666, 8)
```

Logical operators for comparing quantities

```
In [17]: 2 > 3, 3 > 2
Out[17]: (False, True)

In [18]: 3 >= 3, 3 <= 3
Out[18]: (True, True)

In [19]: # Checking for equality
         2 == 2
Out[19]: True

In [20]: # Checking for equality
         [2, 3] == [2, 3]
Out[20]: True
```

Here, first we entered a series of mathematical operations. As you can see, Python does not care if you put them all on a single line, separated by commas. It understands that each of them is a separate operation and provides you with answers for each of them.

Most programming languages use logical operators such as >, <, >=, and <=. Each of these should make sense, as they are exact representations of how we would use them in regular math or logic studies. What you may find a little surprising is how we represent comparison of two quantities (using ==) and negation (using !=). Use of logical operations result in **Boolean** values – `true` or `false`, or 1 or 0. You can see that in the above output 2 > 3 is false and 3 >= 3 is true. Go ahead and try other operations like these.

Python, like most other programming languages, offers a variety of data types. What is a **data type**? It is a format for storing data, including numbers and text. But to make things easier for you, often these data types are hidden. In other words, most of the time in Python we do not have to explicitly state what kind of data type a variable is going to store.

```
Data types

In [3]: x=1

In [4]: type(x)
Out[4]: int

In [5]: y=2

In [6]: z=x/y

In [7]: z
Out[7]: 0.5

In [8]: type(z)
Out[8]: float

In [9]: test = (z>1)

In [10]: test
Out[10]: False

In [11]: type(test)
Out[11]: bool

In [ ]:
```

As you can see above, we could use the `type` operation or function around a variable name (e.g., `type(x)`) to find out its data type. Given that Python does not require you to explicitly define a variable's data type, it will make an appropriate decision based on what is being stored in a variable. So, when we tried to store the result of a division operation – `x/y` – into variable `z`, Python automatically decided to set the data type for `z` to be "float," which is used for storing real numbers such as 1.1, −3.5, and 22/7.

> **Try It Yourself 2.1: Basic Operations**
>
> Work on the following exercises using Python with any method you like (e.g., directly on the console, using Spyder, using IPython notebook).
>
> 1. Perform the arithmetic operation, 182 modulo 13 and store the result in a variable named `output`.
> 2. Print the value and data type of `output`.
> 3. Check if the value stored in `output` is equal to zero.
> 4. Repeat steps 1–3 with the arithmetic operation 182 divided by 13.
> 5. Report whether the data type of `output` is the same in both cases.

2.4 Control Structures

To make decisions based on meeting a condition (or two), we can use `if` statements. Let us say we want to find out if 2020 is a leap year. Here is the code:

```
year = 2020
if (year%4 == 0):
    print ("Leap year")
else:
    print ("Not a leap year")
```

Here, the modulus operator (%) divides 2020 by 4 and gives us the remainder. If that remainder is 0, the script prints "Leap year," otherwise we get "Not a leap year."

What if we have multiple conditions to check? Easy. Use a sequence of `if` and `elif` (short for "else if"). Here is the code that checks one variable (`collegeYear`), and based on its value, declares the corresponding label for that year:

```
collegeYear = 3
if (collegeYear == 1):
    print ("Freshman")
elif (collegeYear == 2):
    print ("Sophomore")
elif (collegeYear == 3):
    print ("Junior")
elif (collegeYear == 4):
    print ("Senior")
else:
    print ("Super-senior or not in college!")
```

Another form of control structure is a loop. There are two primary kinds of loops: `while` and `for`.

The `while` loop allows us to do something until a condition is met. Take a simple case of printing the first five numbers:

```
a, b = 1, 5
while (a <= b):
    print (a)
    a += 1
```

Here is how we could do the same with a `for` loop:

```
for x in range(1, 6):
    print (x)
```

Let us take another set of examples and see how these control structures work. As always, let us start with an if–else arrangement. You probably have guessed the overall structure of the if–else block by now from the previous example. In case you have not, here it is:

```
if condition1:
    statement(s)
elif condition2:
    statement(s)
else:
    statement(s)
```

In the previous example you saw a condition that involves numeric variables. Let us try one that involves character variables. In a multiple-choice questionnaire you are given four choices: A, B, C, and D. Among them, A and D are the correct choices and the rest are wrong. So, if you want to check if the answer chosen is the correct answer, the code can be:

```
if ans == "A " or ans == "D":
    print ("Correct answer")
else
    print ("Wrong answer")
```

Next, let us see if the same problem can be solved with a `while` loop:

```
ans = input("Guess the right answer: ")
while (ans!= "A ") and (ans!= "D"):
    print ("Wrong answer")
    ans = input("Guess the right answer: ")
```

The above code will prompt the user to provide a new choice until the correct answer is provided. As evidenced from the two examples, the structure of the `while` loop can be viewed as:

```
while condition:
    statement(s)
```

The statement(s) within the `while` loop are going to be executed repeatedly as long as the condition remains true. The same programming goal can be accomplished with the `for` loop:

```
correctAns = ["A", "D"]
for ans in correctAns:
    print(ans)
```

These lines of code will print the correct choices for the question.

Try It Yourself 2.2: Control Structures

Pick any number within the range 99–199 and check whether the number is divisible by 7 using Python code. If the number is divisible, print the following: "the number is divisible by 7"; otherwise, print the number closest to the number you have picked which *is* divisible by 7. Using a `while` loop, print all the numbers within the same range that are divisible by 7.

2.5 Functions

A big appeal of programming is asking the computer to do repetitive things. One way to do this is to put some code in a special module, called a function, and call that whenever needed without having to write that code all over again. In other words, functions are used to provide reusability of code. They also make the code a lot more readable and sharable. We have already used many of Python's built-in functions (e.g., `print`, `input`), but now we will learn how to create our own functions.

We will start by calling functions that are already written but available in some packages. Functions such as `print` are readily available in the core distribution of Python. But at times we need more specialized functions, which tend to be available in special packages. For example, if you want to find the square root of a number, there is a function called `sqrt` available in a package called "math." To use it you need to `import` that package in your code and then call that function as follows:

```
import math
x = math.sqrt(123)
print(x)
```

In this example we imported the whole "math" package, but sometimes we could be more precise and import specific functions from that package that we want to use. For example, the following lines import `sin` and `cos` functions and use them in the code:

```
from math import sin,cos
print(sin(1/2))
print(cos(math.pi/2))
```

Now we will write our own function. For this, let us start by taking existing code that we know and packaging it in a function.

```
def welcome():
   print("Hello, World!")
welcome()
```

As you can see, we created the definition for a function named "welcome." It has only one line with a `print` statement. Later, we call that function by issuing `welcome()`. And that is it! Of course, the outcome is not all that exciting. In fact, if all we wanted to do is `print "Hello, World!"` why bother with all this work?

Let us see another example. See if you can figure out what is going on:

```
def cube(x):
   y = x * x * x
   return y

z = cube(5)
print(z)
```

2.5 Functions

We wrote a function named "cube." It takes one argument or parameter, x. Inside the function it multiplies x three times to generate the cube of that number and then returns that value to whosoever is calling this function. Later, we call that function and we store whatever it returns in a variable z. Finally, we print the value of z.

In short, a function takes the following form:

```
def function_name(arguments):
   function body
   return something (optional)

x = function_name(arguments)
```

Ready to try one more? See if you can figure out on your own what the following function does:

```
def rect_area(p,q):
   r = p * q
   return r
a = rect_area(5,6)
print(a)
```

We are not limited to creating or calling functions only for numerical manipulations. The following example shows how to search for a string within a set of strings:

```
def search(list_of_items, item_to_find):
    item_found = False
    i = 0
    while ((item_found==False) and (i<len(list_of_items))):
       if (list_of_items[i]==item_to_find):
          item_found = True
       i = i + 1
    return item_found
groceries = ["apples","yogurt","cheese"]
if (search(groceries,"apples")):
   print ("Item found")
else:
   print ("Item not found")
```

> **Try It Yourself 2.3: Functions**
>
> You are driving from Seattle to Vancouver. As you cross the border and enter Canada, the distances are now shown in kilometers instead of miles. Write a function that converts miles to kilometers. It will take one argument and return one value. From the main part of the program, call that function and show your conversion at work.

2.6 Making Python Interactive

You can make your Python code interactive. A simple way is to provide a prompt to the user for a value you are interested in getting. Let's try it.

Enter the following on your Python console.

```
name = input("Enter your name: ")
```

This will wait for the user to enter something. Whatever they enter will be stored in the variable `name`. Once you have the value in that variable, you can do whatever you like within your code. Let us see another example where we combine a function we wrote before and make it interactive.

```
def cube(x):
    y = x * x * x
    return y
z = int(input("Enter a number you want to be cubed: "))
result = cube(z)
print(result)
```

As you may imagine, this achieves the same as before (cubing a number), but now, rather than hard-coding what that number is, we are taking it from the user at runtime.

> **Try It Yourself 2.4: Interactions**
>
> Newton's second law says that $F = m \times a$ (where F is force, m is mass, and a is acceleration). Write a program that takes inputs from the user about values of m and a to compute and display F. Think about mass as weight. Acceleration is the *change* in speed. Try calculating the force a car has when accelerating at 5 miles/second^2.

2.7 Installing and Using Python Packages

Earlier in this chapter we saw how to construct a function so we could reuse our code. Now, imagine you have a set of such functions. Wouldn't it be nice if they could be packaged together for reuse and even distribution so that others could call them too? Python, like most other programming languages, accomplishes this using packages or libraries. A package is a collection of functions and declarations that can be easily stored and distributed for the purpose of using its functionalities in various programs. For example, a well-known package for Python is Pandas. This package contains many useful functions for loading and processing data in dataframes. We will see its usage later in this chapter and certainly in the later chapters as we load external datasets into our code.

Your version of Python comes with several pre-installed packages, but depending on what that version is and where you are using it, you may not have some of the packages that you need to do your ML work. In this section, we will discover how to install Python libraries. Typically, you can use the command `pip install` to install a library, but where and how you run this command may vary. Let's see it in three popular environments.

2.7.1 Spyder

If you want to install the package Geopandas in Spyder, you can run `pip install geopandas` in the console, as shown in Figure 2.3.

2.7.2 Jupyter Notebook

If you want to install package "flake8," you can run `pip install flake8` in a notebook cell, as shown in Figure 2.4.

2.7.3 Google Colab

To install a library that is not in Google Colab[3] by default, you can use the command `!pip install`. For example, if you want to install the package "flake8," you can run `!pip install flake8` in a Colab cell, as shown in Figure 2.5. We will learn about Google Colab in Chapter 3.

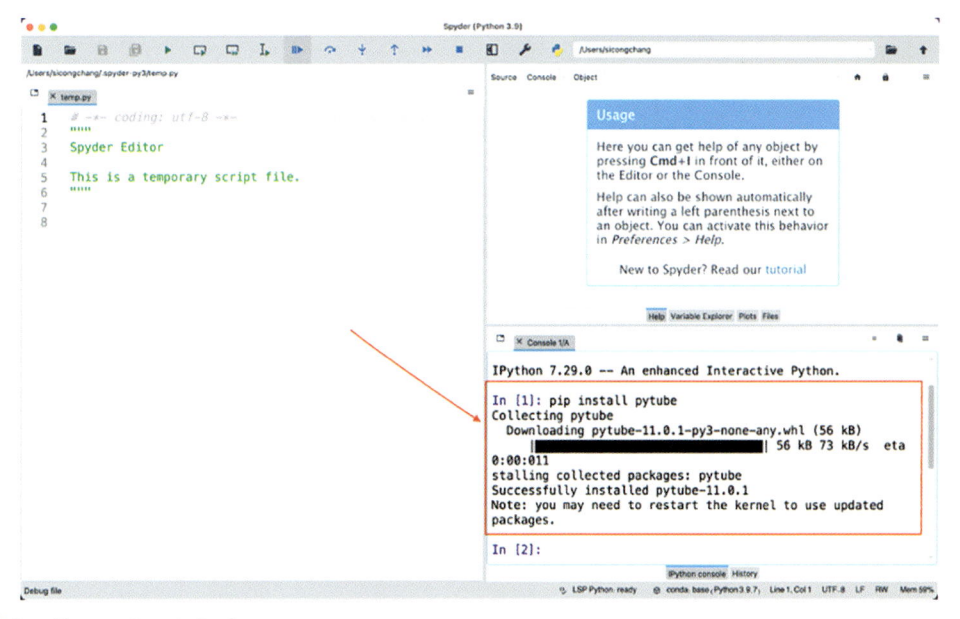

Figure 2.3 Installing a package in Spyder.

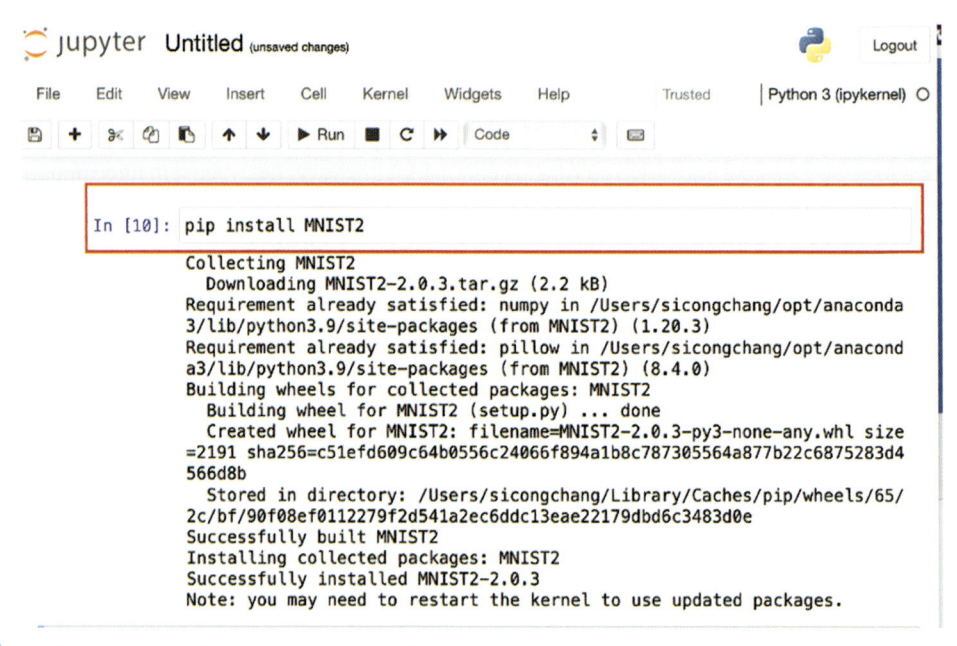

Figure 2.4 Installing a package in IPython or Jupyter notebook.

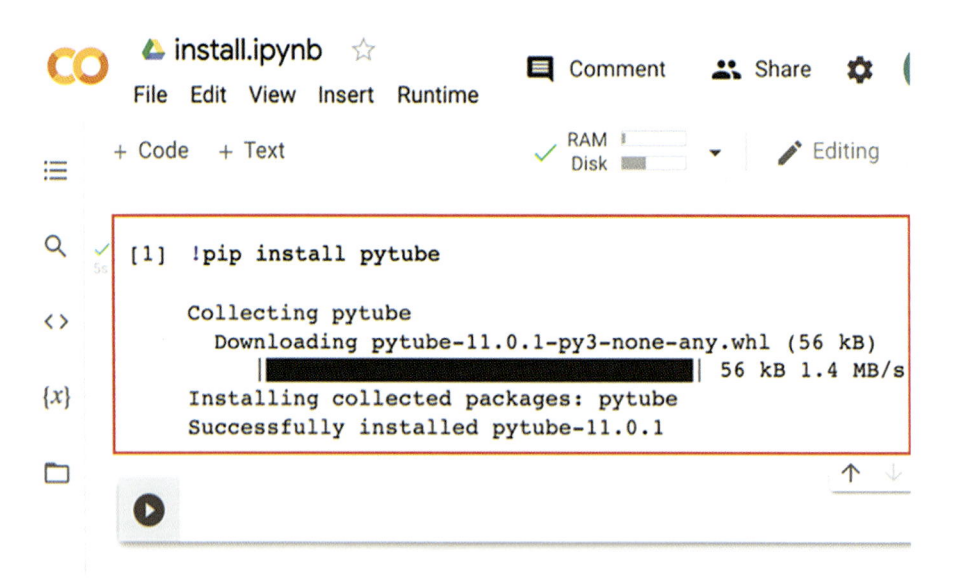

Figure 2.5 Installing a package in Google Colab.

> **Try It Yourself 2.5: Installing a Package**
>
> One of the most important packages for doing ML with Python is "sklearn" or "scikit-learn." Given that we will need this for almost every chapter going forward, let's install it now. Using the guidelines provided above and suitable to the environment you are working in, install the package "scikit-learn."

2.8 Statistics Essentials

In this section we will see how some statistical elements can be measured and manifested in Python. You are encouraged to learn basic statistics or brush up on those concepts using external resources (see Appendix A for some pointers).

Let us start with a distribution of numbers. We can represent this distribution using an array, which is a collection of elements (in this case, numbers). For example, we are creating our family tree and, having put some data on the branches and leaves of this tree, we want to do some statistical analysis. Let us look at everyone's age. Before doing any processing, we need to represent it as follows:

```
data1 = [85,62,78,64,25,12,74,96,63,45,78,20,5,30,45,78,45,96,65,45,74,12,78,23,8]
```

You can call this a dataset. We will use a very popular Python package or library, NumPy, to run our analyses. So, let us import and define this library:

```
import numpy as np
```

What did we just do? We asked Python to import a library called NumPy and we said, internally (for the current session or program), we will refer to that library as "np." This particular library or package is extremely useful for us, as you will see. (Do not be surprised if many of your Python sessions or programs have this line somewhere in the beginning.)

Let us start asking (and answering) questions.

1. What is the largest (**max**) and the smallest (**min**) of these values?

   ```
   max = np.max(data1)
   print("Max:{0:d}".format(max))
   min = np.min(data1)
   print("Min:{0:d}".format(min))
   ```

2. What is the average age? This can be measured using **mean**.

   ```
   mean = np.mean(data1)
   print("Mean:{0:8.4f}".format(mean))
   ```

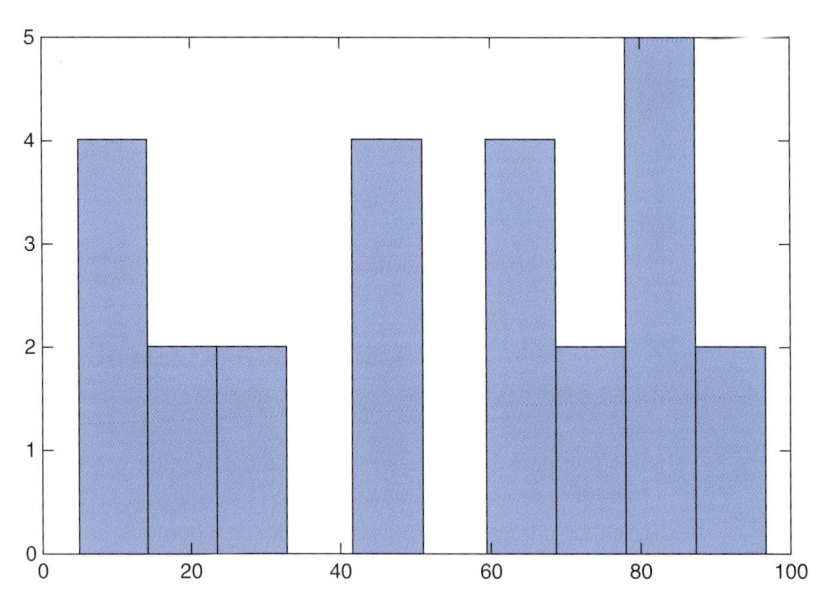

Figure 2.6 Bar graph showing the age distribution.

3. How are age values spread across this distribution? We can use **variance** and **standard deviation** for this.

```
variance = np.var(data1)
print("Variance:{0:8.4f}".format(variance))
standarddev = np.std(data1)
print("STD:{0:8.4f}".format(standarddev))
```

4. What is the middle value of age range? This is answered by finding the **median**.

```
median = np.median(data1)
print("Median:{0:8.4f}".format(median))
```

Finally, we can also plot the whole distribution (a **histogram**) using an appropriate library. Let us import it first:

```
import matplotlib.pyplot as plt
```

Once again, we are importing a package called "matplotlib.pyplot" and assigning a shortcut ("plt") for the purpose of our current session. Now we run the following commands on our dataset:

```
plt.figure()
hist1, edges1 = np.histogram(data1)
plt.bar(edges1[:-1], hist1, width = edges1[1:]-edges1[:-1])
```

Here, `plt.figure()` creates an environment for plotting a figure. Then, we get the data for creating a histogram using the second line. This data is passed to the `plot.bar` function, along with some parameters for the axes to produce the histogram we see in Figure 2.6.

2.8 Statistics Essentials

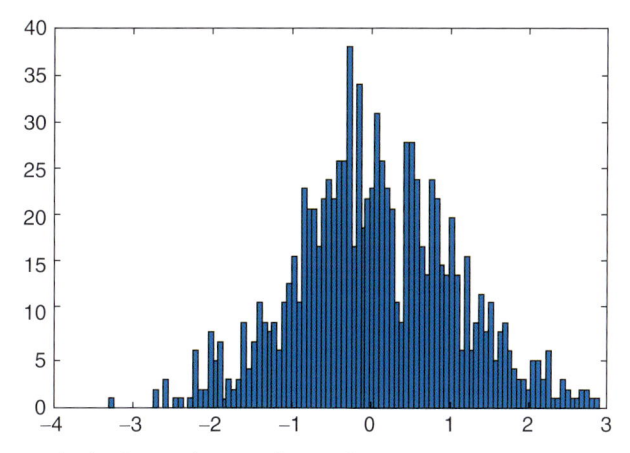

Figure 2.7 Bar graph showing the distribution of 1000 random numbers.

If you get an error for `plt.figure()`, you can just ignore and continue with the rest of the commands. It just might work!

If we are too lazy to type in a whole bunch of values to create a dataset to play with, we could use the random number initialization function of NumPy:

```
data2 = np.random.randn(1000)
```

> **Try It Yourself 2.6: Basic Statistics 1**
>
> Create an artificial dataset with 1000 random numbers. Run all of the analyses we did before with the new dataset. That means finding ranges, mean, variance, and creating a visualization.

If you did this exercise, you would notice that you get bars. But what if you wanted a different number of bars? This may be useful to control the resolution of the figure. Here, we have 1000 data points. So, on one extreme, we could ask for 1000 bars, but that may be too many. At the same time, we may not want to let Python decide for us. There is a quick fix. We can specify how many of these bars, also called "bins," we would like. For instance, if we wanted 100 bins or bars, we can write:

```
plt.figure()
hist2, edges2 = np.histogram(data2, bins = 100)
plt.bar(edges2[:-1], hist2, width = edges2[1:]-edges2[:-1])
```

The result is shown in Figure 2.7. Note that your plot will look a little different because your dataset will be different. Why? Because we are getting these data points using a random number generator. In fact, you may see different plots every time you run your code starting with initializing data2!

> **Try It Yourself 2.7: Basic Statistics 2**
>
> For this hands-on problem you will need the Daily Demand Forecasting Orders dataset from the UCI machine learning repository (OA 2.1), comprising 60 days of data from a Brazilian large logistics company. The dataset has 13 attributes, including 12 predictors and the target attribute, total daily orders. Use this dataset to practice calculating the minimum, maximum, range, and average for all the attributes. Plot the data per attribute in a bar graph to visualize the distribution. You may need to consult the next section to see how CSV data can be imported in your Python code.

We have gathered a few useful tools and techniques in the previous section. Let us apply them to a data problem, while also extending our reach with these tools. For this exercise, we will work with a small dataset available from OA 2.2. This is a macroscopic dataset with seven economic variables observed for the years 1947–1962 ($n = 16$).

2.8.1 Importing Data

First, we need to import the data into our Python environment. For this we will use the Pandas library. Pandas is an important component of the Python scientific stack. The Pandas **DataFrame** is quite handy since it provides useful information, such as column names read from the data source so that the user can understand and manipulate the imported data more easily. Let us say that the data is in a file "data.csv" in the current directory. The following line loads that data in a variable "CSV_data":

```
from pandas import read_csv
CSV_data = read_csv("data.csv")
```

Another way to use Pandas functionalities is the way we have worked with NumPy. First, we import the Pandas library and then call its appropriate functions:

```
import pandas as pd
df = pd.read_csv("data.csv")
```

This is especially useful if we need to use Pandas functionalities multiple times in the code.

> **FYI: DataFrames**
>
> If you have used arrays in a programming language before, you should feel at home with the idea of dataframes in Python. A very popular way to implement a dataframe in Python is using the Pandas library.
>
> We saw above how to use Pandas to import structured data in CSV format into a DataFrame type of object. Once imported, you could visualize the DataFrame object in Spyder by double-clicking its name in the Variable Explorer. You will see that a dataframe is essentially a table or a matrix with rows and columns, which is how you can access each of its data points.
>
> For instance, in a dataframe "df," if you want the first row, first column element you can ask for `df.iat[0,0]`. Alternatively, if the rows are labeled as "row-1," "row-2," etc. and the columns are labeled

as "col-1," "col-2," etc., you can also ask for the same with `df.at["row-1","col-1"]`. You see how such addressing makes it more readable?

Do you ever need to save your dataframe to a CSV file? That is easy:

```
df.to_csv("mydata.csv")
```

There is a lot more you can do with dataframes, including adding rows and columns, and applying functions. But those are out of scope for us. If you are still interested, I suggest you consult some of the pointers at the end of this chapter.

2.8.2 Plotting the Data

One of the nice things about Python, with the help of its libraries, is that it has very easy-to-use functionalities when it comes to visualizing the data. All we have to do is `import matplotlib.pyplot` and use an appropriate function. Let us say we want to do a **scatterplot** of "Employed" and "GNP" variables. Here is the code:

```
import matplotlib.pyplot as plt
plt.scatter(df.Employed, df.GNP)
```

Figure 2.8 shows the result. It seems these two variables are somehow related. Let's explore it further by first finding the strength of their relation using the correlation function, and then performing a regression.

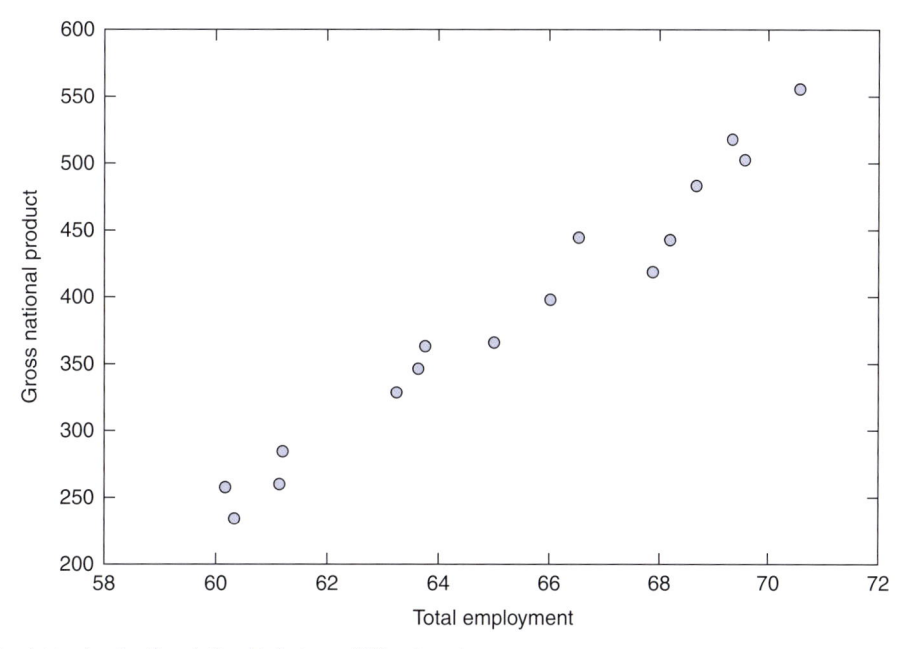

Figure 2.8 Scatterplot to visualize the relationship between GNP and employment.

Before proceeding, note that while you can run these commands on your Spyder console and see immediate results, you may want to write them as part of a program/script and run that program. To do this, type the code above into the editor (left panel) in Spyder, save it as a.py file, and click "Run file" (the "play" button) on the toolbar.

2.8.3 Correlation

One of the most common tests we need to do while solving data-driven problems is to see if two variables are related. For this we can do a statistical test for correlation.

Let us assume we have the data ready in dataframe df, and we want to find if the "Employed" field and "GNP" field are correlated. We could use the `corrcoef` function of NumPy to find the **correlation** coefficient, which gives us an idea of the strength of correlation between these two variables. Here is that line of code:

```
np.corrcoef(df.Employed,df.GNP)[0,1]
```

The output of this statement tells us that there is very high correlation between these two variables as represented by the correlation coefficient of 0.9835. Also note that this number is positive, which means both variables move together in the same direction. If this correlation coefficient were negative, we would still have a strong correlation, but in the opposite direction.

In other words, in this case knowing one variable should give us enough knowledge about the other. Let us ask: If we know the value of one variable (independent variable or predictor), can we predict the value of the other variable (dependent variable or response)? For that, we need to perform regression analysis. This will be covered in Chapter 4.

ML in Practice: Python at Work

I often get asked by my students if the kind of Python we are doing in class is what they get to see and use in their future jobs. The short answer is "yes," but I always have to elaborate. The underlying language of Python will be the same, but you are likely to see a layer of customization on top of it. This is often due to specific off-the-shelf tools or services that your company has bought or subscribed to, or a proprietary solution developed to suit your organization's specific needs. If nothing else, you may find yourself using a different IDE than what you are used to. The good news is that your basic training with Python is still going to be useful. Of course, now you will need something more on top of it, but that is where your onboarding process plays an important role.

In addition to slightly or wildly different tools used for doing Python coding, your organization may also have its own internal standards for coding, which is a common practice across the software development industry. You will be expected to pick up those standards as well. Again, the good news here is that you are not going to start from scratch. You will invariably be paired up with a mentor or be part of a team, from where you can get lots of existing code templates and examples to start.

2.9 Summary

Python has been consistently taking the #1 spot for programming languages – and that is not a surprise. It is an easy-to-learn yet very powerful language. It is ideal for data scientists because it offers straightforward ways to load and plot data, provides a ton of packages for data visualization to parallel processing, and allows easy integration with other tools and platforms. Want to do network programming? Python has got it. Care about object-oriented programming? Python has you covered. What about GUI? You bet!

It is hard to imagine any ML book without coverage of Python, but one of the reasons it makes even more sense for us here is that unlike some other programming languages (e.g., Java), Python does not have a steep learning curve. One can start seeing results of various expressions and programming structures almost immediately without having to worry about a whole lot of syntax or compilation. There are very few programming environments that are easier than this.[4] Not to mention, Python is free, open source, and easily available. This may not mean much in the beginning, but it has implications for its sustainability and support. Python continues to flourish, be supported, and further enhanced due to a large community of developers who have created outstanding packages that allow a Python programmer to do all sorts of data processing with very little work. And such development continues.

Often, students ask for a recommendation for a programming language to learn. It is hard to give a good answer without knowing the context (Why do you want to learn programming? Where would you use it? How long for? etc.). But Python is an easy recommendation for all the reasons above.

Having said that, I recommend not being obsessed with any programming tools or languages. Remember what they are – just tools. Our goal, at least in this book, is not to master these tools, but to use them to solve data problems. In this chapter we looked at Python. In the Appendix you can find an introduction to R. In the end you may develop a preference for one over the other, but as long as you understand how these tools can be used in solving problems, that is all that matters.

Key Terms

- **Integrated development environment (IDE)**: This is an application that contains various tools for writing, compiling, debugging, and running a program. Examples include Eclipse, Spyder, and Visual Studio.
- **Correlation** indicates how closely two variables are related and ranges from −1 (negatively related) to +1 (positively related). A correlation of 0 indicates no relation between the variables.
- **Linear regression** is an approach to modeling the relationship between the outcome variable and predictor variable(s) by fitting a linear equation to observed data.

Conceptual Questions

1. What arithmetic operators can you use with Python?
2. What are three different data types?
3. How do you get user input in Python?
4. Why does Python (or any programming language for that matter) have external packages or libraries?

Hands-on Problems

Problem 2.1

Write a Python script that assigns a value to the variable age and uses that information about a person to determine if he/she is in high school. Assume that for one to be in high school their age should be between 14 and 18. You do not have to write complicated code – simple and logical code is enough.

Problem 2.2

Following are weight values for 20 people:

    164, 158, 172, 153, 144, 156, 189, 163, 134, 159, 143, 176, 177, 162, 141, 151, 182, 185, 171, 152

Using Python, find the mean, median, and standard deviation, and then plot a histogram.

Problem 2.3

Light travels at 186,000 miles/s. The sun is 93,000,000 miles from Earth. Calculate and display how many seconds it takes for light to travel from the sun to Earth.

Problem 2.4

Pythagoras' theorem states that for a right-angled triangle the square of the largest side is equal to the sum of the squares of the other two sides. If the largest side's length is z and the other two sides are x and y, we can say $z^2 = x^2 + y^2$. Or $z = sqrt(x^2 + y^2)$. Write a program that will assign values to *x* and *y* and compute *z* as per Pythagoras' theorem. Print the result.

Problem 2.5

You are used to understanding temperature in Fahrenheit in the United States, but you are on vacation in France, where they use Celsius. Write a function that converts Celsius to Fahrenheit. It will take one argument and return one value. From the main part of the program, call that function and show your conversion at work.

Problem 2.6

You are working on your taxes. One of the things to figure out is the amount of deduction you can have. Write a function that takes two arguments: income and your filing category (1 = single; 2 = married filing jointly; 3 = head of household). The deductions for these three categories are $12,200, $24,400, and $18,350. If you make less than that threshold, then you don't pay any taxes. If you make more, you get that full deduction. So, if the input to your function is $10,000 and "1" (for single), you can declare that no tax is due. But if that amount is $100,000, you can say that the taxable income for that person is $87,800. Make calls to this function from the main program to show how it works.

Problem 2.7

You are part of a team that is building a catalogue for an online retailer. This is a complex project and several people are working on separate parts of it. Your part involves writing a module in Python that interacts with suppliers to get their inventory into your database. There are three parts of this:

1. Getting the initial input from the supplier. Ask them how many items they want to input. This can be done using the `input` function in Python. For example, you can have the following line in your code:

   ```
   n = input("Enter a number: ")
   ```

   This will wait for the user to enter something. Whatever they enter will be stored in variable n.
2. Now initialize a list that is empty at first. Then execute a loop that runs *n* times, each time asking the supplier to enter an item (a string). So, if the supplier had answered "5" for the previous question, the loop would run five times. Each time the supplier enters the name of an item, add it to the list.
3. Print the entire list to the supplier for confirmation.

Problem 2.8

You work for an evil insurance company that likes to reject most of the insurance claims through a complicated set of rules. Here are some of those rules:

- If the customer is male and aged 50–65, reject the claim.
- If the customer is female aged 55–70, reject the claim.
- If the customer is male and aged 41–50, accept the claim.
- If the customer is male or female and aged 25–40, say that you need more information for processing.

Any other claims should be rejected.

Write a program in Python that asks a customer to enter their gender (male/female) and age (a number). Based on those two values and the above rules, declare the status of their claim.

Further Reading and Resources

If you want to learn more about Python and its versatile applications, here are some useful resources, starting with several tutorials on Python.

- www.w3schools.in/python-tutorial/.
- www.learnpython.org/.
- www.tutorialspoint.com/python/index.htm.
- www.coursera.org/learn/python-programming.
- https://developers.google.com/edu/python/.
- https://wiki.python.org/moin/WebProgramming.
- Hidden features of Python: https://stackoverflow.com/questions/101268/hidden-features-of-python.
- DataCamp tutorial on Pandas DataFrames: www.datacamp.com/community/tutorials/pandas-tutorial-dataframe-python.

Notes

1. PyDev: www.pydev.org.
2. Anaconda Navigator: https://anaconda.org/anaconda/anaconda-navigator.
3. https://colab.research.google.com.
4. Yes, there are easier and/or more fun ways to learn/do programming. One popular example is Scratch: https://scratch.mit.edu/.

3 Cloud Computing

What do you need?
- Computational thinking (refer to Chapter 1).
- The ability to install and configure software.
- An internet connection (preferably high-speed).
- Basic experience with Python.

What will you learn?
- The basics of cloud computing.
- An introduction to three big cloud platforms: Google, Microsoft, and Amazon.
- Doing basic machine learning operations with each of these cloud platforms.

3.1 Cloud Computing

It is highly likely that you have at least used the word 'cloud' in the context of computational devices or services. The chances are also good that you use such a *cloud* in your daily life – professionally, personally, or both. But what is a cloud, really? A *cloud* is nothing more than a set of services that are hosted on a remote server and available through an internet connection. What makes these services special is that they are often distributed, have built-in redundancy, and are available on demand. These characteristics make them ideal for many business operations. Think about it – instead of buying your own computational hardware that could be very costly, you borrow hardware (exclusively or shared) as needed. Perhaps for your current needs you would like 100 GPUs (graphical processing units). But tomorrow your needs change and you need 1000 GPUs. The month after, you scale back due to seasonal changes and now you can get away with 300 GPUs. Imagine if you were buying actual hardware. That would be very expensive and cumbersome. But with cloud services, you borrow as much GPU processing and time you need as you like, with dynamic scaling up or down, and pay for what you use. The same goes for storage too. Another benefit of using such services is that you do not have to worry about maintenance or upkeep. The service provider will take care of making sure the services are available and secure as close to 100% of the time as possible with enough redundancy and distributed configuration.

As a user (an individual or an organization), when you sign up for one of these cloud services you can typically configure it to your exact needs and specifications, just as you would do when ordering a new computer or storage device. You can calculate how much it will cost you based on your usage and the kind of contract you sign. Such transparency and accountability are very important for businesses. In other words, cloud services offer some very compelling technical as well as business reasons for adoption. No wonder these services generate tens of billions of dollars in revenue every year, and are constantly growing.

Because of its importance and ubiquity, these days it is almost impossible to work at any organization doing machine learning (ML) or data science without needing to work with one of the cloud services. This is not an optional or an extra thing to do anymore; it is one of the essential skills to have. This chapter will provide an introduction to the three big cloud services platforms: Google, Microsoft, and Amazon. For each, we will see how to access it and do some basic operations. After that, we will see how to use that platform for ML.

3.2 Google Cloud Platform

Google Cloud Platform (GCP) is a host of cloud computing services that runs on the same infrastructure that Google uses internally for its own end-user products, such as Google Search, Gmail, and YouTube. Alongside a set of management tools, GCP provides a series of modular services that includes computing, data storage, data analytics, and ML. Thus, you can use it for infrastructure as a service (IaaS) and for platform as a service (PaaS) services. However, in this section we will mostly cover how to use GCP as a virtual machine and use its PaaS service, which Google calls Compute Engine. To use the services you need to visit https://cloud.google.com, where you can sign in using your Gmail account. If you do not have one, you need to sign up first to create a new account. If this is your first account in GCP you will get $300 worth of credit for signing up, which should be just about enough to complete a small demo project. However, you do need a credit card when you sign up for GCP for the first time, but your card will be charged only after you exhaust your initial $300 sign-up bonus.

After you log in you need to head over to Console, where you will find Compute Engine, Cloud Storage, App Engine, and links to many other cloud service functionalities. To create a virtual machine, click on the Compute Engine link, which should redirect you to your list of projects running on GCP. Assuming this is your first project, you will need to create a project and assign it a name. For this demonstration I have created one with the name "demo-project," as shown in Figure 3.1. Apart from the project name, the project also needs to have some unique project ID. You can use the ID assigned by Google, or you can modify it to some other combination that might be more meaningful to your project. Once you hit the Create button, it usually takes a few minutes to complete this step.

After you create the project it will be displayed under the list of current projects; selecting it will take you to your personal information page. This page contains information that you need to fill out, including your billing information. If it is set up correctly and your account is enabled, you are ready to create your virtual machine on Google's infrastructure (Figure 3.2).

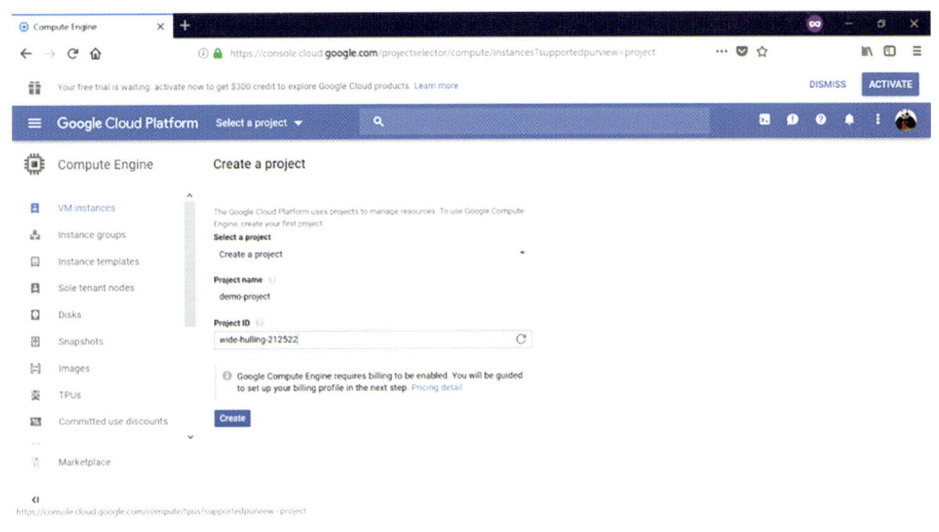

Figure 3.1 Creating a new project in GCP.

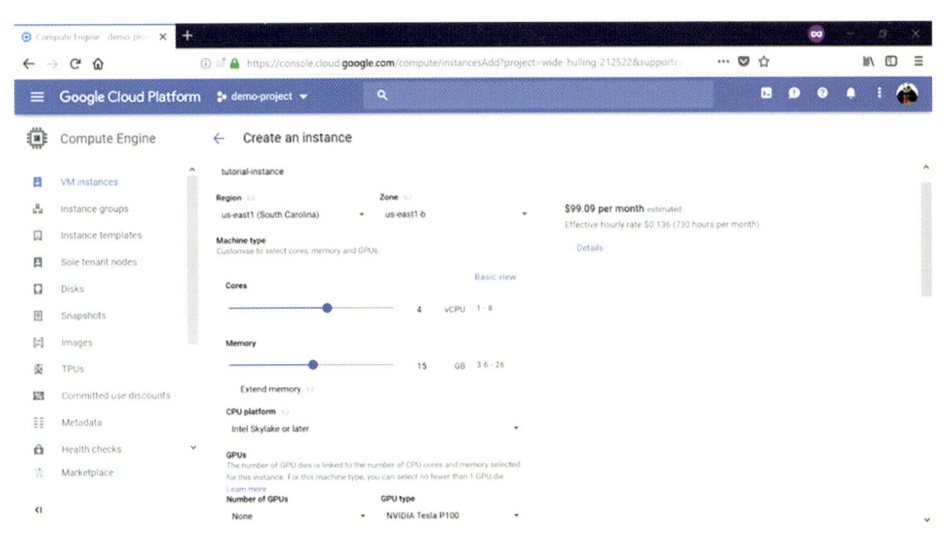

Figure 3.2 Creating a virtual machine on GCP.

To create the virtual instance, click on the VM instances > Create button. This will take you to the instance specification page. You can modify the geographic region, machine type, and Linux distribution of the instance in the specification, as shown in Figure 3.3. You can further customize the machine type in advanced settings by altering the number of CPUs, GPUs, and the amount of memory for your instance. Please note, the more customized and powerful configuration you have for your virtual machine, the higher the cost. As shown in the figure, the configuration I have chosen for this demonstration will cost $99.09 per month to maintain.

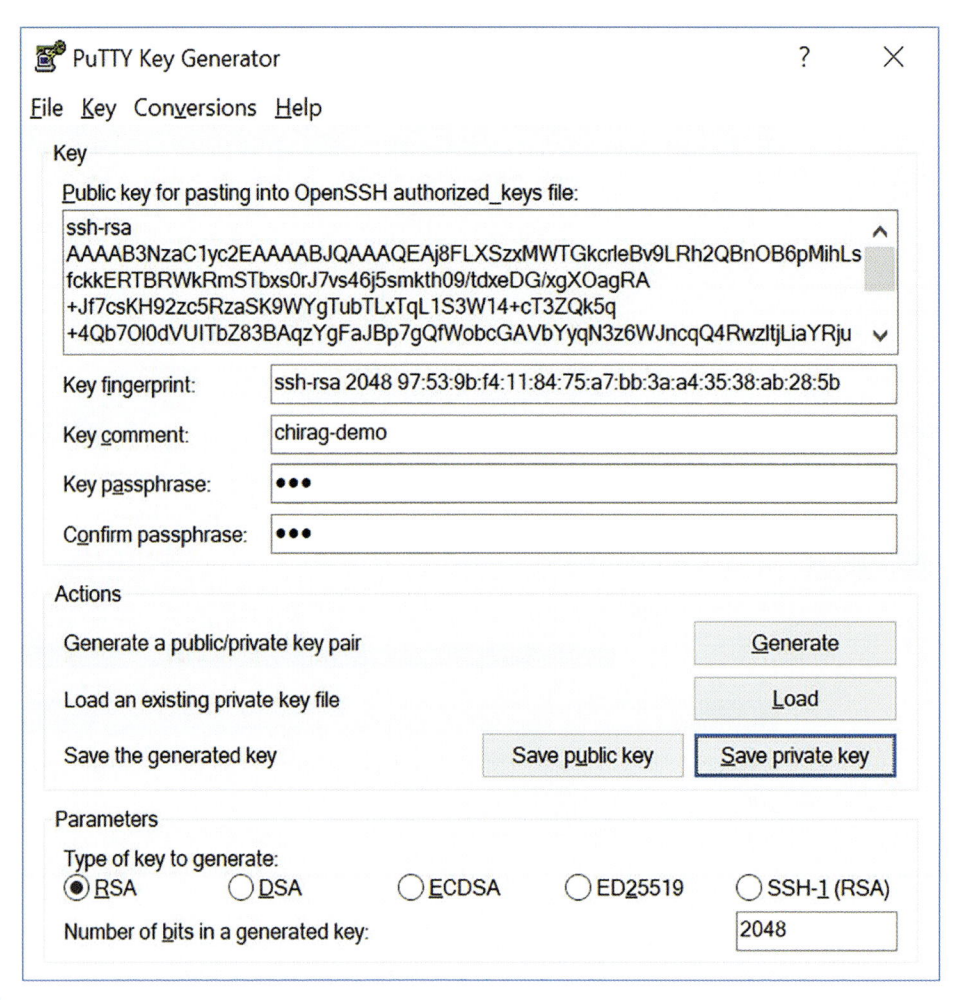

Figure 3.3 Using PuTTYgen to generate the SSH key.

Before you hit the Create button to complete creation of the virtual instance, you need some arrangement to securely access this instance. Since the virtual instance is essentially going to be the equivalent of a UNIX platform, one possible arrangement is to use the secure shell, or SSH. You need a tool to use the SSH client service if you are using a PC. There are plenty of such tools available for free on the Internet. For this exercise I am going to use PuTTY.[1] Once you have downloaded and installed PuTTY, search for PuTTYgen. Run PuTTYgen and move your mouse randomly to generate your unique SSH key. You can modify the key comment, as I did in Figure 3.3, to further personalize your SSH key. Do not forget to save the private key to your local machine and use some passphrase to secure it.

Next, copy the public key from PuTTYgen and add it as the security key to your virtual instance under the "Management, security, disks, networking, sole tenancy" section in

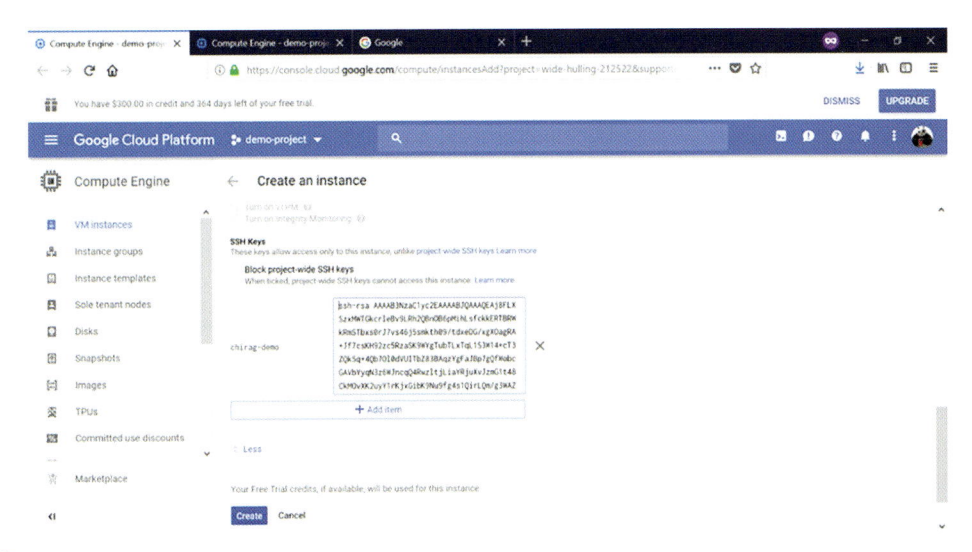

Figure 3.4 Adding the SSH key to your virtual machine.

GCP and hit the Create button, as shown in Figure 3.4. Once setup is complete, it will be shown under the list of virtual instances that have been created under your GCP account. A green tick mark to the left of its name indicates that it is currently running. Its external IP address is also listed. You will need this address to connect to the virtual instance from your local machine.

Since you have the virtual instance up and running, let's connect to it from your local machine. To do this, open PuTTY from your system, go to SSH > Auth, and browse for the private key that you stored earlier. Move back to Session > Host Name (or IP address) and paste the external IP address of your virtual instance here, as shown in Figure 3.5, to open the connection. This should pull up a terminal prompting you for the login name, which should be the same as the key comment in PuTTYgen. In my case, the login name is chirag-demo. Once you provide the login name it should prompt you for the passphrase, which is the same passphrase you used in PuTTYgen to store your private key. Once these two credentials are correctly provided, it should authenticate and let you use the virtual machine. Pretty simple, isn't it? One of the good things about using the virtual instance in GCP is that you can do all sudo operations (those requiring administrative access) without needing an administrative password, meaning you can install all types of packages you might need to handle the data analysis and visualization for your project. How cool is that?

3.2.1 Hadoop

As seen in the previous section, cloud computing services combined with low-cost storage have brought tremendous processing power to our fingertips at a fraction of the cost needed to set up and maintain similar infrastructures on our own. However, large processing capacity is often not enough to solve today's business challenges. For better or worse, the data, both structured and unstructured, that accumulates in a business on a daily basis

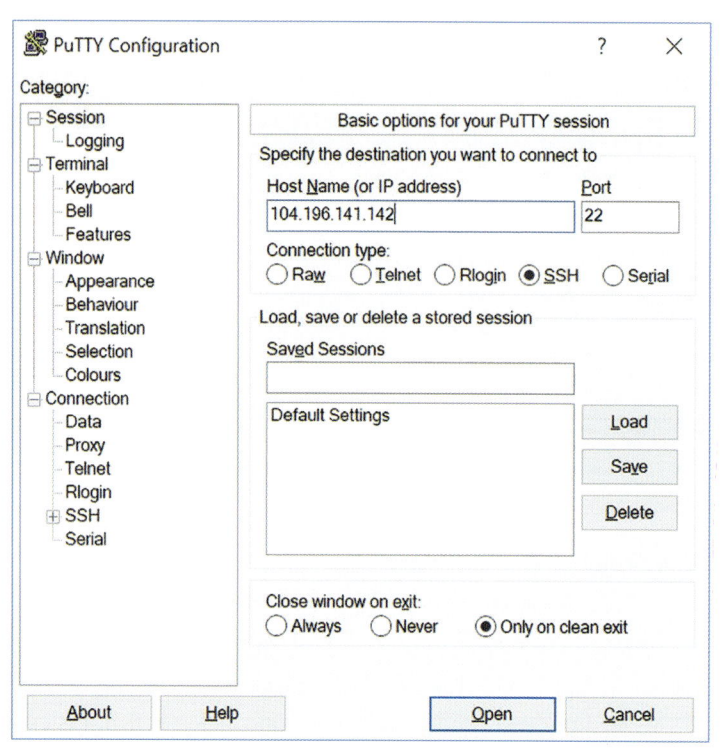

Figure 3.5 Establishing connection to a virtual instance in GCP using PuTTY.

has grown manyfold as well. And it is not just the amount of data, but what the organization does with that data, that matters. Fortunately, there is a set of open source programs and procedures, called Hadoop, that anyone can use as the "backbone" of their large-quantity data (called "big data") operations.

Simply put, Hadoop is a distributed processing framework that manages data processing and storage for big data applications, often running in high-performance clustered systems. The good thing about Hadoop and the principal reason why it is so popular is its modular nature. The whole system consists of four modules, described below, each of which carries out a specific task essential for big data analytics.

Distributed Filesystem

A "filesystem" defines how the computer is going to store any data so it can be found and used later. Normally it is specified by the computer's operating system; however, Hadoop can use its own file system, which sits "above" the file system of the host computer – meaning the data can be accessed using any computer running any supported OS. Thus, Hadoop enables the data to be stored in an easily accessible format, across a large number of linked storage devices, supporting distributed computing.

MapReduce

As the data is distributed into multiple systems in Hadoop, something needs to aggregate it, read it from the database, and put it into a map format suitable for analysis. The MapReduce module does just that. In simple terms, MapReduce refers to two separate and distinct tasks. The first is the map task, which takes a set of data as input and converts it into another set where individual elements are broken into tuples (key–value pairs). The second is the reduce task, which combines the data tuples from the map output into a smaller set of tuples. As the name implies, the reduce task is always performed after the map task.

Hadoop Common

Hadoop Common provides the tools (in Java) required for the user's underlying computer systems (Windows, UNIX, or whatever is installed) to read the data stored in the Hadoop file system.

YARN

The final module is YARN, which manages the resources of the systems that store the data and run the analysis. It is the architectural center of Hadoop that allows multiple data-processing engines, such as interactive SQL, real-time streaming, and batch processing, to handle data stored in a single platform.

Various other libraries or features have been added to the Hadoop "framework" over recent years, but Hadoop Distributed File System, Hadoop MapReduce, Hadoop Common, and Hadoop YARN remain the principle four.

Hands-on Example 3.1: ML with GCP

To develop Python programs we need three resources: storage, processing, and an IDE. When you SSH into a virtual instance, you're using GCP storage and processing, but you're limited to a command line IDE like VIM (unless you configure SSH on a graphical IDE like VSCode). So, is there an easy way to let GCP provide a graphical IDE as well as processing and storage? The short answer is yes. One possible (but not recommended) approach to achieve this is to create a notebooks instance for an existing GCP project. You can do this by selecting your desired project in the GCP console, then searching for notebooks. You should find a page that looks like what is shown in Figure 3.6.

After clicking enable you can navigate to the "Notebooks" page in the GCP console. At this point you will be able to create and configure a new notebooks instance. Once your instance has been created, an Open JupyterLab link will become active. You can follow this link and begin developing on a Jupyter notebook. The code you write here will be run on your provisioned (service assigned) resources for your project, and you will have access to any storage resources from your project as well. However, I would not recommend that most readers use this approach to developing on Google Cloud. First, it is very costly to maintain sufficient resources

Figure 3.6 Interface for notebooks in GCP.

Figure 3.7 Google Colab.

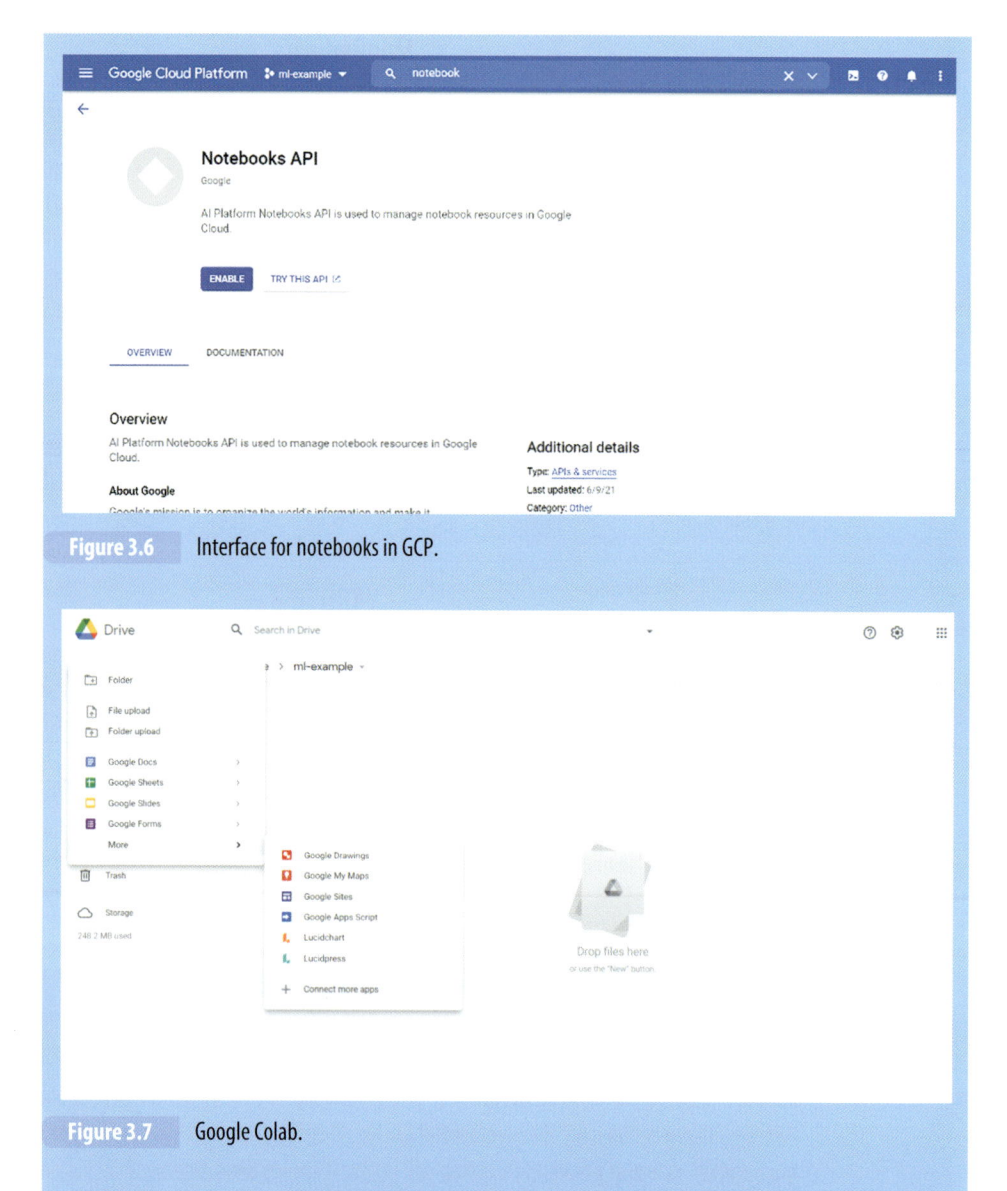

on your GCP project. Second, GCP notebooks have a lot of capabilities that you will likely never use. So, unless you have extremely high processing demands or need to interface with other GCP resources, you should not use GCP notebooks.

Instead, I suggest that you use a completely free alternative: Google Colaboratory (Colab). When you develop in Colab, your code will be run on resources owned by Google, but you do not need to associate any Colab notebook with a GCP project. In fact, you do not even need an active GCP account to start developing on Colab – all you need is an active Google account.

To get started with Colab (Figure 3.7), first navigate to your Google Drive. To see if you have Colab installed, select "New" then hover over "More."

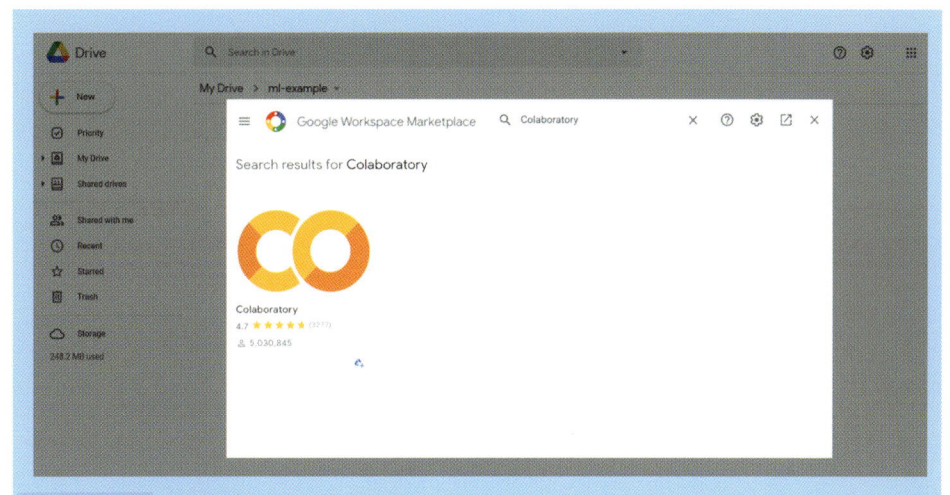

Figure 3.8 Finding the Google Colab app.

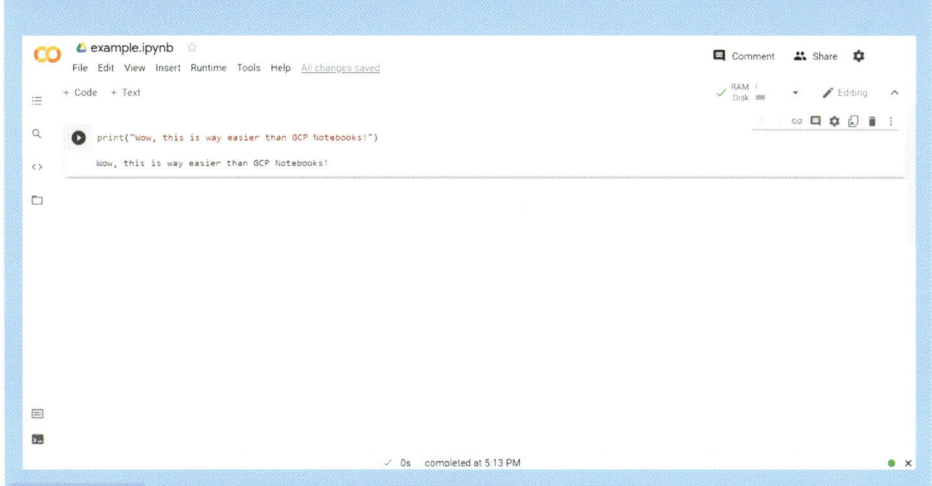

Figure 3.9 Creating a Jupyter notebook in Google Colab.

If Google Colab does not appear as an option, you will need to install the app by selecting "connect more apps" and searching for Colaboratory, which will appear as in Figure 3.8.

After installing Colab you will be able to create a new Colab notebook from the "New" menu. Congratulations, you can now start writing Python3 code in this notebook, as shown in Figure 3.9! In Colab (and in any Jupyter environment), you can split your Python script into cells and then run each cell individually by clicking the Run button at the top-left corner of each cell. This makes it easy to test components of your script as you go: Just press Run, see if it works as expected, and if it doesn't, make changes. You can also delete an unwanted cell using the Trash Can in the upper-right corner.

Colab also comes with many data science libraries, such as Pandas, NumPy, and Scikit-learn, already installed. Moreover, it is easy to use data from your Google Drive in your Colab scripts. As an example, let's pretend you want to follow along with a logistic regression example from Chapter 5. First, you import and

Figure 3.10 Writing code in Google Colab.

Figure 3.11 Running Python code in Google Colab.

Figure 3.12 Running Python code in Google Colab.

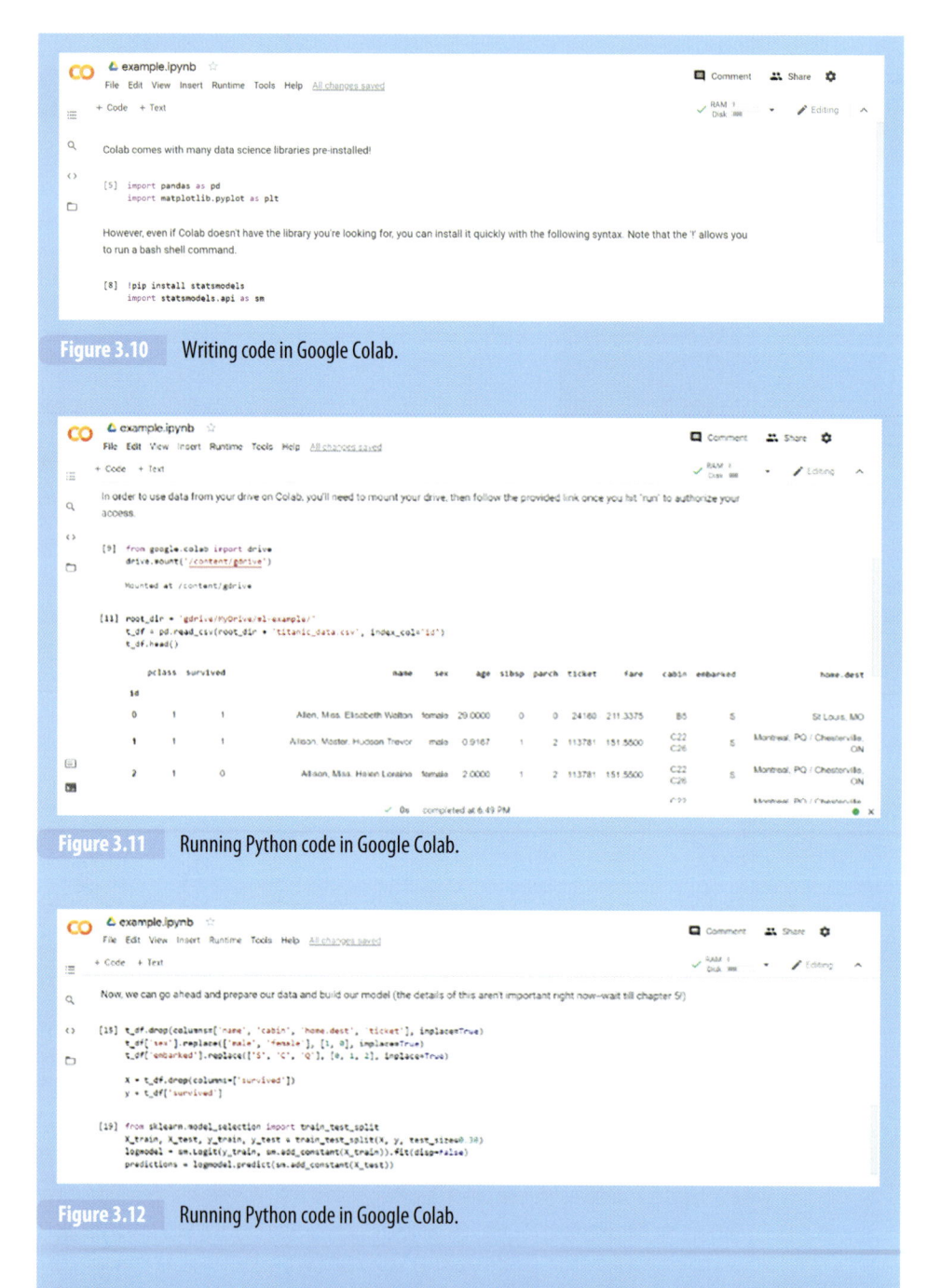

download any necessary libraries (Figure 3.10). Next, you download the necessary data (assuming you have it stored in the same folder you are currently working in – Figure 3.11). Now, you can go ahead and build your model (Figure 3.12). Don't worry if the Python code for this step is not very clear, you will learn about it in Chapter 5. Finally, we can visualize our results (Figure 3.13).

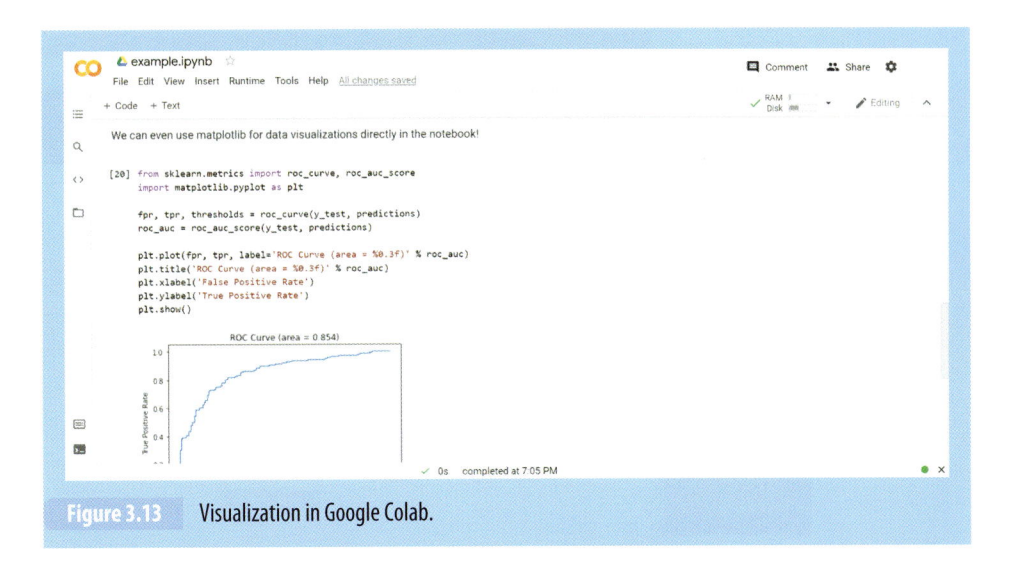

Figure 3.13 Visualization in Google Colab.

As you can see, Google Colab is a simple and powerful tool for developing Python programs, especially when ML is involved. For most readers I would recommend using Google Colab over any alternative options if you plan on developing using the cloud.

> **Try It Yourself 3.1: GCP**
>
> For this exercise, connect to your GCP account and use appropriate tools (e.g., Google Colab) for writing the code in Python. You are visiting Europe from the USA and need to convert your US dollars (USD) to euros (EUR). Write a function that converts USD to EUR using the current conversion rate (you will have to look this up). It will take one argument and return one value. From the main part of the program, call that function and show your conversion at work.

3.3 Microsoft Azure

Now that I have explained the use of cloud services and the Hadoop framework for data storage and processing, it is only logical that I demonstrate Hadoop in the cloud environment. However, for this exercise I am not going to use GCP. I will take this opportunity to introduce you to another cloud platform, Microsoft Azure, which offers similar functionalities and services to GCP. In the following example I am going to demonstrate how to process a big dataset with Hadoop in Azure HDInsight cluster.

If you do not have a current Azure subscription or have never used Azure before, you can sign up for the Visual Studio Dev Essentials program at https://visualstudio.com/dev-essentials, which should give you $25 of Azure credit per month for a year. The HDInsight cluster within the Azure platform is a fully managed cloud service that makes

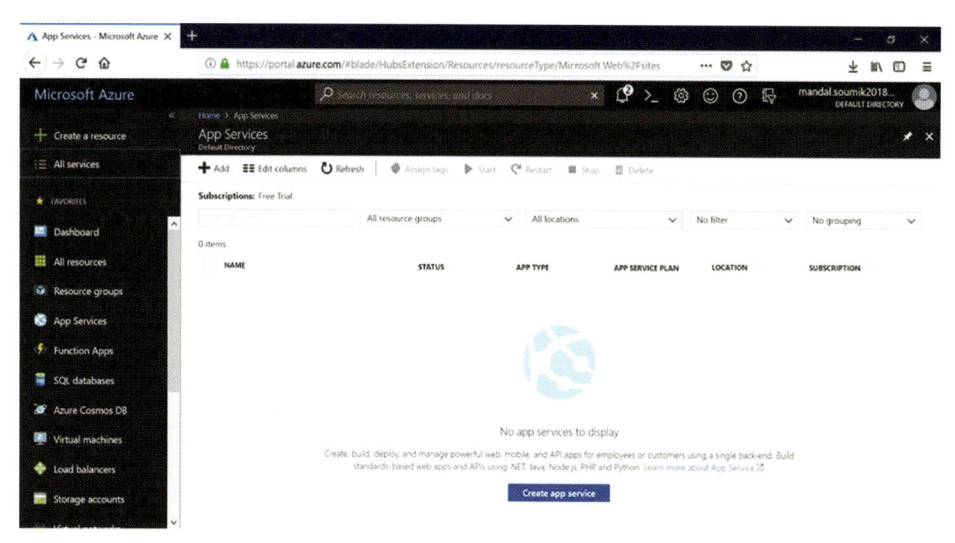

Figure 3.14 Interface of the Azure portal.

massive amounts of data processing easy, fast, cost-effective, and reliable. You can use many popular open source frameworks with HDInsight, including Hadoop, Spark, Hive, LLAP, Kafka, Storm, and R. Note that HDInsight clusters consume credit even when not in use, so make sure to complete the following exercise as soon as possible, if not in one sitting, and be careful to delete your clusters after each use if you do not intend to put them to immediate use, otherwise you may run out of credit before the month ends.

Alternatively, you can follow the steps below to create a free 30-day trial subscription that will give you enough free credit in your local currency to complete the exercise. Note, you will need to provide a valid credit card number for verification (and to sign up for Azure), but you will not be charged for Azure services just yet.

1. You will need to have a Microsoft account that has not been previously used to sign up for Azure. If you do not have one, you can create one at https://signup.live.com.
2. Once your Microsoft account is ready, visit https://azure.microsoft.com/en-in/free/ and follow the instructions to sign up for a free trial subscription to Microsoft Azure. To complete this step:
   a. First, you will need to sign in with your Microsoft account, if you're not already signed in.
   b. Microsoft will verify your phone number and payment details. As said before, your credit card will not be charged for any services as long you use the services during the trial period.

Once you have set up your Azure account, you should land at the centralized portal dashboard, where you have links to access all the resources and services, as shown in Figure 3.14.

To use the HDInsight cluster, click on Create a resource > Analytics > HDInsight. Within HDInsight there are many custom settings available for tweaking the system according to the project requirements. However, for this tutorial I will stick to the Basic setting.

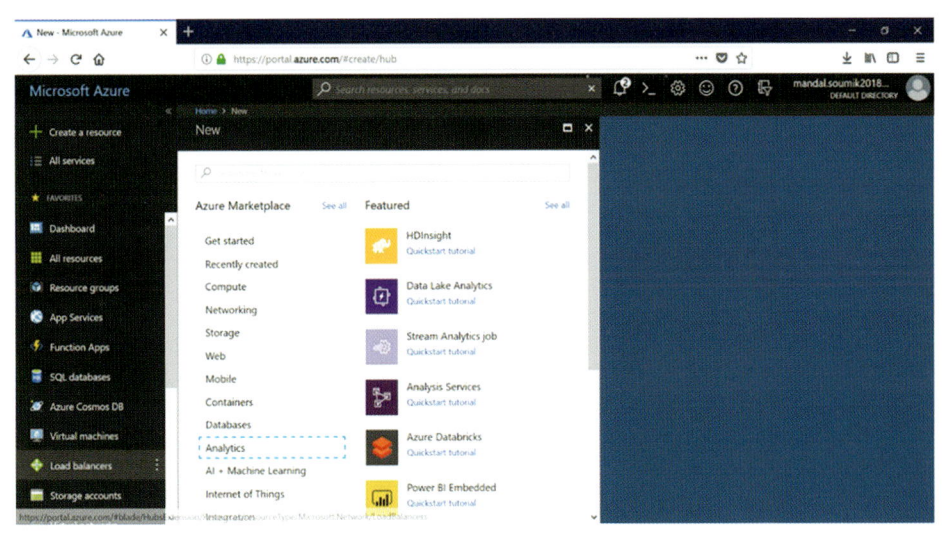

Figure 3.15 Using HDInsight cluster in Azure.

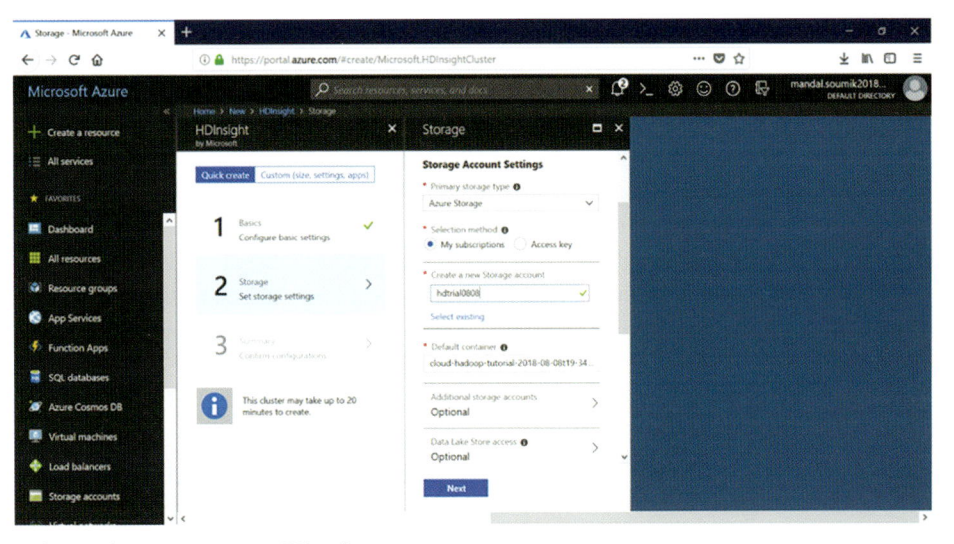

Figure 3.16 Configuring the storage options in HDInsight.

You need to provide a cluster name, in this case "cloud-hadoop-tutorial," as shown in Figure 3.15. Choose Hadoop for the cluster type, go with the default operating system, and select Hadoop version (3.3.3 at the time of writing). Do not forget to provide a resource group name when completing this step. You can use different resource groups for different projects. Alternatively, if two or more projects require the same kind of resource and services in Azure, you can use the same resource group for multiple projects.

In the next step, you will configure the storage setting in Azure. To do this, first select "Azure Storage" for the primary storage type. Use "Create new link" to create a new storage account and provide a name for it. In Figure 3.16 the name is "hdtrial0808." For the

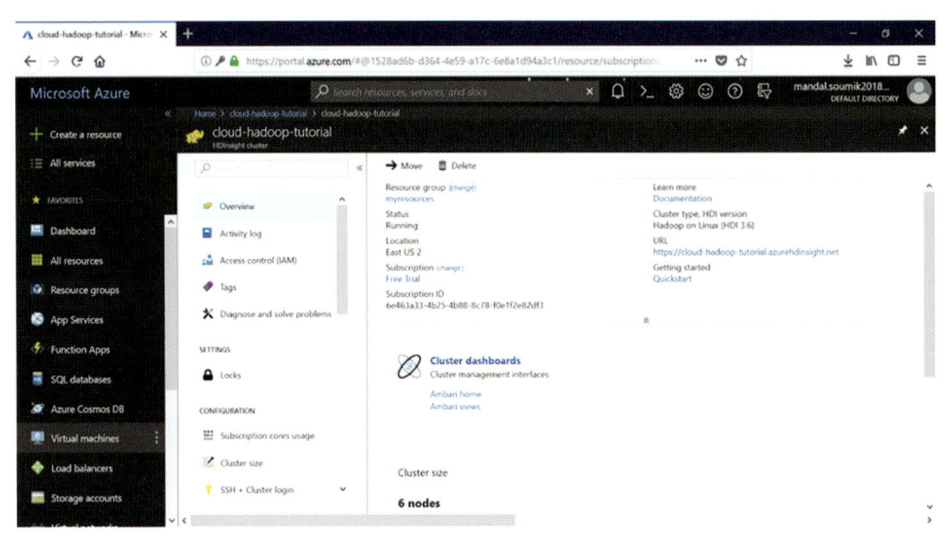

Figure 3.17 Overview of the cluster details.

rest of the settings, stick to the default values. Click Next. On the Summary page you can verify all the major configuration settings that you have chosen, and after you hit the Create button at the bottom it will take roughly 15–20 minutes to create the cluster instance.

Once the cluster creation is complete and successfully deployed, you should be able to see it in the Overview page, as shown in Figure 3.17.

The HDInsight Hadoop cluster that you just created can be provisioned as Linux virtual machines running in Azure. When using a Linux-based HDInsight cluster, as we did in the last setup, you can connect to Hadoop services using a remote SSH session. If you plan to use a PC to access Linux HDInsight, you must install an SSH client such as PuTTY.

To connect to the HDInsight cluster, click on the SSH+ Cluster login option, select the hostname from the dropdown (it should be your_cluster_name-ssh.azurehdinsight.net), and copy it. Next, open PuTTY, go to Session, paste in the Host Name, and click the Open button. This will bring up a prompt that will ask for the SSH username and password you specified when provisioning the cluster (not the cluster login). After it successfully authenticates your credentials you should be able to access the cluster pretty much the same way as in GCP.

To use any functionalities from the Hadoop framework you need to go to "Cluster dashboards" in the Overview page; from the Cluster dashboards click on the Ambari views. This will open a new tab which will prompt you for your Hadoop username and password. The default username is admin, unless you changed it when configuring the HDInsight cluster. Alternatively, you can browse to the link http://<your_cluster_name>.azurehdinsight.net to reach the same page. The Ambari views will have links to all the Hadoop functionalities that you may need to manage your big data, including YARN, MapReduce2, and Hive. If you are curious about any of these specific functions or would like to know more about how to use these components, you can refer to the official Azure documentation.[2]

Hands-on Example 3.2: ML with Azure

Let's see how to develop Python programs in a browser-based IDE with Azure. First, navigate to "All services" from the Azure portal homepage. Select the "AI + machine learning" tab. From there, click on the "Machine learning" resource, as shown in Figure 3.18.

Select the option to create a new ML workspace. Luckily, "Basics" is the only tab you need to worry about in the configuration menu (Figure 3.19). Once the basic information has been filled out, select "Review + create."

After this you will land on the Machine Learning Studio homepage (Figure 3.20). There are a lot of resources here, but for now just click on "Start now" on the "Notebooks" tile. By creating a new notebook you can start to write and run Python code in a Jupyter environment on your browser.

At this point you will likely see a yellow error message about not being connected to a "compute," as shown in Figure 3.21. Essentially, this means that you need to connect your notebook environment to an Azure computation resource. To do so, select an existing compute or press "New compute."

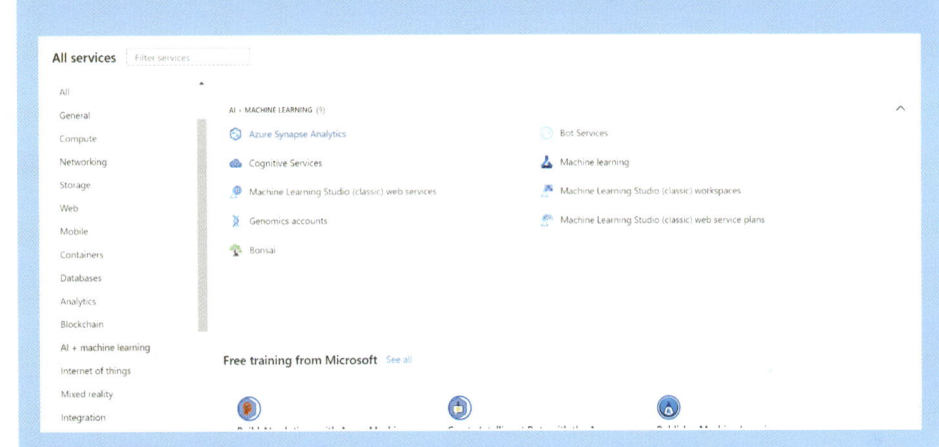

Figure 3.18 Navigating Azure services.

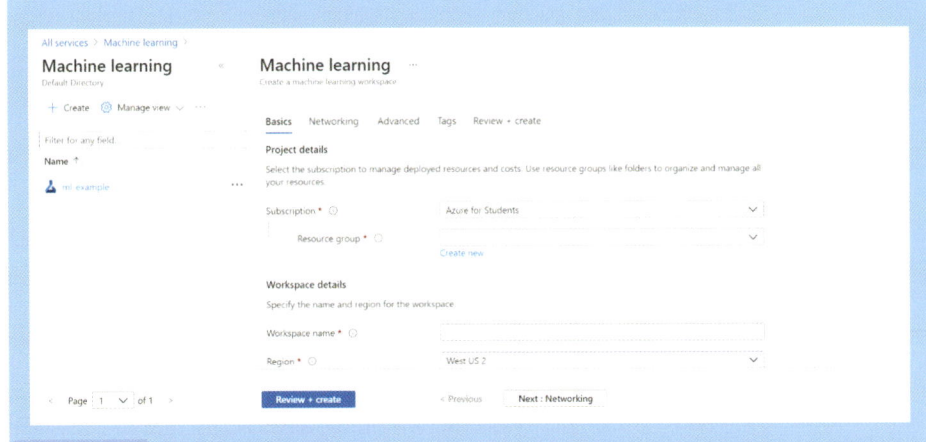

Figure 3.19 ML services in Azure.

Figure 3.20 Azure Machine Learning Studio.

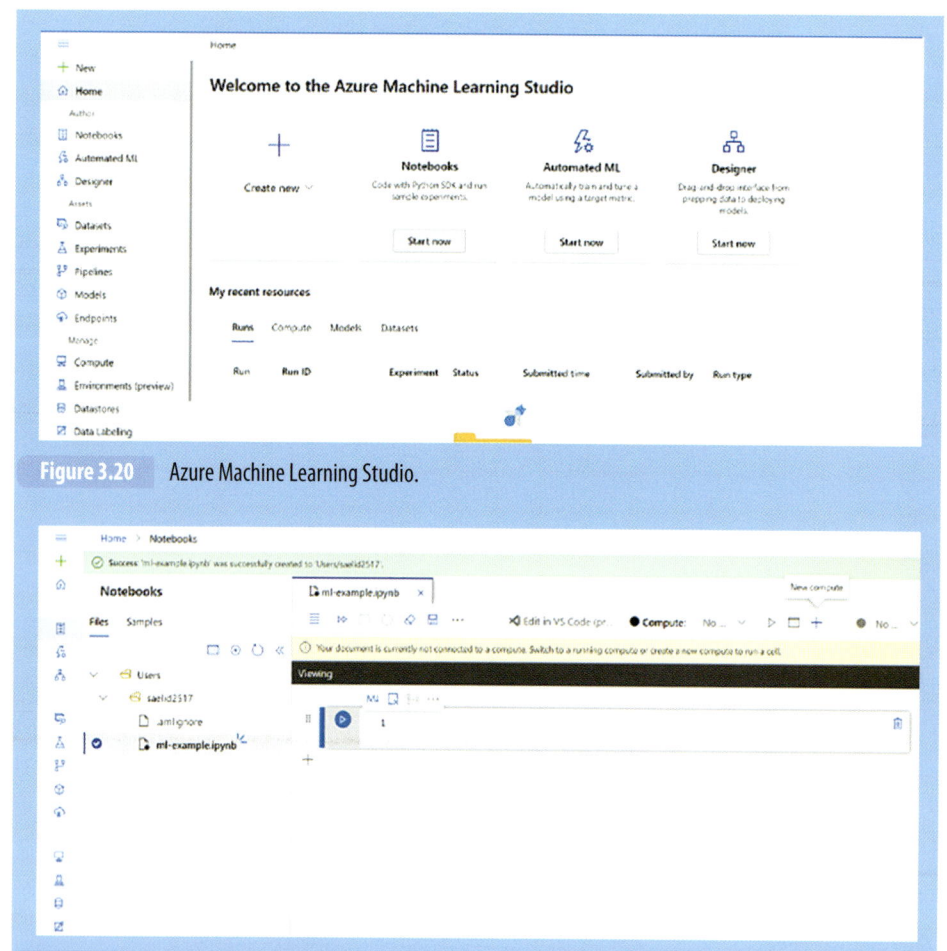

Figure 3.21 Working with Azure ML.

If you are creating a new compute you will see the configuration menu as shown in Figure 3.22. Feel free to select any compute configuration, but note that for most personal/student ML projects the least expensive configuration will be sufficient (even if it is not lightning-fast).

Once you are connected to a compute resource, you can finally start coding! The Azure notebook environment is in many ways a mix of Google Colab and AWS Cloud9 (a browser-based IDE that we will cover later). Like Colab, Azure provides a Jupyter development environment and a Python installation with many data science libraries pre-installed. And, like Cloud9, Azure allows a notebook user to open a terminal and run commands from there. As such, downloading datasets to Azure notebooks works the same way as it does in Cloud9. Simply open a terminal tab by clicking on the terminal icon above the file tree, then `wget` the desired files into your current directory (Figure 3.23).

At this point, everything is in place to train and evaluate a model. Note that since this is a Jupyter environment, like Colab, you do not need to save every matplotlib visualization as a file – visualizations will show up below the notebook tile where `plt.show()` is called (Figures 3.24 and 3.25).

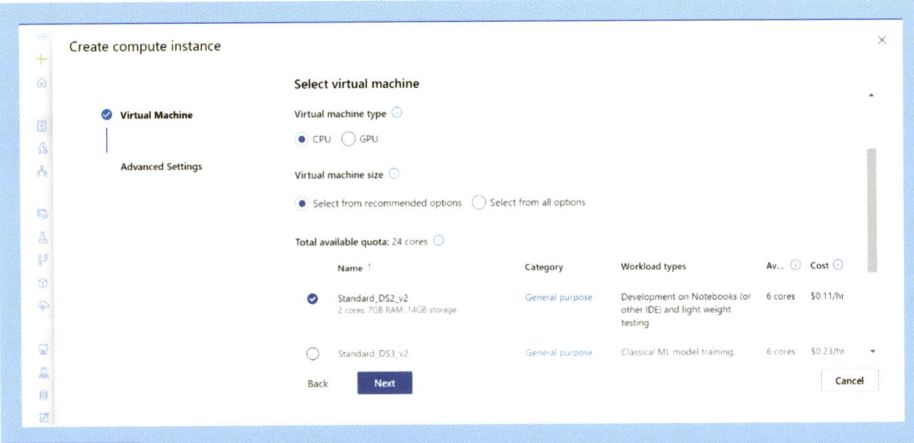

Figure 3.22 Working with Azure ML.

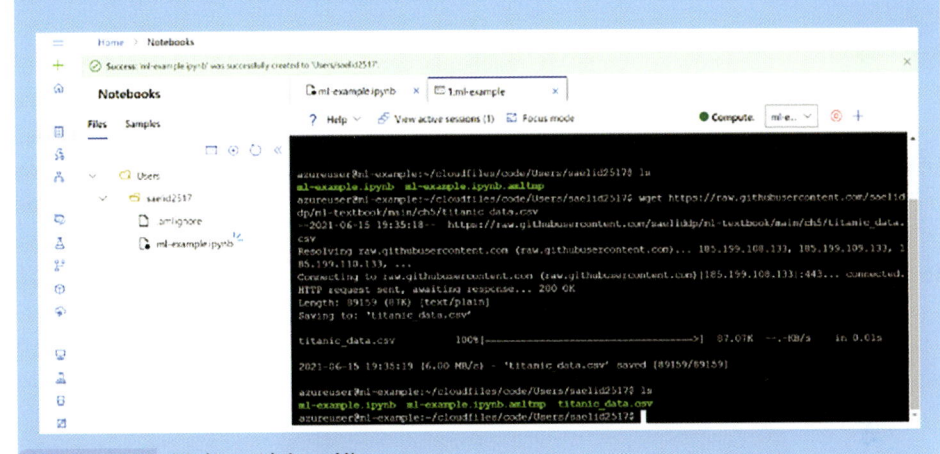

Figure 3.23 Working with Azure ML.

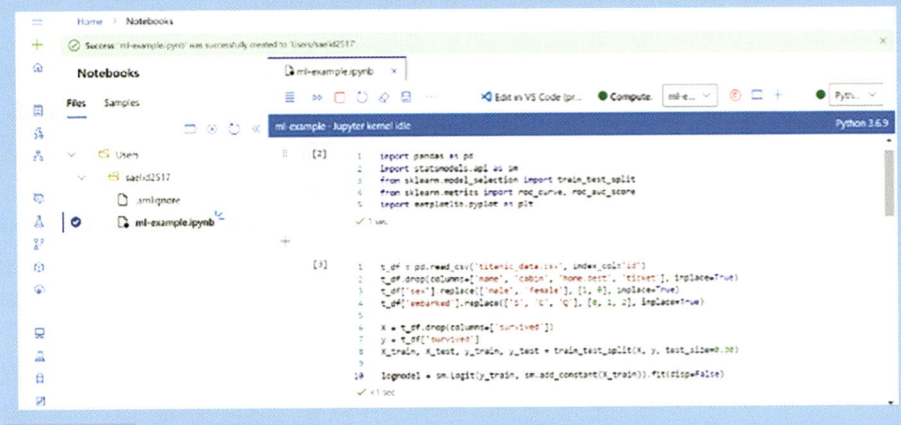

Figure 3.24 Working with Azure ML.

Figure 3.25 Working with Azure ML.

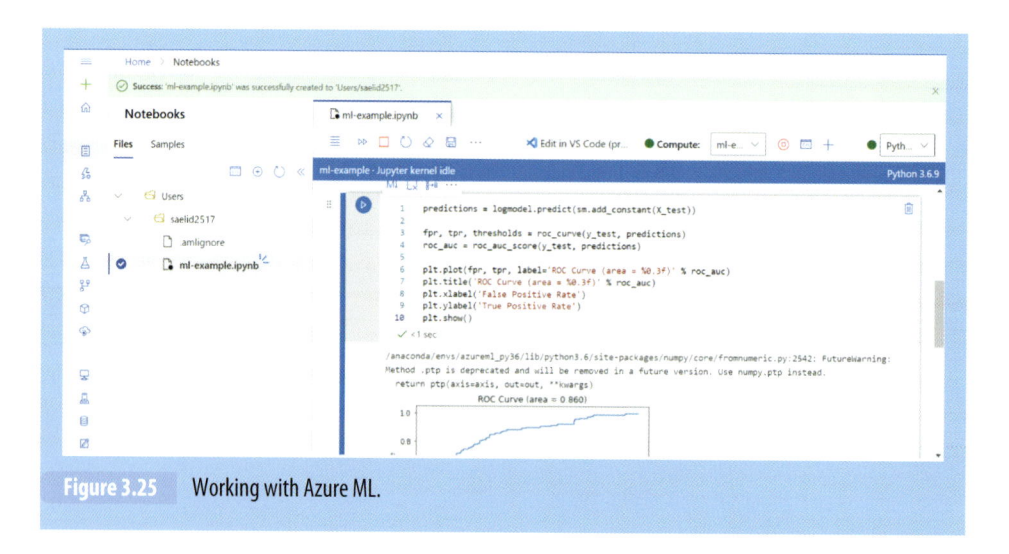

So, how do Azure ML notebooks compare to Google Colab and AWS Cloud9? Azure's development environment combines Colab's notebook style with Cloud9's command line capabilities, which is certainly appealing. However, in most contexts for students, using Azure's ML framework is overkill. Azure provides a plethora of services for ML, the vast majority of which you'll never need as a student. The flipside of this is that there is really no limit on what you can achieve with Azure, so long as you're willing to pay for the resources. Speaking of cost, it's important to note that while Google Colab is always free and Cloud9 can be free, Azure's ML platform is *never* free. It can be effectively free to use the platform when you have Azure credit, but eventually you'll run out of credit and incur costs.

Try It Yourself 3.2: Azure

For this exercise, connect to your Azure account and use appropriate tools to write the code in Python. Light travels at the speed of 186,000 miles/s. Assuming communication messages travel at the speed of light, you want to find out how long it will take for a message sent from Earth to reach various planets. Write a program that interacts with the user, asking the distance. For instance, a user will enter 158,200,000 for Mars (that is the average distance). Then calculate how long a message will take to travel that distance.

3.4 Amazon Web Services

Amazon Web Services (AWS), a subsidiary of Amazon.com, also provides on-demand cloud computing platforms to individuals and organizations on a subscription basis. The cloud service, named Amazon Elastic Compute Cloud (Amazon EC2) provides similar functionalities to GCP and Microsoft Azure. There are several ways to connect to Amazon

EC2, such as through the AWS Management Console, the AWS Command Line Tools (CLI), or AWS SDKs. In this demonstration I will use the AWS Management Console.

1. First, you need to create an AWS account if you do not already have one. To connect to your existing account, or to create a new one, go to https://portal.aws.amazon.com and follow the directions. Note, the later steps will ask for your address, phone number, and credit card details for verification purposes. Like GCP and Microsoft Azure, Amazon will not charge you unless your usage exceeds the AWS free-tier limits.[3]
2. Once you are done setting up your AWS account, navigate to the Amazon EC2 Dashboard and choose Launch Instance to create and configure your virtual machine.
3. When configuring the virtual instance you will have the following options:
   a. Amazon Machine Image (AMI): In step 1 of the wizard (Figure 3.26) you have to choose the preferred OS to install on your virtual machine. If you are not sure about which AMI to go for, the recommended free-tier eligible image is Amazon Linux AMI.
   b. Instance type: In step 2 of the wizard you need to choose the instance type. The recommended instance for free-tier AWS accounts is t3.micro, which is a low-cost, general-purpose instance type that provides a baseline level of CPU performance.
   c. Security group: Use this option if you want to configure your virtual firewall.
   d. Launch instance: In the final step of configuring the instance, review all the modifications you have made before hitting the Launch button.

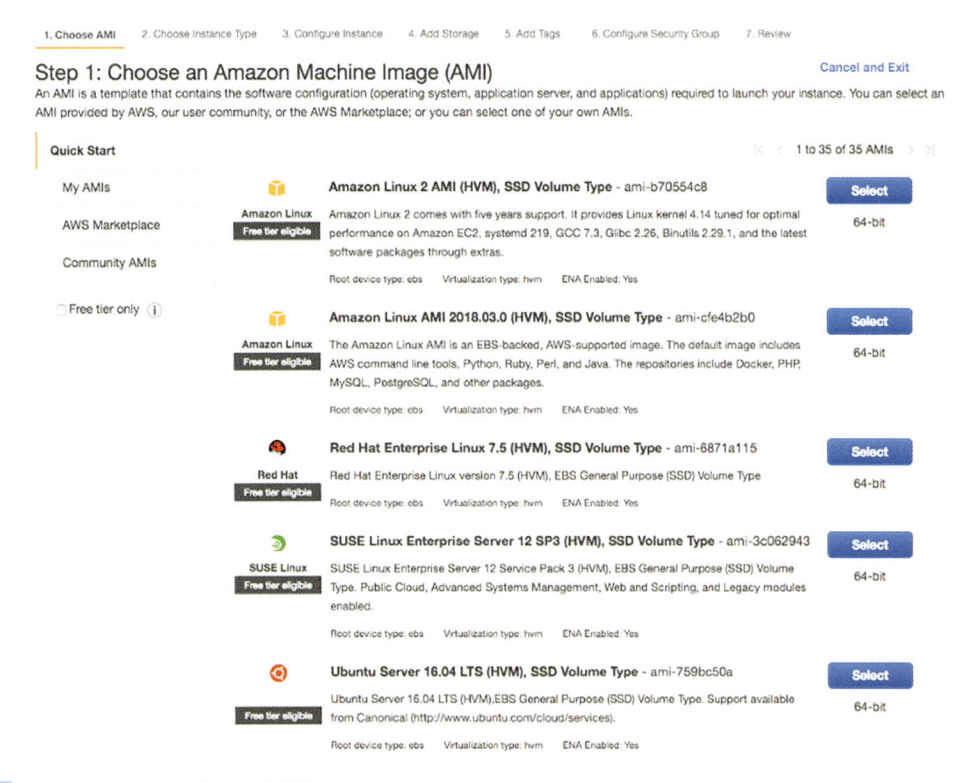

Figure 3.26 Creating a virtual machine with AWS.

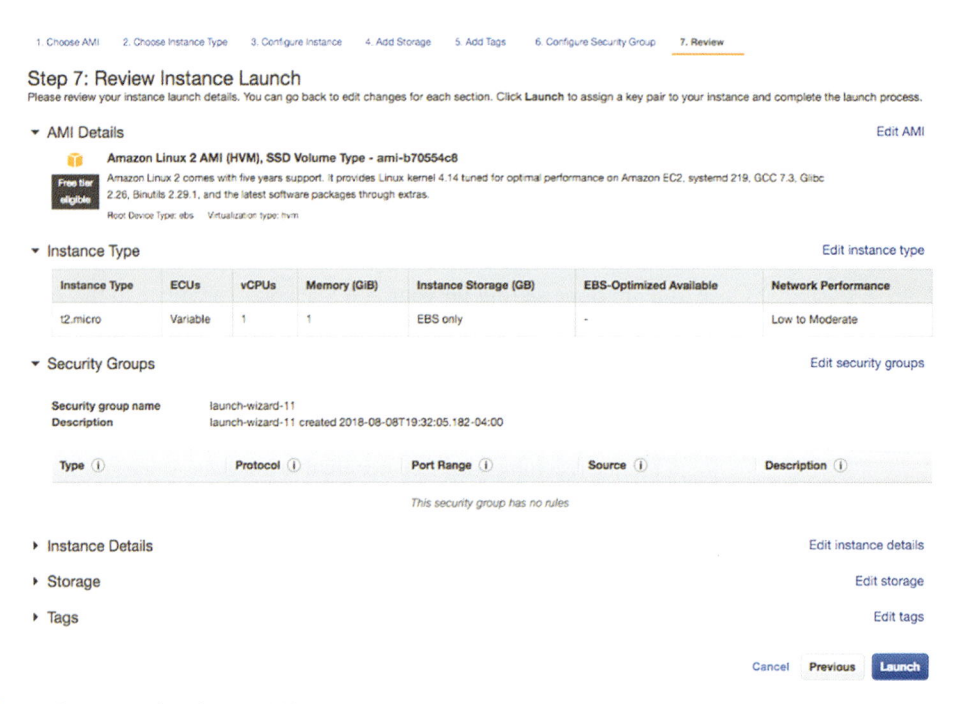

Figure 3.27 Launching a virtual machine on AWS.

e. Create a key pair: To securely connect to your virtual machine, select "Create a new key pair option" and assign a name. This will download the key pair file (.pem). Save this file in a safe directory as you will need it later to log in to the instance.
f. Finally, choose the Launch option to complete set up (Figure 3.27).

Accessing your virtual instance in EC2 from a PC is similar to what we have seen for GCP and Azure. You need to use an SSH client – in this case we use PuTTY. However, there is an extra step involved in accessing an instance in EC2. Since PuTTY does not natively support the.pem format that AWS uses for authentication, you need to convert the. pem file to a.ppk format (PPK = PuTTY Private Key). You can do this using the PuTTY-gen utility. On the PuTTYgen dialog box, click on the Load button, then navigate to the. pem file that you downloaded when setting up your instance – be sure to select All Files in the dropdown list located on the right of the "File name" field. Once loaded, PuTTYgen will convert your file to the.ppk format. To save this.ppk file, click on the "Save private key" option. The utility might yell at you if you try to save the key without a passphrase. Ignore that by selecting Yes, and be sure to provide a name and store it in a directory you will remember.

Now that you have converted the.pem file from AWS to a.ppk file, you are ready to securely log into your instance by using SSH from PuTTY. To do this, start PuTTY, click on Session, and provide the Host Name, which should be in the format user_name@ public_dns_name, as shown in Figure 3.28. The default username for Amazon Linux AMI is ec2-user.

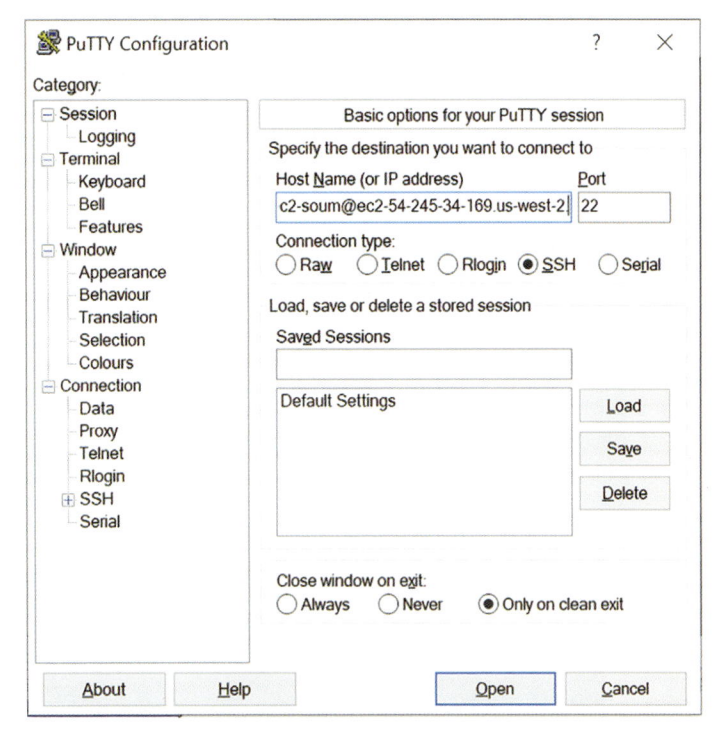

Figure 3.28 Connecting to an AWS EC2 instance from a PC using PuTTY.

Figure 3.29 SSH session connected to an AWS EC2 instance.

Next, navigate to the Auth button under SSH, browse for the private key (the .ppk file) that you saved earlier, and open the connection. If you followed every step above correctly, you should see a new terminal appear displaying your command line SSH session, as shown in Figure 3.29.

Hands-on Example 3.3: ML with AWS

Again, you may be wondering if there is a way to develop Python programs on AWS resources without dealing with SSH. Luckily, AWS provides a browser-based IDE called Cloud9, which fulfills a similar role to Google Colab. To get started with Cloud9, log into the AWS Management Console, select the "Services" dropdown, and click on "Cloud9" under the "Developer Tools" section (Figure 3.30).

When you click on "Cloud9" you will see an option to create a new Cloud9 environment. Go ahead and click on this option, give your environment a name, and proceed to the next step. **It is important that you follow the next instructions closely to avoid unwanted charges.**

When prompted, select a "no-ingress" environment type, a "t2.micro" instance type, and an "Amazon Linux 2" platform. As shown in small print below the t2.micro option, this instance type is the only free-tier-eligible option. So, if you do not want to be charged for your Cloud9 environment, you need to select the t2.micro option. Once you have configured your environment as shown in Figure 3.31, you can keep all other settings on their default options.

Figure 3.30 AWS's Cloud9: a browser-based IDE.

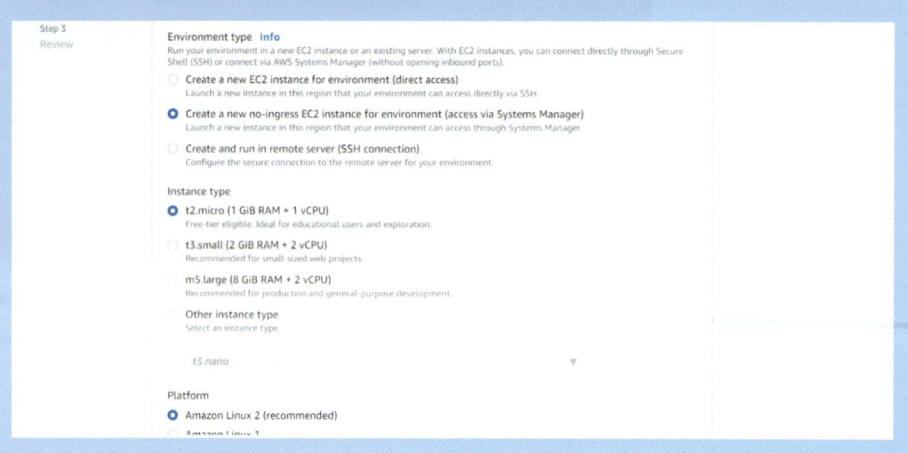

Figure 3.31 Working with AWS.

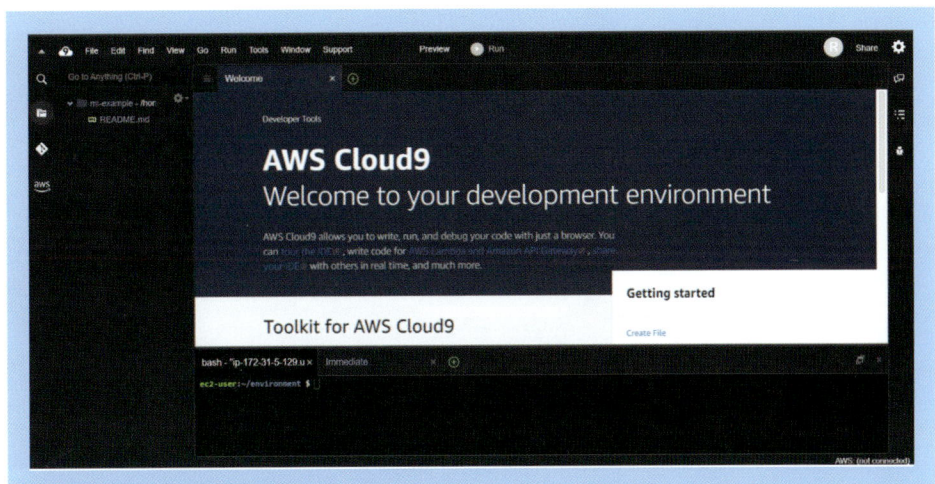

Figure 3.32 Working with AWS through Cloud9.

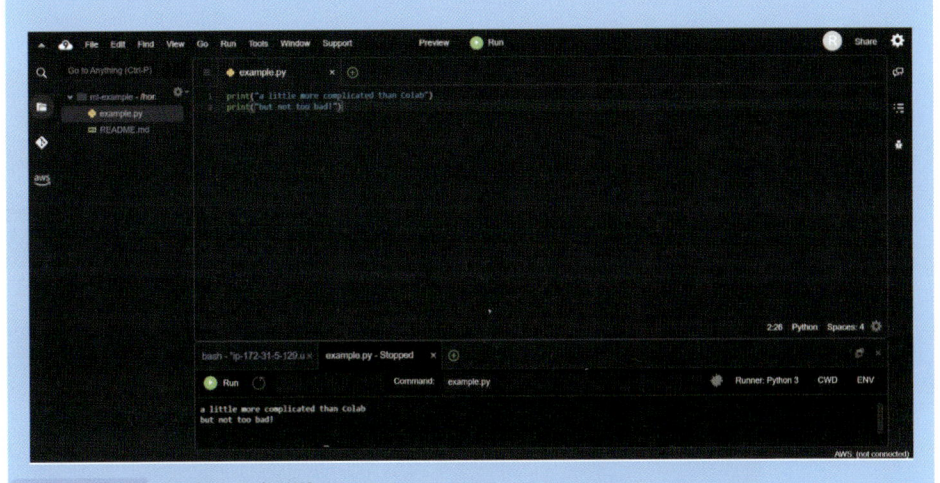

Figure 3.33 Working with AWS.

Once you are done configuring the environment settings, you can go ahead and create your Cloud9 environment. After a few minutes of loading, you will see the browser-based IDE, as shown in Figure 3.32. There are a few important features here to note.

You can create new source files by pressing the green "+" in the central window. Then you can write your programs in that window. The left sidebar displays the working directory, and all created files will show up there. Additionally, in the bottom window, you have access to a bash terminal tab. You can use this terminal the same way you would use a terminal on any Linux machine. Note that when you press Run, your program's console output will show up in a different tab in the terminal window.

Unlike Google Colab, Cloud9's Python installation does not come with data science libraries pre-installed. You'll need to install these libraries yourself from the bash terminal, as shown in Figure 3.34. It's simple – just `pip install` any library you are missing!

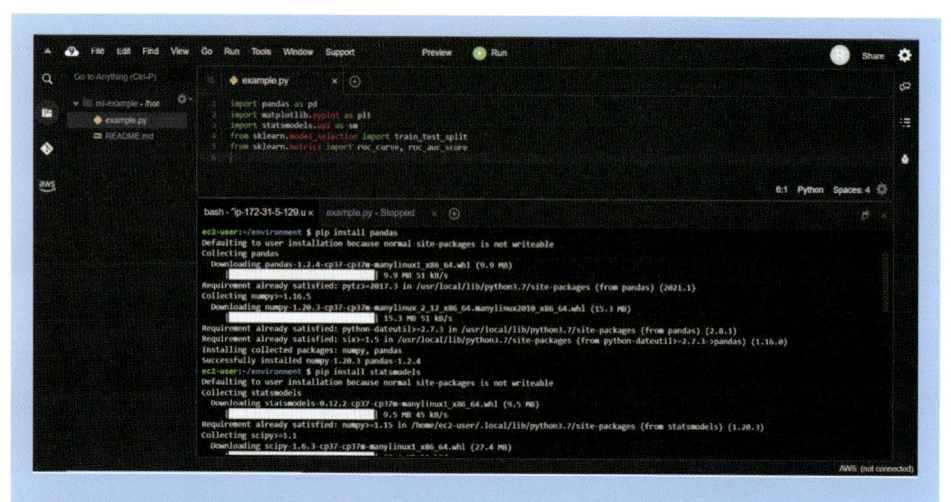

Figure 3.34 Working with AWS.

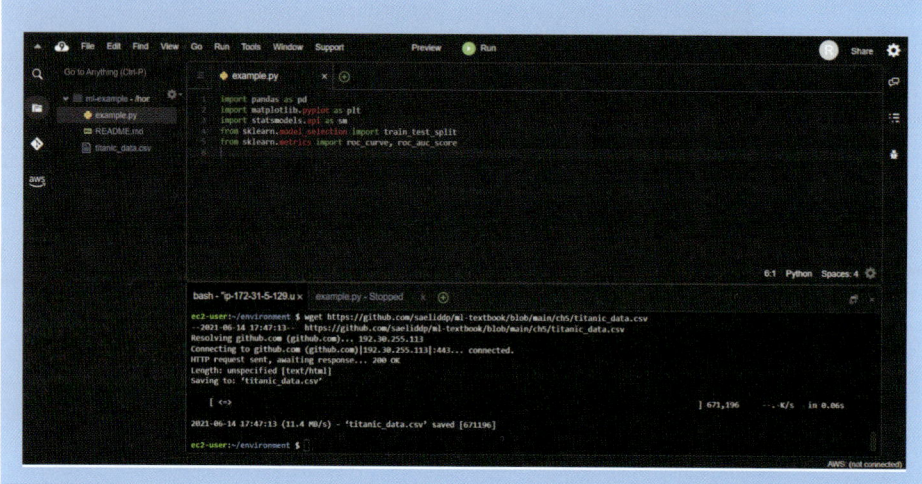

Figure 3.35 Working with AWS.

To build an ML model on Cloud9 you'll also need to access the training data. Again, we'll rely on command line tools to achieve this. To download a dataset from somewhere on the Internet, type `wget` followed by the URL leading to the desired data in the terminal, then press enter (Figure 3.35). By default, the file will be downloaded to your current directory.

Now that you have the necessary libraries and data, you can build your model! However, it is important to note that to view any graphical output of your program on Cloud9 you will have to save the output as a file first. So, if you are using matplotlib, for instance, you'll have to type `plt.savefig(…)` rather than `plt.show()` (Figure 3.36).

To view your visualizations, simply select the file from the browser on the left (Figure 3.37).

Figure 3.36 Working with AWS.

Figure 3.37 Working with AWS.

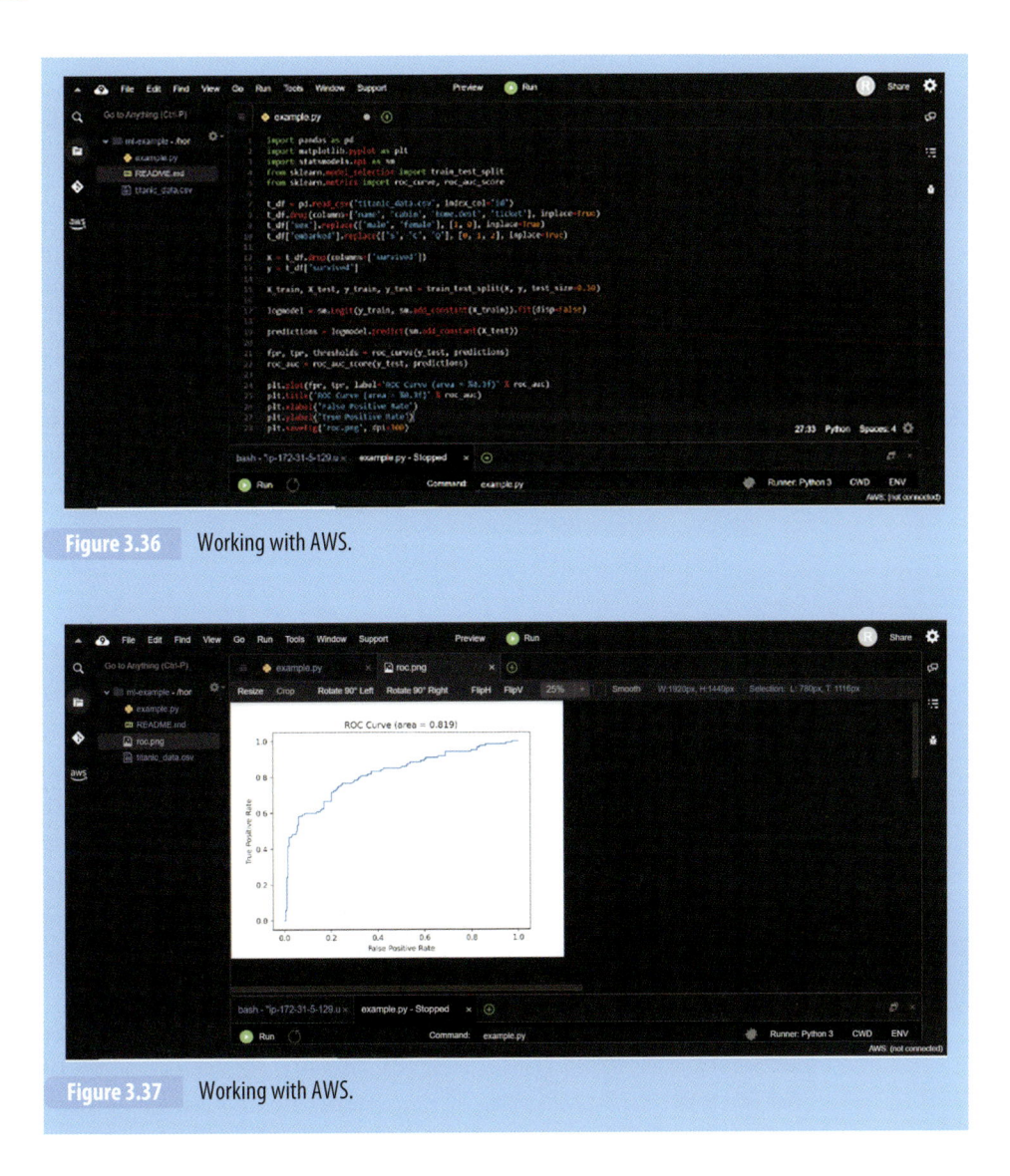

Overall, Cloud9 is an intuitive and powerful development environment from AWS. If you are not a fan of Colab's notebook style or prefer having easy access to a terminal while you work, Cloud9 may be a good option for you. Unfortunately, Cloud9 is only free to a certain storage and processing limit, while Google Colab is always free.

> **ML in Practice: Using Cloud Platforms at Your Job**
>
> In this chapter we are covering the three big options for cloud computing. But of course, there are several other choices, such as IBM, Oracle, SAP, and Alibaba. These platforms are quite comprehensive, in the sense that they provide almost everything you need for your computational needs – processing, storage,

networking, and more. There are also smaller services that are more specific to certain applications – Salesforce for marketing and sales, Workday for human resources (HR) and payroll, and VMware for virtualization and IT support. You can find books and lots of online resources on each of these. But there is no need to sit down and read it all or practice it without a specific purpose.

At your job – whether it is in software development, healthcare, or sales – you will typically have an onboarding phase when you join a company or department (and sometimes before you join), where you will be given a quick, and sometimes rigorous, training for the cloud services your company uses. It is possible that your organization has also built some proprietary solutions on top of a given cloud computing platform, which you will only get to learn and practice once you are inside that organization.

Based on my personal experience and that of my students, I suggest you should familiarize yourself with at least one of the big three platforms presented in this chapter, perhaps go a bit deeper into it, and then leave the rest of the training and practice for your onboarding phase.

FYI: Getting Certified for a Cloud Platform

If you are inclined to go deeper in any of the cloud platforms described here and earn recognition for your skills, you may want to look into getting certification. Each of these platforms has various training courses, exams, and, yes, certificates if you successfully complete them. These certificates can add value to your resumé. Just a word of caution: Do not expect miracles in your job-hunting by simply having one of these certificates. Employers would of course like that you have a deep understanding of a cloud platform, but there is no guarantee that it is their choice for cloud services. Even if it is, there may be so much in-house and proprietary work done on that platform that your certified training only helps you there a little in your first week.

Nonetheless, having such a certificate can show an employer that you are self-driven and serious about learning and getting trained. I can say the same about other certificates and training you could get online. Find links to these certification courses and other learning resources in the "Further Reading and Resources" section at the end of this chapter.

Try It Yourself 3.3: AWS

For this exercise, connect to your AWS account and use appropriate tools to write the code in Python. The Summer Olympics are held every four years (2000, 2004, 2008, etc.). Write a Python script that asks the user to enter a year and prints whether the Summer Olympics were held in that year or not. Note that the 2020 Olympic Games were held in 2021 due to COVID-19 related cancelations, and your program should be able to handle that exception.

3.5 Moving between Cloud Platforms

What if you had all your code and data tied to one of the cloud platforms, and you needed to move it all to a different platform due to policy or contract changes at your organization? There are tools, scripts, and processes available on the Internet that help you do such migration. In fact, most of the time the platform to which you want to migrate will provide such tools and support (they want your business!).

Let's take an example. If you are looking to migrate from AWS to Microsoft Azure, you will find that Microsoft provides a service called Azure Migrate.[4] This service is meant to guide you through the discovery, assessment, and migration of AWS services to Azure. Typically, there are four main steps that you will need to execute:

1. Set up Azure Site Recovery (ASR). This is done on the Azure side through its portal. Here, you will define a source and a target and choose a few more settings related to replication from AWS to Azure.
2. Prepare a process server on AWS. On the other side (AWS) you need to set up an Azure component on your EC2. This component will help you do your migration to Azure. For that, make sure you deploy an EC2 instance and run Azure Process Server on it.
3. Discover EC2 instances and replicate to Azure. Back on the Azure side, you need to perform ASR, which will allow you to identify all of the EC2 instances that you want to migrate to Azure. Once the instances are identified, you can proceed with replication. Depending on how big your resources are on EC2, this could take a while.
4. Failover EC2 instances to Azure. Once the replication process is finished, you need to do a failover action to complete your migration. Make sure to test everything, and when satisfied, delete your EC2 instances so you do not keep incurring costs on AWS.

In practice, such migrations are not done frequently. But it is good to know that you have support if and when you need to move from one platform to another. If you are practicing with more than one platform from this chapter, I suggest you also practice the migration process as a part of your training. Most organizations that use a cloud platform will have committed to using one for multiple years or indefinitely, so migration is not something you'll need regularly. But it helps to know the basics. It is also helpful for freelancers and independent developers who work with multiple organizations, as each of these organizations may have ties to different cloud computing platforms.

3.6 Summary

These days it is almost impossible to do practical data science or ML tasks without using a cloud service. Therefore, in order to be "marketable" in the ML job world, it is imperative that one picks up one or more of these services. What we saw in this chapter is just the tip of the iceberg. These three major cloud services offered by Google, Microsoft, and Amazon are very capable and constantly improving. They offer all the standard tools, services, and languages one needs to do data science or ML, but they go much further than that. Each of them has its own set of specialized tools for doing ML. Often these tools are integrated into other parts of the services, such as storage. For example, Google's BigQuery is connected to its BigData storage service and allows a seamless querying experience from archival or even production data.

Note that for most of what we are going to do in this book, we will not be using any specific cloud service. We will use Python for almost all the exercises, without any assumption about where it is running – your laptop or one of the cloud services. Given that you can run Python easily on all these cloud services, almost everything that follows in this book can be done in the cloud.

Key Terms

- **Cloud computing** is a platform that provides a set of computing and storage services to enable remote data storage and processing. Examples include Amazon Web Services (AWS), Google Cloud, and Microsoft Azure.
- **SSH** is a secure shell, an application or an interface that provides access to various functions and tools of an operating system such as UNIX.

Conceptual Questions

1. When would you recommend moving your ML development work to a cloud service? Think about the limitations of local computing and the advantages of cloud computing.

2. When would you not want to make such a move? Think about costs, privacy, and other implications of cloud computing.

3. After you've had a chance to try out at least two of the cloud services covered in this chapter, compare them in terms of their costs, benefits, and user interfaces.

Hands-on Problems

Problem 3.1

Pick a cloud platform of your choice and find its Python tool or interface (e.g., Google Colab). Write a function in the interface to convert pounds (lb.) to kilograms (kg). Show how you can call that function.

Problem 3.2

Pick a cloud platform of your choice and find its Python tool or interface (e.g., Google Colab). Write a function in the interface calculating the tax deduction from Problem 2.6. Calculate taxable income for someone filing as married and making $123,000.

Problem 3.3

In this chapter we briefly discussed how to move from one cloud computing platform to another (AWS to Azure). Pick any two such platforms to demonstrate how migration between them works. Start by creating a small compute instance with an app, a script, or data associated with one platform. Then, move to the other platform and create a new account. Follow the process for the migration (you may have to look up more specific or detailed instructions from online resources). Provide your documentation of that process with appropriate steps and screenshots.

Further Reading and Resources

- GCP and Python in one minute: https://youtu.be/T_4cGEtHqUs.
- GCP – getting started with Python: https://cloud.google.com/python/docs/getting-started.
- Explore Python on AWS: https://aws.amazon.com/developer/language/python/.
- AWS certification: https://aws.amazon.com/certification/.
- Microsoft Learn for Azure: https://docs.microsoft.com/en-us/learn/azure/.
- Microsoft Certified – Azure Fundamentals: https://docs.microsoft.com/en-us/learn/certifications/azure-fundamentals/.
- An introduction to using Python on Azure: www.microsoft.com/en-us/research/wp-content/uploads/2016/02/an-intro-to-using-python-with-microsoft-azure.pdf.
- Google Cloud certification: https://cloud.google.com/certification.
- Cloud computing costs and comparisons: www.datamation.com/cloud/cloud-costs/.
- The dark side of cloud computing – soaring carbon emissions: www.theguardian.com/environment/2010/apr/30/cloud-computing-carbon-emissions.
- Cloud computing and carbon footprint: www.innoq.com/en/blog/cloud-computing-and-carbon-footprint/.

Notes

1. www.putty.org.
2. Get started with Hadoop and Hive in Azure HDInsight using the Azure portal, available at https://docs.microsoft.com/en-us/azure/hdinsight/hadoop/apache-hadoop-linux-create-cluster-get-started-portal.
3. AWS free-tier details: https://aws.amazon.com/free.
4. https://docs.microsoft.com/en-us/azure/site-recovery/migrate-tutorial-aws-azure.

PART II

SUPERVISED LEARNING

Machine learning has several branches, but supervised and unsupervised learning are the two main ones. This part will cover supervised learning. Here, we can use the data for training with known truth values. If these values of outcome variable are continuous, it falls under regression (Chapter 4), and if it is discrete, we are looking at classification (Chapters 5 and 6). Essentially, most prediction problems fall under supervised learning. Think about predicting rainfall, stock prices, election results, or making hiring decisions.

4 Regression

> **What do you need?**
> - An understanding of how a system learns (see Chapter 1).
> - Basic knowledge of statistical techniques, including correlation (see Appendix A).
> - Introductory- to intermediate-level experience with Python, including installing packages (refer to Chapter 2).
>
> **What will you learn?**
> - Capturing and modeling the relationship between two continuous variables with linear regression.
> - Using one or more variables to predict the value of an outcome variable.
> - Addressing shortcomings of linear regression with ridge and lasso regressions.
> - The gradient descent technique for doing regression, including the derivation of its algorithm and hands-on practice.

4.1 Introduction

Our first topic in machine learning (ML) is **regression**. Think of regression as a much more sophisticated version of extrapolation. For example, if you know the relationship between education and income (the more educated someone is, the more money they make), you could predict someone's income based on their education level. Simply speaking, learning such a relationship is regression.

In more technical terms, regression is concerned with modeling the relationship between two or more variables of interest. We can learn that two variables are related in some way (e.g., correlation), but can we figure out if or how one variable predicts the other? Linear regression allows us to do that.

Imagine you are trying to figure out how age affects income. You observe a few data points that make you think the relationship is *income* = $20,000 × *age*. The chances are this equation is not going to fit perfectly with your observations. So, you revise that equation and check how well it fits the data. You keep repeating this process until you get to a point where your equation that connects age to income does not improve. At this point the relationship equation that you found is still not going to explain everything that you observe, but it is the best you could do. This is one way to perform regression. Once you have used regression to find the linear equation, you are ready to make predictions for someone's income by knowing their age.

In this chapter we will see how to formalize this process. We will start with simple linear regression, trying to learn the relationship between two variables and capturing it in a line equation (thus, "linear"). Then we will expand on this by doing the same with multiple predictors or independent variables. That will be the case of multiple linear regression. Next, we will discuss an apparent shortcoming with linear regression, specifically with how it looks for an optimal solution. To overcome that shortcoming, we will introduce variations, called *ridge regression* and *lasso regression*. All of these can be done neatly with the help of linear algebra that we already know; the chances are that you have done at least some of these things before. But then we will take a step further into the realm of ML and solve the problem of regression using a technique called gradient descent. The gradient descent technique provides us with a more general framework to fit a model to data. Here, our model is a line, but it could be something else. As we will see in a later chapter, gradient descent comes in handy with neural networks and deep learning.

4.2 Linear Regression

Correlation allows us to express the relationship between two variables using a single number. That number has two components: sign and value. The sign indicates the direction of the relationship, and the value provides the magnitude. Correlation allows us to say things like "as A goes up, so does B," "if we increase A, B is likely to change," or "changing A will make little to no difference to B." But we are not able to say more precisely how one change would affect the other. More importantly, this relationship information is not enough for us to make predictions and address questions such as: "if we were to add C to A, what would be the value of B?" Imagine A here is your spending on ads and B is sales. Knowing that more ad spending leads to more sales is not enough to make budgeting decisions. You want to know what kind of sales increase you could expect if you were to increase your ad spending by 50%.

Questions like this call for finding and representing the relationship between A and B in a different way. Instead of a single number, we could find a line. Learning this line that captures the relationship between A and B is what linear regression does. And it is not limited to just two variables. We could have several Bs (predictors or independent variables) affecting A, and we could still find that line. (Technically, a hyperplane in a higher-dimensional space – more on that later.)

For example, in Figure 4.1 we want to predict the annual return of stock using the excess return of stock in a stock portfolio. The line represents the relation between these two variables. Here, it happens to be quite linear (see most of the data points close to the line), but that is not always the case.

Linear regression is the process of finding this line. Specifically, we want to see how a variable X affects a variable y.[1] Here, X is called the **independent variable** or **predictor**; y is called the **dependent variable** or **outcome**. Take a note of the notation here. X is uppercase because it could have multiple feature vectors, making it a feature matrix. If we are dealing with only a single feature for X, we may decide to use the lowercase x. On the

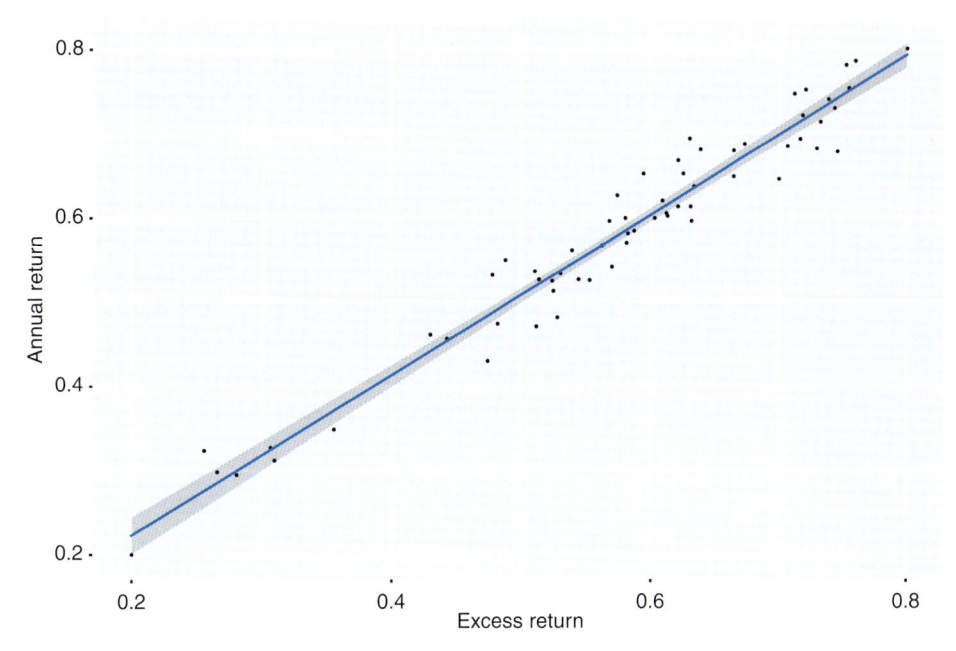

Figure 4.1 An example from the stock portfolio dataset showing the relationship between annual return and excess return of stock using linear regression.[2]

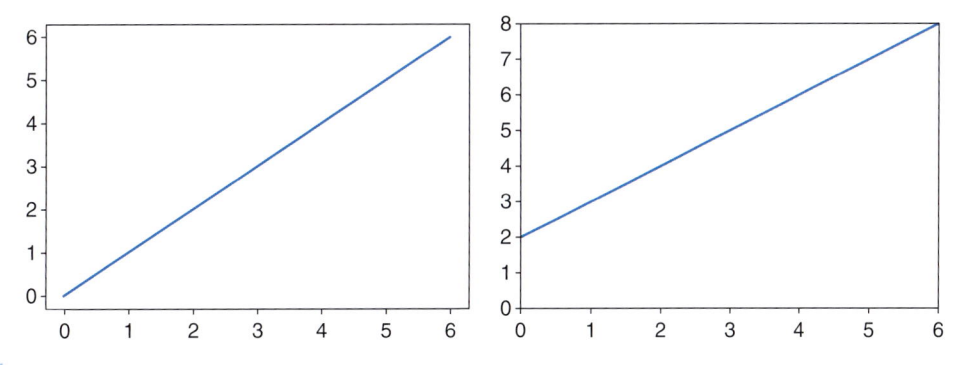

Figure 4.2 Different cases of linear relationships between two variables.

other hand, y is lowercase because it is a single value or feature being predicted. A simple line in a 2D plane can be represented using the equation $y = c + m \times X$. Here, c is a constant or intercept on the y-axis and m is the slope associated with X.

Take a look at Figure 4.2. On the left we see a symmetric relationship between X and y. Using that, it is easy to predict the value of y if we know X. If $X = 3$, $y = 3$. If $X = 100$, $y = 100$. Here, the y-intercept or constant = 0, and the slope of the line is 45°.

The figure on the right tells a different story. Here, the y-intercept is 2 and the slope is gentler than before. In other words, predicting the value of y based on X is not going to be as simple as before, and we will need to know those values of the slope and intercept.

Given that we will hardly ever have a real-life problem where the relationship between two variables is going to be what we see on the left, how do we find the slope and the intercept of a line, given the data? There are many methods for doing so, but perhaps the most common is ordinary least squares (OLS).

To get to OLS, first we need to understand how error is calculated in the case of regression. For simplicity, let's assume we have one predictor variable X, and our outcome variable is y. We have come up with our guess for how these two relate using a line equation: $y = mX + c$. Here, m and c are the parameters we can estimate (or guess). Now, we can plug actual values of X and our guesses for m and c into this line equation for each data point i. This will give us our estimate for y. We will call it $\hat{y}$. But wait, we have the *real* value of y for that data point. We refer to it as y_i. To see how well we did for our prediction for this data point, we can calculate the mean square error (MSE):

$$\text{MSE}_i = \left(y_i - \hat{y}_i\right)^2.$$

Why did we square that difference? Because the difference could be positive or negative, but either of them indicates an error. If we square that, we end up with a positive number. The lowest (best) value we can get here is zero, whereas there is no upper bound to this number. What matters is that we have some measure of error. We can now do this for each data point in our dataset, add them all up, and take the average. That gives us the MSE for a given line function f:

$$\text{MSE}(f) = \frac{1}{n}\sum_{i=1}^{n}\left(y_i - \hat{y}_i\right)^2.$$

Now, imagine we have another line (perhaps a guess) with different values for m and c. That should give us a different value for MSE. Is that value less than what we had before? If yes, then the new line is better than the one before. We can keep repeating this, looking for the line that gives us the lowest MSE. This outcome is what OLS refers to – finding the line with the lowest squared error.

This is a simple-to-understand, yet quite effective, method for finding a fitting line. Let us use a simple example to explore it further.

Hands-on Example 4.1: Linear Regression Using OLS

We will work with the data shown in Table 4.1 about ad spending and sales at a shoe company for the last five years.

We want to find out how ad spending relates to sales. For this we will look for a line. As we know, a line equation is $y = c + mX$. Translating that to what we have here, we get:

$$Sales = Const + Slope \times Ad\ Spending.$$

Now, we start with some guesses. What if *Const* here was 0 and *Slope* was 15,000? Let's plug these values into our line equation and find predictions for sales for each year. Table 4.2 is populated with those numbers.

Table 4.1 Ad spending vs. sales data.

Ad spending (millions)	Sales
2.3	34,221
2.8	36,453
3.2	38,242
3.5	40,231
4.2	43,873

Table 4.2 Calculating the fit for a line, trial 1.

Ad spending (millions)	Sales	Predicted sales	Squared error
2.3	34,221	34,500	77,841
2.8	43,453	42,000	2,111,209
3.2	46,242	48,000	3,090,564
3.5	49,231	52,500	10,686,361
4.2	57,873	63,000	26,286,129
RMSE			2,906.96

Table 4.3 Calculating the fit for a line, trial 2.

Ad spending (millions)	Sales	Predicted sales	Squared error
2.3	34,221	33,500	519,841
2.8	43,453	41,000	6,017,209
3.2	46,242	47,000	574,564
3.5	49,231	51,500	5,148,361
4.2	57,873	62,000	17,032,129
RMSE			2,420.42

Of course, we are going to be off from what the actual sales numbers were. We can compute the error by taking the difference of predicted sales and actual sales and squaring that. We then add it all up, divide by the number of data points (here, five), and take the square-root. That is called root mean squared error or RMSE. All of these values are provided in Table 4.2.

On its own, RMSE does not tell us much. Now, let's go with a different guess. This time, let's assume *Const* is 1000 and *Slope* is 15,000. The new computations are shown in Table 4.3.

This RMSE is lower than what we saw before. In other words, the line created by the new values of *Const* and *Slope* is better. Can we find even better values for those parameters so we could reduce the RMSE? Yes, sure. But we will leave this here, as the possibilities for these values could be endless. What we take away, though, is this process of using OLS, wherein we are looking for a set of values that give us the lowest possible RMSE.

I hope you understand that the hands-on example above is a one-off method for doing regression. In reality, we almost never have the need (or time and effort) to solve regression by hand. But it is still important to go through such an exercise to appreciate the general method for solving regression. Also, OLS is not the only way to find the optimal values for intercept and slope. Other popular methods include least absolute deviation (LAD) and maximum likelihood estimation. These are out of the scope of this chapter, but we will visit maximum likelihood in a later chapter. For now, let's see how we can do linear regression using Python.

Hands-on Example 4.2: Linear Regression

Obtain the "Longley" dataset from OA 4.1 before starting this exercise. Let's begin by importing the packages we will need here.

```
import numpy as np
import pandas as pd
import matplotlib.pyplot as plt
import statsmodels.api as sm
```

Now we will load the data.

```
df = pd.read_csv("longley.csv", index_col = 0)
```

At this point, I suggest you go ahead and explore the data. If you are using an IDE such as Spyder, the easiest way to do this is by going to the Variable Explorer (typically a panel in the top-right corner) and double-clicking the `df` variable. This should bring up a table or a dataframe. You can see that we have two variables of interest here: *GNP* (gross national product) and *Employed*. Let's see if these two have any relationship. We can run the following to find their correlation.

```
print("Correlation coefficient = ",
np.corrcoef(df.Employed,df.GNP)[0,1])
```

That gives us a very high correlation of 0.98. That is positive and large, which means that as one goes up, the other does too. And this is a very strong relationship. That is good for us, because we want to now use one variable (*Employed*) to predict the other (*GNP*). We want to know how change in employment leads to change in GNP. This calls for doing regression analysis. Let's prepare our predictor and output variables.

```
y = df.GNP # response (dependent variable)
X = df.Employed # predictor (independent variable)
X = sm.add_constant(X)   # Adds a constant term to the
                         # predictor
```

What is happening in that last line? Remember, the line equation is $y = c + mX$. Here, X represents the right side of this equation, so we need to add that c (constant) to it. Now we are ready to run the regression process.

```
lr_model = sm.OLS(y, X).fit()
```

Here, `lr_model` is the model built using linear regression with the OLS fitting approach. How do we know this worked? Let's check the results of the model by running the following command:

```
print(lr_model.summary())
```

This generates the output shown below.

```
OLS Regression Results
==============================================================
Dep. Variable:              GNP   R-squared:             0.967
Model:                      OLS   Adj. R-squared:        0.965
Method:           Least Squares   F-statistic:           415.1
Date:          Sat, 15 May 2021   Prob (F-statistic): 8.36e-12
Time:                  09:57:12   Log-Likelihood:       -68.391
No. Observations:            16   AIC:                   140.8
Df Residuals:                14   BIC:                   142.3
Df Model:                     1
Covariance Type:      nonrobust
==============================================================
             coef   std err       t    P>|t|   [0.025    0.975]
--------------------------------------------------------------
const   -1430.4823   89.361  -16.008  0.000  -1622.142 -1238.822
Employed   27.8363    1.366   20.374  0.000     24.906    30.767
==============================================================
Omnibus:                  1.033   Durbin-Watson:           1.530
Prob(Omnibus):            0.597   Jarque-Bera (JB):        0.836
Skew:                    -0.499   Prob(JB):                0.658
Kurtosis:                 2.491   Cond. No.             1.26e+03
==============================================================
```

Somewhere in the output we can find values of coefficients – one for const (constant) and the other for GNP. And here is our regression equation:

```
GNP = const + coeff * Employed
```

Based on our regression analysis we can write the actual equation as:

```
GNP = -1430.4823 + 27.8363 * Employed
```

Let's visualize this line equation. A line is nothing but a collection of points. If we had lots of points we could connect them to draw a line. Conversely, if we have a line (a 2D entity), we could use it to get a full picture of a point, given partial information – that is, given one of its dimensions we could obtain the other dimension. And that is what we are going to do here. We will generate lots of points along the x-axis (*Employed*) and use

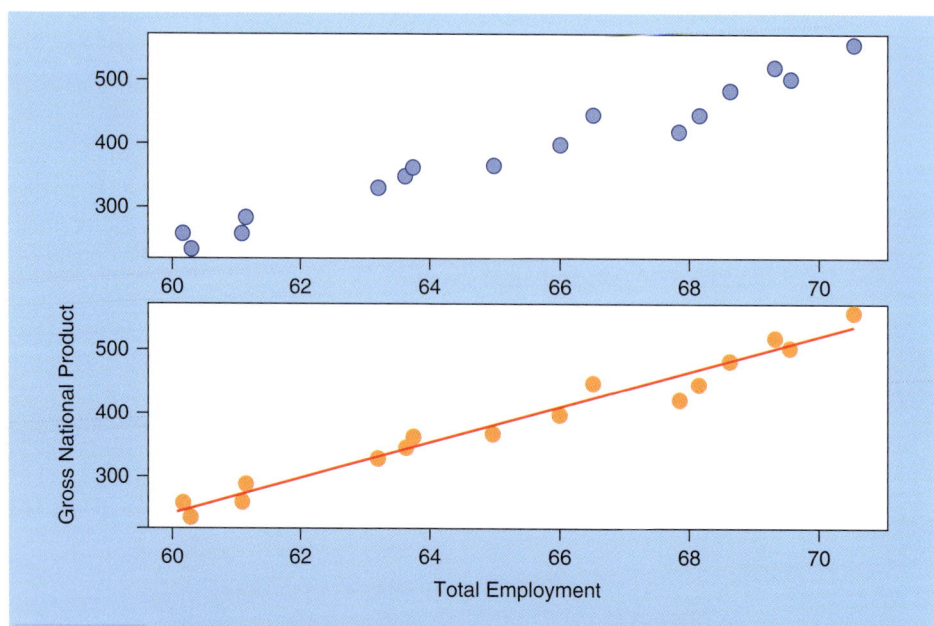

Figure 4.3 Scatterplot of *GNP* vs. *Employed* overlaid with a regression line.

the above equation to find the corresponding values for the *y*-axis (*GNP*). That will give us points with *x* and *y* coordinates.

```
# We pick 100 points equally spaced from the min to the
# max
X_prime = np.linspace(X.Employed.min(), X.Employed.
max(), 100)
X_prime = sm.add_constant(X_prime)   # Add a constant
# Now we calculate the predicted values
y_hat = lr_model.predict(X_prime)
plt.scatter(X.GNP, y)   # Plot the raw data
plt.xlabel("Total Employment")
plt.ylabel("Gross National Product")
plt.plot(X_prime[:, 1], y_hat, "red", alpha = 0.9)
# Add the regression line, colored in red
```

This gives us the visualization shown in Figure 4.3.

If you see something strange in your plots from the above code, the chances are your plotting environments are getting messed up. To address that, change the code for your plotting as shown below:

```
plt.figure(1)
plt.subplot(211)
plt.scatter(df.Employed, df.GNP)
```

```
plt.subplot(212)
plt.scatter(X.Employed, y)  # Plot the raw data
plt.xlabel("Total Employment")
plt.ylabel("Gross National Product")
plt.plot(X_prime[:, 1], y_hat, "red", alpha=0.9)
# Add the regression line, colored in red
```

Essentially, we are creating separate spaces to display the original scatter plot and the new scatter plot with the regression line.

Often, we run through such examples, and while it makes sense, it may still feel a bit abstract. So let's ground this problem a little. Through the regression analysis we obtained the following equation:

```
GNP = -1430.4823 + 27.8363 * Employed
```

This equation gives us predictive powers. All we have to do is substitute a value for *Employed*. We know from the dataset that in 1960 the value of *Employed* was 69.564. We will use our regression equation to calculate the value of GNP. Plugging in the value *Employed* = 69.564 to the above equation, we get:

```
GNP = -1430.4823 + 27.8363 * 69.564 = 505.922
```

Now let's look up the actual value of *GNP* for 1960: It is 502.601. That means we were off by a little (less than 1%). That is not bad for our prediction. And, more important, we now have a model (the line equation) that allows us also to interpolate and extrapolate. In other words, we could even plug in some unknown *Employed* value and find out what the approximate value for GNP would be.

Try It Yourself 4.1: Linear Regression

You are given a dataset named "boston" (OA 4.2). This dataset contains information collected by the US Census Service concerning housing in the area of Boston, MA. The dataset is small, with only 506 cases. The data was originally published by Harrison, D. and Rubinfeld, D.L. (1978). Hedonic prices and the demand for clean air. *Journal of Environmental Economics and Management, 5*, 81–102. Here are the variables captured in this dataset:

```
CRIM - per capita crime rate by town
ZN - proportion of residential land zoned for lots over
25,000 sq.ft.
INDUS - proportion of non-retail business acres per town
CHAS - Charles River dummy variable (1 if tract bounds
river; 0 otherwise)
```

```
NOX - nitric oxides concentration (parts per 10 million)
RM - average number of rooms per dwelling
AGE - proportion of owner-occupied units built prior to
1940
DIS - weighted distances to five Boston employment
centers
RAD - index of accessibility to radial highways
TAX - full-value property-tax rate per $10,000
PTRATIO - pupil-teacher ratio by town
B - 1000(Bk - 0.63)² where Bk is the proportion of
Black people by town
LSTAT - % lower status of the population
MEDV - Median value of owner-occupied homes in $1000s
```

Using appropriate correlation and regression tests, find which of the variables is the best predictor of NOX (nitric oxides concentration). For that model, provide the regression plot and equation.

Using appropriate correlation and regression tests, find which of the variables is the best predictor of MEDV (median home value). For that model, provide the regression plot and equation.

FYI: Bias, Variance, and Overfitting

In basic statistics we learn about the notion of variance (if you are not familiar with it, I suggest you review Appendix A). Variance tells us how much our data is spread out. For example, if I tell you that the average score in an exam in my class is 80, you do not know if every student in my class got 80 or if the scores ranged from 60 to 100. Even if I were to tell you that it was the latter, you still do not know how many were close to 60 and how many were close to 100. Variance allows us to have a greater understanding of how the scores were distributed around that average or mean. The larger the variance, the higher the spread. If all the students got 80, the variance will be 0. A more common way to talk about variance is standard deviation, which is just the square-root of the variance.

A larger variance could also mean we may have a hard time fitting a simple model like a line to the data, or we may need more parameters to fit the data. If we go with a simpler model, it may have large training error, which causes bias. In the first chapter we talked about bias in ML, and in the last chapter we will dive deeper into that issue. But here we are talking about *statistical* bias, which is where we see the expected value differ greatly from the true value. This is a result of trying to fit a simple model to high-variance data. We could overcome it by fitting a more complex model. We could reduce bias that way, but then we may be overfitting the data. This is bad because while we could reduce the training error, we may not do so well on testing data. In other words, while trying to address the bias issue, we lost the robustness of our model.

Is there a way we could address both problems? Yes, and we will see that later in this chapter when we talk about ridge and lasso regressions. But for now, see if you can brush up on these statistical concepts!

4.3 Multiple Linear Regression

What we have seen so far is one variable (the predictor) helping to predict another (the response or dependent variable). But there are many situations in life where there is not a single factor that contributes to an outcome. Therefore, we need to look at multiple factors or variables. That is where we use **multiple linear regression**. As the name suggests, this is a method that takes into account multiple predictors in order to predict one response variable. Let's look at an example.

> **Hands-on Example 4.3: Multiple Linear Regression**
>
> We will start by getting a small advertising dataset from OA 4.3. This dataset contains information about advertising budgets for TV and radio and corresponding sales numbers. We want to learn how much those budgets influence product sales.
>
> Let's first load the dataset in our Python environment:
>
> ```
> # Load the libraries we need - numpy, pandas, pyplot,
> # and statsmodels.api
> import numpy as np
> import pandas as pd
> import matplotlib.pyplot as plt
> import statsmodels.api as sm
>
> # Load the advertising dataset into a pandas dataframe
> df = pd.read_csv("Advertising.csv", index_col = 0)
> ```
>
> We start our analysis by doing linear regression, as we did before, to see how well *TV* predicts *Sales*.
>
> ```
> y = df.Sales
> X = df.TV
> X = sm.add_constant(X)
>
> lr_model = sm.OLS(y,X).fit()
>
> print(lr_model.summary())
> print(lr_model.params)
> ```
>
> In this output what we are looking for is the R-squared value. Roughly speaking, this is a measure of what proportion of the underlying variance in the data is captured by the given model. Here, we see it is around 0.61, which means that about 61% of the variance in this *TV–Sales* relationship can be explained using the model we've built. That's not too bad, but before we move on let's plot this relationship:

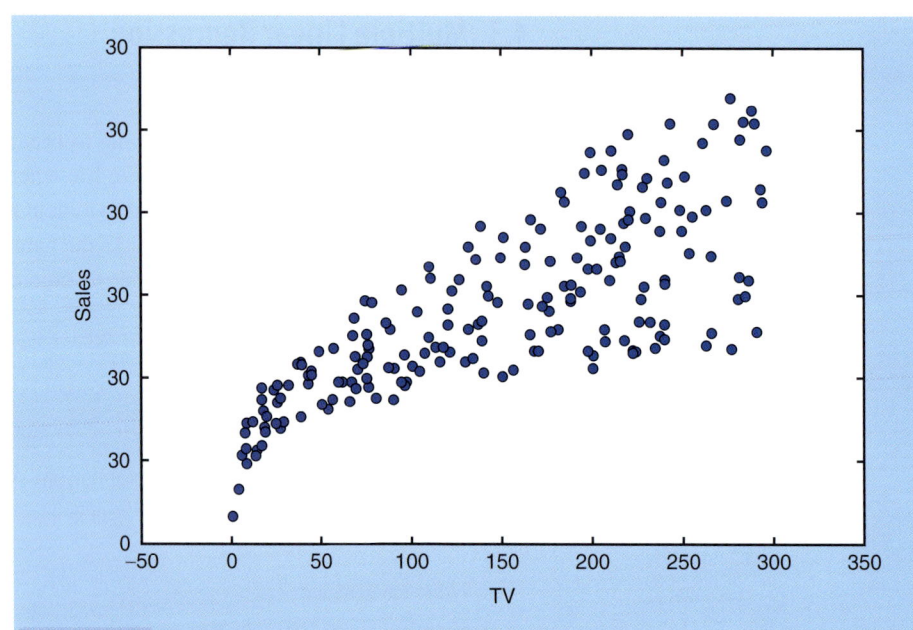

Figure 4.4 Scatterplot of *TV* vs. *Sales* from the advertising data.

```
plt.figure()
plt.scatter(df.TV,df.Sales)
plt.xlabel("TV")
plt.ylabel("Sales")
```

The outcome is shown in Figure 4.4.

Let's repeat the process for radio:

```
y = df.Sales
X = df.Radio
X = sm.add_constant(X)

lr_model = sm.OLS(y,X).fit()

print(lr_model.summary())
print(lr_model.params)

plt.figure()
plt.scatter(df.Radio,df.Sales)
plt.xlabel("Radio")
plt.ylabel("Sales")
```

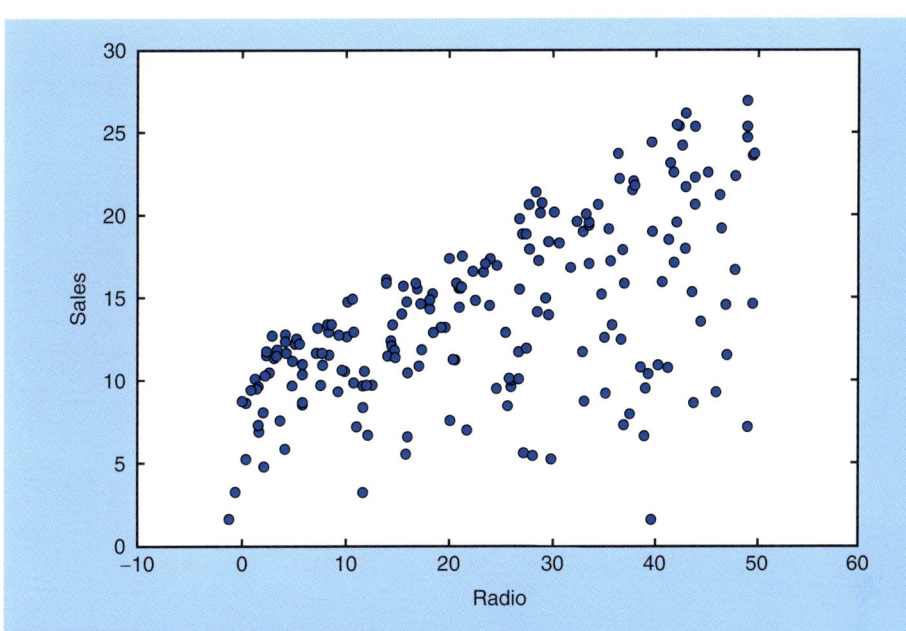

Figure 4.5 Scatterplot of *Radio* vs. *Sales* from the advertising data.

Figure 4.5 is what we get as the result.

This model gives us an R-squared value of around 0.33, which is worse than what we got with TV. Now, let's see what happens if we put both of these independent variables (*TV* and *Radio*) together to predict sales:

```
y = df["Sales"]
X = df[["TV","Radio"]]
X = sm.add_constant(X)

lr_model = sm.OLS(y,X).fit()

print(lr_model.summary())
print(lr_model.params)
```

This comes up with an R-squared close to 0.9. That is much better. It seems that two are better than one!

Here is the code for plotting this regression in 3D, with the result shown in Figure 4.6. Consider this an optional exercise.

```
from mpl_toolkits.mplot3d import Axes3D

# Figure out X and Y axes using ranges from TV and
# Radio
```

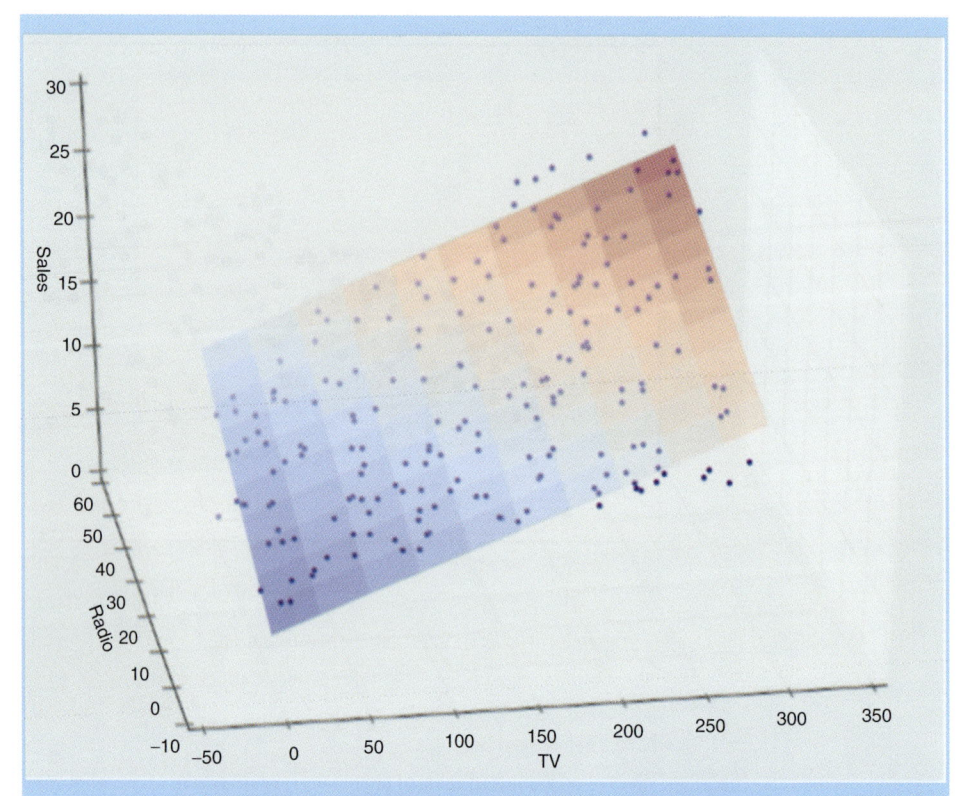

Figure 4.6 3D scatterplot showing *TV*, *Radio*, and *Sales* variables.

```
X_axis, Y_axis = np.meshgrid(np.linspace(X.TV.min(),
X.TV.max(), 100), np.linspace(X.Radio.min(), X.Radio.
max(), 100))

# Plot the hyperplane by calculating corresponding Z
# axis (Sales)
Z_axis = lr_model.params[0] + lr_model.params[1] * X_
axis + lr_model.params[2] * Y_axis

# Create matplotlib 3D axes
fig = plt.figure(figsize = (12, 8))   # figsize refers
# to width and height of the figure
ax = Axes3D(fig, azim = -100)

# Plot hyperplane
ax.plot_surface(X_axis, Y_axis, Z_axis, cmap = plt.
cm.coolwarm, alpha = 0.5, linewidth = 0)
```

```
# Plot data points
ax.scatter(X.TV, X.Radio, y)

# Set axis labels
ax.set_xlabel("TV")
ax.set_ylabel("Radio")
ax.set_zlabel("Sales")
```

> **Try It Yourself 4.2: Multiple Linear Regression**
>
> Let's practice what you have learned about correlation, regression, and visualization with a small dataset that you can obtain from OA 4.4. The All Greens Franchise dataset contains 30 observations about All Greens sales. It has five predictor variables (X1 to X5), as well as an annual net sales figure (X6). Use this dataset to:
>
> 1. determine correlation of annual net sales with money spent on advertising and number of competitors in the area;
> 2. visualize the above correlation in a scatterplot; and
> 3. build a regression model to predict the annual net sales figure using the other five columns in the dataset.

> **ML in Practice: Regression at Scale**
>
> The idea, and hopefully even the implementation, of regression should feel easy after reviewing the material here. But in real life, things may not go as smoothly. A big challenge could be that of scale. Most of the exercises we are doing here are with small datasets — reasonable numbers of rows (data points) and reasonable numbers of columns (variables or dimensions). In many practical situations that may not be the case. In those situations it is important to understand how to optimize your regression analysis.
>
> Ideally, you would be working on a powerful and/or parallel server that allows you to utilize the on-demand memory and processing power you need. But let's say you are not that lucky. What do you do? First, check how large your dataset is. Can it fit in your memory (RAM)? If not, start trimming your data in various ways. Do you need all of those variables? Perhaps not for all of your analyses. Then, load what you need. Sure, you may have to keep reloading different subsets of that dataframe as your analysis demands, but your machine will not crash so much. If the data is still too large, you may also want to take a random sample of it. There are several techniques for such sampling and approximation.
>
> In short, if you are dealing with large datasets and do not have matching infrastructure, you may have to get creative to trim your data to load and process it. Even in cases when you could load and process the whole dataset, some algorithms could take a long time to run. In those cases also, you may want to do such trimming to speed up your experiments, especially if you are just working on some proof of concept or trying to come up with a set of hypotheses.

4.4 Ridge and Lasso Regression

Let's rethink how linear regression works and why it can be problematic. We are trying to draw a line that gets as close to the data points as possible. The way we do that is by minimizing the average distance between these points and the line, as measured through OLS. The examples we worked before seem to do that well. But let's examine an issue with how OLS works.

As we saw before, OLS tries to find a line that gives us the least amount of MSE. On the surface this is a very reasonable approach. But in doing such optimization, OLS can lead to a very rigid model – one that does well on the given data but does poorly on new data. In other words, OLS may lead to a model not being able to capture enough variance or provide enough generalization. (See the FYI box earlier in this chapter for a discussion on bias, variance, and overfitting.)

Mathematically, that process results in large parameter values. Why is this problematic? If a parameter has a very large value, even a slight change in that parameter or variable could result in a big swing in our predictions. We need to somehow build models that discourage large values for parameters. Ridge-based regression uses a modified OLS function to do just that:

$$\text{Ridge Loss}(y, \hat{y}) = \text{MSE}(y, \hat{y}) + \alpha \cdot \sum_{i=1}^{m} \theta_i^2.$$

Here, we have added a term to the usual MSE we use for OLS. This extra term adds a positive value as a penalty to the overall loss function based on values of our parameters (θs). If you are familiar with the concept of norms in statistics, you can identify this extra term as the L_2-norm, and thus, it is also referred to as **L2 regularization**. Here, α is the weight parameter. It allows us to control how much we want to penalize large parameter values. If you set it to 1 you are saying those values matter to you just as much as the errors introduced by data points. Setting it to 0 will result in the usual OLS.

Notice how we squared the parameter values so we do not have negative values potentially reducing the error (because large negative values are just as bad as large positive values here). We did the same in our original MSE calculations. But there is another way to ensure we do not end up with negative values, which is by taking the absolute values. If we do that we end up with a slightly different formulation of regression, called lasso regression:

$$\text{Lasso Loss}(y, \hat{y}) = \text{MSE}(y, \hat{y}) + \alpha \cdot \sum_{i=1}^{m} |\theta_i|.$$

In statistics, the second term (not including the α) is referred to as the L_1-norm or Manhattan norm. It is also called **L1 regularization**.

This idea of adding a penalty to the model evaluation is not restricted to regression. In Chapter 12 we will see that it is often a good idea to go with a simpler model with fewer parameters, even if it means sacrificing some accuracy or fitness. We will cover various metrics that introduce terms like what we saw above in ridge and lasso regressions that penalize models with larger or more parameters. But for now let's get some hands-on practice with ridge and lasso regression.

Hands-on Example 4.4: Ridge and Lasso Regression

For this example we will use the diabetes dataset that comes with Sklearn. Let's begin by importing that dataset, along with other packages we will need here.

```
import numpy as np
from sklearn import datasets, linear_model

# Load the diabetes dataset
diabetes_X, diabetes_y = datasets.load_diabetes
(return_X_y = True)

# Use only one feature
diabetes_X = diabetes_X[:, np.newaxis, 2]
```

Now that we have our *X* and *y*, we are ready to perform various kinds of regression analyses. Note that here we are going to use the linear regression function available within Sklearn's linear_model package. Feel free to use the other functions we used before for doing the same.

```
# Create linear regression object
regr_linear = linear_model.LinearRegression()
regr_Lasso = linear_model.Lasso(alpha = 0.1)
regr_Ridge = linear_model.Ridge(alpha = 0.1)

# Train the model using the training sets
regr_linear.fit(diabetes_X, diabetes_y)
regr_Lasso.fit(diabetes_X, diabetes_y)
regr_Ridge.fit(diabetes_X, diabetes_y)

# The coefficients
print("Linear Coefficients: \n", regr_linear.coef_)
print("Lasso Coefficients: \n", regr_Lasso.coef_)
print("Ridge Coefficients: \n", regr_Ridge.coef_)
```

The output from the above code looks something like this:

```
Linear Coefficients:
  [938.23786125]
Lasso Coefficients:
  [894.0809961]
Ridge Coefficients:
  [849.36296566]
```

In the example above we can see that the values for coefficients (parameters) are smaller with ridge and lasso regressions compared to our usual OLS-based linear regression.

> **Try It Yourself 4.3: Ridge and Lasso Regression**
>
> For this exercise we will take a look at the California housing sample data that you can download from OA 4.5. Apply ridge and lasso models to the dataset to predict housing price using the other attributes as predictors.

4.5 Gradient Descent

Now we will move on to something more general and a lot more useful in ML. For this, we need to take a step back and think about how linear regression is solved. Take a look at Figure 4.1. Imagine we only have those data points and no line. We can draw a random line and see how well it fits the data. Now let's draw another line and repeat the process. If the error of the new line is lower than the previous one, the new line is better. If we keep repeating this until we find a line that gives us the lowest error, we have found our most fitting line, solving the problem of regression.

How could we generalize this process? Imagine we have some function or procedure for finding the error from our data. The objective is to keep adjusting the function by picking different values for its parameters and seeing if that lowers the cost. Whenever we find the lowest cost, we stop and note the values of the parameters. Those parameter values comprise the most fitting model for the data. This model could be a line, a plane, or in general a function. This is the essence of a technique called **gradient descent**.

Let's formalize this by getting back to that line. It is possible to fit multiple lines to the same dataset, each represented by the same equation but with different m and b values. Our job is to find the best one, which will represent the dataset better than the other lines. In other words, we need to find the best set of m and b values.

A standard approach to solving this problem is to define an *error function* (sometimes also known as the *cost function*) that measures how *good* a given line is. This function will take in a (m, b) pair and return an error value based on how well the line fits our data. To compute this error for a given line, we will iterate through each (x, y) point in our dataset and sum the square distances between each point's y value and the candidate line's y value (computed as $mx + b$). Formally, this error function looks like:

$$\in = \frac{1}{n} \sum_{i=1}^{n} \left(\left(mx_i + b \right) - y_i \right)^2.$$

We have squared the distance to ensure that it is positive and to make our error function differentiable. Note that normally we will use m to indicate the number of data points, but

4.5 Gradient Descent

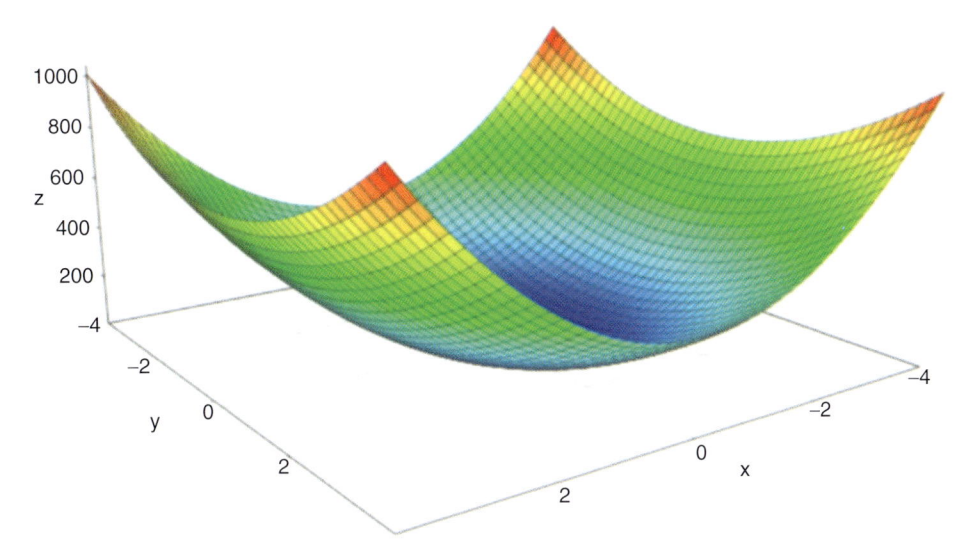

Figure 4.7 Error surface for various lines created using linear regression (*x* represents slope, *y* represents intercept, and *z* is the error value).

here we are using that letter to indicate the slope, so we have made an exception and used *n* for the number of data points. Also note that often the intercept for a line equation is represented using *c* instead of *b*, as we have done.

The error function is defined such that the lines that fit our data better will result in lower error values. If we minimize this function we will get the best line for our data. Since our error function consists of two parameters (*m* and *b*), we can visualize it as a 3D surface. Figure 4.7 depicts what the error surface looks like for our dataset.

Each point in this 3D space represents a line. Let that sink in for a bit. Each point in this 3D figure represents a line. Can you see how? We have three dimensions: slope (*m*), *y*-intercept (*b*), and error. Each point has values for these three, and the *m* and *b* values give us a line. In other words, this 3D figure presents a whole bunch of possible lines we could have to fit the data shown in Table 4.4, allowing us to see which line is the best.

The height of the function at each point is the error value for that line. You can see that some lines yield smaller error values than others (i.e., fit our data better). The more dark blue the color at a point, the lower the error function value, and the better that point fits our data. We can find the best *m* and *b* set that will minimize the cost function using gradient descent.

Gradient descent is an approach for finding minima – points where the error is at its lowest. When we run a gradient descent search we start from some location on this surface and move downhill to find the line with the lowest error.

To run gradient descent on this error function we first need to compute its *gradient* or slope. The gradient will act like a compass that always points us downhill. To compute it, we need to differentiate our error function. Since our function is defined by two

Table 4.4 Data for regression.

x	y
1	3
2	4
3	8
4	4
5	6
6	9
7	8
8	12
9	15
10	26
11	35
12	40
13	45
14	54
15	49
16	59
17	60
18	62
19	63
20	68

parameters (m and b), we need to compute a partial derivative for each. These derivatives work out to be:

$$\frac{\partial \in}{\partial m} = \frac{2}{n}\sum_{i=1}^{n}\left((mx_i + b) - y_i\right)\frac{\partial}{\partial m}\left((mx_i + b) - y_i\right)$$

$$= \frac{2}{n}\sum_{i=1}^{n}\left((mx_i + b) - y_i\right)x_i.$$

$$\frac{\partial \in}{\partial b} = \frac{2}{n}\sum_{i=1}^{n}\left((mx_i + b) - y_i\right)\frac{\partial}{\partial b}\left((mx_i + b) - y_i\right)$$

$$= \frac{2}{n}\sum_{i=1}^{n}\left((mx_i + b) - y_i\right).$$

Now we know how to run gradient descent and get the smallest error. We can initialize our search to start at any pair of m and b values (i.e., any line) and let the gradient descent algorithm march downhill on our error function toward the best line. Each iteration will update *m* and *b* to a line that yields slightly lower error than the previous iteration. The direction to move in for each iteration is calculated using the two partial derivatives from the above two equations.

Let's generalize this. In the above example, *m* and *b* were the parameters we were trying to estimate. But there could be many parameters in a problem, depending on the dimensionality of the data and the number of features available. We will refer to these parameters as θs. It is the job of the learning algorithm to estimate the best possible values of the θs.

Earlier we defined an error function using a model built with two parameters $(mx_i + b)$. Now, let's generalize it. Imagine that we have a model that could have any number of parameters. Since this model is built using training examples, we call it a hypothesis function and represent it using *h*. It can be defined as

$$h(x) \sum_{i=0}^{n} \theta_i x_i.$$

If we consider $\theta_0 - b, \theta_1 = m$, and assign $x_0 = 1$, we can derive our line equation using the above hypothesis function. In other words, a line equation is a special case of the hypothesis function.

Now, just as we defined the error function using the line equation, we can define a cost function using the above hypothesis function:

$$J(\theta) = \frac{1}{2m} \sum_{i=1}^{m} \left(h(x^i) - y^i \right)^2.$$

Compare this to the error function defined earlier. We are now back to using *m* to represent the number of data points. And we have also added a scaling factor of 0.5, which is purely for convenience, as you will see soon.

As before, finding the best values for our parameters means chasing the slope for each of them to reach the lowest possible cost. In other words, we are trying to minimize $J(\theta)$ and we will do that by following its slope along each parameter. Let's say we are doing this for parameter θ_j. That means we will take the partial derivative of $J(\theta)$ with respect to θ_j.

$$\begin{aligned}
\frac{\partial}{\partial \theta_j} J(\theta) &= \frac{1}{2m} \frac{\partial}{\partial \theta_j} \sum_{i=1}^{m} \left(h(x^i) - y^i \right)^2 \\
&= \frac{2}{2m} \sum_{i=1}^{m} \left(h(x^i) - y^i \right) \frac{\partial}{\partial \theta_j} \left(h(x^i) - y^i \right) \\
&= \frac{1}{m} \sum_{i=1}^{m} \left(h(x^i) - y^i \right) \frac{\partial}{\partial \theta_j} \left(\theta_0 x_0^i + \theta_1 x_1^i + \ldots + \theta_j x_j^i + \ldots + \theta_n x_n^i - y^i \right) \\
&= \frac{1}{m} \sum_{i=1}^{m} \left(h(x^i) - y^i \right) x_j^i
\end{aligned}$$

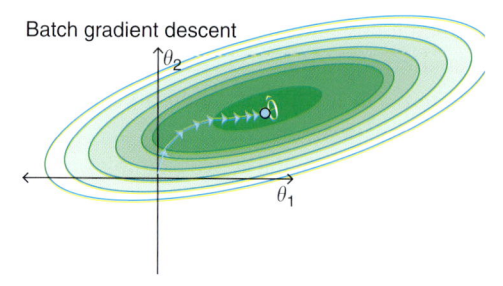

Figure 4.8 Batch gradient descent in action. From Cornell University Computational Optimization Open Textbook.[3]

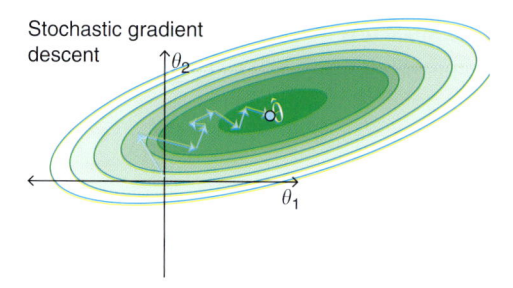

Figure 4.9 Stochastic gradient descent in action. From Cornell University Computational Optimization Open Textbook.[4]

This gives us our learning algorithm, called gradient descent:

$$\theta_j := \theta_j - \alpha \frac{1}{m} \sum_{i=1}^{m} \left(h\left(x^i\right) - y^i \right) x_j^i.$$

This means that in each iteration we update θ (override its existing value) by subtracting a weighted slope or gradient from it. In other words, we take a step in the direction of the slope. Here, α is the learning rate, with a value between 0 and 1, which controls how large a step we take downhill during each iteration. If we take too large a step, we may step over the minimum. However, if we take small steps it will require many iterations to arrive at the minimum.

The above algorithm considers all the training examples while calculating the slope; it is also called **batch gradient descent** (BGD). At times when the sample size is too large and computing the cost function is too expensive we can apply the above algorithm to one data point at a time. That method is called **stochastic gradient descent** (SGD), or *interim gradient descent*. In SGD you can imagine that because we are only looking at one data point at a time we could move around in all kinds of directions – and that is what normally happens. Batch gradient descent operates with quite a bit of grace and smoothness, moving us along the error surface in a focused, almost linear fashion to the point where the cost or the error is the lowest. Figure 4.8 shows what that looks like.

Stochastic gradient descent, on the other hand, bounces around a lot because we are trusting one data point at a time. This leads to us taking lots of steps, many of which may actually be in the wrong direction. Figure 4.9 shows what that looks like. However, with enough inputs we can still converge to the lowest point on the error surface.

This is a clear case of trade-offs. Batch gradient descent takes fewer steps, but each step is quite expensive and could even be prohibitively expensive at times. Stochastic gradient descent takes far more steps but each step is computationally cheap. In this chapter we are only using BGD because our datasets are small and manageable.

> **Hands-on Example 4.5: Regression Revisited**
>
> Before we practice gradient descent in Python, let's see how we would perform regression using what we already know from linear regression. Go ahead and get the dataset from OA 4.6. The following code will allow you to construct a simple linear regression model.
>
> ```python
> import numpy as np
> import pandas as pd
> import statsmodels.api as sm
> import matplotlib.pyplot as plt
>
> df = pd.read_csv("regression.csv")
>
> X = df.x
> y = df.y
>
> X = sm.add_constant(X)
>
> lr_model = sm.OLS(y, X).fit()
>
> plt.xlabel("x")
> plt.ylabel("y")
> plt.title("Linear regression (OLS)")
>
> # define lists of x- and y-axis ticks
> xt = np.arange(0, df.x.max() + 5, 5)
> yt = np.arange(0, df.y.max() + 10, 10)
>
> # set ticks and axis limits for the plot
> plt.axis([xt[0], xt[-1], yt[0], yt[-1]])
> plt.xticks(xt[1:])
> plt.yticks(yt[1:])
>
> # create a scatter plot of the original data
> plt.scatter(df.x, df.y, facecolors = "none", edgecolors = "lightgray")
>
> # define endpoints for regression line based off of
> # x-axis tick limits
> x_prime = [xt[0], xt[-1]]
> ```

Linear regression

Figure 4.10 Linear regression plot.

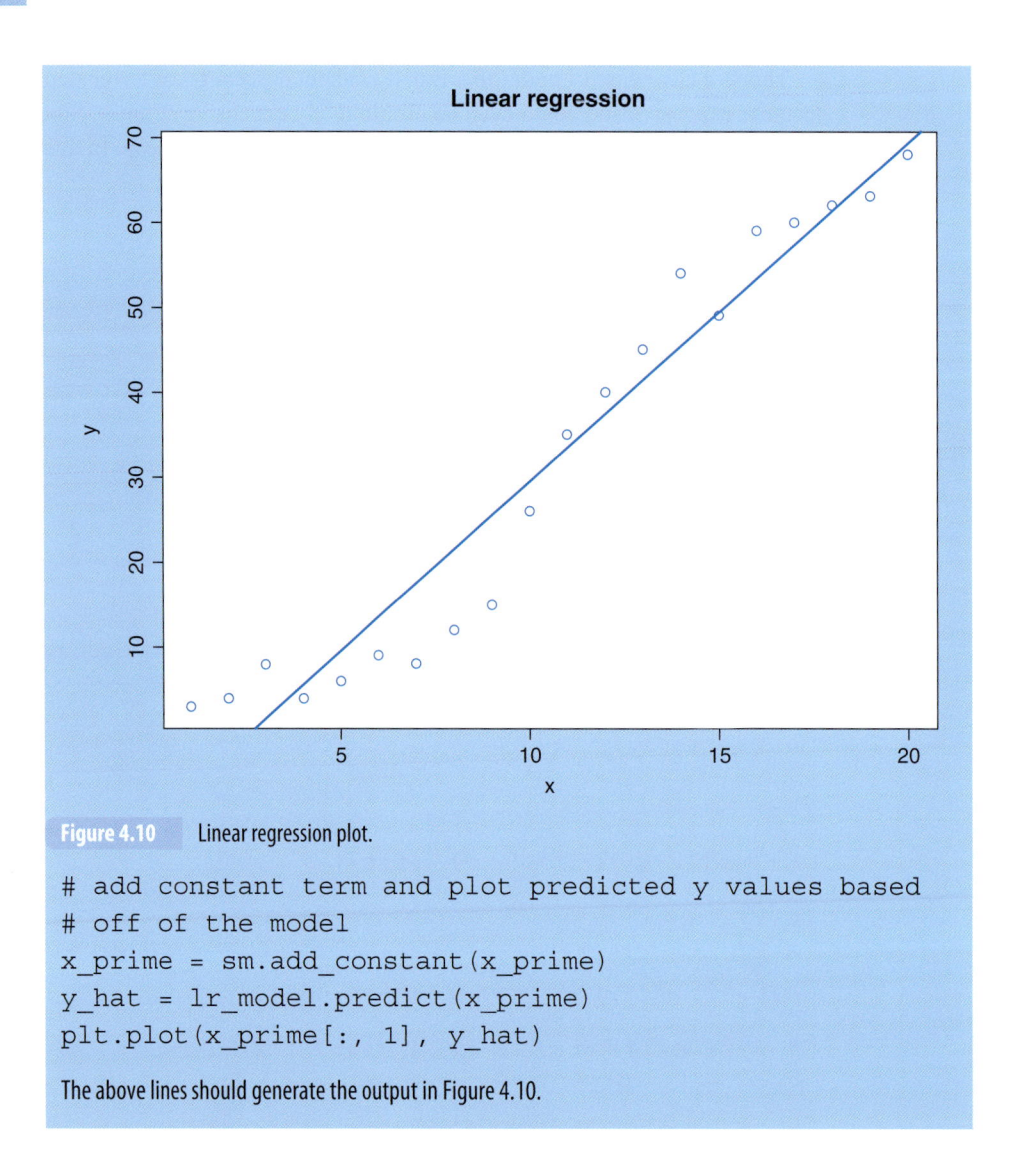

```
# add constant term and plot predicted y values based
# off of the model
x_prime = sm.add_constant(x_prime)
y_hat = lr_model.predict(x_prime)
plt.plot(x_prime[:, 1], y_hat)
```

The above lines should generate the output in Figure 4.10.

None of what we saw above should look unfamiliar. Now we are going to do the same thing, but this time instead of using linear regression we will apply gradient descent (specifically, BGD). This will require us to write our own function for computing gradients.

Hands-on Example 4.6: Gradient Descent

We begin by getting the packages we will need for this exercise.

```
import numpy as np
import pandas as pd
import matplotlib.pyplot as plt
```

Now, let's write a function for running the BGD algorithm. This function will take *X* (independent variables or predictors), *y* (dependent variable or outcome), *alpha* (learning rate), and *epsilon* (minimum change in error or cost for a subsequent step in order to continue). In addition, we will also try to plot how we navigate this error surface. But if you are short on memory (or patience), you may not want to do this (remember, we are going to write a loop that could run hundreds of times). Therefore, we will also have a couple of parameters in this function that will allow us to turn the visualization on or off. The full function is written below with comments at appropriate places to help you understand:

```python
def batch_gradient_descent(y, X, alpha, epsilon,plot_on
= -1, plot_func = None):
    # Initialize our "guess" for each coefficient
    # theta_j to 1 and store these in a single column
    theta = np.ones(shape=(X.shape[1], 1))

    m = X.shape[0] # number of data points

    # Calculate a column of predicted y-values for each
    # data point
    y_hat = X @ theta

    # calculate a 1 by 1 matrix that holds the sum of
    # the squared differences between each y_hat and y
    cost = np.transpose(y_hat - y) @ (y_hat - y)
    # initialize list of costs to contain the cost
    # associated with our initial coefficients (scaled
    # by 1/2m in accordance with the cost formula)
    costs = [cost[0][0] / (2 * m)]

    i = 0 # number of iterations
    delta = 1 # Change in cost

    while (delta > epsilon):
        if (plot_on > 0 and i % plot_on == 0 and
        plot_func is not None):
            plot_func(theta)

        # calculate a column that holds the difference
        # between y_hat and y for each data point
        differences = X @ theta - y

        # Update each theta_j by the partial derivative
        # of the cost with respect to theta_j, scaled by
        # learning rate Note: np.transpose(X) gives us
```

```python
            # the observed values (x_j) for a parameter j in
            # the jth row of a matrix
            theta = theta - (alpha / m) * ((np.transpose(X))
            @ differences)

            # Using the updated coefficient values, append
            # the new cost value
            cost = np.transpose(X @ theta - y) @ (X @ theta - y)
            costs.append(cost[0][0] / (2 * m))
            delta = abs(costs[i + 1] - costs[i])

            if (costs[i + 1] > costs[i]):
                print("Cost is increasing. Try reducing alpha.")
                break
            i += 1
        if (plot_on > 0 and i % plot_on == 0 and plot_func
        is not None):
            plot_func(theta)

    print("Completed in", i, "iterations.")
    return theta
```

Now we are ready to get our data and run gradient descent. Let's go ahead and load the data and identify our *X* and *y*.

```python
df = pd.read_csv("regression.csv")
X = df[["x"]]
y = df[["y"]]
```

Next, we will set up our plotting environment.

```python
plt.xlabel("x")
plt.ylabel("y")
plt.title("Batch Gradient Descent")

xt = np.arange(0, df.x.max() + 5, 5)
yt = np.arange(0, df.y.max() + 10, 10)

plt.axis([xt[0], xt[-1], yt[0], yt[-1]])
plt.xticks(xt[1:])
plt.yticks(yt[1:])
```

What does our original data look like? Given that we have only two variables, we can easily create a scatter plot:

```
plt.scatter(df.x, df.y, facecolors = "none", edgecolors = "lightgray")
```

Next, we will define endpoints for regression lines using *x*-axis tick limits:

```
x_prime = [xt[0], xt[-1]]
```

Now we can plot a current fit using the passed-in column of coefficient values (theta). For simplicity, we will assume that theta has only one element:

```
def plot_model(theta):
    y_hat = [xp * theta[0] for xp in x_prime]
    plt.plot(x_prime, y_hat, color = "dimgrey")

X = X.to_numpy()
y = y.to_numpy()
```

Finally, we call the function that we wrote for computing (and plotting) gradient descent:

```
batch_gradient_descent(y = y, X = X, alpha = 0.01, epsilon = 10**-4,plot_on=1, plot_func=plot_model)
```

The output should look like what you see in Figures 4.11 and 4.12.

We can also visualize how the cost function changes in each iteration by doing the following steps:

```
import numpy as np
import pandas as pd
import matplotlib.pyplot as plt

# Perform batch gradient descent, as in the previous
# example, but plot the evolution of cost as opposed to
# the evolution of the regression line
def batch_gradient_descent(y, X, alpha, epsilon):
    theta = np.ones(shape=(X.shape[1], 1))
    m = X.shape[0]

    cost = np.transpose(X @ theta - y) @ (X @ theta - y)
```

Figure 4.11 Regression lines produced using the gradient descent algorithm.

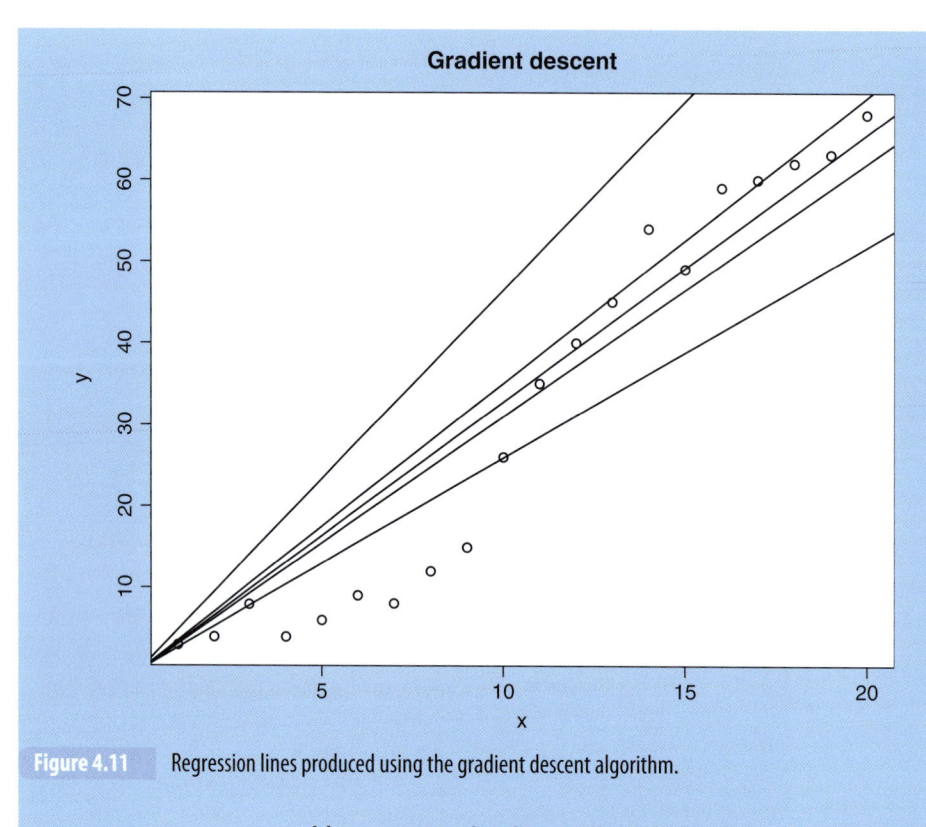

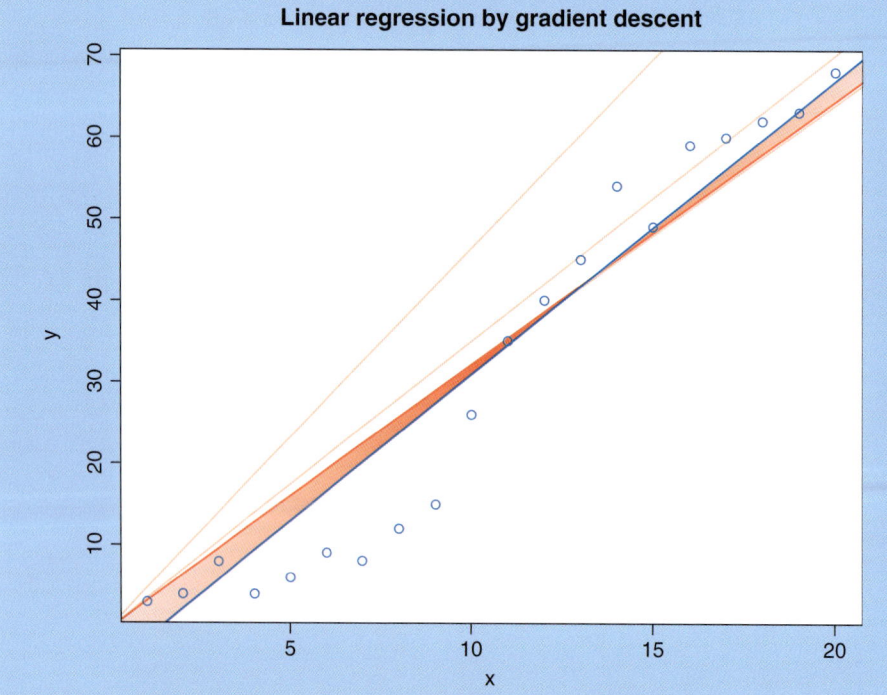

Figure 4.12 Finding the best regression line using the gradient descent algorithm.

```python
    costs = [cost[0][0] / (2 * m)]
    i = 0
    delta = 1
    while (delta > epsilon):
        theta = theta - (alpha / m) * ((np.transpose(X))
        @ (X @ theta - y))

        cost = np.transpose(X @ theta - y) @ (X @ theta - y)
        costs.append(cost[0][0] / (2 * m))
        delta = abs(costs[i + 1] - costs[i])

        if (costs[i + 1] > costs[i]):
            print("Cost is increasing. Try reducing alpha.")
            break
        i += 1
    print("Completed in", i, "iterations.")
    # Plot the cost versus iteration
    plt.plot([i for i in range(len(costs))], costs)
    return theta
# Set up our predictor / response columns
df = pd.read_csv("regression.csv")
X = df[["x"]].to_numpy()
y = df[["y"]].to_numpy()

# Set up our plotting environment
plt.xlabel("iteration")
plt.ylabel("cost")
plt.title("Cost Function")
batch_gradient_descent(y = y, X = X, alpha = 0.01,
epsilon = 10**-4)
```

The output is shown in Figure 4.13.

As we can see, the cost quickly jumps down in just a few iterations, giving us a very fast convergence. That is to be expected because we have only a couple of parameters and a very small sample size. Try practicing this with another dataset (see the below homework exercise). Play around with things like number of iterations and learning rate. If you want to have more fun and try your coding skills, see if you can modify the algorithm to stop when the change in the cost function is low enough, rather than running it for a fixed number of steps.

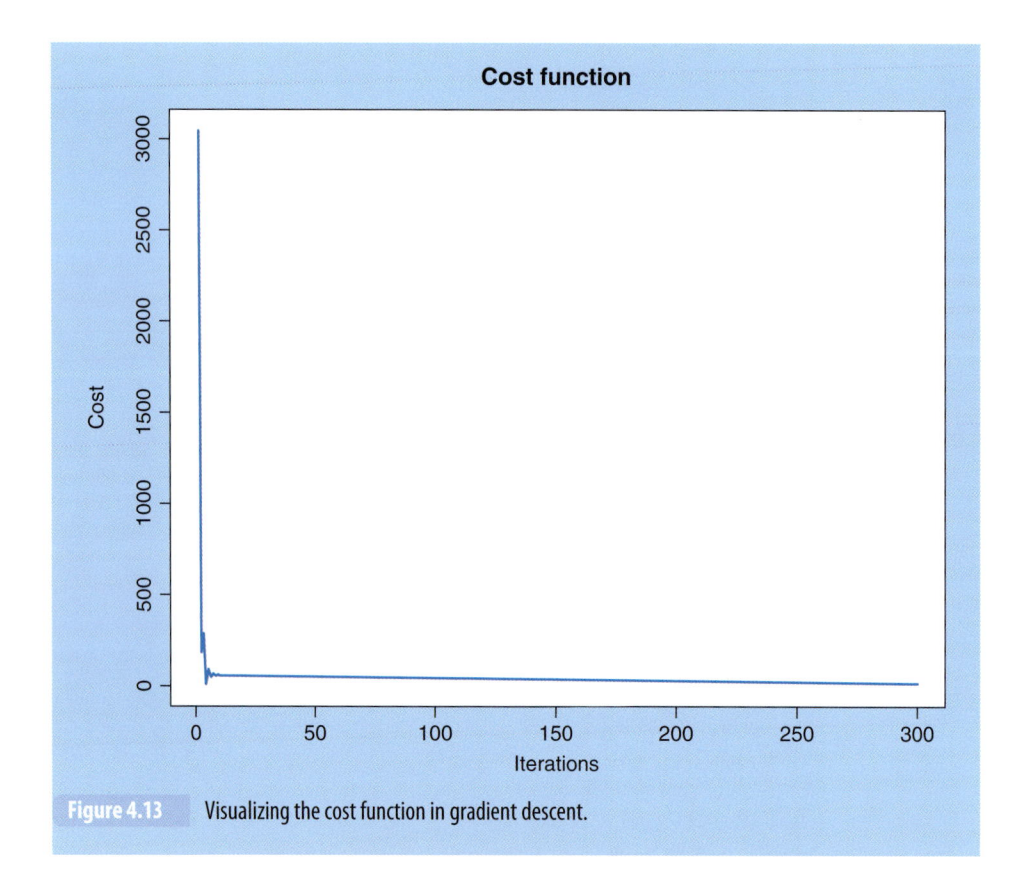

Figure 4.13 Visualizing the cost function in gradient descent.

> **Try It Yourself 4.4: Gradient Descent**
>
> In this exercise you are going to use the kangaroo nasal dimension data (download from OA 4.7) to build a linear regression model to predict nasal length from nasal width. Next, use the gradient descent algorithm to predict the optimal intercept and gradient for this problem.

4.6 Considerations for ML Modeling

In this chapter we explored a host of new tools and techniques, collectively parked under the umbrella of ML, which we can use to solve various data science problems. While it is easy to understand individual tools and methods, it is not always clear how to pick the best one(s) for a given problem. There are multiple factors that need to be considered when choosing the right algorithm for a problem. Some of these factors are discussed below.

4.6.1 Accuracy

Most of the time beginners in ML incorrectly assume that the best algorithm for any problem is the most accurate one. However, getting the most accurate answer possible is not always necessary. Sometimes an approximation is adequate, depending on the problem. If so, you may be able to cut your processing time dramatically by sticking with more approximate methods. Another advantage of more approximate methods is that they naturally tend to avoid overfitting. We will revisit the notion of accuracy and other metrics for measuring how good a model is later in this book.

4.6.2 Training–Testing

In this chapter we used all the data we were given to build a model in most of our examples. However, in supervised learning we often use a portion (typically 70–80%) of the data for training and the rest (typically 20–30%) for testing. These two partitions are created by random sampling of the full data. What does this look like for regression? Assuming 70% for training, we will randomly pick about 70% of the rows with all the variables. Using this data we build the model as we did throughout this chapter. This is called training. Then, we take the remaining 30% of the original data, input the predictors into the model we built and produce our estimates for the outcome variable. We then compare these estimates to actual outcome values (because we still have that in the original data) and ask how close we came to those true values. If we are looking for one number to indicate the error in our estimates, we can use the OLS measurement. This is called testing. It is common to repeat this process multiple times – each time with a different set of randomly sampled training and testing data – and calculate testing success (the lower the error generated through OLS, the greater the success). In the next chapter we will see how to do this training–testing procedure in a systematic way.

4.6.3 Training Time

The time necessary to train a model varies between algorithms. Training time is often closely tied to accuracy – one typically accompanies the other. In addition, some algorithms are more sensitive to the number of data points than others. A limit on time can drive the choice of algorithm, especially when the data set is large.

4.6.4 Linearity

Lots of ML algorithms make use of linearity. Linear classification algorithms assume that classes can be separated by a straight line (or its higher-dimensional analog). These include logistic regression and support vector machines. Linear regression algorithms assume that data trends follow a straight line. These assumptions are not bad for some problems, but on others they bring accuracy down.

4.6.5 Number of Hyperparameters

Hyperparameters are the knobs a data scientist gets to turn when setting up an algorithm. They are numbers that affect the algorithm's behavior, such as error tolerance, number of iterations, or options between variants of how the algorithm behaves. The training time and accuracy of the algorithm can sometimes be quite sensitive to getting just the right settings. Typically, algorithms with a large number of hyperparameters require more trial and error to find a good combination.

Some off-the-shelf applications or service providers may include extra functionalities for hyperparameter tuning. For example, Microsoft Azure (see Chapter 3) provides a parameter sweeping module block that automatically tries all hyperparameter combinations at whatever granularity the user wants. While this is a great way to make sure you have tried every possible combination in the parameter space, the time required to train a model increases exponentially with the number of hyperparameters.

The upside is that having many hyperparameters typically indicates that an algorithm has greater flexibility. It can often achieve high accuracy, provided you find the right combination of hyperparameter settings.

4.6.6 Number of Features

For certain types of data, the number of features can be very large compared to the number of data points. This is often the case with genetics or text data. The large number of features can bog down some learning algorithms, making training time unfeasibly long. Support vector machines are particularly well suited to this case (see Chapter 6).

4.6.7 Choosing the Right Estimator

Often the hardest part of solving an ML problem can be finding the right estimator for the job. Different estimators are better suited for different types of data and different problems. How do we learn when to use which estimator or technique? There are two primary ways: (1) developing a comprehensive theoretical understanding of different ways we could develop estimators or build models; and (2) through lots of hands-on experience. As you may have guessed, in this book we are doing the latter.

If you are looking for a comprehensive and theoretical treatment of various ML algorithms, you will have to use other textbooks and resources. You can find some of those resources at the end of this chapter. But if you are open to working with different data problems and trying different techniques in a hands-on manner in order to develop a practical understanding of this matter, you are holding the right book. In the next two chapters we will go through many ML techniques by applying them to various data problems.

4.7 Summary

Regression is often an entry point to ML if you are coming from statistics. That's because almost any basic statistics course will cover regression. It is such a simple yet powerful and useful method. Many real-life problems call for regression analysis. They range from rainfall prediction to voter turnout on an election day. Another reason regression makes a good entry point to ML is that it allows for us to start adjusting to the ML terminology while still working with familiar concepts from statistics. For example, we start equating coefficients to parameters. While the process or the results may not change, such distinctions are important to consider. Machine learning can be understood, at times, as the process of tuning the parameters for their optimal values, or where the overall error of the model is the lowest.

While the basic idea of regression is easy to grasp, it is important to understand that without a careful treatment we could overfit the data, which is good for memorizing, but not for learning. In other words, we may do really well on the training data but poorly on the testing data. Various forms of regularization can help. This is where we saw ridge and lasso regressions. These methods allow us to penalize complex models that try overfitting the data. Again, while you may have come across these regression methods in statistics, it is important to contextualize them in ML because this idea of working with parameters will keep coming up. Typically, the more parameters a model has, the better it can capture the underlying variance in the data. But more parameters also mean the possibility of overfitting and the need for more training data.

Finally, we learned about the gradient descent technique. While we used it for solving a linear regression problem, it is important to realize that gradient descent is a more general-purpose and powerful approach for optimization or finding a solution in a multi-dimensional space. Studying this technique also allowed us to pick up some more ML terminology such as the idea of error or cost function and learning rate. As we start going deeper and broader with ML techniques, it is important to carry these concepts with us.

Key Terms

- **Machine learning**: A field that explores the use of algorithms that learn from data and uses that knowledge to make predictions on new data.
- **Supervised learning**: A branch of ML that includes problems where a model can be built using the true labels of the data.
- **Model**: An artifact created by the training process on a dataset (called the training set) that is representative of the population.
- **Linear model**: The relationship between a continuous response variable and one or more predictor variable(s) that can be represented using a linear equation.

- **Parameter**: Any numerical quantity that characterizes some aspect of a given population.
- **Feature**: An individual measurable property or characteristic of a phenomenon or object being observed.
- **Independent/predictor variable**: A variable that is thought to not be affected by other variables.
- **Dependent/outcome/response variable**: A variable that depends on other variables (most often independent variables).
- **Gradient descent**: An ML algorithm that computes a slope down an error surface in order to find a model that provides the best fit for the given data.
- **Batch gradient descent**: A gradient descent algorithm that considers all the training examples while calculating the gradient.
- **Stochastic/incremental gradient descent**: A gradient descent algorithm that considers one data point at a time while calculating the gradient.
- **Learning rate**: In many of the ML algorithms a learning rate is a real value between 0 and 1 that determines how much change should be done in subsequent steps. This rate can be fixed or changing throughout the process.

Conceptual Questions

1. There is a lot around us that is driven by some form of ML, but not everything is. Give an example of a system or a service that does not use ML and one that does. Use this contrast to explain ML in your own words.

2. Many ML models are represented using parameters. Use this idea to define ML.

3. How do supervised learning and unsupervised learning differ? Give an example for each.

4. Why is it bad to have large values for regression parameters?

5. Explain how ridge and lasso regression address shortcomings with regular linear regression.

6. Compare batch gradient descent and stochastic gradient descent using their definitions, and pros and cons.

Hands-on Problems

Problem 4.1 (Linear Regression)

A popular restaurant review website has released the dataset you can download from OA 4.8. Each row represents the average rating of a restaurant's different aspects as provided by previous customers. The dataset contains the following attributes: ambience, food, service, and overall rating. The first three attributes are predictor variables, and the last one is the outcome. Use a linear regression model to predict how the predictor attributes impact the overall rating of the restaurant.

First, express the linear regression in mathematical form. Then, try solving it by hand. Here, you will have four parameters (the constant and the three attributes), with one predictor. You do not have to actually solve this with all possible values for these parameters. Rather, show a couple of possible sets of values for the parameters with the predictor value calculated. Finally, use Python to find the linear regression model and report it in appropriate terms (do not just dump the output from Python).

Problem 4.2 (Linear Regression)

For the next exercise you are going to use the Airline Costs dataset available to download from OA 4.9. The dataset has the following attributes, among others:

- airline name
- length of flight in miles
- speed of plane in miles per hour
- daily flight time per plane in hours
- customers served (in thousands)
- total operating cost in cents per revenue ton-mile
- total assets in $100,000s
- investments and special funds in $100,000s.

Use a linear regression model to predict the number of customers each airline serves using the length of the flight and daily flight time per plane. Next, build another regression model to predict the total assets of an airline from the customers served by the airline. Do you have any insight into the data from the last two regression models?

Problem 4.3 (Multiple Linear Regression)

We used the boston dataset earlier in this chapter (OA 4.2). At that time we were looking for a single variable that could help us best predict the variables of interest. To be specific, we were interested in outcome variables NOX and MEDV. Now we want to see if multiple variables could help us build a better model.

Identify two or three variables that can serve as the predictors for NOX and build a linear regression model. Do the same for MEDV as the dependent variable. Hint: We already did some correlation-based analysis to see which of the variables could have most associations with the outcome variables. Use that analysis to determine which of the two or three variables you would use for regression.

Problem 4.4 (Multiple Linear Regression)

Download the dataset from OA 4.10. This dataset contains information about real estate attributes and their values. Using this dataset:

1. determine the correlation of house price of unit area with transaction date and house age;
2. visualize the above correlation in a scatterplot;
3. build a regression model to predict the house price of unit area using all the attributes in the dataset. Do you think this model is a good enough model? Why?

Problem 4.5 (Ridge and Lasso Regression)

Download the Fish Market dataset from OA 4.11. Use all the attributes except for species to predict the weight of the fish. Report the coefficients returned by lasso and ridge models.

Problem 4.6 (Gradient Descent)

Download the data from OA 4.12, which was obtained from BP Research, with image analysis by Ronit Katz at the University of Oxford. This dataset contains measurements on 48 rock samples from a petroleum reservoir. Twelve core samples from petroleum reservoirs were sampled in four cross sections. Each core sample was measured for permeability, and each cross section has a total area of pores, total perimeter of pores, and shape. As a result, each row in the dataset has the following four columns:

1. area: area of pores space, in pixels out of a 256×256 grid;
2. peri: perimeter in pixels;
3. shape: perimeter/sqrt(area);
4. perm: permeability in millidarcies.

First, create a linear model and check if the permeability has a linear relationship with the remaining three attributes. Next, use the gradient descent algorithm to find the optimal intercept and gradient for the dataset.

Problem 4.7 (Gradient Descent)

For this exercise you are going to work again with a movie review dataset. In this dataset, the ratings, budgets, and other information on popular movies released in 2014 and 2015 were collected from social media websites such as YouTube, Twitter, IMDB, etc. The aggregated dataset can be downloaded from OA 4.13. Use this dataset to answer the following questions:

1. What can you tell about the rating of a movie from its budget and aggregated number of followers in social media channels?
2. If you incorporate the type of interaction the movie has received (number of likes, dislikes, and comments) in social media channels, does it improve your prediction?

3. Among all the factors you considered in the last two models, which one is the best predictor of movie rating? With the best predictor feature, use gradient descent to find the optimal intercept and gradient for the dataset.

Further Reading and Resources

If you are interested in learning more about the topics discussed in this chapter, the following few links might be useful:

- http://rstatistics.net/linear-regression-advanced-modelling-algorithm-example-with-r.
- www.analyticsvidhya.com/blog/2017/06/a-comprehensive-guide-for-linear-ridge-and-lasso-regression.
- www.kdnuggets.com/2017/04/simple-understand-gradient-descent-algorithm.html.
- https://machinelearningmastery.com/gradient-descent-for-machine-learning.
- http://ruder.io/optimizing-gradient-descent.
- Ridge regression explained, step by step: https://machinelearningcompass.com/machine_learning_models/ridge_regression.
- Lasso regression explained, step by step: https://machinelearningcompass.com/machine_learning_models/lasso_regression.
- Advanced regression models: http://r-statistics.co/adv-regression-models.html.
- When, why, and how you should standardize your data: https://machinelearningcompass.com/dataset_optimization/standardization.
- Why stochastic gradient descent works: https://towardsdatascience.com/https-towardsdatascience-com-why-stochastic-gradient-descent-works-9af5b9de09b8.

Notes

1. Notice that the predictor variable X is in uppercase and the outcome y is in lowercase. This is on purpose. Often, there are multiple predictor variables, making X a vector (or a matrix), whereas most of the time (and perhaps for us all of the time), there will be a single outcome variable.
2. Stock portfolio dataset: https://archive.ics.uci.edu/ml/machine-learning-databases/00390/stock%20portfolio%20performance%20data%20set.xlsx.
3. https://optimization.cbe.cornell.edu/index.php?title=File:Visualization_of_stochastic_gradient_descent.png.
4. https://optimization.cbe.cornell.edu/index.php?title=File:Visualization_of_stochastic_gradient_descent.png.

5 Classification 1

> **What do you need?**
> - A good understanding of statistical concepts (see Appendix A), probability theory (see Appendix C), and functions.
> - The basics of differential calculus (see Appendix B for a few handy formulas).
> - Introductory- to intermediate-level experience with Python, including installing packages or libraries (refer to Chapter 2).
>
> **What will you learn?**
> - Solving data problems when truth values for training are available.
> - Performing classification using various machine learning techniques, such as *k*-nearest neighbors, decision trees, and random forest.

5.1 Introduction

In Chapter 1 we talked about how learning happens – not just for machines, but for humans as well. Think about the case of learning that fire is not to be touched. Imagine that nobody is there to ever teach us not to do that. How do we figure this out? Perhaps once or twice we touch an open fire and learn that it causes pain. Given that pain is not a good outcome for us, we decide not to do it again. But it does not stop there. We can associate "very hot" to "pain" easily and start avoiding anything that looks too hot – campfire, burning candles, active stovetops. In effect, we have learned how certain features of a class (in this case, very hot stuff) are associated with a label (in this case, "painful"). This is a case of **classification**. More importantly, this is the process of **supervised learning**. Supervised learning problems are a class of problems where we have training examples with correct labels. In other words, we have data for which we know the correct outcome value.

Supervised learning algorithms use a set of examples from previous records to make predictions about the future. For instance, existing car prices can be used to make guesses about the price of future models. Each example used to train such an algorithm is labeled with the value of interest – in this case, the car's price. A supervised learning algorithm looks for patterns in a training set. It may use any information that might be relevant – the season, the car's current sales records, similar offerings from competitors, consumers' brand perception of the manufacturer – and each algorithm may look for a different set of information and find different types of patterns. Once the algorithm has found the best pattern it can, it uses that pattern to make predictions for unlabeled testing data – tomorrow's values.

There are several types of supervised learning that exist within machine learning (ML). Among them, the two most commonly used algorithm types are regression and classification. We covered regression in the previous chapter. In this chapter and the next we will cover classification. There are two chapters because we have so many classification techniques and important details to cover. This is not by accident. So much of what we need to do with ML involves classification, and we need this space and time to learn and work through many possible methods.

In this chapter we start with one of the most popular and easy-to-understand techniques for classification: *k*-nearest neighbors (kNN). This is an easy-to-understand algorithm. Next, we will look at the decision tree technique, which has the great advantage of being very intuitive and offers visual explanation. Finally, we will cover the random forest method that will allow us to overcome some of the limitations of decision trees.

5.2 Classification with *k*-Nearest Neighbors

The task of classification is this: to learn how a given set of data points and their corresponding labels are classified so that when a new data point comes we can put it in the correct class. Typically, we would take existing data with labels to build a model – referred to as "training," as we discussed in the previous chapter. Using this model we can then perform classification on new data – referred to as "testing." One algorithm – kNN – makes the training part very easy, allowing us to move to testing almost immediately.

Let's look at how kNN works by listing the major steps of the algorithm:

1. As in the general problem of classification, we have a set of data points for which we know the correct class labels.
2. When we get a new data point we compare it to each of our existing data points and find similarities.
3. Take the most similar k data points (k-nearest neighbors).
4. From these k data points, take the majority vote of their labels. The winning label is the label/class of the new data point.

k is usually a small number between 2 and 20. As you can imagine, the higher the number of nearest neighbors (the value of k), the longer it takes us to do the processing.

Let's see this with an example. In Figure 5.1 we have plotted our existing data about three types of automotive along two dimensions: length and weight. These three types are sedan, SUV (sports utility vehicle), and minivan. Of course, there are many other features or dimensions for these vehicles, but for simplicity and the possibility of a visualization we will stick to just two here.

What you see in this figure is already a *trained* model. There is nothing specific to do here for training as the data is already organized along the considered dimensions with their corresponding labels. We can, therefore, move to the testing phase. Imagine we have

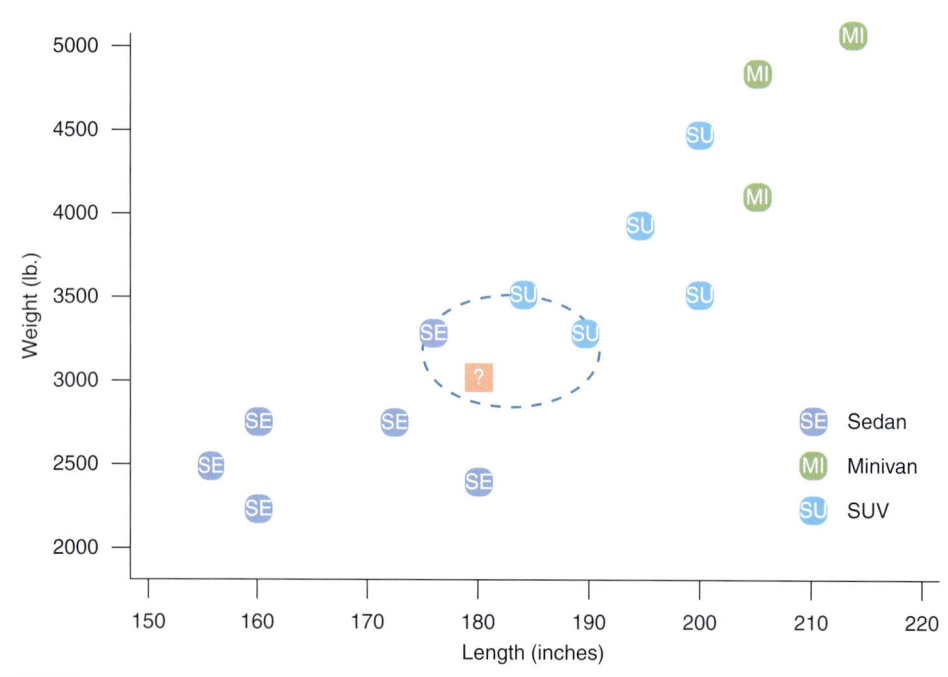

Figure 5.1 Three types of vehicles plotted along length and weight dimensions.

a new vehicle that we want to classify based on its length and weight. We place it on the same plane (shown with a "?" in Figure 5.1). Now, we look at its neighbors. Applying kNN with $k = 3$, we see that the nearest three neighbors are one sedan and two SUVs. Taking the majority vote, we can now declare that the new vehicle can be classified as an SUV.

For classification it usually does not get easier than this. But do you see the shortcomings of this approach? First, our approach is highly sensitive to the raw features we can capture and consider. The technique itself does not tell us which features to consider or weigh. Second, we are assuming that the classes are distinguishable using the features we are considering. If members of different classes are too close to one another, we may have difficulty identifying testing points that fall within that overlap. The decision can be too sensitive to the number of neighbors we look at. And there is the third shortcoming – the value of k being small can mean possible bias as we take inputs from very few neighbors, but a large k could mean more processing power (remember, we need to search for those nearest neighbors).

Despite these shortcomings, kNN is by far one of the easiest to understand and implement techniques for classification. If you have clear enough data (a small number of features helping to distinguish the classes, like we see in Figure 5.1), kNN may give you one of the best results at the lowest cost. It is not a bad idea to start with kNN as your first technique to try classification. So let's go ahead and do just that.

> **Hands-on Example 5.1: kNN**
>
> We will use a wine dataset available from OA 5.1. This data contains information about various attributes of different wines and their corresponding qualities. Specifically, the wine is classified as high quality or not. We will consider these attributes (high quality, low quality) as class labels and build a classifier that learns (based on other attributes) how a wine is classified in one of these two classes.
>
> We start by importing the different libraries we need. After that we load the data, train a classifier on 70% of the total data, test that classifier on the remaining 30% of the data, and calculate the accuracy of the classifier.
>
> ```python
> import numpy as np
> import pandas as pd
> import matplotlib.pyplot as plt
> from sklearn.neighbors import KNeighborsClassifier
> from sklearn.model_selection import train_test_split
>
> df = pd.read_csv("wine.csv")
>
> # Mark about 70% of the data for training and use the
> # rest for testing We will use "density", "sulphates",
> # and "residual_sugar" features for training a
> # classifier on "high_quality"
> X_train, X_test, y_train, y_test = train_test_split(df[["density","sulphates","residual_sugar"]], df["high_quality"], test_size = .3)
>
> # Define the classifier using kNN function and train it
> classifier = KNeighborsClassifier(n_neighbors = 3)
> classifier.fit(X_train, y_train)
>
> # Test the classifier by giving it test instances
> prediction = classifier.predict(X_test)
>
> # Count how many were correctly classified
> correct = np.where(prediction == y_test, 1, 0).sum()
> print (correct)
>
> # Calculate the accuracy of this classifier
> accuracy = correct/len(y_test)
> print (accuracy)
> ```
>
> Note that the above example uses $k = 3$ (checking on the three nearest neighbors when doing the comparison). The accuracy is around 76% (you will get a different number every time because a different set of data is used for training and testing every time you run the program). But what would happen if the value of k was different? Let's try building and testing the classifier using a range of values for k, and plot the accuracy corresponding to each k.

```
# Start with an array where the results (k and
# corresponding accuracy) will be stored
results = []

for k in range(1, 51, 2):
    classifier = KNeighborsClassifier(n_neighbors = k)
    classifier.fit(X_train, y_train)
    prediction = classifier.predict(X_test)
    accuracy = np.where(prediction == y_test, 1,
    0).sum() / (len(y_test))
    print ("k = ",k," Accuracy = ", accuracy)
    results.append([k, accuracy]) # Storing the
    # k,accuracy tuple in results array

# Convert that series of tuples in a dataframe for
# easy plotting
results = pd.DataFrame(results, columns = ["k",
"accuracy"])

plt.plot(results.k, results.accuracy)
plt.title("Value of k and corresponding classification
accuracy")
plt.show()
```

The plotting result is shown in Figure 5.2. Note that, again, every time you run this program you will see slightly different results (and so a different plot). In the output you will also notice that after a certain value of k (typically 15), the improvements in accuracy are hardly noticeable. In other words, we reach the saturation point.

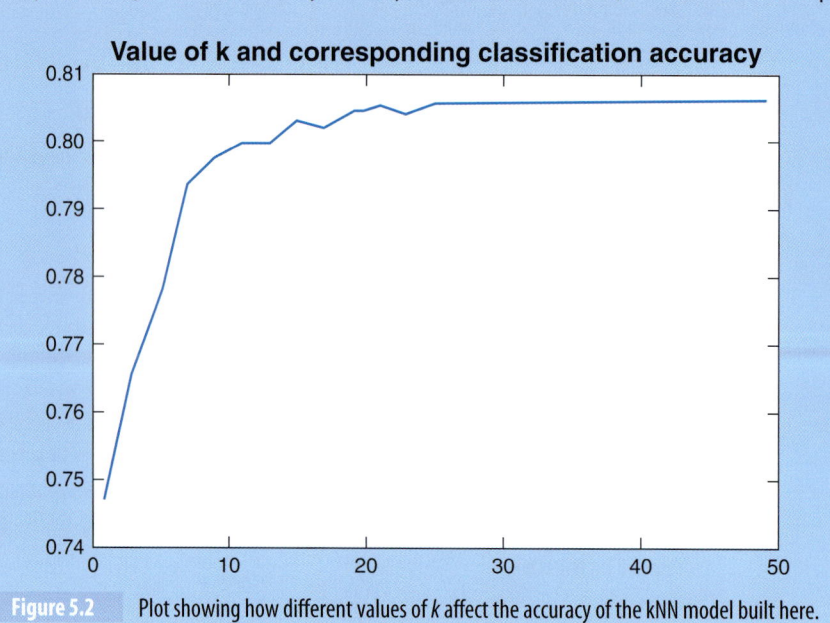

Figure 5.2 Plot showing how different values of k affect the accuracy of the kNN model built here.

> **Try It Yourself 5.1: kNN**
>
> Let's try what you just learned about classification with another dataset. The wheat dataset in UCI's repository (get it from OA 5.2) comprises data about kernels belonging to three different varieties of wheat: Kama, Rosa, and Canadian. For each wheat variety, with a random sample of 70 elements, high-quality visualization of the internal kernel structure was detected using a soft X-ray technique. Seven geometric parameters of wheat kernels were measured. Use these measurements to classify the wheat variety.

5.3 Decision Tree

In ML a decision tree is used for classification problems. In such problems, the goal is to create a model that predicts the value of a target variable based on several input variables. A decision tree builds classification or regression models in the form of a tree structure. It breaks down a dataset into smaller and smaller subsets while at the same time an associated decision tree is incrementally developed. The final result is a tree with decision nodes and leaf nodes. But this is not your "regular" tree that grows with roots at the bottom and branches and leaves at the top. This is an upside-down tree that starts with a root at the top and grows downward with branches splitting off. Each split is a decision point. Each node or leaf provides a decision (class label). In short, a decision tree is a hierarchical, top-down tree built from a root node to leaves and involves partitioning the data into smaller subsets that contain instances with similar values (homogeneous).

The idea here is to build/learn this tree from the training data, so that when we get testing data, for each given data point we can move through that decision tree and check for conditions at each branch, ending up in a node that gives us the class label.

Consider the balloons dataset from OA 5.3, presented in Table 5.1. The dataset has four attributes: color, size, act, and age. It also has one class label: inflated (*True* or *False*). We will use this dataset to understand how a decision tree algorithm works.

Several algorithms exist that generate decision trees, such as ID3/4/5, CART, and CLS. Of these, the most popular is ID3, developed by J. R. Quinlan. ID3 employs *entropy* and *information gain* to construct a decision tree. Before we go through the algorithm, let's understand these two terms.

Entropy is a measure of disorder, uncertainty, or randomness. If I toss a fair coin there is an equal chance of getting a head or a tail. In other words, we would be very uncertain about the outcome, so we would have high entropy. The formula of entropy is:

$$E = -\sum_{i=1}^{k} p_i \log_2(p_i)$$

Here, k is the number of possible class values and p_i is the number of occurrences of the class $i = 1$ in the dataset. In the "balloons" dataset the number of possible class values is 2 (True or False). The reason for the minus signs is that logarithms of the fractions $p_1, p_2, \ldots, p_n$ are negative, so the entropy is actually positive. Usually the logarithms are expressed in base 2, and then the entropy is in units called bits.

Table 5.1 Balloons dataset.

Color	Size	Act	Age	Inflated
YELLOW	SMALL	STRETCH	ADULT	T
YELLOW	SMALL	STRETCH	ADULT	T
YELLOW	SMALL	STRETCH	CHILD	F
YELLOW	SMALL	DIP	ADULT	F
YELLOW	SMALL	DIP	CHILD	F
YELLOW	LARGE	STRETCH	ADULT	T
YELLOW	LARGE	STRETCH	ADULT	T
YELLOW	LARGE	STRETCH	CHILD	F
YELLOW	LARGE	DIP	ADULT	F
YELLOW	LARGE	DIP	CHILD	F
PURPLE	SMALL	STRETCH	ADULT	T
PURPLE	SMALL	STRETCH	ADULT	T
PURPLE	SMALL	STRETCH	CHILD	F
PURPLE	SMALL	DIP	ADULT	F
PURPLE	SMALL	DIP	CHILD	F
PURPLE	LARGE	STRETCH	ADULT	T
PURPLE	LARGE	STRETCH	ADULT	T
PURPLE	LARGE	STRETCH	CHILD	F
PURPLE	LARGE	DIP	ADULT	F
PURPLE	LARGE	DIP	CHILD	F

Figure 5.3 shows the entropy curve with respect to probability values for an event. As you can see, it is at its highest (1) when the probability of a two-outcome event is 0.5. If we are holding a fair coin the probability of getting a head or a tail is 0.5. Entropy for this coin is the highest, which reflects the highest amount of uncertainty we will have with this coin's outcome. If, on the other hand, our coin is completely unfair and flips to "heads" every time, the probability of getting heads with this coin will be 1 and the corresponding entropy will be 0, indicating that there is no uncertainty about the outcome of this event.

Information gain: If you thought it was not going to rain today and I tell you it will indeed rain, you have gained some information. On the other hand, if you already knew it was going to rain, then my prediction will not really impact your existing knowledge much. There is a mathematical way to measure such **information gain**:

$$IG(A, B) = Entropy\ (A) - Entropy\ (A \mid B)$$

The information gain achieved by knowing B along with A is the difference between the entropy (uncertainty) of A and the entropy of A conditional on B. Keep this in the back of your mind and we will revisit it as we work through the next example.

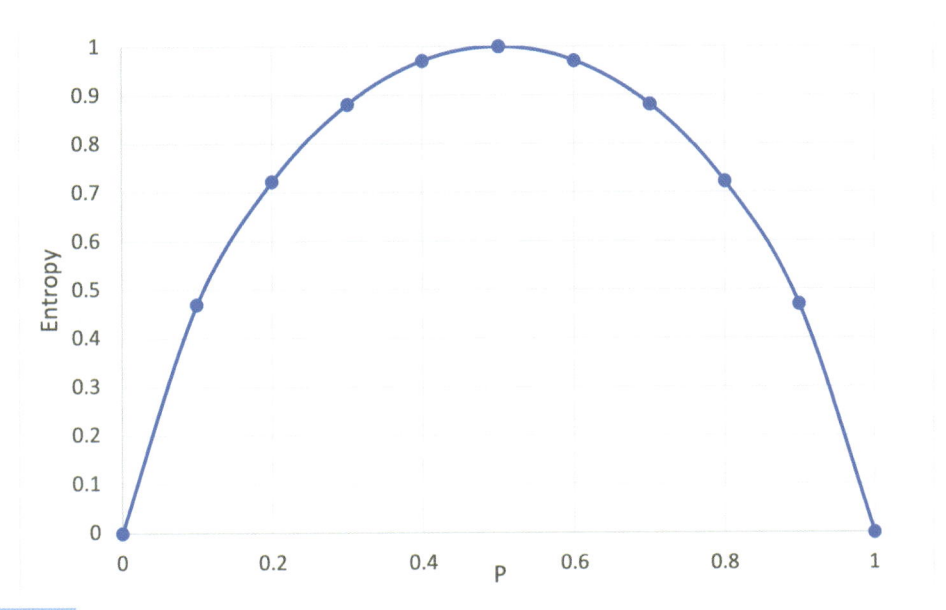

Figure 5.3 Depiction of entropy.

But first, let us get back to that decision tree algorithm. The ID3 algorithm uses entropy to calculate the homogeneity of a sample. If the sample is completely homogeneous, the entropy is 0; if the sample is split equally between two values, the entropy is 1.

To build the decision tree we need to calculate two types of entropy using frequency tables, as follows:

1. *Entropy using the frequency table of one attribute:*

Inflated	
True	False
8	12

Therefore,

$$E(Inflated) = E(12,8)$$
$$= E(0.6, 0.4)$$
$$= -(0.6\log_2 0.6) - (0.4\log_2 0.4)$$
$$= 0.4422 + 0.5288$$
$$= 0.9710$$

2. Similarly, entropy using the frequency table of two attributes is:

$$E(A,B) = \sum_{k \in B} P(k)E(k)$$

Here's the explanation. Let's take a look at Table 5.2.

Table 5.2 Frequency table of act and inflated.

		Inflated		
		T	F	
Act	Dip	0	8	8
	Stretch	8	4	12
Total				20

Therefore,

$$E\ (Inflated\ |\ Act) = P(Dip) \times E(8,0) + P(Stretch) \times E(4,8)$$

$$= \left(\frac{8}{20}\right) \times 0.0 + \left(\frac{12}{20}\right) \times \{-(0.3\log_2 0.3) - (0.7\log_2 0.7)\}$$

$$= \left(\frac{12}{20}\right) \times (0.5278 + 0.3813)$$

$$= \left(\frac{12}{20}\right) \times 0.9090$$

$$= 0.5454$$

The entropy in this case is reduced from the first case. This decrease of entropy is called information gain. Here is the information gain for this case:

$$= E(Inflated) - E(Inflated\ |\ Act)$$
$$= 0.9710 - 0.5454$$
$$= 0.4256$$

If entropy is disorder, then information gain is a measurement of the reduction in that disorder achieved by partitioning the original dataset. Constructing a decision tree is all about finding an attribute that returns the highest information gain (i.e., the most homogeneous branches). The following are the steps to create a decision tree based on entropy and information gain:

Step 1: Calculate the entropy of the target or class variable, which is 0.9710 in our case.
Step 2: The dataset is then split on the different attributes into smaller sub-tables, such as Inflated and Act, Inflated and Age, Inflated and Size, and Inflated and Color. The entropy for each sub-table is calculated. Then, it is added proportionally to get total entropy for the split. The resulting entropy is subtracted from the entropy before the split. The result is the information gain or decrease in entropy.
Step 3: Choose the attribute with the largest information gain as the decision node, divide the dataset by its branches, and repeat the same process on every branch.

If you follow these guidelines step by step you should end up with the decision tree shown in Figure 5.4.

```
                            Act
                    =STRETCH    =DIP
                Age                F (8.0)
         =ADULT     =CHILD
        T (8.0)        F (4.0)
```

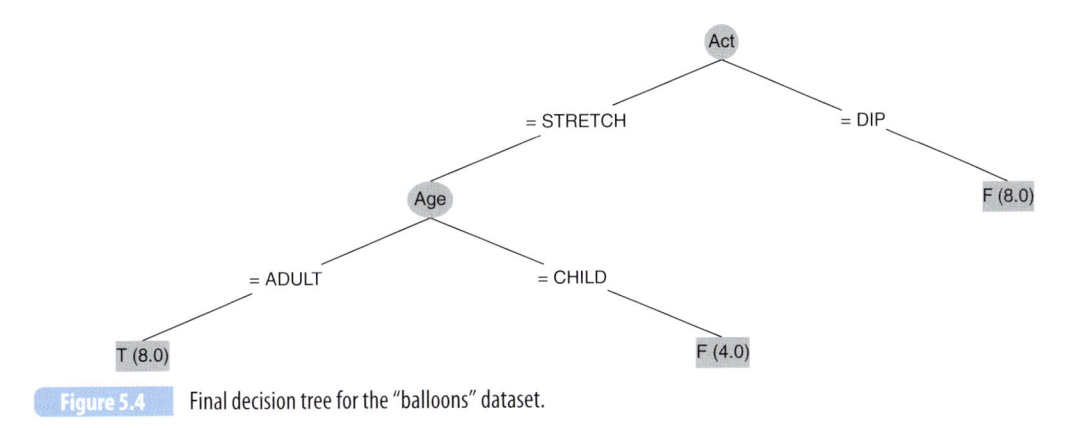

Figure 5.4 Final decision tree for the "balloons" dataset.

5.3.1 Decision Rule

Rules are a popular alternative to decision trees. Rules typically take the form of an {IF:THEN} expression (e.g., {IF "condition" THEN "result"}. Typically for any dataset, an individual rule in itself is not a model, as this rule can only be applied when the associated condition is satisfied. Therefore, rule-based ML methods typically identify a set of rules that collectively comprise the prediction model or the knowledge base.

To fit any dataset, a set of rules can easily be derived from a decision tree by following the paths from the root node to the leaf nodes, one at a time. For the above decision tree the corresponding decision rules are shown on the left-hand side of Figure 5.5.

Decision rules yield orthogonal hyperplanes in the n-dimensional space. What that means is that for each of the decision rules we are looking at a line or a plane perpendicular to the axis for the corresponding dimension. This hyperplane (a fancy word for a line or a plane in a higher dimension) separates data points around that dimension. You can think about it as a decision boundary. Anything on one side of it belongs to one class, and those data points on the other side belong to another class.

5.3.2 Classification Rule

It is easy to read a set of classification rules directly off a decision tree. One rule is generated for each leaf. The antecedent of the rule includes a condition for every node on the path from the root to that leaf, and the consequent of the rule is the class assigned by the leaf. This procedure produces rules that are unambiguous in that the order in which they are executed is irrelevant. However, in general, rules that are read directly off a decision tree are far more complex than necessary, and rules derived from trees are usually pruned to remove redundant tests. Because decision trees cannot easily express the disjunction implied among the different rules in a set, transforming a general set of rules into a tree is not quite so straightforward. A good illustration of this occurs when the rules have the same structure but different attributes, such as:

If a and b, then x.
If c and d, then x.

R1: IF (Act = Stretch) AND (Age = Adult) THEN Inflated = T

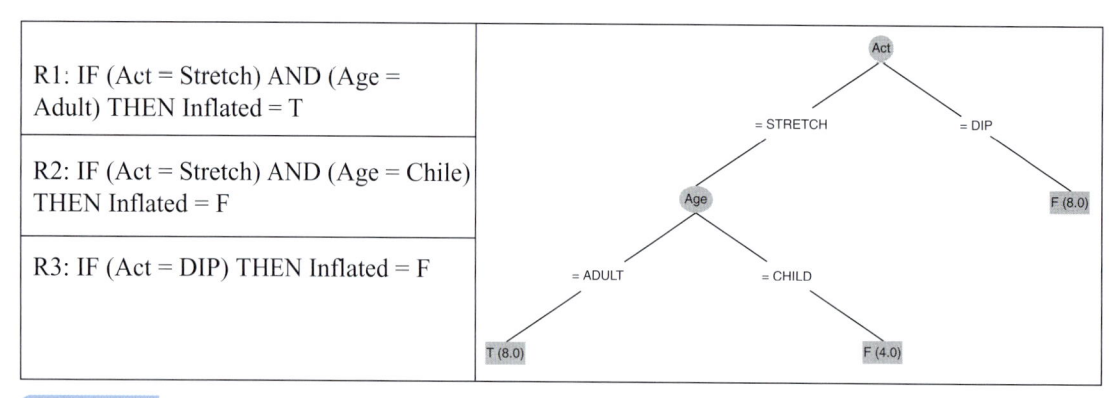

R2: IF (Act = Stretch) AND (Age = Chile) THEN Inflated = F

R3: IF (Act = DIP) THEN Inflated = F

Figure 5.5 Deriving decision rules using a decision tree.

Then, it is necessary to break the symmetry and choose a single test for the root node. If, for example, *a* is chosen, the second rule must, in effect, be repeated twice in the tree. This is known as the replicated subtree problem.

5.3.3 Association Rule

Association rules are no different from classification rules, except that they can predict any attribute, not just the class, and this gives them the freedom to predict combinations of attributes, too. Also, association rules are not intended to be used together as a set, as classification rules are. Different association rules express different regularities that underlie the dataset, and they generally predict different things.

Because so many different association rules can be derived from even a very small dataset, interest is restricted to those that apply to a reasonably large number of instances and have a reasonably high accuracy on the instances to which they apply. The **coverage**, or support, of an association rule is the number of instances for which it predicts correctly. Its **accuracy** – often called confidence – is the number of instances that it predicts correctly, expressed as a proportion of all instances to which it applies.

For example, consider the weather data for playing golf in Table 5.3, a training dataset of weather and the corresponding target variable "Play" (which codes whether or not it is possible to play golf in that day's weather).

The decision tree and the derived decision rules for this dataset are given in Figure 5.6.

Let's consider this rule: If *temperature = cool* then *humidity = normal*. The coverage is the number of days that are both cool and have normal humidity (four in the data of Table 5.3), and the accuracy is the proportion of cool days that have normal humidity (100% in this case). Some other good-quality association rules for Figure 5.6 are:

- If *humidity = normal* and *windy = false* then *play = yes*.
- If *outlook = sunny* and *play = no* then *windy = true*.
- If *windy = false* and *play = no* then *outlook = sunny* and *humidity = high*.

5.3 Decision Tree

Table 5.3 Weather data for playing golf.

Outlook	Temperature	Humidity	Windy	Play
Sunny	Hot	High	FALSE	No
Sunny	Hot	High	TRUE	No
Overcast	Hot	High	FALSE	Yes
Rainy	Mild	High	FALSE	Yes
Rainy	Cool	Normal	FALSE	Yes
Rainy	Cool	Normal	TRUE	No
Overcast	Cool	Normal	TRUE	Yes
Sunny	Mild	High	FALSE	No
Sunny	Cool	Normal	FALSE	Yes
Rainy	Mild	Normal	FALSE	Yes
Sunny	Mild	Normal	TRUE	Yes
Overcast	Mild	High	TRUE	Yes
Overcast	Hot	Normal	FALSE	Yes
Rainy	Mild	High	TRUE	No

R1: IF (Outlook = Sunny) AND (Windy = False) Then Play= Yes

R2: IF (Outlook = Sunny) AND (Windy = True) Then Play= No

R3: IF (Outlook=Overcast) THEN Play = Yes

R4: IF (Outlook = Rainy) AND (Humidity = High) THEN Play = No

R5: IF (Outlook = Rainy) AND (Humidity = Normal) THEN Play = Yes

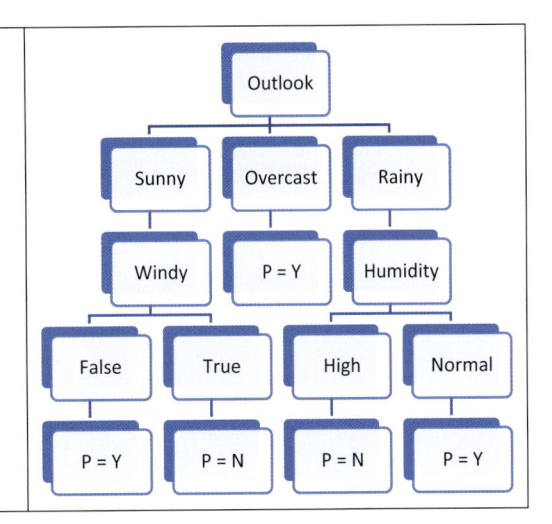

Figure 5.6 Decision rules (left) and decision tree (right) for the weather data.

See if these rules make sense by going through the tree in Figure 5.6 as well as logically questioning them (e.g., if it is sunny but very windy outside, will we play?). Try deriving some new rules.

> **Hands-on Example 5.2: Decision Tree**
>
> Let's see how a decision-tree-based classifier can be implemented with Python. For this demonstration we are going to use the balloons dataset that you can download from OA 5.3. This is from the repository that we used in the earlier example (see Table 5.1).
>
> ```
> import pandas as pd
> from sklearn.model_selection import train_test_split
> from sklearn.tree import DecisionTreeClassifier
> from sklearn import tree
> from sklearn.metrics import accuracy_score, confusion_
> matrix
> # for graphviz on windows
> import os
> # replace with path to your graphviz executables
> os.environ["PATH"] += os.pathsep + "/Users/anaconda3/
> Library/bin/graphviz/"
> ```
>
> Note that we need to know where our Graphviz program is installed. What I put above is a typical path on a Mac OS, but you may have a different operating system. I suggest checking the Graphviz site at https://pypi.org/project/graphviz/ for the documentation pertaining to the latest version and your specific OS.
>
> Next, we load the dataset and do some data transformations:
>
> ```
> bal_df = pd.read_csv("balloons.csv")
> 
> # convert categorical data to int representations of
> # unique categories
> for col in bal_df.columns:
>     labels, uniques = pd.factorize(bal_df[col])
>     bal_df[col] = labels
> 
> X = bal_df.drop(columns = "inflated")
> y = bal_df["inflated"]
> X_train, X_test, y_train, y_test = train_test_split(X,
> y, test_size=0.3)
> ```
>
> We are now ready to start constructing our decision tree. Once the tree is constructed using the training data, we can test it on the test data. The testing will yield our predictions for the class labels. These predictions can then be compared to the ground truth of that test data to calculate classification accuracy:
>
> ```
> dtree = DecisionTreeClassifier()
> dtree.fit(X_train, y_train)
> predictions = dtree.predict(X_test)
> print(accuracy_score(y_test, predictions))
> print(confusion_matrix(y_test, predictions))
> ```

Finally, we create a visualization of our decision tree. Do not worry if your Graphviz installation does not work, this visualization is an optional step. We have already built and tested our classifier above.

```
import graphviz
dot_data =
    tree.export_graphviz(dtree, out_file = None,
                         feature_names = ("Color",
                         "size", "act", "age"),
                         class_names = ("0","1"),
                         filled = True)
graph = graphviz.Source(dot_data, format = "png")
graph.render("balloons_dt", view = True)
```

If you have correctly followed the steps you should see a tree like the one in Figure 5.7.

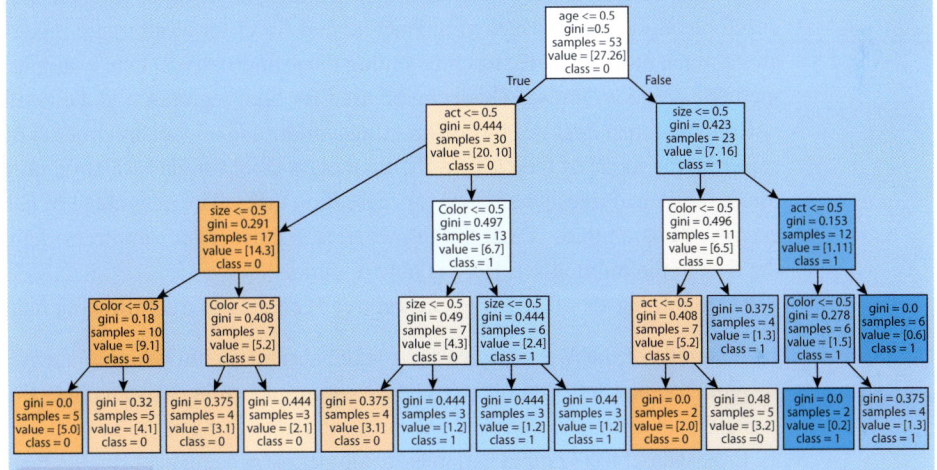

Figure 5.7 Plotting the decision tree.

Try It Yourself 5.2: Decision Tree

Let's test your understanding of the decision tree algorithm with all categorical variables. The dataset you are going to use is about contact lenses (download from OA 5.4), and it has three class labels:

1. the patient should be prescribed hard contact lenses;
2. the patient should be prescribed soft contact lenses;
3. the patient should not be prescribed contact lenses.

Build a decision-tree-based classifier that would recommend a class label based on the other attributes from the dataset.

5.4 Random Forest

A decision tree seems like a nice method for doing classification – it typically has good accuracy and, more important, provides human-understandable insights. But one big problem the decision tree algorithm has is that it could **overfit** the data. What does that mean? It means it could try to model the given data so well that while the classification accuracy on that dataset would be wonderful, the model may find itself crippled when looking at any new data; it learned *too much* from the data!

One way to address this problem is to use not just one, not just two, but many decision trees, each one created slightly differently, and then take some kind of average from what these trees decide and predict. Such an approach is useful and desirable in many situations, and there is a whole set of algorithms that apply them. They are called **ensemble methods**.

In ML, ensemble methods rely on multiple learning algorithms to obtain better prediction accuracy than any of the constituent learning algorithms can achieve. In general, an ensemble algorithm consists of a concrete and finite set of alternate models but incorporates a much more flexible structure among those alternatives. One example of an ensemble method is random forest, which can be used for both regression and classification tasks.

Random forest operates by constructing a multitude of decision trees at training time and selecting the mode of the class as the final class label for classification or mean prediction of the individual trees when used for regression tasks. The advantage of using random forest over decision trees is that the former tries to correct decision trees' habit of overfitting the data to the training set. Here is how it works.

For a training set of N, each decision tree is created in the following manner:

1. A sample of the N training cases is taken at random but with replacement from the original training set (Figure 5.8). Here, "with replacement" means the same sample could be drawn again. This sample will be used as a training set to grow the tree.
2. If the dataset has M input variables, a number m (m being a lot smaller than M) is specified such that at each node, m variables are selected at random out of M. Among this m, the best split is used to split the node. The value of m is held constant while we grow the forest.
3. Following the above steps, each tree is grown to its largest possible extent and there is no pruning.
4. We predict new data by aggregating the predictions of the n trees (i.e., the majority votes for classification, the average for regression).

Let's say a training dataset, N, has four observations on three predictor variables, A, B, and C. The training data is provided in Table 5.4.

We will now work through the random forest algorithm on this small dataset.

Step 1: Sample the N training cases at random (here, $N = 4$). These subsets of N, n_1, n_2, n_3, ... n_n (as depicted in Table 5.5) are used for growing (training) the n decision trees. These samples are drawn as randomly as possible, with or without overlap between them. For example, n_1 may consists of the training instances 1, 1, 1, and 4. Similarly, n_2 may consist of 2, 3, 3, and 4, and so on.

5.4 Random Forest

Table 5.4 Training dataset.

	Independent variables		
	A	B	C
Training instances	A_1	B_1	C_1
	A_2	B_2	C_2
	A_3	B_3	C_3
	A_4	B_4	C_4

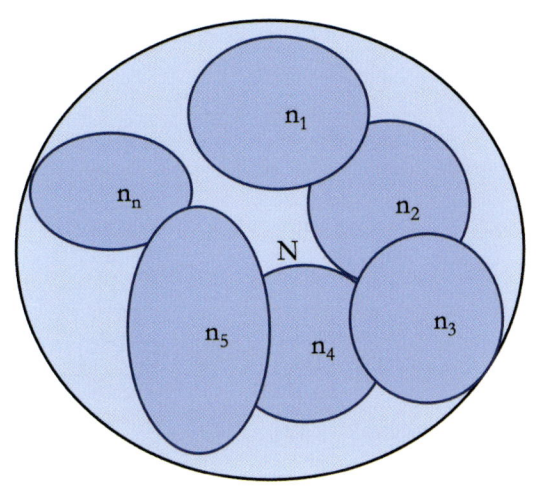

Figure 5.8 Sampling the training set.

Step 2: Out of the three predictor variables, a number $m < 3$ is specified such that at each node m variables are selected at random out of M. Let's say that m is 2; n_1 can be trained on A, B. n_2 can be trained on B, C, and so on.

The resultant decision trees may look something like what is shown in Figure 5.9.

Random forest uses a bootstrap sampling technique, which involves sampling of the input data with replacement. Before using the algorithm, a portion of the data (typically one-third) that is not used for training is set aside for testing. This happens with each individual decision tree, not for the random forest algorithm as a whole. These are sometimes known as **out-of-bag samples**. An error estimation on this sample, known as **out-of-bag error**, provides evidence that the out-of-bag estimate can be as accurate as having a test set of equal size to the training set. Thus, use of the out-of-bag error estimate removes the need for a set-aside test set here.

So the big question is: Why does the random forest as a whole do a better job than the individual decision trees? Although there is no clear consensus among researchers, there are two major theories:

1. As the saying goes, "Nobody knows everything, but everybody knows something." When it comes to a forest of trees, not all of them are perfect or accurate. But most of

Table 5.5 Selection of attributes for the tree.

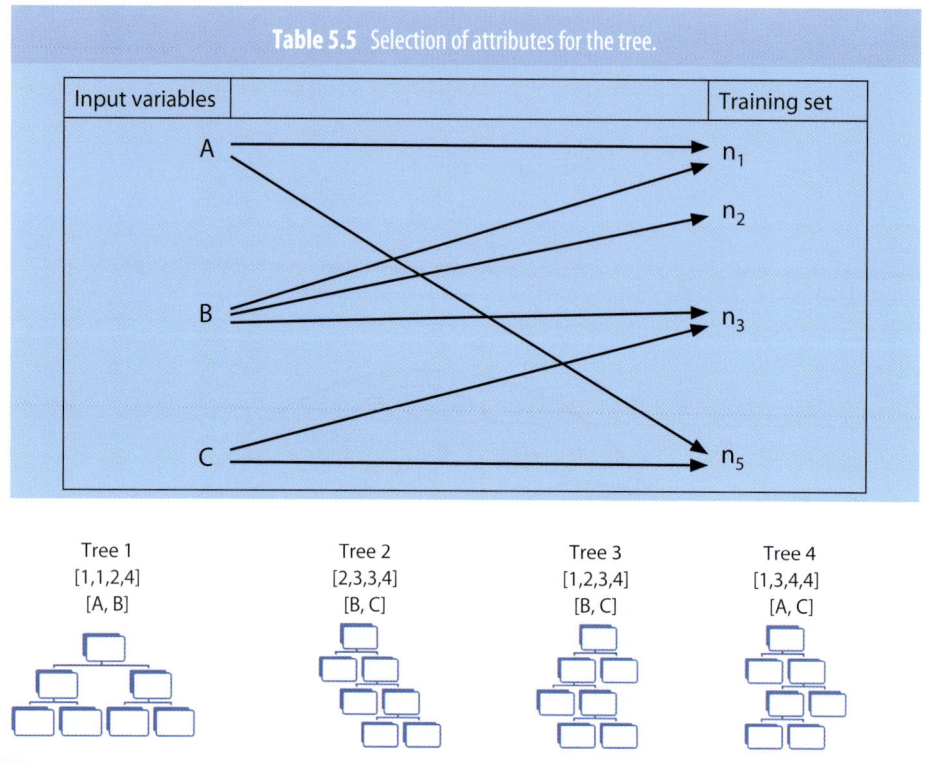

Input variables	Training set
A	n_1
	n_2
B	n_3
C	n_5

Tree 1
[1,1,2,4]
[A, B]

Tree 2
[2,3,3,4]
[B, C]

Tree 3
[1,2,3,4]
[B, C]

Tree 4
[1,3,4,4]
[A, C]

Figure 5.9 Various decision trees for the random forest data.

the trees provide correct predictions of class labels for most of the data. So even if some of the individual decision trees generate incorrect predictions, the majority predict correctly. And since we are using the mode of output predictions to determine the class, it is unaffected by those wrong instances. Intuitively, validating this belief depends on the randomness in the sampling method. The more random the samples, the more uncorrelated the trees will be, and the lower the chances of one tree's incorrect predictions affecting the others.

2. More important, different trees are making mistakes at different places and not all of them are making mistakes at the same location. Again, intuitively this belief depends on how randomly the attributes are selected. The more random they are, the less likely the trees will be to make mistakes at the same location.

Random forest is considered a panacea for all ML problems among most of its practitioners. There is a belief that when you cannot think of an algorithm, irrespective of the situation, you should use random forest. It is a bit irrational, since no algorithm strictly dominates in all applications (one size does not fit all). Nonetheless, people have their favorite algorithms. And there are reasons why, for many data scientists, random forest is the favorite:

1. It can solve both classification and regression problems, and does a decent estimation for both.

2. Random forest requires almost no input preparation. It can handle binary features, categorical features, and numerical features without any need for scaling.
3. Random forest is not very sensitive to the specific set of parameters used. As a result, it does not require a lot of tweaking and fiddling to get a decent model; just use a large number of trees and things will not go terribly awry.
4. It is an effective method for estimating missing data and maintains accuracy when a large proportion of the data is missing.

So, is random forest a silver bullet? Absolutely not. First, it does a good job at classification, but not as well for regression problems since it does not give precise continuous predictions. Second, random forest can feel like a black box approach for statistical modelers, as you have very little control of what the model does. At best, you can try different parameters and random seeds and hope that will change the output.

Hands-on Example 5.3: Random Forest

We will now take an example and see how to use random forests in Python. For this, we are going to use the Bank Marketing dataset from the University of California, Irvine ML dataset, which you can download from OA 5.5. Here, the goal is to predict whether the client will subscribe (yes/no) given a term deposit (variable y).

```
import pandas as pd
import matplotlib.pyplot as plt

bank_df = pd.read_csv("bank.csv", delimiter = ";")
y = bank_df["y"]

# plot bar graph
plt.bar([1, 2], [len(y[y == "yes"]), len(y[y ==
"no"])], tick_label = ["yes", "no"])
```

This code generates the barplot shown in Figure 5.10.

As the barplot depicts, the majority of the data points in this dataset have the class label "no." Before we build our model, let's separate the dataset into training and test instances.

```
from sklearn.model_selection import train_test_split
from sklearn.ensemble import RandomForestClassifier
from sklearn.metrics import accuracy_score, confusion_
matrix

# convert categorical data to int representations of
# unique categories
for col in bank_df.columns:
    labels, uniques = pd.factorize(bank_df[col])
    bank_df[col] = labels
```

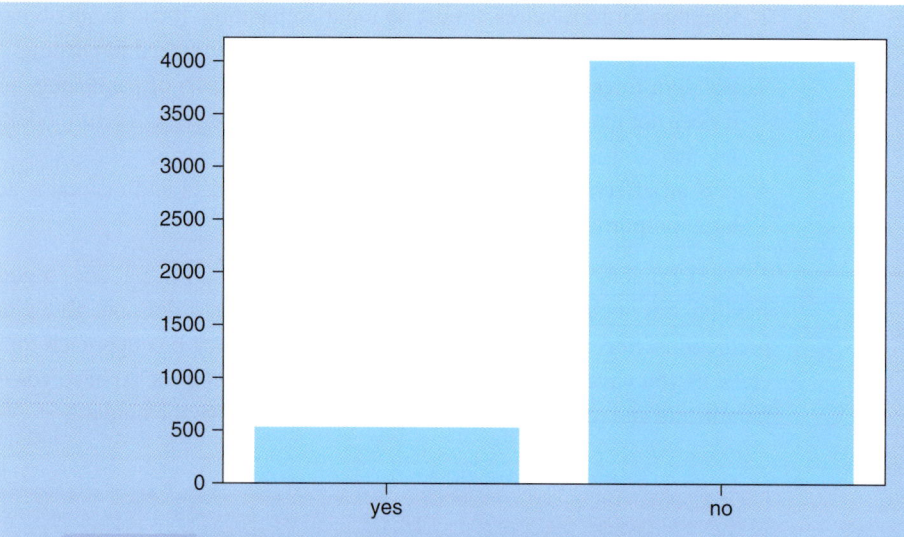

Figure 5.10 Barplot depicting data points with "no" and "yes" labels.

```
y = bank_df["y"]
X = bank_df.drop(columns = "y")
X_train, X_test, y_train, y_test = train_test_split(X, y, test_size = 0.25)
```

The dataset is split into two parts: 75% for training purposes and the remainder to evaluate our model. To build the model we will use RandomForestClassifier from Sklearn's ensemble library. Next, use the training instances to build the model.

```
rfc = RandomForestClassifier(n_estimators = 500)
rfc.fit(X_train, y_train)
```

We can use the n_estimators parameter to specify the total number of trees to build (default = 500). Let's test the model to see how it performs on the test dataset:

```
predictions = rfc.predict(X_test)
print(accuracy_score(y_test, predictions))
print(confusion_matrix(y_test, predictions))
```

The following output is produced:

```
0.8885941644562334
[[986   25]
 [101   19]]
```

There you have it. We achieved about 89% accuracy with a very simple model. We can try to improve the accuracy by feature selection, and also by trying different values for n_estimators.

> **Try It Yourself 5.3: Random Forest**
>
> Get the balloons dataset presented in Table 5.1 and downloadable from OA 5.3. Use this dataset and create a random forest model to classify whether the balloons are inflated or not from the available attributes. Compare the performance (e.g., accuracy) of this model against that of one created using a decision tree.

5.5 Summary

Classification is one of the most active areas of research and development within ML. Many problems we encounter that call for ML fall under classification. Not surprisingly, over the last several decades we have seen many algorithms and techniques being developed, tested, and applied in the real world that address classification. These range from kNN and decision trees (what we saw in this chapter) to support vector machines (SVM) and neural networks – which we will see in the coming chapters.

Building a classifier typically requires training data, where we know the correct class labels. Using this data we could learn a model. This is where we see the first big difference among different classification techniques. In the case of kNN this learning essentially means representing the data along available features or dimensions. In the case of decision trees learning refers to figuring out the set of decision rules based on which features provide the most discriminable configuration of the input space. Finally, we can take test data and run it through the learned model (a classifier) to produce our decision.

There are many ways we can think about and present how well we are doing with these classifiers. The most common measure is accuracy. But it is important to note that accuracy does not provide a complete picture. In fact, at times, using accuracy could be very misleading. For that reason we should use multiple metrics for presenting the *goodness* of our classifiers. Even when reporting accuracy, it is more meaningful to do multiple runs of training and testing for a classification task and report average accuracy. We will discuss these issues of measurement at length in Chapter 12.

Key Terms

- **Supervised learning**: Supervised learning algorithms use a set of examples from previous records that are labeled to make predictions about the future.
- **Data overfitting**: When a model tries to create decision boundaries or curve fitting that connects or separates as many points as possible at the expense of simplicity. Such a process often leads to complex models that have very little error on the training data, but may not have an ability to generalize and do a good job on new data.
- **Training–validation–test data**: Training set consists of data points which are labeled and are used to learn the model. A validation set, often prepared separately from the training set, consists of observations that are used to tune the parameters of the model, such as to test for overfitting. The test set is used to evaluate the performance of the model.

- **Entropy** is a measure of disorder, uncertainty, or randomness. When the probability of each event in a given space happening is the same, entropy is the highest for that system. When there are imbalances in these probabilities, the absolute value of entropy goes down.
- **Information gain** is the decrease in entropy, and is typically used to measure how much entropy (uncertainty) is reduced in a certain event, knowing the probability of another event.
- **Ensemble models** contain a combination of concrete and finite sets of alternate models, each perhaps with its own imperfections and biases, which are used together to produce a single decision.

Conceptual Questions

1. What is supervised learning? Give two examples of data problems where you would use supervised learning.

2. What are the pros and cons of kNN? Discuss.

3. What are two advantages of decision trees?

4. What is a disadvantage of decision trees?

5. What is an ensemble model? Give an example.

6. How does random forest address the issue of bias or overfitting?

Hands-on Problems

Problem 5.1 (kNN)

Obtain the 'hsbdemo' dataset from OA 5.6. Create a kNN-based classifier from the reading, writing, mathematics, and science scores of the high school students. Evaluate the classifiers' accuracy in predicting which academic program the student will be joining.

Problem 5.2 (kNN)

Download weather.csv from OA 5.7. Entirely fictitious, it supposedly concerns the weather conditions that are suitable for playing some unspecified game. There are four predictor variables: outlook, temperature, humidity, and wind. The outcome is whether to play ("yes," "no," "maybe"). Use kNN to build a classifier that learns how various predictor variables could relate to the outcome. Report the accuracy of your model.

Problem 5.3 (kNN)

The dataset shown in Table 5.6 is from "Project 16P5" in Mosteller, F. and Tukey, J. W. (1977). *Data analysis and regression: a second course in statistics*. Addison-Wesley,

Table 5.6 Project 16P5 dataset.

	Fertility	Agriculture	Examination	Education	Catholic	Infant mortality
Courtelary	80.2	17	15	12	5.96	22.2
Delemont	83.1	45.1	6	9	84.84	22.2
Franches-Mnt	92.5	35.7	5	5	93.4	20.2
Moutier	85.8	36.5	12	7	33.77	20.3
Neuveville	76.9	43.5	17	15	5.16	20.6
Porrentruy	76.1	35.3	9	7	90.57	26.6
Broye	83.8	70.2	16	7	92.85	23.6
Glane	92.4	67.8	14	8	97.16	24.9
Gruyere	82.4	53.3	12	7	97.67	21
Sarine	82.9	45.2	16	13	91.38	24.4
Veveyse	87.1	64.5	14	6	98.61	24.5
Aigle	64.1	62	21	12	8.52	16.5
Aubonne	66.9	67.5	14	7	2.27	15.1
Avenches	68.9	60.7	19	12	4.43	22.7
Cossonay	61.7	65.3	22	5	2.82	18.7
Echallens	68.3	72.6	18	2	24.2	21.2
Grandson	71.7	34	17	8	3.3	20
Lausanne	55.7	15.4	26	28	12.11	20.2
La Vallee	54.3	15.2	31	20	2.15	10.8
Lavaux	65.1	73	19	9	2.84	20
Morges	65.5	55.8	22	10	5.23	18
Moudon	65	55.1	14	3	4.52	22.4
Nyone	56.6	50.9	22	12	15.14	16.7
Orbe	57.4	54.1	20	6	4.2	15.3
Oron	72.5	71.2	12	1	2.4	21
Payerne	74.2	58.1	14	8	5.23	23.8
Paysd'enhaut	72	63.5	6	3	2.56	18
Rolle	60.5	60.8	16	10	7.72	16.3
Vevey	58.3	26.8	25	19	18.46	20.9
Yverdon	65.4	45.5	15	8	6.1	22.5
Conthey	75.5	85.9	3	2	95.71	15.1
Entremont	65.3	84.9	7	6	95.68	15.8
Herens	77.3	85.7	5	2	100	18.3
Martigwy	70.5	78.2	12	6	98.96	15.4
Monthey	75.4	64.9	7	3	98.22	20.2
St Maurice	65	75.9	9	9	95.06	17.8
Sierre	92.2	84.6	3	3	95.46	16.3

Table 5.6 (cont.)

	Fertility	Agriculture	Examination	Education	Catholic	Infant mortality
Sion	75.3	63.1	13	13	96.83	18.1
Boudry	70.4	38.4	26	12	5.62	20.3
La Chauxdfnd	65.7	7.7	29	11	13.79	20.5
Le Locle	72.7	16.7	22	13	11.22	18.9
Neuchatel	64.4	17.6	35	32	16.92	23
Val de Ruz	77.6	37.6	15	7	4.97	20
ValdeTravers	67.6	18.7	25	7	8.65	15.5
V. De Geneve	35	1.2	37	53	42.34	18
Rive Droite	44.7	46.6	16	29	50.43	18.2
Rive Gauche	42.8	27.7	22	29	58.33	15.3

pp. 549–551, who indicate their source as "Data used by permission of Franice van de Walle." You can download it from OA 5.8.

The dataset represents standardized fertility measures and socio-economic indicators for each of 47 French-speaking provinces of Switzerland, circa 1888. Switzerland, in 1888, was entering a period known as the *demographic transition*; that is, its fertility was beginning to fall from the high level typical of underdeveloped countries. The dataset has observations on six variables, each of which is in percent (i.e., in the range [0, 100]).

Use the kNN algorithm to find the provinces that have similar fertility levels. For this, you will need to convert the continuous variable "fertility" to a categorical one. Given that "fertility" values are between 21 and 100, we can map that range of 80 values to four categories using the following code:

```
import pandas as pd
data = pd.read_csv("swiss.csv")
ranges = [21, 40, 60, 80, 100]
categories = ["c1", "c2", "c3", "c4"]
data["FertilityCategory"] = pd.cut(data["Fertility"],
ranges, labels = categories)
```

This will load the original data in a dataframe and then add a column "FertilityCategory" that will have a label. You can now run a classification algorithm with five of the original columns (other than "Fertility") as features and the newly created "FertilityCategory" as the category.

Problem 5.4 (kNN)

For this exercise you will work with the NFL 2014 Combine Performance Results data available from OA 5.9, which contains performance statistics of college football players at the NFL, February 2014, in Indianapolis. The dataset includes the following attributes, among others:

- overall grade: lowest 4.5, highest 7.5
- height: in inches
- arm length: in inches
- weight: in pounds (lb.)
- 40 yard time: in seconds
- bench press: reps at 225 lb.
- vertical jump: in inches
- broad jump: in inches
- three-cone drill: in seconds
- 20-yard shuttle: in seconds.

Use kNN on this dataset to find the players who have similar performance statistics. Once again, you will need to convert the continuous variable "Overall grade" to a categorical one. You can use the code given in the previous problem and decide what ranges make sense. For example, you could label 4.5–5.5 as "c1," 5.6–6.5 as "c2," and 6.6–7.5 as "c3."

Problem 5.5 (Decision Trees)

Obtain the dataset from OA 5.10, which was collected from Worthy, S. L., Jonkman, J. N., and Blinn-Pike, L. (2010). Sensation-seeking, risk-taking, and problematic financial behaviors of college students. *Journal of Family and Economic Issues, 31*, 161–170.

For this dataset, the researchers conducted a survey of 450 undergraduates in large introductory courses at either Mississippi State University or the University of Mississippi. There were close to 150 questions on the survey, but only four of these variables are included in this dataset. (You can consult the paper to learn how the variables beyond these four affect the analysis.) The primary interest for the researchers was factors relating to whether or not a student had ever overdrawn a checking account.

The dataset contains the following variables:

Age:	Age of the student (in years)
Sex:	0 = male or 1 = female
DaysDrink:	Number of days drinking alcohol (in past 30 days)
Overdrawn:	Has the student overdrawn a checking account? 0 = no or 1 = yes

Create a decision-tree-based model to predict the student overdrawing from the checking account based on *Age*, *Sex*, and *DaysDrink*. Since *DaysDrink* is a numeric variable you may have to convert it into a categorical one. One suggestion for that would be:

if (no. days drinking alcohol < 7) = 0
   (7 <= no. days drinking alcohol < 14) = 1
   (no. days drinking alcohol >= 14) = 2

Table 5.7 Attributes in the Abalone dataset.			
Name	Data type	Measurement unit	Description
Sex	Nominal	–	M, F, and I (infant)
Length	Continuous	mm	Longest shell measurement
Diameter	Continuous	mm	Perpendicular to length
Height	Continuous	mm	With meat in shell
Whole weight	Continuous	grams	Whole abalone
Shucked weight	Continuous	grams	Weight of meat
Viscera weight	Continuous	grams	Gut weight (after bleeding)
Shell weight	Continuous	grams	after being dried
Rings	Integer	–	+1.5 gives the age in years

Problem 5.6 (Decision Trees)

Download the dataset from OA 5.11 for this exercise, which is sourced from the study Gueguen, N. (2002). The effects of a joke on tipping when it is delivered at the same time as the bill. *Journal of Applied Social Psychology, 32*, 1955–1963.

Can telling a joke affect whether or not a waiter in a coffee bar receives a tip from a customer? This study investigated this question at a coffee bar at a famous resort on the west coast of France. The waiter randomly assigned coffee-ordering customers to one of three groups: When receiving the bill one group also received a card telling a joke, another group received a card containing an advertisement for a local restaurant, and a third group received no card at all. He recorded whether or not each customer left a tip. The dataset contains the following variables:

> *Card*: type of card used: Ad, Joke, or None
> *Tip*: 1 = customer left a tip; 0 = no tip
> *Ad*: indicator for Ad card
> *Joke*: indicator for Joke card
> *None*: indicator for no card

Use a decision tree to determine whether the waiter will receive a tip from the customer from the predictor variables.

Problem 5.7 (Random Forests)

This exercise is based on the Abalone dataset, which can be downloaded from OA 5.12.

The task is to predict the age of abalone from physical measurements. The age of abalone is determined by cutting the shell through the cone, staining it, and counting the number of rings through a microscope – a boring and time-consuming task. Other measurements, which are easier to obtain, are used to predict the age. Table 5.7 shows the list of attributes that are available in the current dataset.

The original data examples had a couple of missing values, which were removed (the majority having the predicted value missing), and the ranges of the continuous values have been scaled for use with an ANN (by dividing by 200).

Use this dataset to predict the age of abalone from the given attributes.

Problem 5.8 (Random Forests)

In this exercise you will work with the Blues Guitarists Hand Posture and Thumbing Style by Region and Birth Period data, which you can download from OA 5.13. This dataset has 93 entries of various blues guitarists born between 1874 and 1940. Apart from the name of the guitarists, that dataset contains the following four features:

Regions: 1 = East, 2 = Delta, 3 = Texas
Years: 0 for those born before 1906, 1 for the rest
Hand postures: 1 = extended, 2 = stacked, 3 = lutiform
Thumb styles: between 1 and 3, where 1 = alternating, 2 = utility, 3 = dead.

Using random forest on this dataset, how accurately you can tell the guitarist's birth year from their hand postures and thumb styles? How does it affect the evaluation when you include the region while training the model?

Further Reading and Resources

If you are interested in learning more about supervised learning or any of the topics discussed above, the following might be useful:

- Decision trees in machine learning, simplified:
  https://blogs.oracle.com/bigdata/decision-trees-machine-learning.
- Ensemble methods – combining multiple models to improve the desired results:
  https://corporatefinanceinstitute.com/resources/knowledge/other/ensemble-methods.
- Probability, entropy, and inference: www.mathcs.emory.edu/~whalen/Hash/Hash_Articles/Probability_Entropy_and_Inference.pdf.
- A simple explanation of information gain and entropy:
  https://victorzhou.com/blog/information-gain.

6 Classification 2

What do you need?
- A good understanding of statistical concepts (see Appendix A), probability theory (see Appendix C), and functions.
- The basics of differential calculus (see Appendix B for a few handy formulas).
- Introductory- to intermediate-level experience with Python, including installing packages or libraries (refer to Chapter 2).

What will you learn?
- Solving data problems when truth values for training are available.
- Performing classification using various machine learning techniques such as logistic regression, softmax regression, naïve Bayes, and support vector machine.

6.1 Introduction

In the previous chapter we saw a few basic techniques for performing classification. Just to be clear – "basic" does not mean weak or bad here. On the contrary, k-nearest neighbor (kNN), decision trees, and random forest are some of the most popular and often most effective techniques for doing classification. But given that classification is such an important problem and there are many different types of situations that call for classification, we are going to learn a few more important methods for building classifiers. We will start with logistic regression. Do not let the name "regression" fool you; this is a classification technique. Going beyond an option for doing classification, some of the concepts and the terminology we pick up with logistic regression are going to be very helpful in machine learning (ML). One such concept is that of *likelihood*. So, as we go through the explanation for logistic regression, and more precisely, the gradient ascent algorithm, pay extra attention to that. Similarly, we will do softmax regression, which is also a classification technique despite having "regression" in its name. While a typical logistic regression allows us to address two-class problems, softmax regression can be used for multinomial (multiple class) problems.

Then we will see two more very popular and important methods for classification: naïve Bayes and support vector machine (SVM). As we pick up this whole new set of classification techniques, make sure to think through not just a given algorithm or its application, but also how it differs from other techniques. This thinking will help you decide (at least partially) when you would consider which ones of them, given a classification task. Of course, it is also very common to build classifiers using multiple techniques and report their costs and benefits.

6.2 Logistic Regression

One thing you may have noticed by now about linear regression is that the outcome variable is continuous. A **continuous variable** is one that can have an infinite number of values between any two values. So, the question is what happens when the outcome variable is not continuous. For example, if you have a weather dataset with the attributes humidity, temperature, and wind speed, each is describing one aspect of the weather for a day. And based on these attributes, you want to predict if the weather for the day is suitable for playing golf. In this case, the outcome variable that you want to predict is categorical ("yes" or "no"). A **categorical variable** is a type of variable that can have two or more discrete values or categories. As we saw before, for predicting discrete values we can use classification techniques. Specifically, we will use a technique that is uniquely designed for two-class problems: logistic regression. We will see how this technique allows us to convert a continuous output to a categorical output for solving classification.

Let's think of this in a formal way. Before, our outcome variable y was continuous. Now, it can have only two possible values (labels). For simplicity, let's call these labels 1 and 0 ("yes" and "no"). In other words, $y \in \{0,1\}$.

We are still going to have continuous value(s) for the input, but now we need to have only two possible values for the output. How do we do this? We can use the sigmoid function, defined as follows:

$$g(z) = \frac{1}{1+e^{-z}}. \tag{6.1}$$

Figure 6.1 contains a visual representation of the sigmoid function.

As you can see in Figure 6.1, for any input the output of this function is bound between 0 and 1. In other words, if it is used as the hypothesis function, we get the output in the 0 to 1 range, with 0 and 1 included:

$$h_\theta(x) \in [0,1]. \tag{6.2}$$

The nice thing about this is that it follows the constraints of a probability distribution and should be contained between 0 and 1. And if we can compute probability that ranges from 0 to 1, we can draw a threshold at 0.5 and say that any time we get an outcome value from a hypothesis function h greater than that, we put it in class 1, otherwise it goes in class 0. Note that 1 and 0 are labels and not numerical values. You could turn them into "Y" and "N" or "Red" and "Blue" or whatever you like. They are just class labels that make sense for a given application. But let's stick to 1 and 0 for now. Formally:

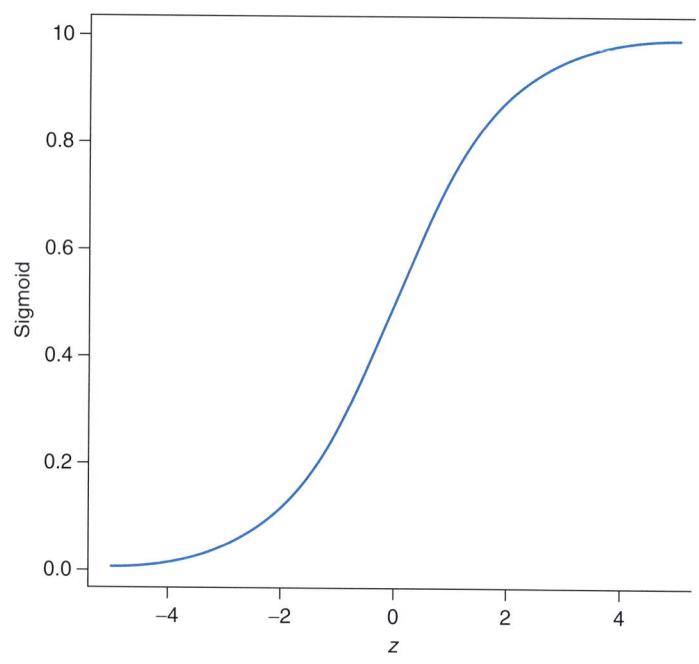

Figure 6.1 Sigmoid function.

$$P(y=1|x;\theta) = h_\theta(x)$$
$$P(y=0|x;\theta) = 1 - h_\theta(x) \qquad (6.3)$$
$$P(y|x;\theta) = h_\theta(x)^y (1 - h_\theta(x))^{1-y}.$$

The last formulation is the result of combining the first two lines to form one expression. See if that makes sense. Try putting $y = 1$ and $y = 0$ in that expression and see if you get the previous two lines.

Now, how do we use this for classification? We want to input the features from the data we have into the hypothesis function (here, a sigmoid) and output a value between 0 and 1. Based on which side of 0.5 it is, we can declare an appropriate label or class. This is a very important step as it allows us to convert a continuous value of probability (between 0 and 1) into a discrete value of 1 and 0.

But before we can do this (called testing), we need to train a model. Just to recap from before, **training** in ML refers to use of some data or observations with appropriate attributes or features to build a model. **Testing**, on the other hand, is where the same model is applied to new data for prediction.

For training and model building we need some data. One way we could build a model from such data is to assume a model and ask if that model can explain or classify the training data and how well. In other words, we are asking how *good* our model is, given the data.

To understand the *goodness* of a model (here, the model is represented by the parameter vector θ), we can ask how likely it is that the data we have was generated by the given model. This is called the **likelihood** of the model and is represented as $L(\theta)$. Let's expand this likelihood function:

$$L(\theta) = P(y|X;\theta)$$
$$= \prod_{i=1}^{m} P(y^i|x^i;\theta) \quad (6.4)$$
$$= \prod_{i=1}^{m} \left(h_\theta(x^i)\right)^{y^i} \left(1-h_\theta(x^i)\right)^{1-y^i}.$$

To achieve a better model than the one we guessed, we need to increase the value of $L(\theta)$. We will do this iteratively, with each iteration trying to increase the value of $L(\theta)$, ultimately ending up with the maximum possible value. But look at that function above. It has all those multiplications and exponents. So, to make it easier for us to work with this function, we will take its log. We can do this because the log is an increasing function (as x goes up, $\log(x)$ also goes up). This will give us a log likelihood function:

$$l(\theta) = \log L(\theta)$$
$$= \sum_{i=1}^{m} \left[y^i \log\left(h_\theta(x^i)\right) + (1-y^i)\log\left(1 - \left(h_\theta(x^i)\right)\right)\right]. \quad (6.5)$$

Once again, to achieve the best model we need to maximize this log likelihood. For that, we do what we already know – take the partial derivative, one parameter at a time. In fact, for simplicity, we will even consider just one sample data at a time:

$$\frac{\partial}{\partial \theta_j} l(\theta) = \left(y \frac{1}{h_\theta(x)} - (1-y)\frac{1}{1-h_\theta(X)}\right) \frac{\partial}{\partial \theta_j} h_\theta(x)$$
$$= \left(y(1-h_\theta(x)) - (1-y)h_\theta(x)\right) x_j \quad (6.6)$$
$$= (y - h_\theta(x)) x_j.$$

The second line in (6.6) follows from the fact that for a sigmoid function $g(z)$, the derivative can be expressed as: $g'(z) = g(z)(1-g(z))$.

Considering all training samples, we get:

$$\frac{\partial}{\partial \theta_j} l(\theta) = \sum_{i=1}^{m} \left(y^i - h_\theta(x^i)\right) x_j^i. \quad (6.7)$$

This gives us our learning algorithm:

$$\theta_j = \theta_j + \alpha \sum_{i=1}^{m} \left(y^i - h_\theta(x^i)\right) x_j^i. \quad (6.8)$$

Notice how we are updating θ this time. We are moving up the gradient instead of moving down. And that is why this is called **gradient ascent**. It does look similar to gradient descent, but the difference is the nature of the hypothesis function. Before, it was a linear function. Now, it is a sigmoid or logit function. And because of that, this regression is called **logistic regression**.

Hands-on Example 6.1: Logistic Regression

Let's practice logistic regression with an example. We are going to use the Titanic dataset. Different versions of this dataset are freely available online; however, I suggest using the one from OA 6.1, since it is almost ready to be used and requires minimal preprocessing. In this exercise we are trying to predict the survival chances of the passengers on the *Titanic*.

We begin by loading various packages and then importing the data.

```
import pandas as pd
import statsmodels.api as sm
from sklearn.model_selection import train_test_split

t_df = pd.read_csv("titanic_data.csv", index_col = "PassengerId")
```

Figure 6.2 shows a sample of the data.

We will now get rid of columns that cannot reasonably be converted into numeric values. After that, we will convert non-numeric columns into numeric ones.

```
t_df.drop(columns = ["Name", "Cabin", "Ticket"], inplace = True)

t_df["sex"].replace(["male", "female"], [1, 0], inplace = True)
t_df["embarked"].replace(["S", "C", "Q"], [0, 1, 2], inplace = True)
```

In the lines above, `inplace = True` indicates that the dataframe will be updated without returning anything. Let's now extract our independent variables or predictors and the dependent variable or outcome ("survived"):

```
X = t_df.drop(columns = ["Survived"])
y = t_df["Survived"]
```

pclass	survived	name	sex	age	sibsp	parch	ticket	fare	cabin	embarked	home.dest
1	1	Allen, Miss. Elisabeth Walton	female	29	0	0	24160	211.338	B5	S	St Louis, MO
1	1	Allison, Master. Hudson Trevor	male	0.9167	1	2	113781	151.55	C22 C26	S	Montreal, PQ / Chesterville, ON
1	0	Allison, Miss. Helen Loraine	female	2	1	2	113781	151.55	C22 C26	S	Montreal, PQ / Chesterville, ON
1	0	Allison, Mr. Hudson Joshua Creighton	male	30	1	2	113781	151.55	C22 C26	S	Montreal, PQ / Chesterville, ON
1	0	Allison, Mrs. Hudson J C (Bessie Waldo Daniels)	female	25	1	2	113781	151.55	C22 C26	S	Montreal, PQ / Chesterville, ON
1	1	Anderson, Mr. Harry	male	48	0	0	19952	26.55	E12	S	New York, NY
1	1	Andrews, Miss. Kornelia Theodosia	female	63	1	0	13502	77.9583	D7	S	Hudson, NY
1	0	Andrews, Mr. Thomas Jr	male	39	0	0	112050	0	A36	S	Belfast, NI
1	1	Appleton, Mrs. Edward Dale (Charlotte Lamson)	female	53	2	0	11769	51.4792	C101	S	Bayside, Queens, NY
1	0	Artagaveytia, Mr. Ramon	male	71	0	0	PC 17609	49.5042	?	C	Montevideo, Uruguay
1	0	Astor, Col. John Jacob	male	47	1	0	PC 17757	227.525	C62 C64	C	New York, NY
1	1	Astor, Mrs. John Jacob (Madeleine Talmadge Force)	female	18	1	0	PC 17757	227.525	C62 C64	C	New York, NY
1	1	Aubart, Mme. Leontine Pauline	female	24	0	0	PC 17477	69.3	B35	C	Paris, France
1	1	Barber, Miss. Ellen 'Nellie'	female	26	0	0	19877	78.85	?	S	?
1	1	Barkworth, Mr. Algernon Henry Wilson	male	80	0	0	27042	30	A23	S	Hessle, Yorks

Figure 6.2 Sample from the Titanic dataset.

Once we have the appropriate variables captured, it is time to split the data into training and testing sets. This is a process that we will almost always follow when building classifiers – using 70–80% of the data for training and the rest for validation or testing:

```
X_train, X_test, y_train, y_test = train_test_split(X,
y, test_size = 0.30)
```

Take a moment to understand what is going on in this line. We are asking Python to split both *X* and *y* into subsets with roughly 70% for training and 30% for testing. At this point, assuming that you ran the code so far, you can check your Variable Explorer and see that you have distinct sets for `X_train`, `y_train`, `X_test`, and `y_test`. Look at their sizes and perhaps open up their corresponding dataframes to see what is in them.

And with that, we are ready to build our classifier. For this, we will only use the training data (`X_train` and `y_train`). After that, we will print the summary of the model we built.

```
logmodel = sm.Logit(y_train, sm.add_constant(X_train)).
fit(disp = False)
print(logmodel.summary())
```

This generates the following table.

```
Logit Regression Results
==============================================================
Dep. Variable:                survived   No. Observations:         730
Model:                           Logit   Df Residuals:             722
Method:                            MLE   Df Model:                   7
Date:                 Sat, 15 May 2021   Pseudo R-squ.:         0.2833
Time:                         14:16:22   Log-Likelihood:        -352.39
converged:                        True   LL-Null:               -491.70
Covariance Type:             nonrobust   LLR p-value:         2.211e-56
==============================================================
              coef    std err       z      P>|z|    [0.025    0.975]
--------------------------------------------------------------
const       4.0903     0.550    7.442     0.000     3.013     5.168
pclass     -0.8845     0.149   -5.920     0.000    -1.177    -0.592
sex        -2.3844     0.201  -11.854     0.000    -2.779    -1.990
age        -0.0375     0.008   -4.943     0.000    -0.052    -0.023
sibsp      -0.4146     0.132   -3.148     0.002    -0.673    -0.156
parch       0.1121     0.128    0.876     0.381    -0.139     0.363
fare        0.0022     0.002    0.910     0.363    -0.003     0.007
embarked    0.1839     0.172    1.067     0.286    -0.154     0.522
==============================================================
```

From the result it is clear that *Parch*, *Fare*, and *Embarked* are not statistically significant as the value of their corresponding *p* is greater than 0.05.[1] That means we do not have enough confidence that these factors contribute all that much to the overall model. As for the statistically significant variables, we can see that *sex* has a strong association with survival. The negative coefficient for this predictor suggests that all other variables being equal, a male passenger is less likely to have survived than a female passenger (reminder: here, male = 1 and female = 0). At this time we should pause and think about this insight. As the *Titanic* started sinking and the lifeboats were being filled with passengers, priority was given to women and children. And thus, it makes sense that a male passenger, especially a male adult, would have a lower chance of survival. Take a look at the *age* variable in this table. What can you say about it?

We will see how good our model is at predicting values for test instances. For this, we will need a few more packages from Sklearn. Note that for a better flow of the explanation, I sometimes include import statements in the middle of the code, but it is usually a good practice to have all your import statements at the top of your program.

```
from sklearn.metrics import accuracy_score, confusion_
matrix

# form our predictions, convert continuous [0, 1]
# predictions to binary
predictions = logmodel.predict(sm.add_constant(X_test))
bin_predictions = [1 if x >= 0.5 else 0 for x in pre-
dictions]
```

Multiple things are happening here. On the right side of = we are checking the condition `if x > 0.5`. If yes, the output is 1, otherwise it is 0. And this is happening for the entire vector of `predictions`. I suggest you go ahead and print both `predictions` and `bin_predictions` to see what is going on here.

We can now assess the accuracy and print out the confusion matrix:

```
print(accuracy_score(y_test, bin_predictions))
print(confusion_matrix(y_test, bin_predictions))
```

This produces the following outcome:

```
0.7955271565495208
[[161   29]
 [ 35   88]]
```

Your outcome may look different. Why? Because splitting our data into training and testing sets has a random component, leading to slightly different sets being used for training and testing every time you run this. Yes, this means you may get different results every time you run this code. Regardless, the chances are you will get an accuracy of around 80%, which suggests that the model performed decently. After that line for accuracy (0.7955), we see a confusion matrix, which shows how well we did for each class. Cell (1,1) indicates the times we predicted a passenger survived and they also did in reality. Cell (2,2) indicates the times we predicted a passenger did not survive and they also did not in reality. These two cells, in other words, indicate how often we are correct in our predictions. The other two cells indicate how often we were wrong – false positive and false negative. If you add the top-left to bottom-right diagonal in a confusion matrix and divide by the total number of instances in this table, you get your prediction accuracy.

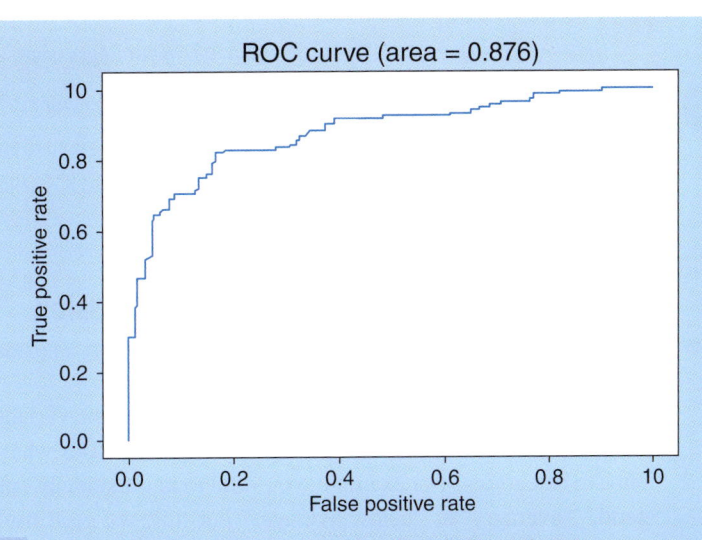

Figure 6.3 Receiver operating curve for the classifier built on the Titanic dataset.

As the final step we are going to plot the receiver operating curve (ROC) and calculate the area under the curve (AUC), which are typical performance measurements for a binary classifier. The ROC curve is generated by plotting the **true positive rate** (TPR) against the **false positive rate** (FPR) at various threshold settings, while the AUC is the area under the ROC curve. The TPR indicates how much of what we detected as 1 was indeed 1, and FPR indicates how much of what we detected as 1 was actually 0. Typically, as one goes up, the other goes up too. Think about it – if you declare everything 1 you will have a high TPR, but you would have also wrongly labeled everything that was supposed to be 0, leading to high FPR. We will cover more detail about these measures in Chapter 12. For now, let's run the code and examine the ROC curve and show the result in Figure 6.3.

```
from sklearn.metrics import roc_curve, roc_auc_score
import matplotlib.pyplot as plt

fpr, tpr, thresholds = roc_curve(y_test, predictions)
roc_auc = roc_auc_score(y_test, predictions)

plt.plot(fpr, tpr, label = "ROC curve (area = %0.3f)" % roc_auc)
plt.title("ROC Curve (area = %0.3f)" % roc_auc)
plt.xlabel("False positive rate")
plt.ylabel("True positive rate")
```

As a rule of thumb, a model with good predictive ability should have an AUC closer to 1 than to 0.5. In Figure 6.3 we can see that the area under the curve is quite large – covering about 87% of the rectangle. That is quite a good number, indicating a good and balanced classifier.

> **Try It Yourself 6.1: Logistic Regression**
>
> First, obtain the social media ads data from OA 6.2. Using this data, build a logistic regression-based classifier to determine whether the social media user's demographics can be used to predict the user buying the product advertised. Report your model's classification accuracy as well as ROC value.

6.3 Softmax Regression

So far we have seen regression for a continuous outcome variable as well as regression for a binary ("yes" or "no"; 1 or 0) categorical outcome. But what happens if we have more than two categories? For example, you want to rate a student's performance as "excellent," "good," "average," or "below average." For this, we need **multinomial logistic regression**. Multinomial logistic regression, or softmax regression, is a generalization of regular logistic regression to handle more than two classes.

In softmax regression we replace the sigmoid function from the logistic regression by the so-called softmax function. This function takes a vector of n real numbers as input and normalizes the vector into a distribution of n probabilities. That is, the function transforms all the n components from any real values (positive or negative) to values in the interval (0,1). How it does that is a discussion beyond this book; if you are interested, you can check the further reading resources at the end of this chapter.

> **Hands-on Example 6.2: Softmax Regression**
>
> We will explore softmax regression through an example in Python. In this example we will use the "hsbdemo" dataset available from OA 6.3. The dataset is about entering high school students who make program choices among general programs, vocational programs, and academic programs. Their choices can be modeled using their writing scores and their socio-economic status. The dataset contains attribute values for 200 students. The outcome variable is *prog*, which is the program type chosen by the student. The predictor variables are social economic status, *ses*, a three-level categorical variable, and writing score, *write*, a continuous variable. We begin by importing packages that will help us with this exercise:
>
> ```
> from sklearn.linear_model import LogisticRegression
> from sklearn.model_selection import train_test_split
> from sklearn.metrics import accuracy_score
> ```
>
> If you get an error while importing LogisticRegression, try installing Imbalanced-learn by issuing the following command on your Python console:

```
!pip install -U imbalanced-learn
```

After that, make sure to restart the runtime then try again.

It is time to load the data and separate *X* and *y*.

```
import pandas as pd
hsb_df = pd.read_csv("hsbdemo.csv")
X = hsb_df[["ses", "write"]]
y = hsb_df["prog"]
```

We will now replace the category labels of "low," "middle," and "high" with 0, 1, and 2.

```
X["ses"].replace(["low", "middle", "high"], [0, 1, 2],
inplace = True)
y.replace(["general", "vocation", "academic"], [0, 1,
2], inplace = True)
```

Finally, let's split the data into training and testing sets, and build a classifier in the same fashion we did for logistic regression:

```
X_train, X_test, y_train, y_test = train_test_split(X,
y, test_size = 0.30)

# Specify that we will perform non-binary
# classification
logmodel = LogisticRegression(multi_class = "multino-
mial")
logmodel.fit(X_train, y_train)
print(accuracy_score(logmodel.predict(X_test), y_
test))
```

This will print your overall accuracy on the test data. You will most likely get a value in the 50s or 60s. Yes, that is not very good, but we have very little data here to be able to learn something reasonably well. One proof of this inadequacy is the fact that for multiple runs of this code your accuracy will vary a lot – from 53% to 65%. In other words, our classifier here is quite sensitive to the data it gets for training and testing. Having more data would improve our model.

Try It Yourself 6.2: Softmax Regression

Download the Car Evaluation dataset from OA 6.4. Build a softmax regression model to classify the car acceptability class from other attributes of the class.

6.4 Naïve Bayes

We now move on to a very popular and robust approach to classification that uses Bayes' theorem. Bayesian classification is a supervised learning method as well as a statistical method for classification. In a nutshell, it is a classification technique based on Bayes' theorem with an assumption of independence among predictors. Here, all attributes contribute equally and independently to the decision.

In simple terms, a **Naïve Bayes classifier** assumes that the presence of a particular feature in a class is unrelated to the presence of any other feature. For example, a piece of fruit may be considered to be an apple if it is red, round, and about 3 inches in diameter. Even if these features depend on each other or upon the existence of the other features, all of these properties independently contribute to the probability that this fruit is an apple. The assumption of independence is why it is known as *naïve*. It turns out that in most cases, even when such a naïve assumption is found to be not true, the resulting classification models do amazingly well.

Let's first take a look at Bayes' theorem, which provides a way of calculating posterior probability $P(c|x)$ from $P(c)$, $P(x)$, and $P(x|c)$. Look at (6.9):

$$P(c \mid x) = \frac{P(x \mid c) P(c)}{P(x)}. \tag{6.9}$$

Here:

- $P(c|x)$ is the posterior probability of *class* (c) given *predictor* (x).
- $P(c)$ is the prior probability of *class*.
- $P(x|c)$ is the likelihood, which is the probability of *predictor* given *class*.
- $P(x)$ is the prior probability of *predictor*.

Here is that naïve assumption: We believe that evidence can be split into parts that are independent:

$$P(c \mid x) = \frac{P(x1 \mid c) P(x2 \mid c) P(x3 \mid c) P(x4 \mid c) \ldots P(xn \mid c) P(c)}{P(x)}, \tag{6.10}$$

where $x_1, x_2, x_3, \ldots, x_n$ are independent a priori.

The Naïve Bayes algorithm uses these two ideas to capture the relationship between a set of features for an object and its class label. Specifically, using Bayes' theorem, it breaks down the probability of a class label, given a feature, and using the assumption of independence of features it breaks down a single joint probability distribution into several individual conditional probability distributions. Both of these steps allow the process to be computationally very efficient, while retaining its effectiveness in classifying.

To understand Naïve Bayes in action, let's revisit the golf dataset to see how this algorithm works step-by-step. This dataset is repeated in Table 6.1 and can be downloaded from OA 6.5.

As shown in Table 6.1, the dataset has four attributes, *Outlook, Temperature, Humidity*, and *Windy*, which are all different aspects of weather conditions. Based on these four attributes, the goal is to predict the value of the outcome variable, *PlayGolf* (yes or no) – that is,

Table 6.1 Weather dataset.

Outlook	Temperature	Humidity	Windy	Play
overcast	hot	high	FALSE	yes
overcast	cool	normal	TRUE	yes
overcast	mild	high	TRUE	yes
overcast	hot	normal	FALSE	yes
rainy	mild	high	FALSE	yes
rainy	cool	normal	FALSE	yes
rainy	cool	normal	TRUE	no
rainy	mild	normal	FALSE	yes
rainy	mild	high	TRUE	no
sunny	hot	high	FALSE	no
sunny	hot	high	TRUE	no
sunny	mild	high	FALSE	no
sunny	cool	normal	FALSE	yes
sunny	mild	normal	TRUE	yes

Temperature	Play
Hot	no
Hot	no
Hot	yes
Mild	yes
Cool	yes
Cool	no
Cool	yes
Mild	no
Cool	yes
Mild	yes
Mild	yes
Mild	yes
Hot	yes
Mild	no

Frequency Table

Temperature	No	Yes
Hot	2	2
Mild	2	4
Cool	1	3
Total	5	9

Likelihood Table

Temperature	No	Yes		
Hot	2	2	4/14	0.29
Mild	2	4	6/14	0.43
Cool	1	3	4/14	0.29
All	5	9		
	5/14	9/14		
	0.36	0.64		

Figure 6.4 Conversion of the dataset to a frequency table and to a likelihood table.

whether the weather is suitable for playing golf. Following are the steps of the naïve Bayes classification algorithm through which we could accomplish that goal:

Step 1: Convert the dataset into a frequency table (Figure 6.4).
Step 2: Create a likelihood or probability table by computing the probabilities for various quantities. For example, *Hot* probability can be computed using the fact that 4 out of 14 times it was hot (probability = 0.29). Similarly, 9 out of 14 times, we played golf (probability = 0.64). The full table is shown in Figure 6.4.
Step 3: Use Bayes' theorem to calculate the posterior probability for each class. The class with the highest posterior probability is the outcome of prediction.

How does this help in a practical application? Let's say we need to decide if one should go out to play golf when the weather is mild based on the dataset. We can solve it using the above-discussed method of posterior probability. Using Bayes' theorem:

$$P(Yes\mid Mild) = \frac{P(Mild\mid Yes) \times P(Yes)}{P(Mild)}$$

Here we have:

$P(Mild|Yes) = 4/9 = 0.44$;
$P(Mild) = 6/14 = 0.43$; and
$P(Yes) = 9/14 = 0.64$.

Now, $P(Yes \mid Mild) = 0.44 \times 0.64 / 0.43 = 0.65$. In other words, we derived that the probability of playing when the weather is mild is 65%, and if we wanted to turn that into a yes–no decision we can see that this probability is higher than the mid-point (50%). Thus, we can declare "yes" for our answer.

Naïve Bayes uses a similar method to predict the probability of different classes based on various attributes. This algorithm is mostly used in text classification and with problems having two or more classes. One prominent example is spam detection. Spam filtering with Naïve Bayes is a two-class problem – that is, to determine a message or an email as spam or not. Here is how it works.

Let's assume that there are certain words (e.g., "viagra," "rich," "friend") that indicate a given message is spam. We can apply Bayes' theorem to calculate the probability that an email is spam given the email word content:

$$P(spam\mid words) = \frac{P(words\mid spam) \times P(spam)}{P(words)}$$

$$= \frac{P(spam) \times P(viagra,\ rich,\ldots,\ friend\mid spam)}{P(viagra,\ rich,\ldots,\ friend)}$$

$$\propto P(spam) \times P(viagra, rich,\ldots,\ friend\mid spam).$$

Here, $\propto$ is the proportion symbol. It signifies that one expression is proportional to another.

According to Naïve Bayes, the word events are completely independent; therefore, simplifying the above formula using Bayes' formula would look like:

$$P(spam|words) \propto P(viagra|spam) \times P(rich|spam) \times \cdots \times P(friend|spam)$$

We can calculate $P(viagra|spam)$, $P(rich|spam)$, and $P(friend|spam)$ each individually if we have a sizeable training dataset of previously categorized spam messages and the occurrences of these words in the training set. So, it is possible to determine the probability of an email from the test set being spam based on these values.

Naïve Bayes works surprisingly well even if the independence assumption is clearly violated because classification does not need accurate probability estimates so long as the greatest probability is assigned to the correct class. Naïve Bayes affords fast model building and scoring and can be used for both binary and multiclass classification problems.

Hands-on Example 6.3: Naïve Bayes

We are going to work with a bank dataset that you can download from OA 6.6. This data has more than 4500 records containing 17 different attributes of bank customers. Of course, we will start by getting the required packages:

```
import pandas as pd
from sklearn.naive_bayes import MultinomialNB, GaussianNB
from sklearn.model_selection import train_test_split
```

Next, we will import the data:

```
bank_df = pd.read_csv("bank.csv", delimiter = ";")
```

Go ahead and explore the data. Does anything stand out? You see the column with "y"? That is our outcome variable, indicating whether a customer stayed with the bank or not. Perhaps we could see the attributes of customers and predict whether they are likely to stay or not. Let's go ahead and turn human-readable labels into numerical labels that are easy for Python to process. This calls for factorizing the data. This is where we get the numeric representation of an array by identifying distinct values. For example, if we have an array ["a," "b," "b," "c"], factorizing will result in two things: labels, which are "a," "b," and "c" here; and unique numerical representations, which will come out as 0, 1, 1, and 2. In other words, Python (more specifically, Pandas) learned to associate "a" with 0, "b" with 1, and "c" with 2. Let's factorize our bank data, and don't forget to examine what labels and unique values you find.

```
for col in bank_df.columns:
    labels, uniques = pd.factorize(bank_df[col])
    bank_df[col] = labels
```

Now we are ready to identify our X and y and split the data into training and testing sets:

```
y = bank_df["y"]
X = bank_df.drop(columns = "y")
X_train, X_test, y_train, y_test = train_test_split(X, y, test_size=0.3)
```

We will now build the classifier using the naïve Bayes algorithm in two ways – multinomial and Gaussian:

```
# Multinomial naïve Bayes assumes categories follow
# multinomial distribution
nb_multi = MultinomialNB()
nb_multi.fit(X, y)

# Gaussian naïve Bayes assumes categories follow normal
# distribution
```

```
nb_gauss = GaussianNB()
nb_gauss.fit(X, y)
```

Let's see how well both of these approaches did.

```
from sklearn.metrics import accuracy_score, confusion_
matrix
multi_preds = nb_multi.predict(X_test)
print("Results for multinomial distribution assump-
tion:")
print(accuracy_score(y_test, multi_preds))
print(confusion_matrix(y_test, multi_preds))

print("Results for Gaussian distribution assumption:")
gauss_preds = nb_gauss.predict(X_test)
print(accuracy_score(y_test, gauss_preds))
print(confusion_matrix(y_test, gauss_preds))
```

This will produce an outcome similar to this:

```
Results for multinomial distribution assumption:
0.5504789977892409
[[648 552]
 [ 58  99]]

Results for Gaussian distribution assumption:
0.8356669123065585
[[1088  112]
 [ 111   46]]
```

This contains two sets of outputs: the classification accuracy and a confusion matrix. We can see that the Gaussian distribution assumption with naïve Bayes in this case does far better than the multinomial distribution assumption.

Try It Yourself 6.3: Naïve Bayes

Use the contact lenses dataset (OA 6.7) from the decision-tree problem under Try It Yourself 5.2 to build a Naïve Bayes classifier to predict the class label. Compare the accuracy between the Naïve Bayes algorithm and the decision tree.

6.5 Support Vector Machine

One thing that has been common in all the classifier models we have seen so far is that they assume linear separation of classes. In other words, they try to come up with a decision boundary that is a line (or a hyperplane in a higher dimension). But many problems do not have such linear characteristics. **Support vector machines** are a method for the classification of both linear and nonlinear data. They are considered by many to be the best stock classifier for doing ML tasks. By "stock," here we mean in its out-of-the-box form and not modified. This means you can take the basic form of the classifier provided by one of the ML packages and run it on the data, and the results will have low error rates. Support vector machines make good decisions for data points that are outside the training set.

An SVM is an algorithm that uses nonlinear mapping to transform the original training data into a higher dimension. Within this new dimension it searches for the linear optimal separating hyperplane (i.e., a decision boundary separating the data points of one class from another). With an appropriate nonlinear mapping to a sufficiently high dimension, data from two classes can always be separated by a hyperplane. The SVM finds this hyperplane using support vectors and margins (defined by the support vectors).

To understand what this means, let's look at an example. Let's start with a simple two-class problem, as shown in Figure 6.5.

Let the dataset D be given as $(X_1, y_1), (X_2, y_2), \ldots, (X_{|D|}, y_{|D|})$, where X_i is the set of training tuples with associated class labels, y_i. Each y_i can take one of two values, either $+1$ or -1 (i.e., $y_i \in \{+1, -1\}$), corresponding to the classes represented by the hollow red cubes and blue circles (ignore the data points represented by the solids for now), respectively in Figure 6.5. From the graph, we can see that the 2D data are linearly separable (or "linear," for short), because a straight line can be drawn to separate all the tuples of class $+1$ from all the tuples of class -1.

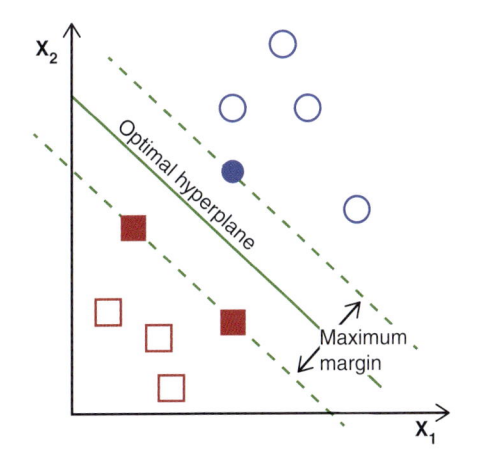

Figure 6.5 Linearly separable data. From OpenCV, "Introduction to support vector machines."[2]

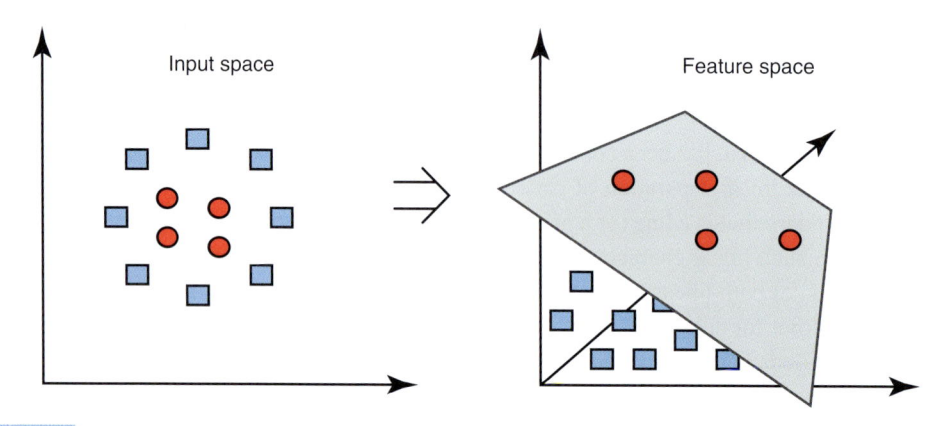

Figure 6.6 From line to hyperplane. From Jiawei Han and Micheline Kamber (2006). *Data Mining: Concepts and Techniques*. Morgan Kaufmann.

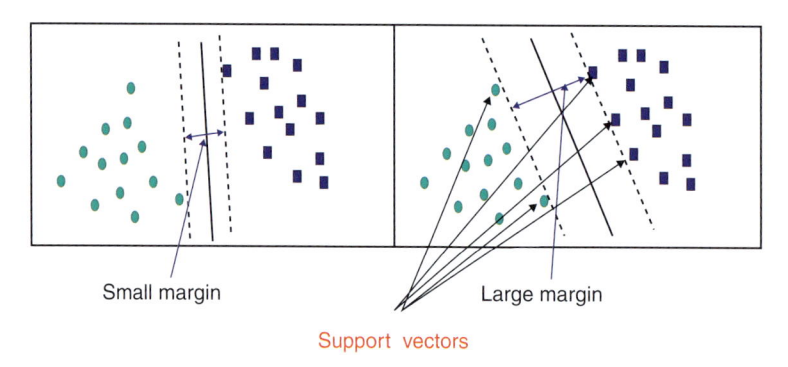

Figure 6.7 Possible hyperplanes and their margins. From Jiawei Han and Micheline Kamber (2006). *Data Mining: Concepts and Techniques*. Morgan Kaufmann.

Note that if our data had three attributes (two independent variables and one dependent), we would want to find the best separating plane (a demonstration is shown in Figure 6.6 for a linearly non-separable dataset). Generalizing to n dimensions, if we had n attributes we want to find the best $n-1$ dimensional plane, called a **hyperplane**. In general, we will use the term *hyperplane* to refer to the decision boundary that we are searching for, regardless of the number of input attributes. So, in other words, our problem is: How can we find the best hyperplane?

There are an infinite number of separating lines that could be drawn. We want to find the "best" one – that is, one that (we hope) will have the minimum classification error on previously unseen tuples. How can we find this best line?

An SVM approaches this problem by searching for the **maximum marginal hyperplane** (MMH). Consider Figure 6.7, which shows two possible separating hyperplanes and their associated **margins**, which is the distance to the closest point. Here, both hyperplanes can correctly classify all the given data tuples. Intuitively, however, we expect the hyperplane with the larger margin to be more accurate at classifying future data tuples than the hyperplane with the smaller margin. This is why (during the learning or training phase) the SVM searches for the hyperplane with the largest margin – that is, the MMH. The associated margin gives the largest separation between classes.

Roughly speaking we would like to find the point closest to the separating hyperplane and make sure this is as far away from the separating line as possible. The points closest to the separating hyperplane are known as support vectors. We want to have the greatest possible margin, because if we made a mistake or trained our classifier on limited data, we would want it to be as robust as possible. Now that we know that we are trying to maximize the distance from the separating line to the support vectors, we need to find a way to solve this problem. Consider this: A separating hyperplane can be written as

$$f(x) = \beta_0 + \beta^T x, \tag{6.11}$$

where T is a weight vector, namely, $T = \{1, 2, \ldots, n\}$; n is the number of attributes; x symbolizes the training examples closest to the hyperplane; and β_0 is a scalar, often referred to as a bias.[3] The optimal hyperplane can be represented in an infinite number of different ways by scaling of β and β_0. As a matter of convention, among all the possible representations of the hyperplane, the one chosen is:

$$\beta_0 + \beta^T x = 1. \tag{6.12}$$

The training examples that are closest to the hyperplane are called support vectors. This representation is known as the canonical hyperplane.

We know from geometry that the distance d between a point (m, n) and a straight line represented by $Ax + By + C = 0$ is given by:

$$d = \frac{|Am + Bn + C|}{\sqrt{A2 + B2}}. \tag{6.13}$$

Therefore, extending the same equation to a hyperplane gives the distance between a point x and a hyperplane $(, 0)$:

$$d = \frac{|\beta_0 + \beta^T x|}{\|\beta\|}. \tag{6.14}$$

In particular, for the canonical hyperplane, the numerator is equal to 1 and the distance to the support vectors is:

$$d_{support\ vectors} = \frac{1}{\|\beta\|}. \tag{6.15}$$

Now, the margin M is twice the distance to the closest data points. So:

$$M = \frac{2}{\|\beta\|}. \tag{6.16}$$

Finally, the problem of maximizing M is equivalent to the problem of minimizing a function $L()$ subject to some constraints. The constraints model the requirement for the hyperplane to classify correctly all the training examples x_i. Formally,

$$\min_{\beta,\beta_0} L(\beta) = \frac{1}{2}\|\beta\|^2 \text{ subject to } y_i\left(\beta^T x_i + \beta_0\right) \geq 1\ \forall i, \tag{6.17}$$

where y_i represents each of the labels of the training examples. This is a problem of Lagrangian optimization that can be solved using Lagrange multipliers to obtain the weight vector and the bias β_0 of the optimal hyperplane.

This is the SVM theory in a nutshell, which is given here with the primary purpose of developing intuition behind how SVMs and other maximum marginal classifiers work. But this is a book that covers hands-on machine learning, so let's see how we can use SVM for a classification or a regression problem.

Hands-on Example 6.4: SVM

We are going to work with skin data available from OA 6.8. The goal here is to use the available attributes to predict skin type. Given that we have already built several classifiers before, I will not describe every line of the code here. Building an SVM-based classifier is quite easy using Sklearn. In addition to SVM, let's also build a classifier using logistic regression and compare these two as a way for us to come full circle in our journey to learn classification.

```
import pandas as pd
from sklearn.svm import SVC
from sklearn.linear_model import LogisticRegression
from sklearn.model_selection import train_test_split
from sklearn.metrics import accuracy_score, confusion_matrix

# Read in a small version of the skin dataset
skin_df = pd.read_csv("Skin_NonSkin_small.txt", names = ["b", "g", "r", "skin"], delimiter = "\t")
X = skin_df.drop(columns = "skin")
y = skin_df["skin"]
X_train, X_test, y_train, y_test = train_test_split(X, y, test_size = 0.3)

# Creating a logistic model will take much less time
# but will ultimately be less accurate for this data
print("starting logistic fit")
log_model = LogisticRegression()
```

```
log_model.fit(X_train, y_train)
print("finished logistic fit\n")

# Train an SVM model
# note that if the full skin dataset is used, the fit
# time becomes impractical
print("starting SVM fit")
svm_model = SVC()
svm_model.fit(X_train, y_train)
print("finished SVM fit")

log_preds = log_model.predict(X_test)
svm_preds = svm_model.predict(X_test)

print("Logistic Regression Results: ")
print(accuracy_score(y_test, log_preds))
print(confusion_matrix(y_test, log_preds))

print("SVM Results: ")
print(accuracy_score(y_test, svm_preds))
print(confusion_matrix(y_test, svm_preds))
```

This will produce outcome like the following:

```
Logistic Regression Results:
0.9208068227968051
[[1204  254]
 [ 331 5598]]

SVM Results:
0.9952619466630567
[[1458    0]
 [  35 5894]]
```

These are quite high accuracy values, but you can see that SVM consistently outperforms logistic regression. Try running the code several times to see if you get different results.

Try It Yourself 6.4: SVM

The dataset you are going to use for this work comes from a combined cycle power plant and the measures were recorded for a period of six years (2006–2011). You can download it from OA 6.9. The features in this dataset consist of hourly average ambient variables and include:

- temperature (*T*) in the range 1.81–37.11 °C;
- ambient pressure (*AP*) in the range 992.89–1033.30 millibar;
- relative humidity (*RH*) in the range 25.56–100.16%;
- exhaust vacuum (*V*) in the range 25.36–81.56 cm Hg; and
- net hourly electrical energy output (*EP*) in the range 420.26–495.76 MW.

Create an SVM-based model that can be used to classify the data based on EP from the other four attributes. Note, (1) EP is a continuous variable that you will need to convert to a categorical one using the instructions in Problem 5.3 (suggested ranges: 420–440, 441–460, 461–480, 481–500); and (2) none of the features in this dataset are normalized.

Here, we used SVM to construct a linearly separable set of classes. But many situations do not have such clearly separable classes. In those situations we need nonlinear shapes to separate the classes. One of the advantages of SVM is that it can take in different functions to create such shapes. Such functions are called kernels. A **kernel** is nothing but a function that allows the data to be mapped in a high-dimensional space, where separating the classes becomes much easier using SVM. This kernel could be a simple linear one, the more sophisticated polynomial kernel, or the quite popular radial basis function (RBF). Further discussion of these kernels is out of scope for us, but when we work on some problems at the end of the chapter we will see at least how to call various kernels while implementing an SVM classifier. Often, the use of a kernel is dependent on the nature of the problem, specifically how the data points in different classes are spread out. It is not uncommon to try different kernels and see which gives the best results in terms of classification accuracy or other metrics we care about.

FYI: Anomaly Detection

In ML, **anomaly detection** (also called outlier detection) is used to identify items, events, or observations that do not conform to the pattern of other items in a dataset. Typically, the anomalous items signify some kind of problem. Such algorithms are used in a broad range of contexts, such as identifying fraud in bank transactions, a structural defect in alloys, potential problems in medicals records, or errors in a text. For example, any highly unusual credit card spending patterns are suspect. Because the possible variations are so numerous and the training examples so few, it is not feasible to learn what fraudulent activity looks like. The approach that anomaly detection takes is to simply learn what normal activity looks like (using a history of non-fraudulent transactions) and identify anything that is significantly different. Anomalies in other subjects are also referred to as outliers, novelties, noise, deviations, and exceptions. Supervised approaches for anomaly detection include kNN, Bayesian networks, decision trees, and SVMs.

To illustrate anomaly detection, let's run through the process with the kNN clustering algorithm. To detect outliers using kNN, first you have to train the kNN algorithm by supplying it with data clusters you know to be correct. Therefore, the dataset to be used to train the kNN algorithm has to be a different one from the data

> that will be used to identify the outliers. For example, you want to cluster the house listings that are similar in price range in your chosen locality. Now, all the current listings that you have collected from the Web may not reflect the correct price of the listings. This may happen for several reasons: Some of the listings may be outdated, some may have unintentional mistakes in listing price, and some may even contain intentional lower prices for clickbait reasons. You want to do a kNN clustering to discriminate such anomalies from the correct listings. One way to do this would be to collect all the previous correct records of list prices of the current listings and train the kNN clustering algorithm on that dataset first. Since I have covered kNN clustering with examples earlier, I will leave this part to you. Once the trained model is generated, it can be used to identify the data points in the current listings dataset that do not properly fit any cluster and thus should be identified as anomalies.

6.6 Summary

Supervised learning, and classification in particular, covers a big portion of today's data problems. Many real-world problems require us to analyze data to provide decision-making insights. Which set of features will be acceptable to our customers for the next version of our app? Is an incoming message spam or not? Should we trust that news story or is it fake? Where should we place this new wine we are going to start selling – premium (high quality), great value (medium quality), or great deal (low quality)?

In this chapter we started with logistic regression as a popular technique for doing binary decision-making; such two-class classification happens to cover a large range of possibilities. But of course, there are situations that require us to consider more than two classes. For them, we saw several techniques between this and the previous chapter: softmax regression, kNN, and decision trees. A problem with some of these techniques is that they can overfit the data, leading to biased models. To overcome this we could use random forest, which uses a large set of decision trees, with each tree intentionally and randomly created imperfectly, and then combines their outputs to produce a single decision. This makes random forest an example of an ensemble method.

We saw naïve Bayes – a very popular technique for binary decision-making problems. It is based on a very naïve assumption that the presence of a particular feature in a class is unrelated to the presence of any other feature. This is often not true. For example, think about the previous sentence: It has a structure. It has a logical flow and a particular word is preceded by a certain word and followed by another. For example, "is" is more likely to be followed by an adjective like "based" and preceded by a noun or pronoun like "it." Naïve Bayes assumes that the order of these words is not important, and the appearance of a word has nothing to do with the appearance of any other word in the sentence. Surprisingly, despite this simple and flawed assumption, naïve Bayes classification works very well. That independence assumption makes complex computations quite simple and feasible.

And so, we find naïve Bayes used in many commercial applications, especially information filtering (e.g., spam detection).

Finally, we dipped our toes into SVM. I say "dipped our toes" because SVM can be much more sophisticated and powerful than what we were able to cover in this chapter. The power and sophistication come from SVM's ability to use different kernels. Think about kernels as transformation functions that allow us to create nonlinear decision boundaries. There are situations where data seems hard to separate using a line or hyperplane, but we could perhaps draw a linear boundary in a higher dimension that looks like a curve in the current space. The full explanation of this process is beyond the scope of this book, but hopefully a few references provided at the end of this chapter will help you explore and learn more about this powerful technique.

Key Terms

- **Supervised learning** is a class of algorithms that use a set of examples from previous records that are labeled to make predictions about the future.
- **Anomaly detection** refers to identification of data points, or observations that do not conform to the expected pattern of a given population.
- **Training–validation–test data**: The training set consists of data points that are labeled and are used to learn the model. A validation set, often prepared separately from the training set, consists of observations that are used to tune the parameters of the model – for example, to test overfitting. The test set is used to evaluate the performance of the model.
- **True positive rate (TPR)** indicates how much of what we detected as 1 was indeed 1.
- **False positive rate (FPR)** indicates how much of what we detected as 1 was actually 0.

Conceptual Questions

1. Relate the likelihood of a model given data and the probability of data given a model. Are these two the same? Different? How?

2. Compare gradient descent and gradient ascent algorithms. Specifically, discuss what kind of functions they use and what their objectives are.

3. How is softmax regression different from logistic regression in terms of its applicability?

4. Bayes' theorem shows us how to turn $P(E|H)$ to $P(H|E)$, where E = evidence and H = hypothesis. But what does that really mean? Imagine you have to explain this to someone who doesn't understand ML or probability at all.

5. Here are the past seven governors of New Jersey based on their party affiliations (Democratic, Republican): R, D, D, D, D, R, D. Using the Naïve Bayes classification

technique we learned in this chapter, calculate the probability of the next governor being a Republican. Show your calculations.

6. What are support vectors?
7. What is a kernel in the context of SVM?

Hands-on Problems

Problem 6.1 (Logistic Regression)

Download crash.csv from OA 6.10, which is an auto-accident dataset portal for the USA hosted by data.gov (crash data for individual states can be searched). The data contains passengers' (not necessarily the driver's) age (in years) and the speed of the vehicle (mph) at the time of impact, as well as the fate of the passengers (1 represents survived, 0 represents did not survive) after the crash. Use logistic regression to decide if the age and speed can predict the survivability of the passenger.

Problem 6.2 (Logistic Regression)

An automated answer-rating site marks each post in a community forum website as "good" or "bad" based on the quality of the post. The CSV file, which you can download from OA 6.11, contains the various types of quality as measured by the tool. The following are the type of qualities that the dataset contains:

- *num_words*: number of words in the post
- *num_characters*: number of characters in the post
- *num_misspelled*: number of misspelled words
- *bin_end_qmark*: if the post ends with a question mark
- *num_interrogative*: number of interrogative words in the post
- *bin_start_small*: if the answer starts with a lowercase letter (1 means yes, otherwise no)
- *num_sentences*: number of sentences per post
- *num_punctuations*: number of punctuation symbols in the post
- *label*: the label of the post (G for good and B for bad) as determined by the tool.

Using the features available, build a logistic regression-based classifier to classify a post's label (G or B). Make sure to create appropriate training and testing sets from the available data and report your accuracies and confusion matrix.

Problem 6.3 (Logistic Regression)

In this exercise you will use the Immunotherapy dataset, available from OA 6.12, which contains information about wart treatment results of 90 patients using immunotherapy. For each patient the dataset has information about the patient's sex (either 1 or 0), age in years, number of warts, type, area, induration diameter, and result of treatment (a binary variable). Build a logistic regression model that predicts the result of treatment from the remaining features, and then evaluate the accuracy of your model.

Problem 6.4 (Softmax Regression)

The Iris flower dataset, or Fisher's Iris dataset (built into Python or downloadable from OA 6.13), is a multivariate dataset introduced by the British statistician and biologist Ronald Fisher in his 1936 paper. The use of multiple measurements in taxonomic problems is an example of linear discriminant analysis. The dataset consists of 50 samples from each of three species of Iris (*Iris setosa*, *Iris virginica*, and *Iris versicolor*). Four features were measured from each sample: the length and width of the sepals and petals, in centimeters. Based on the combination of these four features, create a prediction model using softmax regression for the species of *Iris*.

Problem 6.5 (Softmax Regression)

For this softmax regression problem you will work with Horseshoe crab data, available from OA 6.14. This dataset has 173 observations of female crabs, including the following characteristics:

- *Satellites*: number of male partners in addition to the female's primary partner.
- *Yes*: a binary factor indicating if the female has satellites.
- *Width*: width of the female crab in centimeters.
- *Weight*: weight of the female in grams.
- *Color*: a categorical value having range of 1–4, where 1 = light color and 4 = dark color.
- *Spine*: a categorical variable valued 1–3 indicating the goodness of spine of the female.

Use softmax regression to predict the condition of the spine of female crabs based on the remaining features in the dataset and report the accuracy of your predictions.

Problem 6.6 (Naïve Bayes)

Download the YouTube spam collection dataset available from OA 6.15. It is a public set of comments collected for spam research. It has five datasets composed of 1956 real messages extracted from five videos. These five videos are popular pop songs that were among the 10 most viewed of the collection period. All five datasets have the following attributes:

- *COMMENT_ID*: unique id representing the comment
- *AUTHOR*: author ID
- *DATE*: date the comment is posted
- *CONTENT*: the comment
- *TAG*: for spam 1, otherwise 0.

For this exercise use any four of these five datasets to build a spam filter and use that filter to check the accuracy on the remaining dataset.

Problem 6.7 (Naïve Bayes)

The dataset for the following exercise is sourced from the *Journal of Interdisciplinary History*. It contains statistics on teachers who were members and non-members of the Nazi party by religion, cohort, residence, and gender. It can be downloaded from OA 6.16. Following are the attribute values and their meaning:

- *Religion*: 1 = Protestant, 2 = Catholic, 3 = none
- *Cohort*: 1 = Empire, 2 = Late Empire, 3 = Early Weimar, 4 = Late Weimar, 5 = Third Reich
- *Residence*: 1 = rural, 2 = urban
- *Gender*: 1 = male, 2 = female
- *Membership*: 1 = Yes, 0 = No.

Use the Naïve Bayes algorithm on this dataset to determine the likelihood of teachers being a member of the Nazi party from their religion, cohort, residence, and gender.

Problem 6.8 (SVM)

The dataset to use for this assignment is the Iris dataset, which is a classic and very easy-to-use multiclass classification dataset. It consists of the petal and sepal lengths of three different types of irises (*setosa*, *versicolor*, and *virginica*), stored in a 150 × 4 numpy.ndarray. The rows are the samples and the columns are *Sepal Length*, *Sepal Width*, *Petal Length*, and *Petal Width*.

You can load the Iris dataset through this Python code:

```
from sklearn import datasets
iris = datasets.load_iris()
```

We will use SVM here, but with different kernels. In the chapter we only briefly talked about what a kernel is. Essentially, a kernel is a function that allows the data points to be mapped in a higher-dimensional space to create a separating boundary between classes. This transformation could be as simple as linear. Here is how you can build an SVM with a linear kernel:

```
from sklearn.svm import SVC # importing the package
SVC(kernel="linear") # building the classifier
```

The second line will give you a classifier that you can store and process further, just like you do with a kNN-built classifier. Here we are saying that we want to use a linear kernel for our SVM. Other options are "rbf" (radial basis function) and "poly" (polynomial). Try each of these and see what accuracies you get. Note that every time you run your program you may get slightly different numbers, so try running it a few times:

- For the classification, take only the first two columns from the dataset.
- Split the dataset into 70% for training and 30% for testing.
- Show the resulting accuracies for the three variations of SVM.

Problem 6.9 (SVM)

For this exercise we have collected a sample of 198 cases from NIST's AnthroKids dataset, which is available from OA 6.17. The dataset comes from a 1977 anthropometric study of body measurements for children. Subjects in this sample are between the ages of 8 and 18 years old, selected at random from the much larger dataset of the original study.

Use the SVM to see if we can use mass, height, waist, foot, sittingHeight, upperLegLength, kneeHeight, forearmLength, and age to determine the gender of the child.

Problem 6.10 (SVM)

In this exercise you will use the Portuguese sea battles data from OA 6.18, which contains outcomes of naval battles between Portuguese and Dutch/English ships between 1583 and 1663. The dataset has the following features:

- Battle: name of the battle place
- Year: year of the battle
- Portuguese ships: number of Portuguese ships
- Dutch ships: number of Dutch ships
- English ships: number of English ships
- Ratio of Portuguese to Dutch/English ships
- Spanish involvement: 1 = Yes, 0 = No
- Portuguese outcome: 1 = defeat, 0 = draw, 1 = victory.

Use an SVM-based model to predict the Portuguese outcome of the battle from the number of ships involved on all sides and Spanish involvement.

Further Reading and Resources

If you are interested in learning more about supervised learning or any of the topics discussed above, following are a few links that might be useful:

- Further topics on logistic regression: https://onlinecourses.science.psu.edu/stat504/node/217.
- Common pitfalls in statistical analysis – logistic regression: www.ncbi.nlm.nih.gov/pmc/articles/PMC5543767.
- A practical explanation of a Naïve Bayes classifier: https://monkeylearn.com/blog/practical-explanation-naive-bayes-classifier.
- Softmax regression: http://deeplearning.stanford.edu/tutorial/supervised/Softmax Regression.
- 6 easy steps to learn the Naïve Bayes algorithm: www.analyticsvidhya.com/blog/2015/09/naive-bayes-explained.

Notes

1. At this point I am assuming you have a basic background in statistics and have already come across this idea of a p-value. If not, or if you need a quick refresher, I suggest this resource: www.ncbi.nlm.nih.gov/pmc/articles/PMC6532382.
2. https://docs.opencv.org/2.4/doc/tutorials/ml/introduction_to_svm/introduction_to_svm.html.
3. See "Introduction to support vector machines": http://docs.opencv.org/2.4/doc/tutorials/ml/introduction_to_svm/introduction_to_svm.html.

PART III

UNSUPERVISED LEARNING

In the previous section of this book we saw scenarios where we learn something from existing data and then try to make predictions about new observations or situations. But there are times when we are simply trying to figure out what's going on with what we have – either for our own understanding or for explaining to someone else. In such cases we do not have truth labels or correct values. Instead, we are looking for a structure or a model that can fit the underlying data. And if we can do that reasonably, we can not only understand and explain what's going on, but even start figuring out what may be missing or what may happen in unknown parts of that landscape. We have come to another very important branch of machine learning: unsupervised learning. A lot of what happens under this branch involves organizing, grouping, or clustering the data. We have a whole chapter dedicated to clustering (Chapter 7). Then there are situations where we can't or don't want to assign data points to any specific clusters. Instead, we want to describe how data is distributed across different regions. That brings us to doing density estimation (Chapter 8). In the end, we can see that often unsupervised learning problems can be turned into supervised learning, and vice versa, with certain assumptions and some effort, if it is suitable to do so.

7 Clustering

> **What do you need?**
> - A good understanding of statistical concepts (see Appendix A), probability theory (see Appendix C), and functions.
> - The basics of differential calculus (see Appendix B for a few handy formulas).
> - Introductory-to intermediate-level experience with Python, including installing packages or libraries (see Chapter 2).
>
> **What will you learn?**
> - Solution of data problems when truth values for training are not available.
> - Using unsupervised clustering methods to provide an explanation of data.
> - Performing clustering using various machine learning techniques.

7.1 Introduction

In the previous chapter we saw how to learn from data when the labels or truth values associated with them are available. In other words, we knew what was right or wrong and we used that information to build a regression or classification model that could then make predictions for new data. Such a process defined supervised learning. Now we will consider the other big area of machine learning (ML), where we do not have true labels or values with the given data, and yet we will want to learn the underlying structure of that data and be able to explain it. This is called **unsupervised learning**.

In unsupervised learning data points have no labels associated with them. Instead, the goal of an unsupervised learning algorithm is to organize the data in some way or to describe its structure. This can mean grouping it into clusters or finding different ways of looking at complex data so that it appears simpler or more organized.

Clustering is the division of a set of observations into subsets (called clusters) so that observations in the same cluster are similar in some sense. It is a method of unsupervised learning, and a common technique for statistical data analysis used in many fields. While clustering covers a bit of unsupervised learning, it is not the only unsupervised learning method. In the next chapter we will see density estimation that allows us to create soft boundaries and provide probability distribution for membership of data points into different groups. But for now, let's focus on clustering.

We will look at two types of clustering algorithms in this chapter: agglomerative (going bottom to top) and divisive (going top to bottom). In addition, we will also discuss a very important technique, called expectation maximization (EM), which is used in situations where we have too many unknowns and not enough guidance on how to explain or fit the data using a model. All of these are examples of unsupervised learning, as we do not have labels for data and yet we are trying to understand some potential underlying structure.

Let's begin by reviewing a couple of techniques for clustering the data as a way to explain such a structure.

7.2 Divisive Clustering

The reverse of the agglomerative technique, divisive clustering works in a top-down mode where the goal is to break up the cluster containing all the objects into smaller clusters. The general approach is:

1. Put all the objects in one cluster.
2. Repeat until all clusters are singletons:
   - Choose a cluster to split based on some criterion.
   - Replace the chosen cluster with subclusters.

This may seem fairly straightforward, but there are issues to address, including deciding how many clusters we should split the data into, as well as how to do the split. We will revisit this problem of determining the number of clusters later, but for now let's work on a hands-on example for divisive clustering.

Hands-on Example 7.1: Divisive Clustering

Consider the dataset shown in Table 7.1, which represents the scores (between 0 and 7) that a student received in their last two quizzes.

At present, all seven students are grouped into a single cluster. Let's divide the dataset into two clusters. A sensible approach for separation is parting the *A* and *B* values of the two students furthest apart into two groups. Let's plot these seven points on a 2D plane (Figure 7.1).

Table 7.1 Example dataset for divisive clustering algorithm.

Student	A	B
1	1.0	1.0
2	1.5	2.0
3	3.0	4.0
4	5.0	7.0
5	3.5	5.0
6	4.5	5.0
7	3.5	4.5

Table 7.2 Initialization of two clusters.

	Student	Mean vector (centroid)
Cluster 1	1	(1.0, 1.0)
Cluster 2	4	(5.w0, 7.0)

Table 7.3 First step-through with divisive clustering algorithm.

		Cluster 1		Cluster 2
Step	Student	Mean vector (centroid)	Student	Mean vector (centroid)
1	1	(1.0, 1.0)	4	(5.0, 7.0)
2	1, 2	(1.2, 1.5)	4	(5.0, 7.0)
3	1, 2, 3	(1.8, 2.3)	4	(5.0, 7.0)
4	1, 2, 3	(1.8, 2.3)	4, 5	(4.2, 6.0)
5	1, 2, 3	(1.8, 2.3)	4, 5, 6	(4.3, 5.7)
6	1, 2, 3	(1.8, 2.3)	4, 5, 6, 7	(4.1, 5.4)

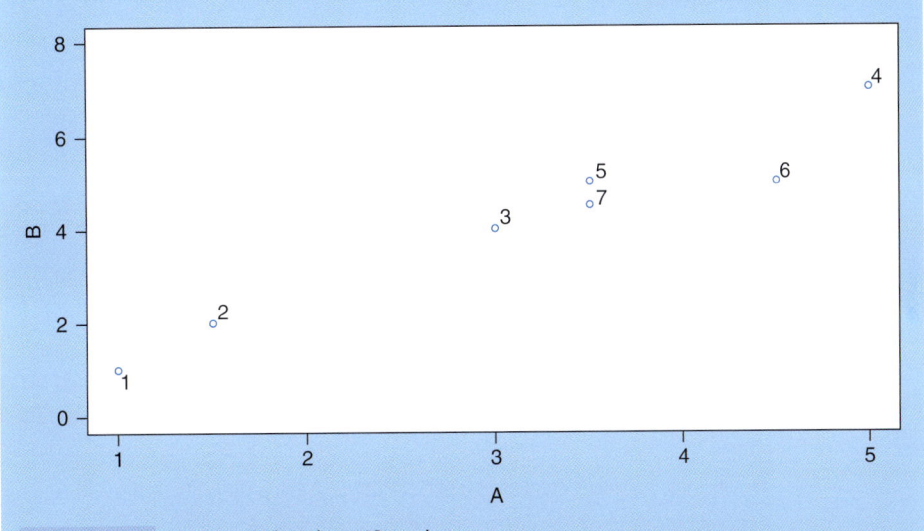

Figure 7.1 *A* against *B* plotted on a 2D graph.

As we can see from Figure 7.1, students 1 and 4 are the furthest apart, making them ideal candidates for partitioning. Therefore, we call them the centers of two different clusters, or centroids, as shown in Table 7.2.

The remaining students are examined in sequence and allocated to the cluster to which they are closest in terms of Euclidean distance to the cluster mean. The mean vector of the cluster has to be recalculated each time a new member is added. This step is repeated until there are no more students to be added. Table 7.3 shows how this is done step-by-step.

Now the initial partition has been changed, and the two clusters at the end of the previous step are turned into the clusters we see in Table 7.4.

Table 7.4 Result of the first step-through with the divisive clustering algorithm.

	Student	Mean vector (centroid)
Cluster 1	1, 2, 3	(1.8, 2.3)
Cluster 2	4, 5, 6, 7	(4.1, 5.4)

Table 7.5 Second step-through with divisive clustering algorithm.

Student	Distance to mean (centroid) of Cluster 1	Distance to mean (centroid) of Cluster 2
1	1.5	5.4
2	0.4	4.3
3	2.1	1.8
4	5.7	1.8
5	3.2	0.7
6	3.8	0.6
7	2.8	1.1

Table 7.6 Result of the second step-through with divisive clustering algorithm.

	Student	Mean vector (centroid)
Cluster 1	1, 2	(1.3, 1.5)
Cluster 2	3, 4, 5, 6, 7	(3.9, 5.1)

However, we cannot yet be sure that each student has been assigned to the right cluster, so we compare each student's distance to its own cluster mean and to that of the opposite cluster. The result is shown in Table 7.5.

As Table 7.5 shows, student #3 is part of cluster 1, yet it is closest to cluster 2. Therefore, it makes sense to relocate 3 to cluster 2. The new partition is shown in Table 7.6.

This iterative relocation would continue from this new partition until no more relocations are required.

> **Try It Yourself 7.1: Devising Clustering**
>
> Age and income for 10 individuals are presented in Table 7.7. Using this data, apply the divisive clustering technique to group these individuals.
>
> **Table 7.7** Age and income data for different individuals.
>
> | Individual | Age | Income |
> |---|---|---|
> | 1 | 22 | $34,542 |
> | 2 | 25 | $47,400 |
> | 3 | 23 | $45,000 |
> | 4 | 43 | $76,140 |
> | 5 | 38 | $74,500 |
> | 6 | 23 | $35,000 |
> | 7 | 56 | $86,000 |
> | 8 | 49 | $82,450 |
> | 9 | 36 | $70,500 |
> | 10 | 52 | $85,000 |

7.2.1 Divisive Clustering with k-Means

Earlier we discussed the difficulty in deciding the number of clusters. Fortunately, there is a simple and effective algorithm to carry out the general approach described in divisive clustering method: k-means. This allows us to more effectively experiment with different values for the number of clusters. One of the most frequently used clustering algorithms, k-means clustering is an algorithm to classify or to group objects based on attributes or features into k number of groups, where k is a positive integer.

The grouping is done by minimizing the sum of squares of distances between data (n) and the corresponding cluster centroid (k). Here is how it works:

Step 1: Begin with a decision on the value of k = number of clusters. It is okay if you do not have a clear way to determine this; you can experiment with different values.

Step 2: Put any initial partition that classifies the data into k clusters. You may assign the training samples randomly or systematically, as in the following:
- Take the first k training sample as single-element clusters.
- Assign each of the remaining ($n - k$) training samples to the cluster with the nearest centroid. After each assignment, recompute the centroid of the gaining cluster.

Step 3: Take each sample in sequence and compute its distance from the centroid of each of the clusters. If a sample is not currently in the cluster with the closest centroid, switch this sample to that cluster and update the centroid of the cluster gaining the new sample and the cluster losing the sample.

> **Hands-on Example 7.2: *k*-Means Clustering**
>
> Let's run through an example to see how the *k*-means algorithm works. To help us with this we will work with artificial data at first, but rest assured we will get to work with *real* data as well. The idea here is to automatically generate a bunch of data points on a 2D plane and see if we can identify their inherent structure or organization. Why do this? Two reasons: (1) we want to control what these data points are, with their grouping and distributions; and (2) knowing how the data was generated will give us a ground truth when we want to assess our clustering outputs. So, let's start by importing various packages:
>
> ```
> # Import libraries needed
> import matplotlib.pyplot as plt
>
> from sklearn.datasets import make_blobs
> from sklearn.cluster import KMeans
> import matplotlib.pyplot as plt
> ```
>
> We will now generate some random data. Let's create 200 data points on a 2D surface that are randomly distributed in six groups:
>
> ```
> # Create 2D data with six clusters
> data = make_blobs(n_samples = 200, n_features = 2,
> centers = 6, cluster_std = 3)
> ```
>
> In that *data* variable we are holding 200 data points that were randomly generated with *x* and *y* coordinates with six different origins. That is the ground truth, but in real-life situations we do not get to know such information about the origin of the data. Instead, we are simply given those 200 data points and asked if we could organize them in some way.
>
> We will now go ahead with clustering the data points into six clusters. Of course, it may seem like we are cheating here, but this example will help us illustrate how the *k*-means process works – from initial random assignment of clusters to the final, converged clustering. For this, we will write a loop that takes us through many iterations of *k*-means and examine (visualize) how the clustering looks at various stages. The following code will accomplish that:
>
> ```
> c = d = 0
> fig, ax = plt.subplots(2, 2, figsize=(10,10))
> for i in range(4):
>     ax[c,d].plot(c,d)
>     ax[c,d].title.set_text(f"{i * 25 + 1} iteration
>     points:")
>
>     # Build a model with fix random_state
>     kmeans = KMeans(n_clusters = 6,max_iter = i * 5 +
>     1, random_state = 4)
> ```

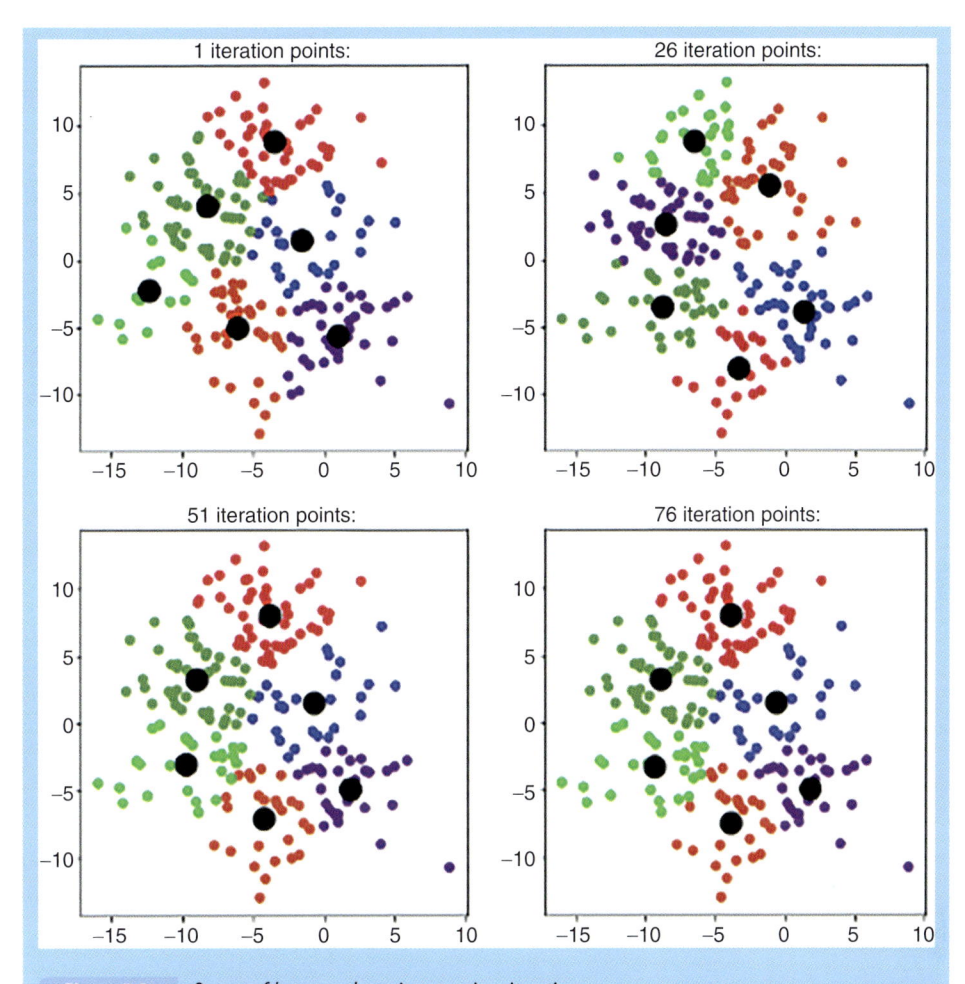

Figure 7.2 Output of *k*-means clustering at various iterations.

```
        # Predict the clusters
        kmeans.fit(data[0])
        centroids = kmeans.cluster_centers_

        # Plot the clusters
        ax[c,d].scatter(data[0][:,0],data[0][:,1],c =
        kmeans.labels_,cmap = "brg")
        ax[c,d].scatter(kmeans.cluster_centers_[:, 0],
kmeans.cluster_centers_[:, 1], s = 200, c = "black")

        d += 1
        if d == 2:
            c += 1
            d = 0
```

The output from this code is shown in Figure 7.2. As we can see, at iteration 1, k-means starts out by randomly placing the six cluster centers (centroids), but as the process continues those centroids shift, and so do the cluster assignments for many of the data points. In the end we have achieved clustering that roughly corresponds to the original data.

Of course, in a real application we are most likely not going to know the ground truth (how many clusters, which point belongs to which cluster). If we treat the given example like that, we should experiment with different numbers of clusters and examine which number for k makes sense. In this example we have the luxury of having a visual representation of our data and clustering. That allows us to qualitatively make a decision about how many clusters may be appropriate. But what if we cannot visualize the data? There are several methods for doing a quantitative assessment for that. One of them is called the "elbow method." See the FYI box for more details.

Try It Yourself 7.2: k-Means Clustering

Let's work with Iris dataset available from OA 7.1.

First, load the data and extract the first two features. Now, do flat clustering using k-means. You can decide how many clusters are appropriate. For this, you may like to plot the data first and see how it is scattered. Show the plot with clusters marked.

If you have also used this data for doing classification, what can you say about this data and/or the techniques you used? Write your thoughts in one or two paragraphs.

Repeat step 3 until convergence is achieved – that is, until a pass through the training sample causes no new assignments. Now, let's do what we normally do in this book: take a hands-on approach and work through an example.

7.2.2 Divisive Clustering with k-Modes

k-means is surely one of the most popular and easy-to-understand techniques for doing clustering. But it is based on an important assumption that the variables or features being considered are numerical. But what if they are categorical? We can use a similar algorithm, called k-modes, which uses mode instead of mean to calculate its centroids. We do not need to rewrite the k-means algorithm to indicate that change. Instead, let's go ahead and do a hands-on example where clustering is done with categorical variables.

Hands-on Example 7.3: k-Modes Clustering

We will start by making sure we have access to the Kmodes package. Go ahead and run an appropriate command to install it with Python. For example, the following command can be run on Spyder or the Google Colab console:

```
!pip install kmodes
```

Table 7.8 Output data table.

person	hair_color	eye_color	skin_color
P1	blonde	amber	fair
P2	brunette	gray	brown
P3	red	green	brown
P4	black	hazel	brown
P5	brunette	amber	fair
P6	black	gray	brown
P7	red	green	fair
P8	black	hazel	fair

Once that is done we can begin writing our code. As always, we import the libraries or packages we will need for this work:

```
# Import necessary libraries
import pandas as pd
import numpy as np
from kmodes.kmodes import KModes
```

For this exercise we will create our own data about eight different people. We will describe these people using their hair, eye, and skin colors.[1]

```
# Create the data we need
hair_color = np.array(["blonde", "brunette", "red",
"black", "brunette", "black", "red", "black"])
eye_color = np.array(["amber", "gray", "green",
"hazel", "amber", "gray", "green", "hazel"])
skin_color = np.array(["fair", "brown", "brown",
"brown", "fair", "brown", "fair", "fair"])
person = ["P1","P2","P3","P4","P5","P6","P7","P8"]
data = pd.DataFrame({"person":person, "hair_
color":hair_color, "eye_color":eye_color, "skin_
color":skin_color})
data = data.set_index("person")# Our data is indexed
# on the "person" attribute
data
```

The last line of the code above prints out the data table, shown here as Table 7.8.

Table 7.9 Output data table with cluster.

person	Cluster	hair_color	eye_color	skin_color
P1	0	blonde	amber	fair
P2	2	brunette	gray	brown
P3	1	red	green	brown
P4	2	black	hazel	brown
P5	0	brunette	amber	fair
P6	2	black	gray	brown
P7	1	red	green	fair
P8	0	black	hazel	fair

Now that we have the data, let's go ahead and perform clustering using the *k*-modes algorithm:

```
# Building the model with three clusters
kmode = KModes(n_clusters = 3, init = "random", n_init = 5, verbose = 1)
clusters = kmode.fit_predict(data)
data.insert(0, "Cluster", clusters, True)
data
```

Once again, the last line of the code above prints out the data table, but this time we have inserted a new column called "Cluster," which contains cluster assignment for each of the data points. It may look something like Table 7.9.

As we can see, we have been able to group these eight people into three clusters. I will leave it up to you to decide if these groups make sense. Better yet, why not try other numbers of clusters?

As we come out of the example, let's make a couple of notes that will help us beyond this specific exercise. Notice here how we extracted and stored cluster assignment information. In most clustering processes, the outcome is cluster assignment. When we have only a few data points, as in this example, that information may be easy to understand. But when we have a large amount of data, printing out the cluster information is not going to be useful. Instead, we should follow the kind of process we did above – create an additional column with the original data and store the cluster information.

Another thing to note is that when we are given a clustering problem, we may not be told what algorithm to use. We need to make a choice based on several factors, one of which should be based on examination of the types of variables we are dealing with. If they are numerical or can be converted to numerical, we could proceed with *k*-means. But if they are categorical, *k*-modes will be a good choice. Of course, there are other factors to consider as well, and perhaps some of them will become clear as we work through more clustering techniques. For now, let's make sure we practice what we have just learned.

> **Try It Yourself 7.3: k-Means with Categorical Variables**
>
> Using the data from Table 7.10 (10 data points with three features or variables) to create two clusters. Explain your process (how you define centroids, find cluster memberships, etc.).
>
> **Table 7.10** Data for Try It Yourself 7.3.
>
> | Record | v1 | v2 | v3 |
> |--------|----|----|----|
> | 1 | M | Q | X |
> | 2 | M | Q | Z |
> | 3 | N | P | Z |
> | 4 | O | Q | W |
> | 5 | O | R | Y |
> | 6 | N | P | X |
> | 7 | N | P | W |
> | 8 | N | R | Y |
> | 9 | M | O | X |
> | 10 | N | P | Y |

> **FYI: Determining Optimal Number of Clusters Using the Elbow Method**
>
> As noted during our discussion and hands-on example of k-means, determining k (the number of clusters or centroids) can be done experimentally, especially if we lack any prior knowledge or intuition about the optimal number of clusters to achieve. But given that k could be anything (from two to the size of the dataset), we could be signing up for an expensive process to get to that optimal k.
>
> To help with this, we could refer to early work by Thorndike, R. L. (1953). Who belongs in the family?. *Psychometrika, 18*(4), 267–276. What is described in this work can be easily implemented, visualized, and used for our decision-making. It is called the "elbow method." If you look at Figure 7.3, it will become apparent why. Here, you can see different values for k on the x-axis, plotted against the amount of variance explained on the y-axis. We could also plot the sum of squared distances on the y-axis using `km.inertia_` in Python, where "km" is our KMeans object. As shown in Figure 7.3, with increasing number of k we are able to explain more variance, but at $k = 4$ the line creates an "elbow." In other words, the performance increase does not keep increasing linearly. We could use that point to settle for our optimal k. Note that if you are using the sum of squared distance instead, you would have a line going down, but you would still be looking for that elbow effect to find a good value for your k.

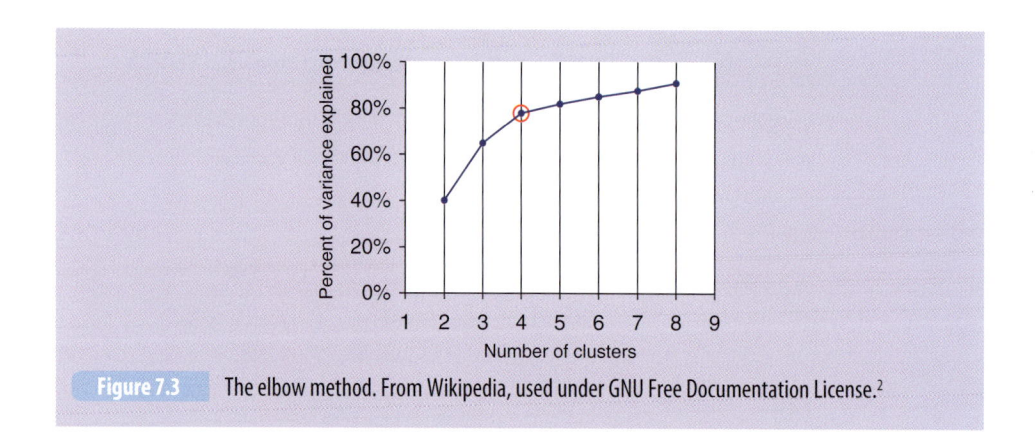

Figure 7.3 The elbow method. From Wikipedia, used under GNU Free Documentation License.[2]

7.3 Agglomerative Clustering

In the divisive clustering method, and through subsequent practice of the *k*-means and *k*-mode techniques, we learned about some basics of clustering. For example, we learned that similarity between two data points can be calculated using a measure of distance. Similar data points tend to be close to one another, and in the same cluster. Of course, how close is close enough for two data points to be in the same cluster is an open question. There is usually no objective answer for this; instead, we rely on how the distance between two given points compares to their distances from other data points, how many other data points there are, and how many clusters we are looking to form. Typically, we do not want too many clusters. We also would want to avoid clusters with only one data point in them.

All of these could be obtained using different methods. Before, we saw how we could do this by a top-down approach – that is, taking the whole dataset as belonging to a single cluster and then keep splitting until we achieve the qualities or characteristics we listed above. Now we will go the other way: bottom-up, or agglomerative. Here, we will start by assuming each data point belongs to its own cluster and then start collapsing points or clusters that are similar. The following is a general outline of how an agglomerative clustering algorithm runs:

1. Use any computable cluster similarity measure $sim(C_i, C_j)$ – for example, Euclidean distance, cosine similarity, etc.
2. For *n* objects $v_1, \ldots, v_n$, assign each to a singleton cluster $C_i = \{v_i\}$.
3. Repeat until there is just one cluster:
    - Identify the two most similar clusters C_j and C_k (these could be tied – chose one pair).
    - Delete C_j and C_k and add $(C_j \cup C_k)$ to the set of clusters.
4. Use dendrograms to show the sequence of cluster merges.

Hands-on Example 7.4: Agglomerative Clustering 1

We will now work with a toy example to understand how agglomerative clustering works. For this example we will use five data points. Distances between every pair of the data points is given in the distance matrix shown in Table 7.11. Do not worry about what the data means here; this table is simply to show you how the algorithm works.

Table 7.11 Computation of distance matrix.

	1	2	3	4	5
1	0				
2	8	0			
3	3	6	0		
4	5	5	8	0	
5	13	10	2	7	0

As expected, the distance matrix is symmetric. This is because the distance between x and y is the same as the distance between y and x. It has zeros on the diagonal as every item is distance zero from itself. As the matrix is symmetric, only the lower triangle is shown in the table. The upper triangle would be a reflection of the lower one.

Since we have distances for each pair of points, let's start clustering by grouping the smaller distances. As shown in the table, data points 3 and 5 are closer than any others, as their distance, 2 (shown in red), is the minimum between all the pairs. So, first we will merge this pair into a single cluster "35." At the end of this step the cluster has four data points: 1, 2, 4, and 35. Since the data points have changed, now we must recalculate the distance matrix. We need a procedure to determine the distance between 35 and every other data point. This can be done by assigning the maximum of the distance between an item and 3 and this item and 5. The distance is calculated as:

$$dist_{35,i} = \max\left(dist_{3,i}, dist_{5,i}\right). \tag{7.1}$$

Using the formula in (7.1), the distance matrix is calculated as shown in Table 7.12.

Table 7.12 Next iteration of distance matrix.

	35	1	2	4
35	0			
1	13	0		
2	10	8	0	
4	9	5	5	0

If we continue this step using (7.1) until all the data points are grouped into a single cluster, we will end up with the cluster shown in Figure 7.4. On this plot, the y-axis represents the cluster height, which is the distance between the objects at the time they were clustered.

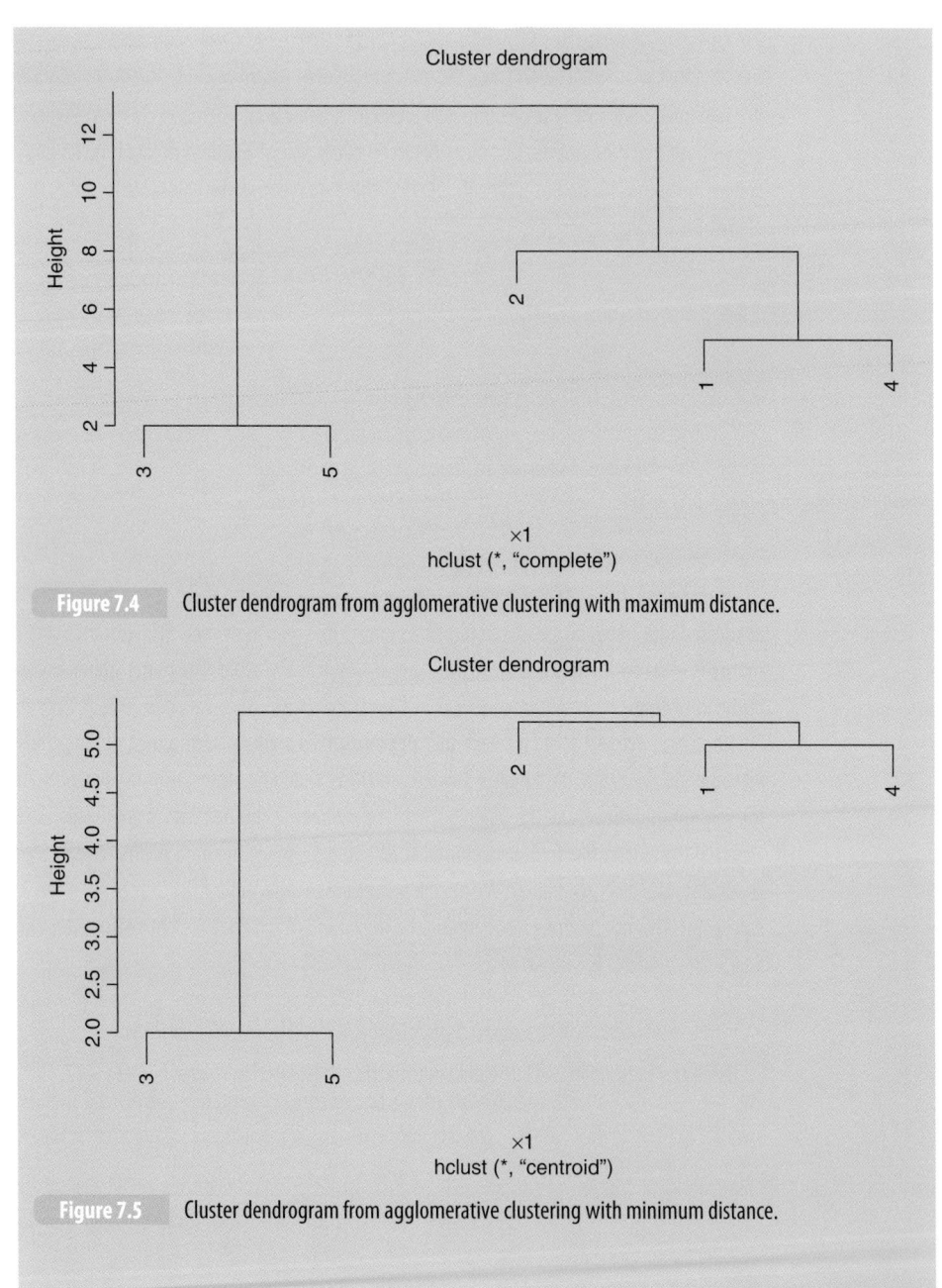

Figure 7.4 Cluster dendrogram from agglomerative clustering with maximum distance.

Figure 7.5 Cluster dendrogram from agglomerative clustering with minimum distance.

Important note: The distance calculation formula for the matrix can vary from problem to problem, and depending on the formula chosen we may end up with completely different clustering. For example, for the same dataset, if we calculate the distance as:

$$dist_{35,i} = \min\left(dist_{3,i}, dist_{5,i}\right) \tag{7.2}$$

then the cluster we will end up with is shown in Figure 7.5.

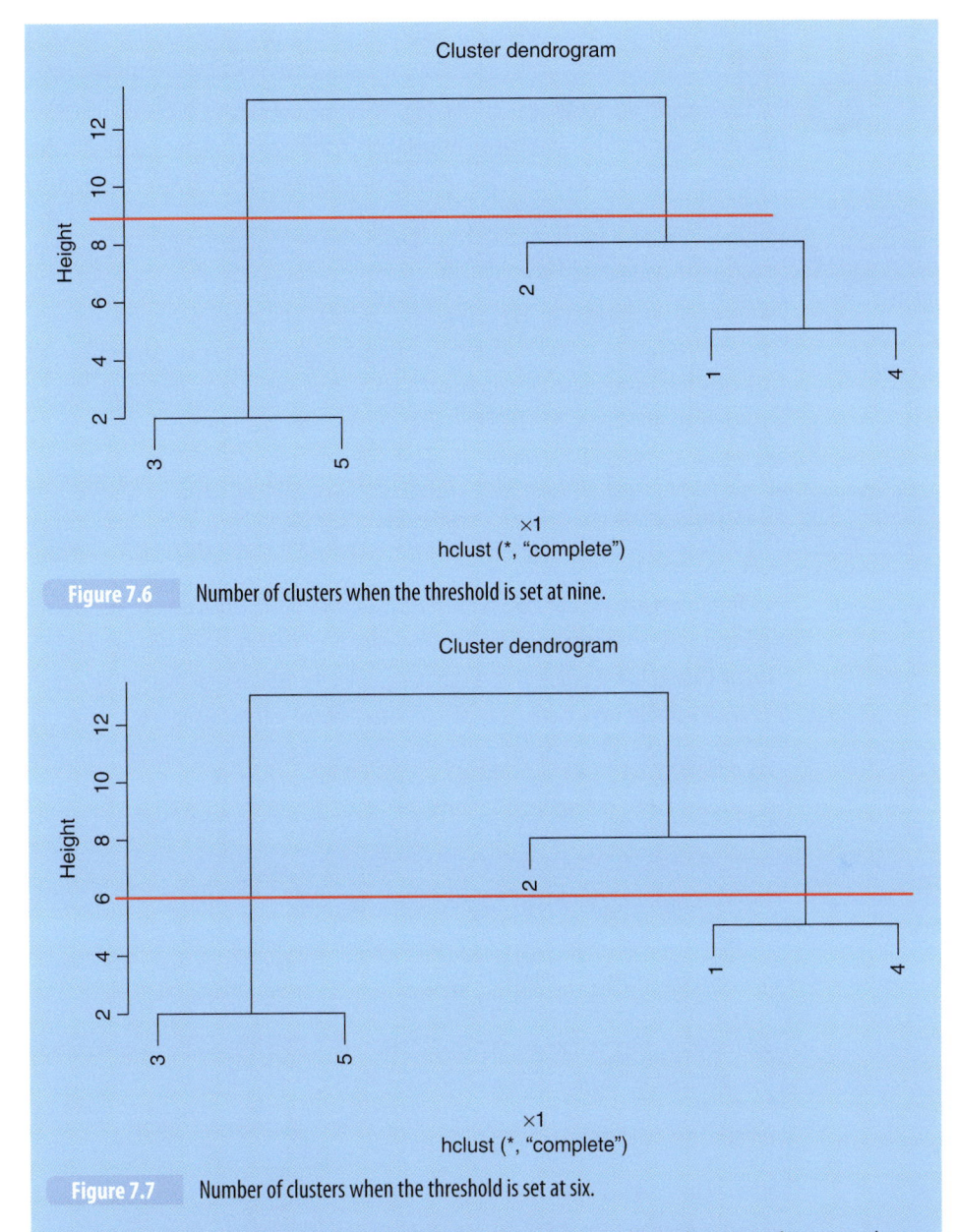

Figure 7.6 Number of clusters when the threshold is set at nine.

Figure 7.7 Number of clusters when the threshold is set at six.

One of the common problems with such clustering is that there is no universal way to say how many clusters there are. It depends on how we define the minimum threshold distance between two clusters. For example, in the first single linkage tree, also called a **dendrogram**, if we set the threshold at nine we will cut the tree into two clusters as shown by the red line in Figure 7.6, and we will end up with two clusters (1,2,4) and (3,5).

On the other hand, if we set the threshold at six the number of clusters will be three, as shown in Figure 7.7. It might be helpful to note that in dendrograms that have values grounded at the x-axis, the number of clusters is the number of vertical lines your horizontal line crosses.

> ## Hands-on Example 7.5: Agglomerative Clustering 2
>
> In this example you are going to use the StoneFlakes dataset from OA 7.2, which contains measurements of the flakes that are the waste products of prehistoric crafting processes. We will use this dataset to cluster the data points that are similar using the agglomerative method. Note, you may need to format the data before you can import the file into Python as a CSV.
>
> ```
> import pandas as pd
> import matplotlib.pyplot as plt
> from sklearn.cluster import AgglomerativeClustering
> from sklearn.preprocessing import StandardScaler
> import scipy.cluster.hierarchy as sch
>
> # We'll use a preprocessed version of the data which
> # contains no N/A values
> flakes_df = pd.read_csv("StoneFlakes_clean.csv")
> ```
>
> The dataset has a few missing instances (all the zeros and question marks). In this demonstration we are going to remove the missing instances, remove the first attribute as it is non-numeric, and standardize the output dataset before proceeding to clustering. Since the first column contains IDs, which is essentially an unusable variable, we will drop that column. After that, we will do scaling of the remaining variables.
>
> ```
> # drop the non-numeric column
> flakes_df.drop(columns = "ID", inplace = True)
>
> scaler = StandardScaler()
> scaler.fit_transform(flakes_df)
> ```
>
> In the next step we are going to build the clusters in the agglomerative method to perform agglomerative clustering by calculating the distance between clusters *u* and *v* as max(*dist*(*u*[*i*], *v*[*j*])):
>
> ```
> linkage_matrix = sch.linkage(flakes_df, method = "complete")
> ```
>
> Let's plot this dendrogram.
>
> ```
> # plot dendrogram
> dendrogram = sch.dendrogram(linkage_matrix)
> plt.ylabel("height")
> plt.savefig("dendrogram.png", dpi = 300)
> ```
>
> Your visualization should look like Figure 7.8.

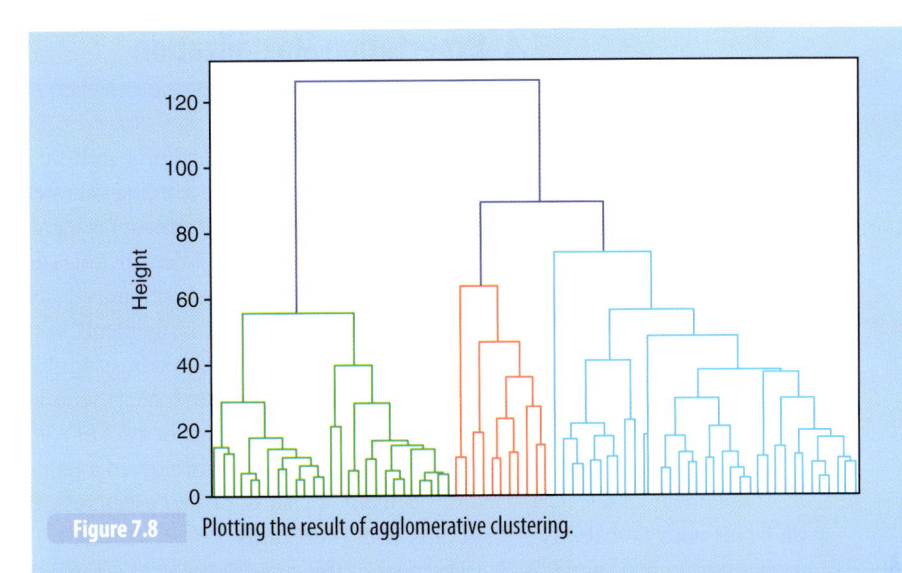

7.3 Agglomerative Clustering

Figure 7.8 Plotting the result of agglomerative clustering.

Technically we are done at this point. But if you are interested in using this for making predictions, you could use the Sklearn implementation of agglomerative clustering:

```
cluster = AgglomerativeClustering(n_clusters = 4, linkage = "complete")
cluster_preds = cluster.fit_predict(flakes_df)
print(cluster_preds)
```

This will generate an output like the following:

```
[3 2 2 0 2 2 2 2 2 0 2 1 2 2 0 1 1 1 1 1 1 1 1 2 0 2 2
 2 2 1 1 1 1 2 0 2 2
 0 2 2 2 1 1 1 2 0 1 1 1 1 1 1 1 0 1 1 2 2 1 2 0 2 2
 2 0 2 2 2 0 2 2 2]
```

What is going on with this series of numbers? These are labels (0, 1, 2, 3) corresponding to the four clusters we asked for. Each label represents a data point.

Try It Yourself 7.4: Clustering

To practice more on clustering, obtain the User Knowledge Modeling dataset from OA 7.3, which contains five numeric predictor attributes and one categorical target attribute, which is the class label. Use both divisive and agglomerative clustering on this dataset and compare their accuracy in predicting the class label from the predictor attributes. How many clusters do you create? Why? Explain the various design decisions you make.

7.4 Expectation Maximization

So far we have seen clustering, classification algorithms, and probabilistic models that are based on the existence of efficient and robust procedures for learning parameters from observations. Often, however, the only data available for training a model is incomplete. Missing values can occur, for example, in medical diagnoses, where patient histories generally include results from a limited battery of tests. Alternatively, in gene expression clustering incomplete data arise from the intentional omission of gene-to-cluster assignments in the probabilistic model. Expectation maximization is a fantastic approach to addressing this problem. The EM algorithm enables parameter estimation in probabilistic models with incomplete data. This can be quite useful for clustering with partial knowledge or a set of features.

Consider an example of tossing coins. Assume that we are given a pair of coins, A and B, of unknown biases, θ_A and θ_B, respectively. (That is, on any given toss, coin A will land on heads with probability θ_A and tails with probability $1 - \theta_A$. Similarly, for coin B, the probabilities are θ_B and $1 - \theta_B$.) The goal of this experiment is to estimate $\theta = (\theta_A, \theta_B)$ by repeating the following steps five times: randomly choose one of the two coins (with equal probability) and perform 10 independent coin tosses with the selected coin. Thus, the entire procedure involves a total of 50 coin tosses.

During this experiment we count two vectors: $x = (x_1, x_2, \ldots x_5)$ where $x_i \{0, 1, \ldots, 10\}$ is the number of heads observed during the ith round of tosses. Parameter estimation of this experiment is known as the *complete data case* in the instance that the values of all relevant random variables in our model (that is, the result of each coin toss and the type of coin used for each toss) are known.

A simple way to estimate θ_A and θ_B is to return the observed proportions of heads for each coin:

$$\theta_A = \frac{\text{number of heads using coin } A}{\text{total number of flips using coin } A} \quad (7.3)$$

and

$$\theta_B = \frac{\text{number of heads using coin } B}{\text{total number of flips using coin } B}. \quad (7.4)$$

This intuitive guess is, in fact, known in the statistical literature as **maximum likelihood estimation** (MLE). Roughly speaking, the MLE method assesses the quality of a statistical model based on the probability it assigns to the observed data. If $\log P(x,y)$ is the logarithm of the joint probability (or **log likelihood**) of obtaining any particular vector of observed head counts x and coin types y, then the formulas in (7.3) and (7.4) solve for the parameters ($= A, B$) that maximize $\log P(x,y)$.

The EM algorithm is used to find (locally) MLE parameters of a statistical model in cases where the equations cannot be solved directly. Often, these models involve latent variables in addition to unknown parameters and known data observations. That is, either missing values exist among the data or the model can be formulated more simply by assuming the existence of further unobserved data points.

7.4 Expectation Maximization

Hands-on Example 7.6: EM

Let's take an example and see how this works in Python. For this experiment, we will use the Diabetes dataset available as part of the Scikit-learn package. Let's go ahead and import the required packages and this dataset:

```
import matplotlib.pyplot as plt
from sklearn.datasets import load_diabetes
from sklearn.mixture import GaussianMixture

# load the included diabetes dataset
diab = load_diabetes(as_frame = True)
```

We can print out some useful information about this dataset by issuing a summary command:

```
print(diab.DESCR)

Diabetes dataset
----------------

Ten baseline variables, age, sex, body mass index,
average blood pressure, and six blood serum
measurements were obtained for each of n = 442 diabetes
patients, as well as the response of interest, a
quantitative measure of disease progression one year
after baseline.

**Data Set Characteristics:**

    :Number of Instances: 442

    :Number of Attributes: First 10 columns are numeric
predictive values

    :Target: Column 11 is a quantitative measure of
disease progression one year after baseline

    :Attribute Information:
        - age      age in years
        - sex
        - bmi      body mass index
        - bp       average blood pressure
        - s1       tc, total serum cholesterol
        - s2       ldl, low-density lipoproteins
```

```
            - s3      hdl, high-density lipoproteins
            - s4      tch, total cholesterol / HDL
            - s5      ltg, possibly log of serum
                      triglycerides level
            - s6      glu, blood sugar level
```

Note: Each of these 10 feature variables have been mean centered and scaled by the standard deviation times 'n_samples' (i.e. the sum of squares of each column totals 1).

Source URL:
www4.stat.ncsu.edu/~boos/var.select/diabetes.html

For more information see:
Bradley Efron, Trevor Hastie, Iain Johnstone and Robert Tibshirani (2004) "Least Angle Regression," Annals of Statistics (with discussion), 407-499.
(https://web.stanford.edu/~hastie/Papers/LARS/LeastAngle_2002.pdf)

Let's extract the appropriate data to apply the EM algorithm to:

```
diab_df = diab.data
print(diab.target)

# since we are not performing regression, we can add
# the target column
diab_df["s7"] = diab.target

# print a summary of our data
print(diab_df.describe())
```

This will generate an output that shows a table with 8 rows and 11 columns.

Now that we have the right kind of data in the right kind of format, we are ready to run EM on it. Specifically, given that we are going to use EM as a clustering mechanism, we will need to pick some number of clusters and decide how they are initialized. Let us go with four, initialized in a random fashion. This is an easy, one-line task. Once we do that, we will extract cluster assignments for each data point and plot them along the dimensions of *bmi* and *bp*.

```
em_gaussian = GaussianMixture(n_components = 4, init_params = "random", covariance_type = "full")
```

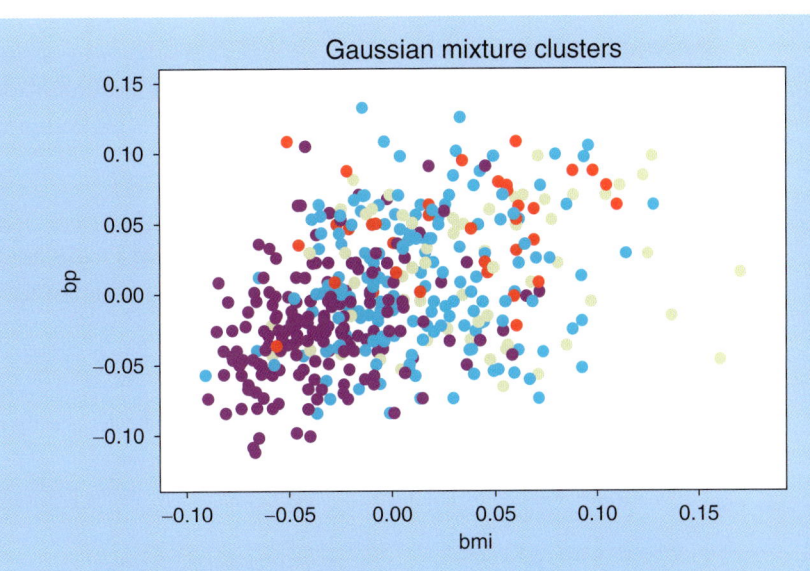

Figure 7.9 Clustering plot for diabetes data.

```
cluster_preds = em_gaussian.fit_predict(diab_df)
plt.title("Gaussian mixture clusters")

# We can pick two dimensions of the input data in order
# to visualize clusters in R^2. Note that this output
# will look different depending on which dimensions you
# choose to plot
plt.xlabel("bmi")
plt.ylabel("bp")
plt.scatter(diab_df["bmi"], diab_df["bp"], c = cluster_
preds, cmap = "rainbow")
plt.savefig("simple_diabetes_clusters.png", dpi = 300)
```

This should generate a clustering plot as shown in Figure 7.9.

Note that our data consists of many dimensions, but because we are able to create such visualizations in two dimensions only, we picked *bmi* and *bp*. Go ahead and pick some other dimensions to do the above plot. It may seem that our clustering has not worked so well because we see lots of overlaps. But this is due to the fact that we are plotting high-dimensional data onto very low (two) dimensions. In other words, do not read much into this visualization.

So, if visualization does not help, how can we ensure that the clusters are good? EM does not have a clear way to assess how well the model is built, like we are able to do for our classification models. To overcome this there are ways we can look into the *goodness* of the model. There are several criteria for evaluating this, such as the **Akaike information criterion** (AIC), the **Bayesian information criterion** (BIC), and the **log**

likelihood. The AIC provides an estimate of the relative information loss by a given model when representing the process that generated the data. Let's say a model has been generated from a model where *k* is the number of estimated parameters. If $\hat{L}$ is the maximum value of the likelihood function for the model, then the AIC value is calculated as:

$$\text{AIC} = 2k - 2\ln(\hat{L}). \tag{7.5}$$

The BIC, on the other hand, estimates the posterior probability of a model being true from a certain Bayesian setup. A lower BIC means that a model is considered more likely to be a better model. The formula for BIC is:

$$\text{BIC} = \ln(n)k - 2\ln(\hat{L}). \tag{7.6}$$

Both AIC and BIC are penalized-likelihood criteria. This means that the higher the number the worse the model. The only difference between AIC and BIC is the choice of log *n* versus 2.

For the clustering model we just created we can easily find out its AIC and BIC values with the following:

```
# View the Akaike information criterion
print(em_gaussian.aic(diab_df))

# View the Bayesian information criterion
print(em_gaussian.bic(diab_df))
```

These lines will print out two different numbers. Do not overthink these. They are not like a correlation coefficient or a slope of a line; there is no physical interpretation of them in isolation. What you could do is compare AIC (or BIC) values of different models generated using different parameters on the same data. For instance, we created four clusters here. Want to find out if three or five clusters is better? Go ahead and create those models and find out their AIC and BIC values. Whichever gives the lowest AIC and/or BIC is the best model.

Try It Yourself 7.5: EM

Use the User Knowledge Modeling dataset from OA 7.3. Use the EM algorithm to find the MLE parameters of the model. Report the AIC and BIC values.

7.5 Density Estimation

One way to think about clustering when we do not know how many clusters we should have is to let a process look for data points that are densely located and use that density information to form a cluster. One such technique is *MeanShift*.

Let's first understand what density information or function is. Imagine you are trying to represent the likelihood of finding a Starbucks in an area. You know that if it is a mall or a shopping district there is a good probability that there is a Starbucks (or two or three!), as opposed to a less populated rural area. In other words, Starbucks has higher density in cities and shopping areas than in less populated or less visited areas. A density function is a function (think about a curve on a graph) that represents a relative likelihood of a variable (e.g., the existence of Starbucks) to taking on a given value.

MeanShift is an algorithm that locates the maxima (maximum values) of a density function given a set of data points that fit that function. So, roughly speaking, if we have data points corresponding to the locations of Starbucks, *MeanShift* allows us to figure out where we are likely to find a Starbucks; or on the other hand, given a location, how likely are we to find a Starbucks.

Hands-on Example 7.7: Density Estimation

To see this in action we will define a density function, have it generate a bunch of data points that fit that function, and then try to locate centroids of these data points using density estimation. This almost seems like a self-fulfilling prophecy! But it allows us to practice and see how unsupervised clustering works when we do not even know how many clusters there should be.

Here is the code for this example, along with inline comments. The visual output as a 3D plot is also shown at the end (Figure 7.10):

```
import numpy as np
from sklearn.cluster import MeanShift
from sklearn.datasets import make_blobs
import matplotlib.pyplot as plt
from mpl_toolkits.mplot3d import Axes3D
```

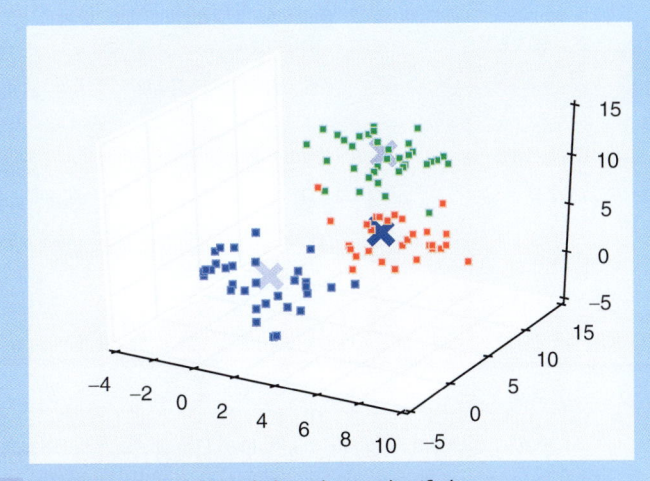

Figure 7.10 Density estimation plot with three clusters identified.

```python
# Import style class from matplotlib and use that to
# apply ggplot styling
from matplotlib import style
style.use("ggplot")

# Let's create a bunch of points around three centers
# in a 3D space
# X has those points and we can ignore y
centers = [[1,1,1],[5,5,5],[3,10,10]]
X, y = make_blobs(n_samples = 100, centers = centers,
cluster_std = 2)

# Perform clustering using MeanShift algorithm
ms = MeanShift()
ms.fit(X)

# "ms" holds the model; extract information about
# clusters as represented by their centroids, along
# with their labels
centroids = ms.cluster_centers_
labels = ms.labels_

print(centroids)
print(labels)

# Find out how many clusters we created
n_clusters_ = len(np.unique(labels))
print("Number of estimated clusters:", n_clusters_)

# Define a colors array
colors = ["r","g","b","c","k","y","m"]

# Let's do a 3D plot
fig = plt.figure()
ax = fig.add_subplot(111, projection = "3d")

# Loop to go through each data point, plotting it on
# the 3D space with a color picked from the above list-
# one color per cluster
```

```
for i in range(len(X)):
    print("Coordinate:",X[i], "Label:", labels[i])
    ax.scatter(X[i][0], X[i][1], X[i][2], c = colors[-
    labels[i]], marker = "o")

ax.scatter(centroids[:,0],centroids[:,1],cen-
troids[:,2], marker = "x", s = 150, linewidths = 5,
zorder = 10)
plt.show()
```

The plot in Figure 7.10 shows three clusters, but try running the program multiple times and you may find a different number of clusters. And, you guessed it, that is because the data points may be slightly different, and how and where we start applying the *MeanShift* algorithm may differ.

> **Try It Yourself 7.6: Density Estimation**
>
> Let's try to cluster and analyze the location of Starbucks in the state of Washington. The data we need are:
> Starbucks locations: www.kaggle.com/starbucks/store-locations
> With this data, create clustering (density estimation) of Starbucks in Washington. As a bonus challenge, you can visualize this using the map. For this, you would need the following US map data: https://github.com/kjhealy/us-county/raw/master/data/geojson/gz_2010_us_040_00_5m.json

7.6 Summary

Machine learning often is just as much about art as it is about science. That means, at times, we do not have a clear and systematic way to address a problem and we have to get creative. Several techniques we saw in unsupervised learning in this chapter fall under that category. Essentially, you are given some data or observations without clear labels or true values, and you are asked to understand, organize, or explain that data. Such scenarios leave you in a position where you have to make design choices.

For instance, when working with StoneFlakes data we had to make choices about where to draw different thresholds for clustering. And that is not all. Often, we do not even know that clustering is the right technique to use for a given problem. Using ML for solving data problems is much more than simply running a classifier or a clustering algorithm on a dataset; it requires first developing an understanding of the problem at hand and using our intuition and knowledge about various ML techniques to decide which of them to apply. This takes practice, but I hope the chapters in this part of the book, along with dozens of hands-on examples and practice problems, are a good head start.

Key Terms

- **Unsupervised learning**: A problem where the outcomes of test cases are based on the analysis of training samples for which explicit class labels are absent.
- **Clustering**: The assignment of a set of observations into subsets (called clusters) so that observations in the same cluster are similar in some sense.
- **Dendrogram**: A representation of a tree structure.
- **Maximum likelihood estimator (MLE)** is a way to assess the quality of a statistical model based on the probability that the model assigns to the observed data. The model that has the highest probability of generating the data is the best one.
- **Log likelihood** is a measure of estimating how likely (or with what probability) a given model generated the data we observed. In other words, it is a measure of the goodness of a model.
- **Akaike information criterion (AIC)** is similar to log likelihood, except it penalizes a model for having a higher number of parameters.
- **Bayesian information criterion (BIC)** is similar to AIC, except it also includes a penalty related to the sample size used for the model.

Conceptual Questions

1. What is unsupervised learning? Give two examples of data problems where you would use unsupervised learning.

2. How is divisive clustering different from agglomerative clustering?

3. Expectation maximization seems like a typical clustering approach, but it is not. What is so special about unsupervised learning with EM? (Hint: Think about the nature of the data and the problem.)

Hands-on Problems

Problem 7.1 (Clustering)

Under the life cycle savings hypothesis as developed by Franco Modigliani, the savings ratio (aggregate personal savings divided by disposable income) is explained by per-capita disposable income, the percentage rate of change in per-capita disposable income, and two demographic variables: the percentage of population less than 15 years old and the percentage of the population over 75 years old. The data is averaged over the decade 1960–1970 to remove the business cycle or other short-term fluctuations.

The following data were obtained from Belsley, Kuh, and Welsch (1980).[3] They in turn obtained the data from Sterling (1977).[4] You can download it from OA 7.4.

The dataset contains 50 observations with five variables:

- *Sr*: numeric, aggregate personal savings
- *pop15*: numeric, percentage of population under 15
- *pop75*: numeric, percentage of population over 75
- *dpi*: numeric, real per-capita disposable income
- *ddpi*: numeric, percentage growth rate of dpi.

Use a clustering algorithm (agglomerative and/or divisive) to identify the similar countries.

Problem 7.2 (Clustering)

For this clustering exercise you are going to use the data on women professional golfers' performance on the LPGA 2008 tour. The dataset can be obtained from OA 7.5 and has the following attributes:

- golfer: name of the player
- average drive distance
- fairway percent
- greens in regulation: in percentage
- average putts per round
- sand attempts per round
- sand saves in percent
- total winnings per round
- log: calculated as (total win/round)
- total rounds
- Id: unique ID representing each player.

Use clustering (agglomerative and/or divisive) on this dataset to find out which players have similar performance on the same season.

Problem 7.3 (Clustering)

Let's try to apply *k*-means clustering on the Starbucks dataset we talked about during our discussion of density estimation. You can obtain the data from OA 7.6. Make sure you have installed Geopandas package if you want to visualize the clustering on a map.

Problem 7.4 (Clustering)

For this exercise you need to work with the breast cancer Coimbra dataset. The dataset has 10 features including the class label (1 or 2). First download the dataset from OA 7.7 and load the data. Next, you need to round off the Leptin feature values to two decimal places. Having done that, use the first nine attributes (the dataset minus the class label) to group the data points into two clusters. You can use any clustering algorithm of your choice, but the number of clusters should remain the same across them. Once the clustering is complete, use the class labels to evaluate the accuracy of the clustering algorithm that you chose.

Problem 7.5 (Clustering)

For this exercise you are going to use the travel reviews dataset (see OA 7.8) in UCI's repository, which was created by crawling travelers' reviews from TripAdvisor.com. Reviews on destinations across East Asia are considered in 10 categories. Each traveler's rating for each category is labeled as Terrible (0), Poor (1), Average (2), Very Good (3), or Excellent (4). Use the clustering method you just learned to group the destinations that have similar ratings.

Problem 7.6 (Clustering)

With the accidents involving Boeing's 737 Max there has been speculation and concern about airline safety. There was also the crash of a helicopter involving Kobe Bryant. Academic studies have found that high-profile crashes can shift passenger demand away from the airlines involved in disasters. Should travelers avoid flying with airlines that have had crashes in the past? That is the question we will try to address in this exercise. The dataset for this is sourced from the Aviation Safety Network and is available from OA 7.9.

The dataset has the following list of attributes:

- *airline*: airline (asterisk indicates that regional subsidiaries are included)
- *avail_seat_km_per_week*: available seat kilometers flown every week
- *incidents_85_99*: total number of incidents, 1985–1999
- *fatal_accidents_85_99*: total number of fatal accidents, 1985–1999
- *fatalities_85_99*: total number of fatalities, 1985–1999
- *incidents_00_14*: total number of incidents, 2000–2014
- *fatal_accidents_00_14*: total number of fatal accidents, 2000–2014
- *fatalities_00_14*: total number of fatalities, 2000–2014.

Use this dataset and two different clustering approaches (agglomerative and divisive) to group the airlines with similar safety records. Do these two approaches lead to the same/similar results? Provide appropriate visualizations, clustering summaries, and your interpretations.

Problem 7.7 (Density Estimation)

For this problem you are going to use the wine dataset in UCI's repository, available from OA 7.10. The dataset contains 178 records on wine; the attributes are the analysis results of different chemicals. Use the MeanShift algorithm to group the wines that have similar chemical components. Report the number of clusters and numbers of wine records in each type.

Problem 7.8 (Density Estimation)

For this task you are going to use the human development data collected by the UNDP. The Human Development Index (HDI) is computed using several components, described at http://hdr.undp.org/en/content/human-development-index-hdi. The UNDP divides the HDIs into four tiers. Use the MeanShift algorithm to group the countries that have similar human development levels. Do you find any difference between the groups you generated and the tiers UNDP proposes?

Problem 7.9 (EM)

Obtain the slump dataset available from OA 7.11. The original owner of the dataset is I-Cheng Yeh.[5] This dataset is about the concrete slump test. Concrete is a highly complex material. The slump flow of concrete is determined by numerous factors. There are seven such attributes in the dataset:

- cement (component kg in one cubic-meter [m^3] concrete)
- slag (component kg in one cubic-meter [m^3] concrete)
- fly ash (component kg in one cubic-meter [m^3] concrete)
- water (component kg in one cubic-meter [m^3] concrete)
- SP (component kg in one cubic-meter [m^3] concrete)
- coarse aggregate (component kg in one cubic-meter [m^3] concrete)
- fine aggregate (component kg in one cubic-meter [m^3] concrete)
- slump (cm)
- flow (cm)
- 28-day compressive strength (MPa).

The task is to predict maximum slump, flow, and compressive strength (each separately) from the amount of ingredients. Use the Mclust algorithm to run EM on this data and comment on how well you are able to explain those three outcome variables using the seven ingredients. Note that this is a typical clustering problem, and you are encouraged to use some other methods for clustering as well. We are using EM for practice as well as comparing it with other clustering methods.

Problem 7.10 (EM)

For this problem the dataset to be used is on SGEMM GPU kernel performance (download it from OA 7.12), which was measured in terms of the runtime required to compute a matrix–matrix product $A \times B = C$, where all matrices have dimension of 2048 × 2048. For each tested combination four runs were performed, and the results of each run were reported. All four runtimes were measured in milliseconds. Apart from these four output performance measurements, the dataset also contains the following features that describe the parameter combination:

- input features 1 and 2. MWG, NWG: per-matrix 2D tiling at workgroup level
- input feature 3, KWG: inner dimension of 2D tiling at workgroup level
- input features 4 and 5, MDIMC, NDIMC: local workgroup size
- input features 6 and 7, MDIMA, NDIMB: local memory shape
- input feature 8, KWI: kernel loop unrolling factor
- input features 9 and 10, VWM, VWN: per-matrix vector widths for loading and storing
- input features 11 and 12, STRM, STRN: enable stride for accessing off-chip memory within a single thread: {0, 1} (categorical)
- input features 13 and 14, SA, SB: per-matrix manual caching of the 2D workgroup tile: {0, 1} (categorical).

From the four runtimes, how would you determine which ones seem more accurate than others at measuring the GPU kernel performance in this experiment? Simply eyeballing the data? Building a classifier or a regression model? Report your process for deciding this. Next, use EM on this dataset to predict the runtimes from the input parameter combinations.

Problem 7.11 (EM)

Under the life cycle savings hypothesis as developed by Franco Modigliani, the savings ratio (aggregate personal savings divided by disposable income) is explained by per-capita disposable income, the percentage rate of change in per-capita disposable income, and two demographic variables: the percentage of population less than 15 years old and the percentage of the population over 75 years old. The data are averaged over the decade 1960–1970 to remove the business cycle or other short-term fluctuations.

The following data were obtained from Belsley, Kuh, and Welsch (1980). They in turn obtained the data from Sterling (1977). You can download it from OA 7.13.

The dataset contains 50 observations with five variables:

- *Sr*: numeric, aggregate personal savings
- *pop15*: numeric, percentage of population under 15
- *pop75*: numeric, percentage of population over 75
- *dpi*: numeric, real per-capita disposable income
- *ddpi*: numeric, percentage growth rate of dpi.

Use EM to cluster "similar" countries. Report how many groups you got and why you chose that number with the help of AIC and BIC.

Further Reading and Resources

If you are interested in learning more about unsupervised learning methods, the following are a few links that might be useful:

- Data mining cluster analysis – advanced concepts and algorithms: www-users.cs.umn.edu/~kumar001/dmbook/dmslides/chap9_advanced_cluster_analysis.pdf.

- Advanced clustering methods: www.cse.psu.edu/~rtc12/CSE586/lectures/meanshiftclustering.pdf.
- An advanced clustering algorithm for clustering large datasets to achieve high dimensionality: www.omicsonline.org/open-access/an-advanced-clustering-algorithm-aca-for-clustering-large-data-jcsb.1000115.pdf.
- Expectation maximization algorithm for clustering multidimensional numerical data: https://engineering.purdue.edu/kak/Tutorials/ExpectationMaximization.pdf.
- Spectral clustering: the intuition and math behind how it works: https://towardsdatascience.com/spectral-clustering-82d3cff3d3b7.

Notes

1. It is one thing to use such characteristics to group people and it is another to use that kind of grouping to make judgments or decisions. That issue is not relevant for the technical topic here, but we do need to discuss it somewhere. We will revisit it in Chapter 13 in the context of responsible AI.
2. https://commons.wikimedia.org/wiki/File:DataClustering_ElbowCriterion.JPG#filelinks.
3. Belsley, D. A., Kuh. E., & Welsch, R. E. (1980). *Regression diagnostics*. Wiley.
4. Sterling, A. (1977). Unpublished BS thesis, Massachusetts Institute of Technology.
5. Yeh, I-Cheng (2007). Modeling slump flow of concrete using second-order regressions and artificial neural networks. *Cement and Concrete Composites, 29*(6), 474–480.

8 Dimensionality Reduction

What do you need?
- A good understanding of statistical concepts (see Appendix A), probability theory (see Appendix C), and functions.
- The basics of differential calculus (see Appendix B for a few handy formulas).
- Introductory- to intermediate-level experience with Python, including installing packages (refer to Chapter 2).
- Understanding of the concept of unsupervised learning and practice of clustering from the previous chapter.

What will you learn?
- Problems associated with dimensionality.
- Selecting important features from a large set of available features.
- Doing component analysis to map higher dimensional data to lower dimensions.
- Linear discriminant analysis to reduce dimensionality of data.

8.1 Introduction

If we look at how we have applied machine learning (ML) to solving various problems in previous chapters, a pattern emerges. We have some data with features, and using those data points and features we build a model. The model could be regression, classification, or clustering, depending on the nature of the problem we are trying to solve. Most, if not all, of the practice problems had datasets with a manageable amount of data that could fit into any reasonable computer's memory. More importantly, the number of features we were dealing with was small. Why does this matter more than the size of the dataset itself? Because the complexity of our ML models largely depends on how many (and what kind of) features we use. Many problems get increasingly difficult to solve, at least using conventional computational methods, as the number of features increases. So, while having more features is often a desirable thing, it can also lead to the *curse of dimensionality*.

The curse of dimensionality refers to unexpected errors or difficulties that happen as the number of features increases. As the number of features grows, the dimension space grows exponentially. This exponential growth causes high data sparsity and increases the storage space and processing time required for ML tasks.

Think about a high-resolution image. A typical image with 1280×720 resolution will have 921,600 pixels. If we want to represent the color of each pixel in a black-and-white image, we need 921,600 cells, each storing 1 or 0 for white or black. Now imagine we want to store a grayscale color value between 0 and 255. For that, we are looking at 235,929,600 possibilities. If we want to check whether two images are the same, we need that many cells per image to store the information. That may not be too bad. After all, that is only about 225 MB. But now we need to compare one image with many other images. Doing a pairwise comparison means carrying out a matrix multiplication on these large matrices (or very large vectors). Suddenly, computational cost becomes an issue.

But let's say we do not care about the computational cost (even though we should). Even then, there are times when such operations are simply not feasible due to a large feature space. Consider web search. Assuming 100,000 words in English and one billion web pages in the world, we are looking at a giant matrix of one billion by 100,000. We get a query that is represented as a 100,000-element vector (or a 100,000 × 1 matrix). In theory, to rank the web pages in response to this query we need to do a matrix multiplication of these two matrices in real time. No matter how much memory or computational power we have, this is simply not going to happen. We need these matrices to be smaller.

Beyond the computational cost and the feasibility of carrying out computational operations in real time, there is also a concern about overfitting. If we have too many features, the chance of overfitting also increases, and this generally reduces the performance of ML models.

How do we combat the curse of dimensionality? Dimensionality reduction is a method of converting high-dimensional spaces into lower-dimensional spaces without losing the major information of the variables. In the following sections we will introduce three dimensionality-reduction approaches: feature selection, principal component analysis (PCA), and linear discriminant analysis (LDA). Each of these operates differently, but with the same broad goal of reducing the number of features.

8.2 Feature Selection

One way to address high-dimensionality problems is to reduce the number of features. But we cannot just throw away features at random, and it may not be feasible to manually pick a subset of the available features. We need a way to systematically select appropriate features.

Feature selection is one of the key techniques in ML that impacts your model's performance. Irrelevant features can decrease the accuracy of ML models because spurious features are not understood as such by most ML models, leading them to read into such features the same way they read into useful and relevant features. Therefore, selecting appropriate features is often considered the first and most crucial step of model design. Feature selection reduces training time, since it uses fewer features. It also improves your training model accuracy and reduces overfitting.

This section will introduce three widely used feature selection techniques: removing features with low variance, univariate feature selection, and feature importance. We will explore each of these using hands-on examples.

> **Hands-on Example 8.1: Removing Low Variance Features**
>
> Removing features with low variance is a baseline method of feature selection. It operates on the simple idea that features that do not have enough variance are not very important in model building. For instance, in your data about insurance, if all the entries (persons) are marked as having a high school diploma, then high school education is a useless feature for most model building and can be safely removed. Of course, this was a simple example with a categorical variable, but the same can be said about continuous variables as well, except that in the case of continuous variables we need to establish a threshold and remove features whose variance is below that threshold.
>
> This is a very simple technique, so we will practice it with simple, synthetic data. We will start by importing the package needed here – VarianceThreshold:
>
> ```
> # Import package VarianceThreshold
> from sklearn.feature_selection import VarianceThreshold
> ```
>
> Next, let's create a dataset with three features:
>
> ```
> # X is a Boolean dataset with three features
> X = [[0, 1, 0], [1, 0, 0], [0, 1, 1], [0, 1, 0], [0, 1, 1]]
> ```
>
> Finally, we will set our desired threshold for variance and remove the features that do not meet that:
>
> ```
> # Set variance threshold as 0.2
> sel = VarianceThreshold(threshold = 0.2)
> # Perform feature selection
> X_new = sel.fit_transform(X)
> print(X_new)
> ```
>
> This produces the following output:
>
> ```
> [[0]
>  [0]
>  [1]
>  [0]
>  [1]]
> ```
>
> This is a 4 × 1 matrix, indicating four data points with one feature or dimension. Compare this with the original data that contained three variables. With this technique, we were able to remove two of those three variables.

Now we will see a slightly more sophisticated method. Before, we removed features that lacked enough variance to be useful. In other words, we associated a feature's importance with having enough variability. Another way we can measure the importance of a variable is by how much it helps us in understanding, explaining, or predicting the outcome variable. That is how **univariate feature selection** works.

Univariate feature selection selects the features with the strongest relationship with the outcome variable based on univariate statistical tests. You can choose different scoring functions to estimate the statistical dependency between the features and the output variable. A popular choice for this function is Chi-square (χ^2). For each variable or feature we have, a Chi-square test is conducted to see how well it explains the outcome variable. If you remember your statistics, you know that Chi-square is used for hypothesis testing. We are doing the same here behind the scenes. For a given independent variable x_i and outcome variable y, we have a null hypothesis (H_0) and a test hypothesis (H_1):

- H_0: x_i has no impact on outcome y (the feature is not important).
- H_1: x_i has an impact on outcome y (the feature is important).

When we conduct a Chi-square test we can reject one of the above hypotheses. If we end up rejecting H_0, the feature is removed; otherwise, it stays. Alternatively, we can simply do Chi-square tests for all features and rank them based on their Chi-square scores. Then, we pick the top *n* features.

Hands-on Example 8.2: Univariate Feature Selection

Let's see how this works using an example. For this example, we will use the Breast Cancer dataset available from OA 8.1. This dataset contains data on 569 tumors, of which 357 are benign and 212 malignant. There are 30 real-valued input features. The main 10 features are:

1. radius (mean of distances from center to points on the perimeter)
2. texture (standard deviation of grayscale values)
3. perimeter
4. area
5. smoothness (local variation in radius lengths)
6. compactness (perimeter²/area – 1.0)
7. concavity (severity of concave portions of the contour)
8. concave points (number of concave portions of the contour)
9. symmetry
10. fractal dimension ("coastline approximation" – 1)

The mean, standard error, and "worst" or largest (mean of the three largest values) of these features are computed for 10 different characteristics of the digitized cell nuclei, resulting in 30 features. For instance, field 0 is Mean Radius, field 10 is Radius SE, field 20 is Worst Radius.

We begin by importing the necessary packages:

```
#import package feature_selection
from sklearn.feature_selection import SelectKBest
from sklearn.feature_selection import chi2
```

In addition to the coding packages we will also import the Breast Cancer dataset package:

```
# import breast cancer dataset
```

```
from sklearn.datasets import load_breast_cancer
```

Let's go ahead and load the dataset. We will also print out its dimensions:

```
# load breast cancer dataset
data = load_breast_cancer()
X, y = data.data, data.target
# The original X has 30 features.
print(X.shape)
```

This should print (569, 30), indicating 569 data points (rows) and 30 features (columns). Now we will use Chi-square scoring to find out the top 10 features and remove the rest:

```
# Here we adopt chi2 as a scoring function and set K to 10
# SelectKBest removes all but the highest-scoring features
X_new = SelectKBest(chi2, k = 10).fit_transform(X, y)
# Show the dimensions after selection
print(X_new.shape)
```

The output (569, 10) shows the new *X* has 10 features. You can examine this new dataframe to see which of the features (columns) made it.

What we saw in this example is a way to rank the importance of features in affecting the outcome variable. This importance was calculated per feature, independent of other features or the full model. One could argue that this approach ignores possible interactions among the features as they relate to the model. We can rectify this by building the model with all the features and then asking how important each feature is to the whole model. This is equivalent to building a house and then asking what will happen to its integrity if we remove one of the bricks, or a combination of bricks. Any change that does not cause any significant damage to the structure can then be carried out.

Feature importance gives a score for each feature. The higher the score, the more important the feature is. For example, tree-based classifiers have a built-in class that can compute impurity-based feature importance and can be used to discard irrelevant features with low feature importance. Let's see this with a hands-on example.

Hands-on Example 8.3: Feature Importance

We will once again work with the Breast Cancer dataset. Let's begin by importing the various packages we will need here, plus the dataset:

```
import matplotlib.pyplot as plt
```

```
import numpy as np
from sklearn.ensemble import ExtraTreesClassifier

# import breast cancer dataset
from sklearn.datasets import load_breast_cancer
data = load_breast_cancer()
X, y = data.data, data.target
print(X.shape)
```

This should print (569, 30) as before, once again confirming the size of our original dataset. Next, we will use these features to build a tree-based classifier. Once built, we can have it print importance scores for its features:

```
# Build a tree classifier
clf = ExtraTreesClassifier(n_estimators = 100, random_
state = 42)
clf = clf.fit(X, y)
print(clf.feature_importances_)
```

This should produce an outcome like the following.

```
[0.06332666 0.02127486 0.03460791 0.05209977 0.01049334
 0.02841893
 0.05655667 0.0721787  0.00765354 0.00717852 0.02817644
 0.00468379
 0.02100093 0.03687671 0.00559261 0.00754089 0.00655527
 0.0104857
 0.00553549 0.00674571 0.11382619 0.02251086 0.09066648
 0.07906783
 0.0211418  0.02709816 0.04675776 0.08921408 0.01285512
 0.00987928]
```

As you can see, this vector has 30 values, corresponding to the 30 features we have. We can sort these in descending order and choose a threshold for removing less important features.

We will first create a visualization of these importance scores:

```
# Visualize feature importances
tree_importance_sorted_idx = np.argsort(clf.feature_
importances_)
tree_indices = np.arange(0, len(clf.feature_impor-
tances_)) + 0.5
fig = plt.figure(figsize = (8,8))
ax1 = fig.add_subplot(1,1,1)
```

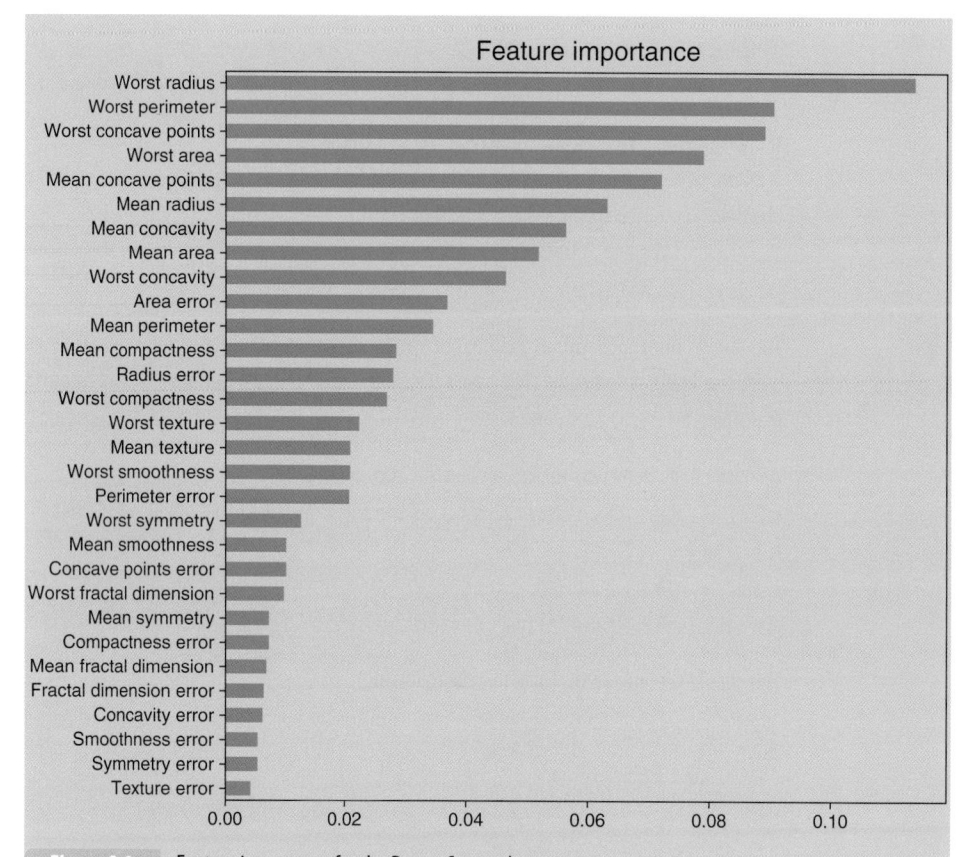

Figure 8.1 Feature importance for the Breast Cancer dataset.

```
ax1.barh(tree_indices,
         clf.feature_importances_[tree_importance_
         sorted_idx], height = 0.7)
ax1.set_yticks(tree_indices)
ax1.set_yticklabels(data.feature_names[tree_importance_
sorted_idx])
ax1.set_ylim((0, len(clf.feature_importances_)))
ax1.set_title("feature importance", fontsize = 20)
```

Figure 8.1 shows ranked feature importance of the tree classifier based on the impurity of each feature. Feature importance values are computed using the mean, and standard deviation of the accumulation of impurity decreases within each tree.

The function `SelectFromModel()` selects features that are considered unimportant and they are removed if the corresponding importance of the feature values is below the provided threshold parameter. Apart from specifying the threshold numerically, there are built-in heuristics for finding a threshold using a string argument. Available heuristics are "mean," "median," and float multiples of these, such as `0.1 * mean`. In combination with the threshold criteria, one can use the `max_features` parameter to set a limit on the number of features to select:

```
from sklearn.feature_selection import SelectFromModel
# Here we use the default feature selection criteria
model = SelectFromModel(clf, prefit = True)
X_new = model.transform(X)

# Show the dimensions after selection
print(X_new.shape)
```

The output (569, 11) shows that the new *X* has 10 features.

FYI: Maximum Likelihood Estimation

A lot of what we are trying to do with dimensionality reduction, or for that matter with clustering, is trying to approximate or guess a compact representation of the data. Think about it as a population distribution. You know there are dense clusters of populations in cities and suburbs, while many rural areas may have very thin distributions of people. Not only that, but you also have a sense of various demographics of these populations. For example, you may know that younger working-class people are more likely to be concentrated in the cities, whereas middle-income families are mostly in the suburbs. What you are doing here is applying a form of maximum likelihood estimation (MLE).

We have come across this notion before when we worked on the gradient ascent algorithm. There, we were looking for a model that would have generated the given data. Similarly, here we are asking about the population that would have generated the samples or observations we have. Maximum likelihood estimation is a method for estimating the parameters associated with a distribution, given some data or observations.

Imagine going through an *n*-dimensional parameter space looking for a point that provides just the right combination of those parameter values that maximizes the chances of explaining the underlying distribution. That point is our MLE. Think about this for a second and reflect on how this idea relates to three things we have done so far in this book: gradient ascent (for solving logistical regression), clustering, and dimensionality reduction. In each of the cases we are trying to estimate, guess, or approximate something – the population, the model, or both. We acknowledge that either we can't know the whole truth or study the whole population or have access to the true model, but we want to approximate and get as close to those things as possible.

Try It Yourself 8.1: Feature Selection

Obtain the Boston House Prices dataset from OA 8.2. There are more than a dozen features in it. Use one or several methods of feature selection on this dataset for predicting house prices. Report your findings (how many and which features you were able to remove).

8.3 Principal Component Analysis

Principal component analysis is probably the most popular dimensionality-reduction technique. It reduces features by projecting the data into a lower-dimensional subspace. For example, a 2D dataset could be reduced to one dimension and a 3D dataset could be reduced to two dimensions, as Figure 8.2 shows. To compress the data with minimal information loss, PCA transforms original covariate dataset variables into the independent factors with the most variability. These independent factors are called **principal components**, which provide the most discriminative features of the original data. As Figure 8.2 shows, if we want to reduce 3D data to two dimensions, what PCA does is find a projection direction (a vector u) to minimize the projection error. In general, when reducing n-dimensional data to k dimensions, PCA discovers k vectors ($w_1, w_2, \ldots w_k$) that minimize the projection error.

Let's learn a mathematical explanation for how PCA works. Knowledge of basic eigenvectors and eigenvalues is necessary for understanding PCA (there are some pointers at the end of the chapter). Data point x_i has a projection $W^T x_i$ in a new space. To keep data points in the projection space as far apart as possible, we need to maximize the variance of the data points in the projection space. Therefore, PCA is an optimization problem.

The optimization goal is to find $\max \operatorname{tr}(W^T X X W^T)$. Here, $W^T X$ is the data matrix after projection and $W^T X X W^T$ is the covariance matrix. We will now see the formal process for performing PCA.

PCA Algorithm
Input: dataset $X = \{x_1, x_2, \ldots, x_m\}$; number of principal components k.
Process:

1. Standardize or scale the data so that all entries of matrix X have similar magnitude, creating standardized matrix Z. Here, standardization makes sure that each column of Z has mean zero and standard deviation 1.
2. Calculate covariance matrix $A = ZZ^T$.
3. Perform singular value decomposition (SVD). Decompose ZZ^T into WDW^{-1}, where W is the matrix of eigenvectors and D is the diagonal matrix with eigenvalues. The eigenvalues on the diagonal of D will be associated with the corresponding column in W. The first element of D is λ_1 and the corresponding eigenvector is the first column of W.

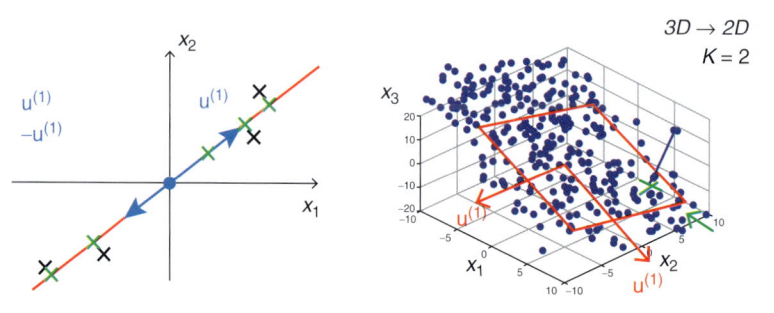

Figure 8.2 PCA at work: 2D and 3D visualization for data.

4. Choose the k eigenvectors $\{w_1, w_2, ..., w_k\}$ of A with the largest eigenvalues. Take the eigenvalues $\lambda_1, \lambda_2, ..., \lambda_p$ and sort them from largest to smallest. Sort the eigenvectors in W accordingly. Call this sorted matrix of eigenvectors W^*.
5. Calculate $Z^* = XW^*$. Z^* is the projection of X in the new space.

There are many applications of PCA. Data compression is a common scenario. We can apply PCA to reduce the memory needed to store data and speed up learning algorithms. It can also be used for data visualization. Real-world data may have hundreds of dimensions, making it difficult to understand. Observations can be visualized easily by reducing them to low dimensionalities such as two or three dimensions. Or we can use PCA to denoise the data. If our original data is noisy, the eigenvectors with the lowest eigenvalues are usually responsible for a lot of the noise. Removing these eigenvectors can reduce the noise. Although PCA is an unsupervised ML technique, because of these applications it is often utilized to analyze data before supervised learning.

FYI: Singular Value Decomposition

Singular value decomposition finds principal components by truncating the less important basis vectors in the original matrix A. Let's introduce some terms that are frequently used in SVD. The eigenvectors of AA^T are denoted u_i and the eigenvectors of A^TA are denoted v_i. These sets of eigenvectors u and v are the **singular vectors** of A. Both AA^T and A^TA have the same positive eigenvalues. The square-roots of these eigenvalues are called **singular values**.

Singular value decomposition diagonalizes a matrix into special matrices that are easy to manipulate and to analyze. It lays the foundation to untangle data into independent components. The SVD theorem states:

$$\mathbf{A}_{nxp} = \mathbf{U}_{nxn} \mathbf{S}_{nxp} \mathbf{V}^T_{pxp},$$

where $\mathbf{U}^T\mathbf{U} = \mathbf{I}_{nxn}, \mathbf{V}^T\mathbf{V} = \mathbf{I}_{pxp}$ (i.e., U and V are orthogonal).

Here, the columns of U are the left singular vectors; S (the same dimensions as A) has singular values and is diagonal; and $\mathbf{V}^T$ has rows that are the right singular vectors. The SVD represents an expansion of the original data in a coordinate system where the covariance matrix is diagonal. Calculating the SVD consists of finding the eigenvalues and eigenvectors of $\mathbf{AA}^T$ and $\mathbf{A}^T\mathbf{A}$. The eigenvectors of $\mathbf{A}^TA$ make up the columns of V, the eigenvectors of $\mathbf{AA}^T$ make up the columns of U. Also, the singular values in S are square-roots of eigenvalues from AA^T or $\mathbf{A}^TA$. The singular values are the diagonal entries of the S matrix and are arranged in descending order. The singular values are always real numbers. If the matrix A is a real matrix, then U and V are also real.

Hands-on Example 8.4: PCA

Let's try to perform PCA on the Wine Recognition dataset in Python. The data is the result of a chemical analysis of wines. There are 178 data points, which include 3 types of wine and 13 numeric features.

- alcohol

- malic acid
- ash
- alkalinity of ash
- magnesium
- total phenols
- flavonoids
- non-flavonoid phenols
- proanthocyanins
- color intensity
- hue
- OD280/OD315 of diluted wines
- proline

For this exercise we will be using the Sklearn PCA package. We start by importing various Python libraries which are useful for our data analysis, data visualization, calculation, and model building:

```
from sklearn.decomposition import PCA
import matplotlib.pyplot as plt
from sklearn.preprocessing import StandardScaler
```

You can get the dataset from OA 8.3. Alternatively, you can load it directly. Once loaded, go ahead and extract *X* and *y*.

```
# Load dataset
from sklearn.datasets import load_wine
data = load_wine()
X_, y = data.data, data.target
target_names = data.target_names
# Original X has 13 dimensions.
print(X_.shape)
```

The first step of preprocessing is to normalize the dataset. Standardization is a critical step toward PCA. Here we will use the `StandardScaler()` function to normalize the dataset.

```
# Standardize all features
X = StandardScaler().fit_transform(X_)
```

Now we are ready to apply PCA to our dataset. Before that, we need to choose the right number of dimensions (i.e., the right number of principal components, *k*). For this exercise we will perform PCA with two dimensions and see how well it captures the variance of the data:

```
# Set number of principal components as 2
pca = PCA(n_components = 2)
```

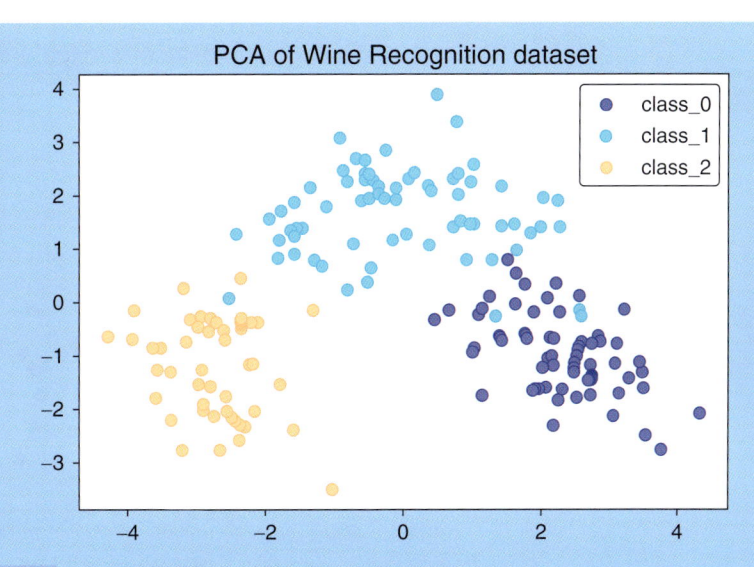

Figure 8.3 Result of the PCA on the Wine Recognition dataset.

```
# Projecting the original data into 2 dimensions
X_r = pca.fit(X).transform(X)
```

Now we will create a 2D scatter plot of the data using the values of the two principal components:

```
plt.figure()
colors = ["navy", "turquoise", "darkorange"]
lw = 2

# Visualize 2D projection
for color, i, target_name in zip(colors, [0, 1, 2],
target_names):
    plt.scatter(X_r[y == i, 0], X_r[y == i, 1], color =
    color, alpha = .8, lw = lw, label = target_name)
plt.legend(loc = "best", shadow = False, scatterpoints
= 1)
plt.title("PCA of Wine Recognition dataset")
print("explained variance ratio (first two components):
%s"
    % str(pca.explained_variance_ratio_))
```

Figure 8.3 shows the visualization of PCA 2D projection. The explained variance ratio (the percentage of the variance explained by the first two components) is [0.36198848 0.1920749].

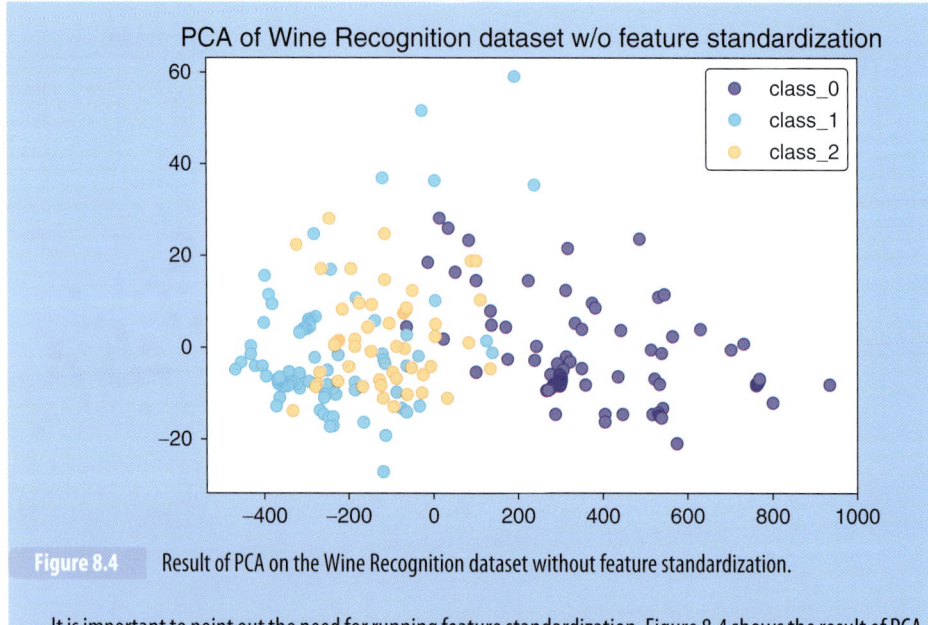

Figure 8.4 Result of PCA on the Wine Recognition dataset without feature standardization.

It is important to point out the need for running feature standardization. Figure 8.4 shows the result of PCA without standardizing. As you can see, the results are not as clear. Therefore, we should always remember to perform feature standardization before PCA.

Try It Yourself 8.2: PCA

Perform PCA on the MNIST dataset available from OA 8.4. Pick digit 7 and try different numbers of principal components (8, 16, 32, etc.). Output the visualization of digits after PCA and report how much information is retained.

8.4 Linear Discriminant Analysis

Linear discriminant analysis is another commonly used dimensionality-reduction technique. The goal of LDA is to project an n-dimensional dataset into a k-dimensional subspace where $k < n$, while maintaining maximum variance between classes. Traditionally, LDA has been used as a linear ML algorithm for multiclass classification. But the resulting linear combination can also be used for dimensionality reduction. Linear discriminant analysis seeks to find a linear projection of the input variables that achieves the maximum

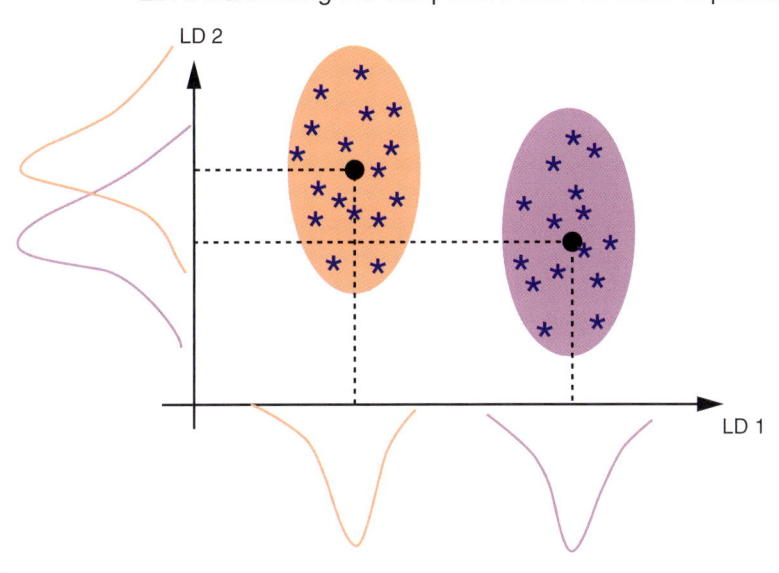

LDA: maximizing the component axes for class separation

Figure 8.5 Conceptualization of LDA.

separation between classes and minimum separation within data points of each class (Figure 8.5). Therefore, LDA is a supervised method.

LDA algorithm

Input: dataset $X^{n \times m}$, where n is the number of samples and m is the dimension of the features; the number of classes Z.

Process:

1. Compute the feature mean vectors $\text{mean}_i = [\mu_{w_{i1}}, \mu_{w_{i2}}, ..., \mu_{w_{im}}]$ for each class i, $i \in Z$.
2. Compute the scatter matrices (between-class and within-class scatter matrix).
3. Compute the eigenvectors $\{e_1, e_2, ..., e_m\}$ and corresponding eigenvalues $\{\lambda_1, \lambda_2, ..., \lambda_m\}$ for the scatter matrices.
4. Sort the eigenvectors by decreasing eigenvalues and choose the k eigenvectors with the largest eigenvalues to form an $m \times k$ dimensional matrix W (where every column represents an eigenvector).
5. Transform the samples onto the new subspace by performing the matrix multiplication $Y = X \times W$.

Output: Y is an $n \times k$ matrix in the new space, where n is the number of samples and k is the dimension of features in the new space.

Linear discriminant analysis projects a dataset onto a lower-dimensional space to avoid overfitting, and to reduce computational costs. It can also be used as a linear classifier or, more commonly, for dimensionality reduction before subsequent classification tasks.

Hands-on Example 8.5: LDA

Let's try LDA on the same Wine Recognition dataset. As before, we start by loading the required packages and the dataset.

```
from sklearn.discriminant_analysis import LinearDiscriminantAnalysis
from sklearn.datasets import load_wine
import matplotlib.pyplot as plt

# Load dataset
data = load_wine()
X, y = data.data, data.target
target_names = data.target_names
```

We are now ready to perform LDA. With the LDA package we have imported, this is quite easy:

```
# Perform LDA
lda = LinearDiscriminantAnalysis()
X_r2 = lda.fit(X, y).transform(X)

colors = ["navy", "turquoise", "darkorange"]
plt.figure()
```

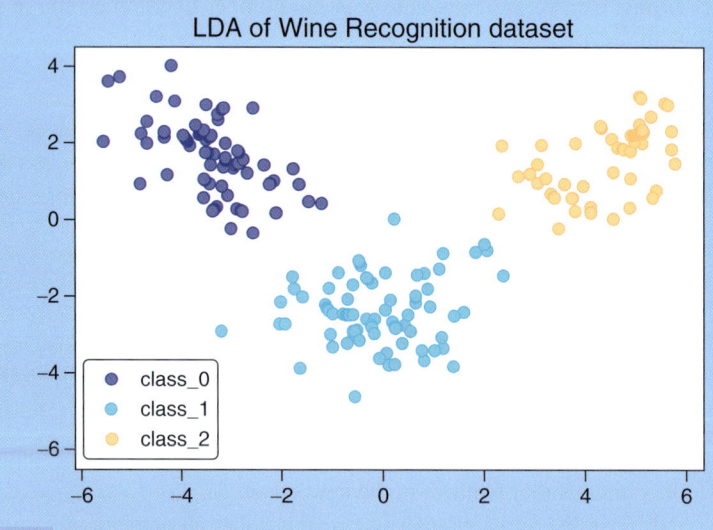

Figure 8.6 LDA result.

```
for color, i, target_name in zip(colors, [0, 1, 2],
target_names):
    plt.scatter(X_r2[y == i, 0], X_r2[y == i, 1], alpha
    = .8, color = color,
            label = target_name)
plt.legend(loc = "best", shadow = False, scatterpoints
= 1)
plt.title("LDA of Wine Recognition dataset")
plt.show()
```

This should produce the outcome shown in Figure 8.6.

Compared to the result generated by PCA (see Figure 8.3), we see that LDA identifies attributes that account for the most variance between classes. The three groups generated by LDA are much farther away from each other than the groups generated by PCA.

> **Try It Yourself 8.3: LDA**
>
> Perform LDA on the MNIST dataset. Pick digit 7 and try different numbers of k. Output the visualization of digits after LDA.

8.5 Summary

In the previous chapters we had small datasets with features that were relevant to building a model. In many practical scenarios we do not have that luxury. Even when we can fit the whole dataset into memory and process it without much delay, we should stop and think about the implications of using all the features. Being selective about the features we use can not only help speed up model building, but can also give us a simpler, more robust, and more transparent model. All of these benefits make reducing dimensionality worthwhile, even if it means sacrificing a little bit of accuracy or adding a bit more error.

In the next part of this book, as we start working with more complex models, specifically neural networks and deep networks, we will see how each additional feature matters. These models, which are already quite complex because they work with nonlinear boundaries, can take a long time to train or converge. Therefore, removing even a few of the features can help tremendously. Using feature selection as a part of your ML pipeline demonstrates that you are putting some care and thought into how you build models, and not simply rushing to get them done.

Key Terms

- **Feature:** A characteristic of a data point. This is typically represented as a column in a dataframe and is equivalent to a variable (more specifically, a predictor).
- **Dimensionality**: The number of dimensions or features of a given dataset. A higher number may indicate richness of the data but could also be problematic for processing and building models.
- **Feature selection**: A technique for removing unwanted or irrelevant features from a dataset, leaving only the most important features.

Conceptual Questions

1. What is the curse of dimensionality?

2. What are three advantages of feature reduction?

3. What are three techniques for selecting or removing features? List these along with their primary method for doing so.

4. Under what circumstances is LDA better than PCA?

Hands-on Problems

Problem 8.1 (Feature Selection)

Pick any dataset from the previous chapters – either a hands-on example or a practice problem – that contains at least 10 features. Run through a feature selection exploration using any of the methods that we have seen. Report your findings.

Now, run your original analysis (regression, classification, clustering) with the new dataset containing fewer features. Compare the original outcomes with the ones you get now. How close or different are they?

Problem 8.2 (Feature Selection)

Download the "Bias correction of numerical prediction model temperature forecast" dataset from OA 8.5. In this dataset the two outcomes are *Next_Tmax* and *Next_Tmin*. Use two methods you learned above to report the five most important features (other than date) for predicting if *Next_Tmax* is greater than 30 or not. (You need to drop all the NaN and negative rows in the dataframe.)

Problem 8.3 (PCA)

Obtain the data about temperature measurements from four corners of a room from OA 8.6. Before doing anything with this data, ask yourself: How much do you expect to see these four features differ? Could some of these be "collapsed" into one another? Go ahead and perform PCA on it. Do the findings make sense with what you expected?

Problem 8.4 (PCA)

Download the USDA nutritional data from OA 8.7. This data is a flattened version of the USDA National Nutrient Database. Each record contains nutrition information about 100 grams of a given product. There are dozens of columns (features) to explore. But perhaps they are not all useful, and we can reduce the dataset to something with fewer dimensions. Apply PCA to this dataset and report your findings.

Problem 8.5 (LDA)

The Bank Marketing dataset available from OA 8.8 is related to direct marketing campaigns (phone calls) of a Portuguese banking institution. The classification goal is to predict if the client will subscribe (yes/no) a term deposit (variable *y*). There are 17 features. Apply LDA to this dataset and visualize the first two major elements.

Problem 8.6 (LDA)

Apply LDA to the USDA dataset described in Problem 8.4. Compare the result with what you got from Problem 8.4 and report your results.

Further Reading and Resources

- A tutorial on PCA: www.cs.princeton.edu/picasso/mats/PCA-Tutorial-Intuition_jp.pdf.
- A tutorial on LDA: www.sci.utah.edu/~shireen/pdfs/tutorials/Elhabian_LDA09.pdf.
- Comparison of PCA and LDA for facial recognition: www.ijert.org/comparison-of-pca-and-lda-for-face-recognition.
- Eigenvalues and eigenvectors:
  - https://byjus.com/maths/eigen-values
  - https://en.wikipedia.org/wiki/Eigenvalues_and_eigenvectors
  - https://math.mit.edu/~gs/linearalgebra/ila0601.pdf.

PART IV

NEURAL NETWORKS

This part is about neural networks. I know students who often think this is something very new or advanced in ML/AI. And I often tell them that it was already pretty old and well established when I was a student. Of course, a lot of new advancements have happened in this field that warrant a fresh look at even the old concepts. Here, we assume no background and start from the beginning – all the way from the 1950s with basic neural architectures. We talk about learning laws and discuss how they are appropriate for different kinds of problems – supervised or unsupervised learning. Then we continue moving through the landscape of various models, all the way to the new ones in deep learning that keep making the headlines, including CNN, RNN, LSTM, and BERT. Once again, the idea here is not to worry about the theoretical depths of these models, but to focus on understanding the intuitions behind them and learn when and how to apply them with lots of hands-on exercises.

9 Neural Networks

What do you need?
- A good understanding of statistical concepts (see Appendix A), probability theory (see Appendix C), and functions.
- The basics of differential calculus (see Appendix B for a few handy formulas).
- Introductory- to intermediate-level experience with Python, including installing packages (refer to Chapter 2).
- Understanding of regression (Chapter 4), classification (Chapters 5 and 6), and clustering (Chapter 7) techniques.

What will you learn?
- How an interconnected network can mimic the human brain.
- Different architectures of neural networks.
- Applying neural networks to problems of regression, classification, and pattern recognition.

9.1 Mimicking the Human Brain

Humankind has always been fascinated by how our brains work. Why do we feel certain ways? What are thoughts? And, above all, what is the purpose of it all? As science fiction writers have been asking for centuries, what is it that makes humans so special? While we still do not have good answers for how our life began on planet Earth, bright minds have been looking at ways to map our consciousness onto an artificial entity. Why? Well, in addition to simply satisfying our curiosity and ego, this may also be a way for us to better understand how our own minds work. Until the middle of the twentieth century this was primarily the domain of biologists and psychologists. But with the advent of computational devices, the age-old question of what makes us so special has resurfaced. Can we understand and map human cognition in a computational way?

In the 1940s, scientists like Warren McCulloh, Walter Pitts, and D.O. Hebb started creating computational structures that mimicked the neural networks that drive the human brain. Over the decades, our fascination with neural networks has grown significantly. Many are attracted to them because such structures, often called artificial neural networks (ANNs), seem to be an obvious way to copy how humans possess and use intelligence. This, however, has not been as straightforward as many believed. Nevertheless, the parallel processing structure that many of these ANNs provide has proven to be very effective in solving complex nonlinear problems. In fact, in the 1980s, a scholarly group emerged, called parallel distributed processing (PDP).[1] This group's distinguished scholars proposed and demonstrated several PDP models that can easily be characterized as ANNs, but they were not interested in mimicking the human brain; instead, they recognized a class of complex problems that could be solved with such structures. Many of these models were capable of memory as well as learning. What is important to note is that PDPs and many subsequent developments in the field of ANN were not directly connected to mimicking or mapping the human brain; instead, they were driven by addressing computational problems of a complex nature. This is how we will discuss ANNs in this chapter – not as a method of creating artificial brains or intelligence, but as a way of solving complex problems. But we will start with the basics, including that of the neural network in the human brain.

9.1.1 Basics of a Neural Network

Artificial neural networks are an information-processing paradigm inspired by the way biological nervous systems (e.g., brains) process information. They are essentially a crude software equivalent of the neuronal structure of our brains. The key element of this paradigm is the novel structure of the information-processing system. It is composed of many highly interconnected processing elements (neurons) working in unison to solve specific problems. We will explore the structures of these neurons in the next subsection. Then we will see how we can connect these neurons to create networks capable of learning, storing, and solving complex problems.

Artificial neural networks, like the human brain, learn by example. They can be trained in a *supervised* or *unsupervised* manner. In a *supervised* ANN, the network is trained by providing matched input and output data samples, with the intention of getting the ANN to provide a desired output for a given input. An example is an email spam filter – the input training data could be the count of various words in the body of the email, and the output training data would be a classification of whether the email was spam or not. If many examples of emails are passed through the neural network this allows the network to *learn* what input data makes it likely that an email is spam or not. This learning takes place by adjusting the *weights* of the ANN connections. We will discuss this process in detail in the next section.

9.1.2 Human vs. Artificial Neuron

Much is still unknown about how the brain trains itself to process information. There are many theories, and some have been more successful than others in explaining brain functions. We're going to assume a few things in this chapter, just to further our exploration of ANNs. In the human brain, a typical neuron collects signals from others through a host of fine structures called *dendrites*. The neuron sends out spikes of electrical activity through a long, thin strand known as an *axon*, which splits into thousands of branches. At the end of each branch, a structure called a *synapse* converts the activity from the axon into electrical effects that inhibit or excite activity in the connected neurons. When a neuron receives excitatory input that is sufficiently large compared with its inhibitory input, it sends a spike of electrical activity down its axon. Learning occurs by changing the effectiveness of the synapses so that the influence of one neuron on another changes. Figure 9.1 shows the structure of a human neuron.

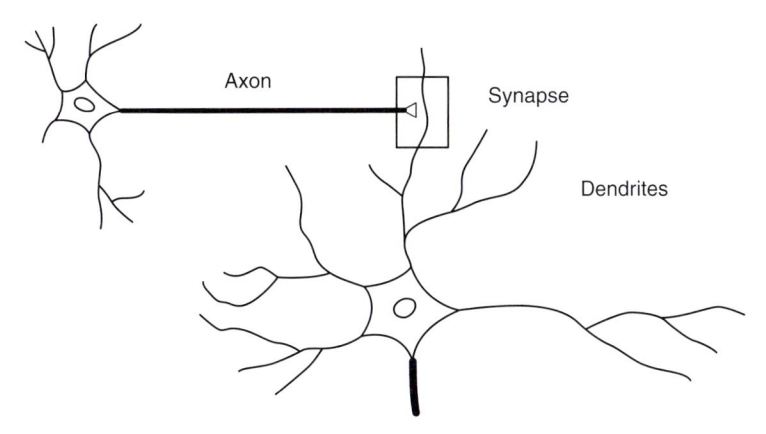

Figure 9.1 Human neuron.

When constructing an ANN, we first deduce the essential features of neurons and their interconnections. We then typically program a computer to simulate these features. However, because our knowledge of neurons is incomplete and our computing power is limited, our models are necessarily gross idealizations of real networks of neurons.

9.2 Architectures of Basic Neural Networks

Consider a supervised learning problem where we have access to labeled training examples (x^i, y^i). Neural networks give us a way of defining a complex, nonlinear hypotheses, $h_{w,b}(x)$, with parameters w,b that we can fit to our data. Here, w is for weights and b is for the bias (think of it like the intercept in linear regression).

To describe neural networks we will begin by describing the simplest possible neural network, one which comprises a single neuron. We will use Figure 9.2 to denote a single neuron. You can view this as a mapping of the biological neuron from Figure 9.1 to an artificial one.

A more sophisticated neuron is the McCulloch–Pitts (MP) model. Here, the inputs are *weighted*; the effect that each input has on decision-making is dependent on the weight of the particular input. The weight of an input is a number which, when multiplied with the input, gives the weighted input. These weighted inputs are then added together; if they exceed a preset threshold value, the neuron fires. In any other case the neuron does not fire. See Figure 9.3 for a schema of the MP neuron model.

In mathematical terms, the neuron fires if and only if

$$x_1 w_1 + \ldots + x_n w_n \ldots > T.$$

A neural network is put together by connecting many of our simple neurons, so that the output of a neuron can be the input of another. For example, Figure 9.4 shows a small neural network. As you can see, there are three layers, each with a different number of neurons, connected through edges from left to right, finally leading to an output.

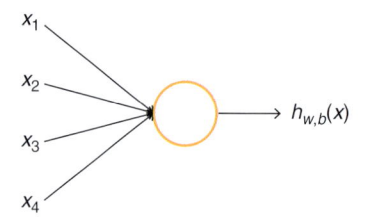

Figure 9.2 Artificial neuron.

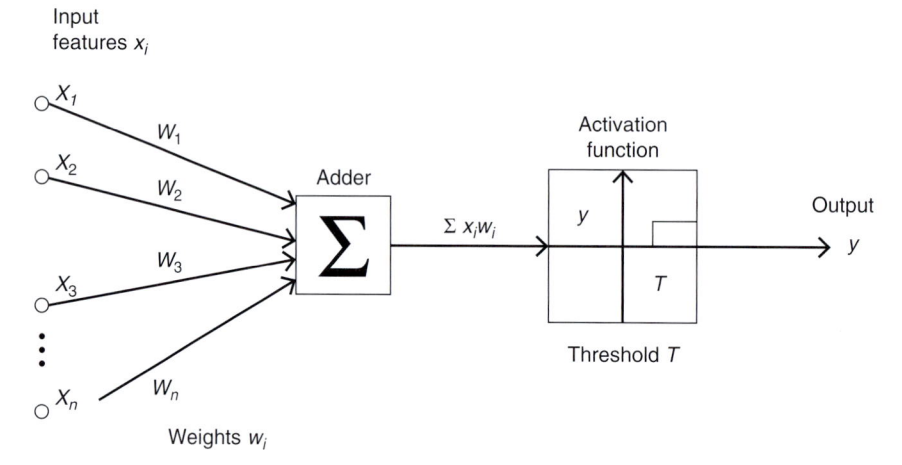

Figure 9.3 McCulloch–Pitts (MP) model of a neuron.

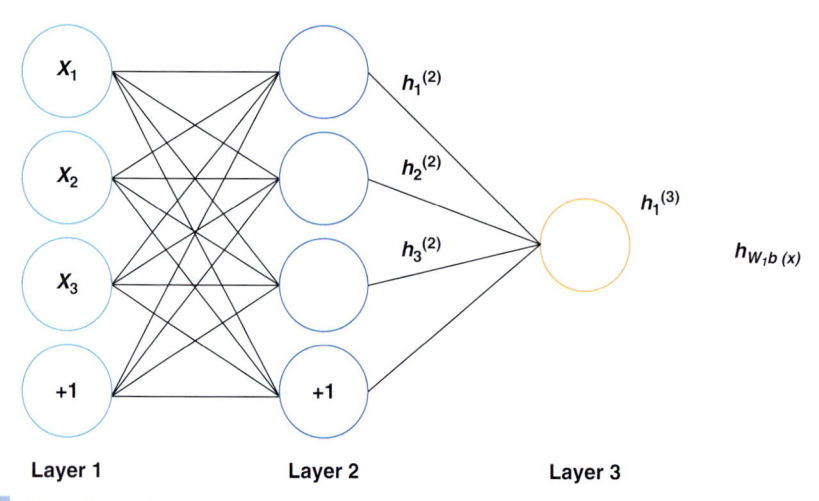

Figure 9.4 A neural network.

Presumably, a human brain consists of similar structures. It is estimated that our brains contain around 100 billion neurons each, which is close to the number of galaxies in the observable universe. Just as a reference, a mouse has 75 million neurons, a cat has 250 million neurons, and a chimpanzee has 7 billion neurons. Clearly, humans have the most processing power. But that is not all. Think about the ways in which these neurons can be connected. It is estimated that there are 100 trillion synapses in a human brain. Our brain is indeed a very complex and a very capable computational structure.

This is the end of our discussion of the human brain and its mapping to ANNs. Moving forward, we will discuss ANNs exclusively, regardless of how accurately they relate to a human brain. We will also drop the "artificial" from the name and simply refer to these structures as "neural networks" (or even just "networks") as the distinction between biological and artificial structures will no longer be needed.

9.2.1 Feed-Forward Network

Let's start with a simple, straightforward neural network structure: *feed-forward networks*. In a feed-forward network, the information flow is unidirectional. A unit sends information to other units from which it does not receive any information. There are no feedback loops.

Feed-forward networks are used in pattern generation, pattern recognition, and pattern classification. These networks have fixed inputs and outputs. Figure 9.5 shows a representation of a feed-forward network.

9.2.2 Perceptrons

The most influential development in neural networks in the 1960s was *perceptrons* – a term coined by Frank Rosenblatt. A perceptron is an MP model (a neuron with weighted inputs) with some additional, fixed, preprocessing (see Figure 9.6 for a representation). Units labeled $A_1, A_2, \ldots, Aj, \ldots, Ap$ are called association units, and their task is to extract specific, localized features from the input images. This is the unique feature of perceptrons in comparison to previous models of neurons. It seems such a simple addition, but it turns out to be a very important way to characterize and provide input information to a network.

Why is the perceptron model of neurons so important? If we think about how humans perceive information, it becomes clear. When we see a hand-drawn digit "1," we recognize

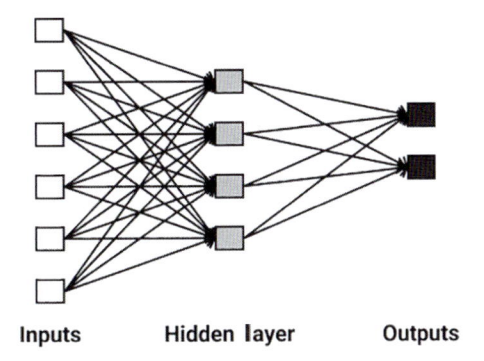

Figure 9.5 Feed-forward neural network.

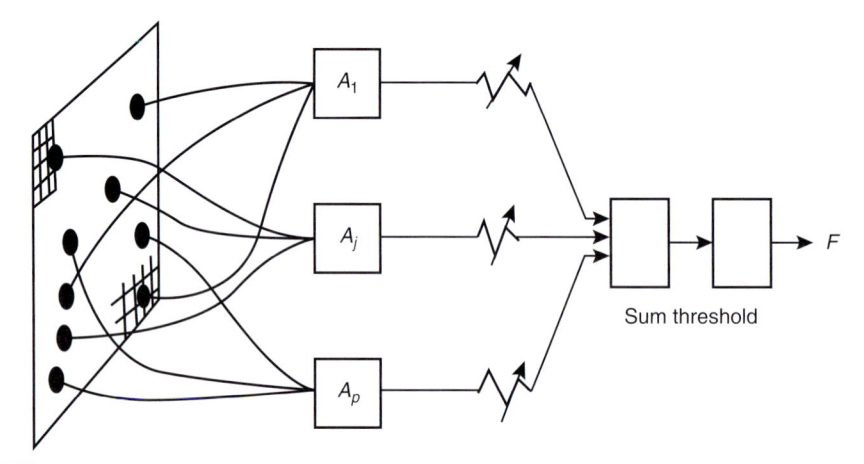

Figure 9.6 Perceptron model of the neuron.

that pattern first. Then, we translate it to data, which is the number 1. Most computational systems will do the opposite. We chop down the rectangle in which that digit is drawn into tiny pixels, feed the information about those pixels to a system as data, and then the system learns to identify that as a pattern depicting the number 1. Pattern recognition is a great ability of human beings (and other animals too), something that often the most sophisticated computational systems struggle with. But perceptrons take us one step closer to doing what humans and other animals do in terms of seeing the inputs as patterns or accepting data points as a part of an underlying pattern.

9.2.3 Single-Layer Perceptron

We will now see perceptrons in action. For that, we will create a simple neural network using perceptrons. A **single-layer perceptron** (SLP) is a feed-forward network based on a threshold transfer function. The SLP is the simplest type of neural network and can only classify linearly separable cases with a binary target (1, 0). You can see an SLP network in Figure 9.7.

Here, we have three neurons at the input layer. Each of these gets their values multiplied by the corresponding weight and summed for the one output neuron. If this sum is greater than some threshold (θ), then the output of the network will be 1. Otherwise, the output will be 0. This output is our prediction. In a supervised learning problem, if the predicted output is the same as the desired output, then the performance is considered satisfactory and no changes to the weights are made. However, if the output does not match the desired output, then the weights need to be changed to reduce the error. This weight change Δw can be calculated as:

$$\Delta w = \alpha \left(y - \hat{y} \right) x$$

where α is the learning rate, which is set between 0 and 1, y is the desired outcome or ground truth, $\hat{y}$ is the predicted value, and x is the input (typically a vector).

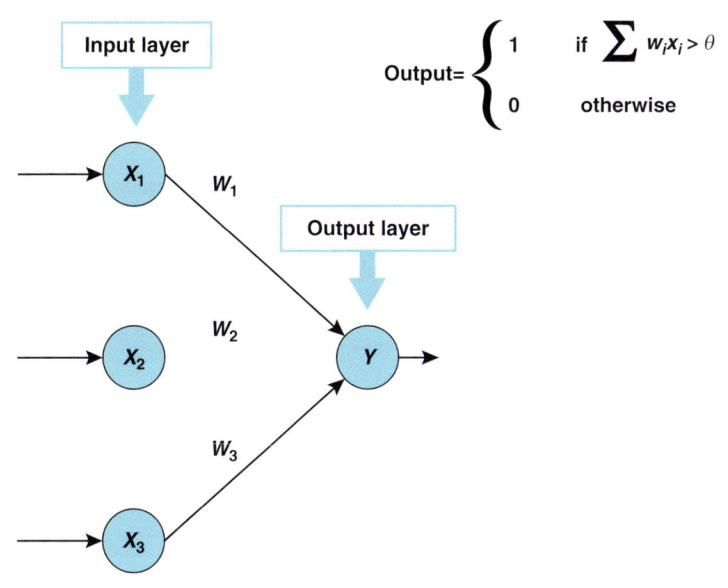

Figure 9.7 Single-layer perceptron network.

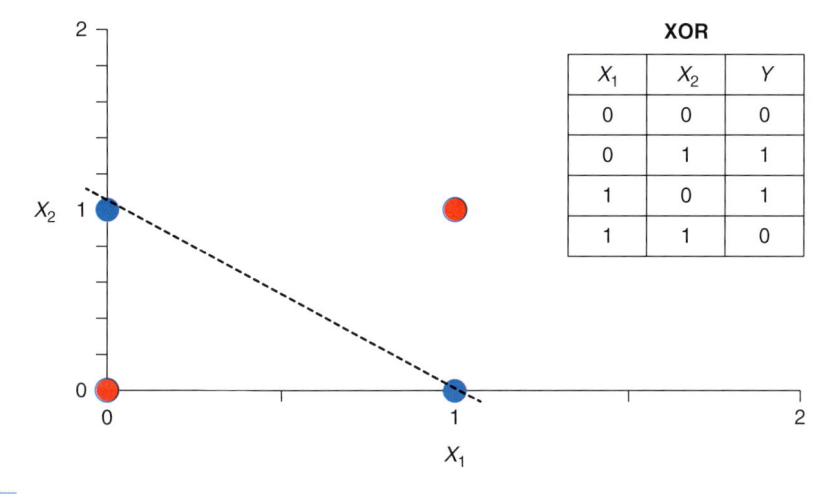

Figure 9.8 Solving an XOR problem using a perceptron neuron.

Since the SLP is a linear classifier, if the cases are not linearly separable the learning process will never reach a point where all the cases are classified properly. In 1969 Minsky and Papert wrote a book[2] in which they described the limitations of SLPs. The most famous example of the inability of perceptrons to solve problems with linearly non-separable cases is the XOR problem. A truth table for XOR is shown in Figure 9.8. Depending on the different binary values of X_1 and X_2, the outcome variable Y will be either 0 or 1. If we want to train a model with this knowledge, we are essentially looking for a classifier that can separate the combinations of (X_1, X_2) with respect to Y (0 and 1). Think of X_1 and X_2 as two neurons that have taken in binary inputs and through their additive unit have output Y. But as we can see from the graph in the figure, no combination of weights for X_1 and X_2 can create a separating line. We will return to this problem of nonlinear separation later. For now, let's practice SLP to see how it can be used for classification.

> ### Hands-on Example 9.1: Single-Layer Perceptron
>
> Let's create a simple SLP network for classification. We will use the famous MNIST dataset available from OA 9.1. This dataset contains a large number of handwritten digits that are often used in testing neural network and deep network models. The dataset contains 60,000 training images and 10,000 testing images. We will use this dataset several times in this and the next chapter.
>
> As always, we start by importing the necessary packages:
>
> ```
> from sklearn.datasets import fetch_openml
> from sklearn.linear_model import Perceptron
> from sklearn.model_selection import train_test_split
> from sklearn.metrics import accuracy_score
> ```
>
> Now, we will load the MNIST dataset and split it into training and testing sets:
>
> ```
> # Load and partition MNIST dataset
> X, y = fetch_openml("mnist_784", version = 1,
> return_X_y = True)
>
> # Create partitions of training and testing data
> X_train, X_test, y_train, y_test = train_test_
> split(X/255., y, test_size = 0.20, random_state = 1)
> ```
>
> In the line above, `random_state` gives a seed for randomizing. Why is this important? Having the same random seed while doing randomized operations allows for better reproducibility of the results. Let's go ahead and create a perceptron. Remember, an SLP is nothing but a weighted linear sum of input signals.
>
> ```
> # Create a perceptron and assign values to various
> # hyperparameters
> perceptron = Perceptron(random_state = 1, max_iter =
> 50, tol = 0.005)
> perceptron.fit(X_train, y_train)
> ```
>
> Here, we went with a maximum iteration of 50 and an error tolerance of 0.005. You can change these and see the effect on runtime and accuracy. Now that we have built the SLP network, we are ready to make predictions on the training and testing sets.
>
> ```
> # We predict with our built perceptron
> yhat_train_perceptron = perceptron.predict(X_train)
> yhat_test_perceptron = perceptron.predict(X_test)
> ```

```
print("Perceptron: Accuracy for training is %.2f" %
(accuracy_score(y_train, yhat_train_perceptron)))
print("Perceptron: Accuracy for testing is %.2f" %
(accuracy_score(y_test, yhat_test_perceptron)))
```

This will print accuracy values for the training set and testing set. You can expect to have very good numbers here. Training accuracy is usually higher than testing accuracy.

> **Try It Yourself 9.1: Single-Layer Perceptron**
>
> Download the Sonar, Mines vs. Rocks dataset from OA 9.2. This dataset contains 111 patterns obtained by bouncing sonar signals off a metal cylinder at various angles and under various conditions. The file "sonar.rocks" contains 97 patterns obtained from rocks under similar conditions. The transmitted sonar signal is a frequency-modulated chirp, rising in frequency. The dataset contains signals obtained from a variety of different aspect angles, spanning 90 degrees for the cylinder and 180 degrees for the rock.
>
> Each pattern is a set of 60 numbers in the range 0.0–1.0. Each number represents the energy within a particular frequency band, integrated over a certain period of time. The integration aperture for higher frequencies occurs later in time, since these frequencies are transmitted later during the chirp.
>
> The label associated with each record contains the letter "R" if the object is a rock and "M" if it is a mine (a metal cylinder). The numbers in the labels are in increasing order of aspect angle, but they do not encode the angle directly.
>
> Using the available features, build a classifier with an SLP model that classifies "R" or "M." Make sure to do a reasonable split of the data for training and testing and then choose appropriate numbers of neurons for your input and output layers.

9.2.4 Multilayer Perceptron

As we noted before, SLPs suffer from the inability to work with nonlinear boundaries. But if we add another layer between the input and output layers, we can deal with more complex learning problems. This additional layer is called a **hidden layer**. A **multilayer perceptron** (MLP) has the same structure as an SLP, with the addition of one or more hidden layers. So how does having these hidden layers help? It turns out that by introducing these additional layers, we can decompose a complex problem into multiple sub-problems, each solved by one of the layers. For example, in a problem of object detection in a picture, perhaps one of the layers learns to detect straight lines and another learns to capture curves. Together, they help to detect a wider variety of objects than either of them could individually. Of course, in reality, things are not that simple. But we will disregard that problem for now and focus on understanding how to build and train an MLP.

An MLP has at least three layers: an input layer, a hidden layer, and an output layer. Should we have more than one hidden layer? Well, it depends on the kind of problem we are trying to solve. We will revisit this in the next chapter when we look at deep networks. For now, let's stick to one hidden layer and see how we could train this network.

If you recall, training or learning in an SLP meant changing weights on the edges leading from input layer neurons to output layer neurons. Here, we have edges (and weights) going from input neurons to hidden neurons and from those neurons to the output neuron (assuming for now only one neuron in the output layer). How do we change all of those weights? For that, we will use weight propagation in two phases: the forward phase, where the activations are propagated from the input to the output layer, and the backward phase, where the error between the observed actual and the requested nominal value in the output layer is propagated backward to modify the weights and bias values.

Forward Propagation

As the name suggests, forward propagation methods propagate inputs by adding all the weighted inputs and then computing outputs using a sigmoid threshold. This is shown in Figure 9.9. This is what we are already familiar with and have used while training SLP models. Forward propagation allows us to use inputs to come up with a prediction. At the output layer we can compute errors if we know what the true output value for those inputs should be. These errors can then be used to change the weights from input layer to output layer, or in other words, to propagate the effects of the errors backward (from output layer to input layer). We did this before with SLP. But now we have at least one hidden layer as well. For that, we need a different process for changing the weights.

Backward Propagation

Backward propagation, often referred to as backpropagation, is trickier than forward propagation, but it is very helpful in many current neural network models, including deep

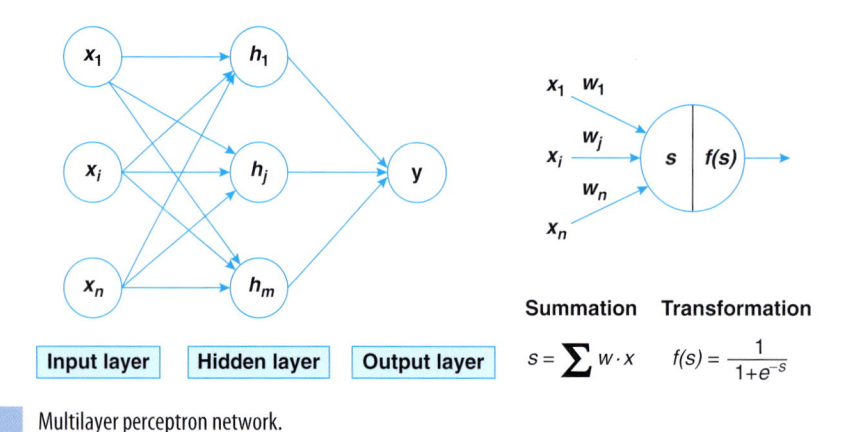

Figure 9.9 Multilayer perceptron network.

learning, as we will see in the next chapter. Backward propagation methods propagate the errors backward by apportioning them to each unit according to the amount of this error the unit is responsible for. The following three steps outline the process:

1. Find out the error in the output neuron. This is where we take the difference between what we see and what we expect to see. Typically, this difference is squared to create the mean squared error, or MSE (see Chapter 4 for more details on this).
2. This difference is then used to find the error for each neuron in the hidden layer.
3. Finally, these errors are used to update the weight matrix.

In other words, the outcome of one run of a backpropagation is a changed weight matrix. This is then repeated until we notice no more or very minimal change in the weight matrix, or we have iterated a certain number of times.

Hands-on Example 9.2: Multilayer Perceptron

Let's go ahead and practice MLP. We will use the same MNIST dataset we used for the previous exercise. As before, we start by importing appropriate packages:

```
from sklearn.datasets import fetch_openml
from sklearn.neural_network import MLPClassifier
from sklearn.model_selection import train_test_split
from sklearn.metrics import accuracy_score
```

And as before, we load the dataset and create training and testing sets.

```
# Load and partition MNIST dataset
X, y = fetch_openml("mnist_784", version = 1,
return_X_y = True)
# Create partitions of training and testing
X_train, X_test, y_train, y_test = train_test_
split(X/255., y, test_size = 0.20, random_state = 1)
```

To build an MLP model we need more configuration parameters than we did for SLP. The activation function is ReLU (rectified linear unit). We will keep the maximum iterations as 50 and `random_state` as 1. Given that there are multiple layers, we also need to define how many units will be in each. As there are 784 features, we will set the input layer size to 784. There are 10 digits or classes for the output, and we can represent them using two units. As far as the middle layer goes, it should be something in between the sizes of the input and the output layers. Let's set it to 100. If you like, you can experiment with different sizes of that layer. But be careful. Having more units creates significantly more connections and it will take a lot longer for the network to converge.

```
# Build an MLP network
```

```
mlp = MLPClassifier(solver = "sgd", max_iter = 50,
                    verbose = True, random_state = 1,
                    learning_rate_init = .1, hidden_
                    layer_sizes = (784, 100, 2))
mlp.fit(X_train, y_train)
```

Keep in mind that this will take several minutes on a typical modern computer. Once the network is trained, go ahead and see how well it does on the training and testing sets:

```
# Make predictions with our new classifier
yhat_train_mlp = mlp.predict(X_train)
yhat_test_mlp = mlp.predict(X_test)

print("Multilayer Perceptron: Accuracy for training is
  %.2f" % (accuracy_score(y_train, yhat_train_mlp)))
print("Multilayer Perceptron: Accuracy for testing is
  %.2f" % (accuracy_score(y_test, yhat_test_mlp)))
```

Once again, we get accuracy scores for training and testing sets. Both should be high, perhaps higher than what we got before with SLP. In other words, while there was a much higher computational cost for building an MLP model compared to the SLP model, it seems to have paid off with higher accuracy values.

One thing to note from the above examples is that there are several ways to construct a neural network in Python. We can build it from scratch, writing long functions for building layers and training the network – something that we accomplished with just a couple of lines above! Or we could use one of the existing packages or frameworks. In the examples above, we used our familiar Sklearn package. Another popular package is PyTorch. As you build networks with many layers (such as deep networks, which we will see in the next chapter), you may find Keras or TensorFlow more useful. Finally, all the cloud service platforms we saw in Chapter 2 not only support these libraries, but often have their own version or implementation of these packages. You can also find more native versions of their support functions, but be careful using them in your applications; if you ever move them to a different platform, those functions may not work.

> **Try It Yourself 9.2: Multilayer Perceptron**
>
> Use the Sonar, Mines vs. Rocks dataset from Try It Yourself 9.1. This time, build an MLP model. I suggest going with one input layer, one hidden layer, and one output layer. You will need to make decisions, such as about how many neurons to have in each layer and how long to train the network. Keep in mind that unlike an SLP, an MLP network can take up significant amounts of time and resources.

We will now work with more neural network examples, solving different kinds of machine learning (ML) problems: regression, classification, and clustering.

9.2 Architectures of Basic Neural Networks

> **Hands-on Example 9.3: Neural Networks for Regression**
>
> Let's take an example of a regression problem and see it works with a neural network. For this example, we are going to use the Yacht Hydrodynamics dataset available from OA 9.3. This is the list of attributes:
>
> - longitudinal position of the center of buoyancy, adimensional
> - prismatic coefficient, adimensional
> - length–displacement ratio, adimensional
> - beam–draught ratio, adimensional
> - length–beam ratio, adimensional
> - Froude number, adimensional.
>
> The output variable is the residuary resistance per unit weight of displacement, which is adimensional.
>
> For this exercise on neural networks we will be using the MLPRegressor package available in Sklearn. Let's import all the packages we need:
>
> ```
> import urllib.request
> import numpy as np
> from sklearn.preprocessing import StandardScaler
> from sklearn.model_selection import train_test_split
> from sklearn.neural_network import MLPRegressor
> ```
>
> You can load the data from a local copy if you have downloaded it, or even directly get it from the original URL (often these URLs change so you may want to keep a local copy):
>
> ```
> # We can use the url to load our dataset
> url = "https://archive.ics.uci.edu/ml/machine-learn-
> ing-databases/00243/yacht_hydrodynamics.data"
> raw_data = urllib.request.urlopen(url)
> dataset = np.loadtxt(raw_data)
> print(dataset.shape)
> ```
>
> This will print out (308, 7), indicating that we have 308 data points with the 7 features listed above.
>
> After the data is loaded, the first step of preprocessing is to normalize the dataset. There are multiple ways to do that. Here we will use the StandardScaler() function to normalize the hydrodynamics dataset:
>
> ```
> data_scaled = StandardScaler().fit_transform(dataset)
> ```
>
> Once you are done with normalization, let's separate the data into training and testing sets before training the network. The first six columns are features and the seventh column is the target. Here is how to do it:
>
> ```
> data_scaled = StandardScaler().fit_transform(dataset)
> X_train, X_test, y_train, y_test =
>     train_test_split(data_scaled[:,0:6], data_
>     scaled[:,6], test_size = 0.25, random_state = 1)
> ```

We are going to use two hidden layers with this configuration: 3:5 (three units in the first hidden layer and five in the second one). The input layer has six inputs by default, corresponding to six independent variables. The output layer has, of course, a single output since we are doing regression. We use the `fit()` function to train the neural network:

```
regr = MLPRegressor(hidden_layer_sizes = (3,5), random_
state = 1).fit(X_train, y_train)
```

We can use the `predict()` function with the test data (just the features) to predict the values of the target variable:

```
prediction_result = regr.predict(X_test[2:3,:])
print(prediction_result)
```

This will generate the output [0.26115805].

Now we can use the `score()` function to compute the squared error of our model, which should give us a rough estimate of the goodness of the network:

```
error = regr.score(X_test, y_test)/len(y_test)
print(error)
```

This will print 0.005538275266150961.

We see that the squared error is very low, which shows our model fits the test data quite well. If you are curious (and adventurous), go ahead and use some other regression method that you know and measure its error to compare with this.

Try It Yourself 9.3: Neural Networks for Regression

For this exercise we will build a neural network for doing regression on the Diabetes dataset. Sklearn provides direct access to the Diabetes dataset (`from sklearn.datasets import load_diabetes`). Go ahead and load it. You will find that it has 442 instances and 10 adimensional features. Build a neural network with an appropriate number of layers and neurons in those layers, as we did above. Report your square error.

As a bonus challenge, use the same dataset for regression using some other method you know. Compare its result (square error) with the one obtained through a neural network model.

Hands-on Example 9.4: Neural Networks for Classification

Now we will turn our attention to applying neural networks to a classification problem. For this, we will use the Seed dataset. This dataset contains predictions for three different varieties of wheat using measurements of geometrical properties of kernels. It has 210 instances and 7 real-valued attributes. The attributes are:

- area, A
- perimeter, P
- compactness, $C = 4 \times \pi \times A/P^2$
- length of kernel
- width of kernel
- asymmetry coefficient
- length of kernel groove.

For this exercise we will be using the MLPClassifier package. Let's start with importing the necessary packages:

```
import sklearn
import urllib.request
import numpy as np
from sklearn.preprocessing import StandardScaler
from sklearn.model_selection import train_test_split
from sklearn.neural_network import MLPClassifier
import matplotlib.pyplot as plt
```

You can get the dataset from OA 9.4 or use a direct URL as shown below to download the dataset and import it to Python:

```
url = "https://archive.ics.uci.edu/ml/machine-learning-databases/00236/seeds_dataset.txt"
raw_data = urllib.request.urlopen(url)
dataset = np.loadtxt(raw_data)

# Check the shape of the dataset if you need
print(dataset.shape)
```

Output: (210, 8)

Let's separate the data into training and testing instances before training the network:

```
X_train, X_test, y_train, y_test =
        train_test_split (dataset[:,0:7],dataset[:,7],
        test_size = 0.25, random_state = 42)
```

We are going to use two hidden layers with this configuration: 5:3. The parameter solver has three options: "lbfgs," "sgd," and "adam." Here we choose "sgd" and set the L2 penalty (regularization term) parameter to 1e-5:

```
clf = MLPClassifier(solver = "sgd", alpha = 1e-5,
hidden_layer_sizes = (5,3), random_state = 1)

# We use the fit() function to train the neural network
clf.fit(X_train, y_train)
```

The `predict_proba()` function returns the estimated probability of three classes. We usually choose the class with the highest probability as our prediction:

```
print(clf.predict_proba(X_test[2:3,:]))
```

Output: [[0.28711844 0.42051915 0.29236241]]

The `predict()` function with the test data (just the features) is adopted to predict which class the data points belong to:

```
print(clf.predict(X_test[2:3,:]))
```

output: [2.]

The prediction result is class 2, which is obvious based on the estimated probability of the three classes. If we want to check the performance of our neural network, we can adopt a `score()` function to see the mean accuracy of the given test data and labels:

```
print(clf.score(X_test, y_test))
```

Output: 0.33962264150943394

Try It Yourself 9.4: Neural Networks for Classification

Let's use a neural network for classification on the Wine Recognition dataset. The data is the result of a chemical analysis of wines. There are 178 instances, with 13 numeric features and 1 target variable (type of wine, which has 3 possible values). Sklearn provides direct access to the wine dataset (`from sklearn.datasets import load_wine`).

FYI: Designing Neural Networks

You can see in the hands-on examples in this chapter that I have provided a certain number of layers and certain number of neurons in each of them. How does one decide these numbers? There are some systematic ways, and some that are trial and error. For instance, typically the input layer will have as many neurons as there are features of the data. The output layer will have neurons that correspond to the nature of the problem – typically, one for regression. For classification, it can be one if it is a two-class problem, or k for k-class problems, including $k = 2$. The hidden layers usually have fewer neurons than the input layer. Since we often do not know enough about the latent variables or factors that represent important aspects of the problem, we need to guess how many hidden layers there are and how many neurons are in them. Many times, we can start our exploration by looking at what has worked for other similar problems or situations. Other times, we set these hidden layers and their sizes based on practical considerations such as computational costs and model training time.

> In short, start with your basic training that you get in this chapter and through the exercises. Then, do some trial-and-error experiments to see how varying the number of layers and the neurons in them affects computational cost and model accuracy. This is both science and art!

9.3 Autoencoders

Think about your typical grade-school exam. You are taught some lessons, you are given some material, and you learn or memorize it somehow. Then, in the exam, you are asked questions based on that material. If you were able to capture the original material accurately enough, you are able to answer those questions well. Otherwise, one could say that you were not able to either represent that information (during your exam preparation) or reconstruct that information (during the exam). Now imagine building a neural network to model this exam-taking process – taking in a lot of information, representing it somehow, and then reproducing it. This type of neural network is called an **autoencoder**.

Autoencoders are unsupervised neural networks for data compression. Autoencoders encode the data and learn to simplify the data representation, making reconstructed data as close as possible to the original input. Autoencoders are closely related to the principal component analysis (PCA) algorithm we introduced in Chapter 8. If an autoencoder uses linear activation functions in every layer, the data in the smallest layer in the network is equal to the principal components in the PCA. Generally, autoencoders use nonlinear activation functions such as ReLU and sigmoid.

We will come back to these details later when we look at a hands-on example. But for now, let's talk about the theory of autoencoders. Why would we want to create a structure that simply reconstructs the input? First off, note that an autoencoder is not meant to simply copy the input. It tries to learn the essence of the input and then reconstruct it. This is similar to your exam preparation and exam-taking. Perhaps you memorized the entire textbook, and during the exam you answered questions word-for-word as the answers appeared in the book. But more likely you rephrased the content to construct your answer. In other words, you didn't copy the answer – you reproduced it. The other reason for creating an autoencoder goes back to how we think about ML. An ML model is meant to learn something from the inputs rather than simply memorize them. Here, as an autoencoder captures the essence of the input, it does precisely that – learning rather than memorizing. While we can see how well the autoencoder has learned by asking it to reproduce that input (just like someone asks a question in your exam), the idea is to let it produce other types of patterns or answers from that learned representation. In other words, an autoencoder can be asked to synthesize new data instead of simply reproducing the data it learned from. Again, this is similar to why a student is expected to prepare for and take an exam; not just to do well in the exam, but to be prepared for what they might face outside the classroom.

Let's look at the autoencoder architecture. A simple structure for such a network is shown in Figure 9.10. There are three parts of this structure: the encoder, a bottleneck, and the decoder.

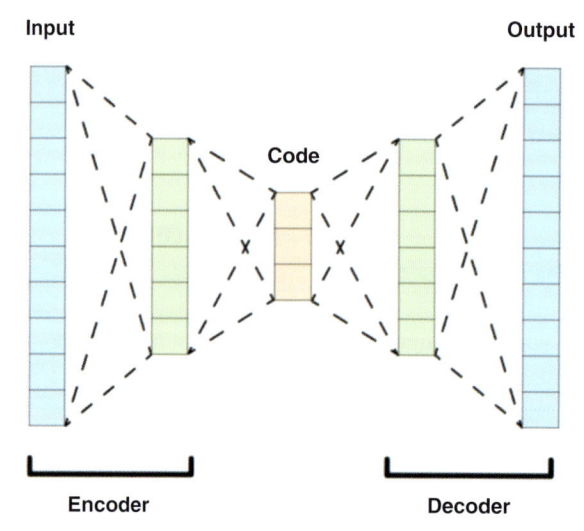

Figure 9.10 Autoencoder structure.

Hands-on Example 9.5: Autoencoders for Unsupervised Learning

We will now see how an autoencoder architecture of neural networks can be applied to an unsupervised learning case. Here, we will implement a simple autoencoder with Keras on the MNIST dataset. Keras is one of the most powerful and easy-to-use Python libraries. It is built on top of popular deep learning libraries like TensorFlow and Theano, which are used for creating deep learning models.[3]

```
import keras
from keras import layers

# This is our dataset
from keras.datasets import mnist
import numpy as np
import matplotlib.pyplot as plt
```

We will begin by defining the size of our encoding layer. Note that our input size is 784 and the encoding dimensions need to be a lot smaller than that. We will go with 32.

```
# This is the size of our encoded representations
encoding_dim = 32
# This is our input image
input_img = keras.Input(shape=(784,))

# "encoded" is the encoded representation of the input
encoded = layers.Dense(encoding_dim, activation =
"relu")(input_img)
```

```
# "decoded" is the lossy reconstruction of the input
decoded = layers.Dense(784, activation = "sigmoid")
(encoded)
```

Finally, we are ready to define the full autoencoder model. This will be done in pieces, one layer at a time:

```
# This model maps an input to its reconstruction
autoencoder = keras.Model(input_img, decoded)
```

```
# This model maps an input to its encoded representation
encoder = keras.Model(input_img, encoded)
```

```
# This is our encoded (32-dimensional) input
encoded_input = keras.Input(shape = (encoding_dim,))
```

```
# Retrieve the last layer of the autoencoder model
decoder_layer = autoencoder.layers[-1]
```

```
# Create the decoder model
decoder = keras.Model(encoded_input, decoder_layer(en-
coded_input))
```

Now that our network is ready, it is time to set up the other parameters, using "adam" (a stochastic optimization method) for optimization and "binary_crossentropy" as the loss function:

```
autoencoder.compile(optimizer = "adam", loss = "binary_
crossentropy")
```

We are now ready to train this network using the MNIST dataset:

```
# Load MNIST dataset and do preprocessing
(x_train, _), (x_test, _) = mnist.load_data()
x_train = x_train.astype("float32") / 255.
x_test = x_test.astype("float32") / 255.
x_train = x_train.reshape((len(x_train), np.prod(x_
train.shape[1:])))
x_test = x_test.reshape((len(x_test), np.prod(x_test.
shape[1:])))
print(x_train.shape)
print(x_test.shape)
```

This should print out the sizes of our training and testing sets. Next, we will train the model:

```
autoencoder.fit(x_train, x_train,
                epochs = 50,
                batch_size = 256,
```

```
                    shuffle = True,
                    validation_data = (x_test, x_test))
```
Let's load up our testing data:

```
# Encode and decode some digits
# Note that we take them from the *test* set
encoded_imgs = encoder.predict(x_test)
decoded_imgs = decoder.predict(encoded_imgs)
```

Finally, it is time to see the reconstruction of our digital images:

```
# Visualizing the digits
n = 10 # How many digits we will display
plt.figure(figsize = (20, 4))
for i in range(n):
   # Display original
   ax = plt.subplot(2, n, i + 1)
   plt.imshow(x_test[i].reshape(28, 28))
   plt.gray()
   ax.get_xaxis().set_visible(False)
   ax.get_yaxis().set_visible(False)

   # Display reconstruction
   ax = plt.subplot(2, n, i + 1 + n)
   plt.imshow(decoded_imgs[i].reshape(28, 28))
   plt.gray()
   ax.get_xaxis().set_visible(False)
   ax.get_yaxis().set_visible(False)
plt.show()
```

Figure 9.11 provides a visualization of the original images and reconstructed images. As you can see, the autoencoder shows a great ability to reconstruct.

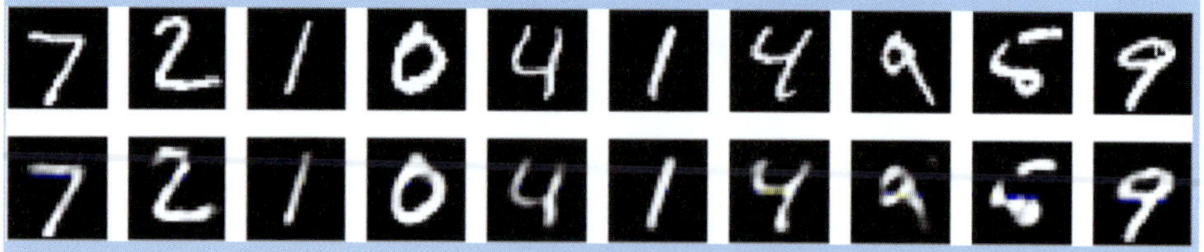

Figure 9.11   The top is the original image and bottom is the image reconstructed by an autoencoder.

> **Try It Yourself 9.5: Autoencoder for Unsupervised Learning**
>
> Let's try an autoencoder on the Fashion-MNIST dataset. Fashion-MNIST is a dataset consisting of 28 × 28 grayscale images of 70,000 fashion products from 10 categories, with 7000 images per category. You can obtain it from OA 9.1. To develop the autoencoder as we saw before, you will need to design a network with appropriately sized layers. Keras should help.

9.4 Convolution Neural Network

Multilayer perceptrons have several drawbacks, especially in image processing. They use one perceptron for every input, so weight numbers will be hard to manage for large images. For example, a black-and-white image with 224 × 224 pixels will have over 50,000 weight parameters. This is problematic when training and could easily lead to overfitting. Another common problem is that MLP regards input images as not transition-invariant. For example, if a cat appears in the top-left corner of image A and the bottom-right corner of image B, MLP will adjust its knowledge (weights) to that position rather than recognizing that a cat has no actual relationship to a given position in the picture. A good object detector should be able to recognize an object no matter where it appears in a given picture.

Now, let's discuss how **convolution neural networks** (CNNs) can solve these sorts of problems. The general idea of CNN is to adapt to attributes of images intelligently. As humans, we know that a typical object, even as small as a pixel, can have some relationship with its neighborhoods. We also know that objects of interest that we are trying to detect can appear anywhere in images. How do we incorporate such understanding into an artificial structure? Let's imagine breaking down the problem into several sub-problems. For example, one sub-problem could be identifying edges, and another sub-problem could be detecting sharp changes in connected parts. Here, each of such sub-problems can be solved using a filter.

If you have used picture editing software or any of the popular photo-sharing apps, you are probably aware of the concept of a filter. Think about applying a "lipstick filter." What does it do? It detects lips in a profile picture and applies a certain color or shade to them. Similarly, we could have different filters that, when combined, help us solve the given complex image problem. A big difference between those photo filters that you have used and the filters we are talking about here is that here we do not have a clear structure or functionality of a filter in mind. We just know we need multiple filters and, somehow, we need to combine these filters to solve the overall problem. This combination process is called **convolution**, which allows multiple filters to be combined to generate one output from

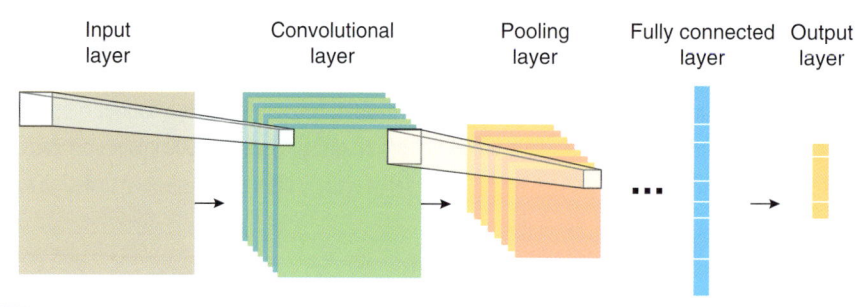

Figure 9.12 CNN structure.

several inputs. Convolution, in mathematics, is a process through which two functions are combined to produce a third function. In statistics, a related concept is cross-correlation. What matters to us here is that convolution allows us to combine multiple filters or layers to produce one output.

A CNN is composed of two basic blocks, as shown in Figure 9.12:

1. Convolution, which consists of a convolutional layer and a pooling layer. These layers are compositions of feature extraction.
2. The fully connected block, which consists of a fully connected simple neural network. This layer does classification tasks based on the input from the convolution block.

Hands-on Example 9.6: CNN

Going deeper into CNN is out of scope for us here, but let's go ahead and practice implementing CNN with Keras. First, let's make sure you have the necessary packages – specifically, TensorFlow. Go ahead and run the following command on your console or terminal if you lack that package:

```
!pip install tensorflow
```

Start by importing TensorFlow and other relevant packages in your Python program:.

```
import tensorflow as tf
from tensorflow.keras import datasets, layers, models
import matplotlib.pyplot as plt
```

We will load training and testing data from the built-in dataset CIFAR. This dataset was created by Alex Krizhevsky, Vinod Nair, and Geoffrey Hinton.[4] The CIFAR-10 dataset consists of 60,000 32 × 32 color images in 10 classes, with 6000 images per class. There are 50,000 training images and 10,000 test images.

```
(train_images, train_labels), (test_images, test_labels) = datasets.cifar10.load_data()
```

9.4 Convolution Neural Network

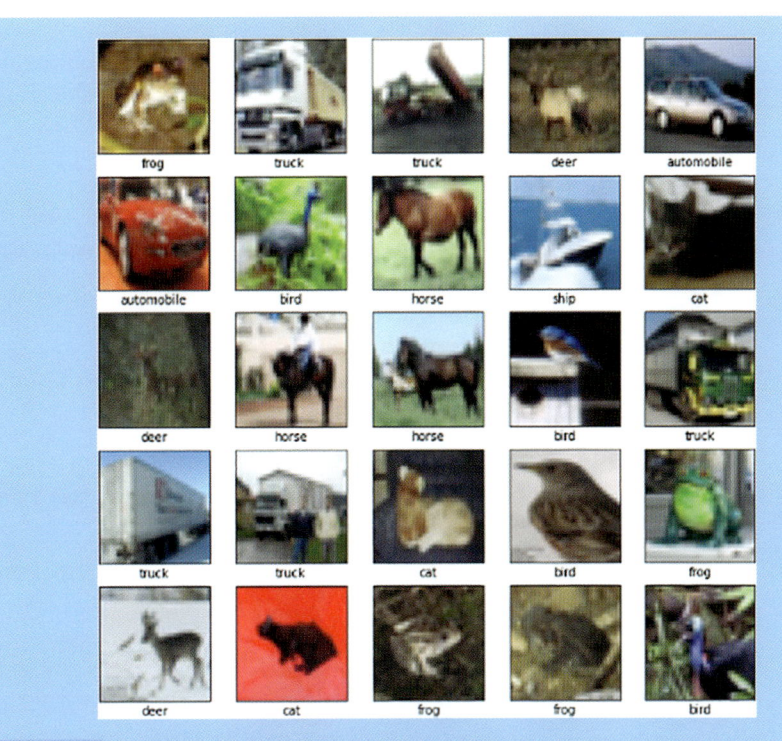

Figure 9.13 The first 25 images and their labels in the training set.

Each of the images contains pixels with 8-bit color information. Let's normalize that information to a value between 0 and 1 by dividing it by 255. Also, we'll initiate the class labels:

```
# Normalize pixel values to be between 0 and 1
train_images, test_images = train_images / 255.0, test_
images / 255.0

class_names = ["airplane", "automobile", "bird", "cat",
               "deer", "dog", "frog", "horse", "ship",
               "truck"]
```

Let's take a look at our training data. The following loop will display the first 25 images with their corresponding labels, as shown in Figure 9.13:

```
plt.figure(figsize = (10,10))
for i in range(25):
   plt.subplot(5,5,i+1)
   plt.xticks([])
   plt.yticks([])
   plt.grid(False)
```

```
    plt.imshow(train_images[i])
    # The CIFAR labels happen to be arrays,
    # which is why you need the extra index
    plt.xlabel(class_names[train_labels[i][0]])
plt.show()
```

Now we are ready to build the CNN-based model. This model will have several multidimensional convolution layers.

```
model = models.Sequential()
model.add(layers.Conv2D(32, (3, 3), activation =
"relu", input_shape = (32, 32, 3)))
model.add(layers.MaxPooling2D((2, 2)))
model.add(layers.Conv2D(64, (3, 3), activation = "relu"))
model.add(layers.MaxPooling2D((2, 2)))
model.add(layers.Conv2D(64, (3, 3), activation = "relu"))

model.add(layers.Flatten())
model.add(layers.Dense(64, activation = "relu"))
model.add(layers.Dense(10))

# Define how we are going to compile the model, how we
# will treat the error and how we will measure the success
model.compile(optimizer = "adam",
      loss = tf.keras.losses.SparseCategoricalCrossen-
      tropy(from_logits = True), metrics = ["accuracy"])

# Retain the history of training epochs
history = model.fit(train_images, train_labels, epochs
                 = 10, validation_data = (test_
                 images, test_labels))
```

At this point our training and testing are done, and we are ready to plot and report both of those phases:

```
plt.plot(history.history["accuracy"], label = "accuracy")
plt.plot(history.history["val_accuracy"], label = "val_
accuracy")
plt.xlabel("Epoch")
plt.ylabel("Accuracy")
plt.ylim([0.5, 1])
plt.legend(loc = "lower right")

test_loss, test_acc = model.evaluate(test_images, test_
labels, verbose = 2)
```

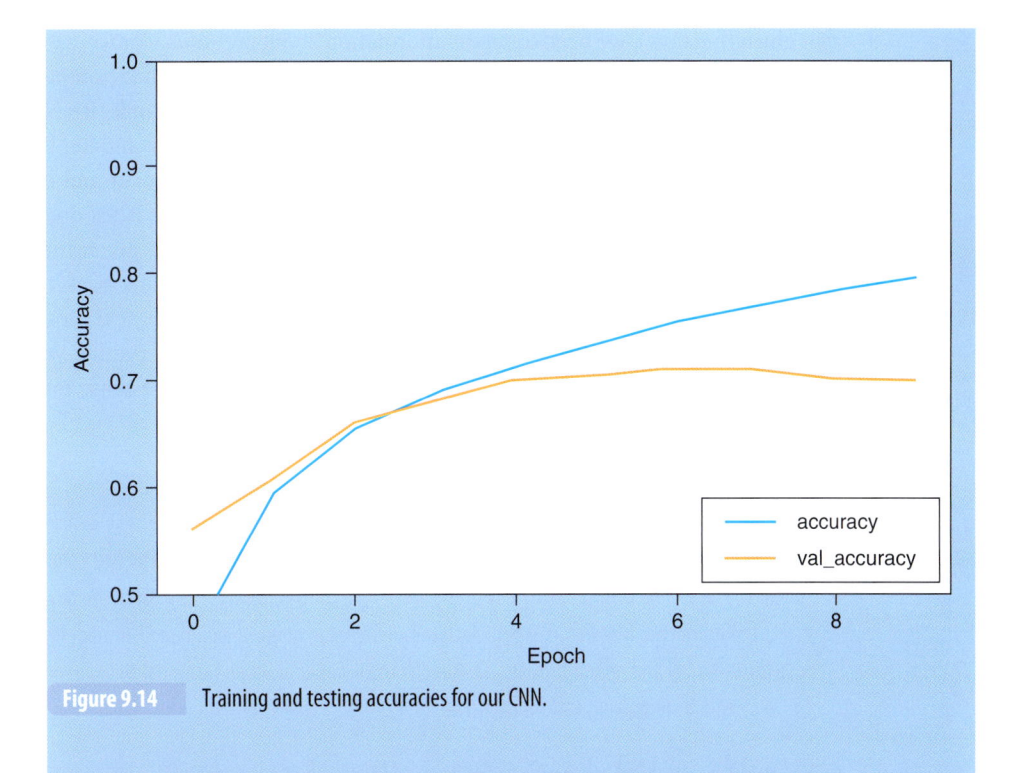

Figure 9.14 Training and testing accuracies for our CNN.

This should print out information for each of the 10 epochs, along with corresponding accuracy and loss values. We will also get a plot for training and testing accuracies, as shown in Figure 9.14.

> **Try It Yourself 9.6: CNN**
>
> In the example above we used the CIFAR dataset available through Keras. There is another popular dataset available – MNIST. Use `keras.datasets.mnist.load_data()` to load the MNIST dataset. This contains hand-drawn image data for 10 digits. Build a CNN to classify the images and report the performance of your model. Plot the accuracy in respect to the number of epochs you train.

9.5 Recurrent Neural Network

With CNN we addressed some of the limitations of an MLP. But one thing that we still assume with all these architectures is that all the inputs and the corresponding outputs are independent of each other. This may not always be the case. For example, think about this sentence – each subsequent word has some connection to what came before it. In other words, as we feed one word at a time as an input to a neural network (for some classification or clustering task), we need to retain information about previous word(s) as well. For this to happen, we need memory. A neural network architecture in which the output from one step is fed as input to the next step is called a **recurrent neural network** (RNN).

Essentially, an RNN is a neural network with a self-loop in its hidden layer. We could unfold the looped RNN with a series of networks that are run over and over again with timed inputs. This is where the "recurrent" name comes from; an RNN does the same task repeatedly, with the output dependent on the previous step in a given time. This allows for what we learn from one pass to influence the next pass. Think back to that sentence example. As you read a sentence, moving from one word to the next, you have to retain your understanding of the previous word (and, in fact, almost everything you have read up to that point). That previous understanding helps you make more sense out of the current word you are reading.

Hands-on Example 9.7: RNN

Download the Bikes dataset from OA 9.5. There are three columns in the data. The first column is the number of bikes. The second column is the day of the week. The third column is the hour of the day. Each row represents the number of bikes at a place in each minute. We are going to build an RNN model with this data and use the weekday and hour information to predict the number of bikes. Note that this is a regression problem.

We begin by importing various packages:

```python
import matplotlib.pyplot as plt
import numpy as np
import time
import csv
from keras.layers.core import Dense, Activation, Dropout
from tensorflow.keras.layers import SimpleRNN
from keras.models import Sequential, load_model
```

Next, we load and clean the data for further processing:

```python
bikes = []
def data_bike_num(path_to_dataset="bike_rnn.csv",
                              sequence_length = 20,
                              ratio=1.0):
    max_values = ratio * 45949
    with open(path_to_dataset) as f:
        data = csv.reader(f, delimiter=",")
        next(data, None)  # skip the headers
        nb_of_values = 0
        for line in data:
            try:
                bikes.append(float(line[0]))
```

```
                nb_of_values += 1
            except ValueError:
                pass
            if nb_of_values >= max_values:
                break
    print ("Data loaded from csv. Formatting...")
    print(len(bikes))
```

Make sure to examine the output from the code so far to ensure you have correctly formatted the data, as the rest of the code assumes that. We are now going to construct our training and testing sets from this data:

```
    result = []
    for index in range(len(bikes) - sequence_length):
        result.append(bikes[index: index + sequence_
        length])
    result = np.array(result)  # shape (2049230, 50)
    result_mean = result.mean()
    result -= result_mean
    print("Shift: ", result_mean)
    print ("Data: ", result.shape)
    row = int(round(0.95 * result.shape[0]))
    train = result[:row, :]
    np.random.shuffle(train)
    X_train = train[:, :-1]
    y_train = train[:, -1]
    X_test = result[row:, :-1] # 2297
    y_test = result[row:, -1]
    X_train = np.reshape(X_train, (X_train.shape[0], X_
    train.shape[1], 1))
    X_test = np.reshape(X_test, (X_test.shape[0], X_
    test.shape[1], 1))
    return [X_train, y_train, X_test, y_test, result_
    mean]
```

Let's define our RNN-based model:

```
# Function to build the RNN-based model
def build_model():
    model = Sequential()
    layers = [1, 50, 100, 1]
    model.add(SimpleRNN(
        layers[1],
```

```
            input_shape = (None, layers[0]),
            return_sequences = True))
    model.add(Dropout(0.2))
    model.add(SimpleRNN(
        layers[2],
        return_sequences = False))
    model.add(Dropout(0.2))
    model.add(Dense(layers[3]))
    model.add(Activation("linear"))
    start = time.time()
    model.compile(loss = "mse", optimizer =
    "rmsprop", metrics = ["mae", "mape"])
    print ("Compilation Time : ", time.time() - start)
    return model
```

We are now ready to train the model we defined on our data:

```
global_start_time = time.time()
epochs = 2
ratio = 1
sequence_length = 20
path_to_dataset = "bike_rnn.csv"
X_train, y_train, X_test, y_test, result_mean = data_
bike_num(
    path_to_dataset, sequence_length, ratio)
print ("\nData Loaded. Compiling...\n")
model = build_model()
model.fit(
    X_train, y_train,
    batch_size = 512, epochs = epochs, validation_split
    = 0.05)
predicted = model.predict(X_test)
predicted = np.reshape(predicted, (predicted.size,))
```

Let's go ahead and evaluate the model using our test data. We will print out evaluation results in terms of MSE, mean absolute error (MAE), and mean absolute percentage error (MAPE). These three quantities are defined as follows:

$$\text{MSE} = \frac{1}{n}\sum_{1}^{n}\left(y_i - \hat{y}_i\right)^2.$$

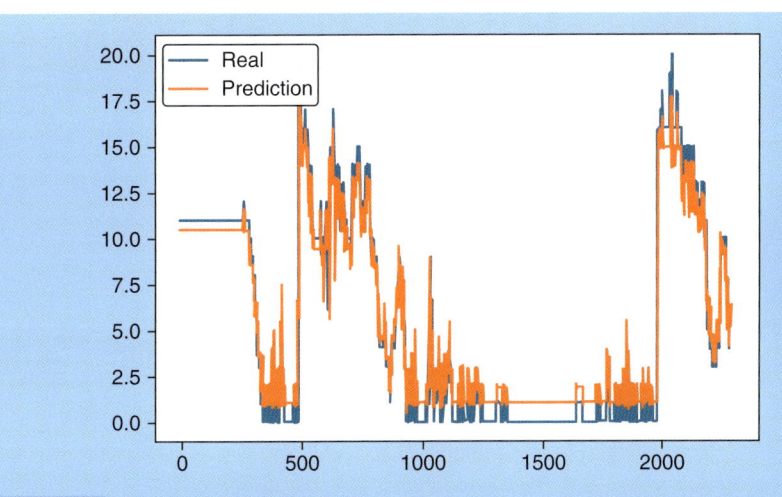

Figure 9.15 Predictions vs. real values of bike numbers.

$$\text{MAE} = \frac{1}{n}\sum_{1}^{n}\left|y_i - \hat{y}_i\right|.$$

$$\text{MAPE} = \frac{100}{n}\sum_{1}^{n}\frac{y_i - \hat{y}_i}{y_i}.$$

Here, y_i is the true value for data point i, and $\hat{y}_i$ is our prediction. In addition to printing these average values, we will also plot out our predictions against the real values of bike numbers (Figure 9.15).

```
# Evaluate
scores = model.evaluate(X_test, y_test, batch_size = 512)
print("\nEvaluation results: \nMSE={:.6f}\nmae={:.6f}\
nMAPE={:.6f}".format(scores[0], scores[1], scores[2]))

# Draw the figure
y_test += result_mean
predicted += result_mean
fig = plt.figure()
ax = fig.add_subplot(111)
ax.plot(y_test,label = "Real")
ax.legend(loc="upper left")
plt.plot(predicted,label = "Prediction")
plt.legend(loc = "upper left")
plt.show()
```

> **Try It Yourself 9.7: RNN**
>
> I hope you are not getting tired of using the MNIST dataset! It is such a useful and important dataset to practice our ML models. So, let's do it one more time. Load up the MNIST data using Keras and build an RNN-based training model. Use it to classify the test images. Since this is a classification problem, you should report the accuracy of your model with each of your epochs.

> **ML in Practice: When to Use a Neural Network?**
>
> These days, neural networks are often an absolutely necessary tool when working on ML problems. In fact, I have seen enough cases in practice where one doesn't even consider anything other than a neural or deep learning architecture. Sure, at times this is warranted because we know the nature of the problem and know that a specific type of neural architecture works best. But what if you are starting out and lack such prior knowledge? In other words, when should you use a neural network and when should you avoid it?
>
> To make such design decisions it is important that you understand some basic characteristics of neural networks. Many neural networks, as we see in this chapter, are great for solving nonlinear problems. Most neural network architectures are also designed to handle parallel processing with multiple units and even multiple layers working concurrently. Finally, most practical neural networks expect a reasonable amount of data and computing power for training. In short, neural networks are powerful and power (and data) hungry. Another cost or disadvantage that people often don't talk about enough is the fact that most neural networks are very opaque. As you add more layers to a neural network (as we will do in the next chapter), it gets even more opaque and complex, making it very difficult to debug and explain.
>
> As we often used to say at Amazon, it's okay to have a simple solution to a complex problem, but not okay to have a complex solution to a simple problem. Neural networks are complex. They are needed for many of today's complex problems, but there are still plenty of real-life problems – both simple and complex – that can be solved without a neural network. So, think before you commit to a complex and expensive solution.

9.6 Long Short-Term Memory

There are two big problems with RNNs: **vanishing gradient** and **exploding gradient**. Rather than going into mathematical details that are out of scope for us, let's explore these problems in simple terms. As an RNN moves forward with its passes, it computes gradients. Think of gradients as a way to figure out how much the error changes with each weight parameter change. Essentially, this is a way to represent our knowledge, which we are carrying from one pass of the RNN to the next. But, if we are not careful, we could end up losing the knowledge from before, or reading too much into it. The former problem is that of vanishing gradient, where the components of our gradient go to zero. The latter problem is that of exploding gradient, where these components increase exponentially. Both of these make it hard for us to learn or retain knowledge.

The exploding gradient issue can be addressed by clipping, which allows us to limit how far and how fast our gradients can grow. But vanishing gradient remains a problem. Enter **long short-term memory** (LSTM) neural networks. An LSTM contains feedback connections, allowing it to process an entire sequence of data, such as a time-series, rather than treating each of the data points in that sequence separately. This allows LSTM to consider the bigger context (long-term memory) while producing the output using the previous input (short-term memory).

In order to execute this process, LSTM uses a set of gates that control how input comes in, how it gets stored, and how it leaves the network. There are three types of such gates: input gates, output gates, and forget gates. The **input gate** allows us to determine what new information should be added to our existing knowledge structure. The **output gate** helps us decide the new hidden state, given the previous hidden state and the new input data. The **forget gate** allows us to control which pieces of the long-term memory should be forgotten (have reduced weights), given the previous hidden state and the new data input. Collectively, these three types of gates provide us with control knobs to guide how our network learns.

Let's consider an example. If you are trying to predict tomorrow's stock prices, you need to consider the levels at which the stock market closed today. But that is not enough. You should also consider weekly, monthly, and seasonal effects. An LSTM-based architecture for learning allows us to control how much we should retain and use in our long-term memory and how much weight we should give to our short-term memory.

Hands-on Example 9.8: LSTM

Let's practice LSTM with a hands-on example. For this, we will work with the IMDB dataset available from Keras.[5] This dataset contains 25,000 movies reviews from IMDB. Each review is labeled as "positive" or "negative." We are going to learn from this review text to classify a given review as positive or negative.

We will start by importing the various packages needed for this example:

```
import numpy
from keras.datasets import imdb
from keras.models import Sequential
from keras.layers import Dense
from keras.layers import LSTM
from keras.layers.embeddings import Embedding
from keras.preprocessing import sequence
```

Since the reviews could have lots of words that are perhaps not important to understand the text, we will use only the top 5000 words from these reviews. Of course, we are also doing this to reduce our processing and memory requirements. For each of these reviews we will consider up to 500 words. Then, we can go ahead and create our training and testing sets:

```
top_words = 5000
(X_train, y_train), (X_test, y_test) = imdb.load_
data(num_words = top_words)

max_review_length = 500
X_train = sequence.pad_sequences(X_train, maxlen = max_
review_length)
X_test = sequence.pad_sequences(X_test, maxlen = max_
review_length)
```

When we are considering textual data such as a movie review, the sequence of words may be important to preserve. We could use RNN for that, but as we saw before, RNN could have some problems with how the gradients are computed. Therefore, we will use LSTM, which will allow us to carry knowledge from the larger sequence while still preserving the local context. We will build an LSTM model here with an input layer of 5000 nodes, an embedding vector of size 32, an LSTM layer of 100 units, and an output layer of one node. As noted before, you can play around with different numbers here, but be careful – these networks can be very expensive to run.

```
embedding_vector_length = 32
model = Sequential()
model.add(Embedding(top_words, embedding_vector_length,
input_length = max_review_length))
model.add(LSTM(100))
model.add(Dense(1, activation = "sigmoid"))
model.compile(loss = "binary_crossentropy", optimizer =
"adam", metrics = ["accuracy"])
print(model.summary())
model.fit(X_train, y_train, epochs = 3, batch_size = 64)
```

This should print a summary of the model that we just built, as shown below. The summary shows the configuration of our model, as well as training results.

```
Layer (type)                 Output Shape              Param #
=================================================================
embedding (Embedding)        (None, 500, 32)           160000
lstm_2 (LSTM)                (None, 100)               53200
dense_4 (Dense)              (None, 1)                 101
=================================================================
```

```
Total params: 213,301
Trainable params: 213,301
Non-trainable params: 0
```

Let's go ahead and test this model. Depending on your parameters and configuration, you may get classification accuracy around 90%.

```
scores = model.evaluate(X_test, y_test, verbose = 0)
print("Accuracy: %.2f%%" % (scores[1]*100))
Model: "sequential_2"
```

> **Try It Yourself 9.8: LSTM**
>
> Use `keras.datasets.cifar10.load_data()` to load the CIFAR-10 dataset. This time, build an LSTM model to classify CIFAR images and report the performance of your model.

9.7 Summary

Neural networks have been around for decades, but it is really in the last few years that they have caught a lot of attention. This is partly due to the large amounts of training data now available (many neural network models need a lot of data), and partly due to the dramatically reduced cost for computation (most neural networks are computationally demanding). On top of that, several new theoretical advancements have been made in recent years that have allowed for very direct and very meaningful applications of neural models. Examples include CNN, RNN, and LSTM, which we saw in this chapter, and various forms of deep networks, which we will introduce in the next chapter.

When it comes to classic ML, neural networks have a definite appeal for solving nonlinear problems. For example, there are several classification problems that are hard to solve with linearly separable classes. Neural networks can be very useful in such situations. Neural networks also make it easy (sometimes too easy) to do feature selection.

Finally, many new frameworks and libraries for neural networks have been developed and are available through open source, making them very easy to implement and experiment with. What we saw in this chapter is just the tip of the iceberg. We have one more chapter to go a bit deeper with deep networks, but there is a lot more to learn and explore beyond that.

Key Terms

- **Neuron**: A unit of processing that takes in a set of inputs and generates an output based on an activation function.
- **Axon**: A long, thin strand which splits into thousands of branches. The neuron sends out spikes of electrical activity through an axon.
- **Synapse**: A structure at the end of each branch of an axon, which converts the activity from the axon into electrical effects that inhibit or excite activity in the connected neurons.
- **Convolution** is a process that allows multiple filters to be combined to generate one output from several inputs.
- **Autoencoder:** An unsupervised neural network that encodes the data and learns to simplify the data representation, making reconstructed data as close as possible to the original input.
- **Recurrent neural network (RNN)**: A neural network architecture in which the output from one step is fed as input to the next step.

Conceptual Questions

1. How does the working of a human brain relate to a computational structure for pattern recognition?
2. Why do perceptrons struggle with solving XOR problems?
3. Why can multilayer perceptrons be exponentially more complex in terms of computational cost than single-layer perceptrons?
4. What are two examples of nonlinear activation functions?
5. What are the three major components of an autoencoder architecture?
6. What are one strength and one weakness of a CNN?
7. When/why would you use an RNN?
8. In your own words, why might we use an LSTM model?
9. How does LSTM address the issues of vanishing gradients and exploding gradients?

Hands-on Problems

Problem 9.1 (Regression)

Download the Air Quality dataset from OA 9.6. This dataset has 9358 instances and 15 attributes. Build a neural network to do regression analysis on this data and report the accuracy. You should have columns that contain "," and use "PT08.S5(O3)" as the target variable.

Problem 9.2 (Regression)

Download the Bias Correction of Numerical Prediction Model Temperature Forecast dataset from OA 9.7. In this dataset the two outcomes are *Next_Tmax* and *Next_Tmin*. Build a neural network model to predict *Next_Tmin* and report the error. Hint: You need to drop all the NaN and negative rows in the dataframe.

Problem 9.3 (Classification)

Download the dataset from OA 9.8 about activity recognition systems. We want to use the input features and predict the activity performed by the user from time-series generated by a wireless sensor network (WSN), according to the EvAAL competition technical annex. Input RSS streams are provided in files named datasetID.csv, where ID is the progressive numeric sequence ID for each repetition of the activity performed.

In each file, each row corresponds to a time-step measurement (in temporal order) and contains the following information: *avg_rss12*, *var_rss12*, *avg_rss13*, *var_rss13*, *avg_rss23*, *var_rss23*. Here, avg and var are the mean and variance values over 250 ms of data, respectively. Target data is provided as the containing folder name.

For each activity, we have the following parameters:

- frequency (Hz): 20
- clock (millisecond): 250
- total duration (seconds): 120.

Using these features, build an SLP that can classify the activity type. Make sure to do a reasonable split of the data for training and testing and then choose appropriate numbers of neurons for your input and output layers.

Problem 9.4 (Classification)

For this assignment, we are going to use the Steel Plates Faults dataset available from OA 9.9. Following are the list of attributes of the dataset:

- Pastry
- Z_Scratch

- K_Scatch
- Stains
- Dirtiness
- Bumps
- Other_Faults

There are 27 independent variables in the dataset. Among the independent variables, only the Steel types (12th and 13th) are categorical variables. The rest are numeric. For this exercise use a neural network to predict the type of faults in steel plates from numeric attributes only. Note: To save time and energy, use the hidden layer numbers and number of nodes in hidden layers that your computer can handle.

Problem 9.5 (Classification)

For this assignment we are going to do weather classification on a multiclass weather dataset, which is used in the research paper "Multi-class weather recognition from still image using heterogeneous ensemble method."[6] You can get it from OA 9.10. The dataset has four different weather conditions: cloudy (300), rain (215), sunrise (357), and sunshine (253). Here "cloudy (300)" means there are 300 images labeled as cloudy. Build a neural network to predict the weather condition. Make sure to reasonably split your dataset into a training set and testing set.

Problem 9.6 (Classification)

Use autoencoders to perform feature extraction on the multiclass weather dataset from Problem 9.5. Then use the same CNN network from Problem 9.5 to do classification. Compare the performance with Problem 9.5 and report your findings.

Problem 9.7 (Unsupervised Learning)

Use an autoencoder to perform unsupervised classification on the IMDB Movie dataset. You can load the dataset from OA 9.11.

Problem 9.8 (Unsupervised Learning)

Design an autoencoder to perform unsupervised classification on the CIFAR-10 dataset. You can load the dataset from OA 9.12. Report the final loss of your model and the number of epochs it takes for the loss to converge.

Problem 9.9 (CNN)

Load the Iris library in Sklearn. You can find the description of the dataset at: https://scikit-learn.org/stable/auto_examples/datasets/plot_iris_dataset.html. Build a CNN to classify the Iris data and report the performance of your model. Hint: You need to explore more types of convolution layers in Keras, such as the Conv1d layer.

Problem 9.10 (RNN)

Download the data from OA 9.13. Build an RNN model to predict sunspots for a given date. The Sklearn MinMaxScaler will allow you to process the time-series dataset.

Problem 9.11 (LSTM)

Load the MNIST dataset from Keras. Build an LSTM model to classify the 10 hand-drawn digits and report the performance of your model.

Further Reading and Resources

- The appeal of parallel distributed processing: https://stanford.edu/~jlmcc/papers/PDP/Chapter1.pdf.
- *Explorations in parallel distributed processing: a handbook of models, programs, and exercises*: https://web.stanford.edu/group/pdplab/pdphandbook/handbook.pdf.
- Sequence modeling: recurrent and recursive nets: www.deeplearningbook.org/contents/rnn.html.

Notes

1. Rumelhart, D. E., McClelland, J. L., & the PDP Research Group (1986). *Parallel distributed processing, volume 1: Explorations in the microstructure of cognition: foundations*. MIT Press.
2. Minsky, M. and Papert, S. (1969). *An introduction to computational geometry*. MIT Press.
3. Tutorialspoint (2019). "Keras." www.tutorialspoint.com/keras/keras_tutorial.pdf.
4. Krizhevsky, A. (2009). "Learning multiple layers of features from tiny images." www.cs.toronto.edu/~kriz/learning-features-2009-TR.pdf.
5. https://keras.io/api/datasets/imdb.
6. Gbeminiyi Oluwafemi, A. and Zenghui, W. (2019). Multi-class weather classification from still image using said ensemble method. In *2019 Southern African Universities Power Engineering Conference/Robotics and Mechatronics/Pattern Recognition Association of South Africa (SAUPEC/RobMech/PRASA)*, pp. 135–140.

10 Deep Learning

What do you need?
- A good understanding of statistical concepts (see Chapter 2), probability theory (see Chapter 3), and functions.
- The gradient descent algorithm (see Chapter 4).
- Introductory- to intermediate-level experience with Python, including installing packages (refer to Chapter 2).
- A good understanding of neural networks, especially perceptrons (Chapter 9).

What will you learn?
- The basics of building deep networks.
- Applying deep learning for pattern recognition.
- Transformer networks for embedding objects.

10.1 Introduction

In the previous chapter we saw how neural networks can be useful in solving complex problems, especially those involving nonlinear boundaries. In some of the most successful architectures of such models, multiple hidden layers are involved. Networks with several hidden layers are called **deep networks.** Training deep networks is challenging, because learning requires changing the weights on all the edges. But how do you change the weights of the internal edges that are not directly connected to inputs or outputs? We saw some strategies in Chapter 9 when we covered multilayer perceptrons (MLPs) and backward propagation learning. Now, imagine performing those strategies over more layers. Even one hidden layer can incur a significant computational cost for learning. We need better ways to do learning with multiple hidden layers. This is where our old friend gradient descent comes to the rescue. Put together all of these – a deep network with backward propagation learning using gradient descent – and you have a **deep learning** framework. In other words, deep learning is nothing but a subset of machine learning, or ML (Figure 10.1), which is done using specialized neural networks and learning methods.

To understand deep learning, we first need to understand artificial intelligence (AI) and ML. Artificial intelligence is about constructing a machine that can think and act like a human. Since we are far from a machine that can think like a real human, AI is best

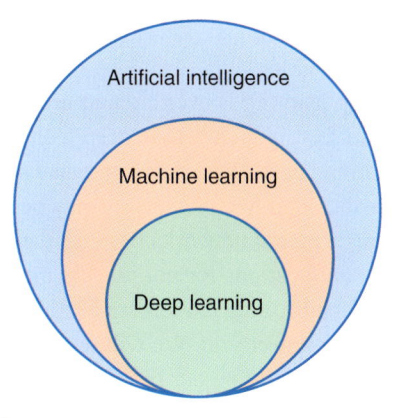

Figure 10.1 Situating deep learning within ML.

described as creating a machine that understands the world and makes decisions reasonably. Machine learning is a subset of AI. It is about teaching computers to learn from data and make reasonable decisions. Deep learning represents the next level of ML; it is a subset of ML.

With ML, machines can learn from data. Programmers could teach computers to recognize cats and dogs by giving them a set of images, some of which contain cats and others of which contain dogs, and training the algorithms on some variables to distinguish between cats and dogs. If the computers return the wrong results, programmers will adjust the code to help the computers learn better. Computers could perform dog and cat classification tasks without being explicitly programmed. However, computers' ability to perform more complex tasks, such as handling large-scale unstructured data like videos, is far below that of humans.

Deep learning mimics the decision-making processes in human brains and needs less ongoing human intervention than traditional ML. It also requires much larger datasets than traditional ML algorithms. Therefore, we do not need to tell algorithms which variables to use to distinguish cats and dogs. Instead, we just give the computer millions of images and let it learn what cats look like.

10.2 When and How to Use a Deep Model

Given the complexity of deep learning architecture, as well as the nature of the problems it is applied on, deep learning works well when there is a substantial amount of data to learn from. It is also ideal for application to a complex problem that typically needs humans' time and energy due to the intricate details or cognitive effort involved. Image processing is a great example. Imagine YouTube paying thousands of employees to flag videos for potentially problematic content. Instead, they can apply deep learning techniques. Translation and speech recognition are other applications. Deep learning is only practical when you have high computational power. If your problem meets these criteria, deep learning may be the ideal solution.

Although deep learning is exciting and impressive, it does not and should not apply to all situations. In fact, in some cases deep learning might be a very bad solution. For one thing, deep learning needs lots of data to make accurate decisions. Therefore, if you do not have enough data, other ML techniques may be more appropriate to use. For another, it is costly to run deep neural networks because they require enormous computational power. This may have implications for not just the money you need to spend, but also our environment. Yes, deep learning models are becoming a major carbon emission concern due to their impact on our power grid. We will revisit this point later in this chapter. But for now, let's get started with building our first deep learning model.

10.3 Building Your First Deep Learning Model with Python

In the following sections we will use one of the most popular deep learning frameworks, PyTorch, to construct deep networks. Unlike TensorFlow, CNTK, and Caffe2, PyTorch uses a dynamic execution graph, creating the computation graph in real time. PyTorch has several special modules like TorchText and TorchVision, and other classes (torch.nn, torch.optim, Dataset, and DataLoader), which help you create and train neural networks.

We will begin by constructing a simple neural network and applying it to the MNIST handwritten digit dataset, like a hello-world program in image recognition. The MNIST dataset, as previously discussed, consists of 60,000 28 × 28 grayscale images with 10 categories. Our workflow is shown in Figure 10.2. We will learn how to associate labels (0, 1, 2, etc.) with different handwritten character shapes using a deep network model. After the model is trained, we will examine a new handwritten character and predict its label.

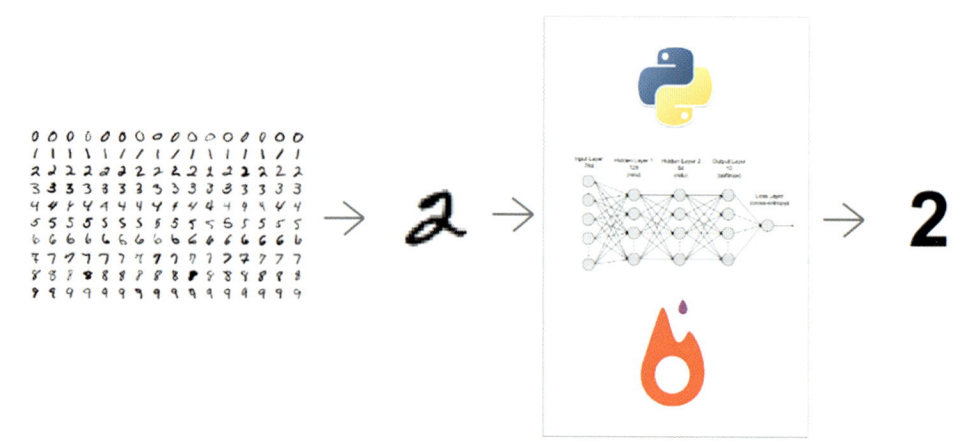

Figure 10.2 Input and output pipeline.

> **Hands-on Example 10.1: Simple Deep Learning Model**

First, we will import some PyTorch functions:

```
from __future__ import print_function
import matplotlib.pyplot as plt
import torch
import torch.nn as nn
import torch.nn.functional as F
import torch.optim as optim
from torchvision import datasets, transforms
from torch.autograd import Variable
```

After importing the necessary libraries, we will define the hyperparameters used in the experiments. Here, *n_epochs* will indicate how many times we will go through the dataset. Learning rate (*lr*) and *momentum* are parameters of the optimizer; *batch size* is the number of items (in this case, images) we want to process at a time.

```
# Training settings
n_epochs = 10
batch_size = 64
lr = 0.01
momentum = 0.5
```

Before we feed the data into the pipeline, there are some transformations we should perform on it. We will edit the images so that all images have the same dimensions and properties. We do that using `torchvision.transforms`. Now, we download the datasets, shuffle the data, and transform them. We load the dataset into DataLoader, which combines the dataset and a sampler and provides single- or multi-process iterators over the dataset:

```
# Load MNIST datasets for training and testing
train_dataset = datasets.MNIST(root = "./mnist_data/",
                               train = True,
                               transform = transforms.
                               ToTensor(),
                               download = True)

test_dataset = datasets.MNIST(root="./mnist_data/",
                              train = False,
                              transform = transforms.
                              ToTensor())

# Create the input pipeline with DataLoader
train_loader =
    torch.utils.data.DataLoader(dataset = train_dataset
                                batch_size = batch_size,
                                shuffle = True)
```

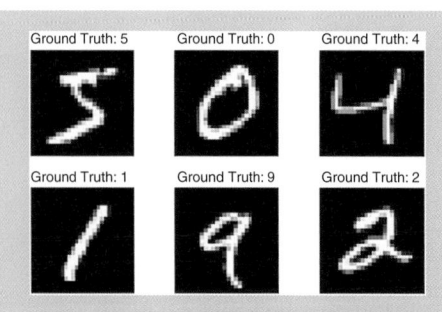

Figure 10.3 Visualizing a few images from the MNIST dataset.

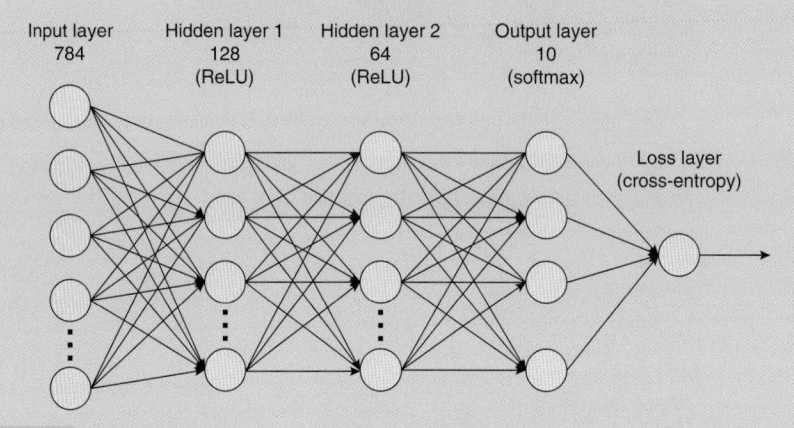

Figure 10.4 Network structure.

```
test_loader =
    torch.utils.data.DataLoader(dataset = test_dataset,
                                batch_size = batch_size,
                                shuffle = False)
```

We now have our data available in training and testing sets. Next, we will plot some images from the datasets. Here, we will draw six images (see Figure 10.3), but feel free to try more:

```
# Visualize some images
fig1 = plt.figure()
for i in range(6):
    plt.subplot(2,3,i+1)
    plt.tight_layout()
    example_data, example_label = train_dataset[i]
    plt.imshow(example_data.squeeze().numpy(), cmap =
    "gray", interpolation = "none")
    plt.title("Ground Truth: {}".format(example_label))
    plt.xticks([])
    plt.yticks([])
fig1.show()
```

We will build the network shown in Figure 10.4, containing an input layer of 784 neurons, an output layer of 10 neurons, and two hidden layers of 128 and 64 neurons each in between. We will set the activation function of the hidden layer to ReLU (rectified linear units). The common way to build a network in PyTorch is to construct a new class. We can also do it using some submodules such as torch.nn and torch.optim.

Let's go ahead and write that network class with those layers, their nodes, and the associated activation functions.

```
# Class for building the network
class Net(nn.Module):
    def __init__(self):
        super(Net, self).__init__()
        self.l1 = nn.Linear(784,128)
        self.l2 = nn.Linear(128,64)
        self.l3 = nn.Linear(64, 10)

    def forward(self, x):
        x = x.view(-1, 784)   # Flatten the data (n, 1,
                              # 28, 28)-> (n, 784)
        x = F.relu(self.l1(x))
        x = F.relu(self.l2(x))
        return self.l3(x)
```

We will now call this function to create an object for a network model:

```
model = Net()
```

Once the model is created, we are now ready to train it. We will set a few parameters, including the learning rate, and define a training procedure:

```
# Set the loss function as cross entropy
criterion = nn.CrossEntropyLoss()
optimizer = optim.SGD(model.parameters(), lr = 0.01,
momentum = 0.5)
```

```
train_losses = []
train_counter = []
test_losses = []
test_counter = [i*len(train_loader.dataset) for i in
range(n_epochs + 1)]

def train(epoch):
    model.train()
    for batch_idx, (data, target) in enumerate(train_
    loader):
```

```
        data, target = Variable(data), Variable(target)
        optimizer.zero_grad()
        output = model(data)
        loss = criterion(output, target)
        loss.backward()
        optimizer.step()
        if batch_idx % 10 == 0:
            print("Train Epoch: {} [{}/{} ({:.0f}%)]\
            tLoss: {:.6f}".format(epoch, batch_idx *
            len(data), len(train_loader.dataset), \
                100. * batch_idx / len(train_loader),
                loss.item()))
        train_losses.append(loss.item())
            train_counter.append(
            (batch_idx*64) +  ((epoch-1)*len(train_
            loader.dataset)))
```

Next, we will create a test function.

```
# Function to run testing
def test():
   model.eval()
   test_loss = 0
   correct = 0
   for data, target in test_loader:
      with torch.no_grad():
         output = model(example_data)
      # sum up batch loss
      test_loss += criterion(output, target).item()
      # get the index of the max
      pred = output.data.max(1, keepdim = True)[1]
      correct +=
      pred.eq(target.data.view_as(pred)).cpu().sum()

   test_loss /= len(test_loader.dataset)
   test_losses.append(test_loss)
   print("\nTest set: Average loss: {:.4f}, Accuracy:
   {}/{} ({:.0f}%)\n".format(
      test_loss, correct, len(test_loader.dataset),
      100. * correct / len(test_loader.dataset)))
```

Finally, we can do an *n*-fold validation by training and testing the model *n* times. Here, we set *n* = 10.

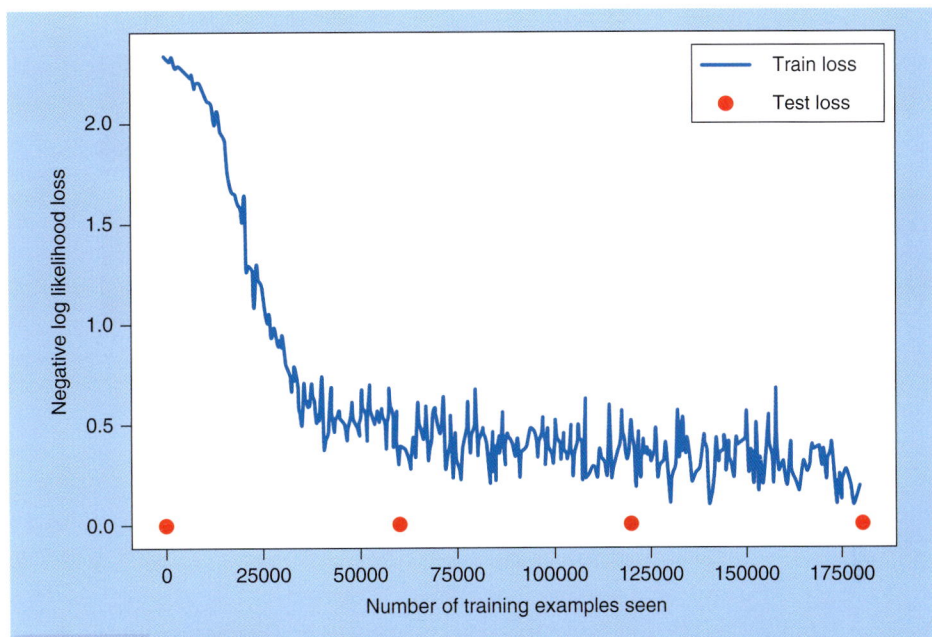

Figure 10.5 Training curve.

```
# Loop for doing n-fold cross-validation
for epoch in range(1, 10):
    train(epoch)
    test()
```

Let's see how well our training did. We will plot our error (here, negative log likelihood loss) with respect to training epochs:

```
# Plot the training curve
fig2 = plt.figure()
plt.plot(train_counter, train_losses, color = "blue")
plt.scatter(test_counter, test_losses, color = "red")
plt.legend(["Train loss", "Test loss"], loc = "upper right")
plt.xlabel("Number of training examples seen")
plt.ylabel("Negative log likelihood loss")
fig2.show()
```

The results are shown in Figure 10.5. As we can see, as we iterate more and increase the number of training samples, our error comes down, and then plateaus. This is a good behavior. This means we could stop at a certain point (maybe around 100,000 training examples) without losing too much.

Let's see how we did with testing. For this, we will write the same visualization loop we wrote at the beginning of this example, only this time with test data:

```
# Visualize the testing data with predictions
fig3 = plt.figure()
```

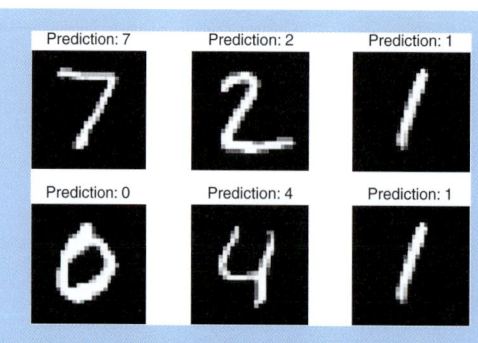

Figure 10.6 Output (test) figures and our predictions for them.

```
for i in range(6):
   plt.subplot(2,3,i+1)
   plt.tight_layout()
   example_data, example_label = test_dataset[i]
   plt.imshow(example_data.squeeze().numpy(), cmap =
"gray", interpolation = "none")
   plt.title("Prediction: {}".format(example_label))
   plt.xticks([])
   plt.yticks([])
fig3.show()
```

The output is shown in Figure 10.6, and as we can see, we were right for all these predictions. Of course, these are only some of our testing data. Go ahead and try plotting other predictions and checking how well we did.

Try It Yourself 10.1: Simple Deep Learning Model

Download the CIFAR-10 dataset from OA 10.1. Similar to what we did with the MNIST data, build a deep learning model for classification on this dataset. You will need to make decisions about how many layers, how many units (neurons) per layer, and how many iterations to go through for learning. Keep in mind that each of these will increase the complexity and running time for your program. So, start small and see how you want to make further adjustments.

10.4 Building a Classifier with Deep Learning

We just saw an example of a deep network model for solving classification. But classification is such an important problem that we can never have enough examples! So, let's do another one, but this time we will go a step further and introduce convolution neural networks (CNNs). We learned the details of CNNs in the previous chapter. Here we will use that architecture for doing deep learning. As you may recall, we used the Keras library while building CNNs. Here, we will use PyTorch.

> **Hands-on Example 10.2: Deep Learning for Classification**
>
> We will build a simple CNN in PyTorch and train it to recognize handwritten digits using the MNIST dataset. We begin by importing the PyTorch libraries we will need here:
>
> ```
> import torch
> import torchvision
> import torch.nn as nn
> import torch.nn.functional as F
> import torch.optim as optim
> import matplotlib.pyplot as plt
> ```
>
> After importing the necessary libraries, we define the hyperparameters used in the experiments:
>
> ```
> n_epochs = 3
> batch_size_train = 64
> batch_size_test = 1000
> learning_rate = 0.01
> momentum = 0.5
> log_interval = 10
> ```
>
> We will set the random seed for doing repeatable experiments and disable cuDNN (CUDA Deep Neural Network) nondeterministic algorithms by setting
>
> ```
> random_seed = 1
> torch.backends.cudnn.enabled = False
> torch.manual_seed(random_seed)
> ```
>
> Now we need data loaders to load the dataset. TorchVision provides an easy way to do it. We will set the training batch size to 64 and the test batch size to 1000. We will use `torchvision.transforms` to normalize the MNIST dataset. The global mean of the datasets is 0.1307, and the standard deviation is 0.3081.
>
> ```
> # Create the input pipeline with DataLoader
> train_loader = torch.utils.data.DataLoader(
> torchvision.datasets.MNIST
>         ("/files/", train = True, download = True,
>         transform = torchvision.transforms.Compose([
>         torchvision.transforms.ToTensor(),
>         torchvision.transforms.Normalize(
>         (0.1307,), (0.3081,))])),
> batch_size = batch_size_train, shuffle = True)
> ```

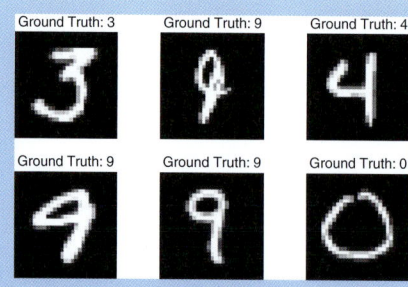

Ground Truth: 3	Ground Truth: 9	Ground Truth: 4
Ground Truth: 9	Ground Truth: 9	Ground Truth: 0

Figure 10.7 Visualizing a few images from the MNIST dataset.

```
test_loader = torch.utils.data.DataLoader(
torchvision.datasets.MNIST
        ("/files/", train = False, download = True,
        transform = torchvision.transforms.Compose([
        torchvision.transforms.ToTensor(),
        torchvision.transforms.Normalize((0.1307,),
        (0.3081,))])),
batch_size = batch_size_test, shuffle = True)
```

Now let's take a look at some examples using `test_loader`. We can plot some of them using `matplotlib`:

```
examples = enumerate(test_loader)
batch_idx, (example_data, example_targets) = next(examples)

# Show what one test data batch consists of
print(example_data.shape)
```

As before, we can print out some of these images along with their labels (Figure 10.7):

```
# Visualize some images
fig1 = plt.figure()
for i in range(6):
   plt.subplot(2,3,i+1)
   plt.tight_layout()
   plt.imshow(example_data[i][0], cmap = "gray",
   interpolation = "none")
   plt.title("Ground Truth: {}".format(example_
   targets[i]))
   plt.xticks([])
   plt.yticks([])
fig1.show()
```

Now let's build our network. We will use two 2D convolutional layers and two fully connected layers. We will set ReLU as our activation function. Then, we will use two dropout layers to regularize our network. We will construct a new class to build our network.

```python
# Class for building the network
class Net(nn.Module):
    def __init__(self):
        super(Net, self).__init__()
        self.conv1 = nn.Conv2d(1, 10, kernel_size = 5)
        self.conv2 = nn.Conv2d(10, 20, kernel_size = 5)
        self.conv2_drop = nn.Dropout2d()
        self.fc1 = nn.Linear(320, 50)
        self.fc2 = nn.Linear(50, 10)

    def forward(self, x):
        x = F.relu(F.max_pool2d(self.conv1(x), 2))
        x = F.relu(F.max_pool2d(self.conv2_drop(self.conv2(x)), 2))
        x = x.view(-1, 320)
        x = F.relu(self.fc1(x))
        x = F.dropout(x, training = self.training)
        x = self.fc2(x)
        return F.log_softmax(x)
```

We will now initialize the network and the optimizer:

```python
network = Net()
optimizer = optim.SGD
        (network.parameters(), lr = learning_rate,
         momentum = momentum)

train_losses = []
train_counter = []
test_losses = []
test_counter = [i*len(train_loader.dataset) for i in
range(n_epochs + 1)]
```

In training mode we iterate over the training set in one epoch. DataLoader will handle loading batches. We need to set `optimizer.zero_grad()` to zero because PyTorch accumulates gradients automatically. Then we generate the output of our network and compute a negative log likelihood loss. We propagate back the gradients into each of the network's parameters using `optimizer.step()`:

```python
# Function to run training
def train(epoch):
```

```
    network.train()
    for batch_idx, (data, target) in enumerate(train_
    loader):
      optimizer.zero_grad()
      output = network(data)
      loss = F.nll_loss(output, target)
      loss.backward()
      optimizer.step()
      if batch_idx % log_interval == 0:
        print("Train Epoch: {} [{}/{} ({:.0f}%)]\tLoss:
        {:.6f}".format(
            epoch, batch_idx * len(data), len(train_
            loader.dataset),
            100. * batch_idx / len(train_loader), loss.
            item()))
        train_losses.append(loss.item())
        train_counter.append(
            (batch_idx*64) + ((epoch-1)*len(train_
            loader.dataset)))
```

In the testing mode we will sum up the test loss and compute the accuracy of the network.

```
# Function to run testing
def test():
 network.eval()
 test_loss = 0
 correct = 0
 with torch.no_grad():
   for data, target in test_loader:
      output = network(data)
      test_loss += F.nll_loss(output, target, size_
      average = False).item()
      pred = output.data.max(1, keepdim = True)[1]
      correct += pred.eq(target.data.view_as(pred)).sum()
   test_loss /= len(test_loader.dataset)
   test_losses.append(test_loss)
   print("\nTest set: Avg. loss: {:.4f}, Accuracy: {}/
   {} ({:.0f}%)\n".format(
   test_loss, correct, len(test_loader.dataset),
```

10.4 Building a Classifier with Deep Learning

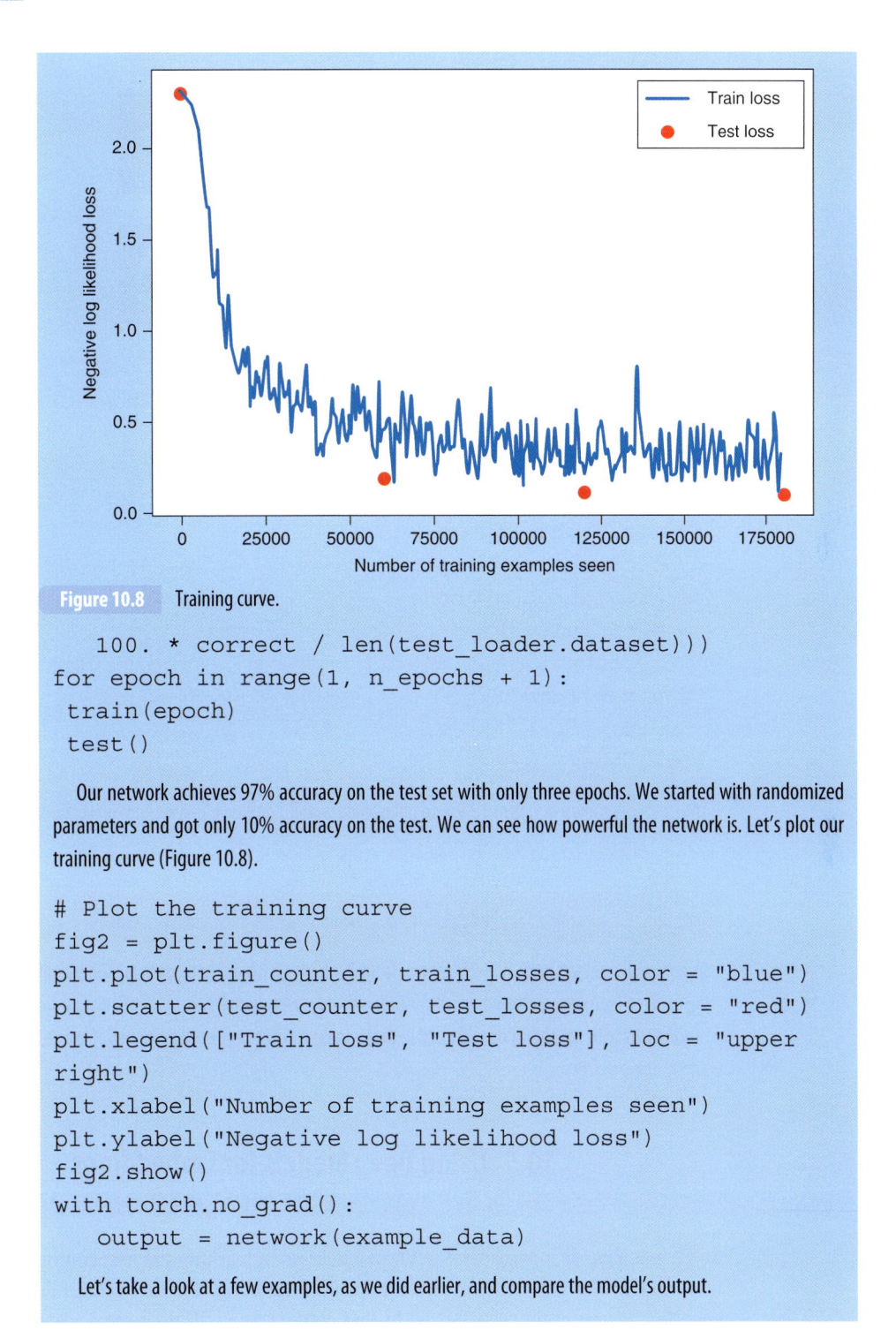

Figure 10.8 Training curve.

```
    100. * correct / len(test_loader.dataset)))
for epoch in range(1, n_epochs + 1):
 train(epoch)
 test()
```

Our network achieves 97% accuracy on the test set with only three epochs. We started with randomized parameters and got only 10% accuracy on the test. We can see how powerful the network is. Let's plot our training curve (Figure 10.8).

```
# Plot the training curve
fig2 = plt.figure()
plt.plot(train_counter, train_losses, color = "blue")
plt.scatter(test_counter, test_losses, color = "red")
plt.legend(["Train loss", "Test loss"], loc = "upper right")
plt.xlabel("Number of training examples seen")
plt.ylabel("Negative log likelihood loss")
fig2.show()
with torch.no_grad():
    output = network(example_data)
```

Let's take a look at a few examples, as we did earlier, and compare the model's output.

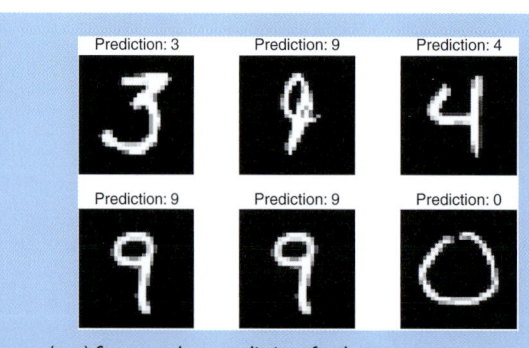

Figure 10.9 Output (test) figures and our predictions for them.

```python
# Visualize the testing data with predictions
fig3 = plt.figure()
for i in range(6):
   plt.subplot(2,3,i+1)
   plt.tight_layout()
   plt.imshow(example_data[i][0], cmap = "gray",
interpolation = "none")
   plt.title("Prediction: {}".format(
      output.data.max(1, keepdim = True)[1][i].item()))
   plt.xticks([])
   plt.yticks([])
fig3.show()
```

The output is shown in Figure 10.9, and once again, we did quite well with these predictions.

> **Try It Yourself 10.2: Deep Learning for Classification**
>
> As before, download the CIFAR-10 dataset from OA 10.1. As we did with the MNIST data above, build a CNN-based deep learning model for classification on this dataset. Remember, this will not be simply substituting one dataset with another. You will need to make some choices here about number of layers, number of units, and training epochs.

10.5 Using Deep Models for Embeddings

So far we have seen how deep networks help us in learning the associations between patterns and labels. This is a big use case for deep learning. Another use for deep networks is encoding or representing patterns. In that context, we will now see a very popular application of deep networks – word embedding. You will hear this term – **embedding** – a lot. It essentially means representing or coding an object or a pattern in a meaningful format. Often this format is a vector.

10.5 Using Deep Models for Embeddings

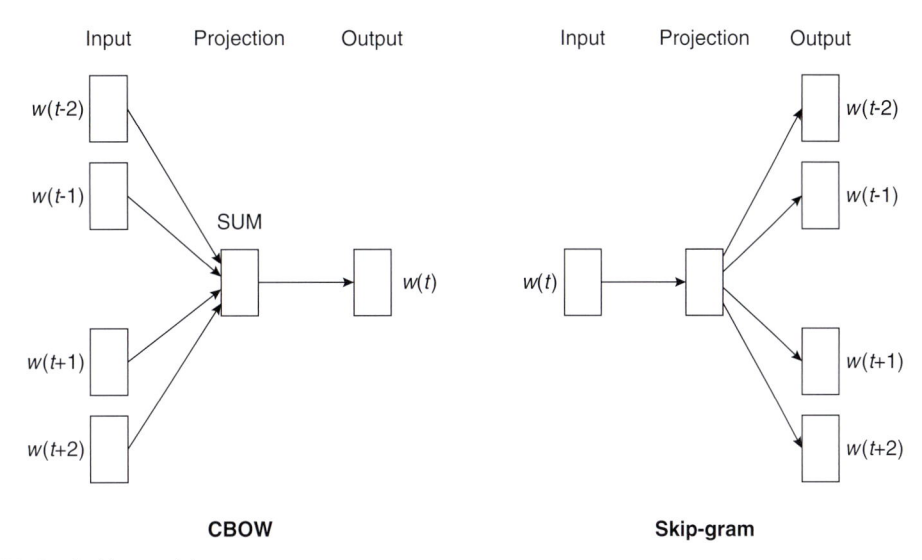

Figure 10.10 Word embedding models.

Word embedding learns real-valued and fixed-size vector representations of a text corpus. It may be considered one of the most critical breakthroughs of deep learning on natural language processing (NLP) problems. It includes two different learning models: the continuous bag of words (CBOW) model and the Skip-gram model (see Figure 10.10). The CBOW model learns word embedding by predicting the current word based on the context. In comparison, the Skip-gram model learns embedding by predicting context words given the current word. The two models both focus on learning words based on local context, where context is defined by the neighborhood word window. The window size is also a configurable parameter of the word embedding model.

Researchers and developers typically use **pretrained word embeddings** for building their applications. Pretrained word embeddings are embeddings that are learned in one task and can then be used for working on a different task. With the appropriate permissions or license, we can use these word embeddings for our academic or business program. For example, the word2vec and GloVe embeddings can be downloaded for free. We can use these pretrained embeddings for our projects rather than training word embeddings from scratch by ourselves. When using pretrained word embedding, we have two primary options: (1) static, where the embeddings are adopted into the model as-is; and (2) updated, where the pretrained embedding is updated jointly during the training of the model.

Hands-on Example 10.3: Creating Word Embeddings

We will now work with a hands-on example to see how we can create word embeddings. We will start by importing the required packages:

```
import torch
import torch.nn as nn
```

Let's define the vector in which the embedding will be stored.

```
def make_context_vector (context, word_to_ix):
    idxs = [word_to_ix[w] for w in context]
    return torch.tensor(idxs, dtype=torch.long)

CONTEXT_SIZE = 2  # 2 words to the left, 2 to the right
EMDEDDING_DIM = 100
```

Here we use a small paragraph as raw text to train a word embedding:

```
raw_text = """We are about to study the idea of a
computational process. Computational processes are
abstract beings that inhabit computers. As they evolve,
processes manipulate other abstract things called data.
The evolution of a process is directed by a pattern
of rules called a program. People create programs to
direct processes. In effect, we conjure the spirits of
the computer with our spells.""".split()
```

First, we need to build a vocabulary.

```
vocab = set(raw_text)
vocab_size = len(vocab)

word_to_ix = {word:ix for ix, word in enumerate(vocab)}
ix_to_word = {ix:word for ix, word in enumerate(vocab)}

# Create our dataset using a combination of context and
# target
data = []
for i in range(2, len(raw_text) - 2):
    context = [raw_text[i - 2], raw_text[i - 1],
               raw_text[i + 1], raw_text[i + 2]]
    target = raw_text[i]
    data.append((context, target))
```

We will be using the CBOW model for developing word embeddings. Let's create a class for that and write the necessary functions:

```
# Class to build CBOW model
class CBOW (torch.nn.Module):
```

```
    def __init__(self, vocab_size, embedding_dim):
    super(CBOW, self).__init__()

        #out: 1 x emdedding_dim
        self.embeddings = nn.Embedding(vocab_size,
        embedding_dim)
        self.linear1 = nn.Linear(embedding_dim, 128)
        self.activation_function1 = nn.ReLU()

        #out: 1 x vocab_size
        self.linear2 = nn.Linear(128, vocab_size)
        self.activation_function2 = nn.LogSoftmax(dim = -1)

    def forward (self, inputs):
        embeds = sum(self.embeddings(inputs)).view(1,-1)
        out = self.linear1(embeds)
        out = self.activation_function1(out)
        out = self.linear2(out)
        out = self.activation_function2(out)
        return out

    def get_word_emdedding (self, word):
        word = torch.tensor([word_to_ix[word]])
        return self.embeddings(word).view(1,-1)
```

Next, we will create the model using the CBOW class:

```
model = CBOW(vocab_size, EMDEDDING_DIM)

loss_function = nn.NLLLoss()
optimizer = torch.optim.SGD(model.parameters(), lr =
0.001)
```

Now we are ready to do training and then testing:

```
# Training
for epoch in range(50):
    total_loss = 0

    for context, target in data:
```

```
        context_vector = make_context_vector(context,
    word_to_ix)
        log_probs = model(context_vector)
        total_loss += loss_function(log_probs, torch.
    tensor([word_to_ix[target]]))

    # Optimize at the end of each epoch
    optimizer.zero_grad()
    total_loss.backward()
    optimizer.step()

# Testing
context = ["People","create","to", "direct"]
context_vector = make_context_vector(context, word_to_ix)
a = model(context_vector)

# Print result
print(f"Raw text: {" ".join(raw_text)}\n")
print(f"Context: {context}\n")
print(f"Prediction: {ix_to_word[torch.argmax(a[0]).
item()]}")
print(f"embedding:{model.get_word_
emdedding("programs")}")
```

This will generate the following output.

```
Context: ["People", "create", "to", "direct"]
Prediction: programs
embedding:tensor([[-1.3032e-03, -1.6272e+00,
-2.5327e-01,  1.2159e+00, -1.7323e+00,..., grad_
fn=<ViewBackward>)
```

The CBOW model uses context words (`"People"`, `"create"`, `"to"`, `"direct"`) to predict the target word programs. We could get the 100-dimensional word embedding from the model.

Try It Yourself 10.3: Creating Word Embeddings

Create a word embedding of the Wikipedia News Corpus dataset available from OA 10.2. The Wikipedia News Corpus contains text from Wikipedia's English-language current events page, with dates. It contains ~25,000 instances in text file format.

10.6 Encoders and Transformers

With the word embedding technique we saw in the previous section, we are able to encode a word using its context, which can provide us with a sense of its meaning. For example, a word embedding can learn that "quarantine" often appears in a close context with "virus," and thus the notion of quarantine has something to do with that of virus. This gets encoded in the representation of "quarantine." But as you can imagine, this encoding may not be sufficient for all decoding purposes. A case in point is translation. When humans translate a sentence from one language to another, we are not simply translating a bunch of words; we are capturing and reconstructing the meaning conveyed by a sequence of those words. Can we extend our word encoding technique to incorporate sequences? In other words, instead of doing word-to-word translation, can we do sequence-to-sequence translation?

Yes, we can – using a **Transformer**. Transformers are deep learning-based models that are breaking many records in machine translation and other NLP tasks. They also have applications in information extraction and synthesis, conversational agents, and various search problems.

The core idea of a Transformer is self-attention. Transformers can attend to different positions of the input sequence to compute the representation of the input. Let's first look at what "attention" means here.

Consider the raw text we used for our hands-on example with word embeddings. It had six sentences, and I bet by the time you finished reading the sixth sentence you forgot exactly what the first sentence was. But in a typical text narrative these sentences are going to be connected and dependent. Therefore, to translate them, or to truly understand them, one needs to retain information about all previous sentences while reading the current sentence. But retaining *all* the information is not feasible for us. Instead, we retain just the *right* kind of information to help us understand the subsequent sentences appropriately. If you watch any TV show with multiple episodes or seasons, you may find that at the beginning of a new episode, they present a synopsis of the previous episode or season, which helps you understand the current episode better. In that synopsis, they are providing you the *right* kind of details that you should pay attention to. The same concept can be applied to sequence-to-sequence mapping. And this is where Transformers excel. They can retain what is important from before and help make better sense out of the current token (word, sentence, sequence).

Attention thus refers to the ability of the output to be influenced by certain parts of the input. Self-attention, to extend this definition, happens when the input can refer to other parts of the input.

Let's consider this in the context of a neural network, specifically an encoder–decoder model. Typically, we would have an encoder going through a sequence of tokens and encode them through multiple passes. Each pass contains a hidden state, but when the encoder hands over the coded sequence to the decoder, the decoder only gets to see the most recent hidden state. An attention mechanism allows the decoder to access all the hidden states rather than just the last hidden state from the encoder.

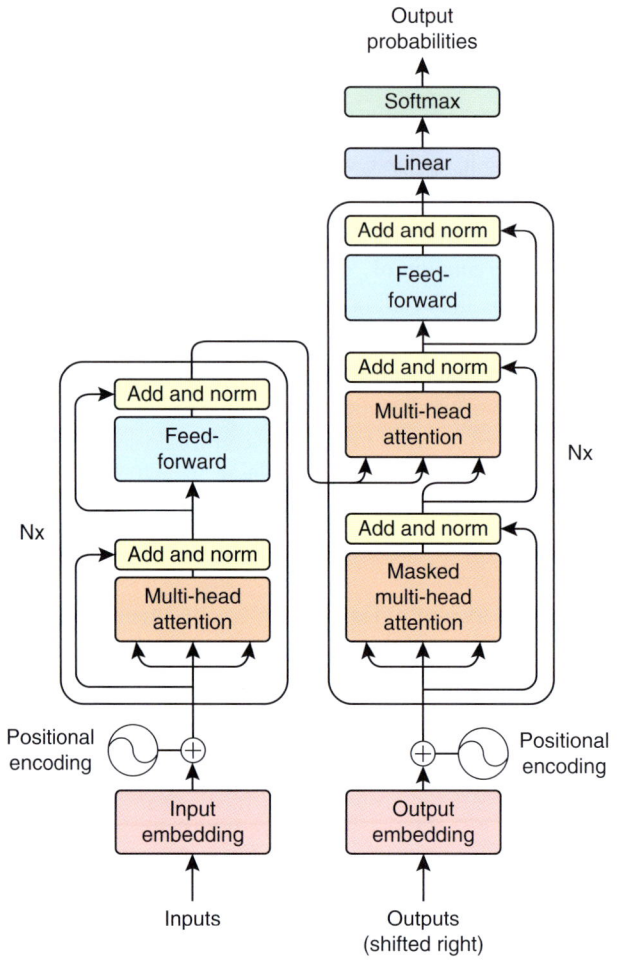

Figure 10.11 Structure of a Transformer. From Vaswani, A., Shazeer, N., Parmar, N., et al. (2017). Attention is all you need. In *Advances in neural information processing systems* (pp. 5998–6008).

Now, let's think about self-attention. According to the original paper on the subject, by Vaswani et al., "Self-attention, sometimes called intra-attention, is an attention mechanism relating different positions of a single sequence in order to compute a representation of the sequence."[1]

Consider this sentence: "I kept drinking the milk from the cup until it was half empty." Here, a human can easily understand that "it" refers to the glass. Self-attention allows us to capture such connections within a given sequence.

Now, let's see how Transformers use self-attention to help us with sequence-to-sequence mapping. Transformers use stacks of self-attention layers. As Figure 10.11 shows, encoders create continuous representations of input sequences in a high dimension. These representations contain all of the information in the input. The decoders use these continuous representations to generate output step by step.

Let's see how Transformers can help with sequence embeddings – specifically, addressing the traditional embedding approach's inability to preserve word position information in a document.

10.6.1 Input Embeddings

The first step is to input our text into a word embedding. Word embedding is a look-up table used to obtain the vector representation of every word. Neural networks learn the mapping from a word to a continuous representation, as we saw before.

10.6.2 Positional Encoding

The next step is to put position information into embeddings. Transformer encoders are not like recurrent neural networks, which are recursive. Therefore, we should embed some position information in our input representations. This is done by positional encoding, as Figure 10.12 shows. To simplify this encoding, we can think about an odd index and an even index for the position. Then we use one kind of function (e.g., cosine function) to create a vector for the odd index and use an opposite kind of function (e.g., sine function) to create a vector for the even index. These index vectors are then appended to their corresponding input vectors, providing us position information for every vector.

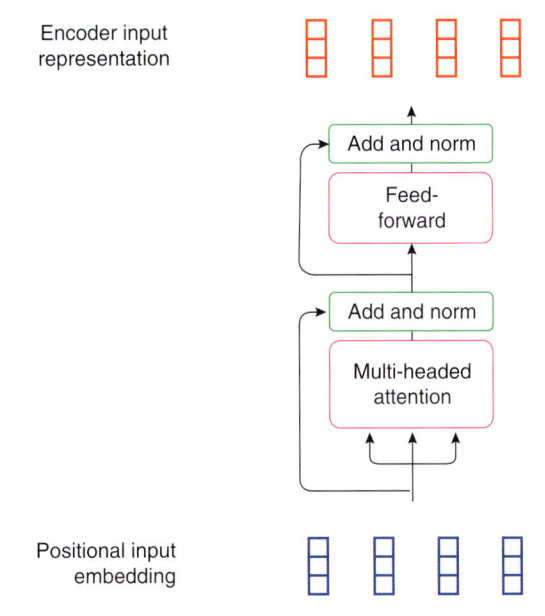

Figure 10.12 Position encoding. From Phi, M. (2020). Illustrated guide to transformers: step by step explanation. *Towards Data Science.*[2]

10.6.3 Encoder Layer

Let's take a look at the encoder layers. An encoder here is designed to map all input sequences into continuous representations. It consists of two submodules: multi-head attention and a fully connected network. The multi-head attention is the secret sauce here.

10.6.4 Multi-headed Attention

In a Transformer, the attention module is repeated multiple times in parallel. This attention module takes *query*, *key*, and *value* parameters and passes them separately through N heads (see Figure 10.13). These updated parameters are then combined to create the final attention score. That is the general idea, anyway. Let's see how this happens in more detail.

1. *Query, key, and value vectors.* In order to realize self-attention, we take our input parameters through three fully connected layers, creating query, key, and value vectors. The concepts of *query* and *key* come from search systems. For example, if you type a query into Google, the search engine will map your query to keywords in the database and then show the best matching document (key).
2. *Product of query and key and scaling down the attention scores.* After putting the query, key, and value vectors into a linear layer, we take the dot product of the query and key vectors to generate a score matrix. The score matrix decides how much attention one

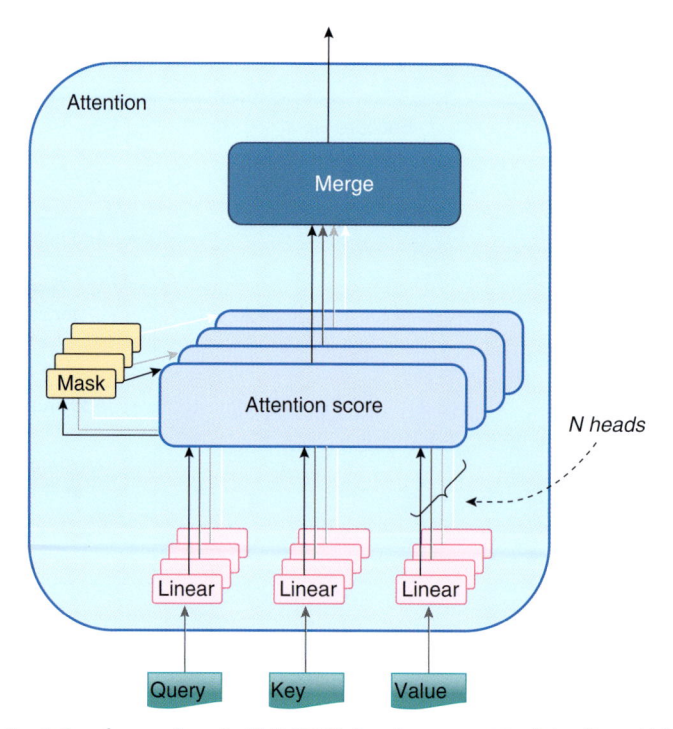

Figure 10.13 Multi-head attention in Transformers. From Doshi, K. (2021). Transformers explained visually: multi-head attention, deep dive.[3]

word should give to other words. Therefore, every word has a score distribution for every other word. The higher the score, the more attention the word gets. We scale down the scores by dividing them by the square root of the dimension of query and key.

3. *Softmax of the scaled scores*. Next, we use a softmax function on the scores to get attention weights, which are values between 0 and 1. With softmax, a high score will get higher and a low score will get lower. A higher softmax score will make a word more valuable, while a lower softmax score will make irrelevant words less important.
4. *Multiply softmax output with value vector*. We then multiply the value vectors by the attention weights to get the output vector.
5. *Computing multi-headed attention*. To compute multi-head attention, we need to split the query, key, and value vectors into N sets of vectors before applying self-attention to each set of vectors. Every self-attention function is called a head. Every head will generate an output vector. Theoretically, every head will learn different things, which gives encoders stronger representation ability. We will concatenate these output vectors into a single vector before feeding that vector into a linear layer.

Multi-head attention is an essential module of Transformers. It computes the input's attention weights and generates output vectors, which contain all of the information about how each word attends to other words in the sequence. We will try to understand many of these elements through practice – specifically, through a popular Transformer model called Bidirectional Encoder Representations from Transformers (BERT).

Hands-on Example 10.4: BERT

Not surprisingly, the main component of BERT is the Transformer. The Transformer consists of two parts: encoder and decoder. The encoder has two modules: the self-attention layer and the feed-forward neural network. The self-attention layer accepts inputs and turns each word into dense representations. Then the feed-forward network passes this representation into the decoder. The decoder has three modules: self-attention, encoder–decoder, and feed-forward layer neural network. This architecture is shown in Figure 10.14.

We often adopt two paradigms to train BERT: pretraining and fine-tuning. During pretraining, the model trains on a large dataset to extract patterns. This is usually an unsupervised learning approach, and the model trains on unlabeled datasets such as the Wikipedia corpus. During fine-tuning, the model trains based on

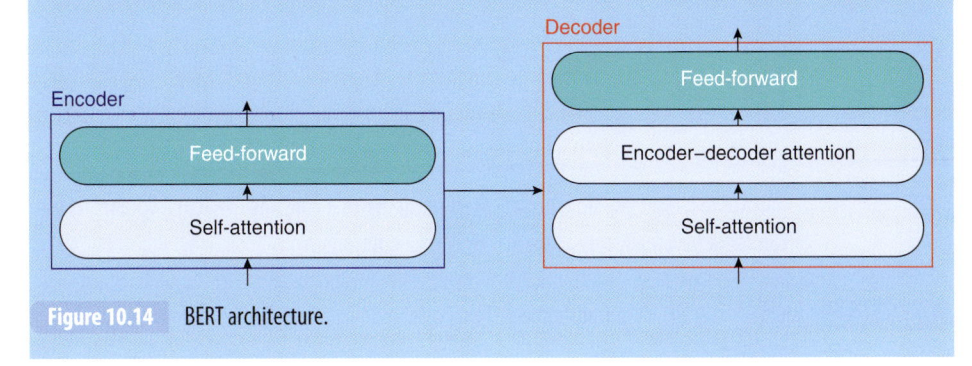

Figure 10.14 BERT architecture.

downstream tasks like question answering, text generation, and machine translation. We could also download a pretrained model and perform transfer learning on our datasets.

BERT comes pretrained with two tasks: the masked language model and next-sentence prediction. The masked language model masks input. For example, "The game is [MASK]" rather than "The game is interesting." It limits the ability of BERT to see more words and helps learn bidirectional representation. Next-sentence prediction predicts whether the two sentences are matchable.

In this section we will use BERT to train a text classifier. Specifically, we will use a pretrained BERT model and append a neural network as a classification layer to train the new model. We will use a multilayer bidirectional gated recurrent unit (GRU) from the Transformer library to get the pretrained BERT, freeze the Transformers' weights, and update the weights of the new appended neural networks.

First, as always, let's import a few packages:

```
import torch
import random
import numpy as np
import torchtext
```

Next, we will set up some random seeds for deterministic results:

```
SEED = 1234
random.seed(SEED)
np.random.seed(SEED)
torch.manual_seed(SEED)
torch.backends.cudnn.deterministic = True
```

The Transformer has already been trained with a specific vocabulary, which means we need to train with the exact same vocabulary and tokenize our data in the same way that the Transformer did when it was initially trained. Luckily, the Transformer library has tokenizers for each of the Transformer models provided. In this case we are using the BERT model, which ignores case (i.e., it represents every word in lower case). We get this by loading the pretrained "bert-base-uncased" tokenizer.

At this point make sure you have an installation of the Transformers package available with your Python. If not, run the following command in your console/terminal:

```
!pip install transformers

from transformers import BertTokenizer
tokenizer = BertTokenizer.from_pretrained ("bert-base-uncased")
```

The "tokenizer" variable has a "vocab" attribute that contains the actual vocabulary we will be using. We can check how many tokens are in it by checking its length:

```
len(tokenizer.vocab)
```

Using the tokenizer is as simple as calling `tokenizer.tokenize` on a string. This will tokenize and lower case the data in a way that is consistent with the pretrained Transformer model:

```
tokens = tokenizer.tokenize("Hello WORLD how ARE yoU?")
print(tokens)
```

We can numericize tokens in our vocabulary using `tokenizer.convert_tokens_to_ids`:

```
indexes = tokenizer.convert_tokens_to_ids(tokens)
print(indexes)
```

The Transformer was also trained with special tokens to mark the beginning and end of the sentence, as well as standard padding and unknown tokens.[4] We can also get these from the tokenizer. The tokenizer does have beginning-of-sequence and end-of-sequence attributes (`bos_token` and `eos_token`), but these are not set and should not be used for this Transformer:

```
init_token = tokenizer.cls_token
eos_token = tokenizer.sep_token
pad_token = tokenizer.pad_token
unk_token = tokenizer.unk_token

print(init_token, eos_token, pad_token, unk_token)
```

We can get the indices of the special tokens by converting them using the vocabulary:

```
init_token_idx = tokenizer.convert_tokens_to_ids(init_token)
eos_token_idx = tokenizer.convert_tokens_to_ids(eos_token)
pad_token_idx = tokenizer.convert_tokens_to_ids(pad_token)
unk_token_idx = tokenizer.convert_tokens_to_ids(unk_token)

print(init_token_idx, eos_token_idx, pad_token_idx, unk_token_idx)
```

Or we can explicitly get them from the tokenizer:

```
init_token_idx = tokenizer.cls_token_id
eos_token_idx = tokenizer.sep_token_id
pad_token_idx = tokenizer.pad_token_id
unk_token_idx = tokenizer.unk_token_id

print(init_token_idx, eos_token_idx, pad_token_idx, unk_token_idx)
```

Another thing we need to keep in mind is that the model was trained on sequences with a defined maximum length – it does not know how to handle sequences longer than it has been trained on. We can get the maximum length of these input sizes by checking the `max_model_input_sizes` for the version of the Transformer we want to use. In this case, it is 512 tokens.

```
max_input_length = tokenizer.max_model_input_siz-
es["bert-base-uncased"]
print(max_input_length)
```

Previously we have used the `spaCy` tokenizer to tokenize our examples. However, we now need to define a function that we will pass to our TEXT field that will handle all the tokenization for us. It will also cut down the number of tokens to a maximum length. Note that our maximum length is two less than the actual maximum length because we need to append two tokens to each sequence, one at the start and one at the end:

```
def tokenize_and_cut(sentence):
    tokens = tokenizer.tokenize(sentence)
    tokens = tokens[:max_input_length-2]
    return tokens
```

Now we define our fields. The Transformer expects the batch dimension to be first, so we set `batch_first = True`. As we already have the vocabulary for our text provided by the Transformer, we set `use_vocab = False` to tell TorchText that we will be handling the vocabulary side of things. We pass our `tokenize_and_cut` function as the tokenizer. The "preprocessing" argument is a function that takes in the example after it has been tokenized. This is where we will convert the tokens to their indices. Finally, we define the special tokens, noting that we are defining them to be their index value and not their string value (i.e., 100 instead of "[UNK]"). This is because the sequences will already be converted into indices. We define the label field as before.

```
from torchtext.legacy import data

TEXT = data.Field(batch_first = True,
                  use_vocab = False,
                  tokenize = tokenize_and_cut,
                  preprocessing = tokenizer.convert_
                  tokens_to_ids,
                  init_token = init_token_idx,
                  eos_token = eos_token_idx,
                  pad_token = pad_token_idx,
                  unk_token = unk_token_idx)

LABEL = data.LabelField(dtype = torch.float)
```

We load the data and create the testing/training/validation splits as before:

```
from torchtext.legacy import datasets

train_data, test_data = datasets.IMDB.splits(TEXT, LABEL)
train_data, valid_data = train_data.split(random_state
= random.seed(SEED))
```

```
print(f"Number of training examples: {len(train_
data)}")
print(f"Number of validation examples: {len(valid_data)}")
print(f"Number of testing examples: {len(test_data)}")
```

We can check an example to ensure that the text has already been numericized:

```
print(vars(train_data.examples[6]))
```

We can use the `convert_ids_to_tokens` method to transform these indices back into readable tokens:

```
tokens = tokenizer.convert_ids_to_tokens(vars(train_
data.examples[6])["text"])
print(tokens)
```

Although we have handled the vocabulary for the text, we still need to build the vocabulary for the labels:

```
LABEL.build_vocab(train_data)
print(LABEL.vocab.stoi)
```

As before, we create the iterators. Ideally, we want to use the largest batch size that we can:

```
BATCH_SIZE = 128
device = torch.device("cuda" if torch.cuda.is_
available() else "cpu")
train_iterator, valid_iterator, test_iterator = data.
BucketIterator.splits((train_data, valid_data, test_
data), batch_size = BATCH_SIZE, device = device)
```

Next, we will load the pretrained model, making sure to load the same model as we did for the tokenizer:

```
from transformers import BertTokenizer, BertModel
bert = BertModel.from_pre-trained("bert-base-uncased")
```

We are now ready to define our actual model. Instead of using an embedding layer to get embeddings for our text, we will be using the pretrained Transformer model. These embeddings will then be fed into a GRU to produce a prediction for the sentiment of the input sentence (e.g., whether it is positive or negative). We get the embedding dimension size (called "hidden_size") from the Transformer via its config attribute. The rest of the initialization is standard. Within the forward pass, we wrap the Transformer in a "no_grad" to ensure no gradients are calculated over this part of the model. The Transformer actually returns the embeddings for the whole sequence as well as a *pooled* output. The pooled output is usually not a good summary of the semantic content of the input, and you are often better off with averaging or pooling the sequence of hidden states for the whole input sequence. Therefore, we will not be using it. The rest of the forward pass is the standard implementation of a recurrent model, where we take the hidden state over the final time-step and pass it through a linear layer to get our predictions:[5]

```python
import torch.nn as nn

class BERTGRUSentiment(nn.Module):
    def __init__(self,
                 bert, hidden_dim,
                 output_dim,
                 n_layers,
                 bidirectional,
                 dropout):

        super().__init__()
        self.bert = bert
        embedding_dim = bert.config.to_dict()["hidden_size"]
        self.rnn = nn.GRU(embedding_dim,
                          hidden_dim,
                          num_layers = n_layers,
                          bidirectional = bidirectional,
                          batch_first = True,
                          dropout = 0 if n_layers < 2 else
                          dropout)

        self.out = nn.Linear(hidden_dim * 2 if
        bidirectional else hidden_dim, output_dim)
        self.dropout = nn.Dropout(dropout)

    def forward(self, text):
        # text = [batch size, sent len]
        with torch.no_grad():
            embedded = self.bert(text)[0]
        # embedded = [batch size, sent len, emb dim]
        _, hidden = self.rnn(embedded)
        #hidden = [n layers * n directions, batch size,
        emb dim]

        if self.rnn.bidirectional:
            hidden = self.dropout(torch.cat((hidden[-2,:,:],
            hidden[-1,:,:]), dim = 1))
        else:
            hidden = self.dropout(hidden[-1,:,:])
        # hidden = [batch size, hid dim]
        output = self.out(hidden)
        # output = [batch size, out dim]
        return output
```

We will now create an instance of our model using standard hyperparameters:

```
HIDDEN_DIM = 256
OUTPUT_DIM = 1
N_LAYERS = 2
BIDIRECTIONAL = True
DROPOUT = 0.25

model = BERTGRUSentiment(bert,
                         HIDDEN_DIM,
                         OUTPUT_DIM,
                         N_LAYERS,
                         BIDIRECTIONAL,
                         DROPOUT)
```

We can check how many parameters the model has. Our standard models have under 5 million, but this one has 112 million! Luckily, 110 million of these parameters are from the Transformer, and we will not be training those.

```
def count_parameters(model):
    return sum(p.numel() for p in model.parameters() if
    p.requires_grad)

print(f"The model has {count_parameters(model):,}
trainable parameters")
```

In order to freeze parameters (not train them) we need to set their "requires_grad" attribute to `False`. To do this, we simply loop through all of the "named_parameters" in our model, and if they're a part of the "bert" Transformer model, we set `requires_grad = False`:

```
for name, param in model.named_parameters():
    if name.startswith("bert"):
        param.requires_grad = False
```

We can now see that our model has under three million trainable parameters, making it almost comparable to the FastText model. However, the text still has to propagate through the Transformer, which causes training to take considerably longer.

```
def count_parameters(model):
    return sum(p.numel() for p in model.parameters() if
    p.requires_grad)

print(f"The model has {count_parameters(model):,}
trainable parameters")
```

We can double-check the names of the trainable parameters, ensuring they make sense. As we can see, they are all the parameters of the GRU ("rnn") and the linear layer ("out").

```python
for name, param in model.named_parameters():
    if param.requires_grad:
        print(name)
```

As is standard, we define our optimizer and criterion (loss function):

```python
import torch.optim as optim
optimizer = optim.Adam(model.parameters())
criterion = nn.BCEWithLogitsLoss()
```

We can place the model and criterion onto the GPU (if available):

```python
model = model.to(device)
criterion = criterion.to(device)
```

Next, we will define functions for calculating accuracy, performing a training epoch, performing an evaluation epoch, and calculating how long a training/evaluation epoch takes.

```python
def binary_accuracy(preds, y):
    """
    Returns accuracy per batch, i.e., if you get 8/10
right, this returns 0.8, NOT 8
    """

    # Round the predictions to the closest integer
    rounded_preds = torch.round(torch.sigmoid(preds))
    correct = (rounded_preds == y).float() # convert into
                                    # float for division
    acc = correct.sum() / len(correct)
    return acc

def train(model, iterator, optimizer, criterion):
    epoch_loss = 0
    epoch_acc = 0
    model.train()

    for batch in iterator:
        optimizer.zero_grad()
        predictions = model(batch.text).squeeze(1)
        loss = criterion(predictions, batch.label)
        acc = binary_accuracy(predictions, batch.label)
        loss.backward()
```

```python
        optimizer.step()
        epoch_loss += loss.item()
        epoch_acc += acc.item()
    return epoch_loss / len(iterator), epoch_acc /
    len(iterator)

def evaluate(model, iterator, criterion):

    epoch_loss = 0
    epoch_acc = 0
    model.eval()

    with torch.no_grad():
        for batch in iterator:
            predictions = model(batch.text).squeeze(1)
            loss = criterion(predictions, batch.label)
            acc = binary_accuracy(predictions, batch.label)
            epoch_loss += loss.item()
            epoch_acc += acc.item()

    return epoch_loss / len(iterator), epoch_acc /
len(iterator)
import time

def epoch_time(start_time, end_time):
    elapsed_time = end_time - start_time
    elapsed_mins = int(elapsed_time / 60)
    elapsed_secs = int(elapsed_time - (elapsed_mins * 60))
    return elapsed_mins, elapsed_secs
```

Finally, we will train our model. This takes considerably longer than any of the previous models due to the size of the Transformer. Even though we are not training any of the Transformer's parameters, we still need to pass the data through the model, which takes a considerable amount of time on a standard GPU.

```python
N_EPOCHS = 5
best_valid_loss = float("inf")

for epoch in range(N_EPOCHS):
    start_time = time.time()
    train_loss, train_acc = train(model, train_iterator,
    optimizer, criterion)
```

```python
    valid_loss, valid_acc = evaluate(model, valid_
    iterator, criterion)
    end_time = time.time()
    epoch_mins, epoch_secs = epoch_time(start_time, end_
    time)

    if valid_loss < best_valid_loss:
        best_valid_loss = valid_loss
        torch.save(model.state_dict(), "tut6-model.pt")

    print(f"Epoch: {epoch+1:02} | Epoch Time: {epoch_
mins}m {epoch_secs}s")
    print(f"\tTrain Loss: {train_loss:.3f} | Train Acc:
{train_acc*100:.2f}%")
    print(f"\t Val. Loss: {valid_loss:.3f} |  Val. Acc:
{valid_acc*100:.2f}%")
```

We will load the parameters that gave us the best validation loss and try these on the test set – which gives us our best results so far!

```python
model.load_state_dict(torch.load("tut6-model.pt"))
test_loss, test_acc = evaluate(model, test_iterator,
criterion)
print(f"Test Loss: {test_loss:.3f} | Test Acc: {test_
acc*100:.2f}%")
```

We will then use the model to test the sentiment of some sequences. We tokenize the input sequence, trim it down to the maximum length, add the special tokens to either side, convert it to a tensor, add a fake batch dimension, and then pass it through our model:

```python
def predict_sentiment(model, tokenizer, sentence):
    model.eval()
    tokens = tokenizer.tokenize(sentence)
    tokens = tokens[:max_input_length-2]
    indexed = [init_token_idx] + tokenizer.convert_
tokens_to_ids(tokens) + [eos_token_idx]
    tensor = torch.LongTensor(indexed).to(device)
    tensor = tensor.unsqueeze(0)
    prediction = torch.sigmoid(model(tensor))
    return prediction.item()

predict_sentiment(model, tokenizer, "This film is
terrible")
```

```
predict_sentiment(model, tokenizer, "This film is great")
```

This results in the following outcome.

```
"This film is terrible" : 0.1025908961892128
"This film is great" : 0.9304782152175903
```

As we can see, the sentiment analysis result is quite good using the BERT model.

> **Try It Yourself 10.4: BERT**
>
> Try to build a BERT-based model to do classification on the Twenty Newsgroups dataset available from OA 10.3. This dataset, as the name suggests, contains information about newsgroups. To curate this dataset, 1000 Usenet articles were taken from 20 different newsgroups. The articles have features like subject lines, signatures, and quotes.

> **FYI: Graph Neural Network**
>
> In the recent years, graph-based neural networks (GNNs) have achieved a lot of attention due to their unique nature in capturing complex relationships among various concepts and representing them.
>
> A graph consists of nodes (V) connected by edges (E). Each of these nodes can have various attributes (e.g., a person node can have name, age, address). The edges can be directed or undirected, and they could have weights on them to indicate how strongly two nodes are connected. Many problems can be represented using graph structures. These include text (words as nodes and their sequence connection for edges), social networks (people as nodes and their ties as edges), and citations (authors or articles as nodes with edges representing who is citing whom).
>
> How does deep learning or GNN come in? For a GNN, a graph is an input. Within the GNN there is typically an MLP that produces embeddings for various parts of the graph (V, E) and creates a new graph. This is similar to inputting a word into word2vec and coming out with an embedding vector. This type of representation done through a deep network allows us to carry out three types of tasks: node prediction, edge prediction, and graph prediction. The details are outside the scope for us here, but if you are interested I recommend reviewing some of the pointers at the end of the chapter.

10.7 Summary

Deep learning has taken the field of ML by storm. There are several reasons for that. As we work with increasingly larger datasets and problems, one of the challenges we find is figuring out which features to use for training our models. Sure, we can use the feature selection and dimensionality reduction techniques that we saw before, but the problem goes deeper than that. Many problems in ML are nonlinear and contain complex relationships among their features. One of the advantages of deep networks is that they can help us figure this out in an automatic way. Of course, this also gets misused a lot, when ML engineers throw all the features they have into a deep network and let the network figure out what features are useful. Such an approach perpetuates the opaqueness of the model. Yes, one big disadvantage of deep learning models is that they are often very closed and hard to explain. They can be attractive for fixing a problem without concern for the number and the quality of features, but the result can lack transparency and fairness. We will revisit this issue in Chapter 13.

My advice to anyone learning and using deep learning is to be mindful of such shortcomings. It is easy to think that deep models can solve almost any problem, and lately, they have shown to do so. But we need to ask at what cost. In addition to the costs of complexity and opaqueness, there is actually real cost for training such models – in terms of money, time, and the climate. Yes, deep learning can have a large carbon footprint,[6] begging us to reconsider and rethink before we dump all our ML problems onto deep learning.

Key Terms

- **Deep network**: A neural network with several hidden layers.
- **Deep learning**: An ML approach for training a deep network with backward propagation and gradient descent (typically).
- **Embeddings**: A vector-based representation obtained by using a deep network with a large input feature vector mapped to a much smaller hidden layer based on known outputs in the output layer.
- **Continuous bag of words (CBOW)**: A deep-network-based technique that learns word embedding by predicting the current word based on the context.
- **Skip-gram models**: A deep-network-based technique that learns embedding by predicting the context given the current word.

Conceptual Questions

1. What is a deep network?
2. What is deep learning? How does it relate to ML and neural networks?
3. What are three different scenarios where deep learning would be appropriate?
4. When or why would you not use deep learning?
5. What, in plain words, does an embedding technique do?
6. What is "attention" in the context of sentence processing?
7. What is "self-attention" in the context of sentence processing?
8. Why do we need an attention mechanism to do a reliable sequence-to-sequence mapping?

Hands-on Problems

Problem 10.1

For this assignment we are going to do weather classification on the multiclass weather dataset that we used for Problem 9.5. The data can be downloaded from OA 10.4. The dataset has four different weather conditions: cloudy (300), rain (215), sunrise (357), and sunshine (253). Here, cloudy (300) means there are 300 images labeled as cloudy. Build a deep multilayer neural network to predict the weather condition. Make sure to reasonably split your dataset into a training set and testing set.

Problem 10.2

Download the Fruits 360 dataset from OA 10.5. This dataset has 90,483 images of different fruits and vegetables (one fruit or vegetable per image). There are 131 different classes of fruit or vegetable. The dataset has been split into a training set of 67,692 images and a testing set of 22,688 images. Build a CNN network to classify the images.

Problem 10.3

Download a set of pretrained English word embeddings (e.g., the GloVe embeddings available at OA 10.6). Use cosine similarity to find the most similar word to each of these words. Report the most similar word and its cosine similarity.

dog
whale
before
however
fabricate

Problem 10.4

For this exercise we will do something that can be a bit challenging because we have not done anything like it in this chapter. But if you are up for this challenge, this could be fun and satisfying work to do!

Use vector addition and subtraction to compute target vectors for the analogies below. This style of evaluation is explained in section 14.6 of the book *Natural Language Processing* by Jacob Eisenstein.[7]

After computing each target vector, find the top three candidates by cosine similarity. Given two vectors x and y, the cosine similarity between them is measured using the following equation:

$$sim(x, y) = \frac{x \cdot y}{\|x\|\|y\|}$$

Report the candidates and their similarities to the target vector.

dog : puppy :: cat : ?
speak : speaker :: sing : ?
France : French :: England : ?
France : wine :: England : ?

Problem 10.5

Try to build a BERT-based model to do classification on the Twitter US Airline Sentiment dataset. This dataset has three kinds of Tweets pertaining to US airlines: positive, neutral, and negative. The dataset can be found at OA 10.7.

Further Reading and Resources

- Eisenstein's *Natural Language Processing*: https://cseweb.ucsd.edu/~nnakashole/teaching/eisenstein-nov18.pdf.
- How do you know when and where to apply deep learning? https://bernardmarr.com/how-do-you-know-when-and-where-to-apply-deep-learning.
- Transformer model for language understanding: www.tensorflow.org/text/tutorials/transformer.
- Illustrated guide to transformers – step by step explanation: https://towardsdatascience.com/illustrated-guide-to-transformers-step-by-step-explanation-f74876522bc0#.
- Alammar, J (2018). The illustrated transformer. https://jalammar.github.io/illustrated-transformer.
- Tan, Z., Wang, M., Xie, J., Chen, Y., & Shi, X. (2018). Deep semantic role labeling with self-attention. In *Proceedings of the AAAI Conference on Artificial Intelligence* (vol. 32, no. 1). https://ojs.aaai.org/index.php/AAAI/article/view/11928/11787.
- How transformers work in deep learning and NLP: an intuitive introduction: https://theaisummer.com/transformer.
- A gentle introduction to graph neural networks: https://distill.pub/2021/gnn-intro.

Notes

1. Vaswani, A., Shazeer, N., Parmar, N., et al. (2017). Attention is all you need. In *Advances in neural information processing systems* (pp. 5998–6008).
2. https://towardsdatascience.com/illustrated-guide-to-transformers-step-by-step-explanation-f74876522bc0.
3. https://ketanhdoshi.github.io/Transformers-Attention.
4. See details at: https://huggingface.co/docs/transformers/model_doc/bert#transformers.BertModel.
5. A detailed solution can be found at: https://colab.research.google.com/github/bentrevett/pytorch-sentiment-analysis/blob/master/6%20-%20Transformers%20for%20Sentiment%20Analysis.ipynb.
6. Manaila, F. (2020). Carbon footprint for training deep learning models. https://aideepdive.medium.com/carbon-footprint-for-training-deep-learning-models-2c574099cfe.
7. Eisenstein, J. (2018). *Natural language processing*. MIT Press. https://cseweb.ucsd.edu/~nnakashole/teaching/eisenstein-nov18.pdf.

PART V

FURTHER EXPLORATIONS

In this last part of the book we will begin with an introduction to reinforcement learning. This branch of ML has always been very important, but in the past it was used more squarely within robotics. In recent years, as we face problems involving large amounts of data and not enough labels or annotations, reinforcement learning has found its way into many interesting and important problems. In this part we will also see how ML is used in research and development – both in academia and industry. We will also look at some of the ways ML systems are evaluated, including A/B testing. The last chapter is one of the most important – it shows where ML fails not on a technical level but at a societal level, where it introduces and propagates biases and lack of fairness and equity. These issues have become very important in recent years and I strongly recommend anyone studying or teaching ML to not ignore them.

11 Reinforcement Learning

What do you need?
- A good understanding of statistical concepts (see Appendix A), probability theory (see Appendix C), and functions.
- The basics of differential calculus (see Appendix B for a few handy formulas).
- Introductory- to intermediate-level experience with Python, including installing packages (refer to Chapter 2).

What will you learn?
- Solution of a simple case of reinforcement learning by hand.
- The Q-learning algorithm.
- A class of learning algorithms involving bandits.
- Practical use cases of reinforcement learning.

11.1 Introduction

So far in this book we have focused on two main types of machine learning (ML): supervised and unsupervised. But there are many situations where neither of them works for framing the problem. Think about a robot navigating an unfamiliar environment – something humans do often and quite well. There are perhaps some known objects around, but there may be many unknown objects. More importantly, the whole environment may be very different than anything this robot has encountered or been taught about. What should it do? Well, what do humans do? We are still able to navigate in that environment by taking one step at a time and evaluating whether it leads to a positive outcome (like not falling off the face of the Earth!). A robot can do the same – look at the environment, choose an action, and evaluate the reward. Keep doing this over and over and you have a walking, navigating robot. If an action leads to something bad, such as hitting a dead-end, you interpret it as a mistake and reverse your action or take steps in the opposite direction until your reward starts getting positive again. This kind of learning-by-doing falls under an area of ML called **reinforcement learning** (RL).

But that is not all that RL does. As the robot navigates through trial-and-error steps in an unknown environment, it can keep track of those trials and errors. Specifically, it tracks the actions taken and the corresponding reward received. This allows it to create a map of the environment with optimal paths from source to destination. As we will see later in this chapter, this process allows an autonomous agent to traverse a puzzle and find a way out or way to a specific point without explicitly being taught it.

Born out of behaviorist psychology experiments performed almost a century ago, RL attempts to model how software agents should take actions in an environment that will maximize some form of cumulative reward.[1]

Let's look at an example. Imagine you want to train a computer to play chess against a human. In such a case, determining the best move to make depends on several factors. The number of possible states that can exist in a game is usually very large. Covering these many states using a standard rules-based approach would mean specifying a lot of hard-coded rules. Reinforcement learning cuts out the need to manually specify rules, because RL agents learn simply by playing the game. For two-player games, such as backgammon, agents can be trained by playing against human players or even other RL agents. In fact, this is what happened when Google introduced the AlphaZero chess bot in 2017.[2] Human chess players had already been defeated hands-down by computer programs for two decades at this point. The game had changed since the beginning of the twenty-first century; it was not about doing better than humans, but doing better than other computer programs. In 2017, Stockfish[3] was arguably the best program in the world at playing chess. It won most world championship games. And then Google (at the time DeepMind) introduced AlphaZero. What was intriguing about AlphaZero was that it was not a chess program. It was a program to learn how to take a series of actions and optimize the reward. That general framework can be applied to chess, but it can also be applied to many other problems. Stockfish could search 70 million positions per second. AlphaZero could do only 80,000 per second. Even more fascinating, AlphaZero did not even know how to play chess nine hours before its first match against Stockfish. And then something incredible happened: Out of 100 games, AlphaZero won 28 and drew 72. Stockfish, the state-of-the-art chess program that had played for years, with much higher computing and specialized training, won nothing.

And that was not all. Next, AlphaZero was trained on shogi, two hours before its first match against the world leader program, elmo.[4] Out of 100 games, AlphaZero won 90, lost 8, and drew 2. After that it moved to the game of Go. Google had a dedicated program called AlphaGo for Go, which was the world leader at the time. AlphaZero, a generic learning program without explicit training of Go, beat AlphaGo 60 out of 100 times.

As you may have guessed by now, the strength of AlphaZero was its ability to apply RL in an unknown environment and figure out the best moves based on the framework we discussed above – taking an action and judging how good it was, over and over until it reached a desired outcome. In the process, it learns the optimal way(s) to achieve that outcome.

11.2 Conceptualizing RL

In RL the algorithm decides the next course of action once it sees a new data point. Based on how suitable the action is, the learning algorithm gets some consequence, positive or negative, a short time later. The algorithm always modifies its course of action toward the highest reward. Reinforcement learning is common in robotics, where the set of sensor readings at one point in time is a data point, and the algorithm must choose the robot's

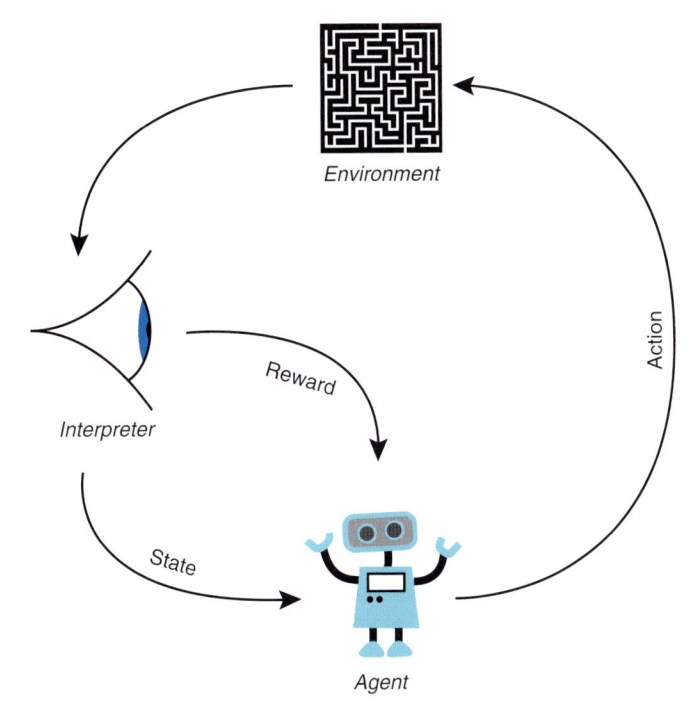

Figure 11.1 The typical framing of an RL scenario (an agent takes actions in an environment that is interpreted into a reward and a representation of the state which is fed back into the agent). From Wikipedia.[5]

next action. Reinforcement learning is also a natural fit for Internet-of-Things (IoT) applications.

The basic RL model consists of (Figure 11.1):

1. a set of environment and agent states S;
2. a set of actions A of the agent;
3. policies (a set of rules and conditions) of transitioning from states to actions;
4. rules that determine the *scalar immediate reward* of a transition; and
5. rules that describe what the agent observes.

An RL agent interacts with its environment in discrete time-steps and in a particular order:

1. At each time t, the agent receives an observation o_t, which typically includes the reward r_t.
2. It then chooses an action a_t from the set of actions available, which is subsequently sent to the environment.
3. The environment moves to a new state s_{t+1} from s_t and the reward r_{t+1} associated with the *transition* s_t, a_t, s_{t+1} is determined.
4. The goal of an RL agent is to collect as high a reward as possible. The agent can choose any action as a function of the history, and it can even randomize its action selection.

Let's take a real-life example to see how RL works. We will follow it up with a simple process to create a model using RL in Python.

First, take a step back and think about how we learn, specifically in a traditional classroom environment. If you are using this book to learn, you could consider me as a teacher and yourself as a student. I have followed the practice of explaining a given concept first and reinforcing the ideas with some follow-up examples. You go through the explanation and follow the examples, and are expected to solve similar questions in the end-of-chapter exercise section. The RL algorithm tries to mimic this process.

So, how do you teach a machine to learn a new concept? To understand this, you need to break down the process of learning into smaller tasks and go through them step by step. For each step you should have a set of **policies** for the machine to follow. A policy, for example in the case of a vacuuming robot, can say that if you detect the edge of a stair coming up, stop moving in that direction (otherwise you would fall down the stairs). A set of reward and penalty rules are defined which the machine uses to assess its performance. The **training limit** specifies the number of trial-and-error experiences that the machine uses to train itself. Within this limit the machine learns by continuously taking each of the possible actions and computing the change in reward after each action. This computation is a **Markov process**, which means that the decision the machine makes at any given state is independent of the decision the machine made at any previous state. Over time, it starts seeking the greatest reward and avoiding the penalties.

> **ML in Practice: Creating a Robot to Do Household Chores**
>
> One area of robotics is devoted to building humanoid robots to do daily life chores, such as cleaning the house and making coffee. Many years ago I spent a summer at Honda Research Institute in Mountain View, California to work on Honda's ASIMO robot. This humanoid robot was being designed to do household tasks. But you cannot simply program a robot for those tasks, as the environment in which it would need to work can be very unpredictable. This is like you going to a friend's place for the first time and figuring out how to cook in their kitchen. You have a general idea what you need to execute the task of cooking, as well as an understanding of how a typical kitchen is organized. Nonetheless, this is a different environment, and you would need to adapt to it to perform your task.
>
> This is where RL can help. It allows an agent to figure out how to do a task in an unknown environment without being explicitly programmed for it. Back to ASIMO, I still hold a patent for teaching the robot how to do household tasks!

11.3 Doing RL by Hand

We will now take Tic Tac Toe as a simple example to demonstrate the working mechanism of RL (Figure 11.2). In Tic Tac Toe we choose an action based on the current configuration and our estimation about the winning probability of the following action. We only get rewards when we make the last action and win. Any step before the final action does not earn rewards. Therefore, we may win not because the final action is a good move, but because some actions before the last one are good moves. The further in the past an action is, the less contribution it makes to the reward. Therefore, we will discount rewards that take place far in the future.

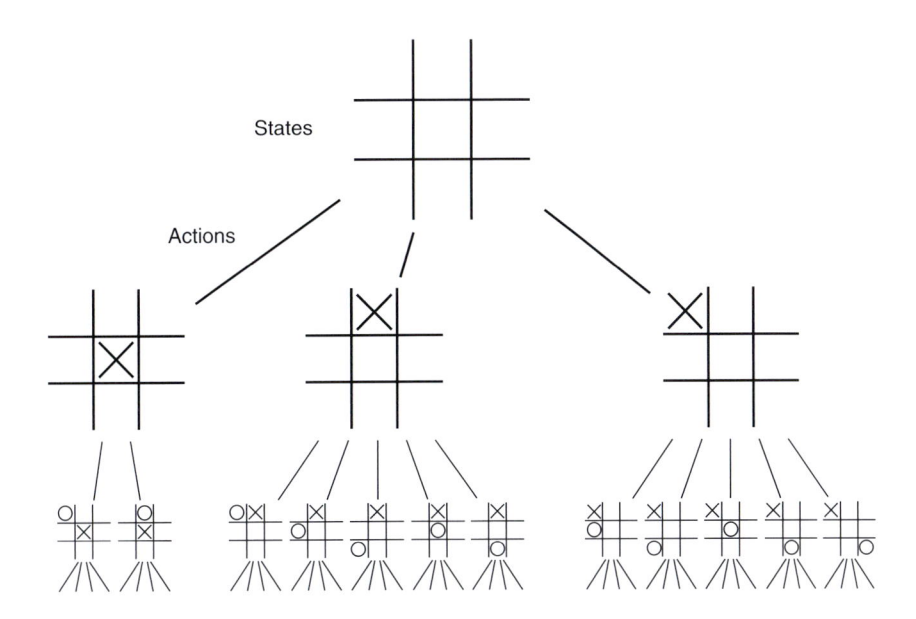

Figure 11.2 Tic Tac Toe in an RL framework.

Hands-on Example 11.1: Reinforcement Learning

Let's understand how RL works by walking through solving a simple maze. Imagine yourself in a 1D maze with six cells, as shown in Figure 11.3.

The game is as follows. You start at a given position, the starting state. From any state you can go left or right or stay in the same position. Each action will take you to a new cell of the grid (a different state). You exit the game if you go to cell 1 or 6. The reward for cells 2, 3, 4, and 5 are 10, 0, 0, and 1. Your goal is to go to a place where you get the most reward. There seems to be an obviously easy solution here. But keep in mind that in a true maze we do not have a picture of the whole maze. All we can see is where we are in each moment. Let's try to solve for the optimal action to take at each cell with RL. Let's first set up the elements we need for a RL problem:

1. **States**. Here, the state is the cell of the maze (1–6). We can store all the states in a list [1,2,3,4,5,6].
2. **Rewards**. We assign the reward to each state in a map. The exit states have a negative reward of −1.

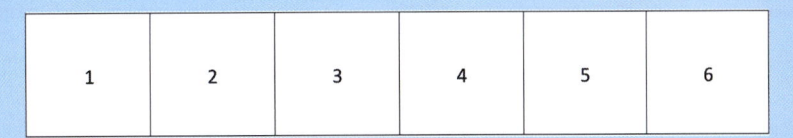

| 1 | 2 | 3 | 4 | 5 | 6 |

Figure 11.3 A 1D maze to traverse.

3. **Actions**. At a given state we can take three possible actions: go left, stay where we are, and go right. Formally, the states we can get to from state i are $i - 1$, i, and $i + 1$ by going left, staying where we are, and going right. Of course, we cannot go left from state 1 or go right from state 6, which are our exit states.
4. The goal here is to learn a policy that optimizes our rewards. We can define an initial policy to start learning with and an initial value function of different states (all zeros for 2, 3, 4, 5 and −1 for exit states).

Let's start coding this. We will import just one package that we need here (NumPy) and initialize a few hyperparameters.

```
import numpy as np

# Hyperparameters
SMALL_ENOUGH = 0.005
GAMMA = 0.9
NOISE = 0.1

# Define all states
all_states = [1, 2, 3, 4, 5, 6]

# Define rewards for all states
rewards = {}
for i in all_states:
    if i == 2:
        rewards[i] = 10
    elif i == 5:
        rewards[i] = 1
    else:
        rewards[i] = 0

# Dictionary of possible actions. We have two exit
# states 1 and 6
actions = {
    2:(1, 2, 3),
    3:(2, 3, 4),
    4:(3, 4, 5),
    5:(4, 5, 6)
    }

# Define an initial policy
policy={}
policy[2] = 1
policy[3] = 2
policy[4] = 5
policy[5] = 6
```

```python
# Define initial value function
V={}
V[1] = -1
V[6] = -1
V[2] = 0
V[3] = 0
V[4] = 0
V[5] = 0
```

With the problem set up, we can solve for the optimal action to take at each cell by updating the initial value and policy while traversing the maze in the way we talked about above:

```python
# Value iteration
iteration = 0
while True:
    biggest_change = 0
    for s in all_states:
        if s in policy:
            old_v = V[s]
            new_v = 0

            for a in actions[s]:
                next = a

                # Choose a new random action to do
                # (transition probability)
                act = np.random.choice([i for i in
                actions[s]])

                # Calculate the value
                v = rewards[s] + (GAMMA * ((1-NOISE)*
                V[next] + (NOISE * V[act])))

                if v > new_v: # Is this the best action so
                              # far? If so, keep it
                    new_v = v
                    policy[s] = a

        # Save the best of all actions for the state
            V[s] = new_v
            biggest_change = max(biggest_change,
            np.abs(old_v - V[s]))

    # See if the loop should stop now
```

```
    if biggest_change < SMALL_ENOUGH:
        break
    iteration += 1
```

After each iteration we can check the updated policy to see if it meets our expectations. Enter `policy` on your console to see what policy emerged. You will get something like the following:

```
{2: 2, 3: 2, 4: 3, 5: 4}
```

Now let's also check our value matrix by printing the value of *V*:

```
{1: -1,
 2: 90.98157507542444,
 3: 80.98340081795058,
 4: 72.88506073615552,
 5: 59.94689919628598,
 6: -1}
```

We could easily choose the shortest way through this matrix by going to a cell that has a higher value. You must admit that this was easy to run. But what do we really take away from this example? Well, in the future if you find yourself needing to use some form of RL, you could construct a dataset such as the one used here, containing states, actions, the new states those actions lead to, and corresponding rewards, which can then be used with a process like the one shown above to build a model.

Try It Yourself 11.1: Reinforcement Learning

Let's expand the maze to 2D with the 3 × 3 configuration shown in Figure 11.4. State 9 (shaded in green) is our ideal state or exit state. In other words, it has the highest reward. State 4 (shaded in red) has a trap. Going there will incur a big penalty (you can decide what that is, but you want to pick a negative number). Try to find the shortest path from a start state to the end state using the RL technique that we used above. Your output should be a matrix with appropriate dimensions that one can use to traverse through this maze and get to the exit state.

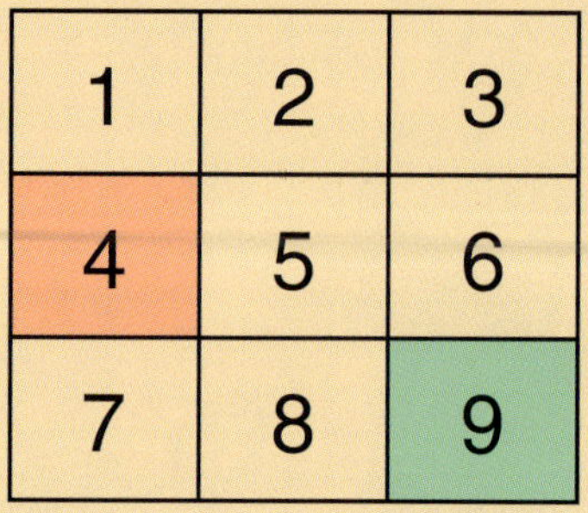

Figure 11.4 A 2D maze to traverse.

11.4 Q-learning

What we saw in the example above is a simplified version of a popular RL algorithm, called **Q-learning**. Q-learning is an off-policy RL algorithm, which finds the best action based on current states. It's called "off-policy" because Q-learning learns from actions that are outside of current policies, like random actions. Specifically, Q-learning aims to learn a strategy to maximize rewards.

The Q in Q-learning means **quality**. An action's quality is the amount of reward we can expect in the future if we take it. We assume that a function to determine quality exists and is deterministic, but we do not know the mapping from states and actions to quality. The goal of Q-learning is to learn the function Q that maps states and actions to quality.

In a deterministic environment, like playing Tic Tac Toe with a player who always adopts the best move, the quality of particular actions under particular states reflects the value of the following states. However, this is not the case when playing with random players. Depending on the random player's actions, we will end up in an unpredictable new state that has a different Q value. Therefore, the Q value of an action is the Q value of all following possible states multiplied by their respective probabilities. This is expressed using the Bellman equation:

$$Q(s,a) = r + \gamma \max_{a'} Q(s',a').$$

Here, s is the current state and a is the action we want to take. $Q(s, a)$ calculates the estimated total reward. As you can see on the right-hand side of the equation, there are two components: r, which is the current reward; and another term that indicates the maximum future reward as we transition to state s'. That second term is calculated recursively. The main idea behind Q-learning is that we can do this recursion in an iterative fashion that can approximate the value of the Q function as follows:

$$Q_{t+1}(s_t,a_t) = Q_t(s_t,a_t) + \alpha \left(r_{t+1} + \gamma \max_a Q_t(s_{t+1},a) - Q_t(s_t,a_t) \right).$$

Here, α is the learning rate that allows us to determine how much we should read into the difference between the previous and new Q value.

Hands-on Example 11.2: Q-learning

Let's dive into an example of Q-learning. Figure 11.5 shows is a node network that we want to traverse to reach node 5, our destination. Thus, going to node 5 gets the highest reward, let's say 100. You can only go to a node if it is connected to the node you are currently in. Let's use Q-learning to find the best paths to node 5 from any given node. First, we work to establish the setup of the problem.

1. The **states** are the six nodes.
2. We also need a 6 × 6 **reward matrix**. Entry [i,j] in this matrix represents the reward for going from node i to node j. We assign −1 if i and j is not connected, 100 if j is 5 and i, j is connected, and 0 otherwise.

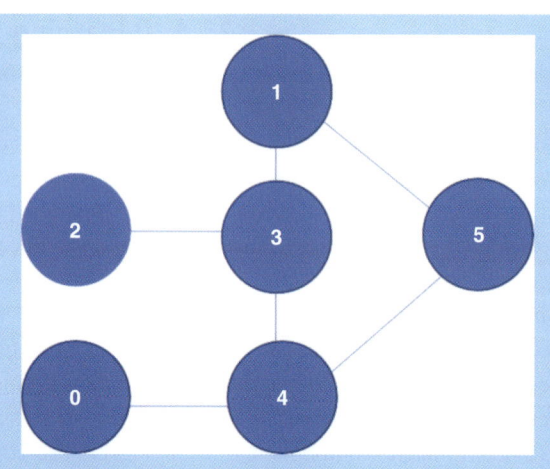

Figure 11.5 Node network to traverse.

3. We also need to set up a **Q matrix** with all values initialized to 0.

Let's start coding this.

```
import numpy as np

# We set up the reward matrix. -1 means not connected,
# 0 means connected, 100 means going to node 5
R = np.matrix([ [-1,-1,-1,-1,0,-1],
    [-1,-1,-1,0,-1,100],
    [-1,-1,-1,0,-1,-1],
    [-1,0,0,-1,0,-1],
    [-1,0,0,-1,-1,100],
    [-1,0,-1,-1,0,100] ])

# We set up the Q matrix and initialize all the values
# to 0
Q = np.matrix(np.zeros([6,6]))

# Gamma is a learning parameter we will use later.
gamma = 0.8
```

Here is our strategy to determine a starting location. We will choose a random, non-terminal starting location. From there, continue choosing random row and column indices until a non-terminal state is identified. The idea is to explore all possible ways we could go from a given state to another state and estimate (and then optimize) the potential reward.

```
# Pick the initial state
initial_state = 1
```

We will now write a function that returns all available actions at a given state. We will use this to choose our next state:

```
# Function to get the available actions, given a state.
def available_actions(state):
    current_state_row = R[state,]
    av_act = np.where(current_state_row >= 0)[1]
    return av_act

# Get available actions in the current state
available_act = available_actions(initial_state)
```

Next, we implement a function that chooses at random which action to perform within the range of all the available actions:

```
# Function to pick the next available action
def sample_next_action(available_actions_range):
    next_action = int(np.random.choice(available_
    act,1)) return next_action

# Sample next action to be performed
action = sample_next_action(available_act)
```

We now need a function that can update the Q matrix according to the path selected and the Bellman equation:

```
# Function to update the Q matrix.
def update(current_state, action, gamma):
    max_index = np.where(Q[action,] ==
    np.max(Q[action,]))[1]

    if max_index.shape[0] > 1:
        max_index = int(np.random.choice(max_index, size
        = 1))
    else:
        max_index = int(max_index)
    max_value = Q[action, max_index]

    # Q-learning formula
    Q[current_state, action] = R[current_state, action]
+ gamma * max_value

# Update Q matrix
update(initial_state,action,gamma)
```

Now we are ready to write our training function:

```
# Training
# Train over 10,000 iterations (re-iterate the process
# above)
for i in range(10000):
    current_state = np.random.randint(0, int(Q.
    shape[0]))
    available_act = available_actions(current_state)
    action = sample_next_action(available_act)
    update(current_state, action, gamma)

# Normalize the "trained" Q matrix
print("Trained Q matrix:")
print(Q/np.max(Q)*100)
```

This will generate a Q matrix such as the following:

```
[[   0.     0.     0.     0.    80.     0.  ]
 [   0.     0.     0.    64.     0.   100.  ]
 [   0.     0.     0.    64.     0.     0.  ]
 [   0.    80.    51.2    0.    80.     0.  ]
 [   0.    80.    51.2    0.     0.   100.  ]
 [   0.    80.     0.     0.    80.   100.  ]]
```

Take a closer look at this updated Q matrix and see if it makes sense intuitively. Remember, this is a 6 × 6 matrix that indicates the estimated rewards for transitioning from one state to another.

This learned matrix can now be used to chart our path from any given state to the destination state. This is our testing. Let's say we are in state 2 and want to find a path to the goal state 5.

```
# Testing
# Goal state = 5

current_state = 2
steps = [current_state]

while current_state != 5:

    next_step_index = np.where(Q[current_state,] == np.
    max(Q[current_state,]))[1]

    if next_step_index.shape[0] > 1:
        next_step_index = int(np.random.choice(next_step_
        index, size = 1))
    else:
        next_step_index = int(next_step_index)
```

```
    steps.append(next_step_index)
    current_state = next_step_index
```

After running this loop, go ahead and print the value of *steps*, which is a list. It should print:

```
[2, 3, 1, 5]
```

Does this make sense? See if you can run through the node graph manually and come to the same conclusion. Specifically, we know that from 2 there is only one possibility: 3. But from 3 you could go to 1 or 4 to reach 5. Would you go 3→1→5 or 3→4→5? Why? Hopefully the solution that we produced here makes intuitive sense. Go ahead and pick a different start state and see if you once again achieve the most reasonable solution.

Try It Yourself 11.2: *Q*-learning

Let's return to that example of Tic Tac Toe. Before, we saw how to solve it by hand. Now that we have a formal structure and code in place, learn to play Tic Tac Toe as the first player using the *Q*-learning algorithm. Start by defining the states and rewards. Then, construct a *Q* matrix. Think about how you would update this matrix as you iterate over possible states and actions. Now, run your training and testing loops and print your learned *Q* matrix. Finally, show the testing part – that is, how, given a start state, you could get to a solution or at least a reasonable end state.

11.5 Bandits

The *Q*-learning approach we saw before is based on doing lots of explorations to learn the best path to a solution. The best path here is defined as the one with the highest reward. But what if the environment is not static? What if there is no specific solution? All we have is an unpredictable (or at least very hard to predict) system, and yet we want to maximize our rewards. This is where we look at bandits.

What is a bandit in this case? The term comes from the old slot machine era. In the nineteenth century, when slot machines were introduced, many looked like a one-armed bandit, as shown in Figure 11.6. To play, you insert a coin into the machine and pull the arm that is holding a gun. It is an interesting visual because these slot machines are designed to take money from the player (in the long run), making them real bandits!

For our purposes, we are going to take the player's side. Imagine we walk into a casino. In this casino there are several known one-armed bandit slot machines where we can try our luck. All bandits behave randomly, and each of them will return some profit. Some bandits have higher returns. How do you find such a bandit? How do you determine a strategy to maximize your profit?

To understand the relationship between bandits and RL, let's quickly recap the latter. Reinforcement learning helps artificial intelligence (AI) agents learn specific environments with exploration, reward, and punishment. If we play games without knowing the rules,

Figure 11.6 One-armed bandit slot machine. © Evans/Stringer/Hulton Archive/Getty Images.

after several moves we will see the result. This is the essence of RL. One of the most well-known challenges of RL is the Exploration–Exploitation dilemma, also known as bandit problems. By exploring, AI agents can improve their understanding of their environment. But they will not directly maximize their reward. At any given point, RL faces the trade-off between exploration and exploitation.

11.5.1 Multi-arm Bandits

Now, imagine you can play multiple slot machines at the same time. You still have limited money, and you are still trying to maximize your rewards. Do you pull on each of the levers with the same frequency? Or do you give some of the levers a higher priority, pulling them more often than the others? How do you figure out the best strategy? This is known as the **multi-arm bandit problem**. The multi-arm bandit is a classic RL problem in which a player is faced with k slot machines or bandits, each with a different reward distribution, and tries to maximize his cumulative reward based on trials.

One typical example of multi-armed bandits is a news website deciding which article to display to a visitor. With no previous information about the visitor, all click results are unknown. The question is, which articles will receive the most clicks? And in which order should they appear? The objective of the website is to maximize engagement. Although they have lots of content, they lack data to help them make strategies. The news website also has the same problem showing advertisements. In this situation they want to maximize advertisement revenue. Which advertisements will bring maximum revenue?

11.5.2 Contextual Bandits

An important component missing from the previous two kinds of bandit problems is that of a context. **Contextual bandits**, also known as associative RL or multi-armed bandits with covariates, address that issue. Let's reimagine the slot machines. When each round starts, the world generates context (a set of covariates of fixed dimensionality) and rewards for each arm relevant to the covariates. The agent chooses one arm for one round and receives the reward for that arm. The goal of the agent is to maximize the long-term reward based on his previous actions.

> **ML in Practice: Displaying Cards**
>
> If you use apps such as Netflix and Spotify, you have seen a card interface. This is where various objects (albums, movies, shows, shopping categories) are shown on cards organized on a grid. Do you ever wonder how these cards are sorted? Each row could have a different logic – most recent, most popular, highest rated, etc. But let's focus on the row that is the system's recommendation. How are those cards sorted? This is where you see a type of bandit algorithm at play. In this set of recommendations, the website wants to show not just the items you are most likely to pick, but also a few that are a bit outside of that comfort zone. But they must find a good balance. You can set the bandit to do 80% exploitation and 20% exploration, which means 8 out of 10 items will be most suitable or relevant to you, but 2 out of 10 will be a bit further from your usual taste. Of course, these are stochastic systems, which means those proportions are probabilistic and targeted in a longer run than just one time. This process not only provides many relevant items, but also provides a way to discover new items. And given that what we like can keep changing, a bit of exploration is good for us. The service promotes diversity in and increases the coverage of our media consumption.

In a real-world scenario we sometimes have the data to help us decide in a multi-armed bandit situation. A contextual bandit makes use of this data: the context and environment. In website optimization, contextual bandits depend on the context data of users, which helps the algorithm make better choices. For example, you can rely on contextual bandits to choose which article or advertisements to show. Context means users' historical or current information, such as browsing history, buying records, device information, or current geolocation. If we know users have visited entertainment news, we can display hot entertainment news on the top of web pages.

There are multiple ways we can solve the multi-armed bandit problem. Three widely used solutions are: epsilon-greedy, upper confidence bound, and Thompson sampling.

1. **Epsilon-greedy**. This is an algorithm that keeps balancing exploration and exploitation. We randomly pull an arm a fraction ε of the time, and pull the arm with the highest rewards $1 - \varepsilon$ of the time.
2. **Upper confidence bound**. This method runs according to the *Optimism in the Face of Uncertainty* principle. It assumes that the highest possible future reward for each arm, given the current data, is the correct one, and pulls the arm whose highest possible future reward is greatest.
3. **Thompson sampling (Bayesian)**. Using a random probability matching strategy, the number of pulls should match the lever's actual probability of being the best.

Here, we will cover the first and perhaps the most popular method for solving multi-armed bandits: epsilon-greedy.

Hands-on Example 11.3: Bandits

This is a hands-on example for solving a multi-armed bandit problem with the epsilon-greedy method. To better understand how the epsilon-greedy algorithm works, we will design a system of multi-armed bandits. This system will have several slots with different (and hidden) reward values. Our objective is to learn a policy that gives us the best rewards through appropriate exploration and exploitation. It helps to think about slot machines in this scenario. If a multi-armed bandit has 10 arms, we can imagine having 10 slot machines lined up. Each of these has a reward function that we do not have access to. We have a limited budget that we can use to pull these 10 levers in whichever order we like. Obviously, we need to do some experimentation. We could randomly start pulling some levers and see what reward we get. If we find a machine that gives out good rewards, maybe we can stick to it (exploitation), but there may be another machine with better reward, and we may exhaust our current favorite. For those reasons, we also need to do some exploration and try other machines occasionally.

Once we have depleted our budget, we can open those 10 machines and look at what reward functions they had. We can compare them to what we learned and see how close we came. That is the general idea here. Let's see how we can implement such a process.

We start by importing a couple of libraries we will need here:

```
import numpy as np
import matplotlib.pyplot as plt
```

Let's write a class to make the bandit work. This class will have several functions. The first one initializes the bandit. The parameters to initialize are how many arms we want in this bandit, the value of epsilon, and the value of alpha (the learning rate). In addition, we will also take an argument for a random seed while creating an object from this class. Note that the set of actions here is the set of arms that can be pulled.

```
class Bandit:
  def __init__(self, arms = 10, epsilon = .3, alpha =
  0.1, seed = None):
    self.arms = arms
    self.actions = range(self.arms) # Possible
    # actions is about which of the arms we could pull
    self.epsilon = epsilon
    self.alpha = alpha
    self.total_reward = 0
    self.avg_reward = []

    self.actualValue = []
    np.random.seed(seed)

    # Initialize reward values corresponding to each
    # arm with random values
```

```
        # with normal distribution. These are "hidden"
        # from the player
        for i in range(self.arms):
            self.actualValue.append(np.random.randn() + 2)

        # Initialized the learned values to zeros
        self.values = np.zeros(self.arms)
        self.times = 0
        self.action_times = np.zeros(self.arms)
```

As you can see, we assigned some actual reward values to each of the arms. These values are hidden from the player, but later we can access them to see how close we came to achieving those rewards. We also initialized the reward gathered for each arm to be zero.

The next function we will write in this class is `chooseAction`, which defines behaviors of exploration and exploitation. Here, exploration means taking actions randomly, while exploitation is choosing the best action (sticking to the arm that has given us the maximum reward so far).

```
def chooseAction(self):
    # Explore stage -- if randomly generated value is
    # less than or equal to epsilon, then pull an arm
    # randomly.
    if np.random.uniform(0, 1) <= self.epsilon:
        action = np.random.choice(self.actions)

     # Exploit stage -- if randomly generated value
     # is greater than epsilon, then stay with the
     # arm that has the highest reward generated so far.
    else:
         action = np.argmax(self.values)
    return action
```

Now we will implement a `takeAction` function that takes an action passed to it and calculates the corresponding reward:

```
def takeAction(self, action):
    self.times += 1
    self.action_times[action] += 1

    # Take action and update value estimates
    reward = np.random.randn() + self.
    actualValue[action] # add randomness to reward
    # Using incremental method to propagate
```

```
        self.values[action] += self.alpha * (reward -
        self.values[action])

        self.total_reward += reward
        self.avg_reward.append(self.total_reward / self.
        times)
```

The last function we will write is for the actual play. To play, we choose which lever to pull (`chooseAction`), pull that lever, and collect the rewards (`takeAction`):

```
def play(self, n):
    for _ in range(n):
        action = self.chooseAction()
        self.takeAction(action)
```

We are done with the hard parts. Let's write the main function. Here, we will create different bandits and run through the simulations a few thousand times to see how well we do. We have a couple of parameters that we can play with here – number of arms and the value of epsilon. For comparison purposes, let's stick to the same number of arms for each bandit (five) and pick different epsilon values for them to see how quickly they can learn the reward function. We will iterate 1000 times with each epsilon, as though we have 1000 coins to play with.

```
if __name__ == "__main__":
    bdt = Bandit(arms = 5, epsilon = 0.1, seed = 1234)
    bdt.play(1000)

    print("\nEstimated values: ", bdt.values)
    print("Actual values: ", bdt.actualValue)
    avg_reward1 = bdt.avg_reward

    bdt = Bandit(arms = 5, epsilon = 0.2, seed = 1234)
    bdt.play(1000)

    print("\nEstimated values: ", bdt.values)
    print("Actual values: ", bdt.actualValue)
    avg_reward2 = bdt.avg_reward

    bdt = Bandit(arms = 5, epsilon = 0.3, seed = 1234)
    bdt.play(1000)

    print("\nEstimated values: ", bdt.values)
    print("Actual values: ", bdt.actualValue)
    avg_reward3 = bdt.avg_reward
```

This should print something like the following.

```
  Estimated values:  [2.29956324 0.74418749 3.62964908
1.56415073 1.49061065]
Actual values:  [2.471435163732493, 0.8090243052935355,
3.432706968426097, 1.6873481039082872,
1.2794112666349884]
  Estimated values:  [2.30500625 0.64920009 3.55960908
1.24693235 1.20763645]
  Actual values:  [2.471435163732493, 0.8090243052935355,
  3.432706968426097, 1.6873481039082872,
  1.2794112666349884]
  Estimated values:  [3.01626983 0.73159104 3.30803198
1.53672378 1.23434972]
  Actual values:  [2.471435163732493, 0.8090243052935355,
3.432706968426097, 1.6873481039082872,
1.2794112666349884]
```

As you can see, our estimates are quite close to the actual values for each of the three bandits. Finally, let's plot how rewards change with the number of iterations for different epsilons:

```
# Reward plot
plt.figure(figsize = [8, 6])
plt.plot(avg_reward1, label = "Epsilon=0.1")
plt.plot(avg_reward2, label = "Epsilon=0.2")
plt.plot(avg_reward3, label = "Epsilon=0.3")

plt.xlabel("n_iter", fontsize = 14)
plt.ylabel("Avg reward", fontsize = 14)
plt.legend()
```

Figure 11.7 is the average reward over time with each epsilon. We can see that after around 500 iterations we are able to get to the maximum possible reward in each scenario. But we can also see that different values of epsilon can lead to different paths to convergence.

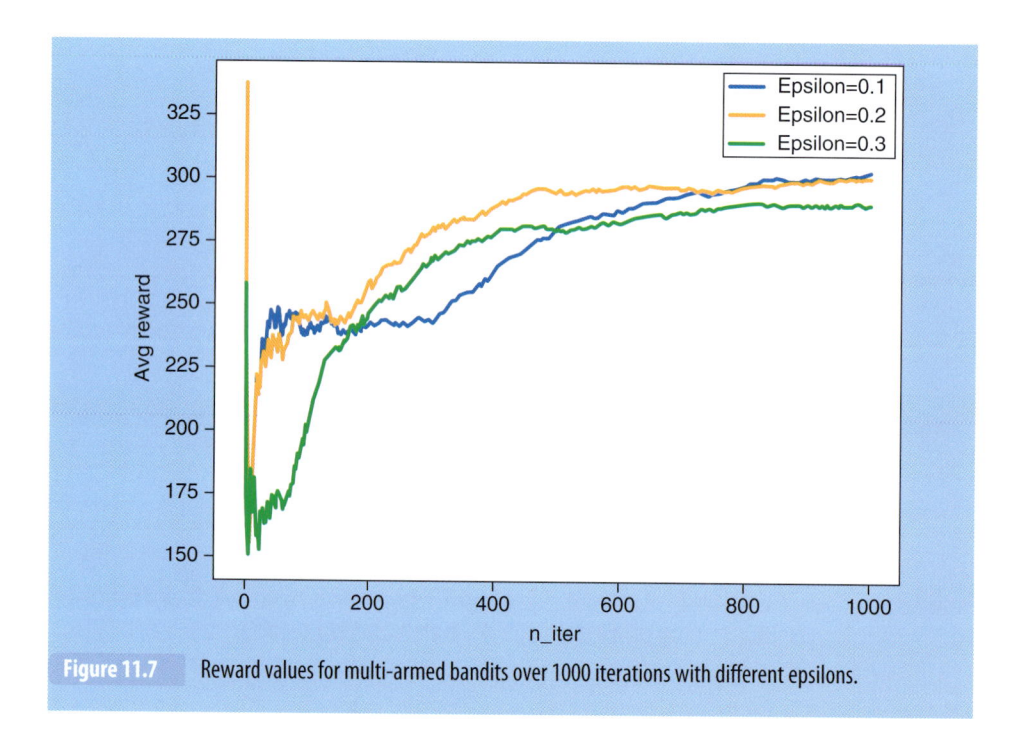

Figure 11.7 Reward values for multi-armed bandits over 1000 iterations with different epsilons.

> **Try It Yourself 11.3: Bandits**
>
> Modify the example we just saw to experiment with different numbers of arms and different epsilons. Report your results as we did with the use of a chart. Provide your interpretations.

11.6 Summary

Reinforcement learning is a computational approach used to learn goals automatically and to make decisions. Unlike other methods, RL emphasizes that agents should interact directly with environments and learn from them without relying on supervision or environment modeling. Reinforcement learning is the first field to learn from interaction with the environment to achieve long-term goals.

Times have changed and we have found many situations where the same approach can be useful. Think about the many natural contexts in which too many possibilities exist to come up with a ground truth to train a supervised learning model. At the same time, we cannot rely on an unsupervised learning method to create a decision-making model. Reinforcement learning offers a very natural and sustainable approach for AI systems. One of the side-effects of this approach, which is not often mentioned in its discussion, is that an RL-based method could also provide a more transparent and explainable solution than many alternatives.

Key Terms

- **Supervised learning**: A class of ML algorithms that use a set of examples from previous records that are labeled to make predictions about future.
- **Unsupervised learning**: A class of ML algorithms where the outcomes of test cases are based on the analysis of training samples for which explicit class labels are absent.
- **Reinforcement learning**: A class of ML algorithms where the objective is to maximize rewards by taking actions in a given context or environment.

Conceptual Questions

1. What is reinforcement learning? How does it differ from supervised and unsupervised learning?

2. What are two examples of situations where you would use reinforcement learning?

3. Explain the intuition of using bandits for reinforcement learning. Think about what makes bandits special and what some of the core elements of reinforcement learning are (context/state, actions, rewards).

4. How does a contextual bandit add value to a multi-arm bandit?

Hands-on Problems

Problem 11.1

You are designing a recommender system for an e-commerce service that presents the user with 10 recommendations for shopping items. You want to figure out what would be a good exploration rate for this system. Use a multi-armed bandit approach to experiment with different exploration rates for this system and provide your insights.

Problem 11.2

We will extend the previous problem. Imagine that you are not set on 10 recommendations. Perhaps 8 is better, or maybe 12. Modify the code to experiment with a range of numbers between 5 and 15 to see where you can find a good sweet spot for maximizing your rewards.

Problem 11.3

You are designing a learning robot vacuum. The room in which it is operating can be configured as follows:

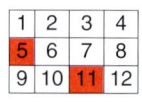

1	2	3	4
5	6	7	8
9	10	11	12

As you can see, there are 12 squares, two of which are colored red, indicating they have pieces of furniture that the robot vacuum cannot go through. But at this point the robot doesn't know all that and needs to learn. Using an appropriate reinforcement learning algorithm, show how your robot would learn this environment so as to avoid those two squares and visit all other squares for cleaning the room.

Problem 11.4

Suppose you face a binary bandit task whose true action values change randomly from play to play. Specifically, suppose that for any play the true values of actions 1 and 2 are respectively 0.1 and 0.2 with probability 0.5 (case A), and 0.9 and 0.8 with probability 0.5 (case B). If you are not able to tell which case you face at any play, what is the best expectation of success you can achieve and how should you behave to achieve it? Now suppose that on each play you are told if you are facing case A or case B (although you still do not know the true action values). This is a contextual bandit task. What is the best expectation of success you can achieve in this task, and how should you behave to achieve it?

Further Reading and Resources

- Sutton, R., & Barto, A. (2018) *Reinforcement learning: an introduction*. MIT Press.
- Python code for Sutton and Barto's *Reinforcement learning: an introduction*: https://github.com/JaeDukSeo/reinforcement-learning-an-introduction.
- RecSys 2020 Tutorial: Introduction to bandits in recommender systems: www.youtube.com/watch?v=rDjCfQJ_sYY.
- Maini, V. (2017). Machine learning for humans, part 5: reinforcement learning: https://medium.com/machine-learning-for-humans/reinforcement-learning-6eacf258b265.
- What's new in recommender systems: https://aws.amazon.com/blogs/media/whats-new-in-recommender-systems.
- How to build a product recommender using multi-armed bandit algorithms: www.offerzen.com/blog/how-to-build-a-product-recommender-using-multi-armed-bandit-algorithms.
- Das, A. (2017). Introduction to Q-learning: https://towardsdatascience.com/introduction-to-q-learning-88d1c4f2b49c.

Notes

1. Reinforcement learning. Wikipedia. https://en.wikipedia.org/wiki/Reinforcement_learning.
2. Chess terms. www.chess.com/terms/alphazero-chess-engine.
3. Stockfish 15. https://stockfishchess.org.
4. elmo (shogi engine). Wikipedia: https://en.wikipedia.org/wiki/Elmo_(shogi_engine).
5. https://en.wikipedia.org/wiki/File:Reinforcement_learning_diagram.svg.

12 Designing and Evaluating ML Systems

What do you need?
- A good understanding of supervised learning algorithms.
- Basic assessment techniques for classification, such as accuracy.
- Understanding of how a simple recommender system works (refer to Chapter 1).

What will you learn?
- To think through a machine learning solution for a given problem, from designing to evaluation.
- Offline and online evaluation techniques.
- A/B testing.
- The counterfactual evaluation technique.

12.1 Introduction

If you have gone through all the previous chapters, you have picked up many tools, techniques, and skills for performing machine learning (ML). But real-life problem-solving with ML is not as *sanitized* as the book so far has appeared. The examples and exercises so far have been clean; there was a clear setup of the problem or the situation, a good, clean dataset was given, and we knew what technique was to be used. In practice, things are never that simple. So, while what we have done so far was a suitable way to learn ML in a classroom setting, it is time we look at how things get done outside of our clean, controlled environment. In this chapter we will do this in two parts: thinking through how, why, and where an ML-based solution is created; and evaluating an ML solution or model. These two steps – design/development and evaluation – are iterative and cyclical.

It is possible that the context or organization in which you work already has an ML solution, and your job is to improve upon it. Or you may be in a situation where things have been done using traditional methods, and you are tasked with coming up with an ML solution. Either way, you need to bring to the table every skill that you have picked up in this book, and then some. In the first chapter we talked about skills needed for doing ML; these include statistics, programming, computer and data literacy, and ML algorithms – all covered so far. But you also need critical-thinking skills. In this chapter and the next we will focus on critical thinking, as we also bring the other skills you've developed into play.

Catalogue

Technique → CBF   CF ←

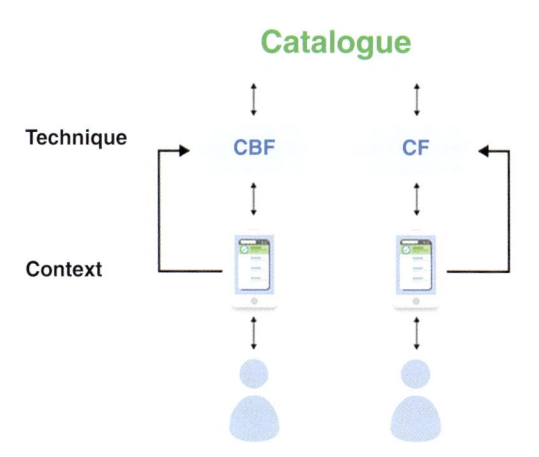

Context

Figure 12.1 Two models of designing a recommender system: CBF = content-based filtering; CF = collaborative filtering.

12.2 Thinking through an ML Solution

Let's take the example from Chapter 1 to walk through developing an ML solution. The example is about a movie recommender system. In Chapter 1 we worked through the example by hand, but now we are ready to think through a larger-scale, more practical system. We will not use our usual data–algorithm–program route for solving this. Instead, we are going to focus on designing an ML solution and understanding the big picture of how such systems are implemented and evaluated. We will also see how data science (DS) and ML relate to each other in an organization. For this example, consider a simple scenario, as shown in Figure 12.1.

Here, the user is looking at a screen where they can see the movies and shows lined up in their queue for watching. There might also be a list of new and popular releases, then a list of recommendations for that user. That list is what we are interested in. In a recommender system, such a page or screen is referred to as **context**. Given this context, the system needs to come up with the most suitable recommendations. There are several ways to do this. We will look at a couple of them, straight out of the recommendation systems literature, and ask which one to use.

> **Hands-on Example 12.1: Designing a Recommender System**
>
> There are three categories of techniques used by recommender systems to come up with recommendations: content-based filtering (CBF), collaborative filtering (CF), and hybrid. The first uses past behavior of the user to filter through possible relevant items, whereas CF uses actions by similar users to come up with objects that the given user will like. Hybrid systems use both. Let's assume that we have access to

the first two techniques implemented: CBF and CF. We want to determine which one is more suitable here.

In Figure 12.1 the context information goes into the technique box, which in turn queries the backend containing the full catalogue. Based on the algorithm used (CBF or CF), the technique box outputs a list of top items to recommend. These items are then sent back to the context (in this case, a screen) for the user to see and interact with.

The lists generated by CBF and CF techniques may be quite different. The question is, which one is better? For that, first we need to have a notion of what defines *better*. In a business setting this is often referred to as a KPI (key performance indicator). A KPI can be anything – the number of interactions the user has with a given set of lists, the amount of time spent, the amount of consumption, etc. The important thing is figuring out what it is that we are trying to monitor and improve. Remember, ML needs a task, a set of observations (data), and a measure for performance. In this case, let's assume that the rank of the first interaction is our KPI. If we present five recommendations to the user in a particular order, we want to see which of the recommendations the user interacts with (clicks on). If they click on the first one, we consider that to be the best case. If they click on the second one, that is slightly worse, and so on. If they do not click on any of the recommendations, that is the worst case.

Now that we have defined our KPI and know our task, we are ready to gather data. Let's begin with CBF for all our users. For a month, everyone who visits the home screen of our movie app gets recommendations produced using CBF. We have a data-logging system that records all the interactions. At the end of the month we can analyze our KPI for the cumulative data for all the users over the one-month period. This analysis is done by the DS team who present the appropriate insights derived (e.g., users were more likely to accept the recommendations later in the day and during the weekends).

In the following month we can swap CBF with CF and do the same analysis. Once again, the DS team jumps in – this time, not only to do and present the analysis for the CF method, but also to compare CBF and CF. Of course, one issue here is our timeframe is different for these two techniques. The content changed from one month to the next, users' behaviors and preferences changed in that time, and there may be many other factors different between these two time windows. So, while we could compare these two methods, it will be hard to create a meaningful causal inference. For that, we should test both systems at the same time. One way to do this is through randomized trials, also called **A/B testing**. We will see how that is done in a later section.

What we have seen so far is more DS than ML. We have not really learned anything new; we simply analyzed and presented what happened. Those insights are definitely very important, and many decisions can be made based on them. But if we are interested in making these systems better, we need some ML. For that, let's assume that we intend to improve interactions with higher-ranked recommendations, as stated in our KPIs. One option is to use something called learning to rank (LTR) or machine learned ranking (MLR). You can check out the FYI box for some details, but the basic idea is simple. If we know the correct ranked list, we can learn a function that produces that list. How do we get the target ranked list? There are several ways, but one way is to take the items that are clicked most in each context and order them according to CBF or CF. The ML part here involves taking the output from the traditional CBF or CF box and figuring out a function that will rank those items in the desired order.

> **FYI: Learning to Rank or Machine Learned Ranking**
>
> Many situations call for a ranked list of items. The most obvious one is web search. But it is also necessary in many other applications we use daily. Whenever there are many possible objects (think of a shopping site) and limited viewing space (think of your mobile screen), we need some form of ordering. Often, this ordering is with respect to a query or a question, in which case we want that order to be based on relevance. The notion of "relevance" is tricky, though. Ordering something by relevance is often not as straightforward as ordering by date, distance, or price. Therefore, there are many different approaches to ranking by relevance. The discussion of these approaches is beyond the scope for us, but we want to look at a category of these approaches that directly connect with ML. What if we turn the ranking problem into an ML problem?
>
> That is what happens in LTR methods. The basic premise is simple. Imagine you have some ground truth about which documents are relevant to a given query. Can we learn the query–document pairs and the probability that they'll be matched by a given function? This is essentially a regression problem. Formally, we want to learn a function $f(.)$ that predicts the relevance score $r_i \in R$ for a given query–document pair (q_i, d_i) so as to minimize the loss function $L(F, q_i, d_i)$. If we do this over all given query–document pairs, it becomes figuring out a line or a polynomial function that minimizes the error. The result is the function that we learned from the training data.
>
> Let's put this in our familiar training–testing framework. For training LTR we need sets, with each set containing a ranking (partial or full) of documents with respect to a given query. How do we know the right ranking or order within each set? Ideally, we want this done by human assessors, but that is not always feasible. Therefore, it is very common to generate such rankings using an existing approach (a baseline). During the training we are trying to learn a function that can generate those rankings with as little error as possible. For testing we get a new set of queries, and we predict their corresponding rankings.
>
> Learning to rank is used extensively in many commercial search engines, enterprise search, and recommender systems. Many advancements have been made over the basic pointwise approach described above, notably pairwise (e.g., RankNet) and listwise (e.g., ListNet) approaches.

This all may seem foreign, so let's do something that we already understand. Let's take the case of testing CBF and CF on the same users, but at different times. For this exercise, let's ignore the issues of confounding variables. The DS team tells us which of the two techniques works the best and perhaps why. More importantly, they provide insights that show that neither of these techniques are perfect. Given that, can we combine them into a hybrid system that automatically switches between the two as appropriate? For example, it is possible that CBF does best during the afternoon and evening hours, whereas CF is better for morning and night. There may be other factors here as well; for example, CF may do better for newer users, whereas CBF may do better for those with a longer history with the service. There are just too many factors for us to analyze manually. This is where ML comes in handy.

Remember the traffic lights example from Chapter 1? This is like that. We want to figure out the best set of rules to pick CBF or CF, given the context and the user. We can start by clustering contexts and corresponding KPIs. For each cluster of these <context, KPI> data points we can analyze which technique was prevalent. In the simplest case we could derive rules from this information and propose a set of hypotheses. These can then be tested on the existing data or through a new A/B test.

> **Try It Yourself 12.1: Designing a Recommender System**
>
> Imagine you are consulting with an e-commerce service about their recommender system module. They are interested in figuring out which of the possible filtering techniques would work best for their users. Propose a plan for figuring this out using either existing data collected through CBF and CF modules, or through a new set of experiments. Show at least two different ML algorithms or techniques that you can apply here to improve their KPIs.

> **FYI: Data Mining**
>
> One phrase you often hear in ML is **data mining**. That is because data mining overlaps with ML quite significantly. Depending on who you talk to, one can be seen as a precursor or entry point for the other. In the end, it does not matter which comes first, as long as we keep our focus on understanding the context and deriving some meaning from the data.
>
> Data mining is about understanding the nature of data to gain insights into the problem that generated the dataset in the first place, or unidentified issues that may arise in the future. Take the case of customers' brand loyalty in the highly competitive e-commerce market. All e-commerce platforms store a database of customers' previous purchases and return history along with customer profiles. This kind of dataset not only helps business owners to understand existing customers' purchasing patterns, but also provides in-depth knowledge about potential new customers.
>
> In today's highly competitive, customer-centered, service-oriented economy, data is the raw material that fuels business growth – if it can be mined properly. Data mining is defined as the process of discovering patterns in data. It uses sophisticated mathematical algorithms to segment the data and evaluate the probability of future events. Data mining is also known as knowledge discovery in data (KDD).[1] In fact, there is a KDD community that holds its annual conference with research presentations as well as the well-known KDD Cup Challenge.[2]
>
> The key properties of data mining are:
>
> - automatic discovery of patterns;
> - prediction of likely outcomes;
> - creation of actionable information; and
> - a focus on large datasets and databases.
>
> From these properties it is evident that ML algorithms can be used for data mining. At this point I must also mention artificial intelligence (AI), the other term often used synonymously with ML. Theoretically, AI is much broader than either ML or data mining. AI is the study of building intelligent agents that act like humans. However, in practice it has been limited to programming a system to perform a task *intelligently*. This may involve learning or induction, but that is not a necessary precondition for developing an AI agent. Thus, AI can include any activity that a machine does, so long as it does not do it *stupidly*. However, it has been our experience that most intelligent tasks require some ability to induce new knowledge from experience.

> This induction of knowledge is achieved through an explicit set of rules or through ML techniques that can extract information automatically (i.e., without constant human moderation). Recently we have seen ML becoming so successful that when we see AI mentioned it almost invariably refers to some form of ML.
>
> In comparison, data mining as a field has taken much of its inspiration and techniques from ML and some from statistics, but with a different goal. Data mining can be performed by a human expert on a specific dataset, often with a clear end goal in mind. Typically, the goal is to leverage the power of various statistical and machine learning to discover insights into a problem where knowledge is limited. Thus, data mining can use other techniques besides or in addition to ML.
>
> Let's take an example to disentangle these two closely related concepts. Whenever you go to Yelp, a popular platform for reviewing local businesses, you see a list of recommendations based on your location, past reviews, time, weather, and other factors. Any such review platform employs ML algorithms in its back end, where the goal is to provide an effective list of recommendations to cater to the needs of different users. However, at a lower level the platform is running a set of data mining applications on the huge dataset it has accumulated from your past interactions with the platform and leveraging that to predict what might be of interest to you. So, for a game day, it might recommend a nearby wings-and-beer place, whereas on a rainy day it might suggest a place where you can get hot soup delivered.

12.3 Evaluation

Throughout this book, whenever we have seen a new technique, we have talked about its *goodness* in some way. Sometimes we did this by looking at how well the data points fit on a line (regression). Other times it was through accuracy (classification). And then there were times when we used a more qualitative assessment (clustering). These are our ways to evaluate how well a given technique is doing in solving the problem at hand. Now that we have studied individual techniques, let's talk about evaluating a whole ML system. Of course, the whole system could be run with a single technique, but even then, we may have multiple ML models that could be applied. Which one is best? We need to assess them using appropriate methods and metrics. In this section we will see several broad approaches as well as specific methods and metrics for doing such evaluations. We will start with something familiar: offline evaluation, which is what we have done most often in this book. The advantage of this method is that the data is already there. Now we get to slice and dice it for DS and build different models with it to enhance the performance of ML methods. But offline testing has limitations. So, we will also cover live testing (user research and A/B testing), as well as a novel way to do offline testing with counterfactual evaluation.

12.3.1 Offline Evaluation

In previous chapters the same weather dataset was used to explain multiple ML algorithms. You have probably realized by now that the same dataset can be used by different algorithms to answer the same set of questions in very different ways. So, you might imagine that when you have a real-world problem with many hundreds of variables and millions of instances, you would want to try multiple models before choosing the most appropriate one. But how would you compare different models to pick the right one for the problem at hand? You can't directly compare the weights of a neural network to the decision rules of a tree and come up with the right answer, especially not with a big dataset. There must be some mechanism to test the goodness of your model to say how well it explains the data. Fortunately, there are plenty of such metrics. Following are a few.

Precision: In any classification problem, precision (also called positive predictive value) is the fraction of classified instances that are classified correctly. Suppose you have designed a program FactChecker that can read any statement and decide whether the statement is true or false. In this case, there are four possible classification scenarios. A statement which is true in reality can be correctly classified as true (known as a **true positive**, TP); a true statement can be misclassified as false (**false negative**, FN); a false statement can be misclassified as true (**false positive**, FP); and a false statement can be correctly classified as false (**true negative**, TN). Precision is defined as:

$$\text{Precision} = \frac{TP}{TP + FP}. \tag{12.1}$$

Precision can be used as a measure of exactness or *quality* of the model.

Recall: What if you have a model with an FP of zero? That model is 100% precise. However, there is no guarantee that minimizing FP results in low FN. Typically, if you decide to create a strict FactChecker, it will be biased toward classifying most instances as false, giving you a low FP, but at the cost of high FN. In those scenarios you can use another evaluation scheme to test the goodness of your model, known as **recall**. Recall is calculated as:

$$\text{Recall} = \frac{TP}{TP + FN}. \tag{12.2}$$

F-measure: Ideally, one would like a model with both high precision and high recall. However, it often happens that precision and recall values are complementary. When the model is designed to have high precision, it typically has low recall, and models with low precision often have high recall. So how do you strike a balance? You take the harmonic mean of the two, also known as the **F-measure**, which is calculated as:

$$\text{F-measure} = 2 \times \frac{\text{precision} \times \text{recall}}{\text{precision} + \text{recall}}. \tag{12.3}$$

Hands-on Example 12.2: Precision and Recall

Let's see how to calculate the various metrics defined above. We will take the results of a classifier, shown in Table 12.1.

The columns – A and B – indicate the real labels. The rows – A' and B' – indicate the predictions. So, cell (1,1) shows the data that was predicted to have label A and was indeed label A. Here, we have 100 samples

> **Table 12.1** Results of a two-class classifier: columns (A, B) indicate ground truth, whereas rows (A', B') indicate predictions.
>
> | | A | B |
> |----|----|----|
> | A' | 32 | 11 |
> | B' | 17 | 40 |
>
> for testing. Of these, 49 are in class A (the sum of the first column) and 51 are in class B (the sum of the second column). Our classifier has identified 43 in class A (the sum of the first row) and 57 in class B (the sum of the second row).
>
> The top-left and bottom-right cells indicate the times we were correct, which is 72. The top-right and bottom-left cells indicate the times we were incorrect, which comes out to be 28. We know how to calculate accuracy from this as we have done that many times before: (#correct)/(#correct + #incorrect) = 72/100 = 0.72.
>
> What about precision? That needs to be defined with respect to a class. Assuming A to be that class, we can ask how precise we were in finding instances that belong to A. Here, true positive (TP) = 32 and false positive (FP) = 11. Therefore, applying (12.1) we get 32/(32 + 11) = 0.74.
>
> Similarly, we can calculate recall using (12.2). Recall is also calculated with respect to a given class. Letting class A be positive, we retrieved 32 out of a possible 49 classifications, so our TP for class A is 32. We mislabeled 17 cases, which is our FN. Plugging these into that equation, we get recall = 32/(32 + 17) = 0.65. With the same logic you can calculate the recall for class B to be 40/(40 + 11) = 0.78.

Try It Yourself 12.2: Precision and Recall

We have built a classifier that does rain forecasting. Table 12.2 shows what it predicted and what really happened over a period of one month.

Using this information, calculate the accuracy of the classifier as well as the precision and recall for both "rain" and "no rain."

Table 12.2 Rain prediction classifier's results.

	Rain	Did not rain
Predicted to rain	9	7
Predicted to not rain	4	10

Not all problems require a high-accuracy solution. In some cases you may want high precision even at the cost of low recall. For example, a bank wants to use their data to design an algorithm to predict loan applicants who may become willful defaulters. In that case, it might be more important that your algorithm has high precision, even at the cost of denying loans to some customers who may not be willful defaulters. Considering this, it

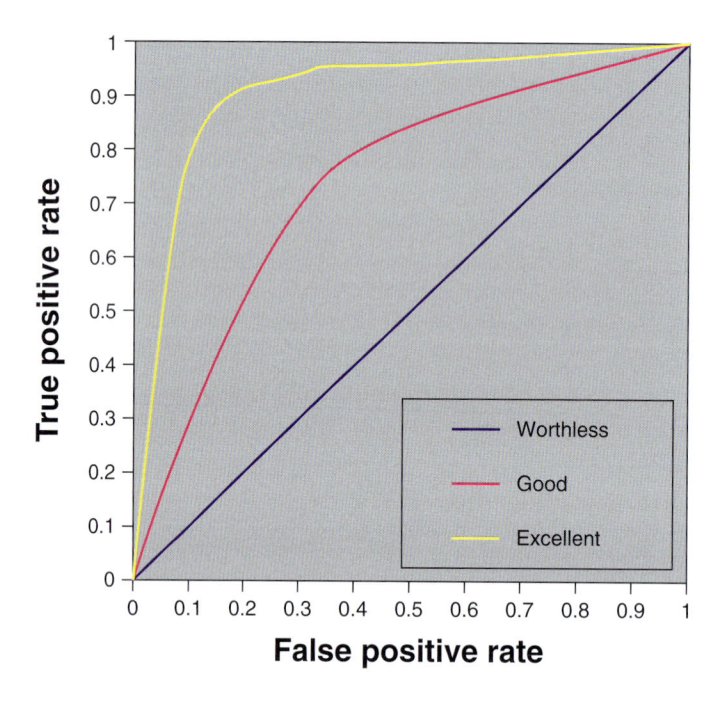

Figure 12.2 ROC curve. From University of Nebraska Medical Center.[3]

might be helpful to have some metric of how the rates of TP and FP change as the settings of the model change.

Fortunately, you can use the **receiver operating characteristic** (ROC) curve for that. In a ROC curve the true positive rate (TPR) is plotted against the false positive rate (FPR) at various thresholds. The area under the curve represents the goodness of the model. To visualize this, consider Figure 12.2.

Figure 12.2 shows three ROC curves representing excellent, good, and worthless models plotted on the same graph. The accuracy of the test depends on how well it separates the group being tested. The yellow line (excellent) has the largest amount of area under the curve, and therefore is the most desired one for the problem.

Akaike information criterion: There are other criteria to compare the accuracy of different models. For example, simple models are less expensive, easier to explain, and less computationally intensive, whereas complex models are more resource-hungry to build and less explanatory, but often provide better performance. So, depending on the problem, you may want to balance the simplicity with the goodness of fit. The Akaike information criterion (AIC), borrowed from information theory, is a measurement of the relative information lost for a model explaining the process that generated the data. It deals with the trade-off between the goodness of fit of the model and its simplicity. Unlike precision and recall, the AIC cannot be used to judge the absolute quality of a model. It can only be used to understand the relative quality of a model compared to other models. Thus, there may not be any difference in results between the case where all candidate models perform poorly, and where all candidate models perform superbly.

Bayesian information criterion: When fitting models it is possible to increase the likelihood by adding more parameters, but doing so may result in overfitting. Both AIC and the Bayesian information criterion (BIC) attempt to solve this problem by introducing a penalty for the number of parameters in the model. Therefore, the more complex the model is, the higher the penalty, and the lower the BIC the better the model. However, the way the penalty is introduced is a little different in the BIC and AIC. The BIC penalizes more severely than the AIC when introducing a new parameter to the model. The AIC approximates a constant plus the relative distance between the actual likelihood function of the data and the likelihood function of the fitted model. So, the lower the AIC, the closer the model is to representing the true nature of the data. Compared to that, a lower BIC also means the model is more likely to be the true model. However, the BIC is calculated as a function of the posterior probability of a model being true, under a certain Bayesian setup.

So, what is the bottom line? In general, it might be best to use the AIC and BIC together to select the most appropriate model. For example, in selecting the number of latent classes in a model, if the BIC points to a four-class model and the AIC points to a two-class model, it makes sense to select from models with two, three, and four latent classes.

12.3.2 User Research

While most systems we design and deploy are for users, we often do not ask all those users if the system is serving their needs. There are good reasons for that. First, doing so is expensive. Imagine if your system is being used by millions of people. How much time and effort (and perhaps money) will you need to talk to each of them? Second, just because you want to talk to them, that does not mean they want to talk to you. In fact, most people are likely to reject your invitation to talk. Even if they do, they may not tell you the truth. Given all of this, why or when would you want to go to real users?

There are two times that one may want to think about going to real users. One is when we are in the early stages of product or feature development. There may be too many variables or open-ended design decisions to consider. Doing user research – whether it is through a survey, interviews, or some other methods – could be a good way to narrow down that design space. Another time for user-based evaluation is when we have a good mockup or a version of a system ready for testing. We can take it to a set of potential users and have them use it for a period and provide us with feedback. Of course, we can do user-based research at any time during the product development cycle, but as noted before, there are costs and limitations.

When we say "user research" or "user-based evaluation," that is a big area. How exactly does one do this research? There are several methods, each with its own set of pros and cons.

Surveys

One user research method is surveys. A survey can be conducted in person, on paper, or online. To get started it is essential that first you know what question or problem you are tackling, and what you want to do with the results. This will allow you to strategize the questions. If you need numbers (how many people think "ABC" or "XYZ"), creating multiple-choice closed-ended questions may be efficient. On the other hand, if you want public opinion about an issue, having respondents provide open-ended free text could be the better option.

A survey offers another angle on your research. You may not want to base your entire thesis on the results as they may be skewed due to the mood the respondents were in, but the results could indicate a direction for you to pursue. What if you get results you did not expect? You may want to do another survey to see if the results were indicative of reality. Some of the initial questions may not get at the "why" behind the answers. Or people may not have answered the questions honestly. You can ask them to be honest, but you cannot force them to be honest. You can boost the probability of honesty by telling them no one will know who answered what – that it is a blind survey – and the responses will be pooled.

It makes sense to mix it up. Give respondents a variety of ways to answer. Try to ask the same question or a couple of questions in different ways, from different angles, if you really need to know something specific. You may want to do a test run of a sample of questions before running the "official" survey to see if the results look promising.

Interviews

Interviews and **focus groups** can deliver rich, targeted information in the exact words of the interviewee. In person and in their own words, respondents may offer nuggets of information you will not get from a survey. And a direct quotation can be a compelling way to conclude a paper if it supports your findings. Interviews are generally done one-on-one, while focus groups are just what they sound like – a group of people responding to focused questions or stimuli. Interviews may be better suited to more intimate questions and focus groups may be ideal for testing something that is easy to talk about in public. There are reasons for using, as well as pros and cons of, each.

Is the interview the most honest of conversations? Perhaps not. As we might do on a first date, we are usually putting forward our best selves. Most people want others to like them. So how would you get an honest answer from someone you are interviewing for a research project? Your best shot is preparation. You are not looking for a relationship with the person, but you want to project warmth and that you are genuinely interested in their answers. Prepare and then practice on your classmates or a friend before the real thing. The first couple of times you interview you will learn as you go what works and what does not.

In focus groups you are going to have the natural dynamic of some people dominating and some being more passive. Some will be tempted to piggyback on what someone else said. But there will be interesting things that develop as a conversation ensues, and sometimes the stimulation of people thinking together, out loud (sometimes called brainstorming), can produce rich fodder for your project. You may find that using a set of interviews or focus groups is a great way to help get a clearer working thesis or data for your ML system design.

User Studies

Actions speak louder than words. The previous two methods we saw are about collecting words – thoughts, ideas, and opinions of potential or real users. But we may learn something very different if we ask them to do something – whether it is using an existing system or a prototype of a new system we designed. For this, you might want a lab-based setting for something that needs supervision or requires confidentiality. How a user interacts with a new product still in the beta stage that may have bugs to be discovered might be moderated in a controlled situation, so you can witness the experience. Of course, there are also computer programs that track a user's experience, so you do not necessarily need to be present, unless witnessing the interaction firsthand is part of your information gathering. Is the artificiality of the lab setting a hindrance to yielding a natural interaction? Possibly, but this may not be important if you are after exacting specifications.

It is common in such studies to use hardware equipment such as an eye-tracker[4] for collecting data about where a user is looking on the screen, heart-rate monitors, electro-conductance monitors to measure emotional responses, and EEG monitors to collect data about brain activity. All of these have become quite sophisticated over time, becoming more powerful, more compact, and able to collect higher-resolution data than in the past.

Often, these tools come with their own software that you can use for analysis. Or they let you export the data in a format (such as XML and CSV) that can be understood by other analysis software. Figure 12.3 shows an example of a heat map that was generated by processing the raw data from an eye-tracker.

In addition to such hardware, you may also need software tools for logging various activities on a system (computer, mobile, etc.). There are several loggers available, and some are free. One such example that my lab uses is Coagmento.[5] (Full disclosure: The author of this book is also the creator of Coagmento.) Coagmento can collect log data (websites visited, queries run, etc.) from within a web browser.

Once you have enough data logged from these studies you can start doing your analysis (DS) and use that interaction data to build a model (ML). Often, such logged data can be instrumental in doing offline and counterfactual evaluations, leading to new A/B testing, which we will see in the next subsection.

12.3.3 A/B Testing

You have seen in various instances in the preceding chapters that once a model is built on training data, it is tested on a test sample. This test sample is usually a smaller dataset compared to the training set, which the model did not see before. The reason behind such a strategy is to test the model's **generalizability**. At its core, generalizability is about making new predictions based on known observations. There are two main types of generalizability.

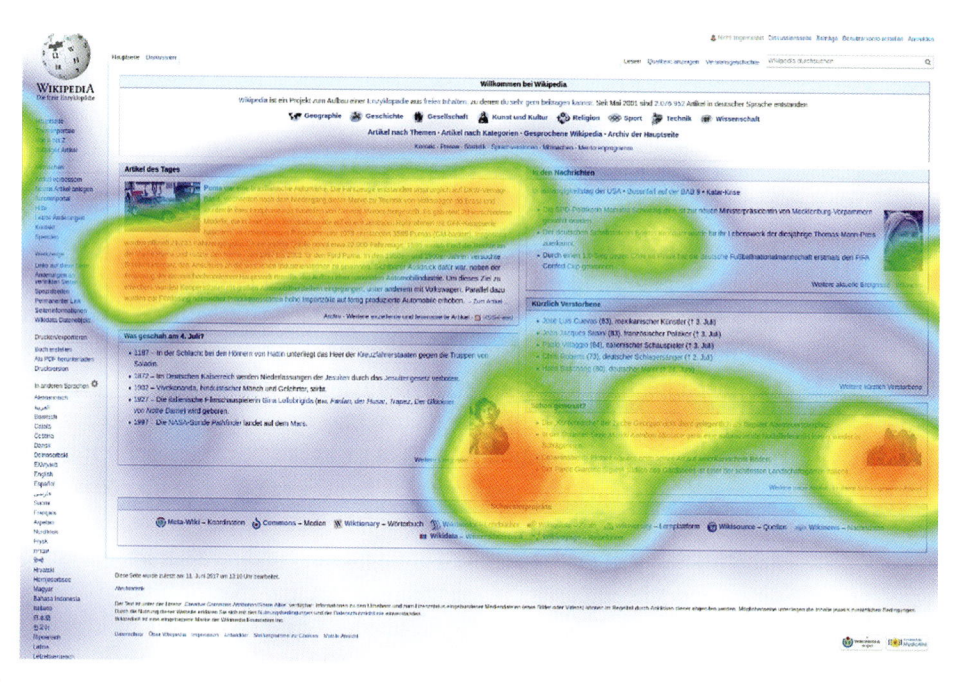

Figure 12.3 An example of a heat map generated from using eye-tracking data. From Holland, J. (n.d.). UX: an art in search of a methodology.[6]

Sometimes when researchers talk about generalizability they are predicting for a larger population from the result of a study on a representative sample. For instance, consider the question, "What percentage of the American population supports the Democratic party?" It would be impossible for the researcher to put this question to every single person who has the right to vote. Instead, the researcher can survey some people and extend their result to the population. In this case, it is important for researchers to survey people who represent the population at large. Therefore, it must be ensured that survey respondents include relevant groups from the larger population in the correct proportions.

Second, the concept of generalizability can help us move from scientific observations to theories or hypotheses. For instance, in the 1940s and 1950s, British researchers Richard Doll and Bradford Hill found that 647 out of 649 lung cancer patients in London hospitals were smokers. This observation prompted many later research studies with larger sample sizes, with different groups of people and different amounts of smoking, and so on. When the results from these studies found similar results across persons, groups, times, and places, the observation was generalized into a theory: Cigarette smoking causes lung cancer.

In the case of A/B testing, the first kind of generalizability is being applied. To test the generalizability of a model, an important step is to separate data into training and testing sets. Typically, when dividing a dataset into a training set and testing set, there are a couple of important factors that need to be considered. First, as demonstrated in various examples in previous chapters, a bigger chunk of the data goes to training, and a smaller portion is set aside for testing. Moreover, the separation must be unbiased. Specifically, the data should be randomly sampled to help ensure that the testing and training sets are similar in terms of variation and representing the population.

Sometimes you may come across other variations of this separation, such as training–validation–testing sets. In this case, the training is done is little bit more rigorously. As you have seen before, some of the data mining models may introduce some form of bias, such as overfitting, while creating the data. To reduce the effect of bias, a validation set is used. Take the example of the decision-tree algorithm. During the training phase the training dataset is used to adjust the decision boundaries. However, such adjustment may introduce overfitting into the model, especially in the case where the model tries to reduce the error in each iteration and does not stop until the error is minimized. While doing so, the model may lose generalizability. This occurs when the decision boundaries are adjusted so well that the model can explain the current dataset but cannot do so for other samples of the same population.

In those cases, a separate validation set is used to reduce the overfitting. This set is not used for training; instead, as the name suggests, this set is used for validating the accuracy of the model before you test it on a larger population. In the example of a decision-tree model you will not use a validation set to further adjust the decision boundaries. Rather, you will verify that any increase in accuracy over the training dataset yields an increase in accuracy over a dataset that has not been shown to the model before, or at least the model has not been trained on it.

The above discussion of training and testing is all about knowing which variables are important for your model and figuring out to what extent they matter. However, often you may come across scenarios where you will not be able to decide or even guess which variable to choose among many, or which version of the same variable is more effective in explaining the response. What then? Fortunately, there is a way to test the importance of competing alternate variables and decide which one is best. This is known as **A/B testing**, typically used with web analytics for figuring out the best online or direct mail promotional and marketing strategies for a business. A/B testing is a controlled experiment with two variants, *A* and *B*, where the subject's response is tested by comparing the response of variable *A* against variable *B*, to determine which of the two variables is more effective. Let's look at an example and see how it works.

A food delivery startup wants to generate sales through its website by running an advertising campaign with discount codes. The company is not sure which is the best channel for customer acquisition: personal email or social media. So it creates two versions of the same advertisement, one meant for its social media channel, "Use this promotional offer code AX! Hurry!" and the other meant for a personal email campaign, "Use this promotional offer code AY! Hurry!" Everything else about the advertisement remains the same. The company can now monitor the success rate of each channel by analyzing the use of the promotional code and come up with better strategies for new client acquisition.

Note that A/B testing does not mean you get to experiment with only two (*A* and *B*) conditions. You can have several conditions/treatments. Of course, having many conditions will increase the complexity of your study design and analysis, and create a greater demand for samples/recruitments. This may become prohibitively expensive for academic research, but for a professional website or a service that has tens or hundreds of millions of users, this may not be a big issue. Not surprisingly, A/B testing is a popular method for evaluation in commercial organizations.

12.3.4 Counterfactual Evaluation

Imagine you built a system based on Algorithm A. Whether that system is working well or not, you wonder how it would do under Algorithm B. Since this is a new algorithm, you do not have any usage data with Algorithm B to be able to compare it with Algorithm A. One option at this point is to do a live A/B test. But as we saw earlier, there are costs and dangers with A/B testing. For example, if we are still in the very early stage of explorations for a new algorithm, we could have too many parameters that we have not been able to tune. Our thinking or approach may not be mature enough to provide a reasonable service to our users, and we do not want to harm our users (too much) in the process. And yet, we want to ask the question, "What if our service was driven by Algorithm B instead of Algorithm A?"

This is a counterfactual question. Simply put, a counterfactual is the alternative of factual; it is a "What if ..." scenario. Currently, our service runs with Algorithm A. That is the fact. Now, we are interested in a counterfact – what if our service ran with Algorithm B? Can we answer this? It seems impossible. We could run our service using Algorithm A for one week and then with Algorithm B for one week and compare our results. But what if things changed between the two weeks? Even if there are no major changes in the world and the system, there may be many small differences that we do not even think or know about. In other words, if we find any differences between the Algorithm A run and Algorithm B run, we cannot say for sure that those differences were due to the differences in those algorithms alone.

Okay, so testing those algorithms back-to-back is not a good idea. What about testing them at the same time, but on different sets of users? This approach is quite common, and is exactly what we saw previously in A/B testing. A/B testing allows you to rule out any temporal effects, but you may still have many other hidden variables confounding your process. A large sample size and careful design considerations can ensure the two randomized groups are well balanced, giving you a better chance of appropriately evaluating the differences between these two algorithms. But as you have already seen, this can get expensive. First, you must invest a lot of time and effort to understand and rule out as many confounding variables as possible. Second, you must get a large sample size. Even after all that, there are going to be imperfections. You just hope they are not as bad. But the more radically different your new algorithm is, the smaller that hope is.

An alternative to either settling for offline evaluation or bearing the cost for A/B testing is **counterfactual evaluation**. This evaluation method is technically a form of offline evaluation, but it typically uses data from a live system and is meant to predict how well a system would do in a live setting.

Counterfactuals are founded on the idea of causality. In a typical data collection system we have our actual data or observations, or facts, for which we can see the effects (user satisfaction, task performance, etc.). We could take such data and build predictive models using techniques such as regression and classification. While doing so, we are inherently extrapolating from correlations to causality. How? For example, suppose in the data we

Table 12.3 The three-layer causal hierarchy.

Level	Typical activity	Typical question	Examples
1. Association $P(y\|x)$	Seeing	What is? How would seeing x change my belief in y?	What does a symptom tell me about a disease? What does a survey tell us about the election results?
2. Intervention $P(y\|do(x), z)$	Doing, intervening	What if? What if I do x?	What if I take aspirin, will my headache be cured? What if we ban cigarettes?
3. Counterfactuals $P(y_x\|x', y')$	Imagining, retrospection	Why? Was it x that caused y? What if I had acted differently?	Was it the aspirin that stopped my headache? Would Kennedy be alive had Oswald not shot him? What if I had not been smoking the past two years?

Source: Pearl, J. (2018) Theoretical impediments to machine learning with seven sparks from the causal revolution. arXiv: 1801.04016v1.

Table 12.4 Treatment for heart attack (fictitious data).

Patient (X_i)	Stent	Drugs	Bypass
1	x	1	x
2	0	x	x
3	x	x	0
4	0	x	x
5	x	1	x
6	x	0	x
7	1	x	x
8	x	x	1

have two quantities x and y that are correlated. We could use regression to build a model that can take in a value of x and predict y. This indirectly implies that x is causing y. But we do not know that for sure. Maybe it is just coincidence. Regardless, most of the time that is alright with us. But this becomes an issue if we want to ask questions about the relationship between x and y. What if y could happen without x? What happens if we take away x? Will y still happen the same way? These are counterfactual questions. And to answer them, we need to establish that there is a causal relationship between x and y. Table 12.3 shows the three levels of causal hierarchy, starting with the "Association" level, which we have explored generously in this book.

Now the question is, how do we use counterfactuals with this understanding of causality? For that, we could write a whole book (and there are books!). So instead, we are going to take a very specific example and work through at least the basics of computing counterfactuals.

Let's take a look at an excellent toy example given by Joachims and Swaminathan in their ACM SIGIR 2016 tutorial.[7] Table 12.4 shows data from treating eight heart attack

Table 12.5 Probability of assigning a patient to a treatment (fictitious data).

Patient (X_i)	Stent	Drugs	Bypass
1	0.3	0.5	0.2
2	0.4	0.4	0.2
3	0.1	0.2	0.7
4	0.2	0.2	0.6
5	0.3	0.6	0.1
6	0.2	0.4	0.4
7	0.2	0.7	0.1
8	0.1	0.1	0.8

patients. There are three possible treatments available: stent, drugs, and bypass. A patient can only be given one of these. In the table the treatment given is indicated using a non-x indicator. 1 or 0 indicate whether the patient survived or not after five years (for example, patient 1 received drugs and survived; patient 2 received a stent and did not survive).

The question is: Which of the treatments is the best? If we simply go with what we are able to observe (facts), we will come out finding each treatment's utility as:

$$\hat{U}(stent) = 1/3, \ \hat{U}(drugs) = 2/3, \ \hat{U}(bypass) = 1/2.$$

But this estimation of utility is suffering from our observation bias. Maybe we are reading too much into these few observations we have. In the absence of what we could not observe, what would help here is to create an estimate of utility that is based on our chances of picking one of the three treatments. First, we assume that the patient was not given a random treatment (if they were, then we are halfway to meeting the requirements for randomized trials and could do a true A/B test). Then, we find out what the chances are that the patient was given one of the three treatments. The probabilities could be based on choosing a given hospital, doctor, or time. The chances are reported in Table 12.5. Yes, in reality these probabilities are perhaps not going to be easy to obtain, but stick with me on this example.

These probabilities, in this context, are called **propensity**. Given that patient 7 had 0.2 propensity to get stent treatment and survived, we should give that survival a higher weight. Similarly, given that patient 3 had 0.7 propensity to get a bypass and did not survive, we should probably not read too much into that. In other words, we should weight the outcomes by the inverse of propensity scores. This inverse is called the **inverse propensity score** (IPS). Taking the IPS into consideration, our utility estimate can now be calculated as:

$$\hat{U}_{ips}(stent) = \frac{1}{8}\left(\frac{1}{0.4}\times 0 + \frac{1}{0.2}\times 0 + \frac{1}{0.2}\times 1\right) = 0.63,$$

$$\hat{U}_{ips}(drugs) = \frac{1}{8}\left(\frac{1}{0.5}\times 1 + \frac{1}{0.6}\times 1 + \frac{1}{0.4}\times 0\right) = 0.46,$$

$$\hat{U}_{ips}(bypass) = \frac{1}{8}\left(\frac{1}{0.7}\times 0 + \frac{1}{0.8}\times 1\right) = 0.16,$$

As you can see, before we thought drugs were the best treatment (0.67), but now we have a better estimator calculation that tells us that a stent is the best treatment. In short, what we have done here is brought what we were not able to observe (counterfactuals) into our calculations of the utility of a treatment.

Now, back to the issue of discovering these propensities. In a medical treatment like the example given here, we may not know such scores. But in many cases we can. Think about three different systems that decide what kind of recommendation to show to a user. We could control or at least know which of these systems get picked with which probability. For counterfactual evaluations we want to start by figuring out these probabilities or propensities. We could have our best system (so far) being picked 80% of the time and the other two systems with lower probabilities that add up to 20%. Then we measure the outcome (i.e., whether the user clicked on the recommendation). If the user clicks on a recommendation from a low propensity score system we give that a higher weight (through IPS). On the other hand, our current system that is picked 80% of the time does not get as much weight for success or failure. Taken together, this estimate allows us to evaluate the effectiveness of different treatments as if we were doing an A/B test.

ML in Practice: Counterfactual Evaluation for Offline Testing

Most tech companies that have user-facing products are invested in doing counterfactual evaluations. The benefits are obvious. There are just too many parameters, too many features, and too many possibilities to work out, and while most of them are almost always doing A/B tests, there are just not enough live tests that can be done to learn about all those possibilities. Not to mention, many of those possibilities or system configurations could be very bad. Therefore, these companies often have a full pipeline for doing counterfactual evaluation.

The pipeline starts by having an appropriate logging policy. As we saw in this chapter, a central piece for doing counterfactual evaluation is having propensity scores. In the production pipeline, as the user requests are served, the system picks different possibilities (algorithms) with different propensities. These propensities are set by a policy that is either handcrafted or learned. As the system serves those requests, it logs which of the algorithms was picked, what was the probability of picking that algorithm, and what was the outcome of serving that request. Later, this data can be used to assess the effectiveness of those algorithms.

This does not necessarily end the need for A/B testing, but it helps narrow down the focus and avoid the mistake of deploying harmful systems that could be costly. The idea of estimating counterfactuals is also helpful in learning. In many systems that offer recommendations or adjust their interface to a given user and a given context (for instance, Netflix and Spotify), it is very common to use similar techniques to learn in real time to optimize the balance of exploitation (give users what they want) and exploration (give them a bit of diversity).

12.3.5 Adversarial Learning

As ML systems get integrated into most aspects of our lives, there are those who want to work against them – sometimes for philosophical or privacy reasons, and other times for maleficence. For example, to avoid detection by spam filters, a spammer can misspell what the filter considers "bad" words and insert many "good" words. This may make the spam filter miss that message as potential spam. Here is a specific example: A machine-manipulated dog image was used to fool an ML system into classifying it as a cat.[8] These techniques and attempts fall under an area of ML called adversarial learning. In essence, the objective here is to learn to evade an ML system.

While these examples may give the impression that adversarial learning is all bad, it can in fact be a useful tool for making ML systems better. For example, adversarial learning techniques are used in auditing algorithms to ensure they do not have leaks or weak spots. We will see this in the next chapter when we talk about accountability and fairness in AI systems. Adversarial learning can also be used for counterfactual situations. For example, in a recommender system, if we want to ask a "what if" question ("What if I want a different outcome than what is recommended?"), we could design an adversarial learning-based approach that tries to generate that counterfactual outcome by learning to change the existing model.

12.4 Summary

Now that we have seen how ML systems are designed, deployed, and tested in real-world applications, let's think about how it all connects. Let's consider an example. Imagine you are building a recommendation service within an e-commerce site. Where do DS and ML come in here?

If this service is already functional, you have an existing algorithm driving it. To understand how effective that algorithm is, the DS team can look at the data behind that algorithm. This could include data about what actions users are taking (clicks, scrolls), what items are being presented to them in what context, and how it all relates to certain business metrics, such as impressions (how often people view an item), interaction rate, and purchase rate. They may also want to look at certain midstream and downstream metrics such as monthly active users, user retention, and user conversion (e.g., how many users sign up for a premium membership). Based on these analyses, the DS team can develop insights and make recommendations. For example, they could come up with an insight that new users tend to spend more time on the site, but less time looking at the recommendations. Based on that insight, they may propose a hypothesis to test about a relationship between a user class (new vs. regular) and the nature of the page or screen layout. This can then be tested using a live A/B test. The DS team can help design this experiment, working closely with the production team of engineers to make sure it meets certain latency requirements, and deploy it. The A/B test could run for a few days to a few weeks. After that, the DS team can analyze the data collected through that test and provide their findings about that hypothesis. This may lead to design changes in the UI or the algorithm driving the recommendations.

The ML team can work very closely with these analyses. In fact, it is now common for a single team to own the whole feature pipeline, with both DS and ML people working on the same team. In the above example, the ML folks can help with the design and training of a new or revised algorithm. They could take the data from the past user interactions with the existing system and feed it into a new approach. For example, they could use the past log data to learn various items' conversion rates – that is, how often an item that was viewed was purchased. Then they could try to come up with a new algorithm that optimizes that conversion rate in various scenarios. This is often done through simulations on existing data. This could then lead to a new algorithm or adjustments in the existing one, ready to be tested.

In cases where we do not have past data (often when we have a completely new algorithm), and an A/B test is considered too expensive or inappropriate, the ML engineers and scientists can design a counterfactual learning and evaluation experiment. For this, they can work with DS folks to create new logging policies and figure out what kind of and how much data will be needed. Once enough data is collected, an analysis using counterfactual evaluation methods can be done. The results could inform us if we need to do an A/B test, and if so, which algorithms and parameters would be the most promising to test.

Key Terms

- **Data mining** involves understanding the nature of the data to gain insight into the problem that generated the dataset in the first place, or what issues may arise in the future.
- **A/B testing**: A live study where there is at least one control group and at least one treatment group.
- **Counterfactuals**: Learning or evaluating alternative facts, such as what would have happened if the same subjects had received different treatments.
- **Propensity** is a probability associated with the likelihood of a data sample being assigned to a treatment or a condition.
- **Inverse propensity score (IPS)** is calculated by inversing the propensity value, and provides a weight of outcomes with respect to a treatment.

Conceptual Questions

1. What is offline evaluation? Give two examples of offline evaluation methods. Focus on what kind of data is being used, how it was collected, and what kind of ML models are built using it.

2. What are two pros and cons of A/B testing?

3. What is a scenario where offline evaluation is better than live A/B testing? Give a scenario where the reverse is true.

4. User research can be expensive, but it could provide the kind of data we may not get from other methods. Describe a scenario where you would have such a need.

5. How can adversarial learning be useful in designing a better ML system?

Hands-on Problems

Problem 12.1

Your bank has made several loans, each of which comes with some amount of risk. This risk assessment is done using an ML system. This system provides a prediction for which of the loans will default and which will not. As you analyze last year's performance you want to figure out how often your system was right. The results are given in Table 12.6.

Using this information, calculate accuracy, precision, and recall for both "default" and "not default." Also calculate the F-measure for your system.

Problem 12.2

Pick a two-class classification problem you have worked on before – perhaps one from an earlier chapter. Briefly describe what the problem is and present the 2 × 2 table indicating how the classifier did on test data. Now, calculate accuracy, precision, and recall for both classes. Also calculate the F-measure for this model.

Table 12.6 Bank loan data for Problem 12.1.

	Defaulted	Not defaulted
Predicted to default	23	9
Predicted to not default	4	132

Further Reading and Resources

- Dandekar, N. (2016). Intuitive explanation of learning to rank (and RankNet, LambdaRank and LambdaMART). https://medium.com/@nikhilbd/intuitive-explanation-of-learning-to-rank-and-ranknet-lambdarank-and-lambdamart-fe1e17fac418.
- www.iro.umontreal.ca/~nie/IFT6255/Books/Learning-to-rank.pdf.

Notes

1. https://docs.oracle.com/cd/B28359_01/datamine.111/b28129/process.htm#CHDFGCIJ.
2. www.kdd.org/kdd-cup.
3. University of Nebraska Medical Center (n.d.). The area under an ROC curve. http://gim.unmc.edu/dxtests/roc3.htm.
4. Wikipedia. Eye tracking. https://en.wikipedia.org/wiki/Eye_tracking.
5. http://coagmento.org.
6. http://johnnyholland.org/2009/10/ux-an-art-in-search-of-a-methodology.
7. Joachims, T., & Swaminathan, A. (2016). SIGIR 2016 tutorial on counterfactual evaluation and learning for search, recommendation and ad placement. www.cs.cornell.edu/~adith/CfactSIGIR2016.
8. *Wired*. AI has a hallucination problem that's proving tough to fix. www.wired.com/story/ai-has-a-hallucination-problem-thats-proving-tough-to-fix.

13 Responsible AI

What do you need?
- A good conceptual understanding of how different classes of ML algorithms work.
- Knowledge of how A/B testing and counterfactual evaluations are done.
- Various metrics for offline evaluation, especially for classifiers.

What will you learn?
- How ML and AI systems introduce bias and unfairness.
- The connections between bias, diversity, and misinformation.
- The principles of responsible AI as they are practiced in academia and industry.
- Technical and regulatory efforts to curb bias and increase transparency in AI/ML systems.

13.1 Introduction

In this book so far we have been concerned with learning new machine learning (ML) tools and techniques to help us solve a variety of problems. Most of the time we made certain assumptions about the problem, the data, and the solution. We assumed that the problem was well-formed and important or necessary to address. We assumed that the data was ethically sourced and free of bias. We assumed that the solution was just and fair. As it turns out, many times these assumptions are flawed. Enter the dark side of ML and artificial intelligence (AI).

In the USA, a tool named COMPAS (Correctional Offender Management Profiling for Alternative Sanctions) is used by judges as well as parole and probation officers to assess the risk of a defendant offending again. Larson et al. found[1] that Black defendants were far more likely than White defendants to be incorrectly judged to be at a higher risk of recidivism, while White defendants were more likely than Black defendants to be incorrectly flagged as low risk. Why is this? This system is essentially a classifier that is using its training data to build a classification model and use that model to make decisions on the test data. The training data it uses contains unfiltered bias and inequality when it comes to representing defendants of different races. In other words, the system is perpetuating the inherent biases and inequalities we have in our society.

In 2016, a company named Beauty AI ran an online beauty competition to be judged by their AI. More than 600,000 people from 100 countries entered the contest, with the AI picking male and female winners from five age categories. But this AI agent seemed to be racist,[2] as almost all the winners it picked were White. The organizers blamed this bias on the data used for training what beauty should look like. White people are disproportionately overrepresented in the labeled data. In fact, this has been the case for much of AI's history so far. Over the decades of AI development, the datasets we have created and used have oversampled, if not exclusively represented, White, male, and Western populations. So many systems and algorithms have been trained on such data, deployed in real-world applications, and adjusted repeatedly to keep confirming the biases that they originally carried.

Most of these models and systems also tend to be complex and opaque, making it difficult to know why they are behaving the way they do. As people (including leaders and policymakers) blindly trust these models to make important decisions for individuals and society at large, it becomes even harder to tease apart the issues with the data, algorithms, and policies, and to assess the part they play in making decisions biased, unfair, and lacking in accountability. In the next section we will run through a specific scenario to understand that this problem is not one that we can fix by simply changing the data or the algorithm. Since many AI systems are tightly integrated in our lives, they can no longer be treated as isolated entities.

This chapter is unique in many ways. You will not find a devoted chapter like this in most ML books, but the set of issues under the broad umbrella of "responsible AI" are becoming increasingly important to study and address everywhere AI and ML systems are developed and used. This chapter also calls for and trains for a different skill than the rest of the book. As you may recall from Chapter 1, for doing ML you need skills such as mathematics, programming, computer and data literacy, communication, and critical thinking. It is that last skill that this chapter will focus on. We started working on that skill in the last chapter, but this is where we go deeper as we question the use of all that we have learned in this book. And given its nature, this chapter will also be light on hands-on practices and heavy on critical-thinking questions and exercises.

Let's begin by asking what responsible AI is. We are not implying that AI can be responsible or irresponsible. What responsible AI really refers to is the responsibility that we all need to take in designing, deploying, and using an AI system. The responsibility is to understand and mitigate the issues of bias, unfairness, accountability, transparency, and privacy. There are also ethical considerations in many cases – asking not just what AI *could* do, but what AI *should* do.

13.2 Diversity vs. Misinformation: A Case Study

A typical search or recommendation algorithm that is taught in a graduate class is quite *innocent*. It typically does some form of similarity matching between a query or a user context (e.g., the page or app screen the user is on) and the available information (e.g., documents, items to sell). It will often have a component for accounting for the user's past behaviors as well as how other users with similar queries and contexts behaved. Finally, it can add some amount of personalization that may include information about the user and his/her location. What such an algorithm does not account for are various anomalies and existing biases present in the data, user behaviors, and user contexts. On top of that, the way these algorithms are evaluated – both in academic settings and in practical applications – is often flawed. For instance, one of the factors contributing to ranking an object is how many people find it relevant, or how often they click on it. We know that people tend to click on sensational headlines, and thus, even when an item that is not relevant to a given situation shows up in search results, many users will click on it. A search algorithm considers this a positive signal and learns that the displayed item should be given higher weight and rank. Thus, that item will keep showing up at higher ranks for many users, and even more people will click on it.

Compounding this problem further is the fact that most people blindly believe in top search results and seldom venture beyond. Thus, the top results get more clicks, which gives the underlying algorithm a positive signal, making it continue to rank these results higher. The algorithm is not wrong here, but it has failed to account for the underlying anomaly in information and human nature. This is an example of a *bias loop*, where one disparity leads to the other, which in turn makes the first one even more pronounced. Many scholars have talked, often very extensively, about data bias, algorithmic bias, and many other forms of biases that exist in almost any computational system. But this notion of a bias loop is often not acknowledged or addressed, as if the whole problem were due to a single form of bias or multiple biases that are acting independently.

To break out of this bias loop, we need to work on both the system side and the user side. For the former, many solutions have been proposed, some of which we will review here. For the latter, very little work has been done, at least in computational sciences. The main reason is that fixing the user side requires more than just coming up with a new algorithm or learning technique; it calls for user education and collaborative actions from multiple parties involved in this loop.

One of the ways scholars have proposed to address various forms of bias in search is by diversifying the information retrieved and presented. This improves the chances for underrepresented and under-clicked objects or topics to arise.

To see if we could fool people with the same technique we used before, we created an online game called "Google or Not." The idea was the same as the one described in the previous section – display two sets of results for a query and ask the user to pick one set. Except, this time, instead of taking any results found through exploration, we manually picked those that contained misinformation (false or debunked information) of some sort (the placement of these results was still picked randomly).[3] Figure 13.1 shows a screenshot for one of these cases.

This game was made available publicly and advertised through various social media channels. Overall, 2100 responses were collected from over 30 countries. When analyzed, we found that about half (52.95%) of the time people chose "google" over the results where one (out of 10) result of misinformation was included, and slightly more (53.93%) times people chose "google" over the case where two results of misinformation were included.[4]

These results are consistent with what we saw before. But the implications here are quite different. Before, we found no statistical difference between the original Google results and those showing some amount of diversity without sacrificing relevance or satisfaction. But now the analysis shows that we could sneak in a couple of results with misinformation or debunked claims, and about half of the people ended up picking the result set that

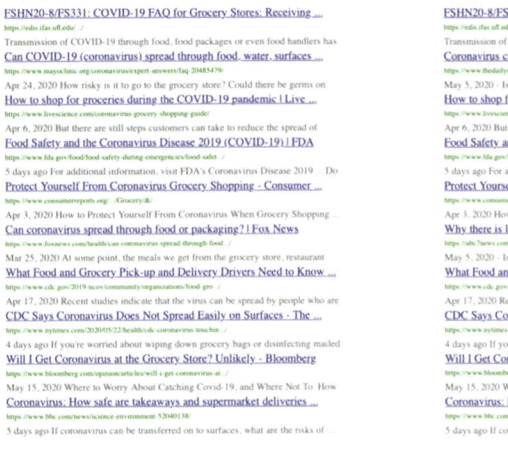

Figure 13.1 A screenshot of the game "Google or Not."

contained those results. Of course, we do not know if these people would have clicked on those malicious results or not, but it does bring up a question about how easy it is to introduce bad content under the pretense of diversity.

It is true that misinformation is a considerable problem on the Web today in general. But what we saw here is more troubling. This is because while not perfect, search engines and other websites can manage to curb many of those bad sites and sources while ranking the relevant results. As we try to introduce diversity in those results, we may end up forcing some information that is harmful but improves our overall standing in terms of diversity and fairness. For example, there are many sites on the Web that deny the Holocaust. Those sites are naturally suppressed by ranking algorithms, preventing them from showing up at higher ranks. But our attempts to bring diversity into search results about the Holocaust may bring some of those sites up to the top 10, giving them attention or clicks that could feed back into the search algorithms as a signal that they are relevant, furthering the positive feedback loop. It is perhaps this danger that triggered Microsoft pulling back on their Bing Multi-Perspective Answers.[5] It is natural for computer and information scientists to look for an algorithmic solution to this problem, but this is more than a computational problem – it is about how we, as a society, think about what is *fair* and *true* and come to an agreement about the basics of fairness and information prevalence.

13.3 Responsible AI in Academia, Industry, and Regulations

The area of responsible AI has received widespread recognition in academia and industry. The programs and groups dealing with this are not always named "Responsible AI," and often they are more specific and purpose-driven, dealing exclusively with one or several of the issues under the broad umbrella of responsible AI. For example, in 2018 I started a research group in my lab called FATE (Fairness, Accountability, Transparency, Ethics) to specifically work on issues of bias and fairness in search and recommender systems.

One of the communities that emerged early on (2018) in this area was the FAT (Fairness, Accountability, Transparency) conference, now called the ACM Conference on Fairness, Accountability, and Transparency (ACM FAccT).[6] As the conference website notes, it is a "computer science conference with a cross-disciplinary focus that brings together researchers and practitioners interested in fairness, accountability, and transparency in socio-technical systems." Many other communities in ML and AI have started hosting workshops, panels, and other events co-located with their conference. For example, the ACM RecSys 2021 conference organized FAccTRec – a workshop on responsible recommendations;[7] the ACM SIGIR 2021[8] conference had two tutorials covering issues of bias and fairness.

Since 2019, NIST (the National Institute of Standards and Technology) in the USA has organized a Fair Ranking track as a part of their annual TREC (Text REtrieval Conference).[9] Through this community-driven forum that provides a platform for competition and cooperation, they have created and provided various datasets and evaluation metrics for assessing fairness in ranking systems.

Many universities and colleges have started developing and running courses, programs, and certificates to address responsible AI. There are also research centers and labs created through university, government, and private funding. Examples include Stanford's Human-Centered AI,[10] MIT's Responsible AI for Social Empowerment and Education,[11] and the University of Washington's RAISE (Responsibility in AI Systems & Experiences),[12] which I had the honor of co-founding and co-directing.

There is an explosion in the growth of ethical and responsible AI in the USA. Companies that explore ethical AI issues received investments totaling more than $100 million in the first half of 2021, following $186 million in 2020.[13] A KPMG survey showed that 77% of government executives aim to increase their use of AI technology, creating new demand for AI ethics training. The academic job market is also being transformed: 47 of 93 job postings returned by a search for *artificial intelligence* mention *bias*, and a search for *responsible AI* returns 18 jobs. Governments, companies, advocacy organizations, and multi-stakeholder groups have published hundreds of ethical AI principles and guidelines in the last few years according to the Berkman Klein Center for Internet & Society and the nonprofit AlgorithmWatch.[14] The National Science Foundation (NSF) and Amazon committed $10 million each toward research, NIST is developing AI standards, and the Department of Defense (DoD) is incorporating responsible AI principles in its work. Several efforts have been made to introduce regulations, though not all have been meaningful or effective. For example, the Algorithmic Accountability Act of 2019, while being well intentioned, has stalled in Congress and has thus far not been shown to be very effective or impactful. But new efforts toward regulations and policymaking have continued, raising the possibility for more progress in this area.

Europe is not behind on this. In fact, one of the first modern responsibility regulations of AI technologies was proposed by the European Union.[15] The regulations include restrictions on mass surveillance and the use of AI to manipulate people. The Federal Trade Commission (FTC) in the USA followed up with its own regulations to address fairness and equity in AI systems.[16] They cite a study in the *Journal of the American Medical Informatics Association* that suggests that if the models for COVID-19 predictions use data that reflect existing racial bias in healthcare delivery, AI that was meant to benefit all patients may worsen healthcare disparities for people of color.[17] Similarly, the Australian government has started building a roadmap for sustainable and fair development of AI, stating that, "For Australia to realise the benefits of AI, people need to be able to trust that AI systems are safe, secure and reliable."[18]

Not to be outdone, many big companies have been laying out their own frameworks for responsible AI. Microsoft created the AI, Ethics, and Effects in Engineering and Research (Aether) Committee, which came up with six AI principles: fairness, inclusiveness, reliability and safety, transparency, privacy and security, and accountability. Google ties their responsible AI practices to that of responsible software development, emphasizing aspects such as fairness, interpretability, privacy, and security. Facebook recognizes the following five pillars for responsible AI: privacy and security, fairness and inclusion, robustness and safety, transparency and control, and accountability and governance. If you look around, most tech companies – big and small – have started acknowledging these issues and laying out a framework, at least in principle, to address them. But the big challenges remain. These frameworks are often incomplete and not accompanied by any measurable action. They also tend to be disconnected from the business objectives these companies have. This makes it hard for employees and partners to take any meaningful actions to accomplish their lofty (and theoretical) goals. As this is an emerging area with lots of attention from regulatory agencies, watchdogs, and governance policymakers, we will continue seeing new developments in the coming years.

13.4 Bias and Fairness

In several places in this book we have discussed the issues of bias and fairness in different contexts. We will continue that topic here as we wrap up our coverage of ML.

13.4.1 Where Does Bias Come From?

Bias in ML may come from the source data, algorithmic or system bias, or cognitive bias. Imagine that you are analyzing criminal records for two districts. The records include 10,000 residents from district A and 1000 residents from district B. In district A, 100 residents have committed crimes in the past year, versus 50 district B residents. Will you conclude that people from district A are more likely to be criminals than people from district B? If you simply compare the number of criminals in the past year you are very likely to reach this conclusion. But if you look at the crime rate you will find that district A's crime rate is 1%, which is less than district B's. Based on this analysis, the previous conclusion is biased toward district A residents. This type of bias is generated due to the method of analysis; thus, we call it **algorithmic bias** or **system bias**.

Does the crime-based analysis guarantee an unbiased conclusion? The answer is no. It could be possible that both districts have a population of 10,000. This indicates that the crime records have the complete statistics of district A, yet only partial statistics for district B. Depending on how the data is collected, 5% may or may not be the true crime rate for district B. As a consequence, we may still arrive at a biased conclusion. This type of bias is inherent in the data we are examining; thus, we call it **data bias**. The third type of bias is **cognitive bias**, which arises from our perception of the presented data. Suppose you are given the conclusions from two crime analysis agencies. You tend to believe one over the other because the former has a better reputation, even though the former may have the biased conclusion.

Read a real-world case of machine learning algorithms being racially biased on recidivism here: www.nytimes.com/2017/10/26/opinion/algorithm-compas-sentencing-bias.html. Can you think of what types of bias exist in this case? Think about the data being analyzed, the algorithms employed, and the decisions people made based on the algorithm's results.

In reality, due to multiple factors such as data distribution, the collection process, and different analysis methods and measurement standards, it is easy to end up with a biased dataset and biased conclusions about the data. We need to be careful when collecting, processing, and analyzing data.

13.4.2 Bias Is Everywhere

With the explosion of data and technologies we are immersed in all kinds of data applications. Think of the news you read every day on the Internet, the music you listen to through service providers, the ads displayed while you are browsing web pages, the products recommended to you when shopping online, the information you found through search engines. Bias can be present everywhere without people's awareness. As the saying goes, "you are what you eat": the data you consume is so powerful that it can shape your views, preferences, judgments, and even decisions in many aspects of your life. Say you want to know whether some food is good or bad for your health. A search engine returns 10 pages of results. The first result and most of the results on the first page say that the food is healthy. To what extent do you believe the search results? After glancing at the results on the first page, will you conclude that the food is beneficial or at least the benefits outweigh the harm? How likely are you to check the results on the second page? Are you aware that the second page may contain results that say the food is harmful – that the first page results are biased? As a data scientist, it is important to be careful to avoid biased outcomes. But as a human being who lives in the world of data, it is more important to be aware of the bias that exists in your daily data consumption.

> **FYI: Simpson's Paradox**
>
> In a classification problem we typically care about the overall accuracy of the classifier. But that single number could be misleading. Imagine you have two classes in your dataset. Class A has 90 instances and Class B has 10 instances. You use these 100 data points to train a classifier. If this classifier ends up labeling all the 100 points as "Class A" during testing, it will achieve 90% accuracy. That seems quite high, and we should be happy with the results. But if you look carefully, you discover that the classifier is right 100% of the time for Class A but wrong 100% of the time for Class B. This phenomenon of having different trends for individual groups and all the groups combined is called Simpson's paradox.
>
> In Figure 13.2 we have two hypothetical groups, blue and red, plotted. If we were learning regression for them individually we would see their lines going upward. But if we combine these two groups to find a regression line for the overall data points, we get the dotted line that is trending downward.

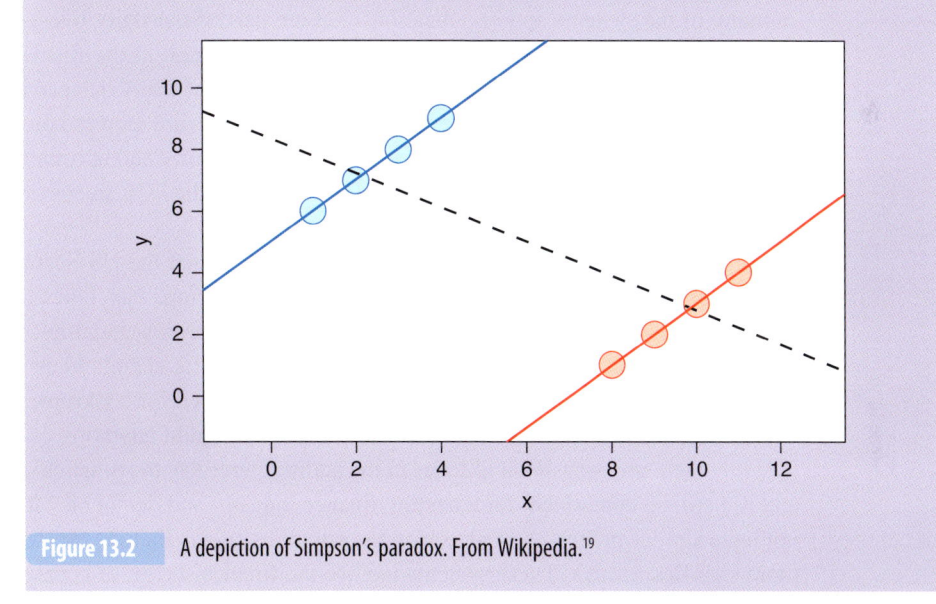

Figure 13.2 A depiction of Simpson's paradox. From Wikipedia.[19]

13.4.3 Bias vs. Fairness

It is possible that bias leads to unfairness, but can something that is biased also be fair? The answer is yes. Consider bias as the skewed view of protected groups (e.g., race, gender, religious beliefs), and fairness as a subjective measurement of the data or the way data is handled. In other words, bias and fairness are not necessarily contradictory. Consider the employee diversity in a US company. All but one employee are US citizens. Is the employment structure biased toward US citizens? Yes, if this is a result of the US citizens being favored during the hiring process. Is it a fair structure? Yes and no. According to the Rooney Rule – which requires that at least one candidate from an underrepresented group be considered for any opening – this is fair since the company hired at least one minority. According to statistical parity this is unfair since the number of US citizens and noncitizens are not equal. In general, bias is easy and direct to measure, but fairness is subtler due to the various subjective concerns. There are just so many different fairness definitions to choose from, some of which are contradictory. But the following three categories of fairness are often used as a benchmark while talking about group or system fairness:

1. statistical parity
2. disparate impact
3. disparate treatment.

13.5 Accountability and Auditing

In many of the systems and organizations that are part of our daily lives, there is often a process for auditing. For example, auditing is very common in the finance and business world. Auditing typically involves an external, independent entity that carries out a review of a business's financial processes. Sometimes these audits are required on a regular basis, such as for a publicly traded company, to show responsibility and accountability. In other cases audits are requested by a regulatory authority (e.g., the FCC in the USA) as a part of an investigation or a settlement.

Auditing has existed for centuries, but it was in 1934 that the US Securities Exchange Act made it a legal requirement for all publicly traded companies. Does it always work? No. One of the most famous cases of its failure is the Enron scandal in 2001, where the company was able to hide important information from its shareholders and regulatory authorities. Once the scandal became public and Enron filed for bankruptcy, the company that was its auditor – Arthur Andersen – lost the right to audit anymore.

While there are occasional glitches in the auditing process, the practice generally works and is a critical component for a healthy finance industry and democracy itself. But we do not have similar processes in place for algorithmic systems that govern our lives in even more significant ways. These systems include the finance sector, of course, but also most other important aspects of our lives, including healthcare, education, and political systems. Why should we not audit them as well? There have been so many cases of misinformation and disinformation in algorithmic systems we use every day, such as Google, Facebook, Amazon, and others, and yet we lack even a simple approach to audit these systems and hold them accountable. There are a few cases of legal processes in the USA and in the European Union going after these and other organizations for the harm caused by their algorithms, but for the most part these companies have remained unaccountable.

Algorithmic accountability refers to assigning responsibility for how an algorithm is designed and deployed, and the harms it causes to individuals and society. This falls under regulations and governmental action in most countries. But there are technological solutions as well. Brent Mittelstadt from the Oxford Internet Institute provides a method of algorithmic auditing based on the idea of discrimination detection in data mining.[20] He argues for functionality auditing of algorithms during development. Taking a segment from p. 4995, an algorithm's functioning can be verified at three stages of development:

1. *Definition*: It should be proven that an algorithm is mathematically correct.
2. *Implementation*: It should be proven that a piece of code correctly implements a well-defined algorithm into a technological system according to its specifications.
3. *Configuration*: It should be proven that the system has been appropriately configured to provide accurate results.

This area is still relatively new and unexplored. A review of algorithmic auditing published in February 2021 by Koshiyama and others[21] provides an overview of some of the recent developments. One of the challenges with algorithmic auditing is that beyond the technical advancements needed to audit an algorithm from outside an organization, we need to be able to channel the findings and recommendations through an enforcement entity (e.g., the FCC in the USA). But such a framework is currently lacking. Many of us who work in this area hope that we can keep making advancements from the technical side and one day the legal system will be ready to leverage them.

Let's look at a case study to understand how auditing works that allows us to point out not only a problem, but also a fix. This case study is based on the work done in the lab that I direct.

Image search engines provide an important information-seeking interface for people to explore the world. According to a recent survey, major image search engines like Google, Yahoo, and Bing process billions of queries every day. Therefore, the quality of image search results can significantly influence how people perceive and view the world. One straightforward but vital image quality measurement is the fairness and unbiasedness of images returned by search engines for given queries. When unfairness and bias are demonstrated in image search results, the public is exposed to an unreal and biased virtual world.

Gender bias is one of the most common and well-studied demographic image biases. For example, an early study by Kay and others[22] reported a problem with how Google image search often characterizes gender stereotypes. Singh and Joachims[23] famously showed an example of a Google image search for "CEO" that contained primarily White men. Since these related studies drew great attention and spawned wide discussion from the public and academia, Google and Bing have fixed such reported gender bias in their returned images. For example, now if you do the Google image search you get something quite different, typically images that show men and women of different color, offering a huge departure from what there was before.

Does that mean Google (and other search engines) fixed the problem? This is what we asked when we started auditing the Google image search. We decided to do this using a technique called adversarial learning (see the FYI box in the previous chapter). In the simplest sense, this meant querying the Google image search system in different ways to see if there is a systematic absence or presence of bias. It turned out that if you query for "CEO" with some other qualifiers, such as the names of countries, the old biases show up again. If you search with a few variations of "CEO," such as "CEO United States" and "CEO UK," you can see that once again we are presented with results primarily showing White men (go ahead, try these queries on your own). In other words, Google seems to have fixed specific instances of queries, but not the underlying algorithm. This has become a common practice among tech companies that fix the high-profile problem on the surface to evade media and government criticism, without fixing the process or algorithm behind the scenes, perpetuating the problem.

We continued with our auditing process and analyzed image search results for 10 different professions. In almost all of them we found that the search results disproportionately represent the actual gender distribution in those professions. In other words, the underlying algorithm is unfair and biased. But we do not want to single out Google here. We looked at other search engines as well – Bing from the USA, Baidu from China, Naver from South Korea, and Yandex from Russia. They all exhibited a similar, deeper underlying problem. Superficially fixing individual queries may be alright for evading media attention, but it does not solve the problem. The question is: Can this problem even be solved?

The short answer is yes. We have proposed several methods for automatically and more objectively balancing the rankings.[24] The description of these methods is beyond the scope of this book, but the point to remember is this: The problem is fixable if we direct our energy to the right places. Instead of doing quick fixes we should study and address the core issues that create biases in AI systems. In this particular case we also saw how auditing can work in practice and at least point out the problems, if not possible solutions.

> **ML in Practice: Addressing Responsible AI**
>
> While most tech organizations have started recognizing the importance of doing socially responsible things with their AI systems, it is still unclear exactly how they are addressing the problem. Some of the efforts we see in the industry stem from regulations and bad publicity surrounding issues of inequality and unfairness in race and gender. Often, these are quick fixes with little to no long-term oversight. Among the big tech companies, Google and Facebook have been more in the news about these issues, but almost no organization is clear of them. A few years ago the main issues under responsible AI that these companies paid attention to were privacy (mostly data privacy) and security. But with the recent developments in AI and high-profile departures of distinguished names from various companies due to lack of recognition of other issues listed in this chapter, there is increased pressure to do more.
>
> On the positive side, this means these companies need more people who can help them do responsible AI in a better way than they have so far. In fact, everybody wants to do better here. That is why we have started seeing more programs, efforts, and funds in this space. For example, the US NSF, a government agency, has teamed up with Amazon to create and support programs related to fairness in AI.

13.6 Transparency and Explainability

Looking back at the earlier days of AI, one could say that things were simpler. Many AI agents were based on rule-based systems. These rules were either handcrafted or derived from data and processes that were well understood. Sure, there were still systems that were complex, nonlinear, and hard to interpret. But if we look at AI and ML development in recent years, the balance has reversed. These days, it is very difficult to find simple and easily interpretable AI systems in practice. Most systems we use that employ some form of AI or ML are complex and opaque. You can blame that on the amount and heterogeneity of the data we use for training, the complexity of the models we are building, or the wide spread of these systems that make it hard to foresee and control how they get used. The chances are it is all of these, and perhaps more.

Arrieta and others[25] provide an excellent review of explainable AI (XAI). They start by defining some of the related terms (p. 84):

1. **Understandability:** The understandability (or equivalently, intelligibility) of a model is how well a human understands its function – how the model works – without any required understanding of its internal structure or the algorithmic means by which the model processes data. Most people understand how a car works without having knowledge of its engine or its battery.

2. **Transparency**: A model is considered to be transparent if it is understandable by itself. Think about a light switch. There is no need for external support or documentation about how it functions; it is usually evident by itself. Since a model can feature different degrees of understandability, transparent models are divided into three categories: simulatable models, decomposable models, and algorithmically transparent models.

3. **Comprehensibility**: When conceived for ML models, comprehensibility refers to the ability of a learning algorithm to represent its learned knowledge in a fashion understandable by humans.

4. **Interpretability**: Interpretability is the ability to explain or to provide the meaning of a model in understandable terms to a human.

5. **Explainability**: Explainability is the ability for a human to understand how a model arrived at its results.

These terms are, of course, defined in the context of ML/AI systems, but they are meant to be user-focused. For example, an AI system can reveal its full code or algorithm, but that is not the kind of transparency or explainability we're interested in. What we really care about here is the end-user being able to understand how that system operates and makes decisions. Take an example of a car. It has a very complex mechanism inside, but most of us do not benefit from having that explained to us. What matters to us is that we understand how the car works on the physical level; how it reacts when we press the gas pedal or the brakes, or when we turn the steering wheel. If a car makes a decision on its own, such as steering itself when accidental lane departure happens, we understand why that behavior happened even though it was not a result of our steering. That level of transparency is sufficient for most use cases. However, now we have entered a new era of (primarily driver-assisted) self-driving cars. These cars can make more complex decisions, including changing lanes, speeding up or slowing down (adaptive cruise control), and braking. As cars start making more decisions for us and move to being completely self-driving, it becomes even more important that we understand their decision-making process, and, when needed (e.g., in the case of an accident), be able to explain in human-interpretable terms why the car made or failed to make certain decisions.

Another place where transparency and explainability have caught a lot of attention is in addressing "what if" questions. Imagine you applied for a bank loan and were denied. You may want to know what you could have done differently to get that loan approved. Perhaps you needed to show more income or collateral. Perhaps if your credit score had been 5% higher the outcome would have been different. You want an explanation – not so much for what you received, but for the alternative. This is the case of **counterfactual explanation**. Here, the goal is to create an explanation for alternative outcomes. This may help people correct mistakes or change their behaviors to achieve their desired objectives. Consider another application – fitness planning. You tried one plan that a healthcare provider or an AI presented, and it did not give you the results you hoped for. Now you are wondering what would have happened if you had tried a different plan. Can your provider or system explain to you what would have happened had you tried the alternative?

Explainability is still an evolving area, with much to be discussed, decided, and discovered. But for now, let's look at a summary table from Arrieta et al.'s work that presents how different types of ML models provide transparency (or not) (Table 13.1).

Table 13.1 Various types of ML models and their associated transparencies.

Model	Simulatability	Decomposability	Algorithmic transparency
Linear/logistic regression	Predictors are human-readable and interactions among them are kept to a minimum	Variables are still readable, but the number of interactions and predictors involved in them have grown to force decomposition	Variables and interactions are too complex to be analyzed without mathematical tools
Decision trees	A human can simulate and obtain the prediction of a decision tree on his/her own, without requiring any mathematical background	The model comprises rules that do not alter data whatsoever, and preserves their readability	Human-readable rules that explain the knowledge learned from data and allow for a direct understanding of the prediction process
k-nearest neighbors	The complexity of the model (number of variables, their understandability, and the similarity measure under use) matches human naive capabilities for simulation	The number of variables is too high and/or the similarity measure is too complex to be able to simulate the model completely, but the similarity measure and the set of variables can be decomposed and analyzed separately	The similarity measure cannot be decomposed and/or the number of variables is so high that the user must rely on mathematical and statistical tools to analyze the model
Rule-based learners	Variables included in rules are readable, and the size of the rule set is manageable by a human user without external help	The size of the rule set becomes too large to be analyzed without decomposing it into small rule chunks	Rules have become so complicated (and the rule set has grown so much) that mathematical tools are needed for inspecting the model behavior

Model	Simulatability	Decomposability	Algorithmic transparency
General additive models	Variables and the interactions among them as per the smooth functions involved in the model must be constrained within human capabilities for understanding	Interactions become too complex to be simulated, so decomposition techniques are required for analyzing the model	Due to their complexity, variables and interactions cannot be analyzed without the application of mathematical and statistical tools
Bayesian models	Statistical relationships modeled among variables and the variables themselves should be directly understandable by the target audience	Statistical relationships involve so many variables that they must be decomposed in marginals to ease their analysis	Statistical relationships cannot be interpreted even if already decomposed, and predictors are so complex that models can only be analyzed with mathematical tools
Tree ensembles	✗	✗	✗
Support vector machines	✗	✗	✗
Multilayer neural network	✗	✗	✗
Convolutional neural network	✗	✗	✗
Recurrent neural network	✗	✗	✗

Source: Arrieta et al. (2020). Explainable Artificial Intelligence (XAI): Concepts, taxonomies, opportunities and challenges toward responsible AI. *Information Fusion*, *58*, 82–115

13.7 Summary

In the previous section we talked about transparency in self-driving cars. The challenge for self-driving cars when it comes to AI systems goes far beyond transparency. Imagine such a car hitting a pedestrian. Who is then responsible for that injury? The car or its driver? Perhaps the car had to make a choice between hitting one pedestrian and hitting two, and it decided to go with the less terrible option. Is that justified? What if that one pedestrian was a kid and the other two pedestrians were adults? These are not AI questions; they are ethics questions. If a human driver had taken the same actions we would have the same deliberation and it would be up to a judge, a jury, or our societal norms to determine how right or wrong this decision was. But now that we have AI systems starting to make such decisions, it is not clear who holds the responsibility and how we make these systems deliberate on ethics.

We stand at a point in human evolution where is possible that in some fields, such as medicine, ML techniques may be in the process of becoming more efficient in clinical settings than the human doctor. One example is in diagnosing disease from the examination of a sample obtained from a single patient. Machine learning is at a place where accuracy may be on par with or better at detecting cancer than a human with a medical degree. But in a macro sense, the overall healthcare system has a subtle systemic racial bias, so ML may not be where it needs to be yet in predicting overall cancer trends. It would be great if someday IBM's Watson could outsmart human doctors in this realm. A philosophical question is: Is that what we want or need? You may want to check out the article by Char and others[26] if you are interested in the role of ML in health, with implications for ethics.

FYI: Federated Learning and Differential Privacy

One reason privacy is tricky with ML systems is that we need data to be collected from many users and devices and analyzed in the cloud. This aggregation of data is needed to train the ML models. Can we build these models without having to share the data? That is what **federated learning** aims to do.

Federated learning allows the data to stay on users' devices or some nearby local storage (called edge devices) and creates local models or trained parameters that can then be exchanged among the devices or a centralized server. Thus, it facilitates building ML models without having to share raw data. Of course, this comes with some trade-offs. There needs to be a layer in between those end or edge devices and the server (in the case of centralized federated learning). That layer needs to smartly coordinate sharing of models and tuning of parameters to arrive at a single model.

This is different from distributed learning. In distributed learning the goal is to do parallel processing so we can build models faster and do computational operations in real time. In the case of federated learning, all the separate threads could be working with their own kind of data, devices, and logic, without necessarily doing it all synchronously. Working on federated learning algorithms requires knowledge of not only ML, but also computer networking.

A related concept is **differential privacy**. Here, the idea is to process the data on a device and share the analysis without sharing private information about the user or the device. For example, differential privacy can be used to understand the demographic distribution in an area without explicitly knowing every individual's personal demographic information. An algorithm is differentially private if an observer seeing its output cannot tell if a particular individual's information was used in the computation.

A deeper dive into these issues is beyond the scope of this book. But as we wrap up this book, it is important that we at least take away this message: AI/ML systems have serious issues of bias, unfairness, and opaqueness. Their ethical development and execution are going to be paramount as we keep building more complex and capable systems. If we are not mindful of our responsibilities and ethics while designing and testing these systems, we may not be able to fix them later.

Key Terms

- **Misinformation**: False information that is spread, regardless of intent to mislead.
- **Disinformation**: False information, such as about a country's military strength or plans, disseminated by a government or intelligence agency in a hostile act of tactical political subversion.
- **Understandability**: The ability of a human to understand a model's function.
- **Transparency**: The understandability of a model by itself.
- **Comprehensibility**: The ability of a learning algorithm to represent its learned knowledge in a human-understandable fashion.
- **Interpretability**: The ability to explain or to provide the meaning of a model's results in understandable terms to a human.
- **Explainability**: The ability for a human to understand how a model arrived at its results.
- **Counterfactual explanation**: An explanation for the alternate outcome from an AI/ML system.

Conceptual Questions

1. Any system, computational or not, can have bias. Why is this issue of bias particularly bad for an AI/ML system?

2. What are at least two examples of an ML system exhibiting potential bias?

3. Think about two different ML systems that lack transparency. Describe them briefly and comment on whether these systems should allow some level of transparency. Give at least one suggestion for each of them of how such transparency should be provided.

4. What is the difference between understandability and comprehensibility in ML systems?

5. Compare interpretability and explainability as two related concepts in an ML system. Give an example of an ML system that provides both of these.

Hands-on Problems

Problem 13.1

Let's practice algorithmic auditing with an ML technique. Pick any classification problem you have solved before. Feel free to pick one from an earlier chapter of this book. Run through the whole exercise (loading the data, building the model, and finding its accuracy). Now, audit this system, with the goal of finding any potential flaws in it.

Start with the data. Are there any biases with respect to any of its attributes? What about the class labels? Are all the classes well balanced?

Next, analyze the classification technique used. Can it or did it overfit the data? Will it give the same results if you use different portions of the data for training and testing (think about *k*-fold evaluations)?

Finally, look at the evaluation metrics. Normally we would focus on the accuracy only, but I suggest you look at the class-wise accuracies to see if we have Simpson's paradox or not.

Report your auditing results with recommendations about how to fix any issues you discovered.

Problem 13.2

Play detective for an AI system! In this chapter we saw how we figured out that Google had not really fixed the gender disparity in the "CEO" query. Instead, they had just done a quick, superficial fix. How did we find it? By running related queries such as "CEO United States" and "CEO UK." Find a similar example where you see inequality in representation based on gender, race, or other attributes. Is this just a single, isolated issue or is there a systematic problem here? This will be primarily a qualitative analysis at this point, but it could open a new area for investigation. Report your findings with supported examples and commentary.

Further Reading and Resources

- Algorithmic accountability: a primer: https://datasociety.net/wp-content/uploads/2019/09/DandS_Algorithmic_Accountability.pdf.
- NSF Program on Fairness in Artificial Intelligence in Collaboration with Amazon (FAI): www.nsf.gov/funding/pgm_summ.jsp?pims_id=505651.
- Bias on the Web: https://cacm.acm.org/magazines/2018/6/228035-bias-on-the-web/fulltext.
- Misinformation vs. disinformation: https://predictiontechnology.ucla.edu/misinformation-versus-disinformation-whats-the-difference/.

Notes

1. Larson, J., Mattu, S., Kirchner, L., & Angwin, J. (2016). How we analyzed the COMPAS recidivism algorithm. www.propublica.org/article/how-we-analyzed-the-compas-recidivism-algorithm.
2. Thubron, R. (2016). Beauty contest's AI judge accused of racism. www.techspot.com/news/66272-beauty-contest-ai-judge-accused-racism.html.
3. Misinformation and disinformation have been receiving a lot of attention in recent years as their spread has intensified through social media and during many important socio-political events in the world, including various elections and COVID-19. Both indicate falsified information, with

disinformation usually referring to intentional and by a higher-level entity like a government or a political party.

4. Han, B., Shah, C., & Saelid, D. (2021). Users' perception of search-engine biases and satisfaction. *Second International Workshop on Algorithmic Bias in Search and Recommendation (Bias 2021)*, April 1, 2021. https://link.springer.com/chapter/10.1007/978-3_030-78818-6_3.
5. Microsoft Bing Blogs (2018). Toward a more intelligent search: Bing Multi-Perspective Answers. https://blogs.bing.com/search-quality-insights/february-2018/Toward-a-More-Intelligent-Search-Bing-Multi-Perspective-Answers.
6. https://facctconference.org.
7. https://recsys.acm.org/recsys21/facctrec.
8. https://sigir.org/sigir2021.
9. https://fair-trec.github.io.
10. https://hai.stanford.edu.
11. https://raise.mit.edu.
12. www.raise.uw.edu.
13. Metz, C. (2021). AI developers give more scrutiny to keeping bias out of the technology. *Seattle Times*. www.seattletimes.com/business/technology/using-ai-to-find-bias-in-ai/.
14. https://inventory.algorithmwatch.org.
15. European Union (2021). Proposal for a Regulation of the European Parliament and of the Council Laying Down Harmonised Rules on Artificial Intelligence (Artificial Intelligence Act) and Amending Certain Union Legislative Acts. https://eur-lex.europa.eu/legal-content/EN/TXT/?qid=1623335154975&uri=CELEX%3A52021PC0206.
16. Jillson, E. (2021). Aiming for truth, fairness, and equity in your company's use of AI. www.ftc.gov/news-events/blogs/business-blog/2021/04/aiming-truth-fairness-equity-your-companys-use-ai.
17. Röösli, E., Rice, B., & Hernandez-Boussard, T.(2021). Bias at warp speed: how AI may contribute to the disparities gap in the time of COVID-19. *JAMA, 28*, 190–192. https://doi.org/10.1093/jamia/ocaa210.
18. Australian Government (n.d.). Artificial intelligence. www.industry.gov.au/policies-and-initiatives/artificial-intelligence.
19. Wikipedia. Simpson's paradox. https://en.wikipedia.org/wiki/Simpson'sdox#/media/File:Simpson'sdox_continuous.
20. Mittelstadt, B. (2016). Automation, algorithms, and politics: auditing for transparency in content personalization systems. *International Journal of Communication, 10*, 12.
21. Koshiyama, A., Kazim, E., Treleaven, P., et al. (2021). Towards algorithm auditing: a survey on managing legal, ethical and technological risks of AI, ML and associated algorithms. https://papers.ssrn.com/sol3/papers.cfm?abstract_id=3778998.
22. Kay, M., Matuszek, C., & Munson, S. A. (2015). Unequal representation and gender stereotypes in image search results for occupations. In *Proceedings of the 33rd Annual ACM Conference on Human Factors in Computing Systems* (pp. 3819–3828).
23. Singh, A., & Joachims, T. (2018). Fairness of exposure in rankings. In *Proceedings of the 24th ACM SIGKDD International Conference on Knowledge Discovery & Data Mining* (pp. 2219–2228).
24. Feng, Y., & Shah, C. (2022). Has CEO gender bias really been fixed? Adversarial attacking and improving gender fairness in image search. In *AAAI Conference on Artificial Intelligence* (pp. 1–9).
25. Arrieta, A. B., Díaz-Rodríguez, N., Del Ser, J., et al. (2020). Explainable Artificial Intelligence (XAI): concepts, taxonomies, opportunities and challenges toward responsible AI. *Information Fusion, 58*, 82–115.
26. Char, D. S., Shah, N. H., & Magnus, D. (2018). Implementing machine learning in health care: addressing ethical challenges. *New England Journal of Medicine, 378*(11), 981–983.

Appendix A: Statistical Techniques

This appendix will cover the basics of statistics, which may be useful if it has been a while since you practiced these concepts.

Variables

- **Nominal variable**: A variable is nominal when there is no natural ordering of the possible values that it stores. For example, colors.
- **Ordinal variable**: If the possible values of a data type are from an ordered set, then the variable is ordinal. For example, grades on a mark sheet.
- **Interval variable**: Interval variables represent numerical values on which we can perform addition and subtraction but not multiplication or division. For example, temperature.
- **Ratio variable**: Ratio variables represent numerical values on which we can perform addition, subtraction, multiplication, and division. For example, weight.
- **Independent/predictor variable:** An independent or predictor variable is one that we don't think is controlled or affected by other variables.
- **Dependent/outcome/response variable:** A dependent, outcome, or response variable is one that depends on other variables (most often independent variables).
- **Continuous variable:** A variable that can have an infinite number of values between any two values.
- **Discrete or categorical variable:** A variable that can have two or more discrete values or categories.

Distributions

Once some data has been collected, it is useful to plot a graph showing how many times each value occurs. This is known as a frequency distribution. Frequency distributions come in different shapes and sizes. Therefore, it is important to have some general descriptions for common types of distributions. The following are some of the ways in which statisticians can present numerical findings.

Histogram: Histograms plot values of observations on the horizontal axis, with a bar showing how many times each value occurred in the dataset. Let's look at an example of how a histogram can be crafted out of a dataset. Table A.1 represents *Productivity* measured in terms of output for a group of data science professionals. Some of them went through extensive statistics training (represented as Y in the *Training* column) while others did not (N). The dataset also contains the work experience (denoted as *Experience*) of each professional in terms of number of working hours.

Table A.1 Productivity dataset.		
Productivity	**Experience**	**Training**
5	1	Y
2	0	N
10	10	Y
4	5	Y
6	5	Y
12	15	Y
5	10	Y
6	2	Y
4	4	Y
3	5	N
9	5	Y
8	10	Y
11	15	Y
13	19	Y
4	5	N
5	7	N
7	12	Y
8	15	N
12	20	Y
3	5	N
15	20	Y
8	16	N
4	9	N
6	17	Y
9	13	Y
7	6	Y
5	8	N
14	18	Y
7	17	N
6	6	Y

> **Try It Yourself A.1: Histogram**
>
> Answer the following questions using Table A.1.
>
> 1. What kind of variable is *Productivity*?
> 2. What kind of variable is *Experience*?
> 3. What kind of variable is *Training*?
> 4. We are trying to understand if by looking at *Productivity* and *Experience* we could predict if someone went through training or not. In this scenario, identify the independent or predictor variable(s) and dependent or outcome variable(s).

A histogram can be created from the numbers in the *Productivity* column, as shown in Figure A.1. Any spreadsheet program, such as Microsoft Excel or Google Sheets, supports a host of visualization options, such as charts, plots, line graphs, and maps. If you are using Google Sheets, the procedure to create the histogram is to first select the intended column, then select "Insert chart," denoted by the icon in the toolbar, which will open up the chart editor. In the editor, select "Histogram chart" in the chart type dropdown. That will create a chart like the one in Figure A.1. You can further customize the chart by specifying the color of the chart, x-axis label, y-axis label, and other attributes.

We will often be working with data that are numerical, and we will need to understand how those numbers are spread. For that, we can look at the nature of that distribution. It turns out that if the data is normally distributed, various forms of analyses become easy and straightforward. What's a normal distribution?

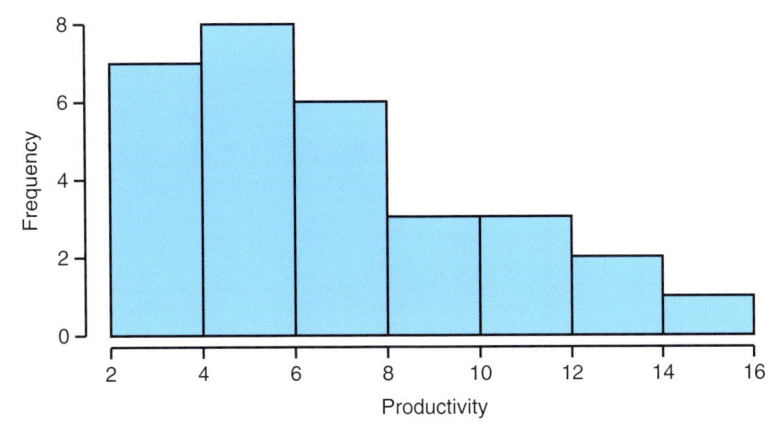

Figure A.1 Histogram using Productivity data.

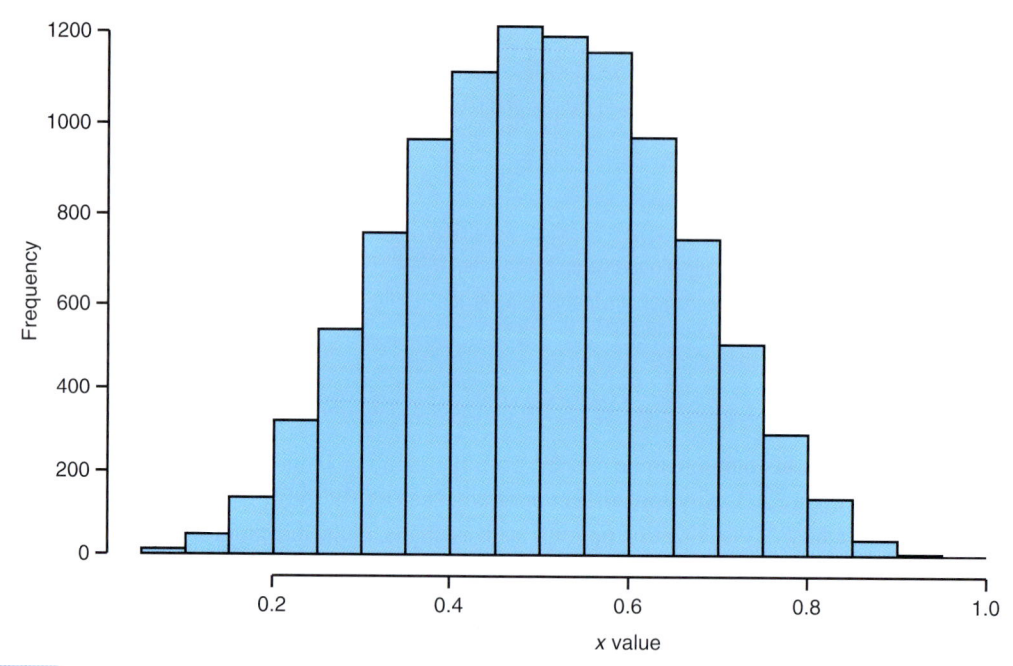

Figure A.2 Example of a normal distribution.

Normal distribution: The normal distribution is characterized by a bell-shaped curve, an example of which is shown in Figure A.2. In a normal distribution, data is distributed symmetrically around the mean. If we drew a vertical line through the center of a distribution, both sides would look the same.

There are two ways in which a similarly shaped distribution can deviate from the normal distribution:

- lack of symmetry (called **skew**);
- pointiness (called **kurtosis**).

A skewed distribution can be either positively skewed (a long tail on the right) or negatively skewed (a long tail on the left), as shown in Figure A.3.

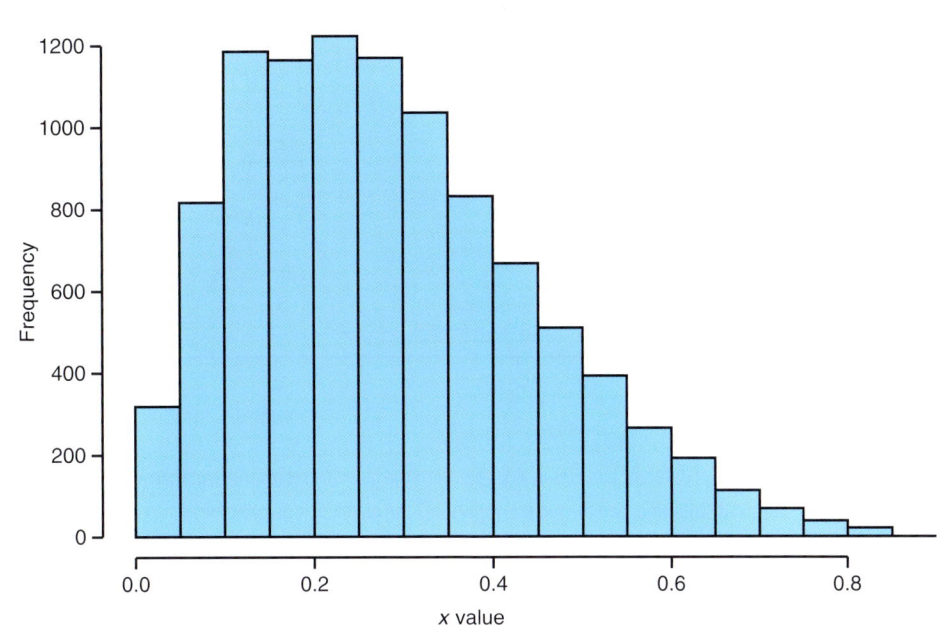

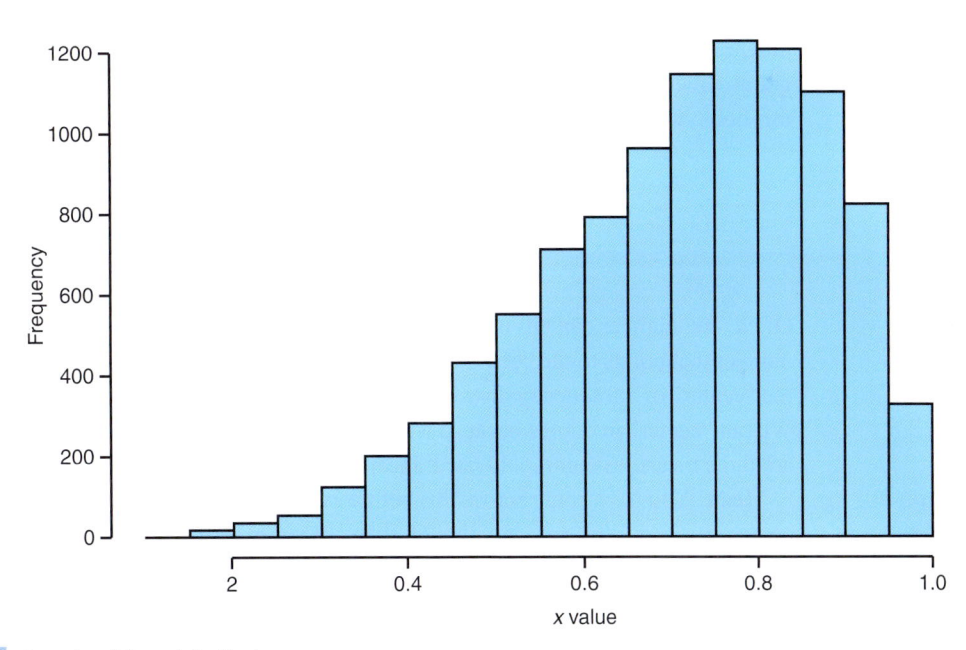

Figure A.3 Examples of skewed distributions.

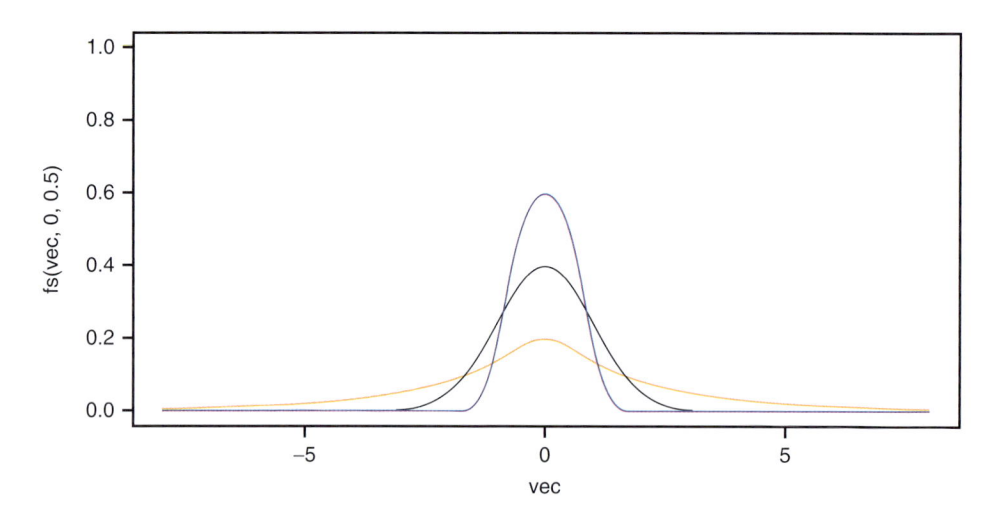

Figure A.4 Examples of different kurtoses in a distribution (the blue line represents leptokurtic, the black line represents the normal distribution, and the red line represents the platykurtic distribution).

Kurtosis, on the other hand, refers to the degree to which values cluster at the end of the distribution versus the center. A flat distribution is *platykurtic*, and a pointy one is *leptokurtic*, as shown in Figure A.4.

There are ways to find numbers related to these distributions to give us a sense of their skewedness and kurtosis, but we will skip that for now. At this point, we will leave the judgment of the normality of a distribution to our visual inspection of it using the histograms as shown above. As we acquire appropriate statistical tools in the next section of this book, we will see how to run some tests to find out if a distribution is normal or not.

Central Tendency

Often, one number can tell us all we need to know about a distribution. This is typically a number that points to the "center" of a distribution. In other words, we can calculate where the "center" of a frequency distribution lies, which is also known as the **central tendency**. We put "center" in quotes because where the center is depends on how it is defined. There are three measures commonly used: mean, median, and mode.

Mean: You have come across this before even if you have never done statistics. Mean is commonly known as *average*, though they are not exactly synonyms. Mean is most often used to measure the central tendency of continuous data. If there are n values in a dataset and the values are $x_1, x_2, \ldots, x_n$ then the mean is calculated as:

$$\bar{x} = \frac{x_1 + x_2 + x_3 + \ldots + x_n}{n}. \tag{A.1}$$

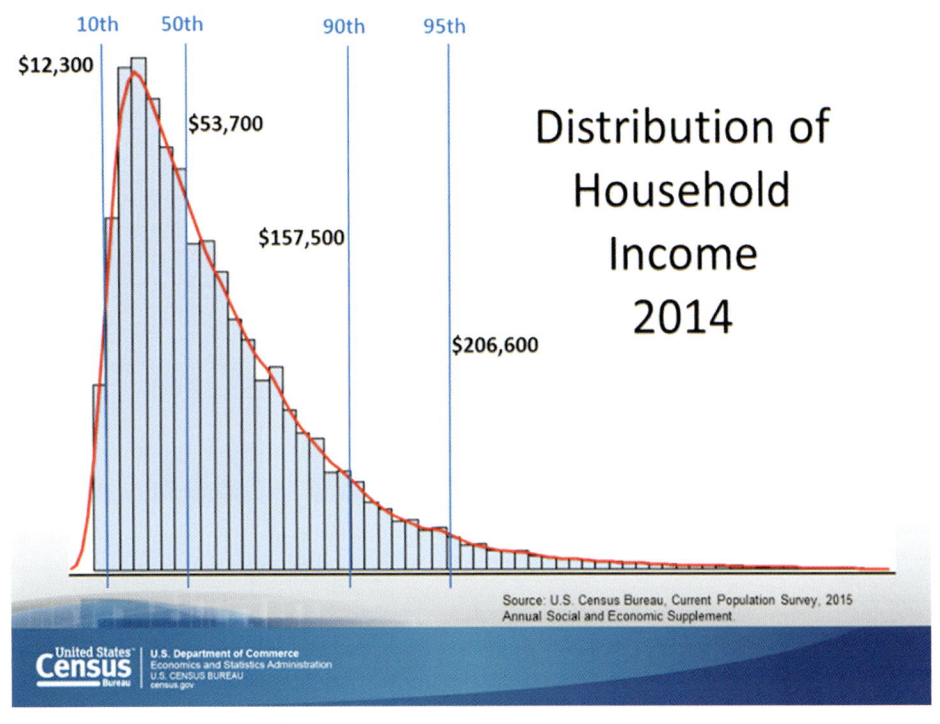

Figure A.5 Income distribution in the USA as of 2014.[1]

Using this formula, the mean of the *Productivity* column comes out to be 7.267. Go ahead and verify this.

There is a significant drawback to using the mean as a central statistic: It is susceptible to the influence of outliers. Also, the mean is only meaningful if the data is normally distributed, or at least close to a normal distribution. Take the distribution of household income in the USA, for instance. Figure A.5 shows this distribution, obtained from the US Census Bureau. Does that distribution look normal? No. A few people make a lot of money and a lot of people make very little money. This is a highly skewed distribution. If you take the mean or average from this data it will not be a good representation of income for this population. So, what can we do? We can use another measure of central tendency: median.

Median: The median is the middle score for a dataset that has been sorted according to the values of the data. With an even number of values, the median is calculated as the average of the middle two data points. For example, for the *Productivity* dataset the median of *Experience* is 9.5. What about the US household income? The median income in the US, as of 2014, is $53,700. That means half the people make $53,700 or less, and the other half make more.

Mode: The mode is the most frequently occurring value in a dataset. In a histogram the highest bar denotes the mode of the data. Normally, mode is used for categorical data (e.g., for the *Training* variable in the Productivity dataset, the most common category is the mode).

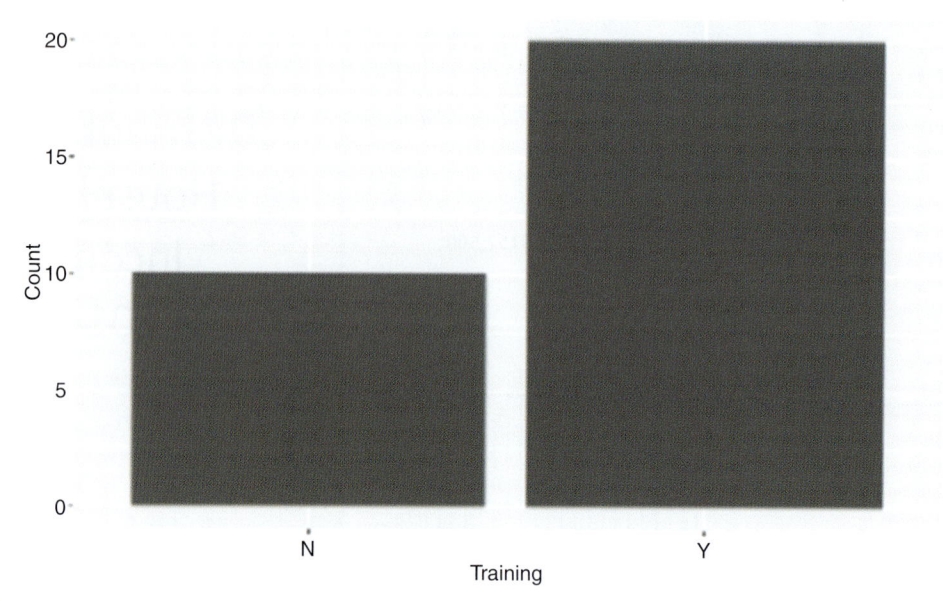

Figure A.6 Visualizing mode for the Productivity data.

As depicted in Figure A.6, in the Productivity dataset there are 10 instances of N and 20 instances of Y values in *Training*. So, in this case, the mode for *Training* is Y. (Note: If the number of instances of Y and N are the same then there would be no mode for *Training*.)

Dispersion of a Distribution

We saw before that distributions come in all shapes and sizes. Simply looking at a central point (mean, median, mode) may not help in understanding the actual shape of a distribution. Therefore, we often look at the spread, or the dispersion, of a distribution. The following are some of the most common measures of dispersion.

Range: The easiest way to look at the dispersion is to take the largest score and subtract it from the smallest score. This is known as the range. For the Productivity dataset, the range of the *Productivity* category is 13.

There is, however, a disadvantage to using the range: Because it uses only the highest and lowest values, extreme scores or outliers tend to result in an inaccurate picture of the more likely range.

Interquartile range: One way around the range's disadvantage is to calculate it after removing extreme values. One convention is to cut off the top and bottom one-quarter of the data and calculate the range of the remaining middle 50% of the scores. This is known as the interquartile range. For example, the interquartile range of *Experience* in the Productivity dataset is 10.

Hands-on Example A.1: Interquartile Range

We can easily find and visualize the interquartile range. Let's revisit the data from Table A.1 and focus on the *Experience* column. If we sort it, we get Table A.2.

Table A.2 Sorted *Experience* column from the Productivity dataset.

Experience
0
1
2
4
5
5
5
5
5
5
6
6
7
8
9
10
10
10
12
13
15
15
15
16
17
17
18
19
20
20

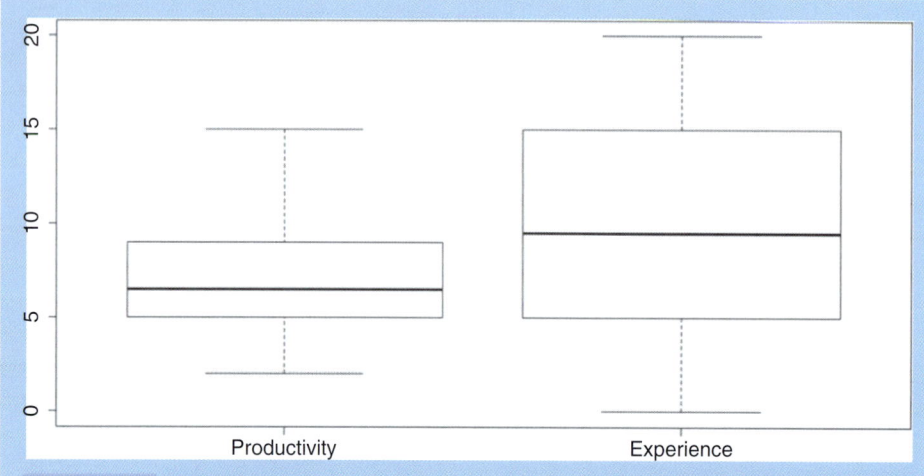

Figure A.7 Boxplot for the *Productivity* and *Experience* columns of the Productivity dataset.

There are 30 numbers here and we are looking for the middle 15 numbers. That gives us the numbers 5, 5, 5, 6, 6, 7, 8, 9, 10, 10, 10, 12, 13, 15, and 15. Now we can see that the range of these numbers is 10 (min. = 5 to max. = 15). That is our interquartile range. We could also visualize this whole process in something called boxplots. Figure A.7 shows boxplots for the *Productivity* and *Experience* columns.

As shown in the boxplot for the *Experience* attribute, after removing the top one-quarter values (between 15 and 20) and bottom one-quarter (between 0 and 5), the range of the remaining data can be calculated as 10 (from 5 to 15). Likewise, the interquartile range of the *Productivity* attribute is 5.

Variance: The variance is a measure used to indicate how spread out the data points are. To measure the variance, the common method is to pick a center of distribution, typically the mean, then measure how far each data point is from the center. If individual observations vary greatly from the group mean, the variance is large, and if individual observations are close to the mean, the variance is small. Here, it is important to distinguish between the variance of a population and the variance of a sample. They have different notations and they are computed differently. The variance of a population is denoted by σ^2, and the variance of a sample by s^2.

The variance of a population is defined by the following formula:

$$\sigma^2 = \Sigma(X_i - X)^2 / N, \tag{A.2}$$

where σ^2 is the population variance, X is the population mean, X_i is the ith element from the population, and N is the number of elements in the population.

The variance of a sample is defined by slightly different formula:

$$s^2 = \Sigma(x_i - x)^2 / (n - 1), \tag{A.3}$$

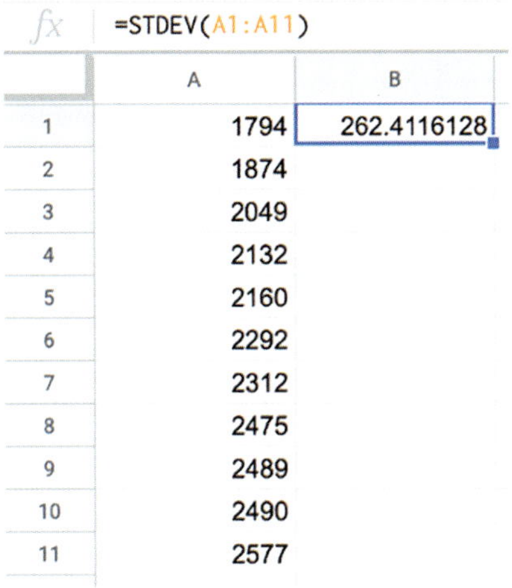

	A	B
	fx =STDEV(A1:A11)	
1	1794	262.4116128
2	1874	
3	2049	
4	2132	
5	2160	
6	2292	
7	2312	
8	2475	
9	2489	
10	2490	
11	2577	

Figure A.8 A snapshot from Google Sheets showing how to compute standard deviation.

where s^2 is the sample variance, x is the sample mean, x_i is the ith element from the sample, and n is the number of elements in the sample. Using this formula, the variance of the sample is an unbiased estimate of the variance of the population.

Example: In the Productivity dataset given in Table A.1 we find by applying the formula in (A.3) that the variance of the *Productivity* attribute is 11.93 (approximated to two decimal places) and the variance of *Experience* is 36.

Standard deviation: There is one issue with variance as a measure of spread. It gives us the measure of spread in units squared. So, for example, if we measure the variance of age (measured in years) of all the students in a class, the measure we get will be in *years*^{2}. However, practically it would make more sense if we get the measure in *years* (not squared). For this reason we often take the square root of the variance, which ensures the measure of average spread is in the same units as the original measure. This measure is known as standard deviation. Figure A.8 shows how to compute standard deviation using Google Sheets.

The formula to compute the standard deviation of a sample is:

$$s = \sqrt{\left(\Sigma(x_i - x)^2 / (n - 1)\right)}. \tag{A.4}$$

Correlation

Correlation is a statistic that describes the *strength* and *direction* of the relationship between two variables. Strength indicates how closely two variables are related to each other, and direction indicates how one variable changes its value as the value of the other variable changes.

Correlation is a simple statistical measure that examines how two variables change together over time. Take, for example, "umbrella" and "rain." If someone who grew up in a place where it never rained saw rain for the first time, this person would observe that whenever it rains, people use umbrellas. They may also notice that on dry days folks do not carry umbrellas. By definition, "rain" and "umbrella" are said to be correlated! More specifically, this relationship is strong and positive. Think about this for a second.

An important statistic, **Pearson's r correlation**, is widely used to measure the degree of the relationship between linearly related variables. When examining the stock market, for example, Pearson's r correlation can measure the degree to which two commodities are related. The following formula is used to calculate the Pearson r correlation:

$$\gamma = \frac{N\sum xy - \sum(x)(y)}{\sqrt{\left[N\sum x^2 - \sum(x^2)\right]\left[N\sum y^2 - \sum(y^2)\right]}},$$

where:
r = Pearson's r correlation coefficient
N = number of values in each dataset
$\sum xy$ = sum of the products of paired scores
$\sum x$ = sum of x scores
$\sum y$ = sum of y scores
$\sum x^2$ = sum of squared x scores
$\sum y^2$ = sum of squared y scores.[2]

Hands-on Example A.2: Correlation

Let's use the formula above to calculate Pearson's correlation coefficient for the height–weight pair with the data provided in Table A.3.

Let's calculate various quantities needed for solving the Pearson's correlation formula:

N = number of values in each dataset = 10
$\sum xy$ = sum of the products of paired scores = 98,335.30
$\sum x$ = sum of x scores = 670.70
$\sum y$ = sum of y scores = 1463
$\sum x^2$ = sum of squared x scores = 45,058.21
$\sum y^2$ = sum of squared y scores = 21,8015

Plugging these into the Pearson's correlation formula gives us 0.39 (approximated to two decimal places) as the correlation coefficient. This indicates two things: (1) *height* and *weight* are positively related, which means that as one goes up, so does the other; and (2) the strength of their relation is medium. Note that the values of Pearson's r correlation range from −1.0 to 1.0.

Table A.3 Height–weight data.

Height	Weight
64.5	118
72.3	143
68.8	172
65	147
69	146
64.5	138
66	175
66.3	134
68.8	172
64.5	118

Further Reading and Resources

There are plenty of good (and mediocre) books on statistics. If you want to develop your techniques in data science, I suggest you pick up a good statistics book at the level you need. A couple of such books are listed below.

- Salkind, N. (2016). *Statistics for people who (think they) hate statistics*. Sage.
- Krathwohl, D. R. (2009). *Methods of educational and social science research: the logic of methods*. Waveland Press.
- Field, A., Miles, J., & Field, Z. (2012). *Discovering statistics using R*. Sage.
- A video by IBM describing the progression from descriptive analytics through predictive analytics to prescriptive analytics: www.youtube.com/watch?v=VtETirgVn9c.

Appendix B: Useful Formulas from Differential Calculus

Generally speaking, for a function $y = x^n$,

$$\frac{d}{dx}x^n = nx^{n-1}.$$

Let's list a few more rules:

$$\frac{d}{dx}cy = c\frac{dy}{dx} \quad (\text{here, } c \text{ is a constant}),$$

$$\frac{d(u+v)}{dx} = \frac{du}{dx} + \frac{dv}{dx},$$

$$\frac{d(uv)}{dx} = u\frac{dv}{dx} + v\frac{du}{dx},$$

$$\frac{d}{dx}\left(\frac{u}{v}\right) = \frac{v\frac{dv}{dx} - u\frac{du}{dx}}{v^2},$$

$$\frac{dy}{dx} = \frac{dy}{du}\frac{du}{dx},$$

If $y = f(u)$, and $u = d(x)$

$$\frac{d}{dx}u^n = nu^{n-1}\frac{du}{dx}$$

Sometimes we have functions with multiple variables. When that happens, we take a derivative with respect to one of the variables and treat other variables as constants. This is called a partial derivative. A partial derivative with respect to x means we regard all other variables as constants, and just differentiate the x parts. Here is an example:

$$f(x,y) = 3y^2 + 2x^3 + 5y,$$

$$\frac{\partial f}{\partial y} = 6x^2$$

Here is what happens if we take a partial derivative of f with respect to y:

$$\frac{\partial f}{\partial y} = 6y + 5.$$

Further Reading and Resources

To learn more about these formulas, their proofs, or some more advanced formulas that are relevant to this book, you can read the following resources.

- Adams, R. A. (2003). *Calculus: A complete course*, 5th ed. Pearson.
- Math is Fun – introduction to derivatives: www.mathsisfun.com/calculus/derivatives-introduction.html.
- University of Texas basic differentiation formulas: www.ma.utexas.edu/users/kit/Calculus/Section_2.3--Basic_Differentiation_Formulas/Basic_Differentiation_Formulas.html.

Appendix C: Useful Formulas from Probability

The probability of an event is calculated as:

$$\text{Probability} = \frac{\text{Number of outcomes in which the event happens}}{\text{Total number of outcomes}}.$$

For mutually exclusive events A and B,

$$P(A \text{ or } B) = P(A \cup B) = P(A) + P(B).$$

For independent events A and B,

$$P(A \text{ and } B) = P(A \cap B) = P(A)P(B).$$

The conditional probability of an event A given B is defined as the probability that A occurs, given the occurrence of some other event B. It is defined as:

$$P(A|B) = \frac{P(A \cap B)}{P(B)}.$$

Here, P(A|B) represents the conditional probability of A given B; P(A∩B) denotes the probability of both A's and B's occurrence, and P(B) is the probability of event B.

Bayes' theorem is a formula that calculates the probability of a hypothesis given some new evidence. It follows simply from the axioms of conditional probability.

Given a hypothesis and evidence, Bayes' theorem states that the relationship between the probability of the hypothesis before getting the evidence and the probability of the hypothesis after getting the evidence is:

$$P(H|E) = \frac{P(E|H)}{P(E)} P(H).$$

Further Reading and Resources

To learn more about these formulas, their proofs, or some more advanced formulas that are relevant to this book, you can read the following pointers.

- Jaynes, E. T. (2003). *Probability theory: the logic of science*. Cambridge University Press.
- Online Statistics Education: An interactive multimedia course of study: http://onlinestatbook.com/2/probability/basic.html.
- Introduction to probability: www.maths.qmul.ac.uk/~bill/MTH4107/notesweek3_10.pdf.
- RapidTables Basic probability formulas: www.rapidtables.com/math/probability/basic_probability.html.

Appendix D: Installing and Configuring Tools

Anaconda

There are plenty of ways to work with Python and Python-related tools. If you already have a favorite tool (e.g., Eclipse), feel free to continue with that. If, however, you are new to Python or want to try something different, I suggest the Anaconda framework.

Anaconda is available from www.anaconda.com/distribution. It provides a host of tools, including Python itself. It also has hundreds of the most popular Python packages, including a large set for doing data science.

Once you install Anaconda, start the Navigator utility. The Navigator will list all the Python-related tools you have on your machine, allowing you to launch and manage them from this one place.

See the screenshot in Figure D.1. A couple of utilities that are very useful for us are Jupyter and Spyder. They are covered next.

Jupyter Notebook

The Jupyter notebook is a nice little utility for trying Python. It allows you to interactively write, execute, and even visualize your Python code. In addition, it helps you document and present your work, so it is good for learning and teaching!

You can get it from https://jupyter.org. Installation instructions can be found at https://jupyter.org/install. Note that Jupyter used to go by the name IPython, so if you ever worked in IPython before, do not let this confuse you.

One nice thing about the notebook is that it runs in your web browser, making it easy to access and compatible with many platforms.

Look at the screenshot in Figure D.2. As you can see, in a Jupyter notebook you can not only write and run your code, but you can also edit and format it.

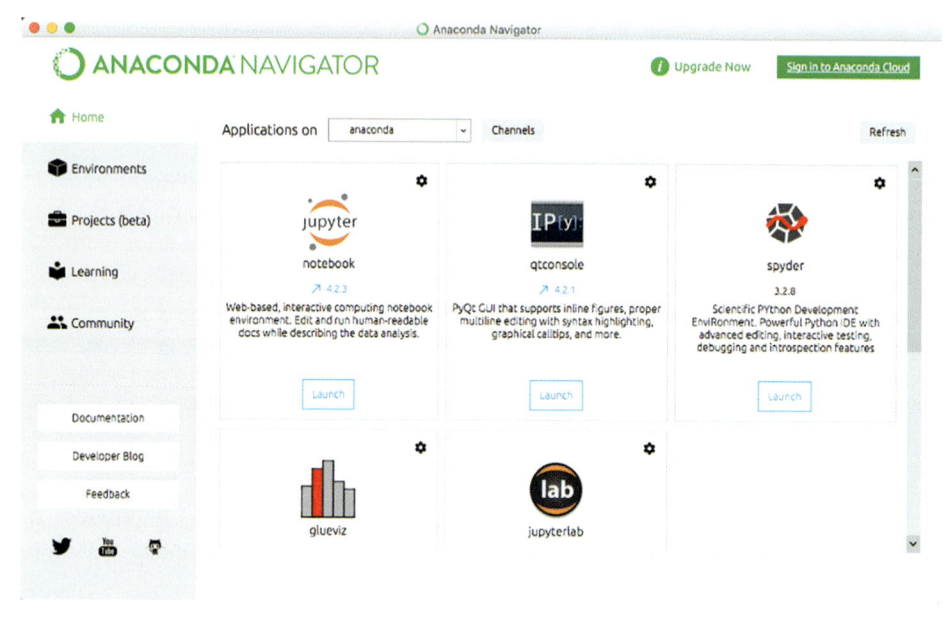

Figure D.1 A snapshot of Anaconda Navigator.

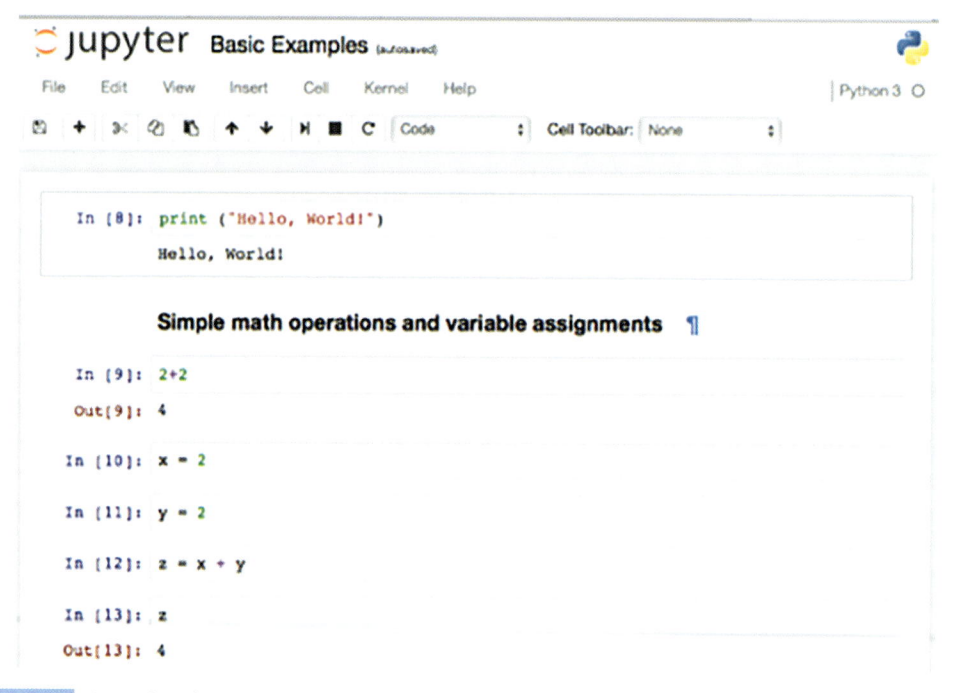

Figure D.2 A snapshot of a Jupyter notebook.

Spyder

Continuing the tradition of switching an "i" with a "y," next we have "Spyder"! This is a fully fledged integrated development environment (IDE) that allows you to write, run, debug, get help, and pretty much do everything you could ever want to do with Python programming.

If you have ever used any IDE, such as Eclipse, this should feel familiar. As you can see in the screenshot in Figure D.3 (taken from Spyder's project page), there are several windows, including one with an editor, one with online help, and another with results (the console).

You can get Spyder from https://github.com/spyder-ide/spyder. Once installed, Spyder, like Jupyter, will also show up in Anaconda.

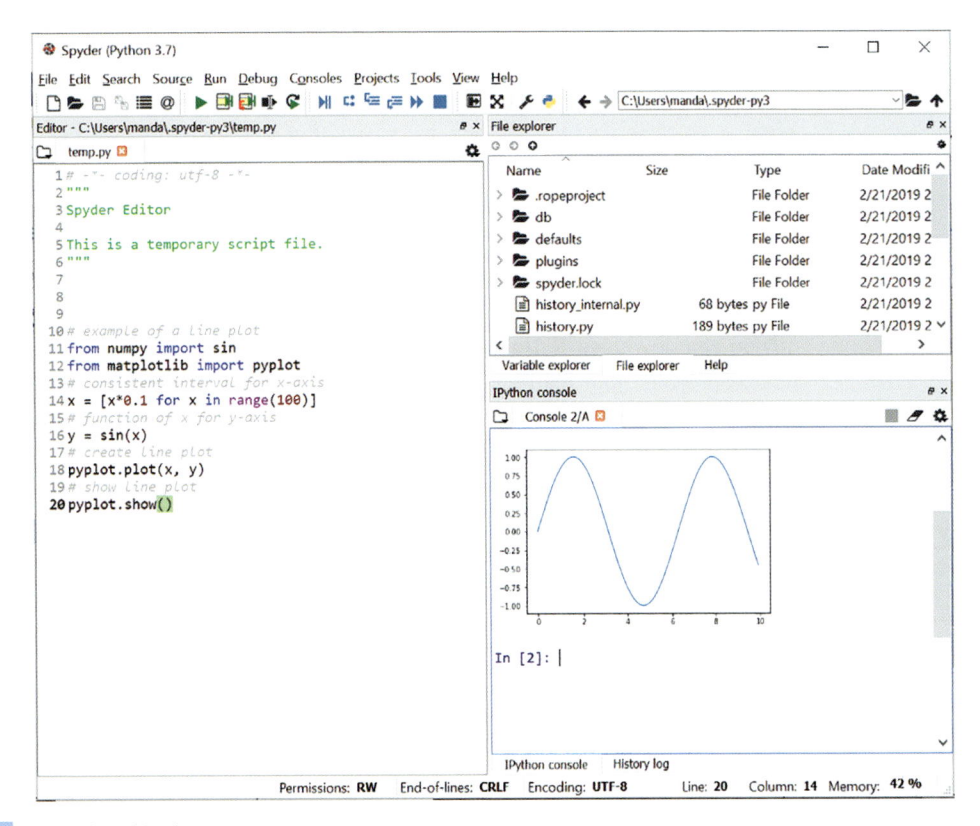

Figure D.3 A snapshot of Spyder.

Appendix E: R for Machine Learning

While Python is the #1 language for doing machine learning (ML), several other languages, tools, and frameworks are also used. If possible, it is a good idea to be familiar with at least one or two of them, in addition to Python. In this appendix we will get a quick introduction to a very popular ML tool: R.

Getting Access to R

R is open source software for statistical computing, and it is available on all the major platforms for free. If you have ever used or heard of MATLAB, SPSS, or SAS, you are familiar with the kinds of things R can do: statistics, data manipulation, visualization, and running data mining and ML algorithms. But R is free and provides an amazing and constantly expanding set of tools. There is also an active community building and supporting these tools. R offers you all the statistical and graphical power that you can handle. No wonder it is becoming an industry standard for scientific computing.

You can download R from www.r-project.org. There, you can also read up on R and related projects, join mailing lists, and find all the help you need to get started and do amazing things.

Once downloaded and installed, start the R program. You will be presented with the R console (Figure E.1). Here, you can run R commands and programs that we will see in the next sections. To leave the program, enter q().

But, as before, instead of using this program directly, we will take advantage of an integrated development environment (IDE). In this case, it is RStudio, which you can get from www.rstudio.com/products/rstudio/download.

Once you have downloaded and installed RStudio, go ahead and start it up. You should see multiple windows or panes (see Figure E.2), including the familiar R console where you can run R commands. As with the regular R, you can enter q() on the RStudio console to exit.

Before proceeding with some ML work, let us make sure we have the appropriate libraries. One library that is quite often used in statistics and data visualization is ggplot2. Let's make sure we have that available. Open RStudio and select Tools > Install Packages. In the dialog box that pops up, make sure CRAN repository is selected for the installation source. Now, type "ggplot2" in the packages box. Make sure "Install dependencies" is checked. Hit "Install" and the ggplot2 package should be downloaded and installed. In the future you can install other libraries through the same process.

Appendices

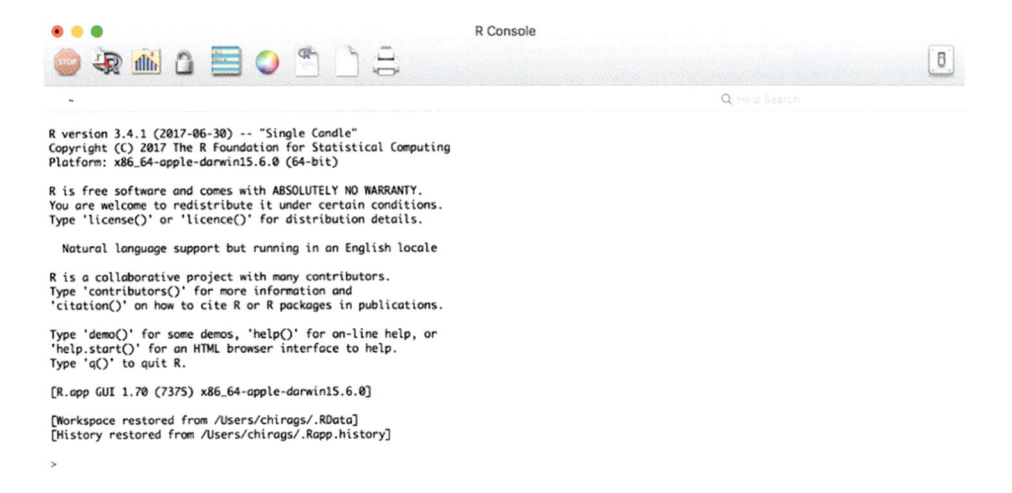

Figure E.1 A screenshot of the R console.

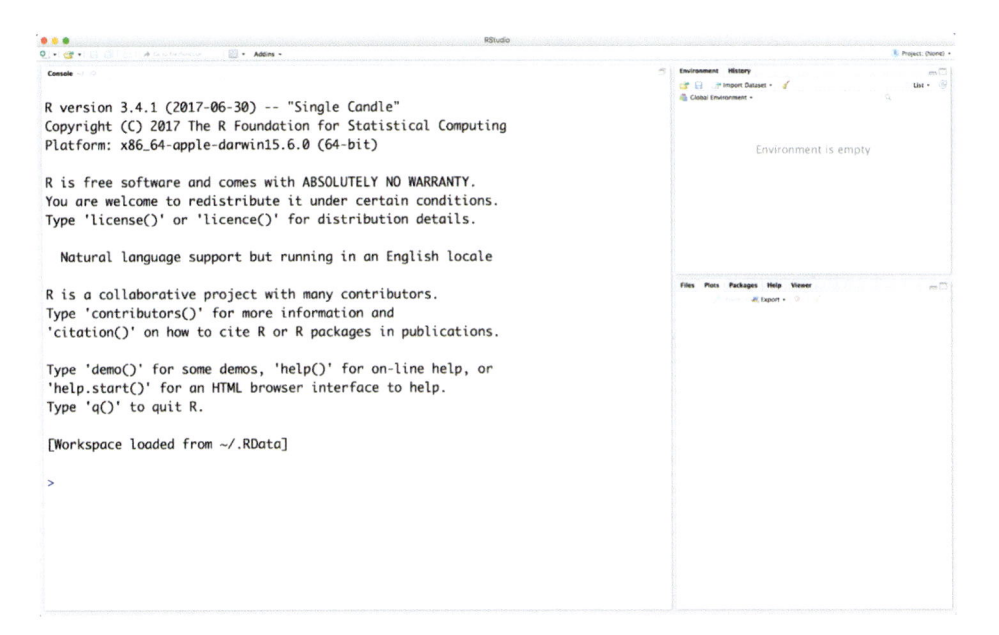

Figure E.2 A screenshot of RStudio.

Basic Statistics

One of the strengths of R is its ability to do many basic math and statistics operations with just a few simple commands. If you have ever worked with or heard about Mathematica, MATLAB, or Stata, you can compare R with them in such capabilities. Rather than reviewing specific commands, we will take a hands-on example and work with a dataset that will help us get some descriptive statistics.

> **Hands-on Example E.1: Classification**
>
> Let us work with the "size.csv" data, which you can download from OA A.1. This data contains 38 records of different people's sizes in terms of height and weight. Here is how we load it:
>
> ```
> size = read.table("size.csv",header=T,sep=",")
> ```
>
> This assumes that the data is in the current directory. Alternatively, you can replace `'size.csv'` with `file.choose()` to let you pick the file from your hard drive when you run this line. Also, while you can run one line at a time on your console, you could type them and save them as a ".r" file so that not only can you run line-by-line, but you can also store the script for future runs.
>
> I am assuming at this point that you have the data loaded. We can ask R to give us some basic statistics about it by running the summary command:
>
> ```
> summary(size)
>      Height          Weight
>  Min.   :62.00   Min.   :106.0
>  1st Qu.:66.00   1st Qu.:135.2
>  Median :68.00   Median :146.5
>  Mean   :68.42   Mean   :151.1
>  3rd Qu.:70.38   3rd Qu.:172.0
>  Max.   :77.00   Max.   :192.0
> ```
>
> The output, as shown above, shows descriptive statistics for the two variables or columns we have here, Height and Weight. We have seen such output before, so I will not bother with the details.
>
> Let us visualize this data on a scatterplot. In the following block, `ylim` is for specifying minimum and maximum values for the *y*-axis:
>
> ```
> library(ggplot2)
> ggplot(size, aes(x=Height,y=Weight)) + geom_point() + ylim(100,200)
> ```
>
> The outcome is shown in Figure E.3. Once again, you have got to appreciate how easy it is with R to produce such professional-looking visualizations.

Figure E.3 Scatterplot of Height vs. Weight.

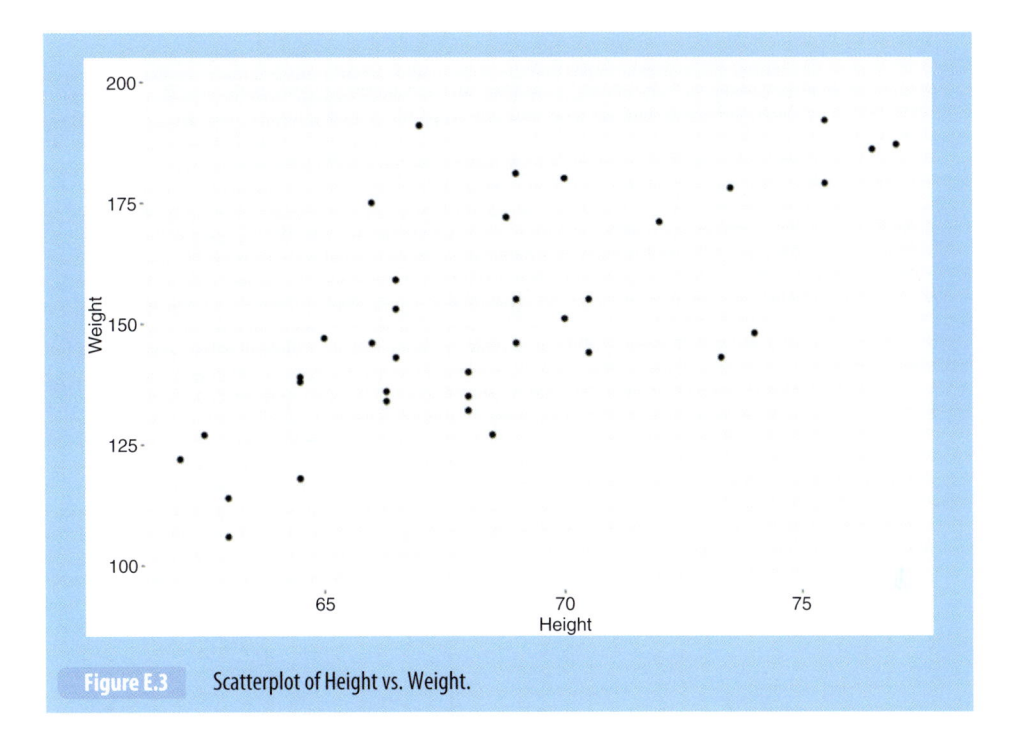

As you can see, R makes it very easy to not only get lots of everyday use statistics, but also provides quick and effective visualization of data. We will now continue with more statistical and ML operations.

Regression

Now that we have a scatter plot, we can start asking some questions. One straightforward question is: What is the relationship between the two variables we just plotted? This question calls for regression analysis, and that is what we will do now with our next hands-on example.

Hands-on Example E.2: Regression

Let's continue working with the previous example. With R you can keep the existing plotting information and just add a function to find a line that captures the relationship:

```
ggplot(size, aes(x=Height,y=Weight)) + geom_point()+
stat_smooth(method="lm") + ylim(100,200)
```

Compare this command to the one we used above for creating the plot in Figure E.3. You will notice that we kept the original plot and simply added a segment that overlaid a line on top of the scatterplot. And that is how easy it is to do basic **linear regression** in R, a form of **supervised learning**. Here, the lm method refers to a linear model. The output is in Figure E.4.

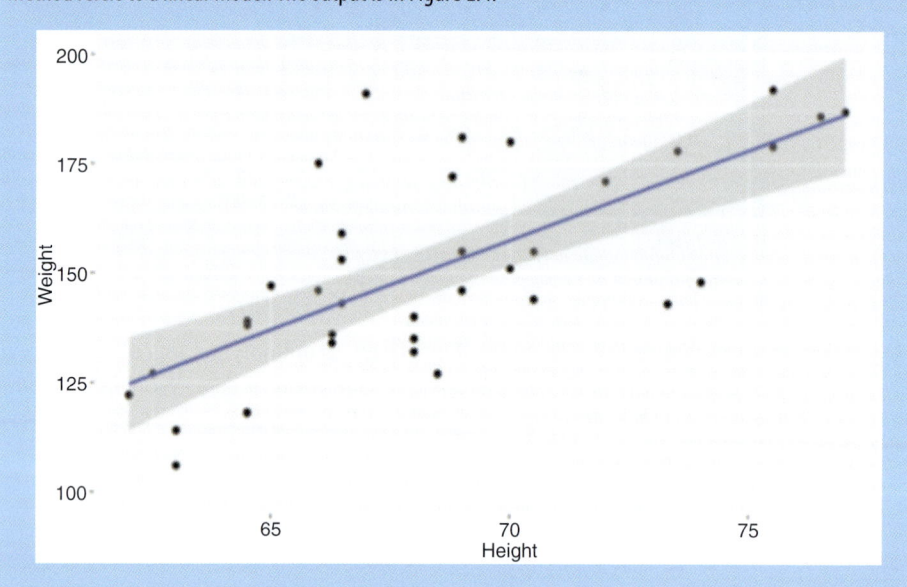

Figure E.4 Linear regression connecting Height to Weight.

You see that blue line? That is the regression line. It is a model that shows the connection between the Height and Weight variables. What it means is that if we know the value of Height, we can figure out the value of Weight anywhere on this line.

Want to see the line equation? Use the lm command to extract the coefficients:

```
lm(Weight ~ Height, size)
```

And here is the output.

```
Call:
lm(formula = Weight ~ Height, data = size)
```

```
Coefficients:
(Intercept)        Height
   -130.354         4.113
```

You can see that the output contains coefficients for the independent variable (Height) and the constant or intercept. The line equation becomes:

```
Weight = -130.354 + 4.113*Height
```

Try plugging different values of Height into this equation. See what values of Weight you get, and how close your predicted values are to reality.

With linear regression we managed to fit a straight line through the data. But perhaps the relationship between Height and Weight is not all that straight. So, let us remove the restriction of the linear model:

```
ggplot(size, aes(x=Height,y=Weight)) + geom_point() +
geom_smooth() + ylim(100,200)
```

The output is in Figure E.5. As you can see, our data fits a curved line better than a straight line.

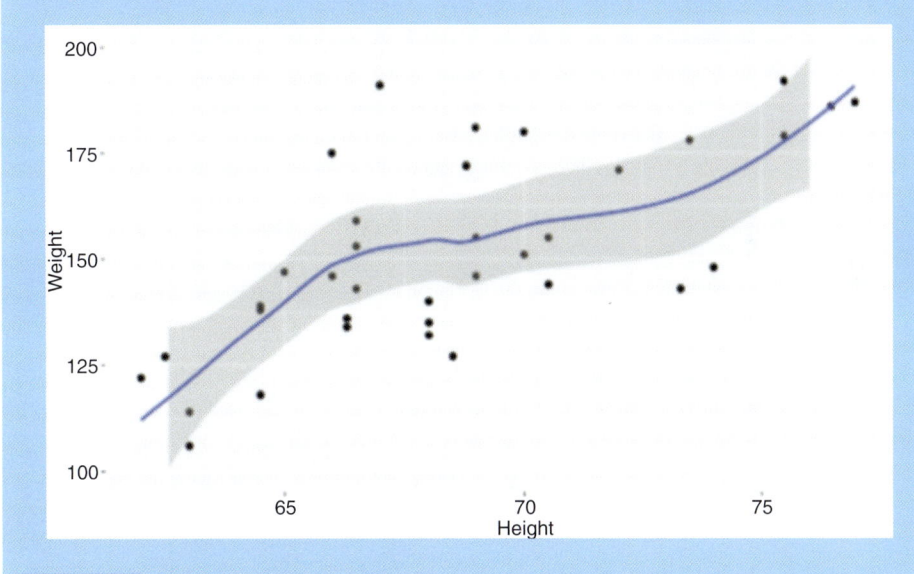

Figure E.5 Regression without a linear requirement.

Yes, the curved line fits the data better, and it may seem like a better idea than trying to draw a straight line through this data. However, we may end up with the curse of *overfitting* and *overlearning* with a curved shape for doing regression. This means we were able to model the existing data really well, but in the process we compromised so much that we may not do so well for new data.

Classification

We will now see how we could do some of the same things we did using Python. Let's start with classification using the kNN method. As you may recall, classification with kNN is an example of **supervised learning**, where we have some training data with true labels and we build a model (classifier) that could then help us classify unseen data.

Before we use classification in R, let's make sure we have a package named "class" available to us. You can find available packages in the Packages tab in RStudio (typically in the bottom-right window, where you also see the plots). If you see "class" there, make sure it is checked. If it is not there, you need to install that package using the same method you did for the ggplot2 package.

Hands-on Example E.3: Classification

Let's begin by loading some data. Download the Wine dataset from OA A.2. Running the following statement in R should bring up a file navigation box that you can use to select the file "wine.csv" from your computer.

```
wine = read.table(file.choose(), header=T, sep=",")
```

Think of "wine" as a dataframe here. From this dataframe or table we want to take all rows and specific columns – *density*, *sulphates*, and *residual_sugar* – as our independent variables, or *X*. Our response/target variable (*y*) remains the same – *high_density*. This can be obtained using the following lines:

```
X_wine <- wine[,c("density","sulphates","residual_
sugar")]
         y_wine <- wine[,c("high_quality")]
```

Now that we have our *X* and *y*, we can split the data into training and testing sets. For that we will use the package "caret," which stands for "classification and regression training." If you do not have this package already installed, you can do so by using the usual method of going to Tools > Install Packages in RStudio, and entering "caret."

Assuming things went okay and you have the "caret" package, let's load it up and use its `createDataPartition()` function to extract 70% of the data randomly for training:

```
library(caret)
set.seed(123)
inTrain <- createDataPartition(y = y_wine, p = 0.7,
list = FALSE)
```

Now let's extract training and testing sets for *X* and *y*:

```
X_train <- X_wine[inTrain,]
X_test <- X_wine[-inTrain,]
y_train <- y_wine[inTrain]
y_test <- y_wine[-inTrain]
```

Here, *X_wine* contains all the rows, but only some of the columns. It is a matrix of size [rows, columns], and when we enter `X_wine[inTrain, ]` we are picking only the rows that are marked in *inTrain*, with all the columns of *X_wine*. In other words, we are generating our training data. The remaining data is in `X_wine[-inTrain, ]`, giving us the testing data.

y_wine, on the other hand, is a vector (many rows but one column). We can similarly split that vector into training and testing sets using `y_wine[inTrain]` and `y_wine[-inTrain]`.

We are now ready to run kNN on this data. For that, we will need to load the "class" library. Then we use `X_train` and `y_train` to build a model, and use `X_test` to find our predicted values for *y*:

```
library(class)
wine_pred <- knn(train=X_train, test=X_test, cl=y_train, k=3)
```

Finally, we want to see how well we were able to fit the model and how good our predictions were. For this, let's load the "gmodels" library[3] and use its `CrossTable()` function:

```
library (gmodels)
CrossTable(x = y_test, y = wine_pred, prop.chisq=FALSE)
```

You should see output that looks something like:

```
Total Observations in Table:   1949
              | wine_pred
       y_test |           0 |           1 | Row Total |
--------------|-------------|-------------|-----------|
            0 |        1363 |         198 |      1561 |
              |       0.873 |       0.127 |     0.801 |
              |       0.836 |       0.623 |           |
              |       0.699 |       0.102 |           |
--------------|-------------|-------------|-----------|
            1 |         268 |         120 |       388 |
              |       0.691 |       0.309 |     0.199 |
              |       0.164 |       0.377 |           |
              |       0.138 |       0.062 |           |
--------------|-------------|-------------|-----------|
 Column Total |        1631 |         318 |      1949 |
              |       0.837 |       0.163 |           |
--------------|-------------|-------------|-----------|
```

You can see, out of 1949 instances for testing, how many times we correctly predicted the label (the upper-left and lower-right quadrants), and how often we failed to predict it (the upper-right and lower-left quadrants).

Note that the last argument `prop.chisq` indicates whether or not the chi-square contribution of each cell is included. The chi-square statistic is the sum of the contributions from each of the individual cells. It is used to decide whether the difference between the observed and the expected values is significant.

Clustering

Now we will switch to the **unsupervised learning** branch of ML. This covers a class of problems where we do not have labels on our training data. In other words, we do not have a way to know which data point should go to which class. Instead, we are interested in somehow characterizing and explaining the data we encounter. Perhaps there are some classes or patterns in them. Can we identify and explain these? Such a process is often exploratory in nature. Clustering is the most widely used method for such exploration and we will learn about it using a hands-on example.

> **Hands-on Example E.4: Clustering**
>
> Here, we will work with the famous Iris dataset. Let's start by loading the "datasets" library and viewing a portion of the Iris data:
>
> ```
> library(datasets)
> head(iris)
> ```
>
> Let's see what this data looks like. First, we will load the ggplot2 library and then do a scatterplot where the color of a data point indicates the species:
>
> ```
> library(ggplot2)
> ggplot(iris, aes(Petal.Length, Petal.Width, color = Species)) + geom_point()
> ```
>
> The outcome is shown in Figure E.6. 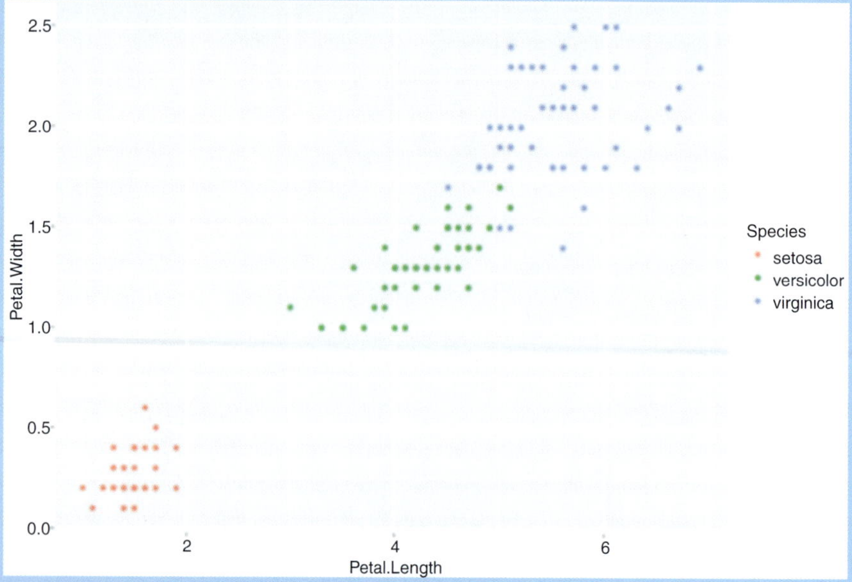
>
> **Figure E.6** Visualization of the Iris dataset according to species.

Now we are ready to start doing clustering. For this, we will generate a random number seed and then use the kmeans function. Note that in the following code we are asking for three clusters:

```
set.seed(20)
irisCluster <- kmeans(iris[, 3:4], 3, nstart = 20)
irisCluster
```

The last line of the code above outputs a nice summary of the clusters generated. We can see how well we were able to cluster data points corresponding to different species by creating a table:

```
table(irisCluster$cluster, iris$Species)
```

Finally, let's recreate the scatterplot using the clustering information:

```
ggplot(iris, aes(Petal.Length, Petal.Width, color = irisCluster$cluster)) + geom_point()
```

In Figure E.7 you can see that the clustering information almost matches the actual classes for the data points, but not quite. There are a few points that you can see are in the wrong class. See if this information corresponds to the table we generated before.

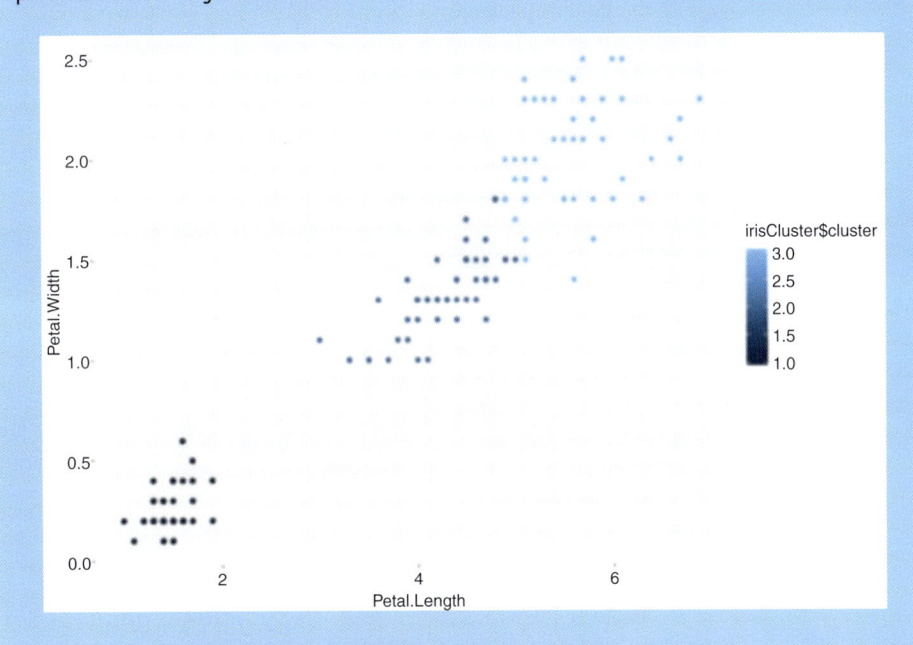

Figure E.7 Visualization of the Iris dataset using predicted clusters.

Appendix F: Connecting with MySQL Databases

Accessing MySQL with Python

Here we will see how to incorporate MySQL into the other data science programming tools and environments we know. This way, instead of retrieving and separately analyzing the data from MySQL, we can create a workflow or a pipeline that integrates data connection to MySQL and data analysis using Python or R.

To access the MySQL database with Python, we will need PyMySQL. You can download it from GitHub.[4] The installation instructions can also be found on that page.

Now that you have PyMySQL installed, let's proceed. We will first import that package, along with the Pandas package:

```
import pymysql.cursors
import pandas as pd
```

Let's provide the MySQL connection parameters to connect to the database:

```
# Connect to the database
connection = pymysql.connect(host="localhost", user="bugs",
password="bunny", db="world", charset="utf8mb4", cursor-
class=pymysql.cursors.DictCursor)
```

Note that we are assuming that your MySQL server is on your local machine (localhost); if it is somewhere else, make sure to change the `host` parameter value in the code above accordingly. Change the values of `user`, `password`, and `db` as well. Once connected we can try running a query; when it is finished, close the database connection:

```
# Try running a query
try:
    with connection.cursor() as cursor:
        sql = "SELECT * FROM City WHERE population>7000000"
        cursor.execute(sql)
        # Extract the data in a dataframe
        df = pd.DataFrame(cursor.fetchall())
finally:
    connection.close()
```

The resulting dataframe (a table or a matrix containing multiple rows and columns) can be found in the `df` variable. Now that you have the dataframe, you can do all kinds of things with the data using Python.

> **Hands-on Example F.1: MySQL with Python**
>
> Let us take another database and see how it can be accessed from Python. For this exercise, we will use a database available from OA A.3. Once you unzip the file, you will see "mysqlsampledatabase.sql." This is an SQL file with the instructions to create data records in your database.
>
> First, we will create a new database:
>
> ```
> create database classicmodels;
> ```
>
> Of course, this was using the SQL query console, but you could also do it using your GUI client. You will need to extract the database file and import it into your MySQL Workbench, SQL Pro, or whichever GUI client you are using. Once the dataset is loaded you should be able to see a list of tables (e.g., customers, employees, offices, order details, to name a few) in your database.
>
> Now, let us try to access some of the tables from Python. Imagine you want to find all the employees who work at the Boston office and retrieve their IDs and first and last names. Below is the code showing how to do it. For this exercise we will assume that your MySQL server is on your local machine (`localhost`), but if it is somewhere else, make sure to change the `host` parameter value in the code below accordingly.
>
> ```
> import pymysql
>
> # Connect to the database
> connection = pymysql.connect(host="localhost",
> user="root", password="*******", db="classicmodels",
> charset="utf8mb4")
> #Initiate cursor
> conn = connection.cursor()
>
> #Write the SQL query to be executed
> sql = """select e.employeeNumber, e.firstName,
> e.lastName from employees e
> inner join offices o on e.officeCode = o.officeCode
> and o.city like "%Boston%";"""
>
> output = conn.execute(sql)
> while True:
>     row = conn.fetchone()
>     if row == None:
>         break
>     print(row)
> ```

```
#Close the connection
connection.close()
```

> **Try It Yourself F.1: MySQL with Python**
>
> Using the database "classicmodels" created in Hands-on Example F.1, write a Python code snippet that will retrieve the phone number (office phone number, followed by the extension) of the president of the company.

Accessing MySQL with R

We will now see how to access MySQL using R. As you might have guessed, to use MySQL through R, we need a package. This time, it is "RMySQL." First, install the package if you do not already have it, and then load it in the environment:

```
> install.packages("RMySQL")
> library(RMySQL)
```

Now, let us connect to our database server and select the database. This is equivalent to specifying the parameters in your MySQL client:

```
> mydb = dbConnect(MySQL(), user="bugs", password="bunny",
dbname="world", host="server.com")
```

In this command we are connecting to a MySQL server "server.com" with user "bugs" and password "bunny". We are also opening the "world" database.

If we want to see the tables available in the database we just opened, we can run the following:

```
> dbListTables(mydb)
```

Now, let us run a query to retrieve some results.

```
> rs = dbSendQuery(mydb, "SELECT * FROM City WHERE popula-
tion>7000000")
```

Here we are working with "mydb" – the database we just opened. We sent it a query that we had tried before and the resulting set is captured in `rs`. To extract the data from this result set we can use the `fetch()` function:

```
> data = fetch(rs,n=-1)
```

Here, n specifies how many records we want to extract: $n = -1$ means we want to extract everything.

That is it. Now you have the data in `data` that you asked for. And once you have the data, you can do all that you did with your R skills before. So, we will just leave it there.

Hands-on Example F.2: MySQL with R

Need more practice? Let's take a similar example to the one used in the previous section for Python. The same "classicmodels" database is going to be used for this exercise. Say you are interested in retrieving the names, IDs, and roles of employees who report directly to the president in the office. The following lines of code should do the job:

```
# Load the package
library(RMySQL)

# Set the connection parameters
connection = dbConnect(MySQL(), user="root", password="*******", dbname="classicmodels", host="localhost")

# Check the connection

dbListTables(connection)

# Write the SQL query
query = dbSendQuery(connection, "SELECT e1.employeeNumber, e1.firstName, e1.lastName, e1.jobTitle from employees e1 where e1.reportsTo = (select e2.employeeNumber from employees e2 where e2.jobTitle like "%President");")

# Store the result
result = fetch(query, n= -1)

# View the result
View(result)

# Close the connection
dbDisconnect(connection)
```

Try It Yourself F.2: MySQL with R

Using the database from Hands-on Example F.2, write an R script that will retrieve the address of all the customers whose first name is Alexander.

Appendix G: Machine Learning Careers

After exploring the key concepts of machine learning (ML) in this book, you might be wondering what jobs are available in the ML field. A search of LinkedIn using the keywords "machine learning" returns over 157,000 job postings, and demand for these skills is only expected to grow. The World Economic Forum stated that "AI, Machine Learning, and automation will power the creation of 97 million new jobs by 2025."[5] Glassdoor reports a salary range of $57,000–$170,000, with an average of $103,000 for ML jobs in the USA. However, Indeed.com reported an average base salary of $146,000 in 2019, a year which also saw a 344% growth in ML jobs, leading Indeed to name Machine Learning Engineer the "Best Job of 2019."[6]

Looking closer at current ML job postings, the most common job titles include Machine Learning Engineer, Data Scientist, Machine Learning Scientist, Software Engineer, Quantitative Analyst, and Machine Learning Researcher. Across these career paths, employers are looking for similar sets of desired skills, especially familiarity with ML frameworks, model building, and model deployment using TensorFlow, JAX, PyTorch, Spark MLib, Scikit-learn, Spacy, Google ML, Google Prediction API, Sagemaker, and Azure ML. Other highly desired skills include Python, natural language processing (NLP), familiarity with cloud-based infrastructures, analytics frameworks, deep learning architecture models, statistical learning algorithms, data pipelines, orchestration platforms, SQL relational databases, and a background in computer science.

There are a wide variety of career pathways, specialties, and industries to choose from in the ML field, with high international demand. Machine learning engineers analyze data to create ML algorithms that learn and make predictions without much human intervention. They often work collaboratively with data scientists, analysts, and administrators to organize large amounts of data and continually optimize the ML algorithms.[7] Data scientists, by comparison, work more closely with business stakeholders, and use analytic technologies including ML to make sense of data and produce actionable insights that inform the business decisions of the company.[8] Quantitative analysts design and employ algorithms to help companies make business and financial decisions, especially in the finance and insurance sectors, where they identify profit opportunities and mitigate risk.[9]

The top five countries for AI and ML are the USA, the UK, Germany, China, and France, and while much of the available data on hiring is from the USA, there is evidence of broad global demand.[10] In the last quarter of 2021, the Asia-Pacific was the "fastest growing region for machine learning hiring among pharmaceutical industry companies."[11] *The Manifest* recently published a list of the top 100 Latin American Machine Learning Consultants,[12] and in Europe ML- and AI-related jobs have tripled in the last three years.[13] China is also investing heavily in ML, with an emphasis on robotics and IT, and India is growing as a hub for ML in IT and software development.[14]

With ML becoming integral to business, technology, and healthcare operations, there are a wide variety of employment arenas to choose from. To demonstrate this, we will dive into four industries and examine the typical job skills required for ML professionals. In the sections below, we will outline roles in finance, healthcare, retail, and tech.

Finance

Machine learning is used in the finance world to automate stock trading, provide investment advice, and detect fraud. Because ML is able to quickly analyze enormous datasets and create optimized predictions, it is becoming more widely applied in finance. In 2019 there was a 60% increase in finance industry job postings that requested these skills.[15] Automated stock trading is a prime example of the benefit of ML to the finance industry. Previously, human stock traders would manually check share prices and make buy and sell orders, but algorithmic trading can process and analyze multiple large datasets, create models that set the conditions for when to buy and sell shares, and increase the total number of trades made per day. Machine learning is also being used in fraud detection, where it is able to continually scan large datasets for anomalous transactions, compare that to the usual spending patterns of the account holder, and place a hold on the withdrawal if the activity seems fraudulent, outsmarting the fraudsters.[16]

The most common job titles for ML professionals in the finance industry are Machine Learning Engineer and Quantitative Analyst, and most hiring platforms allow you to limit your search to the finance industry specifically. These job postings call for skills such as Python, SQL, ML model building, statistical analysis and data analytics, the ability to work as a part of a team, and the ability to communicate technical information to a non-technical audience. For more information, check out the following resources:

1. What is machine learning in finance? https://corporatefinanceinstitute.com/resources/knowledge/other/machine-learning-in-finance.
2. Machine learning in finance: what, why, and how? https://towardsdatascience.com/machine-learning-in-finance-why-what-how-d524a2357b56.
3. Machine learning in finance: 10 companies to know: https://builtin.com/artificial-intelligence/machine-learning-finance-examples.

Healthcare

The healthcare industry might be a surprising place to find ML jobs, but experts predict that 50% of global healthcare companies will be integrating ML into their operations by 2025.[17] Machine learning can sort through and analyze large amounts of patient, facility, insurance, and clinical trial data, which results in faster and more efficient decision-making in developing new drugs and treatments, diagnosing disease, advancing clinical trials, and predicting epidemics.[18] For example, ML is being used to develop new drugs by identifying molecules that failed in a previous trial, and predicting how those same molecules could be recombined and applied to other diseases.[19] Machine learning can also expedite clinical trials by quickly identifying ideal trial candidates using multiple demographic data factors, and more efficiently producing real-time trial results, increasing the pace of medical breakthroughs.[20]

Job postings in this sector use titles such as Machine Learning Scientist, Data Scientist, Research Scientist, and Analytics Lead. While some jobs require a background in the medical field in addition to ML, this is not true for all jobs in this sector. For example, the desired skills listed on current ML job postings in the healthcare industry include: building ML models, familiarity with cloud computing, experience with Python, SQL, statistical analysis, and NLP. Roles in this field also emphasize project management skills and strong communication skills. To learn more about this growing sector for ML, look into the following resources:

1. Machine learning in healthcare: 12 real-world use cases to know: https://nix-united.com/blog/machine-learning-in-healthcare-12-real-world-use-cases-to-know.
2. 16 examples of a healthcare revolution using machine learning: https://builtin.com/artificial-intelligence/machine-learning-healthcare.
3. AI in the pharma industry: current uses, best cases, digital future: https://pharmanewsintel.com/news/ai-in-the-pharma-industry-current-uses-best-cases-digital-future.

Retail

The retail industry is a major employer of ML professionals, with roles ranging from retail forecasting to pricing decisions to sentiment analyses – and much more.[21] The top three ways in which retailers utilize ML worldwide are: (1) customer engagement; (2) supply chain logistics and management; and (3) supply and demand predictions.[22] For example, ML is being utilized by large retailers to predict buyer behavior to target advertisements to individual customers with the goal of increasing sales.[23] Machine learning has become increasingly relevant and important in the retail industry as the popularity of online shopping has expanded, a trend which is expected to continue.

Job postings in this sector use titles such as Machine Learning – Retail Forecasting, Marketing Technology, Retail Decision Automation, Machine Learning Engineering, and Data Science. Due to the wide range of focal areas across industries, positions may require domain-specific knowledge. Most postings include a list of desired skills which tend to contain the following qualifications: experience with programming languages, knowledge of NLP, and an understanding of recommendation systems. Industry positions also often highlight soft skills such as problem-solving, analytical skills, communication, and collaboration.

For additional information regarding the use of ML in retail, check out the following resources:

1. The guide to machine learning in retail: applications and use cases: https://tryolabs.com/guides/retail-innovations-machine-learning.
2. Reinventing the retail industry through machine and deep learning: www.dellemc.com/content/dam/uwaem/production-design-assets/en-gb/solutions/assets/pdf/insideHPC-Report-Reinventing-the-Retail-Industry.pdf.
3. The complete guide to machine learning in retail demand forecasting: www.relexsolutions.com/resources/machine-learning-in-retail-demand-forecasting.

Tech

Artificial intelligence and ML are becoming an increasingly important field of knowledge within the tech industry. Over the next two years it is expected that the number of job postings mentioning AI-related skills will increase 297%.[24] Machine learning is used for chatbots, NLP, and image identification and classification processes.[25] Natural language processing is one of the most exciting areas of growth for tech-related ML jobs. AI-powered devices like Alexa and Siri are just the beginning, and leading tech innovators are working to create seamless communication between humans and machines using voice commands.[26] However, despite the demand for such skills, there is not enough talent to fulfill these roles. Some companies, including Google, have published free courses to train up future employees interested in joining the field.[27]

Typical job postings within the tech sector include Machine Learning Engineer, Data Scientist, Software Engineer, Cloud Support Engineer, and Artificial Intelligence Specialist. Tech employers are seeking the following skills: familiarity with ML model building, NLP, deep learning software frameworks, Python, and SQL. They also mention soft skills relating to teamwork, the ability to work in a fast-paced environment, and a desire to be on the cutting edge of ML development.

For additional information regarding the use of ML in tech, check out the following resources:

1. What tech jobs demand A.I. and machine learning skills in 2022?: https://insights.dice.com/2022/01/04/what-tech-jobs-demand-a-i-and-machine-learning-skills-in-2022.
2. Tech jobs of tomorrow: machine learning: www.pluralsight.com/blog/software-development/tech-jobs-machine-learning.
3. The outlook for machine learning in tech: ML and AI skills in high demand: www.cio.com/article/222015/the-outlook-for-machine-learning-in-tech-ml-and-ai-skills-in-high-demand.html.

Notes

1. www.census.gov/library/visualizations/2015/demo/distribution-of-household-income--2014.html.
2. www.statisticssolutions.com/correlation-pearson-kendall-spearman.
3. I hope you are now comfortable with installing and using libraries/packages. If at any time you get an error regarding a package not found, go ahead and install it first.

4. GitHub for PyMySQL download: https://github.com/PyMySQL/PyMySQL.
5. www.lighthouselabs.ca/en/blog/machine-learning-career-path.
6. www.geeksforgeeks.org/top-career-paths-in-machine-learning.
7. www.techtarget.com/searchenterpriseai/definition/machine-learning-engineer-ML-engineer.
8. www.geeksforgeeks.org/top-career-paths-in-machine-learning.
9. www.investopedia.com/articles/professionals/121615/quantitative-analyst-job-description-average-salary.asp.
10. www.natureindex.com/supplements/nature-index-2020-ai/tables/countries.
11. www.pharmaceutical-technology.com/deals/asia-pacific-is-seeing-a-hiring-boom-for-machine-learning-roles-in-pharma.
12. https://themanifest.com/artificial-intelligence/machine-learning/companies/latin-america.
13. https://analyticsindiamag.com/top-countries-hiring-most-number-of-artificial-intelligence-machine-learning-experts.
14. https://analyticsindiamag.com/top-countries-hiring-most-number-of-artificial-intelligence-machine-learning-experts.
15. www.cnbc.com/2019/09/25/finance-jobs-requiring-ai-skills-are-growing-and-here-are-examples.html.
16. https://corporatefinanceinstitute.com/resources/knowledge/other/machine-learning-in-finance.
17. https://pharmanewsintel.com/news/ai-in-the-pharma-industry-current-uses-best-cases-digital-future.
18. www.forbes.com/sites/cognitiveworld/2020/12/26/the-increasing-use-of-ai-in-the-pharmaceutical-industry/?sh=446a3d504c01.
19. https://pharmanewsintel.com/news/ai-in-the-pharma-industry-current-uses-best-cases-digital-future.
20. https://emerj.com/ai-sector-overviews/machine-learning-in-pharma-medicine.
21. https://spd.group/machine-learning/predictive-analytics-and-machine-learning-in-retail.
22. www.statista.com/statistics/1009599/worldwide-retail-machine-learning-use-cases/.
23. https://builtin.com/artificial-intelligence/machine-learning-ecommerce-retail.
24. https://insights.dice.com/2022/01/04/what-tech-jobs-demand-a-i-and-machine-learning-skills-in-2022.
25. www.cio.com/article/222015/the-outlook-for-machine-learning-in-tech-ml-and-ai-skills-in-high-demand.html.
26. www.cio.com/article/222015/the-outlook-for-machine-learning-in-tech-ml-and-ai-skills-in-high-demand.html.
27. www.cio.com/article/222015/the-outlook-for-machine-learning-in-tech-ml-and-ai-skills-in-high-demand.html.

Index

A/B testing, 3, 328, 337–340, 345
accountability (machine learning), 356–358
accuracy
   association rule, 128–129
   machine learning modeling criteria, 111
ACM Conference on Fairness, Accountability, and Transparency (ACM FAccT), 352
adversarial learning, 344
agglomerative clustering
   defined, 186
   dendogram with maximum clustering, 187
   dendogram with minimum clustering, 32, 188
   steps to create, 186
Akaike Information Criterion (AIC), 195, 196, 200, 334–335
algorithmic accountability, 356–358
algorithmic bias, 353–354
AlphaZero, 304
Amazon Web Services (AWS)
   account set-up, 66–68
   versus Microsoft Azure, 66
   purpose of, 66
Amazon Web Services (AWS) Cloud9
   create Cloud9 environment, 71
   interface, 70
   pricing, 73
   work in Cloud9 environment, 71–72
Amazon Web Services (AWS) connect
   PuTTY, 68–69
   SSH session, 69
Anaconda
   installing and configuring, 383–384
   Python language access, 28
anomaly detection
   approaches for, 164
   defined, 166
   process of, 164–165
   uses for, 164
arithmetic operators (Python), 30
artificial intelligence (AI)
   defined, 20
   differences with machine learning, 10, 19
   responsible, 352–353
artificial neural networks (ANN)
   copying human brain interactions, 227
   versus human neurons, 228–229

   human versus artificial neurons, 228–229
   learning by example, 228
   supervised, 228
ASIMO robot, 306
association rule, 128–129
autoencoder network
   architecture, 243–244
   defined, 243, 260
   unsupervised learning example, 244–246
axon, 228, 260

backward propagation methods
   defined, 237
   process of, 237
bandits (reinforcement learning)
   contextual, 316–317
   exploration–exploitation dilemma, 315–316
   multi-arm, 316–322
   one-armed, 315
batch gradient descent
   in action, 102
   defined, 114
   example, 104–109
   methodology, 20, 102
Bayes' theorem, 382
Bayesian classification
   defined, 154
   Thompson sampling, 317
Bayesian Information Criterion (BIC), 195, 196, 200, 335
Beauty AI, 348–349
bias (machine learning)
   versus fairness, 355–356
   pervasiveness, 354
   Simpson's paradox, 355
bias, statistical, 90
bias, systemic, 353–354
bias types (machine learning)
   algorithmic/systemic, 353–354
   cognitive, 354
   data, 354
bidirectional encoder representations from transformers (BERT), 287–297
Boolean values (Python), 30
bootstrap sampling technique (random forest), 133

categorical variable, 145, 367
central tendency
  defined, 372
  mean, 372–373
  median, 373
  mode, 373–374
classification. *See also* decision tree
  context of, 118
  deep learning, 272–278
  defined, 9
  k-nearest neighbors (kNN), 119–123
  logistic regression, 145–152
  naïve Bayes, 154–158
  neural networks example, 240–242
  as process of supervised learning, 118
  R language, 388–389, 392–393
  softmax regression, 152–153
  support vector machine (SVM), 159–164
classification rule, 45, 127–128
cloud computing
  defined, 49–50
  essential nature of, 50
  Google Cloud Platform (GCP), 50–59
  Microsoft Azure, 59–66
cloud platform
  certification, 74
  defined, 76
  moving between, 75
clustering
  defined, 10, 175, 200
  density estimation, 196–199
  elbow method, 185–186
  expectation maximization (EM), 176, 192–196
  model goodness indicators, 195–196
  R language, 394–395
  in unsupervised learning, 10
clustering algorithms
  agglomerative, 175, 186–191
  divisive, 175–186
cognitive bias, 354
collaborative filtering (CF), 7–8
COMPAS (Correctional Offender Management Profiling for Alternative Sanctions), 348
comprehensibility (machine learning), 359, 363
conditional probability, 382
confidence. *See* accuracy
content filtering, 8–9
context, 327
contextual bandits, 316–317
continuous bag of words (CBOW), 298
continuous variable, 145, 367
convolution, 247–248, 260
convolution neural network (CNN)
  and MLP, 247
  overview, 247
  structure, 248
Correctional Offender Management Profiling for Alternative Sanctions (COMPAS), 348

correlation
  defined, 45, 377
  example, 378
  Pearson's *r* correlation, 378
  Python, 44
counterfactual evaluation, 340–343, 345
counterfactual explanation, 360, 363
coverage (association rule), 128

data bias, 354
data mining, 330–331, 345
data types
  defined, 30–31
  Python, 30
dataframe, Python, 54–55
decision rule, 127
decision tree. *See also* classification
  association rule, 128–129
  classification rule, 45, 128–129
  decision rule, 127
  entropy, 124–125
  information gain, 126
  purpose of, 123–124
  steps to create, 127
deep learning. *See also* machine learning
  classifier building, 272–278
  defined, 264, 298
  embeddings, 278–282
  encoders and transformers, 283–297
  as next level of machine learning, 264–265
  popularity of, 297–298
  Python model, 266
  shortcomings, 298
  simple model, 267–272
  when to use, 265–266
deep networks, 264, 298
dendogram
  defined, 189, 200
  with maximum clustering, 187
  with minimum clustering, 188
dendrites, 228
density estimation
  defined, 10
  Meanshift technique, 196–197
dependent variable (linear regression), 82, 114, 367
differential calculus functions, 380
differential privacy, 362
dimensionality, 222
dimensionality reduction
  curse of, 206–207
  feature selection, 207–213
  linear discrimination analysis (LDA), 388–389, 218–221
  maximum likelihood estimation (MLE), 213
  overfitting, 207
  principal component analysis (PCA), 214–218
discrete variable, 9, 367

disinformation, 363
distributed filesystem (Hadoop), 54
distributed learning, 362
divisive clustering
    with *k*-means, 179–182
    with *k*-modes, 182–185
    steps to create, 176

elbow method (clustering), 185–186
elif command (Python), 32
embeddings
    deep learning and, 278
    defined, 278, 298
    input, 285
    pretrained word embeddings, 279
    word embeddings, 278–279
encoders
    layers in, 286–287
    positional, 285
Enron scandal, 356
ensemble methods, 132, 138
entropy
    decision tree, 124–125
    defined, 138
    types of, 126–127
epsilon-greedy algorithm, 317
estimator choice modeling criteria, 27, 112
evaluation (machine learning)
    A/B testing, 337–340
    adversarial learning, 344
    counterfactual evaluation, 340–343
    goodness and, 331
    offline, 331–335
    user research, 335–337
expectation maximization (EM)
    definition, 192
    log likelihood, 192
    maximum likelihood estimation (MLE), 192
    tossing coin example, 192
    uses for, 192
explainability (machine learning), 359, 360, 363
exploding gradient (RNN), 256
exploration–exploitation dilemma, 315–316

Fairness, Accountability, Transparency (FAT)
    conference, 352
Fairness, Accountability, Transparency,
    Ethics (FATE), 352
fairness versus bias in machine learning, 355–356
false negative statement, 332
false positive rate (FPR), 166
false positive statement, 332
feature, defined, 114, 222
feature selection
    defined, 222
    importance of, 207
    univariate feature selection, 208–210
federated learning, 362

feed-forward neural network, 231
filesystem, 54
F-measure, 332
focus groups, 336–337
for loop (Python), 32
forget gate (LTSM), 257
forward propagation methods (neural networks), 236

generalizability (model), 337
Google biases, 19
Google Cloud Platform (GCP)
    background, 50
    Google Colab, 56–59
    Hadoop, 53–55
    new project creation, 50–51
    SSG key addition, 52–53
    virtual machine creation, 50–51
Google Colab
    accessibility of, 56
    getting started running with Python, 56–59
    installing Python packages, 37–38
    versus Microsoft Azure, 66
Google or Not misinformation, 349–351
gradient ascent, 147
gradient descent, 98–102, 113, 114
graph-based neural networks (GNN), 297

Hadoop
    as backbone of big-data operations, 53–54
    defined, 54
    modules, 54–55
Hadoop Common (Hadoop), 55
HD Insight cluster, 60–61
Hello World program (Java), 14
hidden layer, 235
histogram, 368–369
hyperparameters modeling criteria, 112
hyperplane, 159–160

if command (Python), 32
if–else command (Python), 32–33
incremental gradient descent. *See* stochastic gradient
    descent
independent variable (linear regression), 82, 114, 367
information gain
    decision tree, 125
    defined, 138
input embeddings, 285
input gate (LSTM), 257
integrated development environment (IDE)
    defined, 45
    Python language access, 27–28
interim gradient descent. *See* stochastic gradient
    descent
interpretability (machine learning), 359, 363
interval variable, 367
interviews, 336–337
inverse propensity score (IPS), 342, 345

Java language
    Hello World program, 14
    versus Python, 14
Jupyter Notebook
    installing and configuring, 383–384
    installing Python packages, 37–38

kernels
    decision boundaries, 166
    in SVM, 164
k-means
    divisive clustering, 179–182
    elbow method (clustering), 185–186
k-modes, 182–185
k-nearest neighbors (kNN)
    anomaly detection, 164–165
    easiest to understand and implement technique, 120
    example (trained model), 119–120
    major steps, 119
    reasons for, 119
    shortcomings, 120

learning
    limitations with computer association, 3
    positive change in system or person, 4, 20
learning rate, 30, 114
learning to rank (LTR), 329
likelihood of model, 146–147
linear discrimination analysis (LDA), 219
linear model, defined, 113
linear regression. *See also* regression
    defined, 45
    ordinary least squares (OLS), 84–85
    overfitting, 90
    overview, 90
    process of, 82
    R language, 390–391
    relationship between variables, 83
    statistical bias, 90
    terminology, 82–83
    using Python, 86–89
    variance, 90
linearity modeling criteria, 111
log likelihood, 192, 196, 200
logical operators (Python), 30
logistic regression
    categorical variable, 145
    continuous variable, 145
    defined, 147
    gradient ascent, 147
    likelihood of model, 146–147
    receiver operating curve (ROC), 151
long short-term memory (LSTM)
    defined, 257
    gates, 257

machine learned ranking (MLR), 329
machine learning. *See also* deep learning

algorithms adjusting own parameters, 4–5
defined, 3, 20, 113
differences with artificial intelligence (AI), 10, 30
learn from experience, 4
neural network timing, 256
nomenclature differences with statistics, 9
regression at scale, 95
traditional versus machine learning, 5
machine learning careers
    finance, 401
    healthcare, 401–402
    overview, 400–401
    retail, 402–403
    tech, 403
machine learning design and evaluation
    complexity of, 326
    evaluation, 331–344
    learning to rank (LTR) or machine learned ranking (MLR), 329
    recommender system, 327–328
machine learning example
    collaborative filtering (CF), 7–8
    content filtering, 8–9
    optical character recognition (OCR), 6
    WAYMO car, 5–6
machine learning issues
    fairness, 19
    flawed data, 18
    racial disparity, 18
    user exposure, 19
machine learning modeling criteria
    accuracy, 111
    estimator choice, 27, 112
    features numbers compared to data points, 112
    hyperparameters, 112
    linearity, 111
    training/testing, 111
    training time, 111
machine learning on the job
    certification for cloud platform, 74
    onboarding phase, 74
machine learning problems
    accountability, 356–358
    Beauty AI, 348–349
    bias, 353–356
    Correctional Offender Management Profiling for Alternative Sanctions (COMPAS), 348
    differential privacy, 362
    federated learning, 362
    Google or Not misinformation, 349–351
    responsible AI in academia, industry, and regulations, 352–353
    transparency, 358–360
machine learning, specialized requirements
    skills, 11–13
    tools, 13–14

machine learning taxonomy
    reinforcement, 10
    summary, 9, 20
    supervised, 9
    unsupervised, 10
MapReduce (Hadoop), 55
Markov process (reinforcement learning), 306
maximum likelihood estimation (MLE)
    defined, 200
    dimensionality reduction, 213
    expectation maximization (EM), 192
maximum marginal hyperplane (MMH), 160–161
McCulloch–Pitts model (MP), 229–230
mean (statistics), 372–373
Meanshift technique, 196–197
median (statistics), 373
Microsoft Azure
    account set-up, 59–60
    versus Amazon Web Services (AWS) Cloud9, 66
    cluster details overview, 62
    versus Google Colab, 66
    HDInsight cluster and, 60–61
    interface, 60
    as Linux virtual machine, 62
    machine learning example, 63–65
    storage set-up, 61–62
misinformation, 363
mode (statistics), 373–374
model, defined, 113
multi-arm bandit problem
    background, 316
    solutions, 317–322
multi-headed attention, 286–287
multilayer perceptron (MLP) model
    forward propagation methods, 236
    forward propagation methods example, 237–238
    hidden layer, 235
    layers in, 236
    overview of, 236
multinomial logistic regression, 152. *See also* softmax regression
multiple linear regression, 91
MySQL
    Python and, 396–398
    R language and, 398–399

naïve Bayes
    assumption, 154, 165–166
    defined, 154
    process of, 156
    steps to create, 155
neural networks
    backward propagation methods, 236–237
    basics of, 228
    classification example, 240–242
    construction in Python, 238
    design, 242–243

forward propagation methods, 236
graph-based (GNN), 297
and human brain modeling, 227–228
machine learning timing, 256
regression example, 240
neural networks architecture
    autoencoder, 243–247
    convolution neural network (CNN), 247–251
    feed-forward network, 231
    long short-term memory (LSTM), 256–259
    multilayer perceptron (MLP), 234–235
    perceptron, 231–232
    recurrent neural network (RNN), 251–256
    single-layer perceptron (SLP), 232–235
neuron, defined, 260
neuron network architectures
    McCulloch–Pitts model (MP), 229–230
    single neuron, 230
    small, 229–230
neuron physiology
    axon, 228
    dendrites, 228
    and human processing power, 231
    structure, 229
    synapse, 228
nominal variable, 367
normal distribution, 370–372
NumPy package (Python), 39

offline evaluation metrics, 332–333
one-armed bandits, 315
optical character recognition (OCR), 6
ordinal variable, 367
ordinary least squares (OLS), 84–85
outcome. *See* dependent variable
out-of-bag error (random forest), 133
out-of-bag samples (random forest), 133
output gate (LSTM), 257
overfitting
    decision tree problem, 132
    dimensionality reduction, 207
    linear regression, 90
overfitting, data, 137

Pandas dataframe, 53–54
Pandas packages, 36
parallel distributed processing (PDP), 227–228
parameter, 114
Pearson's *r* correlation, 378
perceptron model
    defined, 231
    importance of, 231–232
    model representation, 232
    multilayer perceptron (MLP), 234–235
    single-layer perceptron (SLP), 232–235

policies (reinforcement learning), 306
positional encoders, 285
positive predictive value. *See* precision metrics
precision metrics
    defined, 332
    example, 332–333
    F-measure, 332
    recall, 332
    receiver operating characteristic (ROC) curve, 334–335
predictor. *See* independent variable
predictor variable, 367
pretrained word embeddings, 279
principal component analysis (PCA)
    algorithm, 214–215
    defined, 214, 214
    process of, 214
    singular value decomposition (SVD), 215
probability formulas
    Bayes' theorem, 382
    conditional probability, 382
    event probability, 382
propensity, 342, 345
PuTTY, AWS connect, 68–69
PuTTYgen, 52
Python language
    basic examples, 29–31
    basic operation, 31–32
    control structures, 32–33
    deep learning model, 266
    and Google Colab, 56–59
    versus Java language, 14
    Jupyter Notebook, 383–384
    linear regression, 86–89
    neural network construction, 238
    overview, 26
    usefulness in a work environment, 44
Python language access
    Anaconda, 28, 383–384
    download/install, 26–27
    MySQL and, 396–398
    platforms, 26
    Spyder, 385, 29
    via console, 27
    via integrated development environment (IDE), 27–28
Python language functions
    form of, 35
    interactive, 36
    write own, 34–35
Python language packages
    matplotlib.pyplot, 40
    NumPy, 34, 39
    Pandas, 36
    using Google Colab, 37–38
    using Jupyter Notebook, 37–38
    using Spyder, 37

Python statistics
    bar graph, 41
    correlation, 44
    data distribution, 39
    histogram, 40–41
    importing data, 42–43
    max, 39
    mean, 39
    median, 40
    min, 39
    plotting data, 43–44
    standard deviation, 40
    variance, 40

Q-learning
    defined, 311
    goal of, 311
    process of, 311
Q-learning set-up
    Q matrix, 312
    reward matrix, 311
    states, 311

R language
    classification, 388–389, 392–393
    clustering, 394–395
    installing and configuring, 386
    linear regression, 390–391
    MySQL and, 398–399
    regression, 389–391
    unsupervised learning, 392–395
random forest
    advantages, 132, 134–135
    bootstrap sampling technique, 133
    versus decision trees, 50, 133–136
    reasons for, 132
    steps to create, 132
ratio variable, 367
recall, 332
receiver operating curve (ROC)
    Akaike Information Criterion (AIC), 334–335
    Bayesian Information Criterion (BIC), 335
    defined, 334
    generation, 151
    graph, 334
recurrent neural network (RNN)
    architecture, 20, 252
    defined, 252, 260
    problems with, 256–257
regression. *See also* linear regression
    defined, 81
    entry point to machine learning, 113
    multiple linear, 91–95
    neural networks example, 240
    R language, 389–391
    Ridge and Lasso, 96–98

at scale, 95
in supervised learning, 9
reinforcement learning
    ASIMO robot, 306
    bandits, 315–322
    as branch of machine learning, 10, 303
    conceptual model, 304–306
    cumulative award maximization, 304
    defined, 20, 323
    Markov process, 306
    policies, 306
    Q-learning, 311–315
    tic tac toe, 306
    training limit, 306
    trial-and-error steps, 303
Ridge and Lasso regression
    batch gradient descent, 20, 102
    gradient descent, 98–102
    reason to use, 98
    stochastic gradient descent, 102

scatterplot (Python), 43–44
self-attention (transformers), 283, 284
Simpson's paradox, 355
single-layer perceptron (SLP) model
    defined, 232
    example for classification, 234–235
    model representation, 233
    overview, 232–233
singular value decomposition (SVD), 215
singular values (SVD), 215
skills for machine learning competence
    computational thinking, 15–18
    computer and data literacy, 12
    critical thinking, 12–13
    machine learning algorithms, 12
    math, 12
    to obtain job, 13
    programming, 12
skip-gram models, 298
Spyder
    installing and configuring, 385
    installing Python packages, 37
    plotting data, 43–44
    Python language access, 29
SSH (secure client), 76
statistical bias, linear regression, 90
statistical distributions
    central tendency, 372–374
    dispersion, 374–377
    histogram, 368–369
    normal distribution, 370–372
statistical variables
    continuous variable, 367
    dependent variable (linear regression), 367
    discrete variable, 367
    independent variable (linear regression), 367

interval variable, 367
nominal variable, 367
ordinal variable, 367
ratio variable, 367
statistics
    log likelihood, 192
    maximum likelihood estimation (MLE), 192
    nomenclature differences with machine learning, 9
    receiver operating curve (ROC), 151
stochastic gradient descent, 102, 114
supervised learning
    ANN, 228
    anomaly detection, 164–165
    classification, 118–138
    decision tree, 123–132
    defined, 9, 20, 113, 137, 166, 323
    discrete, 9
    know truth first in, 9–10
    predictions about future, 118
    R language, 392–393
    random forest, 132–137
    regression, 9, 81–113
support vector machine (SVM)
    defined, 159
    hyperplane, 159–160
    kernels, 164
    maximum marginal hyperplane (MMH), 160–161
    theory, 161–162
    types of data, 159
surveys, 336
synapse, 228, 26, 260
systemic bias, 353–354

test set, 137, 146
Thompson sampling, 317
tic tac toe (reinforcement learning), 306
tools for machine learning competence
    Python language, 14
    R language, 386–395
training limit (reinforcement learning), 306
training time modeling criteria, 111
training–validation–test data, 137, 146, 166
transformers
    Bidirectional Encoder Representations from Transformers (BERT), 287–297
    defined, 283
    input embeddings, 285
    self-attention, 283, 284
transparency (machine learning), 358–360, 363
true negative statement, 332
true positive rate (TPR), 166
true positive statement, 332

understandability, 363
understandability (machine learning), 359
univariate feature selection, 208–210

unsupervised learning
   autoencoder network, 244–246
   clustering, 175–199
   clustering in, 10
   defined, 200, 323
   density estimation, 10
   dimensionality reduction, 206–221
   R language, 394–395
upper confidence bound, 317
user research (machine learning evaluation)
   interviews, 336–337
   surveys, 336
   timing for, 335
   user studies, 337
user studies, 337

validation set, 137
vanishing gradient (RNN), 256
variance (linear regression), 90

WAYMO car, 5–6
while loop (Python), 32, 33
word embeddings, 278–279

YARN (Hadoop), 55